The Economics of John Kenneth Galbraith

The recent financial crisis has once again seen John Kenneth Galbraith return to the bestseller lists. Yet, despite the continued popular success of his works, Galbraith's contribution to economic theory is rarely recognized by today's economists. This book redresses the balance by providing an introductory and sympathetic discussion of Galbraith's theoretical contributions, introducing the reader to his economics and his broader vision of the economic process. The book highlights and explains key features of Galbraith's economic thought, including his penetrating critique of society, his distinctive methodology, his specific brand of Keynesianism, and his original – but largely ignored – contribution to the theory of the firm. It also presents, for the first time, a detailed examination of Galbraith's monetary economics and revisits his analysis of financial euphoria. This unique work seeks to rehabilitate Galbraith's contribution, setting out several directions for possible future research in the Galbraithian tradition.

DR. STEPHEN P. DUNN is Director of Strategy at NHS East of England. He is an international authority on John Kenneth Galbraith and has published numerous articles on Post Keynesian economics and the economics of the firm in leading international journals. In 2000 he received the prestigious K. William Kapp prize from one of Europe's largest economics associations. He is the author of *The Uncertain Foundations of Post Keynesian Economics* (2008) and the editor of the four volume reference collection *John Kenneth Galbraith: The Economic Legacy* (2011).

The Economics of John Kenneth Galbraith

Introduction, Persuasion, and Rehabilitation

STEPHEN P. DUNN

CAMBRIDGE
UNIVERSITY PRESS

CAMBRIDGE UNIVERSITY PRESS
Cambridge, New York, Melbourne, Madrid, Cape Town,
Singapore, São Paulo, Delhi, Tokyo, Mexico City

Cambridge University Press
The Edinburgh Building, Cambridge CB2 8RU, UK

Published in the United States of America by Cambridge University Press, New York

www.cambridge.org
Information on this title: www.cambridge.org/9781107404489

First published 2011
First paperback edition 2011

A catalogue record for this publication is available from the British Library

Library of Congress Cataloguing in Publication Data
Dunn, Stephen P.
The economics of John Kenneth Galbraith : introduction, persuasion, and rehabilitation / Stephen P. Dunn.
p. cm.
Includes bibliographical references and index.
ISBN 978-0-521-51876-5 (hardback)
1. Galbraith, John Kenneth, 1908–2006. 2. Economics–United States. I. Title.
HB119.G33D86 2010
330.1–dc22
2010024615

ISBN 978-0-521-51876-5 Hardback
ISBN 978-1-107-40448-9 Paperback

Praise for The Economics of John Kenneth Galbraith

"Richard Parker's book *John Kenneth Galbraith* is an intellectual and political history nestled inside a biography. Stephen Dunn's book is almost exactly the opposite. Parker's book is about the man. Dunn's is about the structure of what went on inside his brain and what appeared in his major books."

James K. Galbraith, Professor, LBJ School of Public Affairs, The University of Texas at Austin

"This is a remarkably rich and intelligent assessment of John Kenneth Galbraith's place in, and relevance to, modern economics. At a moment when Galbraithian analysis far better explains the global financial crisis than any of the standard models, Stephen Dunn's cogent handling of the richness of Galbraith's authentic originality will help provoke a much-needed debate on where we are heading – and why."

Richard Parker, Official biographer of John Kenneth Galbraith and Senior Fellow at the Shorenstein Center, Kennedy School of Government, Harvard University

"In setting out to rehabilitate J. K. Galbraith, Stephen Dunn has done us all a great favor. This book would be important at any time. In the current global conditions, it is invaluable. It will provide a much needed impetus to encourage a new generation of economists and policy-makers to address the policy questions that so preoccupied Galbraith."

Patricia Hewitt, MP, Former Secretary of State for Health and Secretary of State for Trade and Industry

"Stephen Dunn has produced a timely, insightful and valuable introduction to the economic thinking of J. K. Galbraith. It deserves to be widely read. And it will inform debate in these interesting times."

Alan Milburn, MP, Former Secretary of State for Health and Former Chief Secretary of the Treasury

"In the face of the financial crisis, Galbraith's work on the Great Crash of 1929 has gained particular attention for its many insights into the 'irrational exuberance' of the financial sector. This book demonstrates the vast breadth of Galbraith's work on capitalism, the dominance of large corporations, private affluence and public squalor, technological development, poverty and government policy as well as money, finance and instability. This is all set within an appreciation of Galbraith's methodological approach. A fine monument to the continuing relevance of J. K. Galbraith."

Malcolm Sawyer, Professor of Economics, University of Leeds

"Stephen Dunn has done more than anyone else in the last decade to keep the ideas of John Kenneth Galbraith alive. In this volume Dunn establishes the breadth and depth of Galbraith's vision, and the force and contemporary relevance of his analysis. This work is a timely and engaging monument to one of the greatest economists of the twentieth century."

Geoff Hodgson, Research Professor in Business Studies, University of Hertfordshire

"Stephen Dunn's book on Galbraith is comprehensive and scholarly and an absorbing read. Dunn writes clearly, providing detailed suggestions for further research and developments based on Galbraith's contributions."

Geoff Harcourt, Emeritus Professor, Adelaide University, Emeritus Reader in the History of Economic Theory, University of Cambridge and Emeritus Fellow, Jesus College, Cambridge

To Lucy, Harry, Alexander, and Katie with love

A prophet is only despised in his own country, among his own relations and in his own house.

Mark 6:4

Contents

Figures

Tables

Foreword

JAMES K. GALBRAITH

My father passed his centennial birthday on October 15, 2008. Within two weeks of that milestone, one of his books, *The Great Crash, 1929*, was back on the best-seller lists. That is no doubt mainly because the book is famous as a master narrative, combined with the eerie similarities between the years of Our Lord 1929 and 2008.

But why do the similarities seem so great? One reason, perhaps, is that we understand the events of October 1929 in the first place through a theoretical framework created by *The Great Crash, 1929*. It is a framework that emphasizes the role of speculative euphoria as a catalyst for imaginative fraud, theft, and abuse, and that illuminates the incentives for, and consequences of, complaisance by public authority. But above all, it places the financial sector in context, recognizing, and illustrating its role as a catalyst for prosperity and disaster in the larger spheres of economic life.

None of this was fully clear to economists before Galbraith; much of it has been highly disputed by many economists since. In Milton Friedman's telling, it was the tight policy of the Federal Reserve that converted slump into depression. In Jude Wanniski's, it was the Smoot-Hawley tariff. If Mr. Kevin Hassett of the American Enterprise Institute is to be believed, it was the cartel-friendly policies of the National Recovery Administration and the union-friendly policies of the Wagner Act. But the fact remains, for most readers, the most theoretically coherent and therefore persuasive telling is that of John Kenneth Galbraith. And all the more so today, when the key elements have been so plainly reprised in modern times.

Galbraith's larger work, considered as a whole, is rooted partly in Marshall's theory of the firm, partly in Veblen's economic anthropology, partly in Keynes' macroeconomics, and partly in Schumpeter's vision of technological change. But a consistent theoretical orientation is to the work of students of large organizations, from Weber, to Berle and Means, to Herbert Simon, to James Burnham and others of the American mid century. *The Affluent Society* is my father's reconsideration of what is now called neoclassical economic theory in view of this work, and *The New Industrial State* was his comprehensive effort to bring the large corporation into focus as the centerpiece of economic life and organization.

Needless to say, on all these matters Galbraith met resistance – but not only resistance. At the hands of professional colleagues he met something worse: a studied non-recognition that his work was theory, that it was even economics. The fact that his work was presented in clear English, in elegant style, to audiences of millions, only made it easier for academics to dismiss him from view. To the next generation of economists, it is fair to say, he is today little known, even as in many cases they struggle to reinvent his ideas.

In this book Stephen Dunn begins the task of bringing Galbraith's theoretical achievements into focus. Dunn, a scholar with the most comprehensive grasp of my father's extant published work, is ideally qualified for this task. In a concise, well-ordered argument he takes us through the major critical and constructive elements of Galbraith's thought – the theory of the consumer, of the corporation and of technology, of government and public purpose, of money and financial instability, of poverty and development. Here the work of many books and many years is brought within the reach of a contemporary professional reader.

Beyond that, Dunn does a fine job of capturing Galbraith's frame of mind, his intellectual style and mode of analysis. It is a mode that is fact based and synthetic – an approach that as Dunn recognizes and argues is scientific to the core, in a precise sense. And this is true, even where the eye of the disciplined scientist is concealed, to a degree, behind the pen of a literary master.

Preface

Political economy is an art as well as a science. John Kenneth Galbraith has always been a creative artist in formulating theories of the social world. His fabrications constitute the stuff of economic science.

Paul A. Samuelson (1989: 128)

April 29, 2006 marked the end of an era – it was the day that John Kenneth (Ken) Galbraith died. This was a great loss. Galbraith was a hugely influential figure in shaping and influencing the course of events and intellectual debate over the long twentieth century. Nevertheless, many of the tributes and obituaries that followed identified him principally with a vision of the postwar economy dominated by large bureaucratic corporations, unfettered by the demands of consumers and financiers alike – something unthinkable today. In the days that followed his death, little serious reflection was given to Galbraith's lasting contributions to, and place in, the study of economics. The purpose of this book is to seek to fill this gap and offer an accessible introduction to Galbraith and his ideas, and present some suggestions for further research and analysis in the Galbraithian tradition.

This book draws on previous writings that have been brought together to facilitate Galbraithian scholarship. I have sought to reduce duplication and adopt a more coherent approach to Galbraith's economics, seeking to achieve four principal objectives. First, I have sought to provide an introductory and sympathetic discussion of the salient theoretical contributions of J. K. Galbraith. The second objective is to consider Galbraith's work as a coherent whole – introducing the reader to Galbraith's economics and his vision of the economic process. The consequence of these first two aims is a focus on what I consider to be Galbraith's mature view, rather than an outline of the historical evolution of Galbraith's thought.

The third objective is to evaluate Galbraith's place in the study of economics. I believe that Galbraith was a hugely original theorist, whose contributions are now so widely assimilated that their originality and lasting force is easily overlooked. The argument made here is that Galbraith espoused a distinctive methodological approach that underpinned his highly original and distinctive theory of the firm, his approach to power and development, his study of financial markets, and his ardent Keynesianism. In doing so, I argue that Galbraith should be seen more squarely within the Post Keynesian and Institutionalist traditions of economics – even offering the prospect of integrating them in a foundational vision of the economic process. This aim also links to the fourth objective, which, through reviewing Galbraith's contribution, enables us to establish new directions for future research in the Galbraithian tradition. That is to say, the aim is to contribute to the serious study, rehabilitation, and development of Galbraith's ideas. In doing so critical discussion is focused on development.

Acknowledging these aims explains why I do not dwell on the historical evolution of Galbraith's thought and the discussion and reflection that often surrounded it. But while several excellent critical appraisals have been produced on Galbraith, many fail to get under the skin of his theoretical system or consider its lasting salience. This is the purpose here. I offer two supporting arguments for such a contention. First, I believe the reappraisal of Galbraith's key ideas presented here is profoundly original and typically missed by earlier treatments. As we shall see, Galbraith: espoused an oft ignored and distinctive methodology that underpinned his divergence from the conventional wisdom; made an important contribution to the theory of the firm that anticipated many of the concerns and issues raised by the New Institutional Economics and proponents of a resource–based or capabilities view of the firm; developed a theory of advertising and consumer manipulation that is deeper and more complex than the persuasive view with which he is commonly associated, and; was an avowed Keynesian who anticipated recent developments in macroeconomics, as embodied in the New Consensus, which acknowledges the endogeneity of the money supply. Second, I was personally struck by Galbraith's suggestion, in private correspondence, on the study that forms the basis of chapters 7 and 8 that I "was one of the first to read [*The New Industrial State*] like I hoped might be more generally the case." Such an admission suggests that Galbraith himself believed that the full force of his contribution had not always been fully appreciated.

The book also presents the first attempt at a comprehensive bibliography of Galbraith's works. This has been principally conducted in the excellent library facilities in the Graduate School of Business at Stanford University. In an ideal world I should have liked to triangulate this research with a systematic consideration of the materials deposited in the Galbraith collection at the Kennedy library. This, alas, has not been possible. Nevertheless, I believe I have been sufficiently rigorous in approach and that this represents a major contribution to the renewal of Galbraithian scholarship.

I should also record that I have not sought to emulate Galbraith's masterful prose. One should not try to imitate a master, as it will only invite ridicule and unfavorable comparison. Similarly I have resisted the temptation to attempt to copy his acclaimed wit. Krugman (2008c: 7) argues that "one temptation that often afflicts writers on economics, especially when the subject is so grave, is the tendency to become excessively dignified ... Too often, though, pundits imagine that because the subject is serious, it must be approached solemnly; that because these are big issues, they must be addressed with big words; no informality or levity allowed. As it turns out, however, to make sense of new and strange phenomena, one must be prepared to play with ideas." Although I find both Krugman and Galbraith's incisive wit penetrating, I have nevertheless sought to avoid "the grave risks in a resort to humor" (Galbraith, 1979a: 291). In seeking to highlight Galbraith's economic contributions, I have therefore focused largely on his ideas, and not his invective. Those seeking to be so regaled by Galbraith's wit should read Galbraith for themselves, or look elsewhere (see, for example, Stanfield, 1996: 8–17; 2001: 8–10).

Finally I should apologize for relegating too much scholarship to footnotes. As McCloskey (2000: 48) observes, footnotes are nests for pedants and can detract from the argument and flow. I agree. In an ideal world many of the points made in the footnotes would have been developed in the broader narrative. I am seeking, however, to introduce the general reader to the economics of J. K. Galbraith. This is why I have sought to avoid distracting digressions in the main text and relegated important but peripheral scholarship to endnotes. I would encourage all but the committed professional reader to avoid these. I hope, nevertheless, that the devoted scholar will be rewarded. Many of the endnotes highlight the similarities between Veblen, Knight, Keynes, and Schumpeter, provide evidence for the claims I make, and provide further suggestions for supplementary research.

Acknowledgments

I should first like to convey my thanks and appreciation to the Galbraith family. It was Jamie who strongly encouraged me to bring to his father's attention my work on his contribution to the theory of the firm. This led to a series of unsolicited and supportive correspondence from Ken Galbraith himself on the ideas developed in this book. It resulted in a visit to the Galbraith's home and a hugely enjoyable and instructive afternoon with both Ken and Kitty, the product of which was an interview on the origins of Galbraith's thought, reproduced here as chapter 12. For their warmth and hospitality, I am greatly appreciative.

I should also like to extend my sincere thanks to Malcolm Sawyer. Malcolm continues to be a friend, mentor, and inspiration. Without his advice and instruction over the years, I doubt I would have sustained my interest in both Galbraith and Post Keynesianism. He also commented extensively on several papers and earlier versions of the manuscript, greatly improving the clarity of the argument. I hope he is pleased with the final product. Geoff Hodgson also deserves singling out. Without his encouragement to pursue my ideas on Galbraith while walking in the Czech mountains, I doubt whether I would have resolved to begin to document what I believe is his neglected contribution. Geoff continues to provide advice, support and friendship beyond that which could be reasonably expected from a fellow academic. Paul Davidson also continues to be a major influence on my thinking and his ideas, contributions and correspondence have shaped my understanding of both Keynes and Galbraith. Geoff Harcourt, another warm and supportive scholar, also warrants a special mention. Geoff provided insightful comments on the whole manuscript that has, I hope, resulted in a clearer exposition. Ron Stanfield provided help, support, and copies of books and manuscripts to support the final push and also deserves singling out for a warm thank you. Kate Duncan, Linda Merrill, and Lister Wilson also read and commented on the whole manuscript, greatly improving the final draft and the clarity of argument. For this I am most grateful.

I must also thank my joint authors for their help and support and permission to use and edit material that we have worked on together. Paul Davidson, Steve Pressman, Stacey Anderson, and Andrew Mearman are wonderfully engaging and original scholars who have influenced the development of my ideas on Galbraith and to whom I am profoundly in debt. I hope they are pleased with the resultant book.

I should also like to thank those who provided comment on earlier papers that have been extensively revised here. I would especially like to thank Ben Alamar, Philip Arestis, Dorie Apollonio, David Bunting, Charley Clark, Dan Cook, Paul Davidson, Dan Dohan, Paul Downward, Peter Earl, Eirik Evenhouse, Keith Glaister, Mark Groom, Geoff Hodgson, Jamie Holland-Jones, Christopher Jewell, Graeme Jones, Stefan Kesting, John King, Thorbjoern Knudsen, Tony Lawson, Fred Lee, Hal Luft, Jeff Madrick, Foad Mardukhi, Huascar Pessali, Rick Pollay, Warren Samuels, Suzaynn Schick, John Smithin, Engelbert Stockhammer, Pavlina Tcherneva, Phil Tomlinson, and Joanna Weinberg for their discussions, critical comments, and other assistance in the development of the ideas contained therein. Simon Leary and Ian Wootton, senior partners at PricewaterhouseCoopers, also deserve a mention for encouraging me to continue in my endeavors amidst a busy job, and for discussions on the great crash, 2008. Similarly I am grateful for the encouragement of Sir Neil McKay and Sir Keith Pearson and colleagues in and across the NHS in the East of England to complete this book. Notwithstanding all this help and encouragement, I should point out, however, that I am solely responsible for the views expressed herein.

The Commonwealth Fund, a New York City-based, private, independent foundation, supported part of the research undertaken here. Especially I must thank Karen Davis and Robin Osborn, who continue to be so supportive in all that I do. Nevertheless, the views presented here are those of the author and not necessarily those of The Commonwealth Fund, their directors, officers, or staff. The Royal Economic Society also provided a research grant that enabled me to visit and interview Galbraith in Cambridge, Massachusetts.

Perhaps most importantly I should thank my family. My mother, father, and my brother, Russell, continue to provide the love and common sense that an academic needs. Kate and Roger Duncan also deserve a warm thank you for all their kind support and hospitality. Lucy, my wife and partner, continues to support my interest in intellectual matters with selfless regard. Such pursuits clearly limit the time we have together. Harry, Alexander, and Katie also warrant a special mention for taking me away from the computer to engage in the joys that are part of family life. From this point onwards I promise to devote to them the time they deserve.

Finally I should like to acknowledge the following publishers for permission to use material from previously published articles: M. E. Sharpe, Association for Social Economics, Routledge, and Cambridge University Press.

1 *The eclipse of* The New Industrial State?

Though economic analysis and general reasoning are of wide application ... every change in social conditions is likely to require a new development of economic doctrines.

Alfred Marshall (1920: 37)

If there were justice in the world, John Kenneth Galbraith would rank as the twentieth century's most influential American economist. He has published several books that are among the best analyses of modern US history, played a key role in midcentury policymaking, and advised more presidents and senators than would seem possible in three lifetimes. Yet today, Galbraith's influence on economics is small, and his influence on US politics is receding by the year.

J. Bradford DeLong (2005: 126)

In the tributes and obituaries that followed John Kenneth (Ken) Galbraith's death on April 29, 2006, much was made of his long and varied career, as well as his closeness to power. John Kenneth Galbraith was a distinguished Harvard economist, an accomplished diplomat, a political activist, a confidant and adviser to presidents, a memoirist and novelist, and one of the best-selling economic writers of his time. The conventional reflection noted his colorful life, celebrated his mordant wit and prose, yet generally castigated his theorizing as being obsolete. This is a major travesty. Galbraith was one of the leading progressive intellectuals of the post-World War II period who, though part of the establishment, was happy to point out its self-serving interests and convenient myths.[1] But he was more than just a gadfly. He was an original theorist whose contributions are now so widely assimilated that their lasting force is easily overlooked.

Indeed, in the days and months that followed his death, and for a long time before, little serious reflection has been given to Galbraith's enduring contributions to economic theorizing. Nobel prize-winner

Paul Krugman's (1994: 13–14) comments in *Peddling Prosperity* perhaps capture the standard mainstream assessment of Galbraith:

> Although Galbraith is a Harvard economics professor ... he has never been taken seriously by his academic colleagues, who regard him as more of a "media personality". The contrast between public and professional perception became particularly acute in 1967, when Galbraith made a grand statement of his ideas about economics in *The New Industrial State*, a book that he hoped would come to be regarded as being in the same league as John Maynard Keynes's *General Theory* or even Adam Smith's *Wealth of Nations*. The book was rapturously reviewed in the popular press, but it met with indifference from the academics. Galbraith's book wasn't what they considered real economic theory. Not incidentally, the academics were right in believing that *The New Industrial State* could be safely ignored.

What is remarkable about such comments, however, is that Krugman himself seems to be evolving into a Galbraithian. Over the last twenty years, Krugman has increasingly moved into the space once occupied by Galbraith.[2] In *Peddling Prosperity*, for example, Krugman (1994) attacked "supply siders" and "strategic traders." In *The Return of Depression Economics*, Krugman (2008c) heralded the return of Keynesianism. In *The Conscience of a Liberal*, Krugman (2007) argued that "movement conservatism" has defended and driven inequality, exploiting cultural and racial divisions to its advantage. And throughout he has attacked the misleading fictions promulgated by textbook economics.

This is a conscience that Galbraith would have applauded. Over the course of his major trilogy – *The Affluent Society* (1958a), *The New Industrial State* (1967a), and *Economics and the Public Purpose* (1973a) – Galbraith developed a system of thought that attempted to shed light on many contemporary concerns such as: the overproduction of private goods and the underproduction of public goods; the increasingly superfluous nature of much technical innovation directed at socially irrelevant commodities; the failure of economic growth to ameliorate enduring social problems; the uneven distribution of government expenditure, reflected in excessive spending on the military and other forms of social infrastructure, e.g. roads, to the relative neglect of others, e.g. parks, cultural activities, environmental protection, mass transit, and public housing, which are all public goods whose very legitimacy is hotly disputed; the increasingly skewed income distribution between different sectors and personnel; the enduring distinction between the high-wage and low-wage industries; the unresponsiveness of the modern corporation, governments and international institutions to public pressure and opinion; the problems of economy-wide coordination; and the continuing fear of inflation as opposed to deflation. Many of these concerns remain pressing today.

Indeed Krugman's discussion of contemporary issues in his *New York Times* column increasingly echoes Galbraith's analysis of the new industrial state (Duhs, 2008). Krugman's analysis of contemporary events is increasingly Galbraithian in orientation, concentrating on the major anxieties of our time. Krugman, like Galbraith before him, increasingly focuses on the divergence between the interests of the conservative and corporate elite and the wider public interest in his analysis of: the soaring wealth of the rich and rise of inequality; the bias of the tax system toward the affluent; the rise in obesity and the role of the large food corporation in promoting the consumption of high-fat, energy-dense foods; the need for the good society to deliver a universal health insurance model; the manipulation by oil and automobile companies of governments and popular opinion, obfuscating understanding and limiting global response to the threat of climate change; Enron and their fabrication of the 2001 Californian energy crisis; Iraq, Halliburton, and the cozy relationship between the military industrial complex; the obsession with increased growth at the expense of happiness; and the cronyism of the Bush administration. All are anxieties similar to ones that Galbraith analyzed. What is more all can be explained by Galbraith's theoretical framework.

Nevertheless, in the conventional wisdom, the assessment continues to be that Galbraith's analysis, as exemplified by *The New Industrial State*, has not come to pass. It was either wrong in its time (Solow, 1967; Gordon, 1968, 1969; Demsetz, 1974; Friedman, 1977) or it is wrong for our times (Krugman, 1994, 2008c; McCloskey, 2007). Either way, *The New Industrial State* has been eclipsed and Galbraith must therefore be unceremoniously consigned to the dustbin of history.

A journey through economic time

The standard view is that Galbraith painted a picture of an autonomous bureaucracy that manipulated consumers and society, unfettered by either competition or shareholders. This view has since been eclipsed by the return of the market. Paul Krugman, for example, has suggested that the academics who rejected *The New Industrial State* were right, arguing that:

> History has not treated the book kindly. Galbraith began it in self-conscious imitation of Adam Smith's memorable description of a pin factory, with an account of the 1964 launch of the Ford Mustang. Starting from that example, he argued that technology was pushing us inevitably into an age of ever greater dominance by giant corporations. These corporations would be able, through market research and advertising, to predict and indeed control demand for their products; they would be run by technocratic managers who would be increasingly independent of the stockholders who nominally owned the companies. And like the automobile companies, they would be virtually immune to the vagaries of market forces.
>
> Need it be pointed out that none of this was remotely on target? The role of giant corporations in the US Economy has been shrinking, not rising, for the past two decades, with the great bulk of the job growth among smaller firms. Many of our biggest companies – from Sears to IBM – have been spectacularly unable to get consumers to buy their wares. Those supposedly autonomous managers, far from being able to ignore stockholders, now live in terror of buyouts from investors willing to promise stockholders a higher return. And nobody, least of all the auto companies, has been insulated from the market. (Krugman, 1994: 13)[3]

Galbraith's economist son, James Galbraith (2008a: 115), also appears to agree with this assessment: "When my father published *The New Industrial State* in 1967, the great industrial enterprise seemed a stable, even permanent, and largely self-stabilizing element of the postwar American scene ... But the system of large organizations as my father described it was far less stable than it seemed. Already in the 1970s, it began to suffer the intrusion, on its home markets, of a competing system: the rising industrial colossus of Japan." In one sense both Krugman and James Galbraith are right. The unchanging dominance of the large firm projected in *The New Industrial State* does appear to have been challenged by the information revolution and the emergence of new large and growing firms such as Wal-Mart,

Samsung, Toyota, Honda, Nissan, Sony, Google, Vodafone, Apple, and Microsoft, to name but a few.[4]

This assessment also appears to have been accepted by Galbraith himself. In the fourth edition of *The New Industrial State*, he conceded that he "did not see the development of the foreign, most notably the Japanese, competition to which [the corporation] would be subject ... No one can doubt that in our older industries this competition has substantially impaired the certainty and effectiveness of the planning process" (Galbraith, 1967a: xxxi–xxxii). Similarly, in an important symposium in the *American Economic Review* on "*The New Industrial State* after twenty years," Galbraith (1988: 375) remarked that:

> There have also been some important microeconomic developments that I did not foresee. In 1967, my view was, in some measure, of a closed American-dominated corporate structure extending its reach internationally by way of American multinational or transnational enterprises. I did not foresee the invasive thrust into this structure by Japan and other countries. This, to put it mildly, has introduced a new element, substantially beyond the influence and control of the firms of the corporate or planning system.

This seems to suggest that Galbraith must be appraised in his time and that his analysis is irrelevant for our times. Indeed James Galbraith argues that his father's analysis represents an analysis of the postwar world of that time and should be considered on those terms:

> my father's vision of an economy dominated by large national corporations as of 1967 was not an error. The mid-century was as he said it was. Nor was it a glance at an interlude between two eras when free markets actually prevailed. It was instead the portrait of a way-station, a stage in the evolution of the world business system. The postwar dominance of the large American industrial corporation counterbalanced by government and organized labor was a fact ... It was simply not a permanent fact ... What some interpreted as showing up the failings of a book is more fairly seen as a process of fundamental change, of evolution and of decay, and especially the redistribution of the power in the industrial system itself. (James Galbraith, 2008a: 117)[5]

The facts, however, are not as clear-cut as Krugman and others would lead us to believe. Technology, the coping stone of *The New Industrial*

State, is even more important today than in the midcentury. It is one of *the* decisive factors in national success. This is why another famous Harvard professor, Michael Porter (1990: 638), acknowledges that: "The quality of human resources must be steadily rising if a nation's economy is to upgrade." And it is clear that the large firms that are largely responsible for the research and development that drives technological development no longer dominate national economies, but instead now straddle the global economy (Porter, 1990; James Galbraith, 1998).

General Electric, BP, Toyota, Shell, Exxon Mobil, Ford, Volkswagen, Chevron, Siemens, Nestlé, BMW, IBM, Pfizer, Johnson & Johnson, and Proctor and Gamble continue to dominate the world stage. Large firms that continue to dominate the motor, oil, food, pharmaceutical, electrical, and telecommunications industries, controlling major flows in trade and production – something we discuss below in chapters 7, 8, and 11. Similarly, those industries that have delivered strong economic performance and investment over time – the computer, chemical, aircraft, missile, pharmaceutical, photo, and electronics industries – are also the most technologically advanced and invariably supported by state spending (James Galbraith, 1998: 117–32). Of course the wider financial turbulence of the world economy makes the position of large firms more precarious. But there is no doubt that the dominance of large firms continues to characterize modern economies. This at least deserves further reflection.

As we shall see, the emergence of what is referred to as "global competition," can also be reinterpreted through the lens of *American Capitalism*, *The New Industrial State*, and *Economics and the Public Purpose*. Although many commentators and economists argue that the massive increase in global merger and acquisition activity reaffirms the ascendancy of the market, it also exemplifies the changed nature and dynamics of competition in THE modern economy that Galbraith identified. Competition in the modern economy has been transformed from price competition into other forms of competition such as advertising, mergers and acquisitions, product innovation, as well as the development of new sources of countervailing power. For Galbraith the competition which characterizes the modern economy is markedly distinct from the "perfect" competition depicted and predicted by the conventional wisdom.

Galbraith's analysis of the firms' focus on growth more than ever characterizes the competitive process and the modern economy, as exemplified by the exponential rise in the numbers of mergers and acquisitions (see chapters 7, 8, and 11 below). And much of the talk of global competition also reflects the emergence of new corporate sources of countervailing power. Much of global competition has been driven by the consolidation of the "buy-side" of various global markets, as exemplified by the rise and rise of the retail power of Wal-Mart (see Reich, 2009). This reflects Galbraith's (1952a: 119) thesis in *American Capitalism* that "in the typical modern market of a few sellers, the active restraint is provided not by competitors but from the other side of the market by strong buyers."

What is more, although we have undoubtedly witnessed a rise in the number of small firms over the 1980s and 1990s, this should not be interpreted uncritically as reflecting the increased intensity of global competition. The outsourcing of production, which has reinforced the dominance and position of the large firms that span the global economy, has driven much of this trend. As I highlight below, one of the implications of Galbraith's approach to the firm is that it encompasses subcontracting and market relationships, as well as internal operations that are more clearly under the control of the large corporation (Cowling and Sugden, 1998a, 1998b, 1999; Dunn, 2001a, 2001c, 2008a). Consistent with Galbraith's (1973a) bimodal view of the modern economy, the planning system continues to dominate and exploit the market system, at home and abroad (see chapters 5, 7 and 8 below).

This means that focusing on the traditional boundaries of the firm, relying on conventional measures of concentration, results in an under-appreciation of the power and influence of the modern technostructure. By narrowly focusing on the rise in the number of small firms, we overlook the actual increase in scope of the large firm's influence and power. We underestimate both the extent of its control of production and the subsequent degree of concentration and influence of the multinational enterprise (Cowling and Sugden, 1998b; Cowling, Yusof, and Vernon, 2000; Cowling and Tomlinson, 2005; Granovetter, 1998; Klein, 1999). As Reich (2009: 216) remarks, this "is especially true under supercapitalism, when companies are quickly morphing into global supply chains." Domestic and overseas outsourcing, which in the conventional wisdom is interpreted as a response to global competition, that is reducing the scope and influence of the firm, can instead be viewed as consolidating the power of the technostructure. The subcontracting relationships of the large, brand-managing firm consolidate its global power and reach (cf. Klein, 1999).

Similarly the rise of Japanese and Asian competitiveness, through the rise of Toyota, Honda, Nissan, Mitsui, Mitsubishi, Sony, and Hitachi, can be viewed as consistent with Galbraith's (1967a) thesis in *The New Industrial State*, even if this was something that he did not himself recognize.[6] Cowling and Tomlinson (2000), for example, note that the entrance of large Japanese firms onto the global stage reflected their productive and technological virtuosity, as well as the state support provided to them by the Ministry of International Trade and Industry (MITI).[7] The modern Japanese corporation led to the emergence of a new affluent Japanese society which, towards the end of the postwar period, was approaching saturation point for its products in its domestic economy. It therefore required new outlets to buy its products (cf. Galbraith, 1973a: 180–91). As Cowling and Tomlinson (2000: F367) record: "Initially, surplus production could be satisfied through exporting to Western markets, a policy that resulted in consistently large trade surpluses. However, the threat of retaliatory trade barriers, especially from the United-States, threatened future export growth and, in response, the larger Japanese firms considered the transnational option."[8] This is consistent with Galbraith's (1973a) analysis of the transnational firm, considered in *Economics and the Public Purpose* – something we explore in chapter 8 below. What is more, it is important to note that such a Galbraithian analysis of the emergence of Japanese competition does not rest on the view that Japanese capitalism was a new and superior brand, but rather argues that it reflects the dynamics of the modern firm predicted by the New Industrial State.[9]

The large firms that characterize the planning sector of the economy also continue to spend vast sums on advertising and lobbying, which has become increasingly sophisticated and targeted at eliciting the required consumer and legislative response (Packard, 1957; Gunter and Furnham, 1992; Hawkins, Best, and Coney, 1998; Heath, 1995, 1996; Weinstein, 1994; Dawson, 2003). This process has never been perfect, nor is it determinate, as Galbraith himself acknowledged. But, notwithstanding such imprecision, there is now an increasing recognition that the tobacco, pharmaceutical, oil, automobile, and food industries seek to manipulate public policy and the consumer in a manner that is consistent with Galbraith's hypothesis (Anderson and Dunn, 2006; David, 2006; Monbiot, 2000, 2006, 2007; Krugman, 2005a, 2005c; Sample, 2007; Stiglitz, 2006; Klein, 1999; Glantz *et al.*, 1996; Shamasunder and Bero, 2002; Moynihan, 2003a; Moynihan *et al.*, 2002; Angell, 2004; Avorn, 2004; Goozner, 2004; Greider, 2003; Abramson, 2004; Moynihan and Cassells, 2005; Petersen, 2008; Lang and Heasman, 2004; Patel, 2008; Mayo and Nairn, 2009). Similarly, there have been renewed attempts at testing Galbraith's thesis. Lamdin (2008), for example, presents an important econometric analysis that shows that, consistent with the Galbraithian thesis, advertising and credit both have economically and statistically significant positive influences on consumption. I explore these issues below in chapters 7, 8, 9, and 11.

Finally it is far from clear that the modern firm is now effectively policed by investors and stockholders alike (Stiglitz, 2003; Bebchuk and Fried, 2004). The widely acknowledged explosion in chief executives pay – something we examine below – raises urgent questions regarding the ability of financial markets and their associated institutions to provide effective governance and oversight of the modern firm – be they banks, energy companies, or large motor companies. This is part of what Galbraith (2004: 27) referred to as "innocent" fraud:

> This fraud has accepted ceremonial aspects: one is a board of directors selected by management, fully subordinate to management but heard as the voice of the shareholders. It includes men and the necessary presence of one or two women who need only a passing knowledge of the enterprise; with rare exceptions, they are reliably acquiescent. Given a fee and some food, the directors are routinely informed by management on what has been decided or is already known. Approval is assumed, including for management compensation – compensation set by management for itself. This, not surprisingly, can be munificent ... Legal self-enrichment in the millions of dollars is a common feature of modern corporate government. This is not surprising; managers set their own compensation.

What is more, the accepted practice of linking CEO pay to stock market valuations as opposed to underlying corporate cash flow – to the strength of the underlying business – can drive more serious failures in corporate governance (Bebchuk and Fried, 2004). Stock prices, which are driven by sentiment, convention, and "irrational exuberance," can be inflated and manipulated by "serious" fraud (Forelle and Bandler, 2006). The collapse of Enron and the wrongdoing of WorldCom, Qwest, Tyco, and Xerox provide *prima facie* evidence of the inability of modern financial systems to police effectively large and complex corporations. As James Galbraith (2008a: 124) highlights:

> What they exposed was the complete incapacity of the financial markets to oversee from the outside the inner workings of a complex financial structure. In every case – Enron, Tyco, WorldCom, and the others – financial market pressures encouraged fraud ... Each such collapse was initially rewarded, not punished, by the financial markets. In no case did the financial markets detect the fraud. Quite to the contrary, the markets converted the fraudulent enterprise into a performance standard by which other corporations in the same field were to be judged. Nor did any large accounting or auditing firm blow the whistle; again to the contrary, all the major frauds had their books cleared by reputable accountants. Nor did the ratings agencies, then or later, intervene.

Such "serious" frauds raise important questions about shareholders' ability to prevent managers in "their" corporation from pursuing dubious and illegal strategies. And although recent moves have been taken to improve accounting honesty, increase surveillance and strengthen regulation, the recent sub-prime meltdown and global economic crisis point to the continuing difficulties in effectively policing the modern corporation.[10] The technostructure of the financial services industry appears to have run amok with little effective oversight from boards, banks, regulators, or governments alike. Such considerations reinforce Galbraith's insight that the complexities of modern technologies and firms make it extremely difficult to monitor the activities of the modern army of managers, technical specialists, lawyers, accountants, public relations professionals, and marketing managers, as long as an acceptable level of earnings is posted and projected to the wider financial community (cf. Williamson, 2008).[11] Modern management is not insulated from the wider financial system. But it is not effectively policed by it either. This much is clear. And it must be acknowledged as such.[12]

The economics of John Kenneth Galbraith

So while the grand sweep of Galbraith's analysis is often caricatured as conveying a world of durable, dominant American megacorporations surreptitiously manipulating gullible consumers, one should resist using this as an excuse for dismissing Galbraith's economic contributions without further and deeper consideration. As argued over the course of this book, Galbraith introduced many notions into economics that are now widely accepted by economists. He presented an analysis that reflects, and is consistent with, both the Institutionalist and Post Keynesian traditions. He drew on a distinctive methodology in arguing for a revised view of economics and its purpose. He emphasized the endogeneity of the money supply, which is now an acknowledged cornerstone of the "New Consensus" in macroeconomics. He identified the financial fragility and susceptibility to manias that characterize the modern global financial system. And he developed a vision of the modern economy and firm that continues to provide a compelling explanation of many of the pressing problems of our time.

What is more, Galbraith's theoretical system embodied a view of the firm that in many respects has a degree of similarity and overlap with Knight (1921), Coase (1937), Schumpeter (1943), Penrose (1959), Richardson (1960), Williamson (1975, 1985), Chandler (1962, 1977, 1990), and Hymer (1976). Even though their analysis is, in many respects, also a product of their time, their contributions have nevertheless been subject to further reflection and development. In contrast Galbraith's specific contribution has been overlooked. This needs to be rectified. Galbraith's contribution to the theory of the firm has much to teach us and can and should be subject also to further study and development.[13]

Such considerations should not be taken, however, as implying that I believe that Galbraith was omniscient, nor right for all times. Indeed being criticized as a child of his time would not unduly worry Galbraith. As Galbraith (1958a: 86) writes in *The Affluent Society*: "Most economic philosophers [need] only to be right as regards their own time." For Galbraith the aim of a socially relevant economics was to be in touch with the great problems of our time. And as times change and history moves on, so must analysis. Any system of thought must be continually re-examined and reassessed in light of evolving circumstance and process. It must demonstrate its usefulness in passing the "test of anxiety" through illuminating the major problems of our time. Nevertheless my aim here is to draw attention to the fact that Galbraith's economic contributions are deeper and more extensive than he has traditionally been given credit. It is too early to write Galbraith off as a curiosity of a now passed age. The purpose of this book, therefore, is to begin the process of rediscovering and rehabilitating Galbraith's contribution to economics. But first we must consider the events and influences that shaped them.

Notes

1 In a cover story in the late 1960s, *Time* (1968: 24) magazine referred to him as: "the most quotable – and possibly influential – critic of United States society."

2 It is similarly now forgotten that Galbraith was a serious economist who had published in *The Economic Journal* and *The American Economic Review* long before deciding to write for a more popular audience as he approached the age of fifty (see the bibliography below). In the future we will no doubt witness a new "Young Turk" reproaching Krugman in a manner similar to which he has admonished Galbraith.

3 Compare Holmstrom and Kaplan (2001: 137), for example, who provide a more qualified assessment: "There are two interpretations of the increased influence of markets on corporate decision-making. One view is that, after a period of corporate mismanagement, including misguided experiments with conglomerates in the 1960s and waste of free cash flow in the late 1970s and early 1980s, we have finally seen a return to healthy market capitalism. Shareholder value is back because it is the most efficient form of corporate governance. While such a conclusion is consistent with much of the evidence ... the efficiency hypothesis has its weak spots. Chief among them is the US economic performance of the 1960s. How could productivity and GDP growth be so great at a time when managers supposedly wasted large amounts of money on conglomerates? How could an inefficient governance system produce so much new wealth? And what about all the family firms that became conglomerates in the 1960s? Family firms are subject to fewer agency problems than widely held companies, yet many of them followed the general trend. The 1960s, rightly or wrongly, viewed conglomerates more favorably than we do today. Indeed, stock markets reacted positively to most conglomerates in the 1960s." Williamson (2008) argues that despite numerous past and recent contributions to the literature on the efficacy of corporate boards of directors, a consensus has yet to emerge. He highlights the intrinsic limitations of boards in monitoring and managing,

and in a manner that is consistent with Galbraith's contribution to the theory of the firm, he analyses and proposes a series of reforms which recognize the complexity of technology and decision-making.

4 See also McCloskey (2007), who argues: "In truth the list of companies that Galbraith held in awe as great forces in 1967 looks quaint now. US Steel, AT&T, and General Motors belie his assertion 'of great stability in [a great corporation's] position in the planning system.' Eight years after the first publication of *The New Industrial State*, Bill Gates founded Microsoft. Let creative destruction rip."

5 See also Holmstrom and Kaplan (2001: 123), who implicitly acknowledge the relevance of Galbraith's view of the large corporation as an accurate description for his own time: "The corporate governance structures in place before the 1980s gave the managers of the large public corporations little reason to focus on shareholder concerns ... management was loyal to the corporation, not to the shareholder. The external governance mechanisms that were formally available to shareholders were little used ... Boards tended to be cozy with management, making board oversight weak. Internal incentives from management ownership of stock and options were also modest. In 1980, only 20 percent of the compensation of chief executive officers was tied to stock market performance."

6 In one sense Galbraith (1988) does himself a great disservice in suggesting that he overlooked the rise of German and Japanese competition. In *Economics and the Public Purpose*, Galbraith extended his analysis of *The New Industrial State* to consider the multinational enterprise – something we explore in more depth in chapter 8 below. What is more, he explicitly tied his analysis of the rise in German and Japanese competition to the technocratic nexus: "In the United States ... the symbiotic relationship between the planning system and the public bureaucracy has led to heavy investment in industries, notably weapons production and space exploration, to the neglect of civilian industry for which capital has recurrently been expensive and scarce. Germany and Japan have, by contrast, had abundant funds for modernizing and expanding less powerful civilian industry" (Galbraith, 1973a: 338).

7 As Nathan Rosenberg (1994: 121) has pointed out: "the successes of Japanese firms have been attributed to policies of 'industrial targeting' orchestrated by the Ministry of International Trade and Industry (MITI) usually said to involve extensive government subsidies and coordination of import policy that unfairly tilted what should have been a 'level playing field'." It is important to note the role played by MITI in underpinning the success of Japanese firms underscores the developmental role for the state that Galbraith highlighted as an engine for driving economic development – see chapter 6 below.

8 In *A History of Economics* Galbraith (1987: 294–5) argued that the rise and success of Japanese capitalism would provoke a series of pro-active responses such as a seeking tariff protection, buying overseas firms, aggressively outsourcing production overseas and seeking intervention from the Government. All such protective responses have been variously observed (see Krugman, 1994).

9 As Galbraith (1987: 293) remarks in *A History of Economics*: "A further influence from Japan is and will be a better understanding of dynamics and motivation in the modern great corporation." Indeed MITI and other distinctive features of Japanese capitalism, such as the network of firms and banks – the Keiretsu, can be viewed, consistent with the arguments of *The New Industrial State*, that is, as a set of firm and technology driven institutional responses to reduce market uncertainty. Nevertheless, it is also important to note that although Galbraith's approach can be viewed as providing a rationalization for the emergence of specific institutions this is not the same as endorsing a specific set of institutional responses. That is to say Galbraith does not advocate a detailed set of institutional configurations to secure national comparative advantage. Galbraith's analysis does not stand or fall on the argument as to whether the specific institutional features of Japanese capitalism underpinned its inexorable rise or created an unstable structure of 'crony capitalism' that inevitably would collapse in the context of increasing global competition. But it does help explain why certain institutional arrangements may have emerged – to cope with market uncertainty. In any case, as Krugman (2008c: 56–76) points out, Japan's slump in the 1990s reflected the fact that its institutional structures had evolved to increase, as opposed to reduce, market uncertainty. Similarly Asian economies were more vulnerable to financial panic "not because of crony capitalism, or indeed what would usually be considered bad government policies. Rather, they had become more vulnerable partly because they had opened up their financial markets – because they had, in fact, become better free market economies, not worse" (Krugman, 2008c: 97).

10 In response to such issues, Branston *et al.* (2006a) suggest, in a manner reminiscent and consistent with Galbraith (1973a), that corporate governance should evolve to become better aligned to the public interest.

11 As Parker (2005: 443) notes: "glimmers of Galbraith's insights still shine through today. For example, the consistently greater benefits mergers bestow on the technostructure's senior managers and outside financial advisers than on the corporations shareholders support Galbraith's claim about the ability of managers to optimize their advantage compared to that of the company's legal owners to do so. So,

too, the use of stock options and other incentives in management pay schemes, intended by their proponents to align the divergent interest of managers and owners more closely, has led to managerial practices that have boosted short-term performance at the cost of the long-term health of the stock and company, a recipe for managerial misbehavior and predatory financial market practices. These options, a major element in technostructure compensation, have let managers do spectacularly well even while their companies failed."

12 As Galbraith (1973a: 104) acknowledged in *Economics and the Public Purpose*: "as stockholders are dispersed by some forces, they are aggregated by others – notably insurance companies, pension funds, mutual funds and banks. This does something to arrest the deterioration of the power of the stockholder. However, the effect is easily exaggerated. The tradition of financial institutions in relation to management is usually passive."

13 As I argue in chapters 7, 8, and 9 *The New Industrial State* can also be interpreted as a theoretical contribution to the theory of the firm that links the rise of the modern firm to asset specific technological investments and the mitigation of uncertainty. It offers a conceptualization of the firm that emphasizes the strategic control of the modern firm by the technostructure that links well to the governance approach of the Warwick School (Cowling and Sugden, 1987a, 1987b, 1992, 1994, 1998a, 1998b, 1999; Cowling and Tomlinson, 2000, 2002, 2005; Coffey and Tomlinson, 2003, 2006; Branston *et al.*, 2006a, 2006b; Sugden, 1997).

2 *A life in our times*

What John Kenneth Galbraith's life gives us is more than the chance to see the prodigious career of a single man. It is the opportunity to revisit not only his own views about how modern economies (and governments) should operate, but the larger world of transformed, and still transforming, economic theories of which they are a part and with which they sometimes clash, to gauge the economies they seek to guide, and thus to understand something larger about where we are all now going.

Richard Parker (2005: 14)

Galbraith himself has been immersed in politics almost from the cradle.

Arthur M. Schlesinger, Jr (1999: 29)

John Kenneth Galbraith was one of the leading progressive intellectuals of the post-World War II period. He is principally associated with writing a series of intellectually demanding yet rewarding books, aimed at a general readership. His purpose was to alert the public to the social consequences of the major transformations in the economic structure that were occurring, notably the rise of the modern corporation. His disdain and sarcastic wit targeted abuses of business power and the sometimes unjust accumulation of private wealth, in the context of poor and under-funded public services.

Galbraith's analysis was hugely shaped by the events, circumstance, and political philosophy that influenced him. But Galbraith was more than just an academic. He was a man of practical affairs who enjoyed and benefited from a wide and varied set of roles, ranging from speechwriter, journalist, political advisor, bureaucrat and administrator, government analyst and ambassador. Galbraith did not, it is fair to say, conform to the caricature of an ivory tower academic. As the interview with Galbraith in chapter 12 highlights, his academic contributions were greatly influenced by his close association with events, people, and power.[1] His economic contributions need to be viewed in this context.

The purpose of this chapter therefore is to provide a brief introductory overview of John Kenneth Galbraith's life highlighting the major influences and experiences that shaped his thought. Those desiring a more comprehensive assessment are advised to consult Parker's (2005) excellent biography, which provides more detailed information on the life and times of Galbraith and the development of his thought.

Canadian beginnings

Galbraith was born on October 15, 1908 in Iona Station, a small town on the northern shore of Lake Erie and he grew up in Southern Ontario, part of Scotch Canada. This was an area settled by Scottish immigrants in the 1820s and 1830s (see Galbraith, 1964b). Since childhood, Galbraith went by the name "Ken." He vehemently disliked his given name "John," which came from an uncle after whom he was named. By the time Galbraith was a teenager, his uncle John had become a heavy drinker, and the whole family dropped "John" in favor of "Ken." Galbraith was born into a family of farmers – his parents owned two modest farms totaling 150 acres. In his autobiography – *A Life in our Times* – Galbraith (1981) regrets, however, that his schooling was interrupted frequently by farm work and that his academic record was rather undistinguished.

Parker (1999) highlights how Galbraith's father, Archie, was a major force in his life, especially after his mother died at the age of 49, when Galbraith was only 15.[2] Archie was an educated and opinionated man. Although he was born into a family of farmers, Archie, with his family's support, trained as a teacher. It was only when his father died, that Archie decided to go back into farming – a decision made easier by the fact that he had recently married. Farming was not Archie's only occupation. He was "a man of standing," who "helped establish the local telephone exchange and a cooperative insurance company, and for many years was a township and county official, supervising the auditing of local finances" (Parker, 2005: 27). Archie was active in local politics and a senior official in the county branch of the Canadian Liberal Party. And Galbraith would often travel around the county with his father:

> He has often retold the story of his father striding before a crowd gathered in a neighbor's barnyard and mounting a large manure pile. Galbraith

says his father called for silence from the surprised onlookers, then with a straight face (but a twinkle in his eye), "apologized with ill-concealed sincerity for speaking from the Tory platform." (Parker, 1999: 156)

In the fall of 1926, Galbraith enrolled at Ontario Agricultural College (OAC), which is now the University of Guelph, located about 50 miles west of Toronto. His intent was to study agricultural economics. The curriculum at OAC involved mainly practical instruction in the agricultural arts – how to build a good dairy stable and how to raise quality livestock. To earn extra spending money Galbraith wrote a weekly column describing new and useful agricultural practices for his hometown newspaper. But as the Great Depression began, Galbraith realized it made no sense to improve the quality of livestock if the livestock could not be sold at a decent price. So he switched his field of study to farm economics, seeking to understand the determinants of farm prices. Besides the fact that it let him focus on a practical problem, Galbraith made the switch for pragmatic reasons; he realized that understanding the causes of low farm prices: "might help me get a job. As the Depression continued, there would, logically, be a demand for those with a remedy" (Galbraith, 1981: 15).

Galbraith spent five years at OAC, the fifth year owing mainly to health problems (tuberculosis) and poor preparation for college (Parker, 2005: 33). During his last year there Galbraith noticed a posting for a research assistant position at Berkeley that was sponsored by the Giannini Foundation of Agricultural Economics.[3] It carried a stipend of $60 a month, a princely sum of money during the Great Depression. So he applied for the position, was accepted, and spent his graduate student days at Berkeley (Galbraith, 1971: 259). Galbraith claimed that his years at Berkeley were among the best of his life. In his courses he was introduced to the great economists, both past and present – Smith, Ricardo, Marx, Marshall, the German historical school, Veblen, as well as the early Keynes. The ferment of radicalism was apparent in his contemporaries, promoting an appreciation of Marxism and its wider emancipatory programme:

The graduate students with whom I associated in the thirties were uniformly radical and the most distinguished were communists. I listened to them eagerly and would like to have joined both the conversation and the Party but here my agricultural background was a real handicap. It meant that, as a matter of formal Marxian doctrine, I was politically immature. Among the merits of capitalism to Marx was the fact that it rescued men from the idiocy of rural life. I had only very recently been retrieved. I sensed this bar and I knew also that my pride would be deeply hurt by rejection. So I kept outside. There was possibly one other factor. Although I recognized that the system could not and should not survive, I was enjoying it so much that secretly, I was a little sorry. (Galbraith, 1971: 281–2)[4]

At Berkeley Galbraith, for the first time, experienced knowledgeable teachers such as E. T. Grether, Henry Erdman, and Leo Rogin, who encouraged debate, no doubt influencing his lifelong commitment to academic freedom and plurality.[5] During his second year his stipend was raised to $70 per month. In his third year Galbraith was sent to Davis to head up the Departments of Economics, Agricultural Economics, and Accounting and Farm Management. He was required to teach courses in all of these areas, and his annual pay was increased to $1800 (Galbraith, 1971: 287). The administrative and teaching demands were not that great, however, and Galbraith had enough time to write his doctoral dissertation during the year. His Ph.D. thesis, on the expenditures of California counties, nevertheless: "was without distinction ... The purpose was to get the degree" (Galbraith, 1981: 22).

Cambridge beckons

In the spring of 1933, Galbraith received an offer from Harvard (Cambridge, USA), for an instructorship position at an annual salary of $2,400. With the Harvard offer in hand and ready to bargain, he went to negotiate with his dean, for Galbraith had heard this was how an academic advanced. To his horror, the dean: "congratulated me warmly on my offer, gave me the impression that he thought Harvard was being reckless with its money and said that I should go ... The great love of my life was over" (Galbraith, 1971: 288). And so Galbraith went off to Harvard, where – apart from an unhappy sojourn to Princeton and a stint as an editor of *Fortune* magazine – he spent the rest of his academic life, albeit with much time off to pursue his political and his writing interests.

At Harvard Galbraith quickly became involved in policy issues under the stewardship of the famous agricultural economist John

D. Black. He also began to make important political connections. In late 1933 the Brookings Institution decided to study the operations of the Farm Credit Administration, and Galbraith was put in charge of this study. In the fall of 1935 Galbraith first met Joseph Kennedy, Jr. and two years later John F. Kennedy arrived at Harvard (Galbraith, 1981: 53–60). An important early influence on Galbraith was his work for the Agricultural Adjustment Administration (AAA) beginning in 1934. This early experience in Washington taught Galbraith the importance of power, a theme that appears in much of his more mature work in economics. Owing to oversupply, the government was paying farmers not to grow crops, but this resulted in many surplus tenant farmers and sharecroppers. One key issue was how to divide government payments between farmers and their employees. The farmers, of course, wanted all the government money, but this created problems as their employees became extremely poor and migrated to northern cities. Liberals, like Galbraith, wanted the majority of the money to go to the poor farm workers. The eventual compromise was that money would continue to go only to farmers; but farmers agreed not to get rid of their employees and to provide them with some support.

More importantly, at Harvard Galbraith moved beyond agricultural economics. Several factors were at work in this transformation. The influential work of Berle and Means (1932) analyzed the impact of the large firms that had emerged to dominate the American economy, arguing that power in the firm was increasingly being transferred to managers, leaving shareholders as passive recipients of corporate dividends. At the same time Joan Robinson (1933) and Edward Chamberlin (1933) simultaneously produced a theoretical examination of the emerging industrial structure that was characterizing several industries.[6] These analyses were quickly assimilated by Galbraith and when, in 1935, he began a monograph on the causes of the Great Depression with the industrialist Henry S. Dennison, the argument focused on the macroeconomic impact of monopolistic competition in a manner that echoes Kalecki (1935).[7] However, the major influence on Galbraith occurred following the publication of *The General Theory*, when Keynes: "reached Harvard with tidal force" (Galbraith, 1981: 67). Galbraith, along with the younger Harvard faculty, read Keynes avidly and was an early convert.[8] Keynes inspired Galbraith through his incisive analysis and the fact that he was able to write in a manner that could capture the attention of his colleagues and the general public. Galbraith admired Keynes's pragmatic side – his ability to identify real world problems, analyze them, and develop sensible and relevant policy responses that could be acted on by politicians.

The year 1936 also saw Galbraith's political involvement deepen. He volunteered to help on the Roosevelt re-election campaign and took the message of Keynesiansim to Washington (Galbraith, 1971: chapter 3). At the suggestion of several other Democrats, he decided to apply for American citizenship, which was granted in 1937. In the fall of 1937 Galbraith became an American citizen and married Catherine Merriam Atwater – known as "Kitty." The newlyweds took a ship to England and headed to Cambridge, UK, where Galbraith was to serve as a Rockefeller Fellow. Keynes, who was recovering from his first heart attack, did not meet Galbraith. Instead Galbraith established close and lifelong friendships with Richard Kahn, Joan Robinson, Piero Sraffa, and Michal Kalecki. Once a week he would head to London to attend London School of Economics (LSE) seminars run by Friedrich von Hayek and Lionel Robbins. And on weekends and holidays Galbraith and his new wife would tour the English countryside and continental Europe (Galbraith, 1981: 70–9).

The political Galbraith

Returning to Harvard in 1938, Galbraith was asked to head a commission to review the public works programs of the New Deal. This meant frequent travel to Washington, and deeper immersion in the politics of the time. In 1939 Galbraith had his first face-to-face meeting with FDR (Galbraith, 1981: 95). In 1940 Lauchlin Currie recruited Galbraith to serve as the resident economist for the American Farm Bureau Federation, "a government-organized lobby on behalf of government services for agriculture" (Galbraith, 1981: 98). But Galbraith's talents as a writer were quickly discovered, and he spent most of his time writing political speeches and memos after being asked to be part of the White House speechwriting team for the 1940 election.

In 1941, as the USA was becoming more deeply involved in World War II, Galbraith was asked for his help in facilitating economic stabilization and resource mobilization by controlling prices in the War economy. Galbraith became deputy administrator of the Office of Price Administration (OPA), giving him effective control over the prices of most US goods until 1943 when he was removed from office and replaced by Chester Bowles.[9] Galbraith (1981: 170ff.) argued that his work at the OPA was a great success, largely as a result of the changing institutional structure of the US economy:

> We were successful also because, even in those days, concentration in American industry had gone far beyond the current estimate or appreciation of the textbooks. Oligopoly, the monopoly of the few, which had impressed itself on my classical thoughts at Harvard, was no longer the exception by 1941. For around half of the system it was the rule. Where a few large firms dominated an industry, as they did steel, aluminum, oil, chemicals, pharmaceuticals and many others, prices were already controlled by the seller. The supervening government control, however different in purpose, was not different in kind from what had been done under private auspices before. The administrative task was also greatly simplified. It is far easier to deal with a handful of large firms than with a plethora of small ones. Compliance was also facilitated by industrial concentration. Surveillance was easier. (Galbraith, 1981: 173)

Although national income grew a great deal during the war, shortages were limited to a few items, such as whiskey and gasoline. But when the controls were removed there was only a small increase in prices, offering *prima facie* evidence that inflationary pressures were actively managed and not just kept temporarily under control. Galbraith's work at the OPA also inspired a novel contribution to the theory of price control (see Galbraith, 1952b; Colander, 1984). Even Milton Friedman was moved to acknowledge Galbraith's contribution:

> Kenneth Galbraith has the company of many other people from many other points of view who are in favor of, or have from time to time espoused, wage and price control, but so far as I know, he is the only person who has made a serious attempt to present a theoretical analysis to justify his position, in a book called *A Theory of Price Control.* (Friedman, 1977: 12)

Galbraith (1952b) argued for controls on wages and prices as a way to deal with inflation in the postwar world. What is more, his experience at the OPA cemented his belief that wage and price controls are the most effective solution to the problem of inflation – a view he maintained throughout his life.

As the OPA was disbanded because of mounting political pressure, Galbraith joined the editorial staff of *Fortune* magazine, and worked there from 1943 to 1948. Galbraith credits his experience at *Fortune*, and especially its owner, Henry R. (Harry) Luce, for helping him develop his celebrated ability to write with grace and humor (Galbraith, 1981: 264; 1986: 409–16). Galbraith (1981: 268) also credits his years at *Fortune* with: consolidating his understanding of the dominance of the large corporation in the American economy; instructing him about how large firms actually operate; underscoring the importance of moving beyond the myths of the firm perpetuated in neo-classical textbooks; introducing him to the actual decision-making processes of large corporations; and forcing him to analyze the impact of these decisions on wider society.[10]

In the fall of 1944, George Ball was asked to provide an independent assessment of the results of the air force bombing of Germany. Ball asked Galbraith to join the efforts and to be in charge of assessing the economic effects of both German mobilization and the air attacks. Working under Galbraith was a virtual "who's who" of distinguished economists including Nicholas Kaldor, E. F. Schumacher, Paul Baran, Tibor Scitovsky, and Edward Dennison (who went onto become a major luminary in modern statistical analysis and growth accounting).[11] They began their study believing that the air attacks had greatly damaged the German economy. Much to their surprise they found that the US bombing of Germany actually aided the war effort because it destroyed civilian businesses in the big cities, leaving many people without jobs and in need of employment. But the military factories of Germany were generally located on greenfield sites outside the big cities that were bombed. So the bombing generated an increased supply of labor for producing military goods (Galbraith, 1981: 199–205).[12] This conclusion was inconvenient to the US Air Force and, unsurprisingly, was quietly ignored.

Based on this study Galbraith also concluded that the German war economy was badly run. He made this case in *Fortune* (Galbraith, 1945), despite misgivings from the editors; indeed, its radical thesis was at odds with the dominant interpretation of the German war machine (Galbraith, 1981: 229). According to Galbraith, Hitler's intrusion into technical areas, where he had no competence, resulted in poor decision-making and created serious problems for the German economy. Another problem, Galbraith argued, was German overconfidence at the beginning of the war. After quickly occupying large parts of Europe, Hitler expected that his easy successes would continue. This led to considerable under-mobilization by Germany. Galbraith (1946a) also produced a ten-point plan that anticipated the Marshall Plan for redeveloping Europe that was set forth by Secretary of State George Marshall in the spring of 1947.

During the fall of 1948 Galbraith returned to Harvard and academic life. His teaching responsibilities included agricultural economics and industrial organization, but his focus was more on writing and politics. Soon came two books on power relationships, *American Capitalism* (Galbraith, 1952a) and the aforementioned *A Theory of Price Control* (Galbraith, 1952b), plus a history of the stock market bubble of the 1920s and its subsequent crash, *The Great Crash, 1929* (Galbraith, 1955a). The aim of *American Capitalism* and *The Great Crash, 1929* was partly to explain and justify the then new Keynesian philosophy, which was still viewed with suspicion. *The Great Crash, 1929* sets out a Keynesian analysis of animal spirits and associated stock market instabilities, providing one of the most authoritative expositions of the factors that lead to the 1929 bubble.[13] As White (1990: 67) remarks: "Galbraith's classic book still provides the most commonly accepted explanation of the 1929 boom and crash."[14] But these books also sought to highlight the importance of history and the profound transformation in economic structure that was being observed in the American economy, and how that was underpinning prosperity.

American Capitalism in particular argued that America's large and dominating corporations, though they had power to control their markets, also sustained the modern technological progress fundamental to economic growth. The main argument of *American Capitalism* was, however, that new restraints on private economic power emerged on the other side of the market to limit the power of large firms – what Galbraith labeled countervailing power. Galbraith argued that the emergence of sources of countervailing power challenged the traditional conceptions of competition:

> Competition which, at least since the time of Adam Smith, has been viewed as the autonomous regulator of economic activity and the only available regulatory mechanism apart from the state, has in fact, been superseded. Not entirely to be sure. There are still important markets where the power

> of the firm as (say) a seller is checked or circumscribed by those who provide a similar or a substitute product or service. This, in the broadest sense that can be meaningful, is the meaning of competition. The role of the buyer on the other side of such markets is essentially a passive one. It consists in looking for, perhaps asking for, and responding to the best bargain. The active restraint is provided by the competitor who offers, or threatens to offer, a better bargain. By contrast, in the typical modern market of a few sellers, the active restraint is provided not by competitors but from the other side of the market by strong buyers. Given the convention against price competition, it is the role of the competitor that becomes passive. (Galbraith, 1952a: 119)

Although *American Capitalism* is remembered primarily for its exposition of the theory of countervailing power, it also contains the seeds of *The Affluent Society* and *The New Industrial State.*[15] It is important to note, however, that in his subsequent works Galbraith did not abandon his thesis of countervailing power, but instead sought to move beyond its acknowledged limitations:

> That a countervailing assertion of economic power is the normal answer to original economic power, I still wholly believe. But in 1952 I made it far more inevitable and rather more equalizing than, in practice, it ever is. Countervailing power often does not emerge. Numerous groups – the ghetto young, the rural poor, textile workers, women clerical workers, many consumers – remain weak or helpless. (Galbraith, 1981: 284)

In the summer of 1955 Galbraith arranged for a year-long sabbatical. He used a Guggenheim Fellowship to go to Switzerland in order to write a book on poverty. This he combined with a good deal of travel, including his first trip to India, where he saw the poverty of less-developed countries first hand. Published in 1958, *The Affluent Society*, along with Michael Harrington's (1962) *The Other America*, helped bring the problem of poverty amidst affluence to the attention of the American public, culminating in President Johnson declaring a "war on poverty" in 1964.[16]

The success of *The Affluent Society* made Galbraith a household name.[17] The central argument of *The Affluent Society* was that the prosperity and improvements in income levels brought about by Keynesianism through its general commitment to increased production and consumption, did not fully address all the needs of a great society.[18] Anticipating much of the contemporary backlash against consumerism, globalization, and climate change, Galbraith argued against increased production being the key to solving contemporary social problems, arguing instead for increased spending on social programs to address long-standing social needs and inequalities. Parker (2005: 288–9) summarizes the central thesis of *The Affluent Society* as follows:

1. The central focus of orthodox economics has been (and still was) on "output" efficiency, measured by the rational allocation of resources via the private market.
2. Keynes, to our great advantage, shifted that focus to a second idea, that of a guided "growth" efficiency: the maximization of output through government's efforts at macromanagement of private markets. The resulting full employment helped solve the twin issues of inequality and insecurity, which private markets and "output" efficiency had not.
3. The conventional wisdoms endorsing "this paramount position of production" in both models, however, were taking no account of the resultant postwar prosperity, and remained focused on maximization through private production for private consumption. The result was what Galbraith called "social imbalance," in which the market for privately sold goods and services was being saturated, while the demand for public goods – clean air, more parks and schools, better healthcare, less crime, less crowded transportation systems – remained unfilled.
4. The abundance of private goods and services was all the more anomalous because to a great degree, thanks to large corporations' advertising and market efforts, private "wants" ... which privately sold goods are meant to satisfy, are as much a corporate product as the goods sold to satisfy them ...
5. Finally the "paramount position of production" made persistent inflation the inevitable rule. Operating near full capacity, a production driven economy allowed its powerful actors to pass on wage and price increases to consumers, and resisted conventional fiscal and monetary policies that sought to brake inflation.

In the conventional interpretation of Keynes, it did not matter whether the Government invested in public services, military defense, or used tax policy to increase consumer spending. What mattered was that the Government took action to raise the level of effective demand to stave off recessions. In *The Affluent Society* Galbraith challenged this view. He argued that using Keynesian policy to promote consumption and production would not only increase the supply of private goods, but that it would also require the talents of the Madison Avenue marketers to ensure the ultimate consumption of these goods. That the public needed to be persuaded to consume such goods suggested *prima facie* that they were not needed in a basic way. In contrast the America of that time had few public goods and services, and there was a lack of investment in basic and needed services, such as housing, transportation, and health. That this social imbalance must be rectified was a core argument of *The Affluent Society*.

After finishing *The Affluent Society*, Galbraith went on a lecture tour of Poland and Yugoslavia in May of 1958 at the invitation of Oscar Lange. During the trip he spent a lot of time with Michal Kalecki. In his diary of this trip Galbraith (1958d) focused on the uneven quality of life in Eastern Europe. Galbraith noted both the clean streets and the high educational achievements attained; but he also remarked on the poor quality of workmanship on buildings and roads, and the general drabness of life there. In the fall of 1959 Harvard appointed Galbraith to the Paul Warburg Chair in Economics, established in honor of one of the architects of the Federal Reserve System and one of its original Governors. At the same time, Harvard gave Galbraith two terms off to begin work on the sequel to *The Affluent Society* – what was to become *The New Industrial State*. Work on the book was interrupted when John Kennedy was elected President in November 1960 and appointed Galbraith Ambassador to India.[19]

Notwithstanding his extensive academic activities, the 1950s and the 1960s were also a period of high political activity. Galbraith was one of the founders of the liberal Americans for Democratic Action. He was an adviser and speechwriter for Adlai Stevenson in his two presidential campaigns, and then for John Kennedy in his 1960 presidential campaign. In the 1952 Stevenson campaign, Galbraith wrote on farm policy and economics. John Bartlow Martin (1976) describes some rather tense meetings of Stevenson's speech writers during the heat of the campaign. In an obscure saloon in Springfield, Illinois, where the writers lunched to avoid the press and relax, they sat around a table next to the jukebox. As Martin (1976: 636) reports: "Once when somebody started to put a nickel in the jukebox, Galbraith said to him, 'I'll give you a dime if you don't play it'." Between the 1952 and 1956 presidential campaigns, Galbraith (1981: 296ff.) attempted to teach Keynesian economics to Stevenson, who was skeptical of running budget deficits and thought Keynes a subversive.

Over time his relationship with Stevenson cooled, and Galbraith began to actively support John Kennedy (Reisman, 1980: 170). Surprisingly, Galbraith was more actively involved in the Stevenson campaigns than the Kennedy campaign, even though he was personally closer to Kennedy than to Stevenson. Nevertheless, his Ambassadorial appointment was testament to his political standing and access to the corridors of power. Parker (2005: 348) highlights that Galbraith's preference at that time was to enter into politics: "Galbraith's first choice wasn't the ambassadorship in New Delhi ... his real hope was that Kennedy would arrange his appointment to the President-elect's now vacant Senate seat."[20] Instead the vacant seat was reserved for Teddy Kennedy, and Galbraith was offered other roles in the administration, before settling on India:

> Kennedy, I've always believed, was pleased to have me in his administration but at a suitable distance such as India. This saved him from a too close identification with my now extensively articulated economic views. At his very first press conference in Los Angeles after his nomination he was asked if he and the Democratic Party could now be considered committed to the ideas in *The Affluent Society*. He evaded with skill and grace. A few days after the election he asked Arthur Schlesinger if I wanted to be Chairman of the Council of Economic Advisers. Schlesinger mentioned my interest in India. (Galbraith, 1981: 389)[21]

From India, Galbraith sent Kennedy telegrams advising against the growing US involvement in Vietnam, against the planned (and infamous) Bay of Pigs operation in Cuba, and against clandestine CIA operations in India (Galbraith, 1969a, 1998). Galbraith left India in May 1963 to return to Harvard. After the death of Kennedy in November, Galbraith continued to provide extensive policy advice to the Oval Office. He advised Lyndon Johnson on his misgivings about the escalating war in Vietnam and on the question of reducing poverty in the USA. In 1964, Johnson appointed Galbraith to the White House Task Force that was responsible for formulating a "war on poverty" – part of "The Great Society" agenda.

But as Johnson increased US involvement in Vietnam, Galbraith became a leader of the anti-war movement. In November 1967 Galbraith published *How to Get Out of Vietnam* (Galbraith, 1967b), which argued for pulling US troops back to the cities and coastal areas, setting up some sanctuaries that could be defended, and negotiating a respectable withdrawal with the opposition. Two years later, *How to Control the Military* (Galbraith, 1969b) explained how both the military and the firms supplying their needs, had acquired considerable power and influence over US government policy and the articulation of national interests. It forcefully argued that arms control agreements were necessary, as were elected politicians who would stand up to, what Eisenhower had labeled, the military-industrial complex.[22] He also wrote about revitalizing the Democratic Party and making it a true alternative to the Republican Party (Galbraith, 1970b).

In 1967 Galbraith published *The New Industrial State.* Although widely read this is his most technically demanding and major theoretical work. Many of its themes were outlined in the 1966 Reith lectures a year earlier (Galbraith, 1966a, 1966b, 1966c, 1966d, 1966e, 1966f).[23] Taking forward the arguments of *The Affluent Society*, he focused on the large corporation and its governing scientific elite – the technostructure – that was responsible for the technological and economic advance that underpinned the successes of American capitalism. Parker (2005: 439–41), following Solow (1967), summarizes *The New Industrial State* as advancing six key ideas:

Thesis 1: The giant corporation, for Galbraith is the 'characteristic organization' of modern capitalism ... a thousand or so giants dominate the economic landscape, not only because of their advantages of size (due largely to what economists call "returns to scale") but because complexity and cost of advanced technological investment requires extensive bureaucratic organization ...

Thesis 2: Shareholders, the nominal owners of the corporations, have little power over corporate decision-making compared to the top managers and senior specialists in operations, marketing, and research and development, whom Galbraith calls collectively "the technostructure" ...

Thesis 3: The members of the technostructure for the most part don't own significant blocks of stock themselves and, disliking uncertainty in the company's prospects, seek to reduce risk by giving up classic 'profit-maximizing' principles so beloved by economics in favor of growth with predictable profits. They do this by various means that introduce a new level of corporate-led "planning" into the market as a whole – Galbraith explicitly identifies it collectively as 'the planning system' – which overtly tries to manipulate demand as well as supply ...

Thesis 4: In lieu of classical "profit-maximizing," the giant corporation purses its end of survival and independence by concentrating on steady but maximal sales growth, consistently predictable earnings, technological virtuosity, and insulation from what it considers adverse interference (though not assistance) from Government ...

Thesis 5: Advertising, plus a national ideology that praises the constant growth of privately consumable goods and services, may serve the giant corporation and its technostructure, but it misdirects the collective energies and attention of citizens away from the truth that the United States for the most part is already awash in affluence ...

Thesis 6: The key resource of the modern economy is no longer its huge industrial capacity for producing goods but the capacity to mobilize organized intelligence. (Here Galbraith was anticipating what others were later to christen the new "information economy.") Central to this new economy is the modern "educational and scientific elite": the scholars, teachers, and researchers who work in universities and nonprofit research centers whose innovations in science, technology and social organization are woven into the work of big corporations, which provide research funds, endowed chairs, and lucrative consultancies in exchange for these valuable new technologies.

The most contentious thesis of *The New Industrial State* was that the large investments in advanced technology culminated in the need to control the response of the consumer and to influence the pattern of Government spending. *The New Industrial State* also examined the symbiosis of the military industrial complex with the Government – which was no doubt influenced by Galbraith's role in assessing the strategic impact of bombing in the USA and his well-documented exchanges with Secretary of State Dean Rusk, and the State Department during his time as ambassador to India.

During the late 1960s, the 1970s, and the early 1980s, Galbraith continued to play an active, if somewhat diminished, role in politics. In 1968 he worked in the presidential campaign of Senator Eugene McCarthy (seconding his nomination at the Chicago Democratic convention), and in 1972 he worked for Senator George McGovern, serving as a delegate for McGovern at the Democratic convention in Miami. He then worked in the presidential campaigns of Representative Morris Udall in 1976 and Senator Edward Kennedy in 1980.

A tenured professor

In the 1970s Galbraith continued his efforts to bring economic ideas to a more general public. In *Economics and the Public Purpose* Galbraith completed his major trilogy. Galbraith presented a broader, more comprehensive view of the economy that attempted to set out more clearly the relationship of the planning system to the market and other aspects of social life. There he elaborated the nexus between the economic superstructure and the social roles of men and women, highlighted the increasingly transnational nature of economic life and again pressed the themes of social balance and tackling environmental degradation. Galbraith was more explicit than ever before of the policy implications of his analysis and made a strong case for emancipatory change:

> *Economics and the Public Purpose* advanced a score of ... proposals for a new American economy. For example, he called for an expanded and increased minimum wage; a return to a more progressive taxation system; a guaranteed annual income for the poor; sharply increased revenue-sharing with states and cities; abandonment of "full" employment, narrowly defined, as a federal policy goal; heavily increased funding for the arts; radically diminished power for monetary policy and the Federal Reserve; greater government support for unionization; international commodity price stabilization; the advancement, under certain specified conditions, of a "fair trade" policy, rather than doctrinal support for unqualified 'free trade'; and an effective (rather than Nixonian) wage-and-price-control system. (Parker, 2005: 514–15)

In *Economics and the Public Purpose* Galbraith noted the convergence and similarities of advanced economic development across the USA and Russia, and made the case for the nationalization of parts of the economy and in particular for the development of universal public services, such as healthcare.[24] Again, and reflecting his post-Keynesian approach, he anticipated the widespread stagflation of the 1970s – a consequence of the way the bimodal nature of the American economy responds to external shocks – and once again advocated wage and price controls to subdue the inflation.[25] In doing so *Economics and the Public Purpose* embraced a popular radical sentiment and attempted to capture the zeitgeist, winning a new audience in the process. Galbraith even mischievously described his ideas in terms of "the new socialism" – which both inflamed and confused attractors and detractors alike (Schlesinger, 1984).[26]

In the second half of the decade, Galbraith worked on the British Broadcasting Corporation's (BBC) television series and associated book *The Age of Uncertainty* (Galbraith, 1977a) – which was syndicated in the USA on the Public Broadcasting Service (PBS).[27] Work on that television series also resulted in a much neglected book on money and monetary institutions – *Money: Whence it came, where it went* (Galbraith, 1975). *Money* presented a Keynesian history of money that highlighted the endogeneity of the money supply and the associated speculative manias that banking institutions fuel. And like *The Great Crash, 1929* it also sought to debunk the social elevation of those that are associated with finance and handling money. Similarly his book *Almost Everyone's Guide to Economics* (Galbraith and Salinger, 1978) was geared, as the title proclaimed, to increase general economic literacy. During the 1970s and 1980s Galbraith also received a degree of professional recognition. In 1972 he served as president of the American Economic Association (Galbraith, 1973b); and in 1976 he was honored by the Association of Evolutionary Economics – receiving its Veblen-Commons award (Galbraith, 1977b). In 1982 he was elected to the fifty-member American Academy of Arts and Letters, the first economist to be so honored. Two years later, he became president of the Academy.

Galbraith continued to be professionally active during this period. He provided both the "moral and financial support" to help start the *Journal of Post Keynesian Economics* (King, 2002: 135), which began publishing in 1978 under the joint editorship of Paul Davidson and Sidney Weintraub (see Galbraith, 1978a). Following the untimely death of Weintraub in 1984 (cf. Galbraith, 1985), Davidson – another longstanding friend of Galbraith's – became its sole editor. Immediately the journal became one of the major publishing outlets for post Keynesian economists, with Galbraith serving as the chairman of the Honorary Board of Editors from its inception until his death.

Although retiring from Harvard in 1975, and greatly reducing his active engagement in politics not long after, Galbraith continued to write about economic and policy issues throughout the 1980s and the 1990s. He strongly opposed the conservative trend in the USA and the resurgence of greed as a primary motivation for individual behavior.

He was especially critical of the trickle-down, supply-side policies of Reagan and Bush Senior, which masked the politically aided consolidation of corporate and economic power, fueling the re-emergence of the super rich (cf. Krugman, 2007, 2008c).[28] Galbraith also opposed the Clinton administration's reductions in domestic spending and welfare reform as unnecessary, arguing that it was an undesirable accommodation to conservative Republicans in Congress.[29]

Galbraith's writings in the 1980s and 1990s saliently emphasized the importance of studying history in order to understand the economy, and the importance of understanding the locus of power in order to understand the real world. *The Anatomy of Power* (Galbraith, 1983a) expounded in detail his mature thoughts on the nature of power and its relation to the economic and political system. *A History of Economics* (Galbraith, 1987) attempted an integration of economic history and the history of economic thought to demonstrate the link between the march of events and the impact on ideas.[30] *The Culture of Contentment* (Galbraith, 1992) and *The Good Society* (Galbraith, 1996b) focused on the complacency in addressing the needs of the poor in the late twentieth century. Their aim was to slow and reverse the march of, what Krugman (2007) now calls "movement conservatism". *A Journey Through Economic Time* (Galbraith, 1994a; cf. McCloskey, 1994) provided an overview and history of economic policy making in the USA over the course of the last century. *Name Dropping* (Galbraith, 1999) takes us on a trip through the economic policies of presidents Roosevelt, Truman, Kennedy, and Lyndon Johnson. And *The Economics of Innocent Fraud* (Galbraith, 2004) returned to the central role of the corporation and re-emphasized the shift in authority from shareholders and board members to management.

Finally it is important to note that, like Keynes before him, Galbraith was also a man of letters, biographies, travelogues, and the arts. He was an expert on Indian painting (Randhawa and Galbraith, 1968). He wrote several novels (Galbraith, 1963, 1964b, 1990b) and travelogues (Galbraith, 1973d, 1986: section VII). He penned a series of prefaces and reflections covering such diverse figures as Evelyn Waugh, Anthony Trollope, James Mill, John Steinbeck, and David Niven, as well as compiling a series of biographical sketches of major politicians including de Gaule, Churchill, Roosevelt, Lyndon Johnson, Eisenhower, Richard Nixon, Chairman Khrushchev, Senator Paul

Douglas, among others (Galbraith, 1971, 1979a, 1986; cf. Keynes, 1919, 1972b). Similarly his views of the social imbalance created by the emergence of the modern corporation led to sustained reflection on the role of aesthetics and the artist in modern life (see Galbraith, 1960: chapter 3; 1966f; 1973a: chapter 7; 1986: section IV).

Academia redux

As should be clear from this brief overview, a variety of practical influences and experiences shaped Galbraith and, as we shall see, his subsequent theoretical contributions. Moreover, throughout his long life in both public and academic roles Galbraith was true to his liberal values. He consistently sought to highlight the uneven impact of the economic structure on the blue-collar worker, the poor, and the otherwise disadvantaged. And he encouraged action as both an insider and vocal outsider, through wit, apportionment of guilt, and through the advocacy of a range of practical policy proposals.

Maintaining such a path required considerable intellectual courage and honesty. Galbraith's readiness to criticize injustice and hypocrisy, already visible when he served as the Price Tsar during World War II, almost resulted in his being denied tenure at Harvard. In those early postwar years – at the height of McCarthyism – to be a follower of Keynes and an advocate of government spending to alleviate the unnecessary hardships of recession, could arouse suspicions of subversion – and did.[31] Galbraith also took an early and unpopular stand against American involvement in Vietnam; he continued to press publicly for American withdrawal after leaving office, demonstrating a degree of prescience and courage in the face of powerful and influential vested interests.

In the rest of the book I attempt to summarize Galbraith's principal economic contributions. It is worth reiterating that the purpose here is introduction, exposition, and development, rather than detailing the numerous criticisms and judgments that have been made of the Galbraithian system. The companion four volume reference collection *John Kenneth Galbraith: The Economic Legacy* reproduces Galbraith's seminal contributions, details the mainstream reaction and highlights recent developments in Galbraithian economics (see Dunn, 2012). Readers can also find more details and the numerous criticisms that have been leveled at Galbraith's contributions in the several excellent overviews of his work (Hession, 1972; Sharpe, 1973; Gambs, 1975; Munro,

1977; Pratson, 1978; Reisman, 1980; Stanfield, 1996; Waligorski, 2006). The two Galbraith (1977c, 2001) readers, the three Festschriften (Bowles *et al.*, 1989; Sasson, 1999; Keaney, 2001), as well as the collection of interviews with Galbraith (Stanfield and Stanfield, 2004) also offer an excellent overview and discussion of Galbraith's thought. The interested reader who seeks to explore Galbraith's extensive contributions in more depth would be advised to consult these sources.

Notes

1 On June 22, 2001 I interviewed Professor J. K. Galbraith and his wife and constant companion Kitty at their most agreeable home in Cambridge, Boston. We talked at length about his own intellectual history and origins of his contribution to the theory of the firm and their interconnecting relationships and experiences with the two Cambridges and Post Keynesianism. The interview, which is reproduced in chapter 12, is an edited and abridged version of that discussion.

2 Stanfield (1996: 1–2) suggests that Galbraith's childhood experiences may have influenced his latter psychological problems: "Galbraith recalls having had a happy childhood but there were some bleaker aspects. His mother died when he was fourteen and the family struggled for some time adjusting to the trauma. Galbraith found farm labor boring in large part and no doubt there was much of it to do. He was a gangly youth, without talent in schoolboy athletics, and somewhat prone to sudden mood swings and difficulties with a strict teacher/principal that suggest behavioral adjustment problems. No doubt these are early indications of the 'cloud' of depression for which Galbraith sought psychotherapy in the early 1950s. The experience of therapy revealed a longstanding pattern of cyclical 'euphoria and depression'. The insights gained left Galbraith with an abiding appreciation of the services of psychiatrists" (see also Galbraith, 1981: 304–5). No doubt future research will explore whether this also had an influence on his theorizing, for example on the motivations of the technostructure or the psychology of mass manias. Keynes's thinking on animal spirits and stock market instabilities, for example, was influenced by the theories of Sigmund Freud (see Skidelsky, 1992: 88, 188, 234, 237, 414; Winslow, 1986a, 1986b, 1989, 1990, 1992, 1993).

3 It resulted in a series of three papers published by the Giannini Foundation (see Voorhies, Galbraith, and Todd, 1933a, 1933b; Galbraith, 1934).

4 This reflection comes from Galbraith's engaging essay of his time in California, titled "Berkeley in the Thirties." It also found its way into his FBI file – see Galbraith's lampooning of the incompetence of the intelligence services in his essay, "My Forty Years with the FBI" (Galbraith, 1979a: 155–81).

5 As Galbraith (1971: 278–9) remarked: "At Berkeley I suddenly encountered professors who knew their subject and, paradoxically, invited debate on what they knew. They also had time to talk at length with graduate students ... I first discovered from Henry Erdman ... and Howard Tolley ... that a professor might like to be informed on some subject by a graduate student – might not just be polite but pleased. So profound was that impression that I never stopped informing people thereafter."

6 Galbraith (1981: 64) notes that: "Chamberlin and Robinson showed that a few firms, an oligopoly, could produce the same (or a similar) result as monopoly – prices too high, production too small. The firms did not need to communicate, only reflect rationally on the price and production that was best for all. And Chamberlin went on to argue that almost any producer of a consumer product, by advertising or by otherwise urging the unique features of his product, his location or even his own personality as a seller, could establish a partial monopoly. This was monopolistic competition."

7 More recently Bruce (2000, 2001) has reconsidered the intellectual impact of Henry Dennison on J. K. Galbraith's theorizing. Bruce draws our attention to two monographs written with Dennison (one as a ghost writer) both of which examine the rise, role and relevance of big business for practical policy (see Dennison and Galbraith, 1938; Dennison *et al.*, 1938). Gambs (1975: 40) highlights how these early books contained the seeds of his later contributions: "The Dennison-Galbraith book was published by the Oxford University Press. Galbraith seems not to be very proud of it and would willingly have it forgotten. It no longer appears in the list printed opposite the title page of his recent books ... Yet he concedes that it wasn't so bad as all that. Actually it is nothing to be ashamed of; indeed, it is very good if account be taken of his youth and of the times in which it was written. It popularizes the Berle-Means work on the modern corporation and makes suggestions on how mammoth companies could be controlled in the public interest. The authors do not propose the breaking up of huge firms into little ones. Here are the germs of ideas later developed in *The Affluent Society* and *The New Industrial State*."

8 As Parker (2005: 298) notes: "Galbraith also never doubted that he was firmly grounded in Keynes's own thought in several important ways. First, he willingly embraced the idea that the economist was directly obliged to speak to, and persuade, the nonprofessional public, just as Keynes had done. But in the decades since *The Economic Consequences of the Peace*, no economist but Galbraith came even close to producing such a volume for the public. Second, like Keynes, Galbraith sought to define economics not as a scientific field of

'positive' assumptions that could be distinguished from the messier 'normative' issues of policy but as an instrumental practice that was designed to achieve central moral and political ends and that was at its best when economists educated and persuaded the public. This had been true of Keynes's masterpiece *The General Theory*, despite its admitted complexity, and of many other short, accessible works, such as *How to Pay for the War* and *The Economic Consequences of Mr. Churchill* ... And it was supremely true in Keynes's 'Economic Possibilities for Our Grandchildren,' with its prediction that in a few generations a new and unimaginable level of material abundance would 'lead us out of the tunnel of economic necessity into the daylight,' and release us from the antiquated strictures of 'maximizing' behavior in order to pursue other goals."

9 Galbraith was already deeply involved in World War II planning before Pearl Harbor, which came on December 7 of that year, with war declared the following day. Preparations were by that time deeply underway, and Galbraith was working as the director of the National Defense Advisory Commission, under the Secretary of Agriculture, Chester Davis. Galbraith moved over to the OPA in late 1941. He was sacked from OPA in May of 1943 but controls were not lifted until 1946 and OPA was not disbanded until then. Instead, Chester Bowles (father of Sam) was brought in to run it.

10 Chandler (1977: 482–3) points out that: "In the years after World War II the large managerial enterprise became even more powerful. It acquired control of an increasing share of the nation's economic activities, as well as a growing part of the industrial production of Europe and the rest of the world. In 1947, the two hundred largest industrials in the United States ... accounted for 30 percent of the value added in manufacturing and 47.2 percent of total corporate manufacturing assets. By 1963 ... they were responsible for 41 percent of the value added and 56.3 percent of assets. By 1968, that last figure had risen to 60.9 percent. These giant enterprises generated by far the largest share of nongovernment funds and provided most of the nongovernment personnel involved in industrial research and development."

11 It is important to note that several of these economists become lifelong friends as well making several important economic contributions and pursuing certain themes that are reflected in Galbraith's (1952a, 1958a, 1967a) mature view (see also Galbraith's comments in chapter 12 below). Kaldor's contributions are too extensive to do justice in summary, but as well as being a lifelong Keynesian he made several contributions to the theory of the firm, market imperfections, speculation and economic stability, money supply endogeneity, the role of increasing returns, technical progress, and cumulative causation,

argued for regional policies, and attacked the irrelevance of equilibrium economics, as well as being an advisor to Labour Governments (see Kaldor, 1950, 1970, 1972, 1978, 1983, 1985; see also the essays in Targetti and Thirlwall, 1989). Paul Baran, with Paul Sweezy (whom Galbraith also knew, see Galbraith, 1981: 50, 199, 327) wrote the radical *Monopoly Capitalism* (Baran and Sweezy, 1966). *Monopoly Capitalism* considered the divorce of ownership from control, the self perpetuating role of "inside" management, the internal generation of funds by the large modern corporation, as well as criticizing military Keynesianism and modern imperialism from a radical Marxist point of view. Sweezy (1939), who was one of Schumpeter's doctoral students (and denied tenure at Harvard for his Marxist views), wrote the seminal article on the Kinked Demand Curve, which was part of the re-examination of economic theory ushered in by the emergence of the large corporation. Sweezy (1942) also wrote an exposition of Marx's economics that is still, arguably, one of the best introductions to his thought. Fritz Schumacher's (1973) *Small is Beautiful* questioned the blind pursuit of the profit and progress, which promotes large organizations and specialization at the expense of inequality, inefficiency, and environmental pollution. Similarly Tibor Scitovsky (1943) published an important and much neglected article that started to question whether profits are automatically maximized by firms. Scitovsky's argument was that the entrepreneur in maximizing their utility may seek to trade off profits and income against leisure. In *The New Industrial State* Galbraith (1967a) questioned whether the technostructure automatically maximized profits or pursued other objectives such as technical virtuosity, growth, and prestige. I consider Galbraith's theory of the firm in more detail in chapters 7 and 8 below.

12 The economic report was published as *The Effects of Strategic Bombing on the German War Economy* (US SBS, 1945). Galbraith also participated in an assessment of aerial bombing on the Japanese economy. This study concluded that the Japanese economy was damaged by the US bombing raids (US SBS, 1946).

13 See Dunn (2003a, 2004, 2008a) for an exposition and analysis of Keynes's approach to investment, uncertainty and animal spirits.

14 As Gambs (1975: 47) highlights, *The Great Crash, 1929* "is charmingly written and Mark Van Doren is quoted as having said that it brought the language of poetry to history. Van Doren is, of course, competent to speak in his field; others may be more impressed by the book's virility of style, by its satire and ridicule. With joyous malice Galbraith tells us about the politicians and experts who, combining optimism

with ignorance, were talking though their hats during the frightening months of business collapse."

15 For example: "in the chapter entitled 'The Unseemly Economics of Opulence' (Galbraith, 1952a) ... [Galbraith] asserted that the American economy is wasteful and inefficient in a static sense, but that it can afford this waste because of its dynamic efficiency. The most spectacular waste is advertising and related selling costs which are uniquely characteristic of affluent societies. 'No one would advertise the sound-effects of processed breakfast foods striking the milk to ... [those] who have only the resources to buy oatmeal' (1952a: 106–107)" (Stanfield, 1996: 38). *The Affluent Society* was originally going to be called "The Opulent Society," but Galbraith thought it had a greasy, oily ring to it. Similarly Galbraith's analysis of technological innovation in *American Capitalism* develops many themes that were further explored in *The New Industrial State*.

16 As Hession (1972: 130) highlights, Harrington's *The Other America* is "a powerful and moving book, in which he claimed that there were between 40 and 50 million poor people in the nation. It is notable that Harrington was not as critical as others had been of Galbraith on poverty. He said that the Harvard professor had underestimated the problem, but he also had been one of the first writers to describe the new invisible poverty. Indeed in Harrington's view, Galbraith's achievement had been considerable. 'He was one of the first to understand that there are enough poor people in the United States to constitute a subculture of misery, but not enough of them to challenge the conscience and the imagination of the nation'." Galbraith sought to return and press such issues, which became more acute in the 1990s, in both *The Culture of Contentment* (1992) and *The Good Society* (1996b).

17 Parker (2005: 311) notes that: "*The Affluent Society* made John Kenneth Galbraith America's most famous economist. The book spent nearly a year on *The New York Times* best-seller list – unheard of for a book about economics – and as the title itself swiftly gained a permanent place in the English language, Galbraith was deluged with an almost unimaginable stream of requests for speeches, articles, interviews and TV appearances."

18 As Parker (2005: 660) highlights: "Affluent America in the 1950s was still far from achieving Keynes's post-scarcity ideals. Corporate America with its marketing dominance and massive advertising had chained the country to an endless treadmill of consumption that flooded the market with private goods, while the conservative politics with which the corporation was intimately intertwined left Government unable to fulfill the public's desire for 'public goods' or to achieve a final, permanent

elimination of residual poverty. Galbraith understood that any chance of creating a *liberal* Keynesian future required more than just tinkering at the margins by changing growth-rate assumptions and diverting some of the billions spent on arms to schools, roads and hospitals. Something much larger was called for, something that challenged society's 'conventional wisdom' across the board – from its habits of consumption to its domestic political alignments to its costly international behavior."

19 The history of Galbraith's time in India appears in his *Ambassador's Journal* (1969a).

20 Parker (2005: 348) continues, noting that: "Trial balloons suggesting the idea had appeared in the Boston papers and then in *The New York Times* right after the election. (Galbraith has always insisted that he wasn't the source for them). But reaction to them made him quickly realize that JFK had another candidate in mind; his younger brother Robert. Then, under intense pressure from their father, he appointed Bobby as Attorney General, which left the still younger brother Edward as the designee. But Ted's youth (at twenty eight) stood in the way of his appointment (the constitution set thirty as the minimum age for a US senator), and so Ben Smith an old family friend, was tapped as the seat's place holder until the President's younger brother become old enough to run in 1962."

21 This refutes Krugman's (1994: 14–15) assessment that: "Galbraith's influence never reached into the actual determination of policy. John F. Kennedy brought him into his administration, but literally put him as far from economic policy as possible by making him Ambassador to India. The actual architects of Kennedy's economic program were professors through and through. Indeed Kennedy was the first President to elevate the chairman of the Council of Economic Advisors, an organization staffed by professors on leave, to cabinet rank; and his council contained not one but two future winners of the Nobel Prize (James Tobin and Robert Solow)." Not only was Galbraith considered to Chair this committee it was in fact Galbraith (1981: 389–90) who chose Kennedy's Council of Economic Advisors, with Sargent Shriver and Arthur Schlesinger.

22 However, see Cypher (2008), who argues that although *How to Control the Military* boldly championed political and institutional reforms to curb "the military power," Galbraith's assertion that the military was the dominant force within the "military industrial complex" was never empirically demonstrated. Cypher (2008) also argues that Galbraith did not address adequately the crucial role that military outlays played in advancing major technological innovations which underwrote the

accumulation process. Instead Cypher argues that Veblen offered a more comprehensive analysis of the role of military expenditures. On the institutional origins of the Military Industrial Complex, see Brunton (1988).

23 At the time the Reith lectures were highly controversial. See, for example, the rejoinder by Allen (1967).

24 In terms of the convergence thesis, history suggests that Galbraith, in one sense was mistaken, but in another, he was right. Although the Soviet economy collapsed under the heavy weight of militarism and badly conceived state planning policies, what emerged was a mixed economy that approximated those of the West. This has led many commentators to note that modern economies had converged on a similar mixed economy dominated by large firms: "with the exception of the few absurdly communist states such as North Korea, all of today's many political economies lie along a recognizable spectrum of more-free-market versus less-free-market arrangements" (Kennedy, 2009).

25 In 1971 Richard Nixon imposed price controls on the American economy. These were quickly withdrawn and widely acknowledged as an unmitigated failure. Galbraith continued to defend such controls arguing that Nixon's administration pursued them half heartedly – explaining their failure – and that his experience during World War II showed that economy wide price control could be achieved. As Parker (2005: 565) notes: "Galbraith was not alone in advocating series use of wage and price controls to stem inflation. Barry Bosworth and Bruce McLaury of Brookings, James Tobin at Yale, Francis Bator at Harvard, and Wall Street economist Henry Kaufman all supported such controls, though several still saw the need as ad hoc rather than permanent."

26 According to Galbraith "the new socialism" is quite distinct from "classical" or "old" socialism, which was more ideological (see Galbraith, 1967a: 111–20; 1973a: 237–8, 292–303). For Galbraith (1973a: 296) "the new socialism" was directed at focusing development in areas such as health, housing and mass transportation where the modern corporation has found it difficult to develop: "The new socialism is not ideological; it is compelled by circumstance. The compelling circumstance ... is the retarded development of the market system. There are industries here which require technical competence, related organization and market power and related command over resource use if they are to render minimally adequate service." For such reasons Galbraith (1973a) argued for the development of publicly owned or publicly responsive organizations in areas of under development.

27 The television series was not without controversy: "Before it could be aired in the United States, *The Age of Uncertainty* started drawing

aggressive, bitter denunciation from American conservatives ... Late in 1976, managers at KCET, the Los Angeles PBS affiliate in charge of US distribution, decided that after each hour-long segment of the series a conservative critic must be allowed to 'respond', which the BBC had felt no need to arrange. They did so without telling the show's host or producer, who first learned about it at a private screening in New York just prior to the series' scheduled US debut. Needless to say, both Galbraith and Malone [the producer] were deeply offended, and they both protested vehemently. But when faced with the implicit possibility of cancellation, they grudgingly acceded" (Parker, 2005: 549).

28 As Parker (2005: 570) records: "Its safe to say that virtually everything about 'Reaganomics' and the Reagan Revolution appalled Ken Galbraith ... Two days after Reagan's inauguration in January 1981, Galbraith laid out in detail his concerns not only about Reagan's announced plans but also the broader rightward political and ideological shift under way. In 'The Conservative Onslaught,' a long essay for *The New York Review of Books* ... he derided the coming consequences of the 'Reagan Revolution,' and correctly named Arthur Laffer's supply side ideas, Milton Friedman's monetarism, and William Simon's hyperconservative commitment to tax cutting for the wealthy and corporations, and their shared contempt for the public sector, as the basic concepts that would guide it." Galbraith's criticisms of Reaganomics were shared by many Post Keynesians (see Sawyer, 1982; Kaldor, 1985; Davidson, 1991b; Davidson and Davidson, 1996). This early critique of "movement conservatism" is ignored by Paul Krugman (2007).

29 In many ways Galbraith's critique of the economic analysis underpinning the third way was similar to contemporary Post Keynesians (see Arestis and Sawyer, 2001a, 2001b).

30 This interest and recognition of the importance of the history of economic thought on the problems of our time echoes both the Post Keynesian and Institutionalist approach. Time permitting I would also have liked to have made an assessment of Galbraith as a historian of ideas and events (see Galbraith, 1987, 1994a, 1994b).

31 Parker (2005: 658) highlights Galbraith's intellectual conviction and courage: "If one looks at the direction of Galbraith's life and the choices he made before he was fifty, one sees something fundamental about his character, sees where his separation from mainstream economics and mainstream liberalism would carry him. He had faced more than half a dozen major junctures in his early career: he had given up a safe position in agricultural economics to strike out a new career as a Keynesian macroeconomist; he had chosen to stand by two

young radical colleagues when maintaining a discreet silence might have better served his own academic ambitions; while in government, he'd refused to alter his tough-mined behavior toward powerful business and congressional interests; at *Fortune*, where he might have followed Harry Luce's advocacy of 'American Century' internationalism, he had pressed for a fuller embrace of Keynes; at the Bombing Survey, he had insisted on challenging the claims made by powerful military and civilian individuals for the 'success' of strategic bombing; at the State Department, he had fought against the alleged inevitability of a militarized global confrontation with the Soviet Union; and at Harvard he had refused to trim or apologize or recant in the face of those who wanted to deny him the right to teach there because of his 'radicalism.' In short, he had demonstrated a willingness to choose the harder path, to risk his career, in order to maintain the independence of his own critical judgment. But he had also refused to be marginalized."

3 *The economics of John Kenneth Galbraith*

The ideas of economists and political philosophers, both when they are right and when they are wrong, are more powerful than is commonly understood. Indeed the world is ruled by little else. Practical men, who believe themselves to be quite exempt from any intellectual influences, are usually the slaves of some defunct economist. Madmen in authority, who hear voices in the air, are distilling their frenzy from some academic scribbler of a few years back. I am sure that the power of vested interests is vastly exaggerated compared with the gradual encroachment of ideas.

J. M. Keynes (1936: 383)

Galbraith's work on the modern corporation, and public policy toward it, has been scantily explored in the journals – except for scraps of disavowal on the basis of competitive postulates.

Paul Davidson and Sidney Weintraub (1978: 5)

The economic contributions of John Kenneth Galbraith can be viewed both negatively and positively. On the negative side Galbraith was highly critical of traditional approaches to understanding the way the economy works and the concomitant economic policies that are pursued. He criticized economic theory for ignoring and obscuring the economic power accumulated by large corporations. He has criticized politicians who aligned themselves with the objectives of the large corporation instead of acting in the public interest. And, like Paul Krugman (1998) more recently, he censured those economists who perform sophisticated mathematical analysis but who do not seek to promote deeper understanding of the real world.

On the positive side Galbraith (1952a, 1952b, 1958a, 1967a, 1973a) provided an examination of economic power, analyzing the evolution and dominance of the large firms that characterize the global economy. Galbraith argued that an understanding of the nature of modern production is central for understanding the nature of the firm, which seeks to control and supersede the market in order to expand the influence of its bureaucratic apparatus – what Galbraith labels "the technostructure".[1] A critical appreciation of the nature of modern production also allows us to identify: sources of power; the manner in which it is expressed; the divergences of private and public interests, and; the most appropriate policy responses to its uses, abuses and absences. Galbraith highlighted the role of the large corporation in contributing to both modern day affluence, as well as adverse consequences such as the degradation of the environment. He analyzed the power of the expansive and imperialistic military-industrial complex, with its interest in perpetuating the arms race.[2] Galbraith's analysis also provides a rich examination of the factors that generate and reproduce pockets of poverty amongst more general affluence. Similarly his analysis of power is used to develop economic and social policy that counters the power of firms, and works to improve economic outcomes and the lives of those disenfranchised by modern society.

These critical efforts sought to "emancipate belief," urging the public and educational elite to question the conventional wisdom that dominates economic instruction and underpins much contemporary policy.[3] In *Economics and the Public Purpose* Galbraith (1973a: chapter 22) argued that the dominating influence of accepted beliefs, in excluding the possibility of contrary thought, limits our ability to properly understand and analyze how the economy works. Galbraith argued that the power and prestige of large firms is obscured by the conventional wisdom, which promotes economic analysis that is neither socially relevant nor useful. He criticized the various conventional wisdoms that permeate economic and social thought. His aim was to improve the public's understanding of how the economy actually works and functions in order to promote the acceptability of the necessary policy responses.

Galbraith highlighted the power that ideas have in facilitating social change. He accepted Keynes's contention that "the ideas of economists and political philosophers ... are more powerful than is commonly understood" (Keynes, 1936: 383). But Galbraith went further than Keynes, arguing that outdated economic ideas misinform social policy in a way that supports the corporate power structure, to the detriment of the wider public interest (see Reisman, 1990). In their refusal to yield to the onslaught of circumstance, economic ideas can be socially damaging. Misleading ideas about the firm sustain the prestige of the large corporation and its personnel, as well as goods that they produce and promote (Galbraith, 1958a). Outmoded analyses assessing the relationship between the firm and market obfuscate the proper regulatory response (Galbraith, 1967a, 1973a). They make it easier for large firms to resist government regulation, and they shield firms pursuing practices that may be environmentally unsound and detrimental to national security (Galbraith, 1973a, 2004). Ultimately cherished but erroneous ideas about how the economy works make it harder to win support for effective policies that might improve society. It is therefore necessary to highlight outmoded ideas and point out their obsolescence.

Challenging and developing the conventional wisdom

Galbraith's principal theoretical contribution unfolds most clearly into view in his trilogy: *The Affluent Society*, *The New Industrial State*, and *Economics and the Public Purpose*. His thesis was that the economic ideas that once explained a world of poverty had not adjusted to the world of affluence ushered in by the large and dominant modern corporation.[4] Galbraith's focus was the concentration of economic power in the large corporation, and the social and environmental imbalance that it generated in the successful pursuit of its narrow goals. He sought to explain the factors generating the uneven development associated with modern affluence, and outline a pragmatic case for social change to address the associated inequalities.

In developing his overarching vision of how the economy works, and in recognizing the changing institutional structure of modern economies, Galbraith introduced many new perspectives into economics. As DeLong (2005: 127) observes:

> Lots of ideas in the background of contemporary US political and economic thought are Galbraith's. His work as an economist was a scattered but comprehensive attempt to think through the consequences of the transition from a nation of small farms and workshops to one of large factories and superstores. In doing so, he took on many of the questions most central to the new US economic landscape: How much can advertising shape demand? In a world of passive shareholders, autonomous managers and engineers, and firm decisions that emerge out of internal bureaucratic contests, just what are the objectives that drive big firms?

How does competition work when its principal dimensions are quality and marketing rather than price? And critically, how do the limits of polite discourse allow the system to hold itself together while constraining its flexibility?

Several key themes stand out in the work of Galbraith. He analyzed the economic power held by large firms, and argued that such power is one of the main reasons for the technological success of the US economy in the post-World War II era. As Galbraith (1952a: 93) first pointed out in *American Capitalism*:

> in the modern industry shared by a few large firms, size and the rewards accruing to market power combine to insure that resources for research and technical development will be available. The power that enables the firm to have some influence on prices insures that the resulting gains will not be passed on to the public by imitators (who have stood none of the costs of development) before the outlay for development can be recouped. In this way market power protects the incentive to technical development. The net of all this is there must be some element of monopoly in an industry if it is to be progressive.

But the emergence of the modern large-scale mode of production is not without further consequence. Galbraith was one of the first economists to identify and explore the advent of the consumer society ushered in by the large corporation. Galbraith was also one of the first economists to highlight how the large corporation and the wider economic superstructure influence consumption and work patterns in a way that runs counter to the wider public need. Large firms dominate the food, tobacco, pharmaceutical, oil, automobile, and alcohol industries, for example, and use sophisticated marketing techniques to increase sales (Glantz *et al.*, 1996; Moynihan and Cassells, 2005; Patel, 2008; Mayo and Nairn, 2009; Krugman, 2005a).[5] The resulting consumption patterns can have harmful health and environmental effects (Fine, 2002; Stiglitz, 2006; Klein, 1999; Lang, 2003, 2006; Lang and Heasman, 2004). Likewise social and economic pressures to increase working hours and augment incomes have been linked to the increase in psychological disorders. Indeed many modern health problems should be seen as consequences of consumption and behaviors encouraged by large firms and modern society (see Dunn, 2009). As Galbraith (1973a: 297) presciently argued:

> Virtually *all* of the increase in modern health hazards is the result of increased consumption. Obesity and associated disorders are the result of increased food consumption; cirrhosis and accidents are the result of increased alcohol consumption; lung cancer, heart disease, emphysema and numerous other disabilities are the result of increased tobacco consumption; accidents and resulting mortality and morbidity are caused by increased automobile use; hepatitis and numerous disabling assaults are often caused by increased drug consumption; nervous disorders and mental illness follow from efforts to increase income, observation of the greater success of others in increasing income, the fear of loss of income or the fear of the various foregoing physical consequences of high consumption. At the same time medical and hospital care is not part of the development which induces these disorders. It lags systematically behind – for a large part of the population, including many who are relatively affluent, its availability is uncertain and its cost alarming or prohibitive.

The bias toward consumerism also fuels the emulatory processes that drive the rat race – what Stanfield (1994, 1996) calls the "treadmill syndrome" – resulting in people working harder and harder in order to consume more and more (Schor, 1991; Folbre and Bittman, 2005). This pressure to work and earn even higher levels of income, also explains the increased demand for childcare, which has exploded in recent times.[6] As Galbraith (1958a: 212) argued in *The Affluent Society*:

> In a society which sets large store by production, and which has highly effective machinery for synthesizing private wants, there are strong pressures to have as many wage-earners in the family as possible ... If both parents are engaged in private production, the burden on public services is further increased. Children, in effect, become the charge of the community for an appreciable part of the time. If the services of the community do not keep pace, this will be another source of disorder.[7]

This outsourcing of child rearing therefore raises the prospect of a "nurturance gap," which can result in a range of social and health problems, as parents are unable to foster adequate social and educational development for their children (Folbre, 1994; Stanfield and Stanfield, 1997; Folbre and Nelson, 2000; Ellwood, 2000). And the consequences of inadequate social and educational development, which are compounded by poverty, low aspiration and poor employment prospects, are profound. They are expressed in terms of growing problems of drug abuse, anti-social behavior, knife crime, mental illness, and early sexual activity, which plague certain socioeconomic groups and characterize the rising underclass.[8]

In *Economics and the Public Purpose* Galbraith also sought to analyze the position and role of women, as it related to the theoretical structure developed in *The New Industrial State.* Galbraith argued, in a manner reminiscent of Veblen, that in the modern consumer society, women increasingly assume the role of professional and voluminous consumer.[9] To counteract this tendency Galbraith argued for the emancipation of women and for the opening up of the jobs market in order to increase female participation in the labor market. Indeed over the last fifty years we have witnessed a remarkable rise in female participation in the labor market and higher education. Galbraith anticipated that this would require legislative and institutional change: "Equal access to jobs requires the support of the law. It also requires a series of companion reforms ... (1) Provision of professional care for children ... (2) Greater individual choice in the work week and work year ... (3) An end to the present monopoly of the better jobs in the technostructure by males (4) Provision of the requisite educational opportunity for women" (Galbraith, 1973a: 253–56). Galbraith argued that this might reduce and realign consumption by increasing critical attitudes to advertising and reducing the time spent on shopping and buying and consuming things: "The consequence of the emancipation of women – and the rationalization of the household – will be the substantial change in patterns of life" (Galbraith, 1973a: 257). Nevertheless although much progress has been made, however, there is still a long way to go to deliver a more egalitarian society, freed from the demands of an excessively consumerist society.

Galbraith's analysis resulted in him being one of the first economists to argue against the uncritical use of traditional economic measures of growth, such as GDP or industrial production, to estimate economic and social well-being (cf. Morris, 1979; United Nations, 1952; United Nations Research Institute for Social Development, 1970).[10] For Galbraith that which was measured or traded, was not necessarily superior to that which was not. The "paramount position of production" must be analyzed and challenged, rather than uncritically accepted:

> The quality of life is subjective and disputable. Cultural and aesthetic progress cannot easily be measured. Who can say for sure what arrangements best allow for the development of individual personality. Who can be certain what advances the total of human happiness? Who can guess how much clear air or uncluttered highways are enjoyed? Gross National Product and the level of unemployment, on the other hand, are objective and measurable. To many it will always seem better to have measurable progress toward the wrong goals than unmeasurable and hence uncertain progress towards the right ones. (Galbraith, 1967a: 398–399)

Galbraith argued that many of the goods produced and sold by private firms do not address important social or civic needs, or are harmful if excessively consumed, for example fast food, alcopops, cigarettes, pornography, violent computer games, knives, and guns. Nevertheless all goods produced by the large firm sector, what Galbraith refers to as the planning system, are counted as part of GDP. Galbraith noted the perversity in that activities which pollute the environment and contribute to the manipulation and management of the consumer, as well as those goods that threaten civic society, such as guns, knives and nuclear weapons, count toward GDP, whereas other things that people value, such as more leisure time, safe streets, a clean environment, and a world safe from nuclear destruction, are not properly accounted for in GDP (Stanfield, 1996). And if we acknowledge the fact that the large corporation seeks to manage the consumer, then it also becomes clear that many of the goods and services we are urged to consume may not be needed, or will fail to improve the quality of life (Scitovsky, 1987, 2000).

In presenting his analysis Galbraith (1958a; see also Galbraith, Jarrett and Future, 1958) was also one of the first major economists to address the environmental destruction and degradation that is now widely acknowledged to have contributed to climate change (Stern, 2007).[11] As Galbraith (1971: 227) pointed out in his essay on Richard Nixon in *Life*, to change the environmental direction requires consideration of the wider role of private enterprise:

> There is an even stronger impression that we can retrieve the environment without in any way invading the sacred prerogatives, as they are called, of private enterprise. This is fantastic. The tendency of the modern economy is to service not the wishes of the public but the convenience (and other interests) of the more powerful producers. And it is convenient and in accord with the producer interest to make automobiles that poison the air, and to

dump industrial waste that poisons the waters, and to use chemicals that poison birds, fish and people along with the worms, and to allow the cities to engulf the countryside in an unregulated sprawl, and to give the highways over to billboards and the purveyors of gasoline, exotic inedibles and sundry places of rest and assignation. This, alas, is the nature of unregulated private enterprise ... We have yet to realize that to rescue the environment, we will have to restrict production and consumption of some goods.

Such concerns are now belatedly being addressed through tougher international regulation, and the introduction of emissions trading. The USA however, still lags behind other countries in taking affirmative action on the environment – not least because of the powerful and dominating influence of the large oil and automobile industries who continue to resist scientific consensus (Oreskes, 2004; David, 2006, Sample, 2007; Mother Jones, 2005; Monbiot, 2006, 2007). This points to the larger role for the state that Galbraith identified. The state must counter the power of the large firm. And it must assist in providing goods and services that are not subject to the imperatives of organization and technology, and that are not produced by the large firm. The state must also use its power to mitigate macroeconomic problems such as unemployment, inflation, and poverty (cf. Sachs, 2009). These themes are introduced in chapter 5 and subject to development in chapter 6.

Galbraith advanced several important concepts that are now widely accepted and used by many economists. As I shall argue in chapter 7, Galbraith's (1967a) discussion of the relationship between technology and organization predates and parallels Williamson's (1975, 1985, 2005) recognition of the importance of asset specificity for the study of organizations.[12] According to Williamson, asset specificity is critical in that once an investment has been undertaken the buyer and seller become locked into a transaction for a considerable period, referred to as "*ex post* bilateral dependence." In contrast, Galbraith argued that the imperatives of modern technology and the associated commitments of time, capital, and specialized labor in an uncertain environment, entail that planning supersedes the market: "Planning exists because this [market] process has ceased to be reliable ... the firm ... must replace the market with planning" (Galbraith, 1967a: 41). Galbraith moves beyond the limiting view of "in the beginning there were markets," toward a view that "in the beginning there was an absence of a need for extensive planning as technology was not that sophisticated!"

Another notable aspect of Galbraith's analysis is his identification of the problem of a rising underclass, which received considerable attention in the USA in the 1980s (Auletta, 1982; Wilson, 1987). This problem was first anticipated and analyzed by Galbraith (1958a: 97, 260) in the 1950s.[13] Similarly Galbraith's emphasis on the importance of education in helping solve the problems of poverty, represents one of the earliest statements of human capital theory – something I discuss in chapter 6 below. As he noted in *The Affluent Society*:

> In the earliest states of economic development, from which so many of our economic attitudes are derived, the simple and sufficient way of getting more growth was to have more saving and therefore more material capital ... [W]ith the development of a great and complex industrial plant, and even more with the development of a great and sophisticated body of basic science and of experience in its applications, all of this has been changed. In addition to the entrepreneurs (and perhaps one should add the accountants and clerks) who were more or less automatically forthcoming, more economic activity now requires a great number of trained and qualified people. Investment in human beings is, *prima facie*, as important as investment in material capital. The one, in its modern complexity, depends on the other. (Galbraith, 1958a: 221–2)

Even before the work of Becker (1964) and Schultz (1993), Galbraith (1958a: chapter 18, see also 1962: chapter 4) recognized that education was both an investment good and a consumption good.[14] Galbraith (1958a: 225) also identified the now accepted distinction between general and specific human capital: "Human development, in other words, is what economists have long termed an external economy. Its benefits accrue to all firms; it is not sufficiently specific to any one to be bought and paid for by it." In doing so he lamented that the investment component of education was not generally recognized by the affluent society, arguing that human capital and knowledge was a decisive factor of production underpinning the success of modern economies (cf. Porter, 1990; Hodgson, 1999).[15] Forty years later Anthony Giddens (2000: 52), for many the intellectual leader of "The Third Way," argued, like Galbraith (1958a, 1967a) before him, that: "In the new information economy, human (and social) capital becomes central to economic success."[16]

Another significant aspect of Galbraith's theoretical structure concerns his analysis of savings. Economists have focused on the sharp drop in saving rates in the USA and throughout most of the developed world (Maddison, 1992; Seidman, 1990; Walker, Bloomfield, and Thorning, 1990), and have pointed to rising household debt ratios as a potential problem facing the US economy during the early twenty-first century (Godley, 2000; Scott, 2006, 2007; Pressman and Scott, 2007). Galbraith anticipated such concerns back in the 1950s when he recognized that in order to sustain its production and planning processes, the technostructure requires that consumers are able to buy the goods that are produced: "The process of persuading people to incur debt, and the arrangement for them to do so, are as much a part of modern production as the making of the goods and the nurturing of wants" (Galbraith, 1958a: 167). This results in lower savings rates and higher levels of indebtedness for the household (see Lamdin, 2008). It is no surprise that, as Stanfield (1983: 591) notes: "Easier credit checks, lower down payments, longer repayment terms, and other inducements for people to go further and further into debt are permanent and necessary fixtures of the consumer society described in *The Affluent Society*."

Galbraith's (1958a: 167) analysis explains the recent decline in savings rates and the corresponding rise in consumer debt and bankruptcies: "Viewing this process as a whole, we should expect that every increase in consumption will bring a further increase – possibly a more than proportional one – in consumer debt. Our march to higher living standards will be paced, as a matter of necessity, by an ever deeper plunge into debt." Galbraith acknowledged the role of consumer debt in supporting higher levels of consumption and augmenting demand in the economy.[17] But Galbraith also highlighted how the precarious explosion of debt adds to macroeconomic instability – something we explore in chapters 10 and 11 below (cf. Minsky, 1975, 1982, 1986; Godley, 2000; Davidson, 1994, 2007).

Economics and the art of controversy

Notwithstanding such contributions, many mainstream economists reject, or have forgotten, his system of thought. Mainstream economists typically view Galbraith as a social theorist, rather than an economist. They tend to see him as an ambitious system builder who preferred to substitute generalization for rigorous analysis. On a more personal level, economists tend to regard Galbraith with the same disdain that Galbraith has heaped on them through ridiculing their outdated views of the firm and their inability to explain what is going on in the real world because of an infatuation with unrealistic, formal modeling.

Krugman (1994), for example, is among those who would belittle Galbraith's stature as an economist. In *Peddling Prosperity*, for example, he referred to Galbraith as a "policy entrepreneur" – an economist who writes solely for the public, as opposed to one who writes for other professors, and who therefore makes unwarranted diagnoses and offers over-simplistic answers to complex economic problems.[18] He asserted that Galbraith was never taken seriously by fellow academics, who viewed him as more of a "media personality." Krugman (1994: 13–15) argued that Galbraith's work *The New Industrial State* should not be considered to be "real economic theory," and similarly that *Economics in Perspective* is "remarkably ill-informed." It should therefore be no surprise that, as remarked at the start of this chapter, "Galbraith's work on the modern corporation, and public policy toward it, has been scantily explored in the journals" (Davidson and Weintraub, 1978: 5).

Perhaps more interesting, therefore, is the relationship between Galbraith and two heterodox schools of thought that have expressed a great deal of appreciation for his work – the Institutionalists and the Post Keynesians.[19] Although Galbraith was one of the first Keynesians, he was, like many Post Keynesians, keen to move beyond the static and restrictive ISLM bastardizations of the neo-classical synthesis (Galbraith, 1996a; cf. Shackle, 1955, 1967, 1972; Robinson, 1972, 1974; Davidson, 1972, 1994; Sawyer, 1982, 1995; King, 2002). Moreover his critical and positive contributions were warmly and sympathetically received by heterodox approaches. In 1976 Galbraith received the Veblens-Commons award from the Association for Evolutionary Economics (AFEE) to honor his contributions to Institutionalist thinking (see Galbraith, 1977b), and he was instrumental in the founding and development of the *Journal of Post Keynesian Economics* (see Davidson, 2005). But although the *Journal of Economic Issues* has had retrospective symposiums on *The Affluent Society* and *The New Industrial State* as well as a posthumous symposium in 2008, and the *Journal of Post Keynesian Economics* has had a symposium on Galbraith's theory of the firm in 1984, as well as one more recently appraising his thought in 2005, it would not be unfair to suggest that Galbraith's economic contributions have also been pretty much ignored by both Institutionalists and Post Keynesians. His ideas do not pervade the pages of such journals and opportunities to develop Galbraith's contributions are frequently missed.[20]

Such neglect is unwarranted, given Galbraith's system of thought has much to add to the development of an alternative to the conventional wisdom – something to which both of these schools of thought aspire (Eichner and Kregel, 1975; Eichner, 1978, 1983; Holt and Pressman, 2001). With his focus on the relationships between power, the firm, and the state, the Galbraithian system facilitates the integration of the economics of Keynes, Kalecki, and the Institutionalists into a comprehensive vision of political economy.[21] Although Institutionalists focus on the origins and nature of power, insufficient attention is typically given to macroeconomic processes as they bear down on institutions. Similarly, although Post Keynesians have acknowledged the presence and role of firm power, they have been reluctant to move beyond their models of imperfect competition and aggregate demand, to analyze the impact of organizational power on wider social and economic processes (Peterson, 1989). Galbraith's vision offers a starting point to develop a research agenda along these lines (cf. Dunn, 2000a). Indeed I would argue that Galbraith should be viewed as a foundational figure for integrating Insititutionalist and Post Keynesian economics.[22] Several features of this integration stand out, which I shall explore in greater depth over the course of this book.

First, Galbraith's historical approach shares many methodological concerns with Institutionalists and with Post Keynesians (Stanfield, 1996). As I argue in the next chapter, Galbraith, like both these schools, acknowledged the need to reflect on the nature of reality and consider the implications for scientific study. In doing so Galbraith argued that social processes were inherently transformative – that economic agents were not passive atoms but purposeful social beings that drive social and institutional change through their individual and collective actions (Stanfield, 1994; Hodgson, 2001a, 2004).[23] As a consequence Galbraith argued for a pluralistic and tailored method. He developed provisional and empirically grounded theory, which was marshaled to provide emancipatory critique and underpin the case for social change (Stanfield, 1996).

Galbraith rejected neo-classical orthodoxy because its theoretical core failed to explain real world phenomena. Like both Institutionalists and Post Keynesians Galbraith (1981: 282) argued that economic theory must be realistic and must describe the salient features of real world experience: "To look at the world as it exists is often an informative thing" (cf. Eichner, 1983; Holt and Pressman, 2001; Pressman, 2008). Galbraith, like both schools, rejected abstract equilibrium models based on optimizing behavior. Instead he developed analysis that acknowledged real behaviors, a range of stylized facts, cumulative processes, and the importance of history (cf. Veblen, 1898a; Myrdal, 1957, 1978; Kaldor, 1972, 1985).[24] Galbraith developed a holistic and dynamic analysis of the firm, highlighting the evolutionary consequences for society. And he incorporated cumulative causation processes into his analysis of inequality and poverty – see chapter 6.

Galbraith rejected, on the grounds of realism, the idea that economic analysis must begin with rational atomistic individuals with given desires and preferences.[25] Galbraith developed an analysis that echoes Post Keynesian-Institutionalist views that individual actions are socially conditioned and culturally contingent (Dow, 1996a, 1997b, 2001; Hodgson, 1988, 2001a, 2004). According to Galbraith conventions, mental frameworks, and manufactured habits play an important role in influencing individual, firm, and collective behavior, sometimes resulting in adverse societal outcomes (Stanfield, 1994, 1996; Hodgson, 1997b). For example, emulation and conspicuous consumption, developed and reinforced by advertising, result in low saving rates, high consumer indebtedness, and the neglect of public needs and goods (Galbraith, 1958a). Similarly myriad economic institutions contribute to a wage-price spiral (Galbraith, 1967a, 1973a). And various economic institutions contribute to our wider acceptance of the inevitability of poverty across societies (Galbraith, 1983c, 1992, 1996b). As a consequence Galbraith, like contemporary Post Keynesians and Institutionalists, rejected methodological individualism, and its implication that knowledge of atomistic behavior is sufficient to explain macroeconomic outcomes (cf. Arestis, 1990, 1996; Chick, 1995; Hodgson, 1986, 1988, 2001a, 2007; Stanfield, 1996).

Second, Galbraith presented an analysis of the large firm that reflects the broader Institutionalist tradition, but also brought in Keynesian concerns and insights. Galbraith (1981: 362) himself acknowledged that: "Since the 1930s, the innovative studies of Adolf A. Berle and Gardiner C. Means and the later work of James Burnham and Robert Aaron Gordon had thrown much light on the changing character and role of the corporation." As we shall see in chapter 7 Galbraith develops these analyses, articulating a view of the firm that brings in Coasian, Schumpeterian, Knightian, and Keynesian considerations. Galbraith's analysis of the firm, also offers the prospect of further developing Post Keynesian analysis of uncertainty. Galbraith considered the impact of uncertainty on firm behavior and management coordination. He provides a foundation for the development of a Post Keynesian theory of the firm that is embedded in its recognition of the importance of uncertainty for understanding economic processes (cf. Dunn, 1999, 2000b, 2001a, 2001c, 2008a). Post Keynesian approaches typically begin with Eichner (1976), who presented a determinate view of the firm that largely ignored the problems of uncertainty. Post Keynesians have focused traditionally on uncertainty at the macroeconomic level and have largely neglected uncertainty when it comes to thinking about the firm (Dunn, 2008a).[26] This has led some commentators to point to the apparent inconsistency between Post Keynesian micro-analysis and their macroeconomic insistence on the salience of uncertainty (cf. Reynolds, 1990). As Tarshis (1980: 12; cf. Kenyon, 1980; Harcourt, 1980) notes: "it is hard to reconcile the Post Keynesians' insistence that uncertainty about the future is ever present, with their readiness to forget this whole business when they come to discuss price setting in that very set of market conditions in which uncertainty is likely to be most serious."[27]

Galbraith argued that many of the organizational strategies pursued by the firm, including the use of long-term money contracts, help to reduce the uncertainty faced by it. As production in the new industrial state takes time and planning, money-denominated contracts represent the means by which uncertainties about the future may be mitigated and money enables the discharge of such contractual arrangements.[28] Galbraith's view that price is related to costs, at a level of output determined by aggregate demand, and that price decisions have significant implications for both real wages and inflation is shared by all Post Keynesians.[29] In doing so, Galbraith developed a view of a modern corporation that is consistent with Post Keynesian inflation and monetary theory, offering opportunities for further integration and development (cf. Dunn, 2008a: chapter 10; Davidson, 1992). Chapter 8 develops this analysis by also considering Galbraith's contribution to the theory of the multinational corporation. As we shall see, Galbraith develops a view of the transnational corporation as an institution for coordinating production from one center of strategic decision-making across national boundaries under conditions of uncertainty and should be developed with respect to recent contributions. As such I argue that Galbraith's contribution to the theory of the firm should no longer be neglected by Post Keynesians.

Third, and building on both his methodological approach and view of the firm, Galbraith focused on the social processes by which firms seek to influence and shape consumer demand for their products. In *The New Industrial State* Galbraith famously challenged the doctrine of consumer sovereignty, arguing that large corporations managed and manipulated the demand for their products. Although attracting a degree of attention and notoriety around the time of publication, Galbraith's thesis of the direct manipulation of the consumer has slipped somewhat from view in favor of a view of advertising as "information provision" (although see Dutt, 2008 and Lamdin, 2008, for recent attempts to redress this). In chapter 9 I reconsider Galbraith's theory of "The Management of Specific Demand" and illuminate its salience in the context of the US tobacco industry (see also Anderson and Dunn, 2006; Dunn and Anderson, 2006). This analysis suggests that the US experience is congruent with many of the claims that Galbraith made regarding the manipulation of the consumer by large corporations and thus warrants rehabilitation of the Galbraithian view.

Fourth, Galbraith's bimodal image of the planning and market sectors accords with the Kaleckian view of the modern economy. For both Galbraith and Kalecki, modern economies are characterized by an oligopolistic sector, dominated by the major corporations, and a competitive sector, which covers agriculture and certain input markets, and is in the service of the more dominant sector (cf. Sawyer, 1985b). *A Theory of Price Control* (Galbraith, 1952b; see also Galbraith, 1936; Dennison and Galbraith, 1938) preceded Hicks, Okun, and the New Keynesians, but not Kalecki, in recognizing the salience of classifying the economy into fix and flex price sectors for macroeconomic policy (Colander, 1984). According to Galbraith (1973a: 294), however, this bimodal view of the economy is linked explicitly to technological advance, which conditions both the nature of development and exploitation: "The central problem of the modern economy is unequal development. The least development is where there is the least monopoly and market power; the greatest development is where there is the most."[30]

Like Kalecki, Galbraith presented an analysis of capitalism where organization in addition to income, underpins power, and where the decisions of individual workers, consumers, and households have a subordinate role in determining macroeconomic outcomes (cf. Sawyer, 1985b). As Ray Canterbery (1984: 78) has pointed out, Galbraith's notion of firm power and Kalecki's notion of the degree of monopoly have much in common. Class conflict for Galbraith, however, is different from Kalecki's more traditional Marxist approach, reflecting his analysis of the technostructure and its organization and goals, and the conditions under which these conflict with wider social objectives – see chapters 5 and 6 below. The persuasive power and educational and technical respectability of the technostructure also means that social conflict has become more diffuse and hidden than Marxist analysis would lead us to believe (cf. Klein, 1992). For Galbraith the division between the planning sector and the market sector has more contemporary relevance than the outmoded distinction between the owners of the means of production and workers who must labor for their income (which has been somewhat usurped by the emergence of the technostructure).

Fifth, Galbraith offers an alternative analysis to the Monopoly Capitalist theses espoused by some Post Keynesians (for a survey see Sawyer, 1988; see also Stanfield and Carroll, 1997; Cowling, 1982, 2004, 2006). Monopoly Capital theorists, following Baran and Sweezy (1966), like Galbraith, focus on the impact of the large corporation upon wider society. Indeed in an argument that echoed many Galbraithian themes, Baran and Sweezy focused on the control of "inside" management, the relentless sales effort, and the emergence of a professional class of managers, arguing that it fundamentally changes the way in which capitalism works (Stanfield, 1996). Nevertheless, and in contrast to Galbraith, Baran and Sweezy did not accept that the new managerial class and the nature of advanced technology changed the basic objectives of the firm, which for them remained the maximization of profits. Baran and Sweezy argued that the profit-maximizing modern corporation has ushered in an era of tremendous productive advance, which, in stabilizing costs and fixing prices, creates a tendency for the economic surplus to rise (cf. Stanfield, 1973). Accordingly the surplus, which was defined as the difference between what a society produces and the cost of producing it, needs to be absorbed to prevent crises and underconsumption. Although Baran and Sweezy presented an examination of consumption, advertising, waste, and military expenditure that echoes Galbraith's analysis, it was nevertheless based on a quite different view of the nature of organization, technology, and the firm. This also underscored their divergent policy recommendations.

Similarly Steindl (1945) integrated Marxist and Kaleckian ideas on competition to explain and analyze the increasing concentration associated with advanced capitalist development. Steindl (1952) argued that the emergence of oligopolistic industries stifles (price) competition, resulting in higher prices, reduced sales, higher margins and profits, as well as a degree of excess capacity at the level of the firm to smooth variations in demand. This microeconomic analysis, however, has macroeconomic implications. As the number of oligopolies rises, the increased excess capacity and reduced production observed in individual industries amplify the propensity for the economy to stagnate.

While such theses offer plausible explanations of the Great Depression and stagflation, they provide a less satisfactory explanation of the rise in living standards witnessed over the twentieth century, and the "gilded age" of the post-World War II expansion.[31] For Galbraith it is this that also requires explanation. He seeks to provide one by focusing on the large firm and its nexus to the state, technological advance, and economic growth. Moreover the underconsumptionist and stagnationist arguments of Baran and Sweezy and Steindl, in focusing on consumption and productive capacity, fail to consider adequately the role of the financial system in generating growth and instability – something which Galbraith and contemporary Post Keynesians emphasize.

Sixth, like many Post Keynesians and Institutionalists, Galbraith accepted that in a monetary production economy the level of economic activity is set by the level of effective demand (cf. Davidson, 1994; Chick, 1995; Arestis, 1990, 1992, 1996). Like both these schools Galbraith (1973a: 37) firmly rejected Say's Law. As I highlight in chapter 10,

Galbraith was a lifelong and prominent Keynesian who, like Keynes, acknowledged the primacy of the financial sector, emphasizing the distinctive nature of money in determining macroeconomic outcomes. For Galbraith, as for Keynes, there was little reason to think that the economy would automatically generate a level of effective demand consistent with full employment: "Downward instability – recession – in all normal peacetime circumstances is caused, in the first instance, by an insufficiency of effective demand, i.e. effectively used purchasing power. More goods and services are available or could be produced with available manpower and plant than there is demand for them" (Galbraith, 1973a: 196). Nevertheless Galbraith also argued that the evolution of the modern mode of production adds to the instability of the Keynesian system. The technical and productive superiority of the modern firm increases the supply of goods and services to be consumed. If they are not consumed, then the plant and personnel that produce them risk unemployment. To mitigate this risk, firms seek to manipulate the consumer response so as to ensure high and stable levels of demand for their goods. Firms also seek a protective response from the state – by buying (directly) its goods, for example the defense industries, and lobbying for policies that support the (general) demand for its products, for example pursing Keynesian macroeconomic policies and engaging in road building. But such strategies do not work precisely and do not conspire to reinstitute Say's Law. What is more, the planning system adds to macroeconomic instability:

> Spending on the products of the planning system is extensively the result of persuasion. However effective this management, the resulting consumption is less reliable than that derived from individual discovery based on pressing need for food, shelter, medicine or clothing. When incomes in the planning system fall, people can cut their consumption far more readily than in the market system (Galbraith, 1973a: 198).

Seventh, like all Post Keynesians, Galbraith rejected the monetarist inflation story, whereby increases in the stock of money cause inflation. As I highlight in chapter 10, Galbraith recognized the importance of history, uncertainty, distributional issues, and the relevance of political and economic institutions in determining the level of activity and inflation in an economy. For Galbraith, inflation arises from the real side of the economy, with changes in the stock of money being caused by income conflict among different groups in society (including the technostructure). As noted above, inflation may be controlled by slowing down the economy and increasing unemployment, but Galbraith advances controls on prices as a more civilized response to this problem – a perspective shared by many Post Keynesians (see, for example, Arestis and Sawyer, 2005, Cornwall, 1977, 1994; Davidson, 1972, 1985a, 1994, 2006, 2007). As part of this analysis, Galbraith (1958a: 190) also recognized, long before it was fashionable to do so, that the money supply was endogenous: "The money supply increases or decreases as the result of increases or decreases in commercial bank lending."

Eighth, like many Institutionalists, Galbraith acknowledged profound differences between the workings of technology and the workings of the financial system – which explains why Galbraith's analysis of money, outlined in chapter 10 below, appears in the background of his major trilogy. At the beginning of the twentieth century, Veblen (1904, 1921) distinguished business activities from the technical processes of production, and thus capitalists from engineers. Capitalists, for Veblen, were predators, only interested in making profits. Engineers, who designed processes, were concerned with productivity and efficiency. Somewhat naively, Veblen thought that machine processes would facilitate a greater planning of production and distribution, ultimately superseding the need for a price system, and ending the waste of conspicuous consumption.[32] Such concerns are evident in Galbraith, who analyzed technological development and its nexus to the business enterprise, as well as the consequences of a dual economy that resulted from the uneven development of technology.[33] But Galbraith went much further than Veblen, identifying and analyzing the rise of a new class, the technostructure, as well as outlining the economic and social consequences of a consumerist and bimodal economy that resulted from the uneven import of technology.

Ninth, Galbraith acknowledged and analyzed the financial instability endemic to modern capitalism that links the real and financial sectors (Galbraith, 1955a, 1990a). *The Great Crash, 1929* (Galbraith, 1955a) provides an historical description of the events preceding and accompanying a particular financial crisis, but one with devastating impact.[34] As I highlight in chapter 10, Galbraith presents an analysis that acknowledges the animal spirits and irrational psychology of financial markets and institutions. Reminiscent of Keynes (1936), Davidson (1972, 1994, 2007), and Minsky (1975, 1982, 1986, 1992), he describes how human proclivities of greed, euphoria, frustrated expectations, and panic move financial markets, how percieved changes in the economy provoke heightened expectations of return, and lead to excess, fraud, and eventual collapse – something I dwell on in chapter 11 when considering the recent global financial meltdown.[35]

Finally, Galbraith's system should be viewed as a generalization of *The General Theory*, taking into account institutional processes that have changed the structure and nature of economic society, altering the efficacy of various Keynesian policies. Following Keynes, Galbraith pointed out how certain institutions, such as the stock market and the modern corporation, distort rationality and economic outcomes. And he advocated for the acceptance of the 'Principle of Effective Demand'. But Galbraith also recognized the need to move beyond Keynes and consider the ramifications of wider institutional change upon analysis:

> [Keynes] was right to the extent that economics is concerned with the production of goods and the prevention of depressions ... [but he] did not see that, with economic development, power would pass from the consumer to the producer. And, not seeing this, he did not see the increasing divergence between producer or planning purpose and the purpose of the public. And he did not see that – since power to pursue the planning purpose is unequally distributed – development would be unequal. And therewith the distribution of income. Nor did he see that the pursuit of such purpose would threaten the environment and victimize the consumer. And he did not see that the power which allows producer purpose to diverge from public purpose would ensure that inflation would not yield to a simple reversal of the policies that he urged for unemployment and depression. Nor did he foresee the problems of planning co-ordination, national and international. (Galbraith, 1973a: 342)

Galbraith's analysis underscores the importance of updating theory to reflect social and institutional change. Indeed the central themes of Post Keynesian economics, which include a concern for history, uncertainty, distributional issues, and the importance of political and economic institutions in determining the level of economic activity, are all central tenets of the Galbraithian system. Likewise, the central themes of the Institutionalists – economic power, how institutions affect individual behavior, and the importance of understanding the real world by actually examining it – are all major aspects of Galbraith's economics. Galbraith's system thus allows a marriage of Veblen, Keynes, and Kalecki in a comprehensive and contemporary vision of the modern economy. It should form the foundation of renewed efforts to develop alternatives to the conventional wisdom. The purpose of this book is to begin this process.

Introduction, persuasion, and rehabilitation

Galbraith was a deeply original theorist who introduced many concepts into the economic lexicon. Galbraith recognized the significant economic power held by large firms. And such power is one of the main reasons for the success of the US economy in the post-World War II era. But this concentration of power also creates a range of unintended social and environmental problems. Galbraith highlighted the resultant manipulation of the consumer and the inequitable distribution of income and the provision of social goods. For such reasons the good society must counter the power of the large firm and the wealthy, and ensure the provision of those essential goods and services that are underprovided. The state must also use its power to mitigate the macroeconomic problems of financial instability, unemployment, inflation, and poverty. Galbraith presented an analysis of the substantial economic power that large firms possess, he sought to explain salient contemporary concerns, and outlined a programme of civilized policy responses. It is this focus on the role and ramifications of economic power that embodies Galbraith's principal lasting contribution. The purpose of this book is to explore Galbraith's contribution and begin the process of rehabilitating his economic ideas.

Many of these concerns, which Galbraith addressed and discussed, remain relevant. Individuals do not always act in ways that augment their happiness, which challenges one of the basic building blocks of conventional economics. Indeed recent Nobel prize-winner in economics Daniel Kahneman has shown that individuals do not conform to the rules of economic rationality and make systematic mistakes (see Pressman, 2006). Likewise it has become widely acknowledged, in the aftermath of the recent global economic meltdown, that financial markets are driven by "irrational exuberance" and are not as efficient or rational as many in the conventional wisdom would have us believe (Shiller, 2005; Akerlof and Schiller, 2008). Many are concerned that large firms dominate the setting of prices and wages and shape consumer desires through advertising and marketing and that public goods such as transportation and universal access to healthcare are essential to social welfare and to economic growth (Dunn, 2006, 2008a). And it is now widely recognized that Keynesian fiscal policy – using government spending and changes in tax rates to stimulate growth – can be effective in preventing another Great Depression. For all these reasons, the economic contributions of John Kenneth Galbraith deserve lasting attention. The purpose of this book, therefore, is to make this case, and outline some avenues for further research and development of Galbraith's ideas.

Notes

1 There are many parallels between Galbraith's technostructure, Veblen's soviet of engineers (cf. Gordon, 1968) and Berle and Means' technocracy (1932: 356). Galbraith (1979a: 144), however, explicitly rejected the narrowness of the whole technocracy movement.

2 Such themes are also evident in Veblen (1904), who highlighted the nexus between business interests and military spending (see Baran and Sweezy, 1966: chapter 7).

3 The conventional wisdom refers to the structure of acceptable ideas and those that articulate them. It is not the property of any political group and "must not be thought to have a wholly invidious connotation" (Galbraith, 1958a: 43). In many respects it is similar to Thomas Kuhn's (1970) notion of a paradigm. Galbraith's concept of the conventional wisdom also echoes Veblen's (1899: 191) notion of "habits of thought." As Veblen (1914: 6–7) remarked: "The apparatus of ways and means available for the pursuit of whatever may be worth seeking is, substantially all, a matter of tradition out of the past, a legacy of habits of thought accumulated through the experience of past generations. So that the manner, and in a great degree the measure, in which the instinctive ends of life are worked out under any given cultural situation is somewhat closely conditioned by these elements of habit, which so fall into shape as an accepted scheme of life."

4 In his discussion of the central tradition in economics, Galbraith (1958a: 49) demonstrates a keen understanding of the history of economic thought arguing that: "although Adam Smith is rarely identified with the idea, [*The Wealth of Nations*] was one of the beginnings of perhaps the most influential and certainly the most despairing dictum in the history of social comments, the notion that the income of the masses of the people – all who in one way or another worked for a living and whether in industry or agriculture – could not for very long rise very far

above the minimum level necessary for the survival of the race. It is the immortal iron law which, as stiffened by Ricardo and refashioned by Marx, became the chief weapon in the eventual ideological assault on capitalism."

5 See also Lang and Heasman (2004), who point out that a small number of firms and buyers control the diverse food supply chain. Food supply chains are highly concentrated and dominated by retail power. They also highlight the fact that the large advertising outlays of the food industry overwhelmingly extolling the joys of sweet, fatty foods run counter to public health messages about healthy eating.

6 As Eric Schlosser (2002: 4) points out in *Fast Food Nation*: "Adjusted for inflation, the hourly wage of the average US worker peaked in 1973 and then steadily declined for the next twenty-five years. During that period, women entered the workforce in record numbers, often motivated less by a feminist perspective than by a need to pay the bills. In 1975, about one-third of American mothers with young children worked outside the home; today almost two-thirds of such mothers are employed. As the sociologists Cameron Lynne Macdonald and Carmen Sirianni have noted, the entry of so many women into the workforce has greatly increased demand for the types of services that housewives traditionally perform: cooking, cleaning, and childcare. A generation ago, three-quarters of the money used to buy food in the United States was spent to prepare meals at home. Today about half of the money used to buy food is spent at restaurants – mainly at fast food restaurants."

7 Compare Krugman (2006), who in his *New York Times* article "Our Sick Society" makes a series of similar points that echo Galbraith: "Full-time American workers work, on average, about 46 weeks per year; full-time British, French and German workers work only 41 weeks a year. I've pointed out in the past that our workaholic economy is actually more destructive of the 'family values' we claim to honor than the European economies in which regulations and union power have led to shorter working hours. Maybe overwork, together with the stress of living in an economy with a minimal social safety net, damages our health as well as our families."

8 England, for example, appears to be witnessing an epidemic of knife crime. Investigating this phenomenon the UK House of Commons Home Affairs Committee (2009: 79–80) concluded that: "Individuals born into social deprivation are more likely to commit violence. Key risk factors for becoming involved in street violence include coming from a dysfunctional family with poor parental support, low self-worth, poor school attendance and living in an area where aspirations are low and there are few employment opportunities. Young people who have witnessed

or experienced violence as a child are also far more prone to commit violence ... Extreme parental neglect halts the development of faculties that enable the majority of people to regulate their aggression. Solutions should therefore focus on dealing with dysfunctional and violent families and providing opportunities for young people to develop self-worth." Such an assessment is consistent with Galbraith's theoretical framework outlined in *Economics and the Public Purpose.*

9 As Gambs (1975: 94) notes: "Veblen assigned to her the role of consuming conspicuously for her master. Galbraith updates him in the modern idiom. Galbraith gives woman the further task of consuming voluminously. The idea seems to be that if women were not kept at home by our culture, they would consume fewer of the useless things that flow in increasing volume from the planning system. If women worked or were encouraged to spend their time in worthy activities, they would have less time to see and hear advertisements, to stock the home with dust-catchers and other worthless objects." Reisman (1980: 78) highlights the gender power relation that Galbraith identifies: "the man is the head of the family by virtue of his earning power, while the woman is an unpaid servant who performs the tasks and duties assigned to her ... Such subordination leads Galbraith to dismiss the tendency of economists to speak of the 'household' as a fiction which blinds them to the need to disaggregate: in reality, he argues, 'the household, in the established economics, is essentially a disguise for the exercise of male authority'."

10 See also the United Nations human development index, which is reported now on an annual basis (United Nations Development Program, 1999). For a survey of developments in the worldwide standard of living over the last two centuries, see Easterlin (2000).

11 As Galbraith (1973a: 306) remarked: "Neo-classical economics, as even its most prideful communicants would agree, did nothing to prepare people for the explosion of concern over the environment – something that might be expected from a good and competent science."

12 On the similarities and differences between Williamson and Veblen, see Knoedler (1995).

13 In *The Culture of Contentment* (1992: 180), Galbraith continued to press for action, arguing that: "The present and devastated position of the socially assisted underclass has been identified as the most serious social problem of the time, as it is also the greatest threat to long-run peace and civility."

14 The conceptual ideas underpinning human capital theory also surface much earlier in Marshall (1920: 204–19, 560–6). Galbraith had clearly absorbed Marshall's *Principles* (see chapter 12 below). Galbraith's view

of education, nevertheless, is modern and quite distinct from Marshall's heavily "Victorian" analysis. It has, perhaps, greater similarities with Veblen's (1918, 1919) approach.

15 It is interesting to note that Galbraith (1958a: 229) was also aware of what Marxists would refer to as the internal contradictions associated with the investment in human capital: "Education, therefore, is a double-edged sword for the affluent society. It is essential, given the technical and scientific requirements of modern industry. But by widening tastes and also inducing more independent and critical attitudes, it undermines the want-creating power which is indispensable to the modern economy. The effect is enhanced as education enables people to see how they are managed in the interest of the mechanism that is assumed to serve them. The ultimate consequence is that the values of the affluent society, its preoccupation with production as a test of performance in particular, are undermined by the education that is required in those that serve it."

16 Compare the following passage written forty-two years earlier: "Finally, with better social balance, investment in human resources will be kept more nearly abreast of that in material capital. This, we have seen, is the touchstone for technological advance. As such it is a most important and possibly the most important factor in economic growth" (Galbraith, 1958a: 255).

17 It is important, however, to note that higher consumption and lower saving need not result in debt. In principle an individual could have a high propensity to consume of 0.9999 without necessarily going into debt.

18 Russell Jacoby (1987: 5), in his book *The Last Intellectuals*, makes a positive distinction between "intellectuals" who "cherish thinking and ideas" and the more elite cadre of public intellectuals, "the writers and thinkers who address a general and educated public."

19 John S. Gambs' (1975: 9) short introductory volume on Galbraith: "evaluates the work of John Kenneth Galbraith as a social scientist, particularly as a heterodox economist." Gambs was one of the founders and early presidents of the Association for Evolutionary Economics (AFEE) and was on the editorial Board of the *Journal of Economics Issues* (which is published by AFEE).

20 That is not to say he has been ignored by either Post Keynesians or Institutionalists. See, for example, the papers set out in Laperche and Uzunidis (2006) and Laperche, Galbraith, and Uzunidis (2006). However, his contributions are not subject to the same sort of reverence or detailed development as, say, the ideas of Keynes, Veblen, Commons, Robinson, Kaldor, or Kalecki. The ideas of these authors

continue to permeate contemporary writings of Post Keynesians or Institutionalists, unprompted by celebratory symposiums.

21 Compare the institutionalist John Fagg Foster (1981), who argued that institutionalism complements Keynesianism, in providing the crucial theory of institutional adjustment that is required for Keynesian policies to work.

22 Hession (1972: 26) suggests that in "his general orientation to economics, Galbraith is usually classified as a member of the so-called institutional school of thought." Stanfield (1996: 1) and King (2002: 225) agree with this classification. I would argue, however, that Galbraith is broader, sharing many of the macroeconomic tenets of the Post Keynesian school, as well as its focus on the role of uncertainty. I would thus argue that, technically, Galbraith belongs to both the Post Keynesian and old Institutionalist traditions. The old Institutionalist tradition is different to the approach of the new Institutionalists (see Williamson, 2000, 2005; North, 1981, 1990; cf. Hodgson, 1998).

23 This goes to the essence of "old" institutionalism. According to Hodgson (2004: 257): "Institutionalists do not have a very good record in defining and agreeing among themselves upon the essentials of their approach." Hodgson (2004: 257) argued, however, "that there is a core idea in institutionalism that above all others helps to define its identity. The idea that institutions can be reconstitutive of individuals is arguably the most fundamental characteristic of institutional economics. Clearly, institutions themselves differ, in time and in space. However, individuals themselves are also likely to be radically affected by these differences. Different institutions can act as more than constraints on behavior: they may actually change the character and beliefs of the individual. As a result, much of the 'new' institutional economics of Oliver Williamson (1975) and others is not 'institutional economics' in the stronger sense of involving the reconstitution of individual preferences by institutional circumstances. This is because most 'new' institutionalists cling on to an irreducible notion of the rational individual that Veblen, Commons, Mitchell, Hamilton and others were keen to replace or explain." Based on this definition Galbraith can be viewed clearly as being part of the 'old' institutionalist tradition.

24 Veblen (1898a: 381, 384, 386; 1900: 266; 1904: 67, 313, 314, 365) was one of the first to introduce the concept of cumulative causation into economics. Nevertheless Galbraith's conception is quite distinct from Veblen's. As Hodgson (2004: 152–3) points out: "while Veblen coined the term 'cumulative' causation, he used it primarily to refer to cumulative sequences of cause and effect. With other authors, the term 'cumulative causation' took on the different meaning (in modern

parlance) of non-linear processes of positive feedback. For instance, in his classic article on 'increasing returns' Allyn Young (1928: 533) wrote that: 'change becomes progressive and propagates itself in a cumulative way'. One of his students was Nicholas Kaldor, who made extensive use of Young's positive-feedback notion of 'cumulative causation' (Kaldor, 1985). Gunnar Myrdal (1939, 1957) independently took the idea of cumulative causation from the positive feedback mechanisms in the monetary economics of fellow Swedish economist Knut Wicksell." Galbraith's conception links more clearly to this latter-day conception. It is clear, however, that Galbraith was influenced by Veblen, Myrdal, and Kaldor.

25 This is not to suggest that analysis should start from groups or institutions either. Rather a more sophisticated approach is needed (cf. Hodgson, 1988: 53–72). Veblen (1909: 629), for example, argued that individuals impacted on processes and outcomes, that institutions were a product of individuals in a group, and institutions were sustained by individuals: "The growth and mutations of the institutional fabric are an outcome of the conduct of the individual members of the group, since it is out of the experience of the individuals, through the habituation of individuals, that institutions arise; and it is in this same experience that these institutions act to direct and define the aims and end of conduct. It is, of course, on individuals that the system of institutions imposes those conventional standards, ideals, and canons of conduct that make up the community's scheme of life. Scientific inquiry in this field therefore, must deal with individual conduct and must formulate its theoretical results in terms of individual conduct."

26 A notable early exception is Harcourt and Kenyon (1976).

27 In an uncertain world within which "production and hiring decisions must be made in advance of offer for sale and knowledge of market demand ... (a) a price must be set without the 'correct' price being known; (b) the price could well be set 'too high' or 'too low' [in terms of other competitors] ... and (c) others might do the same" (Chick, 1992: 158–9).

28 As Davidson (1972: 149) notes: "In a world of uncertainty where production takes time, the existence of money contracts permits the sharing of burdens of uncertainties between the contracting parties whenever resources are to be committed to produce a flow of goods for a delivery date in the future."

29 According to Galbraith the expansion of aggregate demand requires credit creation, and liquidity preference considerations impact on the demand for and supply of money, but that is independent of any considerations as to how firms arrive at their pricing decisions.

30 As Sawyer (1985b: 22) points out: "There is a degree of correspondence between the distinction made by Kalecki between cost-determined and demand-determined prices (and price changes) and fix-price/flex-price distinction widely used in macroeconomics, and popularized by Hicks and others." Galbraith's approach mirrors Kalecki's approach in that for both the difference between fix and flex price sectors arises due to differences in industrial structure and not speeds of adjustment (cf. Sawyer 1985b: 22).

31 Compare Baran and Sweezy (1966: 17), who argued: "Marxists have failed to explain important developments, or sometimes even to recognize their existence ... Marxists have [not] contributed significantly to our understanding of some of the major characteristics of the 'affluent society' – particularly its colossal capacity to generate private and public waste and the profound economic, political and cultural consequences which flow from this feature of the system." It is important to note, however, that Baran and Sweezy's *Monopoly Capitalism* was an attempt at rectifying this failure. Baran and Sweezy's analysis represents a heady admixture of Marx, Veblen, Keynes, and Schumpeter exhibiting many parallels with, and some important divergences from, Galbraith (cf. Stanfield, 1996).

32 Veblen (1899: 78) used a specific definition of 'waste' that appears to underpin much of Galbraith's critique of advertising and his theory of social imbalance: "The use of the term 'waste' is in one respect an unfortunate one. As used in the speech of everyday life the word carries an undertone of deprecation. It is here used for want of a better term that will adequately describe the same range of motives and of phenomena, and it is not to be taken in an odious sense, as implying an illegitimate expenditure of human products or of human life. In the view of economic theory the expenditure in question is no more and no less legitimate than any other expenditure. It is here called 'waste' because this expenditure does not serve human life or human well-being on the whole, not because it is waste or misdirection of effort or expenditure as viewed from the standpoint of the individual consumer who chooses it."

33 For a discussion of the Veblenian origins of *The New Industrial State*, see Leathers and Evans (1973, 1980) and Rutherford (1980; see also 1984; 1992). Galbraith (1979a), however, was of the view that much of Veblen's (e.g. 1904) economic writings were not as penetrating as his social observations. As Galbraith (1979a: 144) noted in his essay "Who was Thorstein Veblen": "The basic idea of *The Theory of the Business Enterprise* is a plausible one – I can still remember my excitement when I first read the book in the thirties while a student at Berkeley, where

the Veblen influence was strong. There is a conflict between the ordered rationality of the machine process as developed by engineers and technicians and the moneymaking context in which it operates. The money makers through competition and inter-firm aggression, and the resolution of the latter by consolidation and monopoly, sabotage the rich possibilities inherent in the machine process. But – though some will still object – the idea has been a blind alley. Organization and management are greater tasks than Veblen implies; so is the problem of accommodating production to social need. As so is that of motivation and incentive. All of this has become evident in the socialist economies, where far more difficulties have been encountered in translating the rationality of the machine process into effective economic performance than Veblen would have supposed. In the thirties, after Veblen's death, the political movement (perhaps more properly the cult) 'technocracy' was founded on these ideas by Howard Scott. For a while it flourished. Had the technocrats been given a chance, they would have faced the same problems of management, organization and incentives as the socialist states. Though much read in the first half of the century, *The Theory of the Business Enterprise*, unlike *The Theory of the Leisure Class*, has not similarly survived." Such observations underpin my assessment that while similar economic themes surface in both Veblen and Galbraith there is nevertheless a fundamental difference in approach and vision (cf. Hodgson, 2004: 222). Galbraith should not be relegated to the role of a minor Veblenian (cf. Leathers and Evans, 1973; Evans and Leathers, 1980; see also Kahn, 1974).

34 Galbraith's principal objective in writing *The Great Crash, 1929* was to challenge the conventional wisdom that the financial and manufacturing sectors of the economy were insulated; that is, that money and finance were a veil, behind which real forces determined the level of economic activity. According to Galbraith (1955a: 26): "There is a unity in economic phenomena; no Chinese wall separates the fiduciary from the real. Wall Street – as its prophets for other purposes conceded – is of considerable importance in the American economy. The stock market crash and the speculation that made it inevitable had an important effect on the performance, or rather malperformance, of the economy in the ensuing months and years."

35 Galbraith's analysis again appears superficially similar to Veblen's. For example Hodgson (2004: 207) notes: "Veblen saw business fluctuations and industrial depressions as rooted in the credit mechanism and business psychology, with their cycles of boom, bust and possible recovery. This analysis had business speculations and expectations at the centre, against the counterpoint of the increasing potential

productivity of mechanized industry. Against the prevailing view that industrial recessions in market economies would automatically bring about the mechanisms of recovery, Veblen stressed that the forces that created depressions would feed cumulatively on their own results." Nevertheless, Galbraith (1979a: 144) repudiated his analysis of *The Theory of Business Enterprise*, suggesting his view of financial markets reflected more the influence of Keynes. As Leathers and Raines (2008: 551–2) point out: "While speculative booms and collapses in stock prices played a key role in Veblen's analysis, there was little attention to the internal dynamics of speculative manias. He recognized that individual stock prices were often manipulated, but explained general movements in stock prices as quasi-efficient stock markets capitalizing 'putative' future profits. During the booms, stock prices reflected speculative expectations about corporate profits rather than speculative expectations about stock prices themselves. The expectations of profits were generated by a business prosperity that was initiated by external developments that temporarily stimulated aggregate demand and, subsequently, was magnified by the general speculative psychology about prices and profits."

4 *The methodology of John Kenneth Galbraith*

Evidently an economic inquiry which occupies itself exclusively with the movements of this consistent, elemental human nature under given, stable institutional conditions – such as is the case with the current hedonistic economics – can reach statical results alone; since it makes abstraction from those elements that make for anything but a statical result.

Thorstein Veblen (1909: 628–9)

In considering the image of modern industrial society, one must have clearly in mind two factors that act strongly and persistently to distort the economist's view of that reality. The first of these distorting factors is the very great inclination to think of the ultimate subject matter with which we deal in static terms ... The second factor that distorts understanding is the very great social and political convenience – or so it seems – of the wrong image of economic society.

J. K. Galbraith (1979a: 3–5)

By today's standards many practicing economists would view Galbraith as an economic sociologist rather than as a technical economist. Preferring prose to algebra his efforts are viewed by many as providing insight and challenge, but ultimately he stands accused of lacking rigor and empirical grounding. Like Veblen, Galbraith is often mistakenly regarded as lying outside the purview of economics proper. This is unfair and overlooks significant aspects of Galbraith's contributions and approach. Galbraith's approach reflected his analytical focus. That is to say, Galbraith largely rejected the methods of mainstream economics as inappropriate for the study of historical and institutional change. As Galbraith (1991: 41) argued: "Economics that assumes transformation, change, can never be as tidy, secure and elegant as that which assumes and cultivates unchanging verity."

Galbraith espoused an analytical approach that reflected an historical and evolutionary conceptualization of the economic process and resulted in the adoption and tailoring of methods accordingly.[1] His subsequent theoretical structures embody a range of methodological considerations that accords well with, what contemporary methodologists refer to as, realism (Dow, 1996a; Lawson, 1997, 2003; Hodgson, 2001, 2004). Galbraith's theoretical system develops explanatory critique; analyzing salient societal trends, exposing false beliefs, identifying the social processes that generate those beliefs, and advocating an emancipatory response to the problems and issues identified (Stanfield, 1996).

Nevertheless, although some Institutionalists (e.g. Samuels, 1984; Stanfield, 1996; Hodgson, 2001b, 2003) have attempted to highlight Galbraith's methodological approach, Galbraith's own explicit methodological writings are typically overlooked. This is perhaps because in courting a popular audience, Galbraith's deeper methodological reflections are brief and kept at a general level. Yet, throughout all his major works Galbraith acknowledged the importance of methodological considerations as underpinning the process by which his more substantive contributions and conclusions were developed. Although Galbraith seldom undertook lengthy methodological reflection, he was keen to stress the fact that his analysis "reverses the established method" (Galbraith, 1967a: 14). And in *The New Industrial State*, he felt compelled to insert "An Addendum on Economic Method", to explain why his analysis differed so markedly from that of the mainstream economics profession. For Galbraith his different, but nevertheless legitimate scientific approach, was also a major source of the controversy that his writings generated.

Galbraith was keen to develop an alternative and comprehensive view of the economic system that was in quite fundamental respects – in terms of method, theoretical structure, and policy – at variance with the prevailing economics. Galbraith (1973a: 20) proposed "a revised view of the purpose of the economic system [and] a revised view of the purpose of economics." Such considerations suggest that a detailed examination of Galbraith's view of reality, and how he studied it, is warranted. It is important to note that I am not interested at this point in evaluating the specific content and explanatory power *per se* of Galbraith's contribution. This is considered in more detail in other chapters below. My purpose here is to consider the methodological approach of J. K. Galbraith, its broader underpinnings, and its analytical implications. Before I consider Galbraith's views regarding how social science should be practiced, I examine his reflections on the more general nature of reality – what methodologists refer to as his "philosophical ontology."

Galbraith and the nature of reality

Throughout his long life Galbraith sought to reorient economics to become a more socially useful and relevant discipline, advocating greater engagement with practical and contemporary problems. In doing so Galbraith (1967a: 392–402) acknowledged the need to reflect on the nature of social reality and social science, to consider how it differed from the physical sciences, and to take that into account when developing theory, or conducting analysis. Galbraith was keen to highlight the implicit (philosophical) assumptions about the nature of reality that underpin the conventional wisdom.[2] Following Marx, Veblen, and Keynes, Galbraith recognized that "the economic environment is not homogenous over time" (Keynes, 1973: 289). Galbraith accepted Keynes's argument that economics is a moral science, dealing with creative human agents and social processes. Human decision-making and actions move society onward – the march of events. Social theory also needs to be updated to reflect this march of events. Otherwise outdated social theory loses its scientific status, solidifying into ideology.[3]

In contrast to Schumpeter (1954), who argued that ideology was the pre-analytic vision that was ground out through scientific analysis, Galbraith argued instead that as society changes, the dominant scientific analysis in one period may be inappropriate and misleading in another. Galbraith recognized that when analyzing the real world, researchers are frequently constrained by habitual modes of thought that may be outdated and hide from view new social phenomena. As Galbraith (1958a: 35) pointed out: "The first requirement for an understanding of contemporary economic and social life is a clear view of the relation between events and the ideas which interpret them. For each of these has a life of its own, and much as it may seem a contradiction in terms each is capable for a considerable period of pursuing an independent course."

For Galbraith, science in one period could yield to ideology in another, if underlying change in the economy was not recognized and incorporated into analysis. The reason for this reflects the nature of social science, which deals with change and social processes: "In the physical sciences – chemistry, physics, biology – change is associated only with discovery, with the improving state of knowledge. The matter being studied does not change. In economics, as in other social sciences, there is change both in the state of knowledge and in what is being studied" (Galbraith, 1967a: 400).[4]

In reflecting on such issues Galbraith considered whether social phenomena and processes can be analyzed in the same way as natural phenomena, that is, he focused on what contemporary methodologists call "the question of naturalism". He concluded that: "Physics, chemistry, geology and biology are indubitably sciences; they are mounted on an unchanging subject matter" (Galbraith, 1967a: 401). In drawing attention to the immutable nature of the subject matter of the physical sciences, it is clear that Galbraith recognized the importance and value of reflecting on the methods of the science of economics, that is, what methodologists refer to as its ontological presuppositions. In doing so, Galbraith – like Hayek, Keynes, Kaldor Marshall, Marx, Menger, Robinson, Schumpeter, and Veblen – is unusual among economists. Furthermore, in considering the (ontological) underpinnings of the methods of the natural sciences, which attempt to intervene, insulate and isolate some fixed or relatively stable causal mechanism through experimental methods of control, Galbraith raised the possibility that not all objects of scientific enquiry will be constant, atomic, or free from the influence of the scientist (cf. Dow, 1996a).

Galbraith (1971: 9) argued that the successes associated with the physical sciences are related to the fact that "the natural sciences are not subject to underlying institutional or behavioral change," which underpins their ability to (i) isolate objects of analysis, and (ii) to guarantee their constancy over time.[5] In the first case, the object is considered always to have been affected by the same causal factor, such that every effect has the same cause. In the latter case, the objects and structures of the physical sciences exhibit an immutability, which can be summarized loosely as signifying the fact that a cause, always and everywhere, results in the same effect.[6] Together these assumptions mean that it is possible to assume that the objects of enquiry do not change over time. These assumptions characterize the approach of the physical sciences.

Social phenomena, however, exhibit a degree of flux and change such that social events and processes are not constant over time.[7] Galbraith argued that in contrast to the physical realm, the social realm (including economic science, which itself is a social activity) is both purposeful and subject to change, as a result of transformative and creative human agency. This echoes Keynes (1973: 300), who argued: "One has to be constantly on guard against treating the material as constant and homogenous. It is as though the fall of the apple to the ground depended on the apple's motives, on whether it is worth falling to the ground, whether the ground wanted the apple to fall, and on mistaken calculations on the part of the apple as to how far it was from the centre of the earth." As such, the methods of the physical sciences – as epitomized by either mathematical formalism, or by the laboratory process of experimental control – may obscure from view important social processes that either cannot be captured neatly by algebra or because their causes or effects cannot be conveniently isolated. Accordingly, Galbraith (1967a: 23–4) explicitly recognized the limitations of rooting explanations of social phenomenon in terms of atomized individuals, acknowledging that social change was complex, with the whole often more than the sum of its parts:

> To view [social changes] in isolation from each other, the usual practice, is greatly to minimize their effect. They are related to each other as cause to consequence. All are part of a yet larger matrix of change. In its effect on economic society this matrix has been more than the sum of its parts.

Keynes (1972b: 262) made a similar point in his biographical essay on Edgeworth, arguing:

> Mathematical Psychics has not ... fulfilled its early promise ... When the young Edgeworth chose it, he may have looked to find secrets as wonderful as those which the physicists have found since those days ... this has not happened ... The atomic hypothesis which has worked so splendidly in physics breaks down in psychics. We are faced at every turn with the problems of organic unity, of discreteness, of discontinuity – the whole is not equal to the sum of the parts, comparisons of quantity fail us, small changes produce large effects, the assumptions of a uniform and homogeneous continuum are not satisfied.

In other words, if social reality is complex, constantly evolving and changing, then the employment of methods that are tailored to the study of stable, unchanging processes is likely to throw up misleading accounts of individual and collective human behavior (Eichner, 1983; Dow, 1997b; Stanfield, 1994; Hodgson, 2001a; Lawson, 1997, 2003).[8] It is such reflection, or ontological insight, that underpins Galbraith's (1991: 41) questioning of the relevance of the methods of the physical sciences:

> Are we concerned with a science or subject matter that is essentially static? Does economics explore and serve human motivations, aspirations and institutions that are ultimately constant? Does the subject matter change only as its unchanging context is more deeply explored and understood? ... Or, on the contrary, are we dealing with a subject matter that is in a constant state of transformation? Is the ultimate economic motivation subject to change? And, more particularly, are the economic institutions through which it is expressed and served also in process of change?

Therefore, to the extent that economics is a subject that is characterized by change, and that the subject can in some way affect the object, the methods of natural science, which presuppose a constant and invariable subject matter, cannot be accepted as universal in application (Dow, 1996a; Hodgson, 2001a, 2004).[9] It is for similar reasons that Galbraith (1971: 8) warned against the narrow pursuit of "imitative scientism"' – or what realist's now refer to as "positivistic naturalism" – that is, the mimicking of the methods of the natural sciences, "which is carried further in economics than in any other discipline."

Galbraith argued that the methods of mainstream economics are pursued largely because they facilitate formalistic modeling, rather than because they help us to understand reality. They are accepted for no better reason than that formalist methods are perceived to form the basis of the successful natural sciences, rather than because they illuminate social change (cf. Chick, 1998; Krugman, 1998). As Galbraith (1967a: 401; 1988: 376) pointed out, however, they may in fact hinder such analysis. The consequence of pursuing and employing the methods associated with the physical sciences is the exclusion from consideration of human agency, and its associated change and consequence.[10] Galbraith was concerned that the desire to emulate the hard sciences contributes to the active withdrawal of economists from engaging with reality. What is more, a further consequence of 'imitative scientism' has been the establishment of a well-graded prestige system that accords status to those that mimic the methods and presuppositions of the physical sciences and assigns low regard to those that actively seek to engage with reality:

> The prestige system of economics ... assigns ... the very lowest position to the man who deals with everyday policy. For this individual, in concerning himself with the wisdom of a new tax or the need for an increased deficit, is immediately caught up in a variety of political and moral judgments. This puts him in communication with the world at large. As such, he is a threat to the sharp delineation which separates the tribal group from the rest of society and thus to the prestige system of the profession. Moreover, his achievements are rated not by his professional peers but by outsiders. This causes difficulty in fitting him into the professional hierarchy and argues strongly for leaving him at the bottom. (Galbraith, 1971: 32)[11]

Further:

> At the higher levels, economics divorces itself fully from practical questions and from the influence of other fields of scholarship with the exception of mathematics and statistics. One can think of the full prestige structure of the subject as a hollow pyramid or cone, the sides of which, though they are transparent and with numerous openings at the base, become increasingly opaque and impermeable as one proceeds to the apex. Positions near the apex are thus fully protected from external communication and influence. Work here is pure in the literal sense. Questions of practical application are excluded as also the influence of other disciplines. And this being so, tasks can be accommodated to the analytical techniques which the scholar wishes to use. These techniques may not be mathematical but the absence of extraneous practical considerations is conducive to mathematical techniques ... It is no criticism of this work that it is unrelated to the real world. Such divorce is its most strongly intended feature. (Galbraith, 1971: 33)

The effect is that much of economics operates as a convenient fiction, which serves to reproduce and reinforce the sociology of the profession, rather than illuminating reality (cf. Waller, 2008; Wrenn, Stanfield, and Carroll, 2008).[12] As Krugman (1994: 8) observed in *Peddling Prosperity*, in a manner reminiscent of Galbraith:

> You don't progress as an economics professor by solving the real problems of the real economy, at least not in any direct way. Instead you progress by convincing your colleagues that you are clever. In an ideal world you would demonstrate your cleverness by developing blindingly original ideas or producing definitive evidence about how the economy actually works. But most of us can't do that, at least not consistently. So professors look for more surefire approaches. And thus the most popular economic theories among the professors tend to be those that best allow for ingenious elaboration without fundamental innovation – ways to show that you are smart by putting old wine in new bottles, usually with fancier mathematical labels.

In the same way, a further and related effect of "imitative scientism" has been the disparagement accorded to interdisciplinary social theorizing or practical work. Yet, as Galbraith (1967a: 393) warned: "specialization is a scientific convenience, not a scientific virtue." The consequence of such "imitative scientism" is the inappropriate employment of formalistic (closed system) reasoning which, by its nature, excludes consideration of institutional and behavioral change. The problem is such that applying the methods of natural science to the study of evolutionary and transmutable processes is unlikely to assist in the generation of practical insights and solutions. For Galbraith, this methodological mistake is a source of popular derision habitually leveled at economists:

> This explains why professional economists of the highest standing often come forward with proposals of the most impractical sort – for the abolition of corporations or trade unions, the outlawing of oligopoly, the enforcement of free competition, therapeutic unemployment, cathartic deflation, elimination of central banks, ending of income taxes – with no damage whatever to their reputations. No store is set by ability to assess such measures in their political and social context. On the contrary, such preoccupation is discrediting. (Galbraith, 1971: 33n)

In developing his argument, it is important to note that Galbraith does not reject *per se* formal methods or mathematical deduction on *a priori* grounds. If mathematics can be brought to bear to illuminate reality, then its usefulness should of course be considered (cf. Chick, 1998). Nevertheless, the *a posteriori* lack of practical content of much economic and mathematical reasoning highlights the limitations of an overly formalistic method in illuminating change (see Galbraith, 1971: 9; cf. Chick, 1995, 1998; Dow, 1996a).[13] Thus, to narrow down *a priori* the range of methodological approaches by eschewing those that do not accord with the methods of the natural sciences is clearly unwarranted. Instead a broader more considered view of the appropriateness of a variety of different methods is required (Dow, 1996a; Hodgson, 2001a, 2006).[14]

Why is economics not an evolutionary science?

It is important to note that Galbraith did not reject the possibility of the scientific analysis of social phenomenon. Nor was Galbraith arguing that economics should be dumbed down, or that it should not be technical:

That economics has a considerable conceptual apparatus with an appropriate terminology cannot be a serious ground for complaint. Economic phenomena, ideas and instruments of analysis exist. They require names. No one can reasonably ask a serious scholar in the field to avoid reference to index numbers, the capital gains tax, the consumption function, acceleration effects, circular money flows, inflation, linear programming, the progressive income tax, the pure rate of interest or the European Common Market. Nor should he be expected to explain what these are. Education in economics is, in considerable measure, an introduction to this terminology and to the ideas that it denotes. Anyone who has difficulties with the ideas should complete his education or, following an exceedingly well-beaten path, leave the subject alone. (Galbraith, 1971: 306)

Rather, Galbraith was arguing that economics needs to recognize and explain the underlying change in the economy, which is all too often obscured from view by the methods underpinning the conventional wisdom:

In the last one hundred years the great corporate enterprise, the trade union, depression and war, increasing and increasingly dispersed affluence, the changing nature of money and the new and enhanced role of the central bank, the declining role of agriculture with the counterpart urbanization and growth of urban poverty, the rise of the welfare state the newly assumed responsibility of the government for overall economic performance, the emergence of socialist states, have all dramatically altered, even revolutionized economic life. (Galbraith, 1987: 2)

Galbraith argued that to understand and analyze such institutional change a more relevant view of the nature of scientific method, as applied to economics, was required. Galbraith observed that the dominant scientific approach, in seeking to identify universal and eternal economic truths and patterns, both misleads and obfuscates dynamic and evolutionary social processes. This is why Galbraith (1973a: 23) rejected "imitative scientism" and sought to "revert to the older, more traditional, more scientific, expository purpose which is to seek to understand how things are."[15] From this perspective social science, including economic science, is possible, but its practice will differ from natural sciences owing to the distinct nature of social processes (cf. Veblen, 1898a; Lawson, 1997, 2003; Hodgson, 2001a, 2004, 2006).

Galbraith, in seeking a reorientation of economics, was not rejecting the possibility of scientific understanding – that is the possibility that the study of social processes can be scientific (in the sense of natural science). Specifically, natural science methods, for example excessive and abstract formalism, may be nothing more than an elaborate game, unable to shed light on contemporary problems and issues. Instead Galbraith argued that scientific enquiry and methods must be tailored appropriately and must avoid imitating slavishly the methods and approach of the natural sciences (cf. Lawson, 1997, 2003; Hodgson, 2001a, 2004, 2006).[16] Nevertheless the possibility of a scientific economics remains.

Galbraith argued that the methods of economists should reflect the nature of reality, that is, for a fashioning of methods that reflect what contemporary methodologists refer to as the ontological assumptions of the phenomenon under investigation (cf. Dow, 1997a, 1997b; Lawson, 1997, 2003; Hodgson, 2001a, 2004, 2006). Realism and relevance must be paramount, Galbraith argued, if economists are to be the "guardians of the possibility of civilization." Accordingly the scientific nature of economic ideas should be evaluated against their ability to relate to popular concerns about the economic system rather than the congruence of method with the natural sciences – the aim of "imitative scientism." The value of a useful economics rests on its ability to penetrate and explain contemporary social concerns:

> The ultimate test of a set of economic ideas – a system, if the word be allowed – is whether it illuminates the anxieties of the time. Does it explain problems that people find urgent? Does it bear on the current criticisms of economic performance? Most important, perhaps, does it bear upon the issues of political debate, for these, though many have always preferred to believe otherwise, do not ignite spontaneously or emerge from the mouths of agitators to afflict the comfortable. (Galbraith, 1973a: 215)[17]

Specifically Galbraith argued that the aim of economic science is to identify, and then explain, significant institutional change and social trends (cf. Stanfield and Wrenn, 2005). Methodologically this means first, identify empirical matters of interest and second, make claims about the mechanisms and processes producing these empirical phenomena (Lawson, 2003). Galbraith employed both of these steps, identifying numerous phenomena of interest as well as the causal factors that generated them.[18]

In seeking to understand institutional change, Galbraith, as noted above, "reverses the established method" (Galbraith, 1967a: 14).[19] Throughout all his major theoretical contributions, Galbraith began by identifying emergent trends that call for further investigation and elaboration and then proceeded to analyze their salience (Stanfield, 1996; cf. Kaldor, 1972; Lawson, 1989, 1997).[20] Galbraith sought to move beyond surface phenomena and developed a theoretical system that was concerned with real social structures, as opposed to artificial theoretical constructs, and with the essential and salient aspects of social processes.

There are several emerging social trends that feature throughout Galbraith's principal theoretical contributions and which underpin his broader vision. These trends are summarized in the first chapter of *The New Industrial State*.[21] First, there is the increasingly technologically sophisticated production process that has underpinned productive advance (Galbraith, 1952a, 1967a). Second, there is the unquestionable growth and development of the corporate form of organization with its associated divorce of ownership from control and its diminishing symbiosis with unionism (Galbraith, 1952a, 1967a). The third visible trend is the increasing private affluence of the corporate sector in modern society, as rendered by the productive advance of the modern business enterprise (Galbraith, 1952a, 1958a, 1967a, 1973a).[22] Fourth, there has been a massive increase in the apparatus of "persuasion and exhortation" and an associated rise of consumerism, as evidenced by the continuing preoccupation with increasing the net national output, with its concomitant impact on the environment and the quality of life (Galbraith, 1949b, 1952a, 1958a, 1967a).[23] Fifth, there is the dramatic increase in the extent of state activities in social and economic life especially since the Keynesian revolution (Galbraith, 1958a, 1967a). Sixth, this increase in state activity has typically not resulted in an even and properly funded investment in public goods such as social housing, healthcare, mass public transportation, parks and recreational facilities (Galbraith, 1958a, 1973a, 1992). Similarly, while there has been a drive to ensure that higher education aligns more closely with business needs, the consequence has been that the intrinsic and critical role of higher education has been undervalued, and thus remains underdeveloped (Galbraith, 1967a). Finally, there is the inflationary bias that characterizes the modern economy (Galbraith, 1952a, 1967a, 1973a).

Having established the facts that require further investigation, Galbraith analyzed the underlying causal mechanisms, processes, and institutions that generated them. For Galbraith what was happening on the surface did not necessarily reflect what was going on underneath. Galbraith, like Marx, sought to move beyond appearances and look at underlying trends and processes. In doing so he developed an original analysis of the nature of modern society that considered emerging social trends and concerns, long before many of his fellow academics began to recognize and study that reality.[24]

Change and the industrial system

Galbraith offered a comprehensive view of the modern economy that illuminated contemporary concerns and their underpinning social causes. At its core Galbraith identified the modern corporation, rather than the state or the individual, as the principal locus and driver of change (Galbraith, 1973a: 54). In focusing on the modern firm, however, Galbraith was conscious to avoid engaging in what methodologists refer to as "institutional reductionism" (cf. Hodgson, 1988). Galbraith recognized the emergent and complex nature of social change which affects the way we think and analyze social processes, and noted that:

> all social life is a fabric of tightly interwoven threads. The change of which the corporation is the driving force is a complex process in which many things are altered at the same time and in which cause becomes consequence and cause again. No description is uniquely correct; much depends on where one breaks into this matrix. But a starting point which has application over the whole development is technology and its yet more important counterpart which is organization. (Galbraith, 1973a: 54)

Such considerations highlight how Galbraith used abstraction in developing his theoretical structure. Galbraith recognized that much of what is essential to the explanation of social structures and processes is highly context related. It is still necessary, however, to develop theory to explain and illuminate reality; that is, Galbraith avoided the problems commonly ascribed to the historical school (see Hodgson, 2001a, 2004). Galbraith focused on what he deemed to be fundamental in explaining significant social trends and processes. He argued that it is critical to understand the nature of technology and organization as it relates to the modern corporation, in order to identify the proper social response.[25] He recognized, for example, that abstraction, carefully carried out, enables us to access and understand a complex and dynamic reality (cf. Lawson, 1997: 131–3, 232–7; Hodgson, 2001a). Abstraction for Galbraith was therefore an indispensable part of scientific analysis that could be marshaled to illuminate social change.

Galbraith's (1973a: 54) argument was that advanced "technology – the development and application of scientific or systematic knowledge to practical tasks – is a central feature of modern economic development." And it is advanced technology that calls for organization. The consequence of such modern technology is that it requires detailed specialized knowledge, effective group decision-making and large capital commitments to be conducted and coordinated over long periods of time. Accordingly, it cannot be left to whim and chance and must be sought to be managed:

> Goods being in process for a greater time, the investment in working capital is greater. Steps must be taken to ensure that initial decisions are not ruined and capital lost by events that occur before the results are achieved.

The capital that is now at risk and the organization that now exists must be paid for – are an overhead cost. It is incurred or persists whatever the level of output. Things that might go wrong and jeopardize sales and therewith the return to capital or the revenue that is needed to pay for organization must be prevented from going wrong; things that need to go right must be made to go right. (Galbraith, 1973a: 55)

It is for such reasons that the firm is obliged to engage in extensive planning. Planning promotes the successful organization of production and facilitates the active mitigation of unfettered agency from both within and outside the firm. Planning is an inescapable consequence of advanced technology and the extended, highly specialized, division of labor that is called forth to manage it.

Galbraith focused on the social structures and mechanisms, and the actions of agents within those structures, that seek to transform and reproduce the modern corporation (cf. Courvisanos, 2005). This led Galbraith to identify a class of business specialists that includes management, accountants, lawyers, technicians, marketers, and engineers among others – what is referred to as the technostructure. In doing so, Galbraith articulated a holistic, socially embedded view of the knowledge process upon which corporate success is founded: "Specialized knowledge and its coordination have now, as we have seen, become the decisive factor in economic success. This requires that men work in groups. And power passes to these groups" (Galbraith, 1967a: 151). Anticipating much of the recent discussion on the nature of the learning economy, as well as the postwar expansion in higher education, Galbraith recognized that the requisite technical knowledge associated with modern production is embodied in seasoned experience, tacit knowledge, and intuition and is thus not always explicit or codifiable (see chapter 7 below).[26]

Galbraith's focus on the technostructure is a direct challenge to the conventional wisdom, which espouses an atomistic methodological individualism. In the conventional wisdom individuals are to be the sole explanatory units of analysis. In the conventional wisdom individuals are stripped of their agency and relations to others (cf. Davis, 2003; Dow, 1997b; Hodgson, 2007). In contrast Galbraith offered a socialized view of "practical" knowledge, which is transformed and reproduced through the decisions and planning rules and routines of the modern corporation (cf. Hodgson, 1996, 1999, 2004, 2006).[27]

The salience of the technostructure is that it is involved in and responsible for such investments and is of necessity highly committed to ensuring its success for its own narrow ends:

> An organization acquires power, it uses that power, not surprisingly, to serve the ends of those involved. These ends – job security, pay, promotion, prestige, company plane and private washroom, the charm of collectively exercised power – are all strongly served by the growth of the enterprise. So growth both enhances power over prices, costs, consumers, suppliers, the community and the state and also rewards in a very personal way those who bring it about. Not surprisingly, the growth of the firm is a dominant tendency of advanced economic development. (Galbraith, 1973a: 56)

The simultaneous consequence of technology is therefore that it promotes the consolidation of economic power, as well as requires it: "The larger the firm, the larger it will be in its industry. The greater, accordingly, will be its influence in setting prices and costs. And the greater, in general, will be its influence on consumers, the community and the state – the greater, in short, will be its ability to influence, i.e., plan its environment" (Galbraith, 1973a: 56). The large modern corporation has, therefore, a major impact upon society over time and space:

> This growth, with the associated exercise of power, is the primal force by which economic society is altered. In its practical manifestation, however, it is singularly uneven. In some parts of the economy such growth by the firm is subject to no clear upper limit. In other parts it is subject to severe limits or it proceeds against increasing resistance. Where the growth is stunted, so, of course, is the capacity to persuade consumers as to products, and the state as to products and needs, and so is the technical competence that goes with organization. These are facts of the first importance for understanding the modern economy. That is why, in some parts of the economy, product and the associated blessings are great or excessive and in other parts deficient. It is why the rewards to workers and other participants are far more favorable in some parts of the economy than others. It explains, as we shall see, much else. (Galbraith, 1973a: 56–7)

From this primary abstraction Galbraith (1967a, 1973a) proceeded to explain and clarify the impact, effects and consequences of a number of popular and contemporary concerns such as: the overproduction of private goods (associated with the modern corporation) and the underproduction of merit and public goods (owing to the deficiency of technology and organization); the increasingly superfluous nature of much technical innovation directed at socially irrelevant commodities; the failure of economic growth to ameliorate enduring social problems; the environmental anxiety; the uneven distribution of government expenditure reflected in the spending on the military and other forms of social infrastructure, e.g. roads, to the relative neglect of others, e.g. healthcare and education[28]; the increasingly skewed income distribution between different sectors and personnel; the enduring distinction between the high and low wage industries, that is, the bimodal distinction between the planning and market systems (and the domination of the latter by the former); the problems of economy wide coordination; the continuing fear of inflation as opposed to deflation; the unresponsiveness of the modern corporation and international institutions to public pressure and opinion; the vilification of the multinational corporations and its associated multilateral trade institutions, and so on.

I shall consider such issues in more detail in the chapters that follow. What is important to note, however, is that Galbraith, by focusing on the consequences of technology, the associated size and resultant power of the modern corporation, and the agency of the technostructure, is identifying a series of casual structures. Again, this is consistent with a realist orientation which seeks to identify the processes and mechanisms that give rise to dominant social and economic trends.

The emancipation of belief

Galbraith's theoretical contributions, in analyzing a range of contemporary concerns, sought to identify the existence of relevant shared human objectives and raise self-awareness of such needs and interests such that they feed into policy making and action. The pursuit of explanation and critique was not undertaken, therefore, for its own sake. Galbraith, like Marx, believed that the purpose of economics was not just to understand or explain the economy, but also to change it. As Reisman (1980: 124) notes: "Galbraith believes that social goals need to be revised, and that the precondition for such revision is the emancipation of belief from the chains of outdated ideology." Consequently, Galbraith promoted critical reflection to challenge conventional myths and drive collective and corrective action (see, for example, Galbraith, 1973a: 243). According to Galbraith the purpose of analysis is to develop understanding so as to galvanize action to transform social structures and institutions in a ways that aligns them more closely with societal needs (Reisman, 1980: chapter 7; see also Stanfield, 1996: 118–52). For Galbraith, "the emancipation of belief" must result in action to transform those structures that create false beliefs and obfuscate reality. Galbraith sought to identify those views, structures and institutions that were obsolete, restrictive, or misleading, and to replace them with those that are relevant, necessary, and empowering: "The first step in reform ... is to win emancipation of belief. Until this has happened, there is no chance for mobilizing the public on behalf of its own purposes in opposition to those of the technostructure and the planning system" (Galbraith, 1973a: 239). In so doing, Galbraith arguably goes further than any economist apart from Marx in engaging in what contemporary methodologists refer to as "explanatory critique." Explanatory critique has three key features: it identifies false beliefs in society; it identifies those structures which create them, and; shows how those structures create false beliefs that perpetuate or preserve those structures.[29]

Through his notion of the conventional wisdom Galbraith criticized mainstream economics as a set of false beliefs originating through its neglect of historical and social change (Samuels, 1984).[30] He argued that the conventional wisdoms of society and the economics textbooks, operate as a convenient fiction serving the interests of the technostructure, as well as the business and political elite (cf. Veblen, 1899, 1918, 1919). This, he argued, should be understood and challenged:

> The first step in the assault on belief is to show the sources of the present myth. The next is to identify and render null the specific instruments for perpetuating the myth. These instruments are four, as follows: (1) The present economic pedagogy ... The service of present economic instruction is not to understanding but to the purposes of the planning system ... (2) The present orientation of the educational system ... [which holds] scientific, engineering, business and legal instruction to be useful; instruction in the arts, and notably if it is creative in character, to be decorative or recreational ... (3) The present reaction to overt persuasion. The present reaction to advertising and other forms of producer persuasion is, broadly speaking, one of resigned acceptance. Exaggeration is always assumed and mendacity

normally suspected. But to yield is not thought damaging ... (4) The manufacture of public policy ... The planning system is symbiotically related to the Executive branch of Government ... Emancipation of belief requires that all policy emanating from the Executive and the acolytes of the corporate community be assumed, in the absence of contrary demonstration, to be what serves the needs of the planning system. (Galbraith, 1973a: 244–6)

Galbraith's explanatory critique, unsurprisingly, targeted neo-classical economics and its "imitative scientism." Galbraith argued that the pursuit of such "'imitative scientism" was not neutral in effect (cf. Krugman, 2009). In its neglect of change mainstream economics (unintentionally) excludes urgent as well as politically salient questions from professional consideration (cf. Samuels, 1984; Reisman, 1990; Hodgson, 2001a). The attachment to and acceptability of established ideas is great and resistant to the accommodation of new circumstance into social thought. In terms of the body of economic ideas this reflects both the historical genesis of economics itself and the (deductive) methodological orientation of the mainstream economics project (Galbraith, 1971: 50–72).

The consequence is that an economics that does not accommodate and analyze change, functions not to improve understanding of broader civil society through the development of appropriate social policy, but rather to promote the goals of those who possess power in the economic system. This is what Galbraith refers to as its instrumental role:

The accepted economics models ... have not necessarily been the ones that illuminated reality. They have frequently served to divert attention from questions of great social urgency which, in the established view, had alarming implications for political action. In doing this, they and the subject of economics have served a political function. Economics has been not a science but a conservatively useful system of belief defending that belief as science. (Galbraith, 1971: 53)

In contrast to neo-classical economics, social emancipation and political engagement are thus explicit and intrinsic goals of economic analysis.[31] Galbraith, like many political economists, adopted a view that factual or analytical claims can lead directly to, or constitute, evaluative and value based claims – that the distinction between positive and normative economics is not clear-cut.

Such considerations help to illuminate and explain the recent crises of mainstream economic theory regarding its method, methodology, and social theory associated with the mainstream (as documented and subject to a more extensive philosophical investigation by Lawson, 1997, 2003, among others). Furthermore, the essence of such considerations appears to have been somewhat anticipated by Galbraith. But Galbraith also went further than explanatory critique and sought to set out a theoretical and pedagogical alternative to the conventional wisdom.

Peddling irrelevance

It would come as no surprise to Galbraith that Blaug (1997: 3) argues that: "Economics has increasingly become an intellectual game played for its own sake and not for the practical consequences for understanding the economic world." Nor that the importance of learning esoteric techniques over developing real world understanding continues to be the test of success in the leading economic programs. As Hodgson (2006: 117) summarizes, a recent study of seven top US graduate programmes by David Colander revealed:

> that only 9 per cent thought that having "a thorough knowledge of the economy" was "very important" for professional success. Only 24 per cent thought that it was "moderately unimportant" and 51 per cent thought it was "unimportant". Also ... 89 per cent thought that being smart ... at problem solving was "very important" or "important" and 82 per cent thought that "excellence in mathematics" was "very important" or "important". Colander observed that the teaching of techniques was still dominant, with little attempt in the graduate programmes to show how and why the techniques have been developed.

Such trends highlight the "imitative scientism" that continues to plague the economics profession and generates recurrent crises of confidence (Robinson, 1972; Bell and Kristol, 1981; Parker, 1993; Ormerod, 1994, 2000; Heilbroner and Milberg, 1995; Cassidy, 1996; Lawson, 1997, 2003; Hodgson, 2006; Waller, 2008; cf. Dasgupta, 1998). Blaug (1997, 2003) suggests that formalism has been responsible for the divorce of economics from the pragmatic concerns of the real world. Galbraith's assessment went deeper. In 1988 Galbraith

(1988: 376) surmised that if were he writing *The New Industrial State* again he would be keener to dwell on issues of economic methodology. Indeed it is salient that an author who wrote for the general public, sought to insert an "An Addendum on Economic Method and the Nature of Social Argument" into the second edition of *The New Industrial State*. In recent years, social theory that is committed to elaborating the nature of social being and how we understand and access that reality is also experiencing something of a revival in economics. An increasing number of largely heterodox economists have argued that explicit methodological reflection and an appreciation of history is essential to fashioning a successful social science (Dow, 1996a, 1997a, 1997b, 2001; Lawson, 1997, 2003; Hodgson, 2001a, 2004, 2006).

The salience of reflecting on the nature of the world and what it means for the practice of social science is that it enables analysts to build into their theoretical structure relevant dimensions that would be otherwise overlooked or ignored. Consequently, it is possible to identify many of the problems associated with economics as conventionally practiced as originating from its history of refusing to reflect on the nature of reality and what it means for analysis (Lawson, 1997, 2003).

The failure of mainstream economists to engage in explicit ontological analysis appears to have resulted in many of them adopting methods that appear quite inappropriate for exploring social phenomena. In contrast, it is possible to argue that those who have made lasting contributions to the development of an economics that functions as an explanatory science – such as Hayek, Keynes, Marshall, Marx, Menger, Veblen, Robinson, and Kaldor – can be viewed as adopting an implicit realist orientation even if never using the specific term "ontology" (Lawson, 1997, 2003).

It should now be clear that J. K. Galbraith also shared similar methodological concerns, and that this orientation marks a distinctive, enduring as well as a fundamental aspect of his contribution. Galbraith explicitly recognized the need to theorize about how the practice of social science differed from the physical sciences. He accepted the need to focus on explanation, as opposed to prediction, he considered the implications for the role and nature of theorizing and abstraction, and used theory and analysis to develop a case for real change. What is more while Galbraith's vision and system are offered as enduring contributions to economics and wider social theory, he nevertheless openly acknowledged that, in accordance with his overriding approach, his analysis was cautious, and self-consciously fallible and provisional.

One of the benefits of Galbraith's long life is that many of his works have been subject to several revisions, editions, and retrospectives. Accordingly, he had ample opportunity to revisit his analysis and acknowledged that parts of his analysis may have become redundant by changes in society (Galbraith, 1988, 1989). Galbraith (1988) suggested, for example, that his hypothesis that the pursuit of Keynesian macroeconomic policy would be in the rational interests of the large firm seems to have been somewhat undermined by, what Krugman (2007) now refers to as "movement conservatism," in the 1980s and 1990s.[32]

It can also be claimed that Galbraith developed an approach to social structures and hierarchies which is more broadly consistent with realist social theory.[33] Galbraith's (1967a) analysis of the technostructure and the modern corporation are perhaps the best examples of such structures in his theoretical contributions. It is clear that the professionals within the modern corporation are prime movers in reproducing and transforming institutional structures.[34] This warrants further attention. Galbraith's approach also anticipates and shares the concern of more recent developments, contributions and discussions in the philosophy of science. Additionally, by highlighting the realist orientation of Galbraith's contribution it is possible to identify a shared methodological foundation that contributes to the integration of insights between the Post Keynesianism and Institutionalist schools. This should buttress recent efforts to develop and integrate Post Keynesianism and Institutionalism on the basis of methodology (cf. Lawson, 1995, 2003; Dunn, 2008a).

Galbraith's underlying view of the nature of science, however, is not made fully explicit. Galbraith neither formally accepts, challenges, nor discusses underlying (positivistic or deductivist) conceptions of science. Occasionally he appears to cede a role for positivism in the natural sciences. Sometimes he talks of "reversing the established method," but overall Galbraith is somewhat opaque by contemporary methodological standards. This may reflect the fact that Galbraith was seeking a wide readership, and thus seeking to avoid a potentially distracting discussion on the philosophy of science. Such considerations aside, however, it is noteworthy to record that Galbraith still sought to make explicit his views on methodology and how economics needs to be tailored to the distinctive nature of social process. Furthermore, although Galbraith (1967a) pre-dates realism's emergence in the late 1970s, notable aspects of his contributions share the hall marks of a realist approach; not least his concern with ontology, his pluralistic and tailored method, his provisional and empirically grounded theory, which is marshaled to provide emancipatory critique. As such, those seeking to develop a realist vision of the economy would be wise to further consider the economic and social theory of J. K. Galbraith.

Economics as a system of belief

Galbraith's principal focus was the march of events; seeking to bring them into sharper view and analyzing their ramifications for economic and social analysis. Throughout his major works Galbraith consistently sought to identify *a posteriori* salient changes in the economic structure and elaborate their consequences for economic and social theory. In doing so, Galbraith's approach to economics is realist and historical, with institutional change as his principal focus. The consequence was that this methodology led him to markedly different conclusions than the prevailing mainstream.

Galbraith recognized that all approaches have ontological assumptions, that is, conditions under which their usage is appropriate. Galbraith's approach accords with a realist assessment that a significant reorienting of the modern discipline of economics is warranted. Anticipating much of the recent realist (ontological) enquiry Galbraith argued that the conventional wisdom, or what has become the modern mainstream project, constrains economics from realizing its real potential to be explanatorily powerful and useful:

> Lord Keynes, in a famous forecast, thought the subject would eventually become unimportant – in social significance it would rank about with dentistry ... But, though, in a sense Keynes was right that the subject is in decline, in a larger sense he was wrong ... the future of economics could be rather bright. It could be in touch with the gravest problems of our time. Whether this is so – whether economics is important – is up to economists. They can, if they are determined, be unimportant; they can, if they prefer a

comfortable home life and regular hours, continue to make a living out of the infinitely interesting gadgetry of disguise ...

Or economists can enlarge their system. They can have it embrace, in all its diverse manifestations, the power they now disguise. (Galbraith, 1973a: 341–3)

If the aim of economists is to be socially useful then one must seek to develop an approach to economics, which tailors and modifies its methods, practices, and theories in the light of changes in circumstance and society.

Notes

1 Galbraith's approach is similar to Thorstein Veblen. Galbraith was probably familiar with Veblen's (1898a, 1900, 1906, 1909, 1919) reflections on the limitations of the established method. As Galbraith (1971: 279) remarked of his formative years "Thorstein Veblen was still being read with attention in Berkeley in the thirties." The depth of this influence and its overlap with Keynes and his other life experiences, are difficult, however, to disentangle.

2 This is what the contemporary methodologists refer to as the ontological presuppositions of theory.

3 As Galbraith (1958a: 40) pointed out the enemy of the conventional wisdom was not the import of new ideas but rather the march of events (cf. Reisman, 1990).

4 It is clear from this quotation that Galbraith recognized what is now referred to as the realist distinction between the "intransitive" dimension of reality, that is, the object of analysis; and the "transitive" dimension of the objects of knowledge which condition future knowledge and come to facilitate and actively transform it through the social practice of (economic) science (cf. Lawson, 1997: 23–6). Of course Galbraith would not have articulated it in such a technical manner!

5 In realist terminology, these two clauses are now commonly referred to respectively as the extrinsic and intrinsic conditions of "'closure." In such conditions, a "closed system" exists, in which event regularities are likely to exist (see Lawson, 1997, 2003).

6 This is a strong version of the closure conditions. Alternatively, it is sufficient for closure that the external causes of events operate in a constant, or in a stochastic, way; and that objects change in a constant way.

7 In realist terminology the conditions of closure do not hold, and open systems, in which, consequently, event regularities are unlikely to occur, will result.

8 As Galbraith (1973a: 10) remarked in *Economics and the Public Purpose*: "The traditional economics assumes that economic institutions and the motivation of the people who comprise them change but slowly. As with physics or botany, economic truth, once established, is largely immutable. This is agreeable but not so. Economic institutions change rather rapidly; the large corporation and its relations with the community and state are especially in flux. And with such change comes new information, new insight. In consequence the rate of obsolescence in economic knowledge is high."

9 In realist terminology we might say that Galbraith views the (closure) assumptions and methods conventionally associated with the physical sciences as overly restrictive for the study of social phenomenon. Thus, consideration of other methods that may help access an inherently transformative social reality is warranted (see Lawson, 1997, 2003).

10 As Veblen (1898a: 389–90) famously argued: "The hedonistic conception of man is that of a lightning calculator of pleasures and pains, who oscillates like a homogenous globule of desire of happiness under the impulse of stimuli that shift him about the area, but leave him intact. He has neither antecedent nor consequence. He is an isolated, definitive human datum ... Self-imposed in elemental space, he spins symmetrically about his own spiritual axis ... The hedonistic man is not a prime mover. He is not the seat of a process of living."

11 Similarly and not unlike other tribal modes of behavior, such scientism has resulted in economics developing its own inimical series of logic, rules, rites and rituals that are associated with such ontological presuppositions (see Samuels, 1984).

12 As Sharpe (1973: 1–2) points out Galbraith's concern is with the lower economics – with the economics of the real world: "THE LOWER ECONOMICS referred to in the title of this book was suggested by a figure of speech once used by Galbraith. He pictured the prestige structure of economics as a hollow pyramid or cone. At the base the sides are transparent and have many openings to the outside. As one approaches the apex, the sides become increasingly opaque and impermeable. Economists dealing with practical matters dwell at the base, and they have easy communication with the outside world. Their economics is adulterated by foreign admixtures of politics, moral judgments and sociology. The practitioner at this level merits little esteem. In contrast, economists dealing with pure theory can be found near the top of the pyramid. They are protected from outside influence. Their work is formal and mathematical. It has little or nothing to do with reality, and is very highly regarded by the profession. Galbraith's mockery makes it perfectly clear where he thinks the valuable work in economics is being

done. He himself occupies a position near the base of the pyramid and practices the lower economics, which, far from being a term of opprobrium, must in this view be considered an accolade."

13 Such a realist orientation may, however, explain why Galbraith's economic contributions have typically been dismissed as a less rigorous, literary expression of hypotheses developed more formally elsewhere (see, for example, Marris, 1968: 240). Galbraith's use of "non-economic" data and methods appears realist in orientation. Moreover, Galbraith's alleged vagueness might also highlight his ontological approach. For, as Dow (1996a) and Klaes (2004) argue, in open, complex systems, vague concepts are likely to be more useful than the precise terms required by positivist approaches. For Galbraith it was better to be vaguely right than precisely wrong.

14 This anticipates recent realist-inspired calls for a triangulation of methods (Downward and Mearman, 2007). It also reflects Keynes's approach (see Harcourt, 1987).

15 It is also clear that Galbraith rejects strictly pragmatist conceptions of truth and instead requires empirical adequacy: "We should not test our image of the economic system by its political convenience, or we should not if we are interested in analytically serviceable truths. We should see, instead, whether our image accords with observed circumstance, observed need" (Galbraith, 1979a: 9).

16 That is to say Galbraith rejects the equivalence of the underlying subject matter of the natural and social realms (positivist naturalism) and argues that there are likely to be significant differences in methods appropriate to studying social and natural objects (contra scientism).

17 Stanfield (1996: 154) draws our attention to the fact that: "Close students of Dewey will find the test of anxiety to be reminiscent of the instrumentalist philosopher: 'If ideas, meanings, conceptions, notions, theories, systems are instrumental to an active reorganization of the given environment, to a removal of some specific trouble and perplexity, then the test of their validity and value lies in accomplishing this work ... If they fail to clear up confusion, to eliminate defects, if they increase confusion, uncertainty and evil when they are acted upon, then they are false' (Dewey, 1948: 156)."

18 Technically such steps are referred to as retroduction by realists (see Lawson, 1997, 2003).

19 Rather than deductively tease out the implications of a given set of (fictitious) assumptions, or inductively project history into the future and then admonish reality for its departures there from, Galbraith starts

from nascent facts and features of everyday experience upon which he develops his theoretical system.

20 Kaldor (1972) referred to such trends as stylized facts. Realists following Lawson (1989, 1997) have abandoned the notion of stylized facts, preferring the term "'demi regularities," to denote the fact that such phenomenon are grounded in reality, but still provisional, as opposed to being fictitious creations of the analyst. It is salient to note that Galbraith was good, close friends with Nicky Kaldor (see chapter 12 below).

21 All these trends are present through *American Capitalism*, *The Affluent Society*, *The New Industrial State* and *Economics and the Public Purpose* (Galbraith, 1952a, 1958a, 1967a, 1973a). They nonetheless are subject to different degrees of emphasis. Thus the citations in the paragraph refer to dominance and centrality of the themes in the relevant contributions rather than their appearance *per se*. It is interesting to note that by 1967 these stylized facts were largely uncontroversial. Malcolm Sawyer has suggested to me, however, that the beginning of the decline of the trade union was perhaps far from controversial, especially in Britain.

22 This trend was also identified by Schumpeter (1943: 189), who argued: "it would still be a fact that the actual efficiency of the capitalist engine of production in the era of the largest-scale units has been much greater than in the preceding era of small or medium-sized ones. This is a matter of statistical record."

23 This was also a theme of *Monopoly Capitalism*. As Baran and Sweezy (1966: 120) note: "The tremendous growth of the sales effort and the spectacular intensification of its sway stem from its having undergone a far-reaching qualitative change."

24 In focusing on generative mechanisms, it is clear that Galbraith was practicing what realists refer to as explanatory social science. From a realist perspective Galbraith can be viewed as adopting an inferential logic consistent with the philosophical ontology of depth realism and causal powers and mechanisms; and of offering a scientific ontology of the same character, in which a range of specific mechanisms can be identified.

25 Compare this to Veblen (1904: 1), who argued that: "The scope and method of modern industry are given by the machine. This may not seem to hold true for all industries, perhaps not for the greater part of industry as rated by the bulk of the output or by the aggregate volume of labor expended. But it holds true to such an extent and in such a pervasive manner that a modern industrial community cannot go on except by the help of the accepted mechanical appliances and processes. The machine industries – those portions of the industrial system in

which the machine process is paramount – are in a dominant position; they set the pace for the rest of the industrial system. In this sense the present is the age of the machine process."

26 Gambs (1975: 76) notes that Galbraith's thesis: "gained support from his colleague Daniel Bell, the sociologist. In his book *The Coming of Post Industrial Society*, Bell writes of nineteenth-century industries that were created by 'talented tinkerers' who knew little about science. Innovations today do not depend on the flashes of genius of such men as the Wright brothers, Ford, Bessemer, Ericsson, Bell and Morse. Modern industry depends on basic science, not on gifted mechanics or nineteenth-century chemists."

27 Under Galbraith's conception, "practical" knowledge is both a condition and consequence of social activity; this is again suggestive of his realist concerns (cf. Lawson, 1997: 25–6, 58–61, 177–80).

28 This is not to deny that there has been an expansion of higher education. Rather to clarify that this explosion has been increasingly focused on corporate needs as opposed to developing a more critical and enlightened citizenry (see Reisman, 1980: 136–45). As Stanfield (1996: 65) points out: "Education has grown along with the increased technical sophistication of production, though perhaps it has not done so to a proportional extent. The adequacy of the state's accommodation of education to the dynamics of the economic process is an issue of great and currently growing importance."

29 Indeed Galbraith's (1988, 1989, 1991) willingness to criticize his own conclusions, moreover, conveys his belief that as well as being explanatory, economics, as well as other social sciences, should also be critical (cf. Dewey, 1916).

30 Galbraith's work contains several examples of explanatory critique. For example, in his exposition of the conventional wisdom, Galbraith (1958a: 17–21) discusses how acceptable ideas get reproduced, particularly if they accord with the self-interest of agents; he claims that the complexities (which have been developed over time) of the conventional wisdom are used as a means of defending it; and he claims that the articulation of the conventional wisdom is the: "prerogative of academic, public or business position. Thus, any individual, on being elected president of a college or university, automatically wins the right to enunciate" the conventional wisdom; they are then expected to expound it. In making this argument, Galbraith again demonstrates his conception of the reproduction of social position-practice systems.

31 Moreover, such realist considerations also perhaps explain Galbraith's lifelong engagement in politics (see Schlesinger, 1984; Parker, 2005).

32 Although compare the argument of James Galbraith (2008a) who highlights how conservatives in power no longer take free markets seriously. The policy reaction across the world to the great crash of 2008, moreover, highlights the resurgence and recognition of Keynesian ideas (Krugman, 2008c).

33 More technically realists refer to such structures and hierarchies as position-practice systems. Position-practice systems are sets of relations between hierarchical positions, all of which have common and associated practices, for example teachers and pupils have assigned roles within a broader educational system.

34 As such Galbraith anticipates a central feature of the realist "Transformational Model of Social Activity," developed principally by Bhaskar (1979) more generally and in economics by Lawson (1997, 2003).

5 *The general theory of advanced development*

Galbraith sets out to substitute for Marshall a picture, based on a general observation, of *The New Industrial State*. His account of the behavior of giant firms appears plausible or, at the very least, worth discussing, but it has had no success as an ideological doctrine.

Joan Robinson (1977: 1326)

In many modern business enterprises neither bankers nor families were in control. Ownership became widely scattered. The stockholders did not have influence, knowledge, experience, or commitment to take part in the high command. Salaried managers determined long-term policy as well as managing short-term operating activities. They dominated top as well as lower and middle management. Such an enterprise controlled by its managers can properly be identified as managerial, and a system dominated by such firms is called managerial capitalism.

Alfred Chandler (1977: 10)

At its core Galbraith's thesis was that the economic ideas that once interpreted the world of poverty have made little adjustment to the world of affluence which has been ushered in by the modern corporation.[1] Galbraith's principal theoretical contribution is foreshadowed in *American Capitalism* (1952a), and unfolds more clearly into view in his trilogy: *The Affluent Society* (1958a), *The New Industrial State* (1967a), and *Economics and the Public Purpose* (1973a). Throughout these works Galbraith focused on the concentration of economic power and the control, role, and influence of the technostructure. Galbraith highlighted how the dynamics of the large corporation challenge the doctrine that the consumer is sovereign, and he examined the resultant social and environmental imbalance ushered in by it. Galbraith sought to tease out the implications and paradoxes of the uneven development of modern affluence within countries and across the world, outlining the case for social change.[2]

Galbraith argued that modern advanced economies are dominated by large firms. He noted, however, that such large firms do not conform to the monopolistic and oligopolistic caricatures of the central tradition. The inefficiencies predicted by theory, of higher prices and lower output, have not been borne out in practice. Instead large, powerful corporations have ushered in an era of unprecedented wealth. This is because the planning of the modern firm has enabled enormous technical and productive advance. But such planning involves heavy upfront investment which must be recouped. Hence the modern firm will increasingly seek to manage those factors that threaten such investment, to mitigate the various uncertainties that surround production, consumption and technological development. In doing so large firms seek to influence and control the response of the consumer, workers, and other firms, as well as governments and the media.[3]

The power and nature of the modern corporation influences the nature of wider economic development. Where the application of technology permits, the genius of the industrial system results in strong material advancement. Where lacking, there is weak economic development. Where there is solely original power, then there is exploitation. Where there is countervailing power, then the consumer, the worker or the vulnerable are to some degree protected. Where the goals of the industrial system are aligned to wider social objectives, government support is forthcoming. Where social objectives conflict with firm objectives, then political resistance on behalf of the industrial system is marshaled.

It is the nature of modern production that underscores the problems of social imbalance and uneven global economic development. The modern corporation dominates national and international trade and exploits its power over small firms right across the global economy. The nature of the new industrial state is such that the goals of society are increasingly identified with those of the industrial system – this is what Galbraith referred to as the "principle of consistency". That is the interests of the modern corporation permeate government and public opinion. This results in the pursuit of economic policies that serve the interests of the powerful. To recognize all this, however, is to begin to identify the need for various government policies that will operate in the public interest.

Power and development

In his early work, Galbraith (1936, 1938, 1943, 1947, 1949a; Dennison and Galbraith, 1938) explored the impact of the rise of the large, modern corporation. But although he quickly became a convert to Keynes (see Galbraith, 1971: chapter 3), it was not until *American Capitalism* (Galbraith, 1952a) that he began to make a decisive break from the neo-classical model and to create an alternative theoretical system that captured the wealth and change ushered in by the large firm in advanced economies (Stanfield, 1996). Galbraith acknowledged the tremendous increase in wealth that characterized, and continues to characterize, the USA – see Figure 1. He linked that increase in wealth to the rise of the modern corporation. And he sought to analyze the economic and social consequences of this change. *American Capitalism*, *The Affluent Society*, *The New Industrial State*, and *Economics and the Public Purpose* all analyzed the impact of the emergence of the large corporation on society. In these works Galbraith (1952a, 1958a, 1967a, 1973a) argued that the large firm was not an historical aberration.[4] The modern large corporation was not an exception that proved the competitive rule; rather, he argued that it is a consequence of the evolution of the mode of production that the large firm has come to dominate modern advanced economies. And the consequences and implications of this evolution differ markedly from the conventional analysis of oligopolies presented in economics textbooks.

In the neoclassical model, competition ensures that scarce resources with alternative uses are efficiently utilized. Prices, including the wages of workers, are set by (impersonal) market forces, and power and profits are kept in check by supply-side competition:

> In the neo-classical model prices are primary; they are the intelligence network of the economic system. They signal changes in the wants of the consumers to the producing firms. And, in reverse, they tell the consumer of changes in the costs of production and, therewith, of new opportunities for serving his or her needs. On the basis of the prices thus established the consumer so distributes purchases as to maximize the satisfaction derived from the funds available for expenditure. And since nothing is so important as the consumption of goods, the consumer thus maximizes happiness. The agreeable equilibrium so established has its counterpart in the way

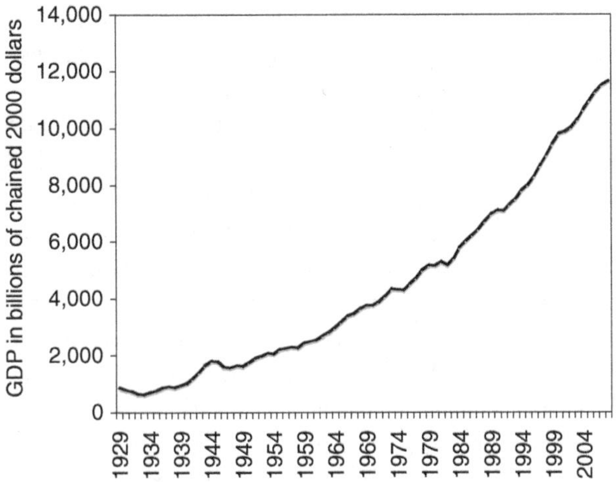

Figure 1. The growth in US gross domestic product, 1929–2008
Source: Bureau of Economic Analysis, National Economic Accounts, www.bea.gov

labor, capital, raw materials and managerial ability are distributed. Prices, including that of labor, are also the signal to these factors of production as to where it can most profitably be used. Their ultimate deployment also reflects the will of the consumer. This use, monopoly and some minor hindrances apart is, from the viewpoint of consumers (and given the distribution of income), the best that is possible. (Galbraith, 1973a: 126)

In this Panglossian world both the market and the consumer are sovereign. This competitive ideal underpins the widespread view, held by many economists, that the sole route to maximize social welfare is to make markets more competitive and promote unfettered private enterprise (Krugman, 2009). This is the underpinning faith that dominates "movement conservatism" (Krugman, 2007). The view of the firm that receives widespread elaboration is one where the individual firm, run by either single entrepreneurial owner or small management executive, seeks to maximize firm profits and their resultant income.[5] Firms that do not seek to maximize profits are driven out of business by other firms that operate more efficiently and grow through the accumulation of profit: "The efficient and the progressive were rewarded with survival and growth. The inefficient and unprogressive were penalized by extinction ... Competition was also the instrument of change. As the tastes of the sovereign consumer altered, the demand for some products rose and so did their prices" (Galbraith, 1958a: 60).[6]

According to Galbraith, this view – which continues to dominate economic instruction – is outmoded, approximating an earlier period in history that has been superseded (cf. Schumpeter, 1943). It is a view that no longer elucidates reality. Instead, it serves to obscure it. Today the firms that produce and sell the majority of the goods and services are large powerful bureaucracies, dominated by professional managers.[7] This was a process that began in the latter part of the nineteenth century, when many of today's dominant brands and firms emerged. Although markets have evolved beyond the mainstream competitive ideal, Galbraith (1952a, 1952b, 1967a) argued that the standard predictions regarding the consequences of this shift – inefficiency and the ruthless exploitation of economic power – have not been supported by the facts. Few customers of large corporations complain of exploitation, anti-trust laws are seldom invoked, and the instances of oligopoly are typically associated with the greatest output and the most robust growth.

Galbraith (1952a, 1958a, 1967a), like Schumpeter (1943), rejected the idea that the perfectly competitive market is the key to the success of capitalism (cf. Swedburg, 1991: 156). Galbraith supplanted the conventional preoccupation with steady state production with an examination of the forces of conscious design that enables large-scale technological change to take place (cf. Rosenberg, 1982, 1994).[8] In sharp contrast to the traditional theories of oligopoly, which depict the large firm as resulting from significant economies of scale in production costs, Galbraith explained the rise of the modern corporation as a means to facilitate technological change by attempting to mitigate the impact of the uncertainties of the market.[9]

For both Galbraith and Schumpeter the process of competition drives both consolidation and concentration, fundamentally changing the dynamics of competition. *American Capitalism* introduced the idea that the USA's large and dominating corporations, though they had power to control their markets, also sustained the modern technological progress fundamental to economic growth (see Galbraith, 1952a). The main argument of *American Capitalism* was, however, that new restraints on private economic power emerged on the other side of the market to limit the power of large firms – what Galbraith labeled countervailing power. In *The New Industrial State* Galbraith (1967: 32–5) further identified the key dynamics that underpin the modern business enterprise. At its core his thesis is that advanced technology requires large dedicated commitments of capital, skilled labor, and time.[10] As the firm grows and as production processes become increasingly complex and technologically more sophisticated, there is an increasing need for a team of dedicated bureaucratic specialists to administer the decisions of the modern business firm. Echoing the notion of bounded rationality (Simon, 1955, 1957, 1959; Earl, 2000; Williamson, 2004), Galbraith noted that the complexities of modern technology mean that one person can no longer be familiar with all the aspects of engineering, procurement, quality control, labor relations and marketing, which are necessary for doing business.[11]

The complexity of modern production moreover makes it increasingly difficult for shareholders to effectively police the modern corporation. As group decision-making and technical expertise become more important, power passes from the individual owner to those people with the requisite knowledge of the relevant business – the technostructure.[12] The technostructure represents a "new class" and a new factor of production.[13] Its pay reflects the power of the corporation and not a series of impersonally determined market rates. The technostructure is composed of the diffuse decision-making structure of the large corporation, and it affects the use and promulgation of modern technology. It encompasses an array of managerial, technical, legal, scientific, engineering, accounting, and advertising expertise (cf. Veblen, 1923; Berle and Means, 1932).[14] And it explains the expansion in the scientific and educational elite, which is an accommodation to this need, exemplifying the "principle of consistency": "The industrial system, by making trained and educated manpower the decisive factor of production, requires a developed educational system" (Galbraith, 1967a: 364).

Organization is the manner by which the technostructure achieves coordination and makes decisions. Organization exists as a necessary response to the imperatives of complex technology and the diffusion of requisite knowledge that needs to be brought to bear in its realization (cf. Simon, 1957, 1959, 1961, 1972, 1976, 1979).[15] The technostructure selects products and chooses production techniques, including the number and type of workers to employ; they develop marketing and pricing policy; they conduct research and development; and they are responsible for organizing access to finance (internally or externally). Its decision-making conventions and governance structures permit informed, reliable, and coordinated decisions, and it enables the pursuit and alignment of common objectives across a range of specialists. Accordingly the decisive factor in economic success is no longer the heroic individual, but rather organized intelligence: "It is not to individuals but to organizations that power in the business enterprise and power in society has passed" (Galbraith, 1967a: 75).[16]

The technostructure will choose those goals and strategies that facilitate its survival and reproduction, such as driving growth, controlling and dominating their supply chain, and lobbying governments and regulators – what Galbraith referred to as "the protective need" – and those that enhance its status and position, such as pursuing technical virtuosity – referred to as "the affirmative need." Similarly the "control of prices by the firm in the planning system, like the other uses of its power, is governed by the protective and affirmative purposes of the technostructure" (Galbraith, 1973a: 128). Unlike owners with a vested interest in maximizing profits, professional managers gain little from direct profit maximization. They are not necessarily interested in profit maximization *per se*, or the maximization of shareholder value, as an end in itself; rather, they seek to maximize their own power, prestige, and affluence. Such motivations are more closely aligned with the growth of the firm.[17] And the growth of the modern firm involves a variety of strategies:

> The first strategy is the expansion of production and sales by the existing corporate entity. This, it is commonly assumed, involves adding products or services which have some technical complementarity – which, in the manner of the rubber manufacturer going into plastics, uses some of the same technical expertise, plant and equipment, marketing outlets, marketing knowledge or managerial skills. But where growth is the goal, such complementarity is not essential ... The second strategy is the acquisition of smaller firms in related or unrelated areas for more or less complete consolidation with the technostructure of the acquiring firm. This allows the superior financial resources of the larger firm to be used for a far more

rapid growth than would generally be possible from the expansion of sales. (Galbraith, 1973a: 119)

Survival for the technostructure means achieving a minimum amount of earnings, so that the independence of these decision-makers can be maintained.[18] As Galbraith (1973a: 110) noted: "Below a certain size there is no absolute defense against a take-over bid to the stockholders. But a favorable earnings performance remains the best protection." Low earnings or losses therefore represent a risk to the autonomy of the technostructure. Firm growth and expansion, however, assures and ensures a minimum level of performance and profits. Growth also serves the "affirmative" or psychological needs of the technostructure – the prestige that generally comes from working for a large well-known firm – reinforcing the "paramount position of production": "If the economic system as a whole is growing, firms in general will be expanding. To the opportunities for promotion with the firm will be added the opportunities from other firms. With so many influential people finding the growth of the economy to their advantage, it would not be surprising if they were not to conclude that economic growth is a good thing" (Galbraith, 1973a: 118). The pursuit of growth and technical virtuosity means more jobs and promotions for members of the technostructure.[19] And the provision of an acceptable level of earnings also facilitates the pursuance of other goals, including socially responsible goals, which "contribute to what is called a sound corporate image and thus help recruiting and worker morale, avoid unwelcome taxes or cultivate a better public attitude toward products" (Galbraith, 1967a: 184).

Of course, profits continue to be necessary to the technostructure's economic and material well-being. But, to reiterate, this need not entail profit maximization.[20] The market is no longer enforcing this goal. And the technical complexities of modern technology mean that ascertaining how to maximize profits is no easy matter.[21] As Galbraith (1967a: 122) argued:

Profit maximization – the only goal that is consistent with the rule of the market – is no longer necessary. The competitive firm had no choice of goals. The monopoly could take less than the maximum; but this would be inconsistent with its purpose of being a monopoly. But planning is the result not of the desire to exploit market opportunity but the result among other factors, of the unreliability of markets. Subordination to the market, and to the instruction that it conveys, has disappeared. So there is no longer, *a priori*, reason to believe that profit maximization will be the goal of the technostructure. It could be, but this must be shown.

What is more, focusing on growth and survival also directs attention to the various policies pursued by the technostructure to make the market more reliable and predictable. The market and the forces of price competition generate considerable uncertainties for the large firm. Inflexibly making large investments over an extended period of time increases the firm's vulnerability to outside threat. As the price of failure is great, it must be avoided at all costs. Thus the firm will seek to mitigate the impact of competition. But this does not necessitate a diminution in competition. Rather competition is transformed from price competition between similarly matched and sized competitors towards other forms of competition such as advertising, mergers, and acquisitions, product innovation and development, as well as the development of new sources of countervailing power. Competition continues. But its nature reflects the complex needs and aspirations of the technostructure:

> The protective purpose of going beyond prices to influence consumer response is to prevent the defection of consumers which would plunge the firm into loss. The affirmative purpose is, of course, to recruit new customers and thus to expand sales – to serve the goal of growth. As sufficiently remarked, the typical industry of the planning system consists of a few large firms. This means that sales can be expanded both by recruiting new users and by persuading customers of other firms to switch. Other firms, for their part, will be engaged in the same effort. The management of the consumer is thus an intricate complex of efforts to recruit new users, win the customers of other firms and hold existing customers in the face of corresponding efforts of the other firms. Since the gain of customers by one firm means their loss by another, the affirmative and protective purposes of consumer management, as they are actually pursued in any consumer industry, are in some degree in conflict. (Galbraith, 1973a: 154–5)

The response to the threat of competition is therefore to mitigate the factors that potentially threaten the technostructure and the pursuit of its objectives. Such considerations continue to characterize the modern firm, as Branston, Cowling, and Sugden (2006: 191) highlight:

Microsoft, for example, made a strategic decision to charge different prices to different corporations manufacturing personal computers, so as to maintain barriers to entry. Similarly, strategic decisions underlay "Microsoft's corporate practice to pressure other firms to halt software development that either shows the potential to weaken the applications barrier to entry or competes directly with Microsoft's most cherished software products". It is also strategic decisions that determine relationships with governments, thus, for example, the way in which corporations respond to antitrust pressures by seeking political assistance. It was said, for example, that Microsoft (like AT&T before it) hoped to avoid break-up by awaiting the arrival of a new President (Bush, as a replacement for Clinton).

That is to say, to thrive, firms seek to control the market, rather than being subservient to it. This is the essence of Galbraith's revised view of the competitive process. New technology is costly and firms wish to avoid the prospect that, after expensive investment, there will be little or no demand for the goods they produce. Large investments of time and money must be protected if the costs of technological change are to be recovered and its benefits realized:

> Technology, with its companion commitment of time and capital, means that the needs of the consumer must be anticipated – by months or years ... By the same token, while common labor and carbon steel will be forthcoming in response to a promise to pay, the specialized skills and arcane materials required by advanced technology cannot similarly be counted upon. The needed action in both instances is evident: in addition to deciding what the consumer will want and will pay, the firm must take every feasible step to see what it decides to produce is wanted by the consumer at the remunerative prices. And it must see that the labor, materials and equipment that it needs will be available at a cost consistent with the price it will receive. It must exercise control over what is sold. It must exercise control over what is supplied. It must replace the market with planning. (Galbraith, 1967a: 41)

This, according to Galbraith, is a primary reason for the observed growth of the large firm and its nexus to the political apparatus. The technostructure, through the modern corporation, must lever its power to ensure its continued operation and, in so doing, reduce the uncertainties to which it is subject.[22] This analysis is reminiscent of Schumpeter's: "According to Schumpeter, monopolistic practices are often very positive for the economy. There are several reasons for this: only big corporations can afford the enormous investments that are needed for a new product, say a car; many risks can only be handled by big corporations; big business tends to attract 'the better brains'; and so on" (Swedburg, 1991: 157). The organizations that are able to emancipate themselves from the vagaries of the market, what Galbraith referred to as "the planning system," account for around half of the total production in modern industrialized economies: "The two thousand industrial corporations comprising the industrial system comprise about half of the non-public sector as measured by their share of total product" (Galbraith, 1967a: 126). Smaller firms populate the other half of the economy, what Galbraith referred to as "the market system." These are firms that resist organization and approximate the neo-classical model:

> Four factors exclude organization, make necessary individual performance or direction. Organization is excluded where the task is unstandardized and geographically dispersed ... The second fact confining the firm to the authority of an individual person is the surviving demand for explicitly personal service ... The third factor limiting the scale of the firm is involvement with art. Scientists and engineers lend themselves well to organization ... The artist lends himself much less well to organization. Accordingly, if the product or service involves original and genuine (as distinct from repetitive or banal) artistic expression, the firm will always be small ... Finally, the firm is on occasion kept small by law, professional ethos or trade union restriction (e.g. group medical practice) that would allow of the growth of the firm. (Galbraith, 1973a: 57–8)

Nevertheless, like the firms that are part of the planning system, firms in the market system also follow pricing conventions and seek to escape the uncertainty of the market. As Galbraith (1973a: 64) stressed:

> The small clothing manufacturer or builder uses the union scale which is common to all plus a conventional mark-up as the basis for pricing his product. So do others, and all thus win control (sometimes tenuous) over prices. Physicians, chiropractors, osteopaths, optometrists, lawyers and the building trades control or influence supply by control of educational requirements, apprenticeship requirements or state licensing. Farmers

persuade the state to fix prices by government purchase and, through acreage or marketing quotas, to limit supply. Small manufacturers seek publicly enforced retail price maintenance ... All of these efforts reflect the tendency of all producing firms, whether in the market or planning system, to control their economic environment and not be subject to it.

The principal difference between the market and planning system is that in the market system firms' power is restrained by what Marshall referred to as "free" competition.[23] Nevertheless, both the market and planning systems are interdependent structures that form part of Galbraith's bimodal view of mature economies. Indeed the resulting distribution of power, dominance, and control of prices by the planning sector means that the terms of trade favor the large corporation. The large firm exploits its power for its own ends, seeking a relatively secure and favorable income (Galbraith, 1973a: 65–6). The consequence is that the market and small firm sector receives lower and less secure income. As Galbraith (1973b: 149) remarked: "The relationship between the planning and the market systems, their unequal development, the exploitation of the second by the first, the resulting inequality in return are central features of the modern economy."

This bimodal view continues to characterize the mature economic systems.[24] According to the most recent economic census in 2002, there are nearly 23 million firms in the USA (table 1). About three-quarters of all US business firms comprise self-employed persons operating unincorporated businesses. And there are nearly 6 million firms that employ personnel. Nevertheless, large firms, (i.e. those that employ more than 2,500 people) account for 97 percent of total firm sales. The top 2,000 firms account for half of total annual sales. And the top 900 firms account for 42 percent of total annual sales.

Of course the precise distribution across firms will change over time. This Galbraith (1973a: 59) recognized: "No agreed level of assets or sales divides the millions of small firms which are half the private economy from the handful of giant corporations which are the other half." What is more, the large firm, through the advance of technology, and in the pursuit of growth, will seek to develop organization in areas previously the preserve of the small firm. It will seek to accommodate the artist. And it will seek to standardize, as well as personalize, its products and services. But there remains, as Galbraith (1973a: 59–60) argued: "a sharp conceptual difference between

Table 1. *The size and distribution of firms in the USA, 2002*

	Firms	Establishments	Employment	Payroll annual ($1,000)	Sales or receipts ($1,000)
Employer firms	5,697,759	7,200,770	112,400,654	3,943,179,606	22,062,528,196
Less than $100,000	1,291,552	1,292,473	1,945,928	26,447,381	64,040,172
$100,000 to $499,000	2,387,780	2,396,006	8,724,876	167,457,202	596,925,336
$500,000 to $999,000	819,513	835,546	6,869,133	166,589,812	576,474,893
$1m to $4.9m	906,936	1,038,624	17,430,229	519,122,708	1,896,143,798
$5m to $9.9m	138,195	225,217	7,054,818	242,369,521	957,896,121
$10m to $49.9m	122,785	350,320	14,465,046	522,395,899	2,504,242,359
$50m to $99.9m	15,895	104,599	5,430,875	203,490,400	1,095,837,221
$100m to $249.9m	8,732	123,220	6,648,609	259,027,065	1,330,102,972
$250m to $499.9m	2,880	93,491	5,201,186	199,189,814	1,006,886,217
$500m to $999.9m	1,544	107,929	5,380,010	204,735,327	1,078,980,045
$1bn to 2.499 bn	1,056	174,666	7,132,953	280,897,627	1,642,368,662
$2.5 bn or more	891	458,679	26,116,991	1,151,456,850	9,312,630,400

Source: Statistics of US Businesses, 2002, www.census.gov/epcd/www/smallbus.html

the enterprise that is fully under the command of an individual and owes its success to this circumstance and the firm which, without entirely excluding the influence of individuals, could not exist without organization." And it is the emergence of the large organization, which has had a profound impact on society, that warrants further examination.

The revised sequence

Perhaps the most contentious part of Galbraith's analysis of the planning system, however, was his argument that the modern corporation sought to manage the response of the consumer. In the conventional wisdom the firm is subservient to the given preferences of consumers. Nevertheless this assumption was being challenged by the massive rise in the apparatus of persuasion and exhortation and required investigation. Indeed as Schumpeter (1949: 380) acknowledged and questioned: "whether we like it or not, we are witnessing a momentous experiment in malleability of tastes – is it this not worth analyzing?" Galbraith accepted this challenge and argued that it is the need to protect the investment of capital and time that creates a strong incentive to ensure what is produced gets sold.[25] If large capital outlays on advanced technology are to be recouped, and if the technical virtuosity of the technostructure is to be maintained, then the response of the consumer must be managed (Galbraith, 1967a: 208). For Galbraith this explained the huge growth in advertising and investment in "brand management" by the modern firm (cf. Dawson, 2003). Accordingly, consumer demand should not be thought of as exogenous, but instead shaped by institutional processes and by particular influences, such as advertising (which is examined in more detail in chapter 9 below).[26]

In identifying the process of want management, Galbraith (1958a) first articulated the notion of a dependence effect.[27] The dependence effect is a portmanteau concept and embodies passive and active aspects. The passive aspect is the process of emulation whereby social norms and localized cultural comparisons induce consumption patterns, that is, the social pressure to "keep up with the Jones's."[28] The active aspect refers to the contriving of specific social wants and, equally importantly, the creation and reproduction of a consumerist

Table 2. *The top twenty global brands*

2008 Rank	Brand	2008 Brand value ($m)	Country of ownership
1	Coca-Cola	66,667	USA
2	IBM	59,031	USA
3	Microsoft	59,007	USA
4	GE	53,086	USA
5	Nokia	35,942	Finland
6	Toyota	34,050	Japan
7	Intel	31,261	USA
8	McDonald's	31,049	USA
9	Disney	29,251	USA
10	Google	25,590	USA
11	Mercedes-Benz	25,577	Germany
12	Hewlett-Packard	23,509	USA
13	BMW	23,298	Germany
14	Gillette	22,069	USA
15	American Express	21,940	USA
16	Louis Vuitton	21,602	France
17	Cisco	21,306	USA
18	Marlboro	21,300	USA
19	Citi	20,174	USA
20	Honda	19,079	Japan

Source: BusinessWeek (2008)

culture (cf. Stanfield, 1973, 1979, 1994, 1996; Fine, 2002; Dawson, 2003). Galbraith accepted that advertising and other attempts at consumer manipulation may not be perfect, but argued that its power, presence and influence must be acknowledged and analyzed – something considered in more detail in chapter 9 below. The success of this advertising, nevertheless, is summarized and epitomized by the valuation of global brands (see table 2).

The dependence effect also identified the various marketing and financing devices that are aimed at the public to encourage them to consume at ever greater levels (cf. Scott, 2006, 2007). In doing so, Galbraith anticipated the emergence of a major anxiety inducing aspect of contemporary economic life – the tying of consumer debt directly to the process of want creation:

> It would be surprising indeed if a society that is prepared to spend thousands of millions to persuade people of their wants were not to take the further step of financing these wants, and were it not then to go on to persuade people of the ease and desirability of incurring debt to make these wants effective. This has happened ... The Puritan ethic was not abandoned. It was merely overwhelmed by the massive power of modern merchandising. (Galbraith, 1958a: 167)

One of the principal deficiencies of the dependence effect, however, was that it did not articulate a clear rationale for the management of the consumer (Hayek, 1961; Johnson, 1960; Stanfield, 1996). In *The New Industrial State* Galbraith (1967a) linked the processes of managing the response of the consumer with the need to protect the upfront investment in technology as well as the interests of the technostructure. This management of the consumer by the firm is referred to by Galbraith as "The Revised Sequence." Rather than just satisfying the wants and demands of the consumer, the modern firm also "accommodates the consumer to the goals of the technostructure and provides a climate of social belief that is favorable to this result" (Galbraith, 1967a: 235). Like the dependence effect, "The Revised Sequence" is broader than just the management of specific consumer demand by the firm – which we shall examine in chapter 9 below. It is the relentless chorus of advertising which conditions society to accept both the paramount position of consumerism and production:

> The advertising of the individual automobile company seeks to win consumers from other makes. But the advertising of all together contributes to the conviction that happiness is associated with automobile ownership. Additionally, make and model apart, it persuades people that the contemporary tendencies in automobile physiognomy and decoration are desirable, that those of the past are obsolete, eccentric or otherwise unworthy. Thus it encourages the general discarding of old vehicles and the purchase of new. Similarly, if one soap manufacturer can establish that white sheets are an index of womanly virtue, this virtue is rewarding to all soap and detergent manufacturers. If one manufacturer can make modest intoxication a mark of suave respectability, so it becomes for all makers of intoxicants ... More important still, the aggregate of all such persuasion affirms in the most

powerful possible manner that happiness is the result of possession and use of goods and that *pro tanto*, happiness will be enhanced in proportion as more goods are produced and consumed. (Galbraith, 1973b: 156)

Consumers must also be able to buy goods as well as desire them, so the technostructure has a vested interest in ensuring the state takes general responsibility for this: "Regulation of aggregate demand is necessary to give certainty to this planning and to protect the technostructure" (Galbraith, 1967a: 229).[29] This underscores the symbiotic relationship between the modern corporation and the state, while also explaining the early appearance of Keynesian policies before the widespread acceptance of the Keynesian theoretical system, and the unacknowledged Keynesianism of the Reagan and Bush eras.

The rise of the modern corporation is thus viewed as undermining Adam Smith's invisible hand and usurping the doctrine of consumer sovereignty (Galbraith, 1967a: chapter 19; cf. Chandler, 1977; Lazonick, 1991). In the conventional wisdom the consumer is king. Wants are given and assumed and they are unaffected by the processes of advertising and consumption. Wants drive the market response, and the flow of instruction is from the consumer to the passive producer, from the market to the firm. Galbraith referred to this as the "Accepted Sequence." Galbraith argued, however, that the nature of modern production, which requires a heavy commitment of time, money, and expertise, necessitates the management of the consumer. The firm increasingly seeks to manage and manipulate wants and reverse the flow of instruction.

Many accused Galbraith of overstatement. Nevertheless Galbraith was keen to point out that producer sovereignty had not replaced consumer sovereignty, rather that reality exhibited aspects of both processes. And this had to be acknowledged:

I do not suggest that the revised sequence has replaced the accepted sequence. Outside the industrial system – beyond the limits of the large corporations – the accepted sequence still rules. Within the industrial system the consumer can still reject persuasion. And, in consequence, through the market he and his fellows can force accommodation by the producer. But consumers, and the prices at which they buy, can also be managed. And they are. The accepted and revised sequences exist side by side in the manner of a reversible chemical reaction. Doubtless it would be neater were it one way or the other. But, again, the reality is plausible but untidy. (Galbraith, 1967a: 217–18)

An important consequence of "The Revised Sequence" is that the goods produced through the planning system are accorded higher privilege and status than other productive and life-affirming activities that are not part of the mass production and mass consumption systems. As such, the elevation of products produced by private firms results in a range of unedifying or superfluous goods and services being implicitly accorded higher social virtue than public goods which seek to meet basic human needs.[30] Moreover the success of the modern firm in raising productive output and persuading the consumer also ushers in the many problems of excess consumption:

More cigarettes cause more cancer. More alcohol causes more cirrhosis. More automobiles cause more accidents, maiming and death; also more pre-emption of space for highways and parking; also more pollution of the air and the countryside. What is called a high standard of living consists, in considerable measure, in arrangements for avoiding muscular energy, increasing sensual pleasure and for enhancing caloric intake above any nutritional requirements. Nonetheless, the belief that increased production is a worthy social goal is very nearly absolute. (Galbraith, 1967a: 172–3)

Similarly the promulgation of mass consumption and the pollution associated with the supporting production creates a variety of environmental challenges:

Damage to the environment, [Galbraith] argued, was a byproduct of systematically related problems: the constant, unreflective quest for technological innovation; an advertising culture supported by big corporations that met accusations of pollution with deceitful paeans to corporate 'green' sensitivities; the dominant, unequal power of the forces of private consumption when compared to the forces that advance the fulfillment of public needs; and the worship of aggregate growth at the heart of modern economic organization and economic theory. Only through an enlightened citizenry who forced its political leaders to pass laws establishing a new system of incentives and regulation could environmental damage be limited; left to themselves, markets would not find the necessary solutions. (Parker, 2005: 516)

The consequence of elevating private production and neglecting the provision of public goods, therefore, is a situation of private affluence amid public and environmental squalor.[31] In a much-quoted passage Galbraith (1958a: 208–9) highlighted this contrast:

> The family which takes its mauve and cerise, air-conditioned, power-steered and power-braked automobile out for a tour passes through cities that are badly paved, made hideous by litter, blighted buildings, billboards, and posts for wires that should long since have been put underground ... They picnic on exquisitely packaged food from a portable icebox by a polluted stream and go on to spend the night at a park which is a menace to public health and morals. Just before dozing off on an air mattress, beneath a nylon tent, amid the stench of decaying refuse, they may reflect vaguely on the curious unevenness of their blessings.[32]

Galbraith was not arguing, however, that growth should not be a social goal. Nor either that productive and technological advance should be curtailed. Rather Galbraith was arguing that we should not be blind to the problems of uneven advance and development. And that the affluence ushered in by the modern corporation could and should enable the widening of social goals to counter the adverse consequences of the modern mode of production.

The public state

Galbraith's bimodal view urged policy makers to understand the nature and extent of the planning system's influence. Galbraith was neither blind to the virtues of the large corporation, nor blind to its vices. For Galbraith the most appropriate policy response is to seek to harness the productive capacity of large corporations, while mitigating clear abuses of their economic and social power. This requires improving the regulation and oversight of the planning system: "This consists in disciplining its purposes – in making these serve, not define the public interest" (Galbraith, 1973a: 240; cf. Reich, 2009).[33] Accordingly, such knowledge may be marshaled to serve the development of new policy and new institutional structures to meet broader social goals (Galbraith, 1973a: chapters 21–31).

In the conventional wisdom issues of governance and the wider public interest are largely hidden from view. As Branston, Cowling, and Sugden (2006: 190) point out: "For all that governance has long been an issue for industrial economists, it has never been the central feature of policy. One reason is that a market-based analysis of the theory and impact of the firm makes markets the principal policy concern – quite appropriately, given its logic – and it cannot give governance that prominence." In contrast Galbraith's analysis placed issues of governance at the centre of policy debate and regulation.[34] Galbraith's analysis of the planning system points to the need to develop appropriate forms of regulation to fetter abuses of corporate power, as well as exploring new ways of making the corporate form more responsive to wider social goals and needs (cf. Davies, 1999; Bailey, Harte, and Sugden, 1994, 1999; Cowling and Tomlinson, 2005; Branston *et al.*, 2006a; Branston, Cowling, and Sugden, 2006; Lang and Heasman, 2004).[35] Such a program of reform, which anticipates recent concern with corporate malfeasance and governance, is necessary to confront the power of the large corporations that continue to dominate the global economy (Reich, 2009).[36]

In advanced economies Galbraith maintained that it is better to limit and regulate the power of large firms than to eliminate that power by breaking it up. In relation to the planning system, Galbraith argued, in a manner that echoes Williamson's (1975, 1985, 1996; see also Joskow, 1991) transaction cost analysis, that there is no sense breaking up the large corporation in the hope of restoring the neo-classical competitive ideal. This would entail rejecting the technology that underpins the escape from the insecurity and uncertainties generated by unfettered markets. Moreover, to break up large corporations would undermine the technical dynamism that provides for much contemporary wealth (even if such wealth is inequitably distributed). Finally, such "trust busting" is unnecessary, not least because in some areas countervailing power develops as a response to original market power, mitigating potential abuses of original power (Galbraith, 1952a; Reich, 2009; cf. Stigler, 1954).[37] Whenever it is difficult or impossible to develop countervailing power, however, the government must itself counter the power of large corporations by making sure there is an adequate supply of those things that have social value, but that are not produced by large corporations – public goods, a clean environment, arms control, full employment, decent incomes for all workers, and relatively low levels of inflation:

> The rule to be followed by government is, in principle, a clear one. There can be very good reason for attacking positions of original power in the

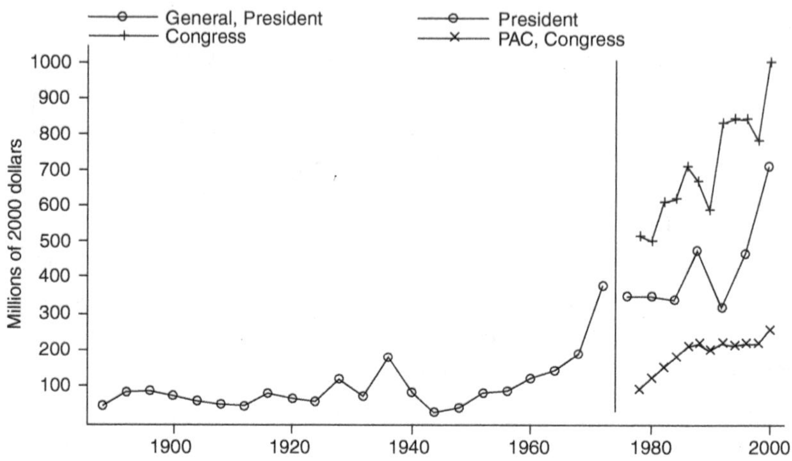

Figure 2. The growth of US campaign spending
Source: Ansolabehere, Figueiredo, and Snyder (2003)

economy if these are not effectively offset by countervailing power. There is at least a theoretical justification for opposing all positions of market power. There is no justification for attacking positions of countervailing power which leaves positions of original market power untouched. On the contrary, damage both in equity and to the operation of the economy will be the normal consequence of doing so. (Galbraith, 1952a: 144)

Governments should seek to encourage the development of countervailing power in the private sector of the economy by, for example, supporting labor unions and smaller competitive businesses (cf. Reich, 2009).[38] Power between the planning and the market systems should be made more equal by implementing policies such as minimum wage legislation, guaranteed minimum incomes, protective tariffs, and support for small businesses (Galbraith, 1973a).

In advocating a strong role for the state, Galbraith (1967a, 1973a, 1983a) highlighted the need to recognize the nexus between big business and the modern state (cf. Monbiot, 2000; Reich, 2009). Galbraith argued that the logic of accumulation, the need to ensure what is invested is ultimately recouped, also means that the large firm will seek to ensure that the policies pursued by the state reflect and protect its needs. It should be no surprise, therefore, that since the 1960s there has been an explosion of campaign spending in US politics (see

Table 3. *Top lobbying spenders, 1998–2009*

Lobbying client	Total
US Chamber of Commerce	$477,005,680
American Medical Association	$204,357,500
General Electric	$187,239,000
American Hospital Association	$167,858,661
American Association of Retired Persons	$158,772,064
Pharmaceutical Research & Manufacturers of America	$154,233,400
Northrop Grumman	$129,955,253
Edison Electric Institute	$126,045,999
National Association of Realtors	$124,117,380
Business Roundtable	$121,840,000
Exxon Mobil	$120,356,942
Lockheed Martin	$114,789,103
Blue Cross/Blue Shield	$114,068,490
Verizon Communications	$112,033,908
Boeing Co.	$106,158,310
General Motors	$101,994,483
Freddie Mac	$96,164,048
Southern Co.	$94,830,694
Ford Motor Co.	$84,319,808
Altria Group	$84,195,000

Source: www.opensecrets.org

Figure 2). And it should be no surprise that: "the largest single source of potential campaign money has been found in corporate political action committees (PACs), corporate executives, and corporate lobbyists who 'bundle' contributions from executives and their business associates" (Reich, 2009: 133).

Galbraith's (1983a: 140–52) analysis explains and anticipates the explosion in lobbying and the symbiotic relationship between big business and the political class. As Robert Reich (2009: 135) observes: "In 1950, fewer than one hundred companies maintained Washington offices. After the mid-1970s the corporate lobbying business exploded ... By the 1990s, more than 500 American companies maintained permanent offices in Washington, and employed more than 61,000 lobbyists, including lawyers who lobbied on their behalf. They were joined by corporate sponsored foundations, centers and institutes, staffed with their own policy experts and marketing personnel." It should be no surprise therefore that the modern state has a tendency to provide and side with those that have a strong powerful lobby behind them (see table 3). For Galbraith this accounted for the large investment in road and defense spending, as well as various forms of support that were provided to the agricultural industry. And it also accounts for the rise in the public relations industry and corporate funded think tanks that seek to influence public policy and opinion:

> Persuasion – advertising and public relations expertise – also allows the direct appeal to the public where support or acquiescence on matters of public policy is sought. A charge that a corporation is polluting water or air, dissipating a natural resource or merchandising an unsafe product brings all but automatically an advertising campaign affirming that company's total devotion to environmental benefaction, resource conservation and the public safety. This is usually considered an effective substitute for more costly substantive action. (Galbraith, 1973a: 174)

Since Galbraith's time of writing, these trends have only intensified (cf. Reich, 2009: 131–67). Modern large firms recognize that they cannot leave to chance regulatory and legislative decision.[39] And they are keen to ensure that broader public policy and spending is channeled to reflect their interests, as was exemplified by the Medicare Prescription Drug and Modernization Act of 2003, the Personal Responsibility in Food Consumption Act of 2004, and the resistance to signing the Kyoto protocol (see Smith and Birnbaum, 2007; Lang and Heasman, 2004; Krugman, 2005a; Stiglitz, 2006, 2007).

The nexus between the technostructure and the state also means that public spending will tend to follow and favor the interests of the large corporation. Elements of public spending that align themselves with the narrow interests of the technostructure receive the requisite sanction from that authority:

> The planning system, it will be evident, exists in the closest association with the state. The obvious core of this relationship is the large expenditure by the government for its products. This pays for the products of those corporations, most notably the large, specialized weapons firms that exist

by selling to the state. And it pays also for the technical development that sustains the cycle of innovation and obsolescence and thus the continuity of the demand (Galbraith, 1973a: 171–72).

But Galbraith also went further, arguing that "the revised sequence" creates an ideological context within which the general interests of the large firm permeate the conventional wisdoms of the legislature. It explains, for example, the nature and distribution of public spending on higher education programs. In his fourth Reith Lecture in 1966, for example, Galbraith argued, that a key function of the state:

> is to provide the specialized and trained manpower which the industrial system cannot supply to itself. This had led in our time to a very great expansion in education, and especially in higher education, and this has been true in all the advanced countries ... As industry has come to need engineers, sales executives, copy writers, computer programmers, personnel mangers, information retrieval specialists, product planners, and executive panjandrums, that is what the educational system has come to provide. (Galbraith, 1966d: 842)

Galbraith further highlighted how higher education spending reflects and supports the wider interests of the modern firm:

> Modern higher education is, of course, extensively accommodated to the needs of the industrial system. The schools and the colleges of business administration ... are preparatory academies for the technostructure. The great prestige of the pure and applied sciences and mathematics in modern times, and the support accorded them, reflect the needs of the technostructure. The ample sums available for research and related graduate training in these areas reflect specific adaptation to such need, whereas the lesser prestige and lesser support for the arts and humanities suggest their inferior role. (Galbraith, 1967a: 364–5)[40]

In relation to the social imbalance generated by the planning system, action is required to encourage the provision of more socially desirable goods and services (see Reisman, 1980: chapter 7). Action is needed to limit the claims of the technostructure and, what Eisenhower referred to as the Military Industrial Complex, on public expenditure (cf. Baran and Sweezy, 1966: chapter 6; see also Cypher, 2008). It requires a more critical and independent higher educational system.

And it also necessitates securing the independence of the state through political reform to ensure that the regulation of corporate power by the state is not subject to industry capture.[41] As Reich (2009: 211) remarks: "Political reforms cannot be achieved as long as public officials and legislators are dependent on the very corporations whose influence is to be limited."

In relation to policy concerning the market system Galbraith (1973a: 295) argued that the state should focus development on areas such as health, social housing, and mass transportation where the modern corporation has found it difficult to develop: "The compelling circumstance ... is the retarded development of the market system. There are industries here which require technical competence, related organization and market power and related command over resource use if they are to render minimally adequate service." For such reasons Galbraith (1967a: 349–56) argued for the development of publicly responsive institutions and organizations in areas of underdevelopment, to address the planning lacunae. Similarly he argued for the continued and, in some cases enlarged, support for the development of the arts and healthcare, as well as the expansion of a more critical and enlightened higher educational curriculum.[42]

The inflationary bias

A major consequence of the revised sequence and the bimodal image of the modern economic system is its inflationary bias. Galbraith argued that it is no coincidence that the emergence and dominance of the modern corporation occurs at the same time that inflation emerges as a major macroeconomic policy issue in developed countries. Galbraith (1952a, 1967a, 1973a, 1977b) argued that the development of power blocs makes the economic system more inflationary. The greater the economic power, the greater the forces in the economy that tend to fuel price increases: "When prices are fully under control, they can be raised to offset increases in costs that are not similarly under control. Wages are the most important example of an uncontrolled cost ... It means also that a general price increase can be expected to follow a general wage increase" (Galbraith, 1973a: 134). It is not in the interests of the planning system to fight increases in wages and costs of production. Such policies have the potential to result in protracted labor disputes, which taint the prestige of the technostructure and undermine the position of the firm. And as the consumer is subject to management by the firm, the effect of an increase in prices is likely to be inconsequential. This too contributes to the inflationary bias of the industrial system. Finally, the modern corporation also has a vested interest in governments maintaining high levels of effective demand, ensuring there is sufficient purchasing power to buy its products. This heightens the inflationary bias of the modern economy. Galbraith argued that there were three potential responses to this inflationary bias:

> There are three ways and only three ways by which inflation, however, induced, can be resisted in the industrial lands. The first is by government budget restraint – by a curtailment of spending and respending from publicly borrowed funds. This is fiscal policy. The second is by the curtailment of spending and respending from bank-borrowed funds. This is monetary policy. The third is by some form of direct intervention to restrain the pressure of trade union wages on corporate prices and of prices on wages, thus stopping the interacting upward spiral. This is an incomes and prices policy, or wage and price control. In an age of organization the problem lies in the choice among these three instruments of economic management and their combination. (Galbraith, 1983c: 70)

Keynes (1940, 1971) argued that the way to control inflation was to manage demand in the economy. This could be done either directly through taxation or reduced spending, or indirectly through higher interest rates. For example, in "How to Pay for the War," Keynes (1940) suggested a policy of forced savings to reduce spending temporarily during World War II. After the war, these savings would be released, and would spark demand when war spending was no longer stimulating the economy. The monetarist counter-revolution, in contrast, argued that inflation is always and everywhere a monetary phenomenon and accordingly control of the money supply is needed to control inflation (Friedman and Schwartz, 1963). With less money, there would be less purchasing power chasing the same amount of goods, thus reducing the inflationary pressures in the economy.

Galbraith advocated neither the monetarist nor the traditional Keynesian solutions to the problem of inflation – arguing that both fail to assimilate the consequences of institutional change in the industrial structure into the conduct of macroeconomic policy. Galbraith argued that monetary policy was an ineffective way to manage aggregate demand and control inflation. Monetary policy works by raising interest rates and thereby impacting on "the cost or availability of credit for capital" (Galbraith, 1958a: 198). Large corporations, who have recourse to retained profits or internally generated funds, are therefore somewhat insulated from such short-run changes. Accordingly "most investment will be extremely unresponsive to moderate increases in the rate of interest" (Galbraith, 1958a: 193). The influence of interest rate changes on aggregate spending is therefore increasingly indirect – thus challenging aspects of the "New Consensus" view of macroeconomics (see chapter 10 below). What is more, anti-inflationary monetary policy discriminates against the firms in the market system. Smaller firms are less insulated from the effects of changes in interest rates. And so another argument against the wholesale use of monetary policy is that it discriminates against the market system.

But Galbraith's main argument against using monetary policy to control inflation was that, to the extent that it does work, it works in socially undesirable ways by reducing demand and increasing unemployment: "Monetary policy does work against inflation ... But it is a policy that works in the highly organized sector of the economy only at the price of severe pain. And while it works better in the market sector of the economy, it is not without pain there also" (Galbraith, 1983c: 72–3). This argument also holds against traditional Keynesian anti-inflation fiscal policies. According to Galbraith, Keynesians were right to argue that tight fiscal policy can control inflation, but what they failed to emphasize is that it does so by imposing unacceptably large costs on the economy or conflicting with other wider social or economic objectives. On this it is worth quoting Galbraith (1958a: 201) at length:

> the most serious problem of fiscal policy is the conflict with other economic goals. It collides, first of all, with the tacit truce ... on income inequality. Taxes are the device by which governments have nakedly sought to influence income distribution. As a result, they have a considerable practical and an even deeper symbolic importance in relation to this issue. Hence a proposal to increase taxes for fiscal reasons automatically provokes a debate on the question of inequality. Liberals, who hitherto had been abiding comfortably by the terms of the truce, are required by their faith to

> rally to the support of taxes which reduce inequality. Conservatives rally to oppose them. In wartime this debate can to some extent be evaded by invoking the doctrine of equality of sacrifice – the rich man can be told that his sufferings at the hands of the tax authorities are roughly the counterpart of those of the soldier under shellfire ... Thus, in wartime, it has been practical to employ the income tax to absorb purchasing excess power. In peacetime such use of taxation will at a minimum be complicated by some argument over the essentially unrelated issue of equality.
>
> Finally, there is the now classic conflict with production. Fiscal policy becomes effective only as the reduced demand brings output below the current capacity of plant and the labor force. Having persuaded ourselves that production is of paramount importance, we must now persuade ourselves to sacrifice it in return for price stability. Moreover, once again the sacrifice may have to be considerable. Where concerns are strongly organized in their markets and deal with strong unions, i.e., where the likelihood of unliquidated gains is great, the slack required ... may have to be quite large. Even though, in fact, the output is not of high urgency, the income to those whom the sack makes unemployed is of utmost interest and importance.

Another anti-inflation policy frequently advocated by economists is to take action to increase competition. Those espousing this view argue that the government should weaken firm and trade union monopoly power, which fuels wage price spirals, and restore the efficacy of the market. In contrast to most economists, and again reflecting his bimodal view of the modern economy, Galbraith rejected the promotion of competition as an effective way to reduce inflationary pressures. Galbraith argued that somewhat perversely, pursuing such policies aids the consolidation of the power of large firms. Reflecting the lobby power of the large firm, efforts to introduce greater competition ultimately yield to dismantling countervailing power, for example attacking trade unions or minimum wage policies, rather than confronting the original power of the large firm. This reflects the political prominence and lobbying effects of the technostructure (Reich, 2009: 131–36). But even if anti-trust policy did help reduce inflationary pressures, there would be a large welfare loss. Policy makers risk losing the dynamism and efficiency that results from large firms undertaking large-scale investment over long time horizons, drawing on technically sophisticated research and development, driving more efficient production.

Instead Galbraith (1952b, 1958a, 1973a, 1977b) argued for the development of appropriate institutions, such as wage and price controls, to minimize inflation. Controls are required, according to Galbraith, because inflation is caused primarily by the pressures of higher incomes on prices and higher prices on incomes.[43] Inflation results because firms and unions have acquired power over the market (cf. Weintraub, 1958, 1963; Davidson 1972, 1985a, 1994; Sawyer, 1982, 1989). What is more, the consequences are more acute the closer to full employment the economy gets: "Wages act on prices and prices on wages as capacity is approached. Controls prevent this interplay. In doing so, they allow the economy to function closer to capacity without price increases" (Galbraith, 1958a: 204). Price controls ameliorate inflationary pressures and allow the expansion of aggregate demand to address the unemployment problem – issues we return to in more detail in chapter 10 below.

The alternative is that a pool of unemployed resources will be needed to discipline wage and price claims and maintain price stability (cf. Kalecki, 1943). The social costs of this solution can, and perhaps should, be avoided. For Galbraith, the only reasonable solution is for the government to step in to prevent the market power of labor unions and large businesses from causing inflation. To achieve the twin goals of full employment as well as price stability, Keynesian macroeconomic policies, which expand effective demand, must be combined with some kind of incomes policy to address the inevitable inflationary pressures that arise when the economy approaches full employment. This radical analysis of inflation echoes Post Keynesian conflict theories of inflation appearing as a hybrid of Keynes, Kalecki, and practical experience (cf. Arestis and Sawyer, 2005; Davidson, 1985a, 1994; Lavoie, 1992; Sawyer, 1982, 1989, 1992b; Wray, 2001).[44]

To many, the control of prices is an anathema to the whole structure of economic theory. Controls induce needless rationing and generate an associated bureaucracy to monitor compliance. Similarly government administered pricing, or interference in the labor market, is viewed as leading to a sub-optimal allocation of resources. Accordingly, it is argued that the most efficient way to allocate scarce resources is to unfetter the market. Galbraith disputed such claims, arguing that in reality large firms were not price-takers. Rather, firms in the oligopolistic sector of the economy are price-makers and thus: "it is relatively easy to fix prices that are already fixed" (Galbraith, 1952b: 17). In the planning system the dominant convention is to fix prices based on some mark-up over the costs of production.[45] Moreover, this mark-up itself is based on a range of social conventions that reflect the interests and objectives of various technostructures.[46]

The fact that prices are set by the corporation to reflect the interests of the technostructure means that prices in the industrial system no longer function as indices of scarcity. As Galbraith (1973a: 127) notes, in the modern economy: "the role of prices is greatly diminished. They are much more effectively under the control of the firm." Accordingly, in the planning system prices play other roles than purely allocative ones. In response to changes in general market conditions, prices may be held constant or altered. Any constancy of price in the face of demand changes is thus rationalized as reflecting the objectives and decisions of firms and the members of the technostructure. Likewise any price changes will reflect the interests of the firm and not the sovereign wishes of the consumer. As a consequence, price controls can be viewed as representing an attempt by governments to align pricing conventions to more socially desirable outcomes.[47] Monitoring such controls is made easier, according to Galbraith, by the fact that prices need to be controlled only in the oligopolistic sector of the economy, since market power exists only in this sector. Consequently, only a thousand or so firms need to be monitored. Enforcement is also assisted by the fact that large oligopolistic firms are all in the public eye.

The valid image of the modern economy

Galbraith's (1973b) presidential address to the American Economic Association (AEA) criticized economists for ignoring power relationships, for failing to analyze the pressing problems of our time, and for failing to identify the required response. He argued that the failure of economists to acknowledge in their core theory the historical evolution of the modern business enterprise and its economic power, meant that attention was diverted away from questions of great social urgency. For Galbraith (1973b: 2): "in eliding power – in making economics a nonpolitical subject – neo-classical theory, by the same process, destroys its relation with the real world."

In eschewing the study of power and change, Galbraith argued that economists were failing to address and illuminate pressing social problems. They were contributing little to contemporary political debates by failing to illuminate many of the serious social concerns of modern society – inequality, unfettered consumerism, environmental decay, and, of course, poverty. Arguably this explains the emergence of the policy entrepreneurs, so reviled by Krugman (1994), who have filled the resultant vacuum. What is more, the consequence of ignoring power in its core theory means that economics functions less as an explanatory science and more as a belief system that is marshaled to promote a conservative agenda (Krugman, 1994, 2007; James Galbraith, 2008a). It should be no surprise that much of the basic economics of the textbooks serves a political or "instrumental" function (Galbraith, 1971: chapter 4).

In contrast, Galbraith (1973a: chapters 20–2) argued that his analysis of the economic power possessed by large firms allows these concerns to be voiced and addressed. Galbraith's view of the nature of the modern economies enables the planning system's impact or absence to be more clearly understood. He argued that the evolution of the modern corporation was not wholly malign; it encouraged technological development and, by so doing, contributes to (uneven) improvements in our standard of living. Breaking up such large corporations, as liberals have conventionally demanded, is not only futile but would also undermine wealth and prosperity. Only big business can make the large-scale investment in new processes, expensive equipment, and basic research required by the modern economy. He nevertheless argued that there was a need to abandon the outmoded view that the large business firm was ultimately subordinate to wider society. It was no longer kept in check by the market and the democratic process. But better to foster and/or limit the power of large firms through regulation, rather than dismantling them and destroying the basis of uneven advance and development.

In analyzing the changing industrial structure, and its consequences and policy implications, Galbraith sought to counter the false beliefs of economists as well as the psychological propensity to accept given ideas. He did this not only by pointing out that received views are erroneous and serve a certain conservative purpose, but also by attempting to offer an alternative theoretical structure that explained both the received wisdom and the underlying reality. In doing so, he insisted that economics must seek to be relevant to the real world.

Notes

1 Those that dispute the notion that we are more affluent today than ever before should consult Easterlin (2000) and Maddison (1995a, 1995b, 2001, 2003).

2 Thus there is a sense in which Galbraith followed both Veblen and Marx in noting the divergence "between the industrial needs of the community and the business needs of the corporation" (Veblen, 1904: 158).

3 In relation to the media Galbraith (1973b: 175) clarified that: "The power of the planning system in relation to media lies not in its forthright control of expression but in its capacity to identify its needs with what, in public policy, seems basic and reputable. Thus, while interesting deviation has no difficulty finding a voice, the needs of the planning system are the norm to which discussion eventually returns ... And this is the norm to which editors, publishers and broadcasters, in the absence of thought to the contrary, also automatically repair. This is not made more difficult by the fact that the needs of the technostructure in general are also those of the larger publishers and broadcasters in their corporate incarnation." It should be apparent from this that Galbraith's analysis of the nexus and influence of the modern firm upon modern media exhibits a degree of similarity with Noam Chomsky's propaganda model (Chomsky, 1989, 2002; Herman and Chomsky, 1998). In the propaganda model the need to maintain advertising revenues means that the large mass media corporations conform to the canons of the conventional wisdoms of the political and business elites – otherwise it risks the loss of the advertising revenue that sustains their business model. This means that the pressures to create a stable, profitable business invariably distort the kinds of news reported, as well as the manner and emphasis, in a way that ultimately furthers the interests of government and business. This is consistent with Galbraith's analysis. What is more Galbraith's analysis also explains and underscores his long and ardent support for public service broadcasting.

4 In his 1925 lectures "Am I a Liberal?" and the "The Economic Transition in England" Keynes, drawing on Commons (1934: 773–88), attempted to develop a non-Marxist conceptualization of the economic process circumscribed by three distinct epochs: the ages of scarcity, abundance, and stabilization. The age of scarcity referred to pre-capitalist modes of governance and coercion, including communitarian, feudal, and medieval power structures. The age of abundance was associated with the dawn of capitalism and the early successes of an individualist liberal economic order. The third age of stabilization is characterized by: "a diminution of individual liberty, enforced in part by governmental sanctions, but mainly by economic sanctions through concerted action, whether secret,

semi-open, or arbitrational, of associations, corporations, unions, and other collective movements of manufacturers, merchants, laborer, farmers, and bankers ... The transition from economic anarchy to a regime which deliberately aims at controlling and directing economic forces in the interests of social justice and social stability, will present enormous difficulties both technical and political" (Keynes, 1931: 303–5). *The Affluent Society* and *The New Industrial State* should be viewed similarly as an attempt to set out the characteristics of a new phase in the evolution of capitalism.

5 Of course Scitovsky (1943) presents a different model where the entrepreneur is treated as an individual and following the standard microeconomic approach treatment to the individual, they are assumed to maximize a utility function (which includes two arguments – leisure and income).

6 This echoes Keynes's (1972a: 282–3) argument in his essay "The End of Laissez Faire": "Economists, like other scientists, have chosen the hypothesis from which they set out, and which they offer to beginners, because it is the simplest, and not because it is the nearest to the facts. Partly for this reason, but partly, I admit, because they have been biased by the traditions of the subject, they have begun by assuming a state of affairs where the ideal distribution of productive resources can be brought about through individuals acting independently by the method of trial and error in such a way that those individuals who move in the right direction will destroy by competition those who move in the wrong direction. This implies that there must be no mercy or protection for those who embark their capital or their labor in the wrong direction. It is a method of bringing the most successful profit-makers to the top by a ruthless struggle for survival, which selects the most efficient by the bankruptcy of the less efficient. It does not count the cost of the struggle, but looks only to the benefits of the final result which are assumed to be permanent. The object of life being to crop the leaves off the branches up to the greatest possible height, the likeliest way of achieving this end is to leave the giraffes with the longest necks to starve out those whose necks are shorter."

7 This was also something Keynes had perhaps begun to notice nearly forty years earlier. In a radio broadcast discussion on "University Men in Business," Keynes (1981: 651–2) noted that a more professional business class was emerging whereby new recruits were no longer selected on the basis of nepotism or aristocratic class but instead: "deliberately chosen on the grounds of their university record, [which] is going to become increasingly important. There has always been a certain number of this type entering business, but it is a comparatively new thing for them to do so in large numbers." In that radio discussion Keynes saliently also went

on to highlight how Shell Group was increasingly drawing upon a university trained and professional class of salaried managers. Nevertheless it is clear that while Keynes noticed the rise of the new class of business managers he did not attempt to theorize about its implications more widely, in contrast to Galbraith.

8 In a footnote in *American Capitalism* Galbraith (1952a: 91) quoted approvingly Schumpeter's (1943) *Capitalism, Socialism and Democracy*, which highlights Schumpeter's influence on his thinking. Equally revealing was that Galbraith (1952a: 91) noted that: "While my analysis is in a tradition of economic theory different from his, and one of which he was frequently critical, the conclusions on this point are similar." I take this to mean that Galbraith was conscious of his own Keynesian-Institutionalist approach, which was different to Schumpeter's own idiosyncratic brand of economics.

9 Keynes also foresaw both the aggregation of business units and the drive to remove the uncertainties and instabilities associated with competition. In his 1927 lectures on "Industry, Economy, Currency and Trade," Keynes (1981: 642) observed that: "the day of the small unit is over, partly for technical reasons, even more for marketing reasons. To get the market is half the task of the modern businessman, and modern methods of capturing markets are hopelessly inapplicable on the small scale of the old competitive industry. In fact, under modern conditions the wastes and expenses of cut-throat competition and the beggar-my-neighbor business, which we used to applaud so whole-heartedly, are so devastating that every go-ahead and prosperous industry spends half its time trying to get rid of them; and those industries which still persist in small units and free competition – like coal and cotton, to take two prominent examples – are rapidly going bankrupt and will continue to go bankrupt until they alter their ways." What is notable about Keynes's assessment of the fate of the coal and cotton industries is that it is remarkably similar to Galbraith's (1952b: 97–8) comparison of the oil and coal industry in *American Capitalism*.

10 The nexus between technology, time, and the need to cover costs was also alluded to by Veblen (1904: 93) who noted that: "the capital invested in any given industrial venture is turned over within a certain, approximately definite, length of time. The length of time occupied by the turnover may vary from one establishment to another, but in any given case the length of the turnover is one of the important factors that determine the chances of gain for the business concern in question."

11 In his autobiography Galbraith (1981: 519n.) acknowledged that: "One of my important sources on motivation, identification in particular, was Herbert Simon of Carnegie-Mellon University. In 1978, he won

the Nobel Prize in economics for ideas that I turned to my use most gratefully."

12 In his 1927 lectures on "The Public and the Private Concern," Keynes (1981: 697) also: "traced the evolutionary process which has been going on in private concerns, bringing about the joint-stock company of diffused ownership and salaried management, which had moved half way from the typical private concern to the public concern." Nevertheless, while Keynes clearly perceived this trend he did not proceed to elaborate its consequences for society, unlike Galbraith.

13 This is an example of a frequent ploy by Galbraith, in which he seeks to update core economic categories. Other examples abound. For example, in *The Affluent Society*, Galbraith (1958a: chapters 3–6) argues that analysis of competition, class, and poverty of the Classical Economists of Smith, Ricardo, Malthus, and Marx needs to be updated for the modern affluent society. See Canterbery (1984) for a consideration of Galbraith's analysis of class and supra surplus, and how it compares to both Piero Sraffa and Michal Kalecki.

14 Schumpeter (1943: 150–2) also recognized the nascent technocratic class which advanced technology calls. Predating Galbraith, Schumpeter (1943: 132) observed that the demands of modern technology were giving rise to a new class of well educated specialists: "Technological progress is increasingly becoming the business of teams of trained specialists who turn out what is required and make it work in predictable ways. The romance of earlier commercial adventure is rapidly wearing away, because so many more things can be strictly calculated that had of old to be visualised in a flash of genius."

15 As Schumpeter (1943: 96) noted: "The first thing a modern concern does as soon as it feels that it can afford it is to establish a research department every member of which knows that his bread and butter depends on his success in devising improvements. This practice does not obviously suggest aversion to technological progress." See also Rosenberg (1982, 1994).

16 Again such themes are evident in Schumpeter (1943: 132) who remarked: "Technological progress is increasingly becoming the business of teams of trained specialists who turn out what is required and make it work in predictable ways. The romance of earlier commercial adventure is rapidly wearing away, because so many more things can be strictly calculated that had of old to be visualized in a flash of genius."

17 This analysis is borne out by history. As Chandler (1977: 10) points out in his authoritative examination of the rise of the modern corporation: "in making administrative decisions, career managers preferred policies that favored the long-term stability and growth of their

enterprises to those that maximized current profits. For salaried managers the continuing existence of their enterprises was essential to their lifetime careers. Their primary goal was to assure continuing use of and therefore continuing flow of material to their facilities. They were far more willing than were the owners (stockholders) to reduce or even forego current dividends in order to maintain the long-term viability of their organizations. They sought to protect their sources of supplies and their outlets. They took on new products and services in order to make more complete use of existing facilities and personnel."

18 As we will discuss in detail in chapter 7, this conception, superficially at least, has much in common with the managerialist theories of the firm (Baumol, 1959; Williamson, 1964, 1970; Marris, 1964; Cyert and March, 1963) that grew out of the recognition by Berle and Means (1932) that large firms were no longer controlled and dominated by their owners, but instead by their managers. Nevertheless, as we shall argue below, Galbraith develops a distinctive view that deserves to be decoupled from this association.

19 As Chandler's (1977: 486) historical study highlights: "the desire of the managers to assure the success of their enterprise as a profit-making institution created strong pressures for its continuing growth. Such growth normally resulted from two quite different strategies of expansion. One was defensive or negative and stemmed from a desire for security. Its purpose was to prevent sources of supplies or outlets for goods and services from being cut off or to limit entry of new competition into the trade. The other strategy was more positive. Its aim was to add new units, permitting by means of administrative coordination a more intensive use of existing facilities and personnel. Such positive growth might be considered as productive expansion and negative or defensive growth as non-productive expansion. One increased productivity by lowering unit costs, the other rarely did." See also the arguments of chapters 7 and 8 below.

20 Nevertheless Galbraith continues to be misunderstood. As Robinson (1977: 1326) was forced to argue: "The stress that John Kenneth Galbraith (1967: 9) lays on the dependence of large corporations on their technostructures has been taken to suggest that they are not governed by the profit motive. This is a misunderstanding. The specialists who serve a particular corporation depend upon it for their incomes and careers and generally develop a kind of patriotism for it. They have just as much motive to promote its profitability as an old-fashioned capitalist. But the complexity of this multidimensional choice in conditions of uncertainty means that maximizing profits, even in the limited sense of preferring more to less profitable policies, is by no means a simple matter."

21 It is also worth comparing Kalecki's analysis of price and investment decisions of the firm. Kalecki (1971) argued that: "in view of the uncertainties faced in the process of price fixing it will not be assumed that the firm attempts to maximize its profits in any precise sort of manner."

22 The parallels with Knight (1921) should be obvious. Knight can be considered as an Institutionalist who studied the ramifications of uncertainty for economic theory in general, and the theory of the firm in particular (see Hodgson, 2004: 322–44, who highlights how Knight can be considered part of the Institutionalist tradition).

23 In recognizing the internal incoherence of the neoclassical competitive model of the firm post-Marshallian authors, such as Richardson (1959, 1960) and Loasby (1976: 173–92), introduce the distinction between free competition used by Marshall and Andrews (cf. Lee *et al.* 1986; Clark, 1940) and perfect competition used in the conventional wisdom. Free competition does not rest on the assumption of perfect information and foresight and is consistent with Galbraith's approach. The concept of free competition refers to the everyday usage of the term to denote rivalry between similar matched competitors (see Marshall, 1920: 337–50). Under free competition competitors do not collude with competitors on either side, that is buyers compete freely with buyers, sellers complete freely with sellers, and it is the free flow of technical knowledge, not the number of competitors, which ensures a conventional and broadly uniform price (cf. Chick, 1992; Davies and Lee, 1988). Galbraith's discussion of the market system appears to reflect Marshall's conception of free competition.

24 In *Economics and the Public Purpose*, Galbraith (1973a: 59) noted that: "In the first quarter of 1971, the 111 industrial corporations with assets of a billion dollars or more had more than half of all the assets employed in manufacturing and received substantially more than half of the earnings on more than half of the sales. The 333 industrial corporations with assets of more than $500 million had a full 70 per cent of all assets employed in manufacturing. In transportation, communications, power utilities, banking and finance, although the concentration is somewhat less, the tendency is similar; in merchandising, the concentration is also high ... Making up the remainder of the economy are around twelve million smaller firms, including about three million farmers, whose total sales are less than those of the four largest corporations; just under three million garages, service stations, repair firms, laundries, laundromats, restaurants and other service establishments; two million small retail establishments; around nine hundred thousand construction firms; several hundred thousand small manufacturers;

and an unspecified number serving the multi-variate interests of an advanced society in what is collectively called vice." Galbraith's figures were drawn from a Senate Testimony and the 1972 *Statistical Abstract of the United States*.

25 Although New Keynesians have increasingly recognized the power of large firms to set their own prices in their employment of the assumption of imperfect competition, they have not yet taken the logical next step to examine the consequences for consumer sovereignty: "The obvious counterpart of the control of prices is an effort to control the response of buyers to those prices. A strategy for protecting established belief which seeks to confine corporate power to the control of prices and costs, however great its service to intellectual vested interest, is also absurd" (Galbraith, 1973a: 151).

26 Indeed as Hodgson (2001a) points out, no author has brought these ideas to the attention of the modern reader more clearly and definitively than Galbraith. Many are inclined to see this as Galbraith's principal conclusion. But as should be clear from this discussion, their nexus to the imperatives of technology and organization are paramount and must not be hidden from view or treated in isolation.

27 For a discussion of the various contemporaneous debates regarding Galbraith's approach to the management of the consumer in *The Affluent Society* and *The New Industrial State* see Hession (1972: 98–106; 180–85) and Reisman (1980: 72–100). Hession and Reisman, however, consider Galbraith's contribution to wider social theory rather than his economic contribution. Chapter 9, below, seeks to evaluate Galbraith's specific economic contribution.

28 This passive effect probably has its origins in *The Theory of the Leisure Class*, where Veblen (1899: 10) noted that: "With the exception of the instinct of self-preservation, the propensity for emulation is probably the strongest and most alert and persistent of the economic motives proper."

29 That is: "Members seek to adapt the goals of the corporation more closely with their own; by extension the corporation seeks to adapt social attitudes and goals to those of the members of its technostructure. So social belief originates at least in part with the producer. Thus the accommodation of the market behavior of the individual, as well as of social attitudes in general, to the needs of producers and the goals of the technostructure is an inherent feature of the system" (Galbraith, 1967a: 217).

30 What is more, firms producing morally questionable products are nevertheless able to attract stock market investment by virtue of their status as private corporations. As Robert Reich (2009: 175) remarks

in *Supercapitalism*: "Social offensiveness is not necessarily financially offputting. Few industries have been more vilified than tobacco but tobacco companies have had no difficulty obtaining funding from investors eager to make a good return. Firms producing alcohol or firearms, companies relying on revenues from gambling, and firms producing lurid magazines and videos have all done reasonably well on Wall Street – most even outperforming the S&P 500 index. Defense stocks, considered morally objectionable by some, have likewise outperformed the S&P 500 index since the late 1980s."

31 One should, moreover, compare this to the latter-day Post Keynesian link between macroeconomics, employment policy and environmental issues including the development of sustainable policies (see Forstater, 2003, 2004, 2006; Lawson, 2007).

32 Again such themes echo Keynes (1982: 242), who noted that: "The same rule of self-destructive financial calculation governs every walk of life. We destroy the beauty of the countryside because the unappropriated splendors of nature have no economic value. We are capable of shutting off the sun and stars because they do not pay a dividend. London is one of the richest cities in the history of civilization, but it cannot 'afford' the highest standards of achievement of which its own living citizens are capable, because they do not 'pay'."

33 Stanfield (1996) traces Galbraith's conception of the public interest to John Dewey. According to Dewey (1927: 244), an act is private when its consequences are affected by the persons directly engaged in it, but if the consequences extend beyond those directly engaged then "the act acquires a public capacity." Dewey (1927: 257) interprets the public as those who are "indirectly and seriously affected for good or for evil" by an act. It is also possible, however, that Galbraith's perspective on the public interest was influenced by Keynes. For example, in his essay "The End of Laissez-Faire" Keynes (1926: 287–8) argued: "The world is not so governed from above that private and social interest always coincide. It is not so managed here below that in practice they coincide. It is not a correct deduction from the principles of economics that enlightened self-interest always operates in the public interest. Nor is it true that self-interest generally is enlightened; more often individuals acting separately to promote their own ends are too ignorant or too weak to attain even these."

34 Branston, Cowling, and Sugden (2006) develop a view and set of policy proposals that seeks, in a manner reminiscent of Galbraith (1967a, 1973a, 2004), to reconcile and align the governance of the modern corporation with the wider public interest.

35 For example see Branston *et al.* (2006a; see also Cowling and Sugden, 1990, 1992, 1993, 1999; Knight and Sugden, 1990), who consider the

various possibilities for widening participation in decision-making to improve the alignment of the objectives of the modern corporation with the public interest – ensuring "making technology serve public not technocratic interest" (Galbraith, 1973a: 240). This approach also underscores the importance of developing a critical educational curriculum to facilitate dynamic processes of learning to increase engagement and participation and democratization around the modern corporation (Sugden and Wilson, 2003, 2005). This is consistent with Galbraith's (1967a: 294) assessment of the role of education in emancipating people from the subservience promulgated by the new industrial state: "The economy for its success requires organized public bamboozlement. At the same time it nurtures a growing class which feels itself superior to such bamboozlement and deplores it as intellectually corrupt."

36 Branston, Cowling, and Sugden (2006: 189–90) similarly argue that: "In modern market economies the desirability of 'good governance' is often advocated or paid lip service. However, what is typically not appreciated is that governance in the public interest requires a form of market economy that is not found in the 'free market'. Whereas the 'free market' implies exclusive interest groups pursuing their own objectives, despite the resistance of others, governance of an economic activity in the public interest requires an inclusive process encompassing all of the public affected by the activity and a constant search for effective democracy."

37 As Gambs (1975: 42) summarizes: "Countervailing power tends to emerge when vast original power is possessed by an economic group. Thus when a steel trust comes into being, countervailing power tends to develop in, say, the automobile or electrical appliance industries, which purchase vast quantities of steel and, as buyers, can match their bargaining power against that of the steel oligopoly ... The development of countervailing power may take other forms. In some nations it may take the form of cooperatives; and in democratic nations, it may take the form of subsidies or other benefits to special groups. This development explains much of the New Deal and especially the Wagner Act and farm price supports. We are not talking here about benefits to consumers but of advantages to workers and suppliers ... To be sure, countervailing power does not always spring into being or, having sprung, does not always remain effective in the public interest ... This theory of countervailing power suggests policy applications. It suggests that liberals should modify their notions about the effectiveness of antitrust or other state programs of reform and should use their talents to help bring about countervailing power where such power has not been able to grow thriftily." As Hession (1972: 36)

points out countervailing power has many antecedents: "In economics, one of the first Americans to stress the importance of bargaining transactions ... was the late John R. Commons. Professors John M. Clark, Edwin G. Nourse, and others have dealt with collective economic action." For other detailed discussions of countervailing power and evaluations of the reactions to *American Capitalism*, see Hession (1972: 30–63), Reisman (1980: 50–71), and Stanfield (1996: 19–40). For a recent study, see Dobson and Waterson (1997). The notion of countervailing power also underpins Robert Reich's (2009) analysis of supercapitalism.

38 Countervailing power is similar to James Madison's idea of dividing up power in government so that no branch of government, or no particular individual, can gain too much power over everyone else. As an economist, Galbraith focuses mainly on economic power rather than political power, although the two never can be neatly separated. From this perspective, the state must serve as another branch of the economy, and must constrain the power of large firms in a similar way that the judiciary constrains the power of the executive branch of government.

39 Indeed as Galbraith (1973b: 176) acknowledged: "Public regulatory bodies, it has long been observed, tend to become the captives of the firms that ostensibly they regulate."

40 Consistent with Galbraith's thesis Sugden (2003, 2004) highlights the recent tendency in Britain to further ensure that universities reflect and anticipate corporate needs. See also, for example, the 2003 Government white paper (UK Government, 2003).

41 As Galbraith (1973a: 246) maintained: "Emancipation of belief requires that all policy emanating from the Executive and the acolytes of the corporate community be assumed, in the absence of contrary demonstration, to be what serves the needs of the planning system. No one should imagine that this service is conspiratorial, wicked or even deliberate. Much of the articulation will be by men of specific unction and well-confined imagination to whom the notion of a divergence between the purposes of the planning system and those of the public is safely unrevealed."

42 Galbraith (1973a: 300) argued, for example, for a range of interventions to support the development of food security and supply: "Public intervention on behalf of agriculture – socialization of agricultural technology, support of agricultural price to encourage and protect investment, co-operative procurement of fertilizer, petroleum and equipment, co-operative or public supply of electricity, subsidy in support of new techniques – is also essential for a balanced development.

In the absence of such social action the supply of food and fibre would be insufficient and unreliable, the cost (like that of housing and medical care) very high." Arguably, as Lang (2003, 2006, 2007; see also Lang and Heasman, 2004) highlights, this state sponsorship of food production in the post-World War II period facilitated the emergence of the large agri-businesses, agrochemical firms, food processors, and food retailers that now dominate the food and retailing industries.

43 As noted above, Galbraith has been interested in the issue of controlling inflation for most of his professional career. He was effectively the US Price Tsar during World War II, and he has continuously advocated wage and price controls to keep inflation in check. In some of his earliest writings, Galbraith (1941, 1952a, 1952b, 1955b, 1958b, 1958c) argued for controlling prices in selected industries. And in testimony before the Joint Economic Committee of Congress on July 20, 1971 he called for permanent wage and price controls in the USA. Even Milton Friedman (1977: 12) was moved to recognize Galbraith's commitment to controlling inflation: "when shortly after he became President, Mr Ford assembled a summit meeting of various groups of people to advise him on inflation, I was fascinated to find that at a meeting of economists Galbraith was one of the few outside of those whom you would expect to take this position – the so-called 'liberal' economists – to take the problem of inflation seriously and to regard it as something which had to be corrected."

44 The conflict theory of inflation developed by Post Keynesians argues that inflation reflects conflict over the distribution of income and is underpinned by the (money) wage demands of workers which are channeled through the pricing and finance process into rising prices.

45 As Galbraith (1958a: 180) notes: "in the characteristic industrial market – those of oligopoly and administered prices – the increase in demand must be implemented by a specific decision by the firm to change its price." It is clear that for Galbraith firms are active price makers and actively coping with history. Moreover Galbraith's analysis stands in direct contrast to the disinterested and disembodied fictional Walrasian auctioneer. It is a conceptualization based on an assessment that typically firms possess power and have the capacity to make real choices that can effect and influence in a real sense: the firm's evolution, the nature of the competitive process and the resulting course of history. According to Galbraith's perspective, which accords with the Post Keynesian view, the allocative role of prices is a residual and by-product of other roles (cf. Sawyer, 1993; Lee, 1990). In the bimodal view: "the role of prices is greatly diminished. They are much more effectively under the control of the firm" (Galbraith, 1973b: 127). Prices reflect

the strategic objectives of the firm. Any constancy of price in the face of demand changes reflects the functions of price and the objectives and decisions of firms themselves. From this perspective it is fallacious to interpret any constancy of prices as rigid prices, that is, fixed by an external agency to induce disequilibrium trading (as typified by the reappraisal of Keynesian economic literature; see Sawyer, 1995). Any constancy of price reflects the decisions of strategic decision-makers within the firm and is likely to reflect the (strategic) costs of making price changes or the fact that the underlying conditions and mechanisms that underpin the pricing process remain unchanged (Means, 1972). As Sawyer (1995: 173) notes: "When producers are price makers, then firms charge the prices they wish to charge even if those prices may not be the ones they would have wished to charge had they been fully informed." From this perspective the prices set are not disequilibrium prices rather they are more akin to equilibrium prices in that firms set prices in the expectation that they will meet whatever demand is forthcoming at that price (with stock changes being a principal means of absorbing any fluctuations).

46 Lee (1998) argues that the diverse contributions of Post Keynesians can be arranged into three non-neo-classical doctrines of administered prices, normal cost prices, and mark-up prices associated with the seminal contributions of Gardiner Means, Philip Andrews, and Michal Kalecki. Together they constitute the foundations of Post Keynesian price theory. Galbraith's contributions reflect this tradition. He frequently refers to the "administered price industries" (cf. Galbraith, 1958a: 181). He was extremely familiar with the work of Berle and Means (1932). Indeed Galbraith (1952a: 37) explicitly acknowledged Berle and Means's modern classic *The Modern Corporation and Private Property* in *American Capitalism*. Moreover A. A. Berle was supportive of Galbraith's approach, arguing that *American Capitalism* was "a square challenge to some of the classic premises on which the current theory of capitalism is based" (Berle, 1953: 81) and subsequently that "*The New Industrial State* will make economic history" (Berle, 1967: 29). Similarly, as I discussed with Galbraith in the interview in chapter 12, Kalecki also was a great influence (even if Andrews was not). Notwithstanding the origins of Galbraith's conception of the price setting processes of the modern corporation it should be clear that Galbraith's vision is influenced by those that made seminal contributions to Post Keynesian price theory, sharing a common heritage.

47 Galbraith also argued that wage and price controls can be used to tackle the large and unjustified income imbalances generated by the

new industrial state: "If greater equality of income distribution is an objective of public policy, greater equality must be an objective in wage and salary control. It must be a goal of the latter to narrow differentials which are a reflection not of function but of hierarchy, tradition and power" (Galbraith, 1973a: 288).

6 *Why people are poor*

In a world where everyone is poor, there is nothing very remarkable about poverty. It becomes remarkable, and also less forgivable, in a community where the great majority of people are well-to-do. And the explanation for poverty in the well-to-do society must be sought in the general and not the particular aspects of the case – not in the nature of the society of the poor but in the nature of a society of the rich which allows or requires some to stay so poor.

J. K. Galbraith (1958a: 20)

Polls also suggest that the public both understand the role of growing inequality and supports government action to do something about it. A massive Pew survey of trends in public opinion found that the fractions of the public agreeing that the rich are getting richer while the poor get poorer, that the government has a responsibility to help those in need, that everyone should be guaranteed enough to eat and a place to live, have all risen to levels not seen since the early 1990s. All this suggests that there's an opportunity for a major push toward policies that address inequality and/or economic insecurity.

Paul Krugman (2007: 202)

In the early 1950s Galbraith obtained a grant from the Carnegie corporation to study the causes of pockets of poverty in substantial areas of the USA. This was the beginning of *The Affluent Society*. The title that Galbraith (1958a: 20) had in mind at that time was "Why people are poor." Nevertheless, for some, *The Affluent Society* was seen as a celebration of affluence that obscured the plight of the poor. Galbraith was accused of ignoring the fact that even one of the richest countries in the world still had a great many poor people. And his attack on the paramount position of production was viewed as callous, given that economic growth offered a means of ameliorating their enduring condition.

This annoyed Galbraith. Quite rightly, it might be said. Although *The Affluent Society* focused on the tremendous wealth of the USA, it also focused on the social and environmental imbalance generated by the modern economy. It argued that a range of policies should be pursued to ameliorate this imbalance, including: establishing a proper system of unemployment compensation; providing access to minimum standards of healthcare; ensuring the provision of adequate social housing; developing targeted education policies; as well as introducing a negative income tax or basic income guarantee to provide a minimum level of security.[1]

Galbraith long focused on the plight of the poor. In *The New Industrial State* and *Economics and the Public Purpose*, Galbraith (1967a, 1973a) sought to explain both the dynamics of modern industrial development as well as identify who benefits from that development, and who does not. In *Economic Development*, *The Nature of Mass Poverty*, and *The Voice of the Poor*, Galbraith (1964a, 1979b, 1983c) considered the problems of global poverty and underdevelopment. And in *The Culture of Contentment* and *The Good Society*, Galbraith (1992, 1996b) argued that contemporary societies have become even blinder to the problems of the poor, at home and abroad. Modern affluence has ushered in a contented majority who have benefited from the modern mode of production; those who are secure in income and existence and who have adequate provision for healthcare and old age.

Galbraith argued, however, that the modern mode of production, in ushering in an age of great wealth, was far from uniform in sharing the spoils of affluence (cf. Myrdal, 1944, 1957, 1968). This central conclusion underpinned Galbraith's analysis of poverty. In *The Affluent Society* Galbraith (1958a) focused on "insular poverty" – the pockets of poverty in developed countries (cf. Myrdal, 1957). This is the problem of poverty amidst plenty, of a minority of households on the cusp of subsistence in rich, vibrant economies. It is the problems of urban slums as well as rural decline and isolation in areas like Appalachia. Galbraith's (1964a, 1971, 1979b, 1983c) analysis of the "mass poverty" of less developed nations, in contrast, considered the poverty of an entire nation, where most of the population lives on the brink of starvation. This is the poverty of vast areas of Africa, of China and India, and of rural areas and urban slums in Latin and South America.

Insular poverty

Galbraith first raised the issue of "insular poverty" in *American Capitalism* (Galbraith, 1952a: chapter 8). There he noted that the affluence created by technological advance can cause problems for those who do not benefit from the new technology, and who are relegated to receiving low wages for work that is no longer in widespread demand. *The Affluent Society* and *The New Industrial State* extended this analysis. Galbraith (1958a: 264–7; 1967a) highlighted the benefits of technology in ushering in modern affluence, but insisted that technology does not in itself help to reduce poverty. The general affluence created by technology and associated management of the consumer blinds us to the situation of the poor, making them powerless and invisible (Galbraith, 1992, 1996b).

The affluent society continues to be blind to the problems of the poor. According to the Agriculture Department, in 2006 nearly 36 million Americans, 4 million more than in 1999, lived in households that could not afford enough food. These households included more than 12 million children. In December 2007 the US Conference of Mayors reported that out of twenty-three major American cities, 80 percent had an increase in people using emergency soup kitchens and food pantries and 43 percent had an increase in the number of homeless children (see Berg, 2008). This poverty, which is concentrated in urban slums as well as areas of rural decline, accords with Galbraith's (1958a: 261) analysis of "insular poverty" – "that which manifests itself as an 'island' of poverty." Nevertheless Galbraith sought to identify the forces that conspire to reproduce such islands of poverty through time and space:

> But the more important characteristic of insular poverty is forces, common to all members of the community, which restrain or prevent participation in economic life at going rates of return. These restraints are several. Race, which acts to locate people by their color rather by the proximity to employment, is obviously one. So are poor educational facilities. And this effect is further exaggerated when the poorly educated, endemically a drug on the labor market, are brought together in dense clusters, by common inadequacy of the schools available to blacks and the poor. So is the disintegration of family life in the slum which leaves households in the hands of women. Family life itself is in some measure a manifestation of affluence. And so, without doubt, is the shared sense of helplessness and rejection and

> the resulting demoralization which is the product of the common misfortune. (Galbraith, 1958a: 262)

In his analysis of "insular poverty" Galbraith (1958a: 258–67) echoed Veblen (1898a), Myrdal (1944, 1968), and Kaldor (1970, 1972, 1985). He viewed poverty as a self-perpetuating cycle of cumulative causation. Those living in poor communities typically receive a poor education and poor public services. They lack the training and good health necessary to improve their economic condition. The poor are also powerless economically and politically, making it hard for them to obtain the government services that might improve their lives and life chances. People living in poor areas also come to accept their poverty and see little means of escape. This reinforces their political powerlessness and contributes to the inadequate provision of public goods that may alleviate their predicament. In this way, poverty reproduces itself in poor areas, and across generations.[2]

Galbraith's (1973a) analysis of "insular poverty" and inequality received its clearest theoretical treatment in *Economics and the Public Purpose*, which described how the bimodal economy consisting of the planning and market systems gives rise to poverty in developed capitalist economies:

> Dominating this book as a drumbeat is the theme of unequal development and the associated inequality in income. The unequal development is unrelated to need; the inequality in income bears no necessary relation to productivity or efficiency. Both are the result of unequal deployment of power. Both are socially damaging ... In *The Affluent Society* I dealt with the starvation of the public services as though all services were alike. I did not see that this deprivation was great where public needs were involved, non-existent where powerful industry pressed its requirement on the state. And perhaps because I was only dealing with the world of the large corporation I did not identify adequately the systemic inequality in product and income as between different parts of the so-called private economy. (Galbraith, 1973a: 10)

Large firms, which are part of what Galbraith calls the "planning system," have acquired enormous economic power. As noted above, they have power to control prices and the resources that enable them to mold public opinion and influence the response of the consumer.

Moreover, the climate of consumerism generated through the management of demand equates happiness with those goods produced by the private sector of the economy.[3] This buttresses the large firms' influence upon the political process.[4] And it underscores the success of the business sector in pursuing political advantage in a way that often conflicts with the needs of the poor and other aspects of the civilized society (Reich, 2009: 131–67).

In contrast, small firms are subject to the dictates of the market. They have little economic power and little ability to sway public opinion or the political process. They are thus disadvantaged relative to the planning system. The result is unequal economic development – the planning system produces too many goods and the market system produces an inadequate supply of goods. Likewise, important public goods that might benefit those in the market system (such as access to high-quality healthcare and education) are likely to be underprovided, as the needs of the planning system predominate and skew public expenditure.

The terms of trade between the market and planning systems are inevitably unequal. The market system "sells a great many things – agricultural products, forest products, other raw materials, numerous services and many parts and components – to the firms of the planning system" (Galbraith, 1973a: 147). Prices, profits, and incomes in the market system are depressed by free competition or the monopsony buying power of the planning system. As a consequence there are powerful forces ensuring that prices and incomes are kept to a minimum in the market system. This situation is then exacerbated by the fact that small firms are nevertheless dependant on buying and supplying goods from the firms in the planning system that have obtained some measure of control over prices. And it follows therefore "that equality is not the tendency between the planning and the market systems; the basic tendency is to inequality" (Galbraith, 1973a: 148).

And just as there is a dual economy, so there is a dual labor market (cf. Doeringer and Poire, 1971; Poire and Sabel, 1984; Sawyer, 1989; Saint-Paul, 1997). Not everyone is employed by large corporations. Some people will choose, for a variety of reasons, to work for the smaller firms that comprise the market system. These people are at a disadvantage compared to planning sector workers and are paid considerably lower wages.[5] So people are more likely to end up poor when they want to work for smaller firms, when they do not have the education or cultural background and are unable to land jobs with firms in the planning or technologically sophisticated sectors. As Galbraith (1973a: 219–20) concluded: "It means that the broadly equalizing assumption of neo-classical economics must be rejected; instead, in the absence of energetic reform, the tendency of the economy is to one comparatively affluent, one comparatively impoverished working force". In order to equalize the power of the market system, Galbraith advocated targeting weak, neglected or impoverished groups for collective and corrective action. To this end Galbraith (1973a: 274–7, italics removed) advanced a series of policy proposals designed to achieve this goal, including:

> (1) General exemption for small businessmen from all prohibitions in the anti-trust laws against combination to stabilize prices and output. Any resulting abuses should be cured by regulation – not by efforts to restore competition ... (2) Direct Government regulation of prices and production in the market system ... Since technology and associated capital investment requires stable prices, the frequent effect of such stabilization will be greater and more efficient production than if firms are left to the unpredictable fortunes of the market ... (3) Strong and effective encouragement to trade union organization ... (4) An extension and major increase in the minimum wage ... (5) A revised view of international commodity organization and a cautiously revised view of tariff protection in the market system ... (6) A strong presumption in favor of government support to the educational, capital and technological needs of the market system.

Another important cause of "insular poverty" is the preoccupation with "private" production and consumption that results from the rise of the modern corporation and its need to plan and advertise – "the paramount position of production." As we discussed in the previous chapter, Galbraith recognized the power held by large corporations over consumers, and their need to manufacture consumer demand. Demand, Galbraith argued, does not originate with the consumer; rather it is increasingly contrived for the consumer by the firm through advertising. Large firms seek increasingly to obtain a degree of influence over the pattern of consumer spending, in order to sustain the prestige and consumption of the goods that they produce and sell (which is considered at length in chapter 9 below). In contrast there is little promotion of the social goals and goods that contribute to the wider development of civil society. There is a systematic underprovision of basic services that would enable more people to escape insular poverty and join the technostructure.

A world of affluence also creates a political bias against taking action to help and address problems of inequality and insular poverty. As Krugman (2007: 70) observes, "people with jobs to do and children to raise have little incentive to pay close attention to political horseraces. In practice this rational lack of interest imparts an upward class bias to the political process: higher-income people are more likely to pay attention to politics, and more likely to vote, than are lower and middle-class Americans. As a result, the typical *voter* has a substantially higher income that the typical *person*, which is one reason politicians tend to design their policies with the relatively affluent in mind." What is more, in a world of rising affluence the poor are increasingly a small, disenfranchised minority. Politicians have little incentive to speak out for them and are unlikely to use the legislature to help them, as this will not garner votes:

> Any politician who speaks for the very poor is speaking from a small and generally inarticulate minority. As a result the modern liberal politician regularly aligns himself not with the poverty-ridden members of the community but with the far more numerous people who enjoy the far more affluent income of (say) the modern trade union member or the intellectual. (Galbraith, 1958a: 263)

In addition, with general affluence, there is a greater tendency to blame the poor for their condition – for if most people can succeed, why should everyone not succeed? This also helps to explain why individualist and social Darwinian explanations of poverty are so popular and prevalent in the affluent society. It also explains why affluent societies often lack the political and economic will to solve problems of "insular poverty" (Galbraith, 1992, 1996b).

Nevertheless, a good society need not accept this. The provision of public goods and services could keep pace with the production of private goods (Galbraith, 1958a). A good society diverts public resources toward helping the poor (Galbraith, 1967a, 1992, 1996b). This is why Galbraith long argued for a strong welfare state, providing benefits such as job protection and basic income guarantees, as well as an acknowledged and legitimate role for unions (even though he acknowledged the decline of the latter).[6] At the end of *The Affluent Society*, Galbraith (1958a: 265) argued for the development of education programs and investing in human and social capital, targeting especially the children of the poor:

> It requires that the investment in children from families presently afflicted be as little below normal as possible. If the children of poor families have first rate schools and school attendance is properly enforced; if the children, though badly fed at home, are well nourished at school; if the community has sound health services, and the physical well-being of the children is vigilantly watched; if there is opportunity for advanced education for those who qualify regardless of means; and if, especially in the case of urban communities, housing is ample and housing standards are enforced, the streets are clean, the laws are kept, and recreation is adequate – then there is a chance that the children of the poor will come to maturity without inhibiting disadvantage.

One such program designed to intervene in such a manner, "Head Start," became a key part of Lyndon Johnson's Great Society program, which, as noted above in chapter 2, Galbraith was involved in. In the UK this idea has been more recently resurrected in the form of the "Sure Start" program, similarly designed to break the vicious cycles of poverty and low aspiration, eliminating child poverty.

Of course, such programs and activities have to be paid for.[7] Funds must be channeled away from supporting the provision of increasingly irrelevant and superfluous private commodities, and instead be used to provide the public goods that address unmet public needs. Toward this end, Galbraith advocated higher sales taxes in order to finance government spending in needed areas, for example public transportation, education, health, and police protection:

> The relation of the sales tax to the problem of social balance is admirably direct. The community is affluent in privately produced goods. It is poor in public services. The obvious solution is to tax the former to provide the latter – by making private goods more expensive, public goods are made more abundant. Motion pictures, electronic entertainment, and cigarettes are made more costly so that schools can be more handsomely supported. We pay more for soap, detergents, and vacuum cleaners in order that we may have cleaner cities and less occasion to use them. We have more

expensive cars and petrol so that we may have more agreeable highways and streets on which to drive them. Food being relatively cheap, we tax it in order to have better medical services and better health in which to enjoy it. (Galbraith, 1958a: 252–3)[8]

Galbraith also advocated greater income taxes on the wealthy, holding that the tax system must be made progressive enough so that the rich protest loudly and vehemently.[9] For Galbraith that was the only way to know that the taxes imposed on the rich are high enough! We return to these issues below.

Mass poverty

The "mass poverty" of less developed countries is quite different than the "insular poverty" of developed nations.[10] It is exemplified by the global skewed distribution of wealth – see Figure 3. The 10th annual UN Development Programme Human Development Report, for example, highlights how the richest 20% of the world produce 86% of world Gross Domestic Product (GDP), while the poorest 20% produce just 1% (UNDP, 1999: 2). The richest 1% of the world's population, around 60 million, now receives as much income as the poorest 57%, while the income of the richest 25 million Americans is equivalent to that of almost 2 billion of the world's poorest people (UNDP, 2003). This skewed distribution means that: "There are still around 1 billion people living at the margins of survival on less than US$1 a day, with 2.6 billion – 40 percent of the world's population – living on less than US$2 a day" (UNDP, 2007: 25).

Poor countries therefore do not have sufficient wealth and income to support the many poor people in need of assistance. This has a devastating human impact: "Around 10 million children die each year before the age of 5, the vast majority from poverty and malnutrition" (UNDP, 2007: 25). In addition, the psychological propensities leading people to accept their condition are even greater than in developed countries (see Sen, 1999). In a poor country, then, a poverty of hope casts its spell on the entire nation, as people come to believe that there is no option other than to adapt to the reality of their circumstances.

Galbraith challenged traditional explanations of "mass poverty." Radical economists, following Lenin, typically argue that imperialist exploitation contributes to economic growth and rising general living

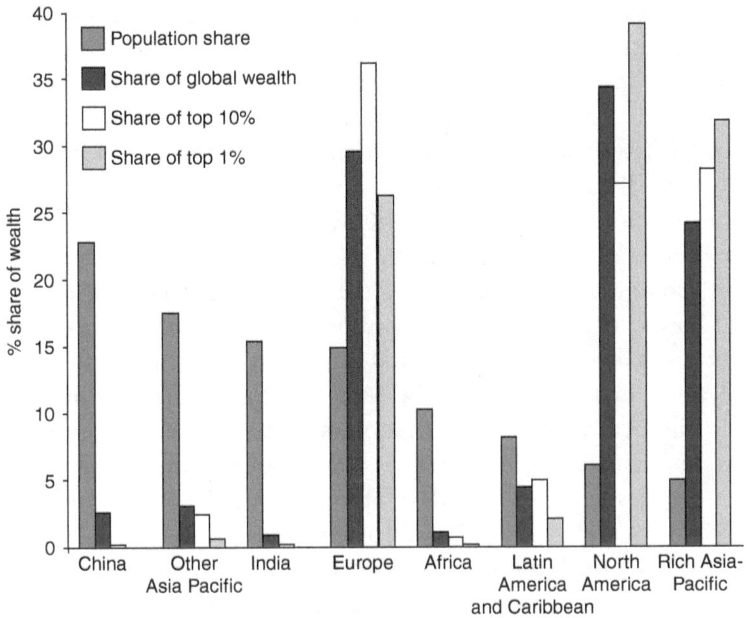

Figure 3. Population and wealth shares by region, 2006
Source: UNU-WIDER (2006)

standards, temporarily ameliorating class conflict, in the advanced and affluent nations:

> Disturbing ideas would emanate from Lenin. One was that the great industrial powers of Europe owed their economic success and well-being to the imperial domains that they had carved out or seized in Africa, Asia and the Pacific. They, and notably also their workers, lived on the backs of the deprived masses of the colonial lands ... And in time it would become a part of the political conscious of the liberal left in the industrial countries, helping, along with declining economic interest, to motivate the inevitable thrust to decolonization. (Galbraith, 1987: 178–9)

In the radical view it is the search and struggle for new markets, raw materials, and colonies that drives war and oppression, further condemning the poor to a world of insecurity and poverty. Accordingly the legacy of colonial systems is that feudal agrarian land systems are perpetuated – most of the land being owned by a small minority, with the majority forced to work on the land for bare subsistence wages.

Galbraith, however, rejected the argument that colonialism was the prime institutional culprit responsible for poverty. In *Economic Development* Galbraith (1964a: 16) pointed out, however, that colonialism was not a recent phenomenon in Latin America, yet most of Latin America was still poor. Nevertheless, Australia, Canada, and the USA were all British colonies at one point and all now experience general prosperity. Similarly Galbraith also rejected the idea that the drive for imperialism and the search for new markets was either an engine of economic development or a counteracting force that helped to stem Marx's "tendency of the rate of profit to fall" in mature capitalist economies. This was because, for Galbraith, much modern international trade is a function of the level of economic development. Although the promotion of international trade and the presence of multinational firms can confer benefits upon poor countries; they are far from engines of economic development. In *Economics and the Public Purpose*, Galbraith (1973a: 180–94) recognized, long before "New Trade Theory," that the majority of trade and competition was between advanced economies. Although he acknowledged that the large firm would seek to secure the sources of supply of necessary raw materials, Galbraith viewed it as an outgrowth of the modern mode of production, rather than a manifestation of class exploitation (see chapter 8 below). The consequence is that foreign investment and modern international trade serves the interests of the large firms and not economic development:

> Where there is a prospect for developing petroleum, bauxite, iron ore or other resources for supply to the United States or Europe, private capital continues to go abroad ... A little capital also goes to develop additional markets, trucks, tires, soap, pharmaceuticals – for European firms. But almost none goes to build the power plants, railroads or factories which are designed to serve the people of the poor countries, as British capital in the last century built the railroads in the United States, Canada and the Argentine to serve Americans, Canadians and Argentinians. (Galbraith, 1971: 178–9)[11]

What is more, in presenting this analysis, Galbraith also highlighted how a weak cultural base, as opposed to imperialism *per se*, contributes to underdevelopment, coups, corruption, and political instability:

> The consequences of an inadequate cultural base are comprehensive – on government, the economy, internal security, communications, even foreign policy. But the most visible manifestation is on the apparatus of government. People with the requisite education, training and honesty for performing the public tasks are unavailable. As a consequence, taxes are collected in haphazard or arbitrary fashion and public funds are spent inefficiently or for no particular purpose except the reward of the recipients. Where this is the case, government will ordinarily be unstable; those who do not have access to public income will have a strong incentive to seek to oust those who do. (Galbraith, 1971: 189)

Galbraith (1979b: 3) similarly rejected other conventional explanations of "mass poverty". He rejected the other conventional wisdom that certain countries, or certain communities, are "naturally poor," that is, poorly endowed with natural resources.[12] Instead Galbraith argued that "mass poverty" was perpetuated by vicious circles of cumulative causation, which were difficult to break and escape from.[13] Accordingly he argued that institutional analysis is required to understand the nature of "mass poverty" (cf. Olson, 2000).

Galbraith (1971: 176) noted that "any purposeful increase in future production requires saving from current consumption." This creates a problem for poor countries because nearly everyone is poor and they do little saving. Living at a bare subsistence level, for example, means that it is difficult to generate savings or get access to finance for agricultural improvements such as irrigation, hybrid seeds, or fertilizer. Likewise, new technologies require a certain minimum educational attainment to adopt and involve significant uncertainties, not least the risk of starvation and premature death from its misapplication:

> The first and most elementary effect of poverty is to enforce the very attitudes and behavior that make it self-perpetuating ... It is regularly observed, often with some surprise, that very poor countries are conservative – that, more than the more fortunate, their people resist change that is in their own interest. Illiteracy, and the limited time horizons it implies, is a partial cause of this; so is the inertia resulting from poor health and malnutrition. But poverty is an even more direct cause of conservatism. If there is no margin to spare, there is no margin for risk. One cannot try a new variety of wheat or rice that promises an additional 20 per cent yield if there is any chance that it is vulnerable to insect pests, disease or drought and thus

in an occasional year might fail altogether. However welcome the extra 20 per cent, it is not worth the risk of not eating for a whole season, the consequences of which tend to be both painful and irreversible. (Galbraith, 1971: 173)

Thus, even if there are savings, it is unlikely that they will be used for improved cultivation methods. If people manage to save out of their subsistence incomes, these savings will be hoarded as a buffer against bad harvests in the future, rather than used to invest in more advanced and efficient means of production. Subsistence farmers are therefore reluctant to invest in any new technology that might increase output but is risky and might threaten starvation during a bad year. The few who are rich are not a very reliable source of saving, preferring lavish expenditure as opposed to investing in farms, factories and power plants.[14] Finally, even if savings are invested and lead to improved agricultural output, or even if landowner revenues are redistributed to the poor, this will not necessarily solve the problem of mass poverty. Greater income will mean the survival of more people, who would have died otherwise, and so family per capita food consumption may be little changed and poverty will persist.

Reinforcing all this is the human tendency to accommodate oneself to one's condition, to accept a life on the edge of starvation rather than seeking to escape it.[15] Galbraith (1979b: 62–3) argued, therefore, that "an equilibrium of poverty" exists in less developed countries:

> People who have lived for centuries in poverty in the relative isolation of the rural village have come to terms with this existence ... Given the formidable hold of the equilibrium of poverty within which they live, accommodation is the optimal solution ... The deeply rational character of accommodation lies back, at least in part, of the central instruction of the principal world religions. All, without exception, urge acquiescence, some in remarkably specific form ... There has long been a suspicion, notably enhanced by Marx, that the contentment urged by religion is a design for diverting attention from the realities of class and exploitation – it is the opiate of the people. It is, more specifically, a formula for making the best of a usually hopeless situation.

Galbraith (1979b) noted that historically there have been three ways to break out of the cycle or equilibrium of "mass poverty" in less developed countries – trauma, migration, and education. Galbraith

(1979b: 116) also identified a fourth route – state-facilitated industrialization: "Industrialization is the counterpart of release from accommodation and escape from the equilibrium of poverty." In terms of the impact of trauma on "mass poverty", Galbraith considered the impact of horrific disasters, such as wars, famines, and tsunamis, that reduce the population to the point that those who remain are finally able to sustain themselves on the land. These are essentially the negative checks to population growth first noted by Malthus (1798) many years ago (cf. Galbraith, 1958a: 50–1). Since this is not a civilized means of reducing "mass poverty", nor a desirable solution to the problem of poverty, it is easy to reject; and so we are left with migration, education, and state-facilitated industrialization as practical solutions.

Among the many successes of migration as a solution to "mass poverty", Galbraith (1979b: chapter 8) pointed to his ancestors, the Scottish Highlanders, who came to the USA and Canada in the nineteenth century, as well as the successful streams of migration from Ireland, Italy, Sweden, and Eastern Europe to North America in the nineteenth and early twentieth centuries. More recently there has been migration from Mexico and Latin America to the USA. There has also been a great deal of migration from poorer parts of Europe to wealthier areas of Europe. Turks, Italians, and Greeks migrated to Germany. Millions of Portuguese, Italians, and Spaniards are living in France, making up around 10 percent of the French labor force. And more recently there has been migration from the transitional economies of Eastern Europe to the wealthier nations of Western Europe:

> In the last forty years in Germany, France and Switzerland, and in lesser measure in Austria and Scandinavia, the provision of outside workers for the tasks for which indigenous laborers are no longer available has been both accepted and highly organized. The factories of the erstwhile German Federal Republic are manned, and broad range of other work is performed, by Turks and Yugoslavs. Those in France are similarly supplied by what amounts to a new invasion of the Moors – the vast influx from the former North African colonies. Switzerland has long relied on Italian and Spanish workers. The industrial north of Italy, in turn, has depended heavily on a reserve army of the unemployed from the south – the more backward Mezzogiorno – and now increasingly from North Africa. The British economy has been sustained in no small part by migrants from the former dominions – India, Pakistan, Bangladesh and the West Indies. (Galbraith, 1992: 34)

Although migration brings cultural tensions and conflicts, it has led historically to a greater standard of living for those who migrate. The countries receiving immigrants have also typically benefited. Besides contributing to their new country by augmenting the labor supply and, in many instances, by performing arduous and tedious work that long-term residents seek to avoid, the reduction in population in their native country makes the problem of survival easier for those who remain and do not migrate.

Besides migration, the other principal policy instrument is the investment in education or the development of human and social capital. In the context of the less developed world, investing in education means ensuring basic numeracy and literacy (Galbraith, 1979b: 100–3). This requires free and compulsory education. Compulsion is needed because otherwise families will tend to keep their children at home where they can help with home production and with chores – a conclusion that perhaps reflects Galbraith's own childhood experiences – see chapter 2. Education helps poor farmers to understand the benefits of adopting technical innovations, which will help reduce "mass poverty". Education is necessary, too, as a means to control population growth. And education is always a good antidote to the psychology of accommodation, especially when the education instructs children about how much better things are in other parts of the world. Finally, education is necessary to underpin an enlightened public administration, free from corruption, which further promotes and develops mass education and channels public funds into other related areas that will sustain further growth, such as transportation, communication, and public health (see Galbraith, 1964a: 66).[16]

Such policies are critical because they work to empower the poor who are living in mass poverty. Education helps people to recognize the things that they need to do to improve the chances of escaping poverty. Education also lets people know that things can be different and that they can do things to make their lives better. And migration allows those people with ambition and desire to move to places where it is more likely that their lives will improve. Finally, in less developed countries, as in the developed world, social balance must be secured by the state, which also must be underpinned by political stability.[17] In *Economic Development*, Galbraith (1964a: 66) noted that the first stage of development requires education, communication and transportation to be provided by the state. In *The Nature of Mass Poverty*,

Galbraith (1979b: 115–16) argued for a third way between unfettered capitalism and state socialism, setting out the essence of what later became identified with the notion of a "developmental state" (see Johnson, 1982; Woo-Cumings, 1999):

No country that has industrialized in modern times, not Japan, Taiwan, Brazil, Mexico, or Iran, has done so without intensive intervention and support by the state. The basic essentials in such intervention and support are also reasonably certain: (1) There must be adequate security for people against physical threat to their property, against expropriation or predacious taxation. (2) There must be a basic and reliable system of roads, ports, electric power supply, and communications. (3) There must be a supply of capital – in practice much of it under public auspices from outside the country – for investment by private and public borrowers, and an intelligent and honest organization for receiving and passing on loans. (4) There probably needs to be some publicly sponsored industries – pilot-fish industries that, much argument to the contrary, have the peculiar merit of bringing others in their wake. Steel, if the country is large enough, and chemicals or petrochemicals, are possible examples.[18]

In addition, state initiatives to improve health and state support for developing heavy industry are prerequisites for economic development. But these are difficult things for a poor nation to do.[19] So, developed Western nations must help redress this social balance with adequate foreign aid (Galbraith, 1961, 1964a).[20]

Notwithstanding the various different ways to break out of "mass poverty", Galbraith argued that the most appropriate developmental path, however, must ultimately be tailored to the individual circumstances and the history of the country in question. In his 1965 Massey Lectures for the Canadian Broadcasting Corporation, for example, Galbraith developed a differential classification of the causes of poverty and a set of tailored policy recommendations (reproduced in Galbraith, 1971: chapters 13, 14, and 15). Over the course of these lectures Galbraith identified three models: (1) the Sub-Sahara African model; (2) the Latin American Model; and (3) the South Asian model. Associated with each was a differential prescription for escaping the equilibrium of poverty that characterized them (see Galbraith, 1971: 199–207). For underdeveloped Sub-Saharan African countries, Galbraith recommended the development of the cultural base to improve education, promote enterprise, and reduce corruption.[21] For

Latin America, which has a developed cultural base, Galbraith recommended that the feudal social structures should be transformed, ideally through an array of liberal reforms, so as to avoid violent and revolutionary struggle. In the more culturally and socially advanced South Asian countries, Galbraith advocated mobilizing internal savings, promoting enterprise, and providing public health advice on birth control. What should be clear, however, from this brief review is that Galbraith's analysis was tailored to the cultural and institutional context. Accordingly it represents a direct challenge to the "one size fits all" developmental prescription of stabilization, liberalization, and privatization that forms the cornerstone of the now intellectually bankrupt Washington Consensus.

The conscience of a liberal

In the central tradition the existence of poverty is typically explained as a consequence of the actions and choices of individuals, or the result of damaging and erroneous government policies. Individualist explanations, for example, have tended to be more prevalent, especially in the USA where Social Darwinism has had a strong hold on the popular imagination (see Hofstadter 1944; Hodgson, 2001a, 2004).[22] According to this doctrine, the economic and social world is characterized by a power struggle in which the inevitable outcome is a "survival of the fittest" (see Galbraith, 1958a: chapter 5; cf. Keynes, 1972a: 272–94). People who pursue education and possess the drive and the desire to be productive succeed – they join the "New Class."[23] In contrast, sloth, the failure to take individual initiative and an unwillingness to learn and develop socially useful skills are choices that relegate individuals to mediocrity or failure. As a consequence, such individuals are more likely to receive low wages and experience frequent bouts of poverty throughout their life. On the standard view, this outcome is the result of individual choices. Galbraith (1958a: 260) referred to such poverty as "case poverty":

> Case poverty is commonly and properly related to some characteristic of the individuals so afflicted. Nearly everyone else has mastered his environment; this proves that it is not intractable. But some quality peculiar to the individual or family involved – mental deficiency, bad health, inability to adapt to the discipline of industrial life, uncontrollable procreation,

alcohol, some educational handicap unrelated to community shortcomings, or perhaps a combination of several of these handicaps – has kept these individuals from participating in the general well-being.

A contemporary variant of "case poverty" focuses on the unintended consequences of an extensive social welfare safety net. Such analyses center on policies that create perverse economic incentives for people, promoting a reliance on generous government benefits, rather than contributing economically to society or economic development (Murray, 1984). Government policies are also identified as failing to encourage the high levels of saving and investment that are thought to be required if the economy and individual incomes are to grow. Large government budget deficits are viewed as discouraging private saving and investment, including investment in human capital (Seidman, 1990).

Galbraith (1958a: 261) accepted that "Case poverty exists." Nevertheless he also highlighted how its existence and causes were frequently accentuated in order to serve the interests of the affluent: "It has also been useful to those who have needed a formula for keeping the suffering of others from causing suffering to themselves" (Galbraith, 1958a: 261). That is, the existence and causes of "case poverty" are frequently marshaled to argue against needed intervention and action:

> Since this poverty is the result of the deficiencies, including the moral shortcomings, of the persons concerned, it is possible to shift the responsibility to those involved. They are worthless and, as a simple manifestation of social justice, they suffer for it. Or, at somewhat higher level of social perception and compassion, it means that the problem of poverty is sufficiently solved by private and public charity. This rescues those afflicted from the worst consequences of their inadequacy or misfortune; no larger social change or reorganization is suggested. Except as it may be insufficient in its generosity, the society is not at fault. (Galbraith, 1958a: 261)

Nevertheless, according to Galbraith the majority of poverty, is explained by his concepts of "mass" or "insular" poverty. And as the causes of "mass" or "insular" poverty are complex and linked to wider, cumulative processes of economic development, there must be determined action by the state to intervene decisively to break the vicious self-reinforcing cycles of poverty. In developed countries action must be funded through taxation, which also serves to make societies more equal and cohesive, as well as supporting macroeconomic stabilization:

> The taxes that serve the goal of greater equality are those that are most efficient for stabilization. The corporation and personal income taxes do most to equalize income. They are also the taxes that increase more than proportionately with increased income and purchasing power and decrease more than proportionately with decreased income and purchasing power. Thus they are the taxes that serve best the goals of stabilization. And the more substantial (within all reasonable limits) the reliance on the corporation income tax and the more progressive the personal income tax, the greater both the stabilization and the equalization effect. (Galbraith, 1973a: 324)

Radical economists similarly identify the socioeconomic processes and institutions that contribute to the vicious circles of cumulative causation that underpin and reinforce poverty. Radical economists point to the functional role played by poverty and an inequitable distribution of income, in that it provides for a cheap, acquiescent, and eager workforce. Radical economists also argue that capitalists in developed countries need a large number of compliant workers who are willing to work hard for low wages (Sweezy, 1942). According to radical economists this "reserve army of the unemployed" is a core and necessary feature of capitalism, making "the sack" an effective sanction (cf. Kalecki, 1943; Bowles, 1985; Bowles and Gintis, 1993; Spencer, 2000a, 2000b, 2008). It functions to discipline workers by holding their economic power in check; but in doing so it also consigns a sizable minority to poverty. In this analysis unemployment is an inevitable feature of contemporary economies: "Helplessness is assured by the industrial reserve army – by the rising and falling but enduring margin of unemployment which is part of the system. Any worker at any time can be flushed into this reserve which ensures that he will be cooperative and will accept the wage that is offered him" (Galbraith, 1958a: 81).

Galbraith, it should be acknowledged, accepted parts of the neoclassical and the radical analyses of poverty. He agreed with the conventional view as to the need to improve access to education and to develop human capital as a means of increasing individual capabilities and individual incomes, as a means of entering "the New Class" (Galbraith, 1958a: 268–78). But like many radicals he recognized the problems created by institutional structures and self-perpetuating processes, which the mainstream characteristically ignores. As Galbraith (1973b: 149) pointed out:

> Neo-classical doctrine ... holds that resources move from lower to better paid employments in an economy homogeneously composed of broadly similar firms. This reduces inequality. This minimizes or eliminates the need for corrective action; one is not moved to remedy what time and the nature of the system itself will cure.

Similarly and again like many radicals, Galbraith also noted the vested interests and unequal contest between the rich and poor:

> Here in briefest form is the modern political dialectic. It is an unequal contest: the rich and comfortable have influence and money. And they vote. The concerned and the poor have numbers, but many of the poor, alas, do not vote. There is democracy, but in no slight measure it is a democracy of the fortunate. A defining issue between these two groupings, as is well recognized, is the role of government. For the poor, the government can be central to their well-being, and for some even to survival. For the rich and the comfortable, it is a burden save when, as in the case of military expenditure, Social Security and the rescue of failed financial institutions, its serves their particular interest. Then it ceases to be burdensome and becomes a social necessity, a social good, as certainly it is not when the government serves the poor. (Galbraith, 1996b: 8)

To reiterate Galbraith stressed the need to intervene and break up vicious circles of cumulative causation through a more progressive taxation policy and a more active welfare state. He argued for the development of new policies, such as basic income guarantees, and new institutions to mitigate both the causes as well as the consequences of poverty. But Galbraith also rejected large parts of both the neo-classical and radical analyses.

Although he accepted that the radical perspective was right to focus on the institutional problems that contribute to poverty, in *The Affluent Society* Galbraith (1958a: 80–90) argued that it failed to correctly identify the institutions that contribute to poverty. And in *The New Industrial State*, Galbraith (1967a: 111–20) argued that the traditional Marxist class analysis of capitalism failed to account for the rise of the technostructure and the associated, albeit uneven, affluence ushered in by the modern corporation. While Galbraith stressed the importance of investing in human capital in addressing poverty, however, his analysis of the modern corporation led him to reject the marginal productivity theory of distribution on which the traditional analysis of poverty rests (cf. Veblen, 1909). In a world of technological advance, where general affluence has been possible, the tradition of despair and scarcity in radical and mainstream economics is made obsolete (see Galbraith, 1958a: chapters 3–6). And the Keynesian revolution challenges the inevitability and cathartic role typically accorded to mass unemployment by the conventional wisdom.

Galbraith challenged the marginal productivity theory of value which is typically marshaled to analyze and explain the distribution of wealth. Galbraith argued that the wealth of the technostructure and the affluent was derived not from their hard work or their direct contributions to economic output, but from their possession of social and economic power (cf. Veblen, 1909; Krugman, 2002, 2007). This analysis underpinned Galbraith's advocacy for a progressive and redistributive income tax policy: "Accordingly, the present analysis supports the most vigorous use of the progressive income tax as an instrument for promoting equality. And it refutes the case for special treatment of what, with much license as applied to higher salary levels, is called earned income. And it similarly denies the need for special pecuniary incentives to executive performance" (Galbraith, 1973a: 288).

Such analysis reflects Galbraith's institutionalist perspective, which recognized the importance and interdependence of political, social and economic factors underpinning economic development. As Galbraith acknowledged in *The Voice of the Poor*:

> To put the matter bluntly, there is in all national development as a sequence in which, with much overlapping, political, cultural, and economic factors are successively important. The economic design appropriate to the later stages of development *cannot*, without waste and damage, be transferred to the early stages. Nor as regards the new countries can the design and emphasis appropriate to a country in one stage of the political, cultural, and economic sequence be applied in a later or earlier stage. (Galbraith, 1983c: 8)

This underscores the importance that Galbraith attached to the study of history in examining problems of economic and social development and clearly links to the methodological approach outlined in chapter 4. Galbraith's analysis also moves beyond with simplistic "markets are good, governments are bad" or "markets are bad, governments are good" analyses, seeking to understand the institutional prerequisites for wider economic development. As Galbraith (1979b: 5–6) noted in *The Nature of Mass Poverty*:

> The economic system as a cause of poverty is invariably cited with passion. The people are poor because they have not perceived the advantages of free enterprise, free competition and the market. Their energies, accordingly, are frustrated by a stupid and costly bureaucracy. Alternatively, they are poor because they are exploited; the surplus that they produce is appropriated by predatory landlords or capitalists. And this poverty persists because since all goes to the owners of property anyway, there is no incentive to improve.

Galbraith argued therefore that it was unwarranted to conclude *a priori* that government intervention will necessarily hinder the workings of the free market and result in lower economic growth, unemployment and poverty. Rather he argued that economic development is a product of overlapping political, cultural, and economic factors which must be examined with reference to history – an approach that reflected his methodological approach (see chapter 4 above).

The humane agenda

For Galbraith it was the presence or absence of the large corporation, which impacts upon and influences the nature of economic development and the extent of poverty.[24] And for Galbraith, poverty is a problem that stems from the lack of economic and social power. In developed countries "case poverty" had largely given way to "insular poverty" – the pockets of poverty. This is the sizeable minority who have been variously excluded from the process of development and the democratic process. This is a poverty that is perpetuated by the social imbalance generated by the affluent society. And it is a poverty that requires determined action:

> Poverty is self-perpetuating because the poorest communities are poorest in the services which would eliminate it. To eliminate poverty efficiently,

we must, indeed, invest more than proportionately in the children of the poor community. It is there that high quality schools, strong health services, special provision for nutrition and recreation are most needed to compensate for the very low investment which families are able to make in their own offspring. (Galbraith, 1958a: 265)

In affluent societies the problems of poverty can and should be addressed. The modern affluence generated by the modern corporation means that there is a large, potentially redistributable, social surplus available for antipoverty efforts. Such redistribution is, nevertheless, obscured by the conventional wisdom and resisted by vested interests, as exemplified by "movement conservatism," which has "played a crucial role in surging inequality" (Krugman, 2007: 9).

Likewise the "mass poverty" of less developed nations also reflects a degree of social imbalance. Many less developed countries spend a disproportionate amount on arms and the military, failing to provide necessary public services like decent healthcare, adequate sanitation, and quality education (Galbraith, 1983c: chapter 4). The consequence is that the poor are trapped in a vicious cycle of cumulative causation that they cannot overcome on their own. The poor lack economic power relative to the technostructures of advanced economies because social processes and insufficient and inadequate social infrastructure undermine their life chances and social mobility. Action is needed. Action can be taken. And Galbraith's analysis continues to be relevant to the pockets of the poor in developed countries, as well as the large number of poor households in less developed countries.

Notes

1 All of which have variously come to pass over the last fifty years. Most recently in the UK, the Labour government has also introduced the essence of a minimum basic income guarantee program in the form of a system of tax credits.

2 It is salient to note that Paul Krugman's (2007: 249) analysis in *The Conscience of a Liberal* is remarkably similar to Galbraith's: "Because American children from low-income families are often uninsured, they're more likely to have health problems that derail their life chances. Poor nutrition, thanks to low income and a lack of social support, can have the same effect. Life disruptions that affect a child's parents can also make upward mobility hard – and the weakness of the US social

safety net makes such disruptions more likely and worse if they happen. Then there's the highly uneven quality of US basic education, and so on. What it all comes down to is that although the principle of 'equality of opportunity, not equality of results' sounds fine, it's a largely fictitious distinction."

3 As Galbraith (1973a: 173) argued: "The public influence of the planning system requires, first of all, a secure public belief in the importance of the things it does. Since it produces goods and services, this means that there must be profound public conviction as to the importance of such goods and services. Much of this ... is a by-product of management of the consumer. That involves a large expenditure on art and money in newspapers, magazines, on billboards and, above all, on radio and television. No other form of communication is even fractionally so ubiquitous. All forms of consumer persuasion affirm that the consumption of goods is the greatest source of pleasure, the highest measure of human achievement. They make consumption the foundation of human happiness."

4 As Galbraith (1973a: 173) highlighted: "The planning system, having prestige as a source of goods and service and thus as a source of public happiness, will have influence as a source of political suggestion."

5 This underscored Galbraith's (1973a: 276) support for a decent minimum wage: "The minimum wage must be more aggressively used than in the past. The test of the appropriate level, a most important point, is not what allows the small firm in the market system to survive. That is because the market system survives in part because of its superior ability to depress wages. Accordingly, a minimum wage that is consistent with survival in the market system is one that eliminates inequality. The ultimate purpose of the minimum wage is to eliminate the wage differential as between the market and the planning systems." For a discussion of the employment impact of minimum wages, see Card and Kruger (1994).

6 For Galbraith (1958a: 240) the importance of basic income guarantees relate to his broader analysis of inflation, want creation and societies' obsession with ever higher levels of production: "So long as we are committed by the imperatives of employment and income to operate at the capacity of plant and labor force and take no other steps, we shall have the threat of rising prices ... The solution, or at least one part of it, is to have some reasonably satisfactory substitutes for production as a source of income. This would break the present nexus between production and income and enable us to take a more relaxed and rational view of output without subjecting individual members of the society to hardship."

7 As Galbraith (1958a: 265–6) remarked: "Much can be done to treat those characteristics which cause people to reject or be rejected by the modern

industrial society. Educational deficiencies can be overcome. Mental deficiencies can be treated. Physical handicaps can be remedied. The limiting factor is not knowledge of what can be done. Overwhelmingly, it is a shortage of money."

8 It is important to note that this analysis may explain the increased use of sales taxes or value-added taxes in the postwar period. The majority of countries in the world now have sales taxes or value-added taxes at various levels. The trend has been for conventional sales taxes to be replaced by more broadly based value-added taxes, and the USA is now one of the few countries to retain conventional sales taxes. At the present time the sales taxes in the USA are administered at the state level, and there is no national sales tax.

9 As Galbraith (1992: 179) argued in *The Culture of Contentment*: "The controlling role of taxation continues. The only effective design for diminishing the income inequality inherent in capitalism is the progressive income tax. Nothing in the age of contentment has contributed so strongly to income inequality as the reduction of taxes on the rich; nothing, as has been said, so contributes to social tranquility as some screams of anguish from the very affluent. That taxes should now be used to reduce the inequality is, however, clearly outside the realm of comfortable thought. Here the collision between wise social action and the culture of contentment is most apparent."

10 See Peach (2008), who argues that Galbraith's numerous works on economic development remain, like so many other aspects of his thought, largely ignored by critics and fans alike. Peach argues that Galbraith approached the economic development problem with a keen understanding of both the economic and political forces shaping the development debate and that his work remains relevant. The developmental literature is only now beginning to recognize that a holistic approach to development is a necessary alternative to single-causation theories of world poverty.

11 As an adjunct to this, it is important to note that Galbraith (1979b: 89) argued that improving the terms of trade between the rich and poor nations would therefore do little in itself to alleviate mass poverty: "what is rhetorically and politically compelling is sometimes a poor guide to practical action. The most drastic imaginable improvement in the terms of trade of primary products – a doubling in the price of agricultural products, metals, other materials – in relation to the products and services of the rich countries would not alleviate the poverty of the masses of India, Pakistan, Indonesia, Egypt, Mexico, or others similarly situated. Price is not decisive if you have little or nothing to sell."

12 As Krugman (1994: 234) observes: "a country's resources do not fully determine what it produces, because the detailed pattern of advantage reflects the self-reinforcing virtuous circles, set in motion by the vagaries of history."

13 As Galbraith (1971: 189–90) noted: "All discussion of economic development involves difficult problems of sequence and circularity. This is an example: how does a country get an education system without an adequate government? How does it get a government with the qualified people that an educational system provides? There is no obvious answer. But it helps to have narrowed the problem to this point. For we then recognize that little is accomplished by action that does not break into this particular circle."

14 As Galbraith (1971: 179) acknowledged: "Some of the poor countries lack the social institutions and manpower which enable them to make effective use of capital and hold out a reasonable promise of repayment. In others the social system is unfavorable to effective capital use; power lies with those for whom government is not an instrument of economic progress but a means to personal enrichment or political aggrandizement."

15 As Galbraith (1971: 182) highlighted in his 1965 Massey Lectures: "Obviously poverty has a penetrating effect on behavior. It affects attitudes towards technical change. It has a controlling effect on the ease or difficulty of economic progress and affects the nature of the country's economic organization. It determines political behavior and international attitudes. It has a profound effect on human reproduction and demography."

16 Galbraith (1971: 189) also recognized how poor educational systems, reinforce an underdeveloped cultural base, resulting in poor and corrupt government: "The inadequacy of government reflects the absence of schools, colleges and cultural environment for producing or preparing people for public tasks."

17 As Galbraith (1983c: 13) argued in *The Voice of the Poor*: "The importance of political stability in the sequence of development cannot be too strongly emphasized. There is today no country with a stable, participatory, and honest government that does not have – or has not had – a reasonably satisfactory state of economic progress."

18 Galbraith (1979b: 116) goes on to add that in this list: "No mention is made of training and specialized education. Opportunity, especially for the latter, is necessary, and it could be added to the list. But, if all else is available, it is reasonable to expect that this will be sought and obtained."

19 It is not, however, impossible. In recent times we have witnessed new multinational competitors springing up from developing countries, and these emerging-market firms are managing to compete successfully, as well as to access, absorb and upgrade technology (Ramamurti, 2004; UNCTAD, 2005, 2006).

20 An underdevelopment of the cultural and entrepreneurial base also supports the "right to press for sensible use of funds that we supply and for economic policies that ensure that they will be effective" (Galbraith, 1971: 181). But Galbraith (1971: 181) also rejected, what would now be referred to as the rigid adherence to the Washington consensus: "we cannot press for a carbon copy of Western capitalism and we cannot hold others even to our sometimes imperfect standards of performance."

21 Galbraith (1971: 200) also recognized that in some despotic Model 1 countries, development may be limited: "All discussion of Model 1 countries must reckon with the possibility that in limiting cases development will be impossible. Predatory and anarchic influence will overwhelm and submerge the small cultural legacy of the colonial period." What is more it is clear from this analysis that Galbraith anticipated the possibility, now widely remarked, that large parts of Africa are being left behind in the accelerating progress of the economic development.

22 In *The Affluent Society* Galbraith (1958a: 67–80, 258–68) explicitly rejected social Darwinianism and its economic variants. One assumes that Galbraith was influenced by Keynes's (1926: 282–3) ridiculing of social Darwinianism in his essay "The End of Laissez-Faire" where he argued that: "Economists, like other scientists, have chosen the hypothesis from which they set out, and which they offer to beginners, because it is the simplest, and not because it is the nearest to the facts. Partly for this reason, but partly, I admit, because they have been biased by the traditions of the subject, they have begun by assuming a state of affairs where the ideal distribution of productive resources can be brought about through individuals acting independently by the method of trial and error in such a way that those individuals who move in the right direction will destroy by competition those who move in the wrong direction. This implies that there must be no mercy or protection for those who embark their capital or their labor in the wrong direction. It is a method of bringing the most successful profit-makers to the top by a ruthless struggle for survival, which selects the most efficient by the bankruptcy of the less efficient. It does not count the cost of the struggle, but looks only to the benefits of the final result which are assumed to be permanent. The object of life being to crop the leaves off the branches up to the greatest possible height, the likeliest way

of achieving this end is to leave the giraffes with the longest necks to starve out those whose necks are shorter."

23 In chapter 23 of *The Affluent Society*, Galbraith identified the burgeoning middle class, what he there referred to as "The New Class" (the incipient technostructure of *The New Industrial State*). Access to "The New Class" is through education: "While virtually no one leaves it thousands join it every year. Overwhelmingly the qualification is education" (Galbraith, 1958a: 275). This underscores Galbraith's commitment to education, both as a means of escaping poverty, by accessing the well paid jobs of the technostructure, as well as developing more critical and aesthetic faculties that facilitate challenge to the social imbalance generated by modern societies.

24 As Galbraith (1979b: 89–90) remarked in *The Nature of Mass Poverty*: "the large multinational corporations, when they operate in poor lands, may well be powerful in their purchase of labor and materials, as also in the sale of their products. But the rural masses do not work for multinational corporations. They would invariably improve their incomes if they did. Nor do they sell to them or in appreciable measure buy from them. Their poverty comes less from their adverse terms of trade than from having so little to trade."

7 Uncertainty and the modern corporation

But more interesting … is the trend of joint stock institutions, when they have reached a certain age and size, to approximate to the status of public corporations rather than that of individualistic private enterprise. One of the most interesting and unnoticed developments of recent decades has been the tendency of big enterprise to socialize itself. A point arrives in the growth of a big institution … at which the owners of the capital, i.e., the shareholders, are almost entirely dissociated from the management, with the result that the direct personal interest of the latter in the making of great profit becomes quite secondary. When this stage is reached, the general stability and reputation of the institution are the more considered by the management than the maximum of profit by the shareholders. The shareholders must be satisfied by conventionally adequate dividends; but once this is secured, the direct interest of the management often consists in avoiding criticism from the public and from the customers of the concern.

J. M. Keynes (1972a: 289)

The role of planning in the modern industrial society remains only slightly appreciated.

J. K. Galbraith (1967a: 41)

A large part of Galbraith's professional career was devoted to examining modern industrial society and the large firms that dominate it. The modern corporation occupies a pivotal role in Galbraith's theorizing in general, and *The New Industrial State* in particular. It is thus perhaps surprising that Galbraith's contribution to the theory of the firm has almost disappeared from view. While theorists like Coase (1937), Penrose (1955, 1959), Marris (1964), and Richardson (1959, 1960, 1964, 1972) have seen a resurgence of interest in their respective theories of the firm, Galbraith's contribution is hardly mentioned.[1] Galbraith is without a doubt a neglected theorist of the firm, ignored by economists of all schools.[2]

There are several possible interrelated reasons for this oversight. Perhaps the main reason for this neglect of Galbraith lies in the fact that he has generally been associated with the managerialist theories of the firm that grew out of the recognition by Berle and Means (1932) that large firms were no longer controlled and dominated by their owners, but instead run by their managers (see also Chandler, 1962).[3] Managerial theories of the firm were rigorously developed by Baumol (1959), Williamson (1964, 1970), Marris (1964), and Cyert and March (1963) and were firmly established by the time that Galbraith published *The New Industrial State* in 1967 (see Gordon, 1968, 1969; Galbraith, 1969c). Moreover the fact that Galbraith was clearly influenced by these theories, and keen to utilize their insights, appears to underscore this fact.[4]

Galbraith, while emphasizing the separation of ownership from control, outlined a view of the modern corporation more complex and subtle than he has generally been given credit for. Indeed Galbraith (1967a: 136) himself observed that while managerial theorists of the firm had gone on to provide explanations of managerial behavior that appear consistent with the separation of ownership and control, these contributions "are still subject to the mystique of the market; were they to accept the full significance of the abandonment of profit maximization they would go on, as here, to examine the modern corporation as an instrument of planning that transcends the market." In any case Galbraith was no newcomer to the study of the large firm. He had long mused on the role and salience of the large corporation in advanced industrialized economies (Galbraith 1936, 1938, 1947, 1952a, 1952b, 1954, 1957, 1958a, 1958b, 1958c, 1959).[5] An initial draft of *The New Industrial State* had been produced by 1961. Only an ambassadorial appointment postponed its revision (Galbraith, 1967a).[6]

A second reason for this neglect of Galbraith is his caustic wit and irreverent, populist, rhetorical style (Solow, 1967; Gordon, 1968, 1969). Since he eschewed the mathematical presentation of more orthodox treatments by Baumol, Williamson, and Marris, theorists of the firm generally view Galbraith's contribution as a less rigorous, literary expression of the managerialist approach and thus tended to ignore it (cf. Marris, 1968; Demsetz, 1974; Galbraith, 1971: chapter 2). Marris's (1968: 240) comments are typical of the general attitude to Galbraith: "for the professional economist it is important to recognize at the outset that Galbraith is dealing in loose but not necessarily unreal concepts, of whose descriptive value he seeks to convince by a mixture of literature and some logic based on casual observation, induction, and selected evidence." This, however, points to the different methodological approach which is employed by Galbraith, an approach which I have argued in chapter 4 above, is realist and broadly falls within the Post Keynesian and Insitutionalist traditions.

The third reason for Galbraith's neglect relates to the widely held perception that, while he was a great synthesizer and an ambitious system builder, he was not wholly original (Solow, 1967; Allen, 1967; Gordon, 1968, 1969; Leathers and Evans, 1973). Gordon (1968: 637) concluded that the "Galbraithian view of the modern economy has innumerable antecedents." Marris, in a review of *The New Industrial State*, similarly remarked that "these conclusions are not exactly new, but they have not previously been drawn in the same way or from so broad a general picture: Galbraith does deserve to be judged on his total effect, and to be given credit for the sweep of his analysis" (Marris, 1968: 245). Economists generally view *The New Industrial State* as an exercise in social philosophy, rather than as an original contribution to economics in general, or the theory of the firm specifically (Gordon, 1968, 1969; Friedman, 1977). Marris (1968: 240), for example, suggested that Galbraith's objectives are "wider than those of traditional 'political economy' ... he aspires to contribute as much in the field of political science as in what is now regarded as the proper field of economic science." For Galbraith the old adage about Marx is more than apt: that philosophers think Marx a bad philosopher but a good political scientist and economist; that political scientists think Marx a bad political scientist but a good philosopher and economist; that economists think Marx a bad economist but a good philosopher and political scientist. The cumulative effect of all these factors has been that Galbraith's vision of the modern corporation has not attracted the attention of contemporary theorists of the firm.

This needs to be redressed. This chapter therefore reconsiders Galbraith's much neglected contribution to the theory of the firm, which occupies a pivotal role within *The New Industrial State*. Galbraith has typically been viewed as a great synthesizer, and system builder, and not as a theorist of the firm. Here I set out in detail his particular view of the firm advanced in *The New Industrial State*, paying particular attention to Galbraith's discussion of how the firm deals with uncertainty, especially with regard to a firm's activities and boundaries. In doing so it will be clear that Galbraith is an original theorist of the firm, who considered many of the key issues raised by Coase, Knight, Schumpeter, and Penrose, among others. Indeed Galbraith anticipates much recent research into the theoretical origins of the firm. Galbraith focuses on the significant uncertainties that surround major investments of time and money, and his work serves as a useful starting-point for future research into how the relationship between uncertainty and the firm should be viewed.

The New Industrial State

Galbraith's central thesis, as noted above, is that the imperatives and nature of advanced technology necessitate the organization of modern industry (see also Galbraith, 1952a). A concentrated market structure is the inevitable counterpart to advanced technology. And modern technology inevitably involves detailed specialized knowledge, effective group decision-making, and the need for large capital commitments to be conducted and coordinated in terms of money denominated contracts over long periods of time. Planning is an inescapable consequence of advanced technology and the extended, highly specialized, division of labor that is called forth to manage it. It is "the increased use of technology and the accompanying commitment of time and capital ... [which force] extensive planning on all industrial communities" (Galbraith, 1967a: 41). Planning enables the mitigation of the impact of unforeseen events and the successful organization of production.[7] Galbraith identified six key consequences of this technology:

> First. An increasing span of time separates the beginning from the completion of any task ... Second. There is an increase in the capital that is committed to production aside from that occasioned by increased output. The increased time, and therewith the increased investment in goods in process, costs money. So does the knowledge which is applied to the various elements of the task ... Third. With increasing technology the commitment of time and money tends to be made ever more inflexibly to the performance of a particular task ... Fourth. Technology requires specialized manpower. To foresee the future in all its dimensions and to

design the appropriate action does not necessarily require high scientific qualification. It does require ability to organize and employ information, or capacity to react intuitively to relevant experience ... Fifth. The inevitable counterpart of specialization is organization. This is what brings the work of specialists to a coherent result. If there are many specialists, this co-ordination will be a major task ... Sixth. From the time and capital that must be committed, the inflexibility of this commitment, the needs of large organization and the problems of market performance under conditions of advanced technology, comes the necessity for planning. (Galbraith, 1967a: 32–5)

Modern technology requires extensive planning because such large investments of time, money, specialized knowledge, and organization cannot be left to whim, chance, and the vagaries of the market. Galbraith (1952a: 91) develops an analysis that is similar to Schumpeter's (1943), arguing that: "modern industry of a few large firms [is] an almost perfect instrument for inducing technical change." This is owing to the fact that large firms are "admirably equipped for financing technical development" and that such "development is costly" (Galbraith, 1952a: 91). Galbraith's thesis helps explain why the majority of Research and Development is carried out in the large firms and buttressed by Government support; why nearly half of all research and development is carried out in firms with more than 10,000 employees – see table 4.

Nevertheless this spending on research and development implies a huge up-front investment. And as the price of failure is great, it should be avoided at all costs. Avoiding failure means avoiding and mitigating the uncertainties and instabilities associated with the competitive process and an autonomous customer response. Modern technology requires highly specialized investment in capital and labor over a long period of time (cf. Dasgupta and Stiglitz, 1980; Rosenberg, 1982, 1994). Thus those involved and responsible for such investments are of necessity highly committed to ensuring its success.

Planning and the technostructure

In *The New Industrial State* Galbraith argued that a key effect of modern technology and the specialized knowledge that is called forth to bear upon it, is that the locus of power has passed from land and capital to organized intelligence (Galbraith, 1967a: 72–3;

Table 4. *Funds expended on industrial R&D in the USA, 2005*

Selected characteristic	$ millions
Total industrial R&D performance	200,602
Source of funds	
Company and other nonfederal	181,169
Federal	19,433
Size of company (number of employees)	
5–24	6,540
25–49	6,642
50–99	6,337
100–249	9,160
250–499	7,228
500–999	12,411
1,000–4,999	31,017
5,000–9,999	16,117
10,000–24,999	29,770
25,000 or more	75,380

Note: Excludes data for federally funded research and development centers.

Source: National Science Foundation, Division of Science Resources Statistics, Survey of Industrial Research and Development, 2005.

see also 1952a: 90–5). It is the nature of modern technology that it requires detailed technical knowledge, a range of problem-solving talents, extensive planning, and, ultimately, its effective coordination (Galbraith, 1967a: 77–8).[8] As noted above, Galbraith referred to such groups, who possess the requisite knowledge of the production process, as the technostructure:

> Eventually not an individual but a complex of scientists, engineers and technicians; of sales, advertising and marketing men; of public relations experts, lobbyists, lawyers and men with a specialized knowledge of the Washington bureaucracy and its manipulation; and of co-ordinators, managers and executives becomes the guiding intelligence of the business firm. This is the technostructure. (Galbraith, 1973b: 98)

It is the knowledge embedded in the planning routines of the organization, and not given atomized entrepreneurial individuals, to which power has passed (Galbraith, 1967a: 75; see also 1973a, 1973b). This echoes Schumpeter (1943: 133), who likewise noted that: "economic progress tends to become depersonalized and automatized. Bureau and committee work tends to replace individual action." Galbraith's conception, however, was broader than a narrow examination of the rise of the corporate bureaucracy, anticipating much of the recent focus on the importance of tacit knowledge and capabilities (see Williamson, 1999; Foss, 1997b). Indeed as early as 1952 Galbraith recognized that:

> firms also acquire – a point somewhat neglected by economists – the economies of experience. The development of an industrial enterprise is a fairly intricate task in organization and administration. It can only be accomplished easily when it is accomplished slowly – when there is the opportunity to search for talent, to try new men out a few at a time, and when there is leisure to reassign, promote to innocuousness, or detach with regrets the inevitable mistakes ... As a result, in an established industry, where the scale of production is considerable, there is no such thing as freedom of entry. On the contrary, time and circumstances combine to bar the effective entry of new firms. (Galbraith, 1952a: 37–8)

Such talent that is to be brought to bear on the processes of production must be assembled into groups. It embodies technical expertise, seasoned experience, tacit knowledge, and intuition, and finds expression within a highly interdependent and organic, social process (Galbraith, 1967a: 76).[9] Such group decision-making represents a sensible response to complex uncertain processes; it "enables members to pool information under circumstances which allow, also, of immediate probing to assess the relevance and reliability of the information offered. Uncertainty about one's information or error is revealed as in no other way" (Galbraith, 1967a: 79). Galbraith outlines an organic, socialized view of the knowledge process upon which corporate success is founded (cf. Freeman and Soete, 1997; Rosenberg, 1982, 1994; Foss, 1996a, 1996b). As Schmookler (1966: 1) noted, technology is the "social pool of knowledge of the industrial arts." It is not individuals who know how to build cars, computers, or airplanes, it is corporations and the groups that comprise it: "No one person has more than a fraction of the knowledge necessary for the design, production or marketing of a new automobile model, missile or detergent. It follows that no one can decide whether one of these should be designed, developed, produced or can be sold ... These matters must be resolved by groups" (Galbraith, 1973a: 100; see also 1967a: 75–6). The comparative advantage of the modern corporation depends upon the differing capabilities of the incumbent technostructures and the successful application of its embedded routines and planning procedures (cf. Foss, 1993, 1996a, 1996b, 1997b; Langlois and Foss, 1999; Langlois and Robertson, 1995).

It is important to note, however, that although Galbraith highlights the role of teams of dedicated specialists in underpinning the success of the modern firm, he also acknowledged three ways in which individuals can shape and influence firm strategy and performance:

> First he can change the participants in the decision-making – he can dismiss, move or replace those who are involved ... Second, he can propose a change in the conceptual framework in which decisions are made. He cannot safely decide to produce a new product or employ a new process or acquire a new subsidiary. This requires the informed participation of specialists who have or can obtain the requisite knowledge. But he can ask consideration of such a new product, process or venture ... Finally, an individual can, by appeal to professional help, appraise the competence of the organization that makes the decisions and the quality of the decisions that are being made. He does not as an individual, command the knowledge to do this. But he can get another organization to do so. This accounts, in modern times, for the great expansion of the management consulting industry. (Galbraith, 1973a: 104–5)

That Galbraith acknowledged the ability of individuals to shape the destiny of firms is frequently ignored by his critics, who mistakenly chastise him for ignoring the role of leadership. Galbraith was not blind, however, to the role of leadership. To suggest so would be a travesty: "These powers – casting of personnel, directing the decision-making process into new areas and placing it under scrutiny – are the principal prerogatives of individuals in the modern corporation, of what is called leadership" (Galbraith, 1973a: 105). For Galbraith, leadership focuses on providing strategic direction, as well as monitoring and metering the principal agent problem. But it does not solve these problems. Internal complexity and external uncertainty are too great.

Galbraith's analysis was drawing attention to the obsolescence of the Victorian entrepreneur and the rise of professional management and leadership. Indeed the routinization of leadership, as exemplified by the huge investment and expansion in the management MBA, highlights how leadership increasingly assumes a technocratic aura. This is something that leaders frequently seek to challenge or refute. This should be anticipated. To suggest that such leadership talent is a function of education and learning, as opposed to heroic entrepreneurial powers, calls into the question the premium that such leaders are typically awarded and rewarded through the rites of boardroom passage. Accordingly the modern-day technocratic leader has a vested interest in perpetuating the conventional wisdoms associated with Darwinian competition, as well as promoting the myth of the heroic entrepreneur who is handsomely and impersonally rewarded for their contribution to society by the market. But, in the new industrial state, as Galbraith (1973a: 282) noted, executive compensation is a function of tradition, hierarchy, power, prestige and peer comparison as opposed to some impersonally determined market rate: "Reward depends not on the market but on determination by human agency."

Planning and the market

Galbraith viewed the firm as an institution that coordinates production and shelters it from the uncertainties that are generated by the market process. Planning, in the Galbraithian system, which embodies both conscious decision and human agency, represents an important means of allocating resources that replaces the market: "The most celebrated feature of the market is that it equates supply with demand at a price ... Planning has within itself, as noted, no similar equilibrating mechanism. The planner must deliberately ensure that planned supply equals planned use. If he fails there will be surpluses or deficits" (Galbraith, 1967a: 58). Planning, however, is not just about coordination; it is also about preparing for unforeseen events (cf. Langlois, 1995b). It is a portmanteau concept:

> Planning consists in foreseeing the actions required between the initiation of production and its completion and preparing for the accomplishment of

these actions. And it consists also of foreseeing, and having a design for meeting, any unscheduled developments, favorable or otherwise, that may occur along the way ... it [also] consists of replacing prices and the market as the mechanism for determining what will be produced, with an authoritative determination of what will be produced and consumed and at what price. (Galbraith, 1967a: 43)

As noted above, planning and the organization of production are linked in essence due to the market uncertainties and the complex, unpredictable nature of modern technology (cf. Gruchy, 1984; Langlois, 1984, 1988, 1995a). "If, with advancing technology and associated specialization, the market becomes increasingly unreliable, industrial planning will become increasingly impossible unless the market also gives way to planning ... Much of what the firm regards as planning consists in minimizing or getting rid of market influences" (Galbraith, 1967a: 43–5). If the uncertainties that surround large commitments of time and money are to be mitigated then the firm must either supersede the market or subordinate it to the requirements of planning:

Technology and the companion commitments of capital and time have forced the firm to emancipate itself from the uncertainties of the market. And specialized technology has rendered the market increasingly unreliable. So the firm controls the prices at which it buys materials, components and talent and takes steps to ensure that the public, other producers or the state take the planned quantities at these prices. So far from being controlled by the market, the firm, to the best of its ability has made the market subordinate to the goals of its planning. (Galbraith, 1967a: 122)

The Galbraithian view of the firm is that it emerges in response to the uncertainties that surround major and complex, long-term investments. Rather than viewing the firm as resulting from a purely instrumental choice of economizing on transaction costs between alternative modes of contracting, Galbraith (1967a), like both Knight (1921) and Schumpeter (1943), saw the firm as an institution for coping with, or getting rid of, market uncertainties (cf. Langlois and Robertson, 1995). It is the large size of the modern corporation – in both relative and absolute terms – that enables the technostructure to engage in more effective planning and to cope with, and absorb, uncertainty (cf. Rosenberg, 1982, 1994). This, according to Galbraith, is a primary reason that helps explain the observed growth of the large firm:

> The most obvious requirement of effective planning is large size. This ... allows the firm to accept market uncertainty where it cannot be eliminated; to eliminate markets on which otherwise it would be dependant; to control other markets in which it buys and sell; and it is very nearly indispensable for participation in that part of the economy, characterized by exacting technology and comprehensive planning, where the only buyer is the federal government. (Galbraith, 1967a: 89)

According to Galbraith the exploitation of economies of scale or the exercise of monopoly power only partly explain the growth of the large firm:

> Economists have anciently quarreled over the reasons for the great size of the modern corporation. Is it because size is essential to reap the economies of large-scale production? Is it, more insidiously, because the big firm wishes to exercise monopoly power in its markets? The present analysis allows both parties to the dispute to be partly right. The firm must be large enough to carry the large capital commitments of modern technology. It must also be large enough to control its markets. But the present view also explains what the older explanations don't explain ... [why does General Motors] produce things as diverse as aircraft engines and refrigerators, which cannot be explained by economies of scale; and why, though it is large enough to have the market power associated with monopoly, consumers do not seriously complain of exploitation. The size of General Motors is in the service not of monopoly or the economies of scale but of planning. And for this planning – control of demand, provision of capital, minimization of risk – there is no clear upper limit to the desirable size. (Galbraith, 1967a: 90–1)

The character of technology, planning, and the associated size and growth of the firm enables the modern corporation to pursue a range of objectives other than profit maximization.[10] A key facet of the size of the large corporation is that as long as the leadership and technostructure ensures that revenues are above some acceptable conventional minimum, which facilitates its continued growth and reproduction, it is unlikely to attract any unwarranted or outside attention.[11] "For any organization, as for any organism, the goal or objective that has a natural assumption of pre-eminence is the organization's own survival. This, plausibly, is true of the technostructure" (Galbraith, 1967a: 175). Attempting to mitigate the uncertainties that threaten the income and prestige of the technostructure is thus paramount.

Galbraith outlined five main strategies used by the technostructure for dealing with the uncertainties that surround the market process. The firm can either ignore market uncertainty or absorb it via growth, diversification, and agglomeration or it can mitigate the impact of the market, by superseding it, controlling it, or suspending it via a network of contracts (Galbraith, 1967a: 44–5). These are strategies that are broader than a simplistic focus on the make or buy decision. And they also include the prospect of control beyond the formal boundaries of the firm. These strategies are analyzed in turn.[12]

First, if an item is relatively unimportant in terms of the production process, then a firm may disregard the market uncertainties that surround its price, availability, and quality. Clearly, General Motors has little need to control the supply of paper clips to its vast organization. In relation to its total activity, its expenditure upon paper clips is tiny and their importance in the production of cars is peripheral. General Motors can ignore such uncertainties that surround the supply of paper clips to its organization. Another approach to mitigating the impact of market uncertainty is to absorb that uncertainty which cannot be ignored by pursuing growth, or combining size with diversification:

> The growth of the modern corporation is a complex process involving a blend of strategies. The first strategy is the expansion of production and sales by the existing corporate entity ... The second strategy is the acquisition of smaller firms in related or unrelated areas for more or less complete consolidation with the technostructure of the acquiring firm. This allows the superior financial resources of the larger firm to be used for a far more rapid growth than would generally be possible from the expansion of sales. (Galbraith, 1973a: 119)

Likewise, producing for several different unrelated markets allows the uncertainties associated with any one particular market to be spread across several markets. As Galbraith (1967a: 45) noted: "We have here a partial explanation of the origins of one of the more notable corporate developments of recent times, the growth of the conglomerate corporation. It combines great size with highly diverse lines of manufacture. Thus it can absorb the adverse consequences of uncertainty that cannot otherwise be eliminated."[13] This is the scale analogue of the maxim "you shouldn't put all your eggs in one basket," which came to be questioned as a successful strategy in the 1980s and 1990s, but might now be coming back into vogue. Of course producing in several markets and industries, while a strategy for spreading risk, can also increase complexity and generate uncertainty (cf. Gatignon and Anderson, 1988; Balakrishnan and Wernerfelt, 1986). So ultimately the assessment will reflect the interests and capabilities of the relevant technostructure, as well as the conventional wisdoms that pervade the business community. Indeed as Galbraith (1973a: 121) pointed out:

> In the late nineteen-sixties, in the so-called conglomerate explosion, there was a large amount of this high risk growth. By no means all reflected the initiative of large firms with highly developed technostructures. A considerable part was on the initiative of individual entrepreneurs operating from a base in a firm of considerably less than the largest size ... Most of the resulting structures did badly; several were subsequently in severe financial difficulties. It is possible that this high-risk, individually sponsored agglomeration was an aberrant development associated with the then-current boom psychology.

The other related strategies for dealing with the uncertainties of the market concern its replacement, control, or suspension.[14] For example, the most common strategy for replacing the market relates to what is typically referred to as horizontal and vertical integration (Williamson, 1971). Horizontally integrating allows the firm to reduce the amount of price competition that it is subject to and facilitates detailed planning – "unless a firm has a substantial share of the market it has no strong incentive to undertake a large expenditure on development" (Galbraith, 1952a: 92). Similarly placing successive stages of production and distribution under the authoritative determination of one centre of control enables the modern corporation to appropriate the profit margin of intermediaries and to secure the sources of supply:

> The planning unit takes over the source of supply or the outlet: a transaction that is subject to bargaining over prices and amounts is thus replaced with a transfer within the planning unit ... To have control of supply – to

not rely on the market but on its own sources of supply – is an elementary safeguard. This does not eliminate market uncertainty; rather the large and unmanageable uncertainty as to the price of ore or crude is replaced by the smaller, more diffuse and more manageable uncertainties as to the cost of labor, drilling, ore transport and yet more remote raw materials. (Galbraith, 1967a: 44–5)

In short, vertical integration represents a means to mitigate uncertainty.[15] The "elimination of the market converts an external negotiation and hence a partially or wholly uncontrollable decision to a matter for purely internal decision. Nothing ... better explains modern industrial policy in regard to capital and labor than the desire to make these highly strategic cost factors subject to purely internal decision" (Galbraith, 1967a: 46). To this end one can also view the mechanization and routinization of the production process as further mitigating uncertainties that surround production:

But to see mechanization and automation purely as a problem in comparative cost is greatly to minimize their role – and to pay further for the error of confining economic goals, and economic calculation, to profit maximization. The technostructure, as noted, seeks technical progressiveness for its own sake when this is not in conflict with other goals. More importantly, it seeks certainty in the supply and price of all the prerequisites of production. And a large blue-collar labor force, especially if subject to the authority of a union, introduces a major element of uncertainty and danger. Its cost is not under the control of the technostructure. Who can assess the likelihood, the costs and consequences of a strike? In contrast, mechanization adds to certainty. Machines do not go on strike. Their prices are subject to the stability which ... is inherent in the contractual relationships between large firms. (Galbraith, 1967a: 239)

This explains the emergence of one of the more recent stylized facts that "at least in developed capitalist countries, wages are certainly no longer the prime cost of production. Services may come closer to 50 percent threshold, but in the relevant manufacturing sectors, wages may make up no more than 20 percent of overall production costs" (Rotheim, 1999: 91).

The large capital commitments necessitated by modern technology must also be insulated from the vagaries of the market and must be protected (cf. Joskow, 1985, 1987). "Control of the supply of savings is strategic for industrial planning. Capital use is large. No form of market uncertainty is so serious as that involving the terms and conditions on which capital is obtained. Apart from the normal disadvantages of an uncertain price, there is danger that under some circumstances supply will not be forthcoming at an acceptable price" (Galbraith, 1967a: 55). With the firm less dependant upon the capital markets for funds, its investment activity is likely to be relatively uninfluenced by the market rate of interest.[16] "If one of the motives for developing internal sources of savings is to free the firm from the uncertainties of the interest rate, it is evident that the decision on this saving will not be affected by the rate of interest. Having contracted out of the money market it will not be affected by the money market" (Galbraith, 1967a: 58–9; cf. Dugger, 1987).[17] Over the last twenty years, the increased availability of credit and capital has reduced this dependence on retained earnings. The consequence has been, however, that this has increased vulnerability and instability of both firms and the wider (global) financial system when the availability of such credit is restricted.

Obtaining the control of markets represents a fourth route for mitigating uncertainty: "This consists in reducing or eliminating the independence of action of those to whom the planning unit sells or from whom it buys ... At the same time the outward form of the market, including the process of buying and selling remains formally intact. This influence and control over markets is the counterpart of large size and large size in relation to the particular market" (Galbraith, 1967a: 46). This involves the large firm controlling and managing smaller firms via subcontracting relationships.[18] This suggests, moreover, that conventional measures of firm size will underestimate the power and influence of the large firm (cf. Cowling and Sugden, 1998a, 1998b; Cowling, Yusof, and Vernon, 2000; Cowling and Tomlinson, 2005).

Securing the control of markets may also include the firm attempting to manage the consumption of its products at the prices that it controls – part of what Galbraith (1967a: 216–23) referred to as "The Revised Sequence." This "need to manage consumer behavior ... arises from the circumstances of modern industrial life – sophisticated technology, large commitments of capital, long-term planning in product development and production and, in consequence, large, inflexible and vulnerable organization. These lead, in turn to the need to control as many as possible of the parameters (costs, prices, demand costs and risks of technical innovation) within which the firm operates" (Galbraith, 1971: 58).[19] The firm must ensure that what is produced is bought and to this end it must manipulate the desires and wants of the consumer (cf. Hodgson, 2001b, 2006: chapter 9). If the large capital outlays on the advanced technologies are to be recouped then the response of the consumer must be managed.[20] This explains the growth in expenditure upon advertising: "The purpose of demand management is to ensure that people buy what is produced – that plans as to the amounts to be sold at the controlled prices are fulfilled in practice" (Galbraith, 1967a: 208). I elaborate further on the implications of this view in chapter 9 below.

The fifth strategy for coping with uncertainty concerns the use of long-term, money-denominated contracts (cf. Davidson, 1972, 2007; Rotheim, 1999).[21] While vertical integration offers the prospect of controlling the price and supply of strategic factors, so too does the contract (Joskow, 1985, 1987, 1988). The firm can enter into large long-term contracts as a strategy for dealing with uncertainty (cf. Davidson, 1972, 1994). Contracts and their enforceability are a major source of stability and security for the modern corporation.[22] In "an economy where units are large, firms can eliminate market uncertainty for each other. This they do by entering into contracts specifying prices and amounts to be provided or bought for substantial periods of time ... In a world of large firms, it follows, there can be a matrix of contracts by which each firm eliminates market uncertainty for other firms and, in turn, gives to them some of its own" (Galbraith, 1967a: 48). The nexus of money-denominated contracts occupies a pivotal role in protecting the prices and costs and safeguarding the sales and supplies at these prices and costs. As production takes time and planning, money-denominated contracts represent a means by which uncertainties about the future may be mitigated (Davidson, 1972: 149). A large and extensive web of money-denominated contracts, cascaded hierarchically downward, greatly facilitates the future planning and stability necessitated by advanced technology.[23] To quote Galbraith at length:

> The contract can be thought of as extending the security which the large ... firm has in its own markets ... throughout the planning system, and to the common advantage of all concerned ... [The large firm] enters into

> contracts with suppliers and they in turn with their supplies extending down through many layers of sub-contracts. These sub-contracts assure the prime contractor on prices and supply. At the same time they give the subcontractor similar assurance on his price and sales; they allow him to make commitments and otherwise undertake the planning requisite to fulfilling his contract ... [T]he more technical the process and product, the longer the period between the original decision to produce and the emergence of the final product in remunerative quantity. And also the more technical the product, the more unlikely that the market can supply either the components, materials or labor that goes into its manufacture. With advancing technology, therefore, contracts increase in importance both for according protection over the longer period between initial decision and pay-off and for ensuring the planning that will, in turn, ensure that needed materials, components and manpower are available when needed. (Galbraith, 1973a: 141–2)

Thus, according to Galbraith, the problems of market uncertainty can either be ignored or absorbed via diversification, or the firm can replace, control or suspend it. The strategies of supersession, control and suspension all "require that the market be replaced by an authoritative determination of price and the amounts to be sold or bought at these prices" (Galbraith, 1967a: 45). It should also be clear that the different strategies available for the mitigation of uncertainty are inextricably bound up with size: "The large organization can tolerate market uncertainty as a smaller firm cannot. It can contract out of it as the smaller firm cannot. Vertical integration, the control of prices and consumer demand and reciprocal absorption of market uncertainty by contracts between firms all favor the large firm" (Galbraith, 1967a: 49).

Galbraith and the theory of the firm

Nobel prize-winner Ronald Coase (1937) provided the now famous definition of the firm that permitted its nature to be more fully understood. According to Coase, markets and firms are alternative means of coordination. Firms represent the internal supersession of the market mechanism by command. Galbraith (1967a: 140) acknowledged this, noting that the "most famous definition of an organization" is of a "system of consciously co-ordinated activities or forces of two or more persons." As markets and firms are alternative mechanisms for resource allocation, a choice is offered. The allocation of resources by planning or command, as opposed to movements in the structure of relative prices, is conditional on the fact that the use of the price mechanism is costly. In finding what are the relevant prices, undergoing a process of negotiation and in engaging in contractual behavior, resources are consumed. Command, with one party obeying the direction of another, reduces the need for costly continual renegotiation and reformulation of contracts. Economic institutions such as the firm economize on, but do not eliminate, contracting costs that arise when using the market.

Williamson (1975, 1979, 1981, 1985, 1987, 1996, 2005) labeled such contracting costs as transaction costs.[24] Williamson (1981) highlighted five core methodological elements associated with the transaction cost approach:

1. The basic unit of analysis is the transaction (that is, exchange);
2. Agents exhibit bounded rationality and act opportunistically;
3. The critical dimensions for describing transactions are (a) the frequency with which they occur, (b) the uncertainty to which they are subject, and (c) the degree to which transactions are supported by specific investments;
4. The criterion employed to explain the choice between alternative modes of contracting is a purely instrumental one of economizing on transaction costs; and
5. The assessment of differences in transaction costs is a comparative institutional undertaking.

A transaction occurs "when a good or service is transferred across a technologically separable interface" (Williamson, 1981: 1544). These transaction costs refer to three sequential aspects of the exchange process, namely search and information costs, bargaining and decision costs, and policing and enforcement costs (Dahlman, 1979).

Galbraith's discussion of the relationship between technology and organization clearly predates, and has many parallels with, Williamson's (1975, 1981, 1985, 1989, 1996) recognition of the importance of asset specificity in the study of organizations. Williamson's discussion of asset specificity refers to the extent to which an asset is specialized and dedicated to a particular task and thus (conversely) can be redeployed to alternative uses without a reduction in its productive value. According to Williamson, asset specificity is critical in that once an investment has been undertaken the buyer and seller become locked into a transaction for a considerable period thereafter, a situation which is referred to as one of *ex post* bilateral dependence. This dependence, according to Williamson, is exacerbated by problems of "information impactedness" that arise in light of the complexity and opportunism that surround transaction-specific investments.[25] While Williamson uses this notion to derive a transaction cost rationalization of the modern corporation, however, Galbraith argued that asset specificity necessitates the need for *planning*:

> From the time and capital that must be committed, the inflexibility of this commitment, the needs of large organization and the problems of market performance under conditions of advanced technology comes the need of planning. Tasks must be performed so they are right not for the present but for that time in the future when, companion and related having also been done, the whole job is completed. And the amount of capital that, meanwhile, will have been committed adds urgency to this need to be right. So conditions at the time of completion of the whole task must be foreseen, as must developments along the way. And steps must be taken to prevent, and to insure that what is ultimately foreseen eventuates in fact. (Galbraith, 1967a: 35)

To reiterate, Galbraith's argument is that the imperatives of modern technology and the associated commitments of time, capital and specialized labor in an uncertain environment entail that planning supersedes the market (cf. Langlois, 1995a). "Planning exists because this [market] process has ceased to be reliable ... [the firm] must replace the market with planning" (Galbraith, 1967a: 41).[26] Galbraith's is not a Williamsonian argument that "in the beginning there were markets," but rather one that "in the beginning there was an absence of a need for extensive planning as technology was not that sophisticated!" Low levels of technology, according to Galbraith, do not require extensive organization or large firms.[27] Similarly Galbraith's focus on the rise of the technostructure and their pursuance of a wider range of goals beyond strict profit maximization is similar to Williamson's stress on bounded rationality and opportunism. That is to say Galbraith's modern corporation is an organization which plans to mitigate and engage the uncertainties that surround advanced technological development.[28]

There are also parallels with Galbraith's approach and the radical re-evaluation of Coase by Cowling and Sugden (1998a; cf. Foss, 1994a, 1994b). As noted, according to Coase, markets and firms are alternative means of coordination.[29] Coase drew attention to the fact that a distinction can be made between coordination through a decentralized price mechanism and coordination by hierarchical centralized decision-making:

> For instance, in economic theory we find that the allocation of factors of production between different uses is determined by the price mechanism. The price of factor A becomes higher in X than in Y. As a result, A moves from Y to X until the difference between the prices in X and Y, except in so far as it compensates for other differential advantages, disappears. Yet in the real world we find that there are many areas where this does not apply. If a workman moves from department Y to department X, he does not go because of a change in relative prices, but because he is ordered to do so. (Coase, 1937: 332–3)

Coase's approach, however, can be reinterpreted as emphasizing the coordinating role of the firm (Cowling and Sugden, 1998a; see also Dunn, 2001a).[30] This is similar to Galbraith's view of the supersession of the market by conscious, coordinating planning. Galbraith's approach to the firm, however, should not be thought of as a variant of the transaction-cost type of story, such that the firm replaces the market on account of its capacity to minimize the uncertainties and thus the transaction costs that engulf markets. Rather, Galbraith's argument is that firms and markets possess different *capabilities* that cannot be broken down and decomposed into their individual elements:

> The small firm cannot be restored by breaking the power of the larger ones. It would require, rather, the rejection of the technology which since earliest consciousness we are taught to applaud. It would require that we have simple products made with simple equipment from readily available materials by unspecialized labor. Then the period of production would be short; the market would reliably provide the labor, equipment and materials required for production; there would be neither possibility nor need for managing the market for the finished product. If the market thus reigned there would be, and could be, no planning. (Galbraith, 1967a: 50)

Conventional interpretations of Coase, moreover, fail to contemplate the control of markets as a strategy for minimizing uncertainty, as suggested by Galbraith (cf. Dunn, 2001a, 2001c, 2006, 2008a). Planning for Galbraith embodies the make, buy, *or control* decision. And it is a creative, as well as a coordinating process. Galbraith's discussion of the firm emphasizes the strategic coordinating role of managers, interest groups and other specialists within the firm, that is, the technostructure and their associated need to plan in an uncertain environment.[31] These are themes which were also highlighted by Edith Penrose:

> Let me stress an obvious fact, but a fact of central importance for the growth of firms: Successful expansion must, in the usual case, be preceded by planning on the part of the firm. Firms do not grow automatically, but in response to human decisions. And if firms act on the basis of plans it follows that they have some degree of confidence in these plans. The question therefore arises how a firm obtains the required degree of confidence. Unless it is assumed that knowledge is perfect and that uncertainty is absent – assumptions that are useless and inappropriate in this context – it is clear that a body of knowledge sufficient to sustain rational plans for action must be developed within the firm. What may broadly be characterized as managerial research will be necessary for the purpose. Consequently, some part of the managerial and entrepreneurial services of the firm must be available to work on the requisite plans whenever expansion is considered. (Penrose, 1955: 532)

There are also several parallels between Galbraith's view of the modern firm and Frank Knight (1921) and Joseph Schumpeter (1943), who also recognized the impact of technology and uncertainty on the evolution of the firm. Knight (1921: 265), for example, argued that:

> Several factors affect the amount of uncertainty to be recognized, and have to be taken into account. The first to be noted is the time length of the production process, for the longer it is, the more uncertainty will naturally be involved. Of very great importance also is the general level of economic life. The lower wants of man, those having in the greatest degree the nature of necessities, are the most stable and predicable. The higher up the scale we go, the larger the proportion of the aesthetic element and of social suggestion there is involved in motivation, the greater becomes the uncertainty connected with foreseeing wants and satisfying them. On the production side, on the other hand, most manufacturing processes are most controllable and calculable as to outcome than are agricultural operations under

usual conditions. We must notice also the development of science and of the technique of social organization. Greater ability to forecast the future and greater power to control the course of events manifestly reduce uncertainty, and of still greater importance is the status of the various devices ... for reducing uncertainty by consolidation.

In his discussion of the technostructure, Galbraith also directs our attention to situations where decisions and power meet, concentrating on the particular processes and structures of decision-making (cf. Dugger, 1980, 1985a, 1988; Cowling and Sudgen, 1998a, 1998b). A much-neglected aspect of Galbraith's contribution is that the locus of power and decision-making is divorced from the formal hierarchy of the firm. And as Tirole (2001: 17) acknowledges, "the allocation of formal control ... cannot be the full story." This represents an important qualification and contribution by Galbraith and should be disentangled from the managerial thesis that it has come to be associated with. The divorce of ownership from control is clearly distinct, although related, to the divorce of hierarchy from control:

> Group decision-making extends deeply into the business enterprise. Effective participation is not closely related to rank in the formal hierarchy of the organization ... decision[s] will require information. Some power will then pass to the person or persons who have this information. If this knowledge is highly particular to themselves then their power becomes great. (Galbraith, 1967a: 80)

Group decision making, for Galbraith, is not solely related to hierarchy, as we might infer from a Williamsonian-type approach, but to specialized (tacit) knowledge and peer review.[32] This is a quite distinct reformulation of the principal agent problem that has preoccupied economists over the last forty years. And it is an aspect of the principal agent problem that is both under analyzed and under appreciated.

A major shortcoming leveled at Galbraith's discussion is that he did not present a clear story as to how the technostructure adapts and changes. For example, there is no discussion of why the U-form mode of organization was replaced by the M-form mode of organization. While all the elements of the modern New Institutional Economics appear to be there – complexity, uncertainty, and asset specificity – orthodox theorists are inclined to dismiss Galbraith's thesis citing the absence of an economizing perspective – which reflects his acknowledgements of the more diffuse objectives of the technostructure (see chapter 5 above). Nevertheless, although Galbraith does not specifically evaluate the reasons for the evolution of certain governance structures, his framework and analysis of the motivations of the technostructure does permit such an explanation – organizational changes that enhance or protect the power of the technostructure are pursued (see Galbraith, 1973a: 109–25). Galbraith's analysis of the affirmative and protective motivations of the technostructure and its resultant strategies offers an alternative theoretical perspective to the narrow economizing perspective that dominates the conventional wisdom.

Similarly Galbraith is often accused of downplaying the role of competition. Galbraith did not minimize the role of competition. But he did highlight its evolution. Complacent technostructures may be challenged by other emerging and rivalrous technostructures seeking to grow.[33] This is an important point and further highlights Galbraith's focus on the evolving nature of the competitive process, which has moved away from price competition toward other forms of competition such as advertising, mergers and acquisitions, product innovation, and development:

> The elimination of price competition as part of the protective purposes of the technostructure does not similarly eliminate other forms of rivalry between firms. Competition in product development, advertising, salesmanship and public ingratiation continues. Unlike price competition the effects of such rivalry are limited. Price-cutting can plunge all firms into disastrous loss. Other forms of rivalry, although they can be expensive, have not similar potential for damage. On the contrary ... each firm's selling efforts do something to sell the products or services of the industry as a whole and to affirm the happiness which derives from consumption in general. In price competition there is damage for all; in other forms of competition there can be benefit for all. (Galbraith, 1973b: 135)

Galbraith's analysis echoes Schumpeter's analysis in *Capitalism, Socialism and Democracy*. There Schumpeter (1943: 80) noted that: "the 'beneficial' competition of the classic type seems likely to be replaced by 'predatory' or 'cut-throat' competition or simply by struggles for control in the financial sphere. These things are so many sources of social waste, and there are many others such as the costs of advertising campaigns, the suppression of new methods of production (buying up of patents in order not to use them) and so on."

It is therefore a mistake to interpret Galbraith's analysis of the large corporation as implying a durable and permanent immortality insulated from financial markets. Galbraith's analysis of the modern firm is an analysis of the dynamics of firm growth, focusing on the increasing importance of mergers and acquisitions. What is more, Galbraith does acknowledge that stockholders *do* possess the ability to intervene. But they are prompted to act only when earnings or rates of return are less than might otherwise be expected: "Given some basic level of earnings, stockholders are quiescent. They become aroused, either individually or collectively, only when earnings are poor or there are losses, and dividends are omitted" (Galbraith, 1973a: 110). This underpins Galbraith's analysis of the dynamics of growth, which focuses on the evolving competitive process of merger and acquisition:

> Low or interrupted earnings make the firm vulnerable, other circumstances being favorable, to a take-over bid. The earnings being low or absent, the stock is cheap; the stockholder is thus open to an offer by another corporation at some price above the going market. From the stock so assembled comes the power to dispense with the senior figures in the technostructure. (Galbraith, 1973a: 110)

For Galbraith the process of corporate mergers and acquisitions, in recent times held up as exemplifying the return of the market, is in fact a fundamental feature of the competitive processes that characterizes the new industrial state. But it is a competitive process driven by the various motivations of differently sized firms, rather than the outmoded view of price competition between small, similarly sized and matched competitors which continues to dominate economic thinking.[34] It is therefore erroneous to suggest that Galbraith was arguing that competition was necessarily diminishing. Rather it was evolving. And it should be acknowledged and analyzed as such.[35]

The nature of industrial planning

In emphasizing the role of planning and the coordinating role of the technostructure in production, Galbraith's analysis of the large firm continues to be interpreted as relating to situations in which product markets are not typically competitive (Solow, 1967; Gordon, 1968; Demsetz, 1974; Krugman, 1994; McCloskey, 2007). Galbraith's concept of planning should not, however, be linked to the structure of the market and the resultant discretion permitted in the conduct of firms and its objectives. Such a view emanates from Galbraith's contribution being viewed as a literary exposition of managerial theories, which are themselves embedded in the structure-conduct-performance paradigm.

Many also continue to interpret Galbraith's (1967a) view of the firm in *The New Industrial State* as suggesting that only large firms can mitigate the impact of uncertainty.[36] But large size is only one strategy for mitigating uncertainty. Large firms, while possessing an array of capabilities that can permit a flexible response to unanticipated events, may in some respects be quite inflexible and cumbersome in dealing with other unanticipated aspects of the uncertain future. *A priori* one cannot rule this out.[37] For Galbraith, however, planning represents a flexible response to an uncertain future (cf. Langlois, 1995b). Small firms plan and, sometimes, through a process of expansion or takeover, grow into big firms (Galbraith, 1973a). What makes sense in one period need not (necessarily) make sense in another (cf. Langlois, 1984, 1988). And in an uncertain world decisions have to be made. If one is to mitigate uncertainties then sensible agents attempt to devise institutions that recognize this fact and seek to ameliorate its impact (cf. Langlois, 1984, 1988, 1995a). It is frequently ignored that Galbraith recognized this. Indeed Galbraith's analysis of uncertainty extends beyond the large corporation. Galbraith (1958a: 111) saw much historical and institutional change as responding to economic insecurity and uncertainty:

> The large corporation has been only the leader in the retreat from risk. Nearly everyone else has participated to the best of his ability and ingenuity, and in the thirties there was a widespread effort to mitigate the economic perils of the average man. The federal government intervened for the first time with relief and welfare funds to protect the individual from

economic misfortune. This was followed by social security – unemployment insurance and old age and survivor's pensions. Farmers, through public payments and support prices, were protected from some of the insecurity associated with competitive market prices. The unions developed rapidly during this decade. Along with their redress of bargaining power, they provided the worker with protection against capricious or adventitious firing or demotion and thus increased his security in his job. Even the smaller businessman, through the Robinson-Patman Act, the Fair Trade laws, legislation against below-cost selling, and through trade associations, won a measure of security from the uncertainties of market competition for which he shared the universal distaste.[38]

Nevertheless, Galbraith, unlike, say, Keynes (1921) or Knight (1921), never sets out in detail his view of uncertainty. This is a pity. Galbraith's approach to time and uncertainty would benefit from further clarification and development. Although Galbraith proposes a historically specific analysis, an understanding of the technical nature of "open" historical time, referred to in the Post Keynesian literature as transmutable (which links to the technical concept of nonergodicity), would, for example, clarify the salience of his focus on planning and uncertainty (Davidson, 1991a, 1994, 1996; see also Dunn, 1999, 2001a, 2003b, 2008a).[39] It would explain why the various "ergodic" mainstream reformulations of the principal agent problem, which theoretically solve the problems of bounded rationality and complexity, do not solve the problem in practice. And it would also more clearly differentiate his approach and contribution to the theory of the firm and link more explicitly to his methodology (see table 5).

From a transmutable perspective planning refers to the process by which firms attempt to anticipate and mould the future, that is, how they attempt to control for as many factors as possible that impact on the success of the firm.[40] The practice of planning is the practice of dealing with uncertainty, *both inside and outside* the firm.[41] What is more, acknowledging and linking Galbraith's concept of planning to a technical definition of uncertainty explicitly links the agency and power of the firm and technostructure to the nature of the environment, of time, and not to "market structure." Agents have to plan how they approach the future – whatever the nature of competition they face. And making flexible provision for an uncertain future represents a sensible response by economic agents: "If ... the concept

Table 5. *Conceptualizations of economic processes*

A. Immutable reality (an ergodic system)

Type 1. In the short run, the future is known or at least knowable. Examples of theories using this postulate are:
(a) Classical perfect certainty models
(b) Actuarial certainty equivalents, such as rational expectations models
(c) New Classical models
(d) Some New Keynesian theories

Type 2. In the short run, the future is not completely known due to some limitation in human information processing and computing power. Examples of theories using this postulate are:
(a) Bounded rationality theory
(b) Knight's theory of uncertainty
(c) Savage's expected utility theory
(d) Some Austrian theories
(e) Some New Keynesian models (e.g. coordination failure)
(f) Chaos, sunspot, and bubble theories

B. Transmutable or creative reality – (a nonergodic system)
Some aspects of the economic future will be created by human action today and/or in the future. Examples of theories using this postulate are:
(a) Keynes's General Theory and Post Keynesian monetary theory
(b) Post-1974 writings of Sir John Hicks
(c) G. L. S. Shackle's crucial experiment analysis
(d) Old Institutionalist Theory

Source: Reproduced from Davidson (1996: 485)

of uncertainty involves important non-ergodic circumstances, then there currently does not exist information (complete, incomplete, distorted or otherwise) that will aid human beings to discover the future. Instead human beings will have to invent or create the future by themselves by their actions within evolving and existing organizations" (Davidson and Davidson, 1984: 329–30). Planning and the taking of crucial decisions are inevitable consequences of a transmutable economic environment. Market structures may indeed affect the responses of strategic decision-makers to an uncertain environment, given that size, both absolute and relative, may help to mitigate the impact of uncertainty on the firm (see above). However, a world that is uncertain and transmutable means that competitive markets do not remove the need for planning. Competition, structural or behavioral, in an uncertain environment cannot force a course of action, a strategic decision to be made, that *ex post* is consistent with loss avoidance or the maximization of any from a range of objective functions we may wish to choose (cf. Dunn, 1999, 2000a, 2000b, 2008a).[42]

The legal fiction of the firm as an individual, allows clusters of economic agents to collectively create structures that allow the uncertainties of the future to be broached, and financial risks to be mitigated. This points to the importance of studying history and the specific path of human decision and institutional change. In transmutable environments the future is not a statistical reflection of the past (see table 5). If we do not know what the future will bring or is likely to bring, history will not tell us what to do. Agents create the future through their own intentional actions (Lawson, 1997, 2003). It helps explain why firms rely on a variety of methods to forecast the future and inform planning. And it also helps explain the poor record of economic forecasting and why policy makers and businessmen continue to rely on them.[43] As Galbraith (1987: 263–64) explained:

> Forecasts are, in fact, inherently unreliable. Were they otherwise, those responsible for them would never give them to the public; that would be an act of unimaginable generosity, for were they kept for the private pecuniary use of the men, women or organizations making them, the resulting accretions of wealth would be nearly infinite ... Nonetheless, a supporting reason for this great economic preoccupation remains. Every day in thousands of different contexts business executives and government officials must make decisions requiring an assumption as to the future – a future that by its nature is unknown. The modern large business enterprise, in contrast with its flexible, quickly accommodating, small entrepreneurial predecessor, must also plan. Planning always involves the future. The forecasts – what the econometric models tell an industry as to prices or costs or probable demand – help establish probable magnitudes and keep decisions within the range of plausibility. But far more important in the modern practice, the forecasts lift from the person who must make decisions as to the future a heavy, even perilous, responsibility ... the forecast allows him to yield his judgment to the forecaster. If the judgment is then wrong, it is not his; instead it is the best professionally available – a significant protection in a world of tense bureaucratic conflict.

It is also important to note that Galbraith's emphasis on the fact that firms are continually dealing with uncertainty reinforces the conclusion that the firm will not necessarily choose Pareto efficient strategies (cf. Zeitlin, 1974). This is not least because in an uncertain environment it is not always possible to assess the future distributional consequences of decisions taken today.[44] Galbraith's recognition of the importance of uncertainty therefore further elevates the importance of control and power. Planning and acquiring control of strategic cost factors is essential in mitigating the impact of an uncertain environment (see also Rothschild, 1947; Dixon, 1996; Hargreaves Heap, 1986–87; Hodgson, 1989, 1998a, 1998b, 2000c). Indeed such considerations underpin Lavoie's (1992: 99–100) assessment that:

> power is the ultimate objective of the firm: power over its environment, whether it be economic, social or political ... The firm wants power over its suppliers of materials, over its customers, over the government, over the kind of technology to be put in use. The firm whether it be a megacorp or a small family firm, would like to have control over future events, its financial requirements, the quality of its labour force, the prices of the industry and the possibility of take-overs. 'The firm is viewed as being able to exercise a degree of control over its environment through R&D, market development, interfirm co-operation, entry deterrence' (Davies and Lee, 1988: 21). In a world without uncertainty, the notion of power dissolves and loses much of its importance.

This exemplifies Galbraith's view that power, as well as the ability to mitigate the impact of uncertainty, are related.[45] Such considerations also suggest that Galbraith's analysis can be further extended in developing a distinctive Post Keynesian view of the firm. Post Keynesian economists are typically associated with the study of uncertainty and the salient institutions of the "real" world (Davidson, 1972, 1994, 2007). However, a moment's reflection reveals a general neglect of the concept of uncertainty in Post Keynesian writings on the firm (Dunn, 1999, 2000a, 2001a, 2008a). While many Post Keynesians acknowledge the pivotal role of money as an institution for coping with uncertainty, they have written little on the fact that the firm is also an institution that deals with, and provides for a flexible response to, uncertainty (Dunn, 2001c).[46]

Coordination, planning, and the prospect

Such a brief review suggests that there is good reason to consider Galbraith's neglected contribution in more detail, not least because of the degree of similarity with many seminal contributions to the theory of the firm. Galbraith offered an approach to the modern firm that links technology, capital, money contracts, power and planning to the problems of uncertainty. For Galbraith the firm is a relatively enduring institutional structure which depends upon the decisions and governance structure that surround the technostructure. But it is not a permanent structure. It means small firms may seek to grow and evolve into large firms. This might improve the chances of survival. But it does not assure it. This must be acknowledged.

Galbraith's analysis shares the concerns of Post Keynesians and Institutionalists (Dunn, 2000b, 2001c, 2008a; cf. Davidson, 1972, 1996). Galbraith's corporation, existing in historical time, represents an enduring institutional response to an uncertain future specifically designed to mitigate its impact. Galbraith presented a rich taxonomy that captures the main strategies open to the firm for coping with uncertainty. Moreover, it anticipates many of the more recent theoretical developments in the transaction cost and knowledge based approaches to the firm. It represents one of the few attempts to examine the nexus between the firm and uncertainty and serves as a useful starting-point for future research into this relationship.

The next task for Post Keynesians is to develop an approach to the firm that elaborates how fundamental uncertainty affects a firm's organizational structure, pricing strategy, size, area of business, range of products, relationship to labor and capital markets, investment procedures, approach toward technology, attitude and inter-firm cooperation, and the motivation of its owners, and so on.[47] In short, Post Keynesians must articulate what a firm dealing with uncertainty looks like. This is a big task and one which will undoubtedly occupy Post Keynesian minds for some time to come. Nevertheless Galbraith offers fertile ground for further reflection and development towards this goal.[48] The next chapter continues the assessment of Galbraith's theory of the firm and considers his approach to the multinational corporation.

Notes

1 Marris and Wood (1971) summarize many of the mainstream analytic reactions to Galbraith's theory of the firm. Notable mainstream attempts at empirically assessing the relevance of Galbraith's distinctive view of the firm include Bower (1970), Caves (1970), Demsetz (1974), Blois (1975), Edwards and Heggestad (1973, 1979) and Christofides and Tapon (1979a and 1979b). But aside from these reviews and the AER symposium on "The New Industrial State after twenty years" in 1988, there is scant mention in the central tradition of any lasting theoretical contribution of Galbraith to industrial economics.

2 Of those that commented upon earlier drafts of this chapter, many took issue with this claim. It was felt that as Galbraith is the most widely read economist after Marx, it was hard to argue that he is neglected. As I pointed out in my defense, Galbraith is *generally viewed as a social* theorist and *not* as a theorist *of the firm.* I cannot stress the italics enough – Galbraith's contribution to the theory of the firm *per se* is generally minimized (James Galbraith, 1984, 1989 is perhaps one of the few exceptions). Moreover, even when Galbraith is considered, it is generally peripheral to the discussion.

3 The term itself entered popular parlance with James Burnham (1941). Burnham was an unacknowledged influence on *The New Industrial State.* As Galbraith (1981: 362) acknowledged in his autobiography *A Life in Our Times*: "James Burnham, partly because he was a stalwart right-winger well out of the political mainstream and partly because he was not a certified academician, never got full credit for his contribution. In my early editions of *The New Industrial State* I was among those in default."

4 Galbraith in chapter 10 of *The New Industrial State* draws heavily on the work of Baumol (1959), Marris (1964), Downie (1958), and Kaysen (1957, 1965) that discusses the managerialist revolution and the separation of ownership from control.

5 See also Galbraith's (1966a, 1966b, 1966c, 1966d, 1966e, 1966f) BBC Reith lectures of 1966 published in *The Listener* and the subsequent rejoinder by Allen (1967).

6 By Galbraith's own admission he revised this draft extensively. It would be interesting to investigate whether this manuscript still survives and the change and continuity between this first draft and its subsequent publication. Galbraith in the interview in chapter 12 suggested that if it does, it is with his papers in the Kennedy Library. Nevertheless it is still clear that many of the themes that were later emphasized in *The New Industrial State* were also emphasized much earlier in *American Capitalism* (1952a).

7 As Frank Knight (1921: 318) noted: "Though we cannot describe a new invention in advance without making it, nor say what quantity and quality of new natural productive capacity will be developed and where, yet it is possible in a large degree to offset ignorance with knowledge and behave intelligently with regard to the future. These changes are in large part the result of deliberate application of resources to bring them about, and in the large if not in a particular instance, the results of such activity can be so far foreseen that it is even possible to hire men and borrow capital at fixed remunerations for the purpose of carrying it on."

8 Compare Veblen (1904: 7–8) who also noted the complex, interdependent and organic nature of the production process: "The whole concert of industrial operations is to be taken as a machine process, made up of interlocking detail processes, rather than as a multiplicity of mechanical appliances each doing its particular work in severalty. This comprehensive industrial process draws into its scope and turns to account all branches of knowledge that have to do with the material sciences, and the whole makes a more or less delicately balanced complex of sub-processes."

9 Organization: "is the arrangement by which specialists combine their information to make decision – decisions that require knowledge, experience or intuition of several or many persons" (Galbraith, 1973a: 100).

10 As Galbraith (1967: 122) points out: "The goal of these planning decisions could still be the greatest possible profit. We have already seen that a high and reliable flow of earnings is important for the success of the technostructure. But the market is no longer specifying and enforcing this goal."

11 It is impossible in a complex and uncertain environment to ascertain what a profit maximizing level of output or prospective yield on an investment is likely to be (see Dunn, 2000b, 2001b, 2008a). As Rotheim (1999: 93) points out: "when the prospective yield on capital assets cannot be known in the future for both epistemological and ontological reasons, entrepreneurs ... must rely on social convention to assess the confidence they have in their predictions of the prospective yield on capital assets."

12 The strategies that Galbraith highlights are somewhat similar to Schumpeter's (1943: 88) assessment: "Practically any investment entails, as a necessary complement of entrepreneurial action, certain safeguarding activities such as insuring or hedging. Long-range investing under rapidly changing conditions, especially under conditions that change or may change at any moment under the impact of new commodities and technologies, is like shooting at a target that is not only

indistinct but moving – and moving jerkily at that. Hence it becomes necessary to resort to such protecting devices as patents or temporary secrecy of processes or, in some cases, long-period contracts secured in advance. But these protecting devices which most economists accept as normal elements of rational management are only special cases of a larger class comprising many others which most economists condemn although they do not differ fundamentally from the recognized ones."

13 One should compare this account with Williamson's discussion (1975: 155–7; see also 1981: 1558–60; cf. Dugger, 1983).

14 Thus there is a sense in which Galbraith anticipated much of the themes evident in Chandler (1977, 1990) and Lazonick (1991).

15 For a variety of empirical studies on vertical integration, see Joskow (1985, 1998), Masten, Meehan, and Snyder (1989, 1991) and Whinston (2003).

16 This argument is again similar to Kalecki who: "argued that the cost of finance will depend upon source, with internal funds usually available at a lower cost than external funds, and on amount with the cost arising with amount borrowed" (Sawyer, 1985b: 102). Kalecki, like Galbraith, argued that retained earnings – past profitability – has a strong influence on investment.

17 Moreover, Galbraith, unlike many latter day theorists highlights the relationship of the technostructure and the firm to the wider economy as it impacts on saving and investment: "The nature of such saving must not, however, be misunderstood. The decisions which provide three fifths of the community's supply of savings are made not by individuals but by authority, in the main by the managements of a few hundred corporations. And from these savings comes the major wherewithal for the growth of the economy" (Galbraith, 1967a: 57).

18 For example, as Cowling and Tomlinson (2000: F364) point out, the Japanese "keiretsu" subcontracting relationships are a mechanism to reduce uncertainty: "A particular feature is that the prime firm, in the corporate group, effectively insures their sub-contractors income stream, against fluctuations in demand. However to counteract the problem of moral hazard, each sub-contractor is given an internal ranking, with poor performance leading to a loss of position and future business."

19 To provide further evidence for this claim: "Price stability also serves the purposes of industrial planning. Prices being fixed, they are predictable over a substantial period of time. And since one firm's prices are another's costs, so costs are also predictable. Thus on the one hand, stable prices facilitate control and minimize the risk of a price collapse that could jeopardize earnings and the autonomy of the technostructure ...

[Prices] must be subject to the authority of the planning unit; otherwise there is risk of loss from uncontrolled price movements and there is no reliable number by which units of product and input can be multiplied to get projected income and outlay. If these estimates are not available in reliable form, there is a large random element in decisions as to what to produce, and with what and by what means, and there is total uncertainty as to the outcome – whether there will be profit or loss and in what dimension. Such error is the antithesis of effective planning. A moment's thought will suggest not only how nearly impossible it would make modern industrial performance but how remote, in practice, such uncontrolled prices are from real life" (Galbraith, 1967a: 200–3).

20 This is again reminiscent of Schumpeter (1939: 73), who observed in *Business Cycles*: "Railroads have not emerged because any consumers took the initiative in displaying an effective demand for their service in preference to the services of mail coaches. Nor did the consumers display any such initiative wish to have electric lamps or rayon stockings or to travel by motorcar or airplane, or to listen to radios, or to chew gum. There is obviously no lack of realism in the proposition that the great majority of changes in commodities consumed has been forced by producers on consumers who, more often than not, have resisted the change and have had to be educated up by elaborate psychotechnics of advertising."

21 Like both Keynes and Galbraith, Schumpeter (1943: 88) also acknowledged the importance of institutions such as sticky wages and long-term money-denominated contracts for facilitating production and mitigating the impact of uncertainty: "Again, if long-period contracts cannot be entered into in advance, other means may have to be devised in order to tie prospective customers to the investing firm."

22 The civil enforceability of contracts ultimately requires the contracting party compensate the other party if the first party does not "choose" to live up to its real contractual commitment (cf. Davidson, 1972).

23 This clearly echoes the Post Keynesian view of contracts. As Davidson (1981: 165) has pointed out, in "all modern market-orientated production economies, production is organized on a forward money-contracting basis ... Since production takes time, the hiring of factor inputs and the purchase of materials to be used in any productive activity must precede the date when the finished product will be at hand. These hiring and material-purchase transactions will therefore require forward contracting if the production process is to be efficiently planned. The financing of such forward production-cost commitments ... requires entrepreneurs [or strategic decision-makers] to have money available to discharge these contractual liabilities at one

or more future dates before the product is sold and delivered, payment received, and the position liquidated."

24 For a discussion of the history and origins of the transaction cost concept, see Klaes (2000a, 2000b). For a variety of surveys of the empirical adequacy of the transaction cost thesis, see Masten (1984, 1996) and Masten and Saussier (2000).

25 As Sawyer (1985a: 202) notes this "rather ugly phrase [of Williamson] refers to cases where relevant information is available to one group but not to others."

26 One should note that Meade (1968) criticized Galbraith for not distinguishing between planning for the market and planning that replaces the market. In the second edition Galbraith (1967a: 18) acknowledged that the "difference was not clear in the first edition" and sought to rectify this lack of clarity.

27 Clearly, higher levels of technology can allow complex tasks to be handled by one or a few people. Computer software is the obvious example in this regard.

28 Balakrishnan and Wernerfelt's (1986) analysis of the links between technical change, competition and vertical integration reveals a correlation between asset specificity and vertical integration. They also present interesting findings with regard to the role played by uncertainty. They find that technological uncertainty is negatively related to vertical integration. In one sense this could be interpreted as refuting Galbraith's hypothesis (although this is not something they explicitly attempt to consider). I would argue, however, that one needs to clearly specify the nature of any empirical testing of Galbraith's theory. Galbraith argues that technological sophistication calls for organization, and that vertical integration is a strategy that can mitigate uncertainty, and not that technological uncertainty leads to vertical integration.

29 Firms represent the internal supersession of the market mechanism by command. As markets and firms are alternative mechanisms for resource allocation, a choice is offered. The allocation of resources by planning or command as opposed to movements in the structure of relative prices is conditional on the fact that the use of the price mechanism is costly. Command, with one party obeying the direction of another, reduces the need for costly continual renegotiation and reformulation of contracts. Firms succeed where markets fail, that is, "in the beginning there were markets."

30 Cowling and Sugden (1998a) return to the notion of strategy, while reflecting on developments in the theory of the firm, stemming from Coase (1937). They return to Coase's original starting point, the notion of economic planning, and provide an alternative approach and

definition of the firm, as a "means of co-ordinating production from one centre of strategic decision making." While Cowling and Sugden's contribution is novel, it is not without problems. I have proposed an extension to this definition of the firm that encompasses the fact that centers of strategic decision-makers coordinating production operate under conditions of fundamental uncertainty (Dunn, 2001a, 2001c). I argue that this extension reinforces many of Cowling and Sugdens' central conclusions and extends and clarifies their underdeveloped notion of strategic decision-making. I believe this approach is consistent with a view of the firm as an institution for mitigating uncertainty, which reflects Galbraith's approach.

31 Emphasizing the coordinating role of the firm may introduce a degree of imprecision in delineating the boundaries (as opposed to the essence) of the firm. As Sawyer (1979: 11) notes: "For example a holding company which owns several units could, under this approach, be regarded as many firms if the holding company did not co-ordinate the activities of its various units and, whilst providing supervision of them, essentially allowed them to operate in an independent manner. Elements of fuzziness would be introduced if the holding company allocated capital between the units but otherwise did not allocate resources between them, or if there was some trading between the units with the prices determined by the holding company. An example from the other end of the spectrum would be where one firm is the major or sole customer of another, and the power of the one firm over the other is such that in many respects resources within the two firms were allocated centrally, even though they were nominally under separate ownership." Cowling and Sugden (1998a, 1998b) propose that this latter situation be thought of as coming under the ambit of the single firm.

32 This echoes many themes identified by Aoki (1990). According to Aoki (1990) the Anglo-American hierarchical approach to governance (H-mode) is typified by a hierarchical separation and specialization between planning and operational decision-making. One of the features of the Japanese mode of governance, what Aoki (1990) refers to as the J-mode, is that these features are less defined with more rotation through the firm's activities, less emphasis on formal job seniority, and greater delegation of power through the organization. Although Galbraith did not analyze these institutional differences, his approach and methodology argues for recognition of such factors in analysis.

33 Accordingly it should not be thought that recognition of Galbraith's *a posteriori* rejection of the assumption of consumer sovereignty entails acceptance of a lessening of competition between firms: "The protective purposes of going beyond prices to influence consumer response is

to prevent the defection of consumers which would plunge the firm into loss. The affirmative purpose is, of course, to recruit new customers and thus to expand sales – to serve the goal of growth. As sufficiently remarked, the typical industry of the planning system consists of a few large firms. This means that sales can be expanded both by recruiting new users and by persuading customers of other firms to switch. Other firms, for their part, will be engaged in the same effort. The management of the consumer is thus an intricate complex of efforts to recruit new users, win the customers of other firms and hold existing customers in the face of corresponding efforts of the other firms. Since the gain of customers by one firm means their loss by another, the affirmative and protective purposes of consumer management, as they are actually pursued in any consumer industry, are in some degree in conflict" (Galbraith, 1973a: 155).

34 Compare Schumpeter (1943: 84), who likewise argued that in reality it is not textbook competition that matters "but the competition from the new commodity, the new technology, the new source of supply, the new type of organization (the largest-scale unit of control for instance) – competition which commands a decisive cost or quality advantage and which strikes not at the margins of the profits and the outputs of the existing firms but at their foundations and their very lives."

35 Galbraith's approach echoes that of Schumpeter (1943: 140), who argued: "A very common type of social criticism which we have already met laments the 'decline of competition' and equates it to the decline of capitalism because of the virtues it attributes to competition and the vices it attributes to modern industrial 'monopolies'. In this schema of interpretation, monopolization plays the role of arteriosclerosis and reacts upon the fortunes of the capitalist order through increasingly unsatisfactory economic performance. We have seen the reasons for rejecting this view. Economically neither the case for competition nor the case against concentration of economic control is anything like as strong as this argument implies."

36 Galbraith (1973a: 9) acknowledged this in the preface to *Economics and the Public Purpose*: "*The New Industrial State* pictures the world of the large corporation as the outgrowth of the neo-classical world of monopoly and oligopoly. At least by implication what was left behind was the world of the competitive market." *Economics and the Public Purpose* sought to rectify this deficiency by elaborating more fully the market system and its nexus to the planning system.

37 To argue otherwise might be construed as invoking a Friedmanite-type Darwinian selection process such that only those organizations

that successfully mitigated the impact of uncertainty survived (Dunn, 2008a).

38 What is more, this is a good illustration of how Galbraith, like contemporary Post Keynesians, focuses on the importance of history, uncertainty, distributional issues and the relevance of political and economic institutions in conducting economic analysis (see Arestis, 1990, 1992, 1996; Arestis, Dunn, and Sawyer, 1999a, 1999b).

39 The resource-based view of the firm that descends from Penrose (1955, 1959), which describes how the access to routines and capabilities enables a flexible response to an uncertain future, may benefit from the technical definition of uncertainty offered by Post Keynesians (see Foss, 1997b, 1997d; cf. Langlois and Everett, 1992). The specific Post Keynesian view of time, nonergodic open system processes, may contribute to a clearer understanding of the need to access routines and capabilities (see Dunn, 2008a; cf. Hodgson, 1999).

40 Galbraith (1973a: 65) appears to recognize this in *Economics and the Public Purpose* where he states: "The difference between the planning and the market systems does not lie in the desire to escape from the constraints of the market and to effect control over the economic environment. It is in the instruments by which these are accomplished and the success with which they are attended."

41 This approach is therefore distinct from Coase, in that this conception of planning entails external and not just internal considerations.

42 Galbraith sometimes slips into the maximize-minimize-optimize vernacular that characterizes ergodic theorizing. For instance Galbraith (1967: 43, n. 3) quotes with approval Marris's (1964) suggestion that "In practice [business management] ... aims to minimize uncertainty, minimize the consequences of uncertainty, or both." Adopting the technical framework utilized by Post Keynesians helps avoid ambiguity.

43 It explains why, as Stiglitz (2003: 61) has observed, that although "Mutual funds spend millions on research ... study after study has demonstrated, most of them do no better at stock picking than they might by throwing darts at a dartboard."

44 As the focus is on the effects and processes of history the assessment of transaction costs by strategic decision-makers must be considered as an evolutionary dynamic judgment as opposed to a comparative static evaluation (Dunn, 1999, 2000b, 2001a, 2001c, 2008a). This means that we must be careful in assessing organizational efficiency in relation to the environment at any point in time because as the environment changes, an organizational mode adapted to the environment of the moment may well be maladapted in a broader larger sense.

45 If, as Malcolmson (1984) argues, firms acquire monopoly power by "economising" on market transaction costs then it follows that the notions of market power, transaction costs and uncertainty are inseparable.

46 Harcourt and Kenyon (1976) represents one of the earliest Post Keynesian attempts to explicitly embed the firm in history, as opposed to equilibrium (to paraphrase Joan Robinson). They still do not, however, fully explore the import of the Keynesian concept of uncertainty within their schema. In many respects Kay (1984) could be considered as one of the first attempts to integrate radical uncertainty into the theory of the firm (although see Dunn, 1999, 2001c, for some caveats). Kay's contribution, in a manner not too dissimilar from Galbraith, has also escaped many Post Keynesians (and Institutionalists).

47 As Lee (1994: 304–5) points out: "post-Keynesians have devoted little energy towards articulating a consistent and realistic microfoundation and have largely ignored 'micro' themes and issues, such as the business enterprise, pricing, the organization, the nature of competitive activities, co-ordinations of economic activity, and innovation and technical change. As a result, there exists no well-grounded cohesive body of economic analysis that could be referred to as post-Keynesian microeconomics." This represents a big challenge to Post Keynesianism and one to which it must rise if it is to present itself as a viable alternative to the conventional wisdom.

48 In a series of articles I have attempted to address this neglect and establish the foundations of a Post Keynesian approach to the theory of the firm that is consistent with its conceptualization of uncertainty (Dunn, 1999, 2000b, 2001a, 2001c). I argue that the essence of the modern corporation lies in its coordination of production from one centre of strategic decision-making under conditions of fundamental uncertainty (Dunn, 2001a, 2008a).

8 A theory of the multinational corporation

The divorce between ownership and the real responsibility of management is serious within a country when, as a result of joint-enterprise, ownership is broken up between innumerable individuals who buy their interest today and sell it tomorrow and lack altogether both knowledge and responsibility towards what they momentarily own. But when the same principle is applied internationally, it is, in times of stress, intolerable.

J. M. Keynes (1982: 236)

The planning system sustains a sizeable priestly class which, for modest compensation, is available for industry meetings, customer and investor indoctrination, sales conventions, executive seminars and other corporate rites, where it combines a slightly extravagant didactic skill with a superficial aspect of deep thought. In recent times the favored topic of all such artisans has been the deeper meaning of the multinational corporation. They picture the multinational corporation – IBM, General Motors, Nestlé – as a major discontinuity in the general process of economic development, something very different that, depending on the preference of the speaker and the need of the audience, is fraught with breathtaking potential for good or, more often, for evil. Standing astride of international boundaries, it is an assault on political sovereignty. Perhaps it is making obsolete the national state. And, since many of the corporations are American in origin, it is singularly a manifestation of American energy, enterprise and power.

J. K. Galbraith (1973a: 180–1)

When theorists of the firm contemplate the multinational enterprise, they have, generally speaking, been happy to draw upon or combine the dominant approaches that exist in the literature encapsulated in the monopoly view (Hymer, 1970, 1976; Kindleberger, 1969; Caves, 1971; Cowling and Sugden, 1987a, 1987b, 1998a, 1998b), the transaction cost, or internalization, account (McManus, 1972; Buckley and Casson, 1976; Buckley, 2004, 2006b; Brown, 1976; Hennart, 1982; Williamson, 1985, 2005), or the emerging resource based perspective (Penrose, 1956, 1959, 1960, 1968; Kay, 2000; Pitelis, 2000, 2004, 2007). What is typically overlooked, however, is the fact that J. K. Galbraith (1967a) advanced a distinctive and innovative contribution to the theory of the firm that predates and anticipates elements of these approaches. Moreover this vision was subsequently extended to advance a distinctive view of the multinational corporation that is embedded in the recognition that international production and trade takes place in uncertain, historical time and is coordinated across national boundaries (Galbraith, 1973a: 180–94). All theorists of the multinational enterprise seemingly overlook this fact.

Theorists of the multinational enterprise may be forgiven, however, for their neglect of Galbraith's contribution.[1] The multinational corporation does not appear in Galbraith's (1967a) major treatise on the modern corporation, *The New Industrial State*, nor in his two main books on economic development (Galbraith, 1964a, 1979b). As Adams (1984) notes the prominence given to issues regarding the multinational corporation, international trade, and economic development appears minimal in comparison to his more general discussion of the nexus between the large modern corporation and the increasing "affluence" of advanced industrial societies. Moreover, when it does appear (Galbraith, 1973a: 138–49, 180–94, 277; 1974: 100; 1977b: 17–19; 1978b; 1979b: 89–90; 1987: 160, 294–7; 1994b: 166–8, 179), it does so fleetingly and is submerged from general view.[2] Such considerations notwithstanding, it is important to acknowledge that Galbraith advanced a distinctive approach to the transnational corporation that is embedded in his general view of the firm, outlined in the previous chapter.[3]

The purpose of this chapter, therefore, is to draw attention to Galbraith's neglected contribution to the theory of the multinational enterprise. Galbraith's theoretical discussion of the multinational enterprise is a development of his broader theoretical contribution to the theory of the firm. This is evident from Galbraith's discussion of how the multinational firm deals with uncertainty, especially with regard to its transnational activities and boundaries. What is more, Galbraith's contribution has much *prima facie* contemporary relevance. Galbraith's theory, for example, helps us to analyze and understand the pharmaceutical and food industries, among others. Accordingly, it should be subject to renewed attention and development.

The Galbraithian theory of the multinational enterprise

Many theorists of the multinational enterprise start from the recognition that there are major uncertainties and distinct and potentially prohibitive costs that arise when strategic decision-makers contemplate engaging in business and organizing production in another country (Buckley and Casson, 1976; Buckley, 2000, 2003, 2004, 2006b). When languages, customs, social networks, business conventions, and legal frameworks, amongst other things, differ, then the costs of operating in a foreign country are likely to be substantial. It is for such reasons that Hennart (1991: 82) suggests that: "it is difficult to understand why firms based in one country would be exploiting their advantages by undertaking production in another country. Why not sell or rent these advantages to local entrepreneurs, who could then combine them with local factors of production at lower costs than those experienced by foreign direct investors?" Contemporary theorists of the multinational enterprise proceed to answer this question in terms of an imperfectionist account of the internalization of financial (the monopoly approach) or non-financial externalities (the transaction cost approach), or in terms of a bundle of dedicated and productive resources (the resource-based view). Galbraith, as we shall see however, advanced a "strategic" view of the multinational corporation which emerges as a response to the particular uncertainties of international production and trade.[4] While, like the literature on the multinational enterprise more widely, Galbraith started from the premise that traditional neo-classical microeconomics has a difficulty in explaining the existence, role and boundaries of the multinational firm, his focus was different. Rather, Galbraith focused on how the firm adapts to the numerous uncertainties that pertain to international trade and production:

> Old-fashioned international trade, as still described with intricacy and sophistication by the neo-classical model, is a system of exchange in which the market remains peculiarly powerful. The firm that engages in such trade is wholly subordinate to an impersonally determined demand and price. The market control by the firm being non-existent, the uncertainty and risk of international trade is exceptionally high. Specifically a firm in

> one country consigns its product, usually through intermediaries, for sale in another country. On leaving the country of origin, the product leaves entirely the influence of the original producer. The latter retains no power over the price at which the product is sold; he is not imagined to influence the preferences of the foreign consumer. The price of the product is subject to the competitive and uncontrolled consequences of domestic production in the country in which it is sold and of competitive imports from other foreign sources. Tariff changes in the recipient country and fluctuations in exchange rates add further uncertainty – both peculiar to foreign trade. If the firm is buying rather than selling – procuring, for example, an important raw material – classical international trade theory depicts a similar uncertainty. Changing costs of supply, changes in the competitive demand from other countries, changes in exchange rates and (on occasion) changes in export taxes are added hazards. In this procurement the firm is also subject to the sole authority of the market. (Galbraith, 1973a: 181)

The nature and extent of a firm's multinational activities, like the domestic firm more generally, are conditioned by the protective need to safeguard the enormous commitments of time and capital from the potentially ravaging and uncertain nature of international competition, as well as reflecting the affirmative objectives of the strategic decision-makers, such as their need to extend their influence and dominance. These needs propel and underpin the expansion of the firm, and the growth in mergers and acquisition both within and across national boundaries.[5] However, in contrast to some explanations of the multinational enterprise, which focus almost exclusively on vertical relations and specialized assets, Galbraith provided a richer discussion which provides for the fact that the majority of multinational growth involves the transfer of intangible assets such as the technostructure's technical and marketing "know-how" into foreign locations (cf. Kay, 1997; Pitelis, 2007; Zanfei 2000; Castellani and Zanfei, 2002). The multinational firm can reproduce and transfer the associated technology, planning routines, and tacit knowledge of the incumbent technostructures to foreign countries in the affirmative and protective pursuit of competitive advantage in a world of uncertainty (Galbraith, 1978b: 58–62; cf. Buckley and Casson, 1976: 36–59; Peteraf, 1993).[6]

It is no coincidence that the multinational firm is large, powerful, and durable. US, German, French, and British transnationals continue to dominate the world stage with the traditional food, motor, oil, electrical, and telecommunications industries controlling major flows in trade and production. As table 6 highlights, multinationals continue to represent a significant and major source of production and trade – with assets and sales in excess of many less advanced countries' GDP. Size clearly facilitates the mitigation of the peculiar uncertainties associated with international trade. As Horst (1972) pointed out long ago, it is the firms that have become dominant in domestic markets that proceed to internationalize (cf. Caves, 1982: 14–15; Kay, 1997; Cowling and Tomlinson, 2000). And as Dunning (1993: 151–2) notes, numerous empirical studies have found that larger firms are more likely to become multinationals (although it can be conceded that that size may be acting as a composite variable for other influences). In the Galbraithian vision both growth and its adjunct, size, are strategies whereby the transnational firm can mitigate the uncertainties of international production and trade: "Transnational operations require organization; they become increasingly feasible the larger the firm. The large firm has or can obtain the financial resources to establish operations or acquire firms in other countries and the managers, scientists, engineers and other specialized talent to re-create itself abroad" (Galbraith, 1973a: 185). And although growth and size are in themselves intrinsically important, especially as it impinges on the power of the firm, it is also important to note that they may also reflect, and be a response to, various uncertainties and threats.

From this perspective a distinctive view of the multinational corporation comes into view – it is simply the accommodation and protection of the planning routines of the modern corporation to the peculiar uncertainties and needs of international trade. It is an extension of the theory outlined in the previous chapter. As Galbraith (1973a: 182) recognized: "In addition to the uncertainties from buying and selling abroad, imports from other countries could prejudice or destroy control and resulting planning in the home country." It is in response to such uncertainties that the multinational corporation emerges:

> It transcends the market internationally as it does nationally. It accomplishes over a world of multiple national sovereignties what it first accomplishes within any one. It minimizes the need for tariffs, quotas and embargoes to reduce uncertainty in national markets. And, needless to say, it is not peculiarly American. It is the common accommodation of all non-socialist planning, whatever the country of origin, to the special problem of international trade. By re-creating itself in other countries the technostructure,

Table 6. *The world's top twenty-five non-financial transnational corporations, 2006*

Corporation	Home economy	Industry[d]	Assets		Sales		Employment		TNI[b] (percent)	No. of affiliates	
			Foreign	Total	Foreign	Total	Foreign	Total		Foreign	Total
General Electric	USA	Electrical & electronic equipment	442,278	697,239	74,285	163,391	164,000	319,000	53	785	1, 117
British Petroleum Company Plc	UK	Petroleum expl./ ref./distr.	170,326	217,601	215,879	270,602	80,300	97,100	80	337	529
Toyota Motor Corporation	Japan	Motor vehicles	164,627	273,853	78,529	205,917	113,967	299,394	45	169	419
Royal Dutch/ Shell Group	UK, Netherlands	Petroleum expl./ ref./distr.	161,122[e]	235,276	182, 538[e]	318,845	90,000	108,000	70	518	926
Exxonmobil Corporation	USA	Petroleum expl./ ref./distr.	154,993	219,015	252,680	365,467	51,723	82,100	58	278	346
Ford Motor Company	USA	Motor vehicles	131,062	278,554	78,958	160,123	155,000[f]	283,000	50	162	247
Vodafone Group Plc	UK	Telecommunications	126,190	144,366	32,641	39,021	53,138	63,394	85	30	130

Total	France	Petroleum expl./ref./ distr.	120,645	138,579	146,672	192,952	57,239	95,070	74	429	593
Electricite De France	France	Electricity, gas and water	111,916	235,857	33,679	73,933	17,185[g]	155,968	35	199	249
Wal-Mart Stores	USA	Retail	110,199	151,193	77,116	344,992	540,000	1,910,000	41	146	163
Telefonica SA	Spain	Telecommuni- cations	101,891	143,530	41,093	66,367	167,881	224,939	59	185	205
E.On	Germany	Electricity, gas, and water	34,304	167,565	32,154	85,007	46,598	80,612	51	273	590
Deutsche Tel- ekom AG	Germany	Telecommuni- cations	93,488	171,421	36,240	76 953	88,808	248,800	49	143	253
Volkswagen Group	Germany	Motor vehicles	91,823	179,906	95,761	131,571	155,935	324,875	57	178	272
France Telecom	France	Telecommuni- cations	90,871	135,876	30,448	64,863	82,148	191,036	52	145	211
ConocoPhilips	USA	Petroleum expl./ref./ distr.	89,528	164,781	55,781	183,650	171,883	38,400	43	118	179
Chevron Corporation	USA	Petroleum expl.ref./ distr.	85,735	132,628	111,608	204,892	33,700	62,500	58	97	226

Table 6. *(cont.)*

Corporation	Home economy	Industry[d]	Assets		Sales		Employment		TNI [b] (percent)	No. of affiliates	
			Foreign	Total	Foreign	Total	Foreign	Total		Foreign	Total
Honda Motor Co. Ltd	Japan	Motor vehicles	76,264	101,190	77,605	95,333	148,544	167,231	82	141	243
Suez	France	Electricity, gas, & water	75,151	96,714	42,002	55,563	76,943	139,814	59	586	884
Siemens AG	Germany	Electricity & electronic equipment	74,585	119,812	74,858	109,553	314,000	475,000	30	919	1,224
Hutchison Whampoa Limited	Hong Kong, China	Diversified	70,679	87,146	28,619	34,428	182,149[g]	220,000	82	115	125
RWE Group	Germany	Electricity, gas, & water	68,202	123,080	22,142	55,521	30,752	68,534	47	221	430
Nestlé SA	Switzer-land	Food & beverages	66,677[a]	83,426	57,234[c]	78,528	257,434[c,g]	265,000	83	467	502
BMW AG	Germany	Motor vehicles	66,053	104,118	48,172	61,472	26,575	106,575	56	138	174
Procter & Gamble	USA	Diversified	64,487	138,014	44,530	76,476	101,220[h]	138,000	59	369	458

Notes: The list covers non-financial TNCs only. In some companies, foreign investors may hold a minority share of more than 10 percent. All figures millions of dollars and number of employees.

[a] All data are based on the companies' annual reports unless otherwise stated. Data on affiliates is based on Dun and Bradstreet's Who owns Whom database.

[b] TNI, the Transnationlity Index, is calculated as the average of the following three ratios: foreign assets to total assets, foreign sales to total sales and foreign employment to total employment.

[c] II, the Internationalization Index is calculated as the number of foreign affiliates divided by the number of all affiliates (note: affiliates counted in this table refer to only majority-owned affiliates).

[d] Industry classification for companies follows the United States Standard Industrial Classification as used by the United States Securities and Exchange Commission (SEC).

[e] Data are for activities outside Europe.

[f] Data are for activities outside North America.

[g] Foreign employment data are calculated by applying the share of foreign employment in total employment of the previous year to total employment of 2006.

[h] Foreign employment data are calculated by applying the average of the shares of foreign employment in total employment of all companies in the same industry (omitting the extremes) to total employment.

Source: UNCTAD (2008). UNCTAD/Erasmus University database.

in effect, follows its product to those countries. In so doing, it enters into the same understanding on prices with the other market participants in the foreign country that it has on its home turf. And the reciprocal movement of foreign firms into its own territory eliminates the hazards of price cutting and allows of the same control there. (Galbraith, 1973a: 183)[7]

That is to say, by following its products abroad the multinational corporation can more easily pursue its various (planning) strategies, such as controlling or suspending or replacing the market, in foreign countries so as to mitigate the potentially damaging impact of international competition: "With the rise of the transnational system, capital, technology and qualified manpower are brought within the authority of a single organization. This authority extends across national frontiers. So does the ability to persuade customers and the community and to win needed support from the state. No such cosmic powers are available to the market system" (Galbraith, 1973a: 190). Producing at home and exporting to foreign markets expose the modern corporation to the whims of foreign consumers, lay it open to domestic competition, subject it to the vagaries of different legal traditions, and court the vicissitudes of foreign governments. Locating abroad enables such hazards to be mitigated and underpins the development of global brands and international marketing. In accompanying its "product to Germany, General Motors can bring its persuasion to bear on the German consumer. And it can press its needs on the German government ... And, by following its product to the USA, Volkswagen is able to influence the responses of American consumers. And it can protect itself and obtain its needs in Washington. None of this would be possible were products consigned through agents in the manner of classical international trade" (Galbraith, 1973a: 183).

The dynamics of transnationalism, however, are not unidirectional. Anticipating the 1980s and 1990s debates on outsourcing, Galbraith considered another countervailing influence, which also motivates the transnational operations of the modern corporation – the potential or real, threat of low cost foreign competition (cf. Ramamurtic, 2004; UNCTAD, 2003, 2005, 2006). For example:

In the past the United States had higher real wages than other countries but better technology and capital equipment. Of late, American civilian industries, formerly important in export or domestic markets, have been

> at a disadvantage in both quality of capital and wage levels in relation to Germany and Japan, where the military development has been much less. American corporations have responded in accordance with the preceding analysis; they have extensively developed lower-cost production abroad. This has enabled them to retain their position not only in overseas markets but in the United States as well. The eminence of the American corporation in transnational operations is a manifestation of both the high development of the American economy and of weaknesses that are associated with the particular form of that development. (Galbraith, 1973a: 186)[8]

Thus, engaging in multinational activities limits the uncertainties associated with the possible entry of new firms that might increase competition. By operating in foreign countries, the multinational can attempt to circumvent the potentially damaging cost advantages which may give rise to foreign competition and its associated uncertainties that impinge upon the processes of production, accumulation and organizational reproduction. As Galbraith (1973a: 183–4) noted:

> This is a matter of great and increasing importance – especially to the United States. Within the United States there is no great danger that one manufacturer of automobiles, television sets, transistor radios, tape recorders, typewriters, or other such products will have an insurmountable cost advantage over its rivals in the same industry. Unions tend to be industry-wide; the productivity of workers and access to capital, technology, qualified manpower and materials, if not the same for all firms, are not permanently and unmanageably different. As between countries, however, this cannot be assumed. In comparison with the United States, labor costs in Japan or Germany may be durably lower, the productivity of labor may be permanently higher, capital costs may be lower and there may be continuing differences in the costs of other requisites of production. In consequence the costs of German or Japanese products may be permanently much lower than their American counterparts. Given the foregoing differences – and given the reduced role of tariffs in the international planning system – the danger to the purely national corporation is evident. The oligopolistic convention under which prices are set serves well for firms that have roughly similar cost functions. But a foreign firm with sharply and durably lower costs might well insist on prices much below those that the domestic corporation finds advantageous. Movements in exchange rates, an occurrence of increasing frequency, add to the hazard. Both the protective and affirmative purposes of the corporation are thus in jeopardy.

With transnational operations this danger is elided. The transnational corporation can produce or arrange production where costs are lowest. The advantage has been extensively and increasingly exploited, especially by American-based corporations, in recent years. Automobiles for all the major American producers are being built in Germany, England, Canada or Japan. Components for models being produced in the United States are assigned, routinely, to the lowest-cost foreign plant.[9]

As this long quotation highlights, it is perhaps prudent for the modern corporation to internalize the cost advantages available in a foreign country, rather than leave the planning routines and large specific capital investments of a solely national organization exposed to challenge: "The threat of lowest-cost foreign production is thus effectively countered by being (or using) the lowest-cost foreign producer. In such fashion does the planning system transcend national boundaries and become transnational" (Galbraith, 1973a: 184).

Similarly the nature of the multinational's imperialistic tendencies, especially in the arena of manufacturing, can be understood as an attempt to gain control over sources of supply. The firm seeks to mitigate the uncertainties that surround the sourcing of the requisite raw materials that feed the complex and extensive production processes that obtain with modern technology (cf. Galbraith, 1973a: 138–49). "The corporation in the planning system, in pursuit of the protective purposes of the technostructure, seeks to secure its sources of important raw materials. This takes it into the less developed countries. And to a limited extent in the case of products such as gasoline, transistor radios and aspirin it finds markets in these countries" (Galbraith, 1973a: 187). Thus the appearance of the multinational in less developed countries reflects the strategy of superseding the market with the planning structures associated with the firm, that is, it reflects a process of vertically integrating to mitigate the uncertainties that surround the obtaining of crucial raw materials. This explains the fact that:

a very significant proportion of international trade – of especial significance to many developing countries – rests with a very few, giant transnational corporations: as examples of particular significance to developing countries, the proportion of commodity trade marketed by three to six of the largest transnationals is 85–90% for coffee, 85% for cocoa beans, 85–90%

for jute, 75–80% for tin. This dominant position of a few transnationals in the whole array of international commodity markets is rarely pointed out in the debates that revolve around access to markets in the developed world by the developing world. (Cowling and Tomlinson, 2005: 3)

However, while Galbraith's approach appears to parallel traditional explanations of the multinational organization it nevertheless explicitly challenges the conventional view that expansion overseas into underdeveloped regions is primarily driven by the incessant need to search for new markets. Rather, from a Galbraithian perspective, the transnational system is a product of the affluent nexus: "the transnational system is primarily a relationship between the developed countries. It is here that the important markets exist; it is here, accordingly, that the protective equilibrium of the planning system must be established" (Galbraith, 1973a: 187; cf. Krugman, 1979).[10] The multinational corporation is neither an expression of modern imperialism (challenging the radical view) nor an engine of economic development (rejecting the conservative perspective). This explains why an extended discussion is not afforded to multinational corporations in Galbraith's (1964a, 1979b) two main contributions to economic development.[11] While the multinational enterprise may in some small way contribute to economic development, its primary preoccupation is with servicing the more established or (rapidly) advancing economies, rather than the more underdeveloped and backward economies (cf. Sugden, 1997; Sugden and Wilson, 2003).[12] This is why, as discussed above in chapter 6, in less advanced countries a developmental state is required to secure free and compulsory basic education, oversee the incubation of domestic firms and technology, and support infrastructure development.

Moreover the adjunct of such discussions, common in many contemporary essays on the future of the multinational system, conflate notions of cultural imperialism with the nature of advanced development more broadly. Many commentators continue to confuse:

the cultural impact of the American corporation with that of the corporation in general. That the planning system, in pursuit of its purposes, has profound influence on the national community in which it operates we have seen. It conducts a powerful propaganda on behalf of its products. Thus it shapes attitudes on behalf of goods in general and makes these central to life. It imposes its intellectual discipline on those associated with its organizations. Its purposes and values become those of the community and the state. But this cultural effect is not peculiarly American. This is imagined only because so many of the multinational corporations have their origins in the United States. (Galbraith, 1973a: 187)[13]

That is to say one of the major implications of the modern technological mode of production is the broad convergence of products, planning routines and the exercise of power. This explains why "hotels, automobiles, service stations, airlines are much alike not because they are American but because all are the products of great organizations" (Galbraith, 1973a: 188).

Perhaps one of the most salient strategies, however, that forms part of the Galbraith vision of the multinational firm is that which pertains to its political nexus to sovereign states. Frequently the multinational is viewed as a deceitful impediment to the democratic processes that should be unceremoniously rejected. Indeed Galbraith (1973a: 188) cryptically remarked, paraphrasing Marx, that the modern state "is not the executive committee of the bourgeoisie, but it is more nearly the executive committee of the technostructure." Similarly Cowling and Tomlinson (2005: 12) note that this continues to be a dominant feature of the transnational system: "The growing influence of corporate power over the state should be seen in the context of globalization and as going hand-in-hand with the emergence of the transnational corporation as the dominant business entity."[14]

While the wielding of power and invasive influences are recognized, however, the motivations, according to Galbraith, are not necessarily Machiavellian. That is to say, the attempt by the modern corporation to secure the requisite response from domestic and foreign governments, forms part of the wider process of mitigating the uncertainties that surround and impinge upon accumulation and production and the affirmative and protective goals of strategic decision-makers (cf. Chandler, 1977, 1990; Porter, 1990; Dunning, 1997). Thus, although the multinational firm greatly impairs the sovereignty of national governments, it "is not because of its transnational character; it is because the impairment of sovereignty – the accommodation of the state to the purposes and needs of the corporate technostructure – is the very essence of the operations of the planning system" (Galbraith, 1973a: 188).[15] Indeed much of the political discussion on the salience of the multinational misapprehends the nature of the planning process. For instance:

> The political case against the multinational firm regularly emphasizes that its wage and price policies are determined in its home country. In consequence workers and consumers are subject to a foreign authority to which they have no access and over which they have no influence. This ... also misapprehends the reality. The multinational firm enters the country to become part of the wage- and price-making process of that country – to protect itself from the wage advantage of domestic producers or to be part of the price equilibrium that ensures it against disastrous price competition. (Galbraith, 1973a: 189)

Similarly the emergence and evolution of the institutions that govern international trade should be viewed as an attempt to accommodate the particular uncertainties of international trade (cf. Scaperlanda, 1992, 1993):

> Since World War II, there has been a marked retreat from what was once called economic nationalism. The visible manifestation has been the General Agreement on Tariffs and Trade (GATT), the European Common Market (EEC), the European Free Trade Area (EFTA), the several efforts between trading countries to reduce tariffs, restrict the use of quotas and, hopefully, forestall competitive currency depreciation. These developments have been attributed to the increasing economic enlightenment of the industrially advanced countries. In fact a matter that will no longer have any large element of surprise – they reflect the needs of the planning systems of the participating countries. (Galbraith, 1973a: 189–90)

Hence the desire of the modern corporation to receive tariffs, diminish quotas, mitigate extreme currency fluctuations, engage in technology transfer, and its manifestation in transnational political and economic institutions can all be viewed as part of the wider process of coordinating production and trade over national boundaries under conditions of uncertainty.

The theory of the multinational enterprise

It should now be clear that Galbraith advanced a theory of the multinational firm that was embedded in the view of the firm developed in *The New Industrial State*. Galbraith's framework extends and facilitates the explicit recognition of the importance and salience of uncertainty within the theory of the multinational firm. Galbraith's analysis of the multinational firm anticipated the great surge in trade, not between complementary nations, not between rich and poor countries, but amongst the advanced trading centers. Galbraith challenged old trade theory long before New Trade Theory emerged. Traditional theoretical explanations of the patterns of international trade focus on the comparative advantage of countries with very different characteristics, such as a poor country exporting agricultural goods to a rich country in exchange for industrial products.[16] However, as Galbraith was keen to point out, increasingly with development, much international trade occurs between broadly similar affluent societies – Sweden exports Volvo cars to Germany while Germany exports BMW cars to Sweden.

Galbraith's analysis also moves beyond New Trade Theory. New Trade Theory, stemming from Paul Krugman (1979), argues first that production which favors economies of scale, drives production, expansion, and internationalization, and second, that consumers prefer a range of choices, which drives diversity. Galbraith's analysis of the large firms is consistent with the first of these propositions. But he reverses the second of these propositions. The dynamics of the modern firm that drive production, expansion, and internationalization also underscore the need to manage the response of the consumer, to promote the global brand image.

What is more, Galbraith's approach provides an original contribution to the study of the strategies and planning routines used by the multinational firm to cope with uncertainty. Strategy is an inevitable consequence of an uncertain environment and the uncertainties and complexities that global markets generate. Market structures may indeed reflect the responses of strategic decision-makers to an uncertain environment, given that size (both absolute and relative) helps to reduce the impact of uncertainty on the firm (see Galbraith, 1967a). And the necessity of planning and acquiring control of strategic cost factors across different countries is essential in mitigating major uncertainties.

Galbraith's contribution to the theory of the firm directs analysis to the nature of control, that is, the power and ability to make strategic decisions and to take a firm in a direction that may or may not be in the interests of others (Galbraith, 1967a; Hymer, 1970, 1976). This vision anticipates recent theoretical contributions that have tried to identify the essence of the modern corporation. Cowling and Sugden (1998a, 1998b) have sought to argue that the essence of the firm is not about economizing a set of transactions – rather it is about strategic decision-making. Cowling and Sugden (1998a: 67) propose a definition of the firm that highlights its essence as "a means of co-ordinating production from one centre of strategic decision making."[17] This approach also provides for a definition of the essence of the multinational enterprise "when this co-ordination takes a firm across national boundaries" (Cowling and Sugden, 1987a: 12; see also Cowling and Sugden, 1987b, 1998b). Cowling and Sugden (1998a: 64) argue that: "the power to make strategic decisions can be equated with the power to control a firm, where control implies the ability to determine broad corporate objectives. Put another way, it may be argued that the power to make strategic decisions is the power to plan the overall direction of production in the firm. This includes the power broadly to determine a firm's geographical location, its relationship with rivals, with governments and its labor force." This links well with Galbraith's focus on the role of firm power set out over the course of this book.[18]

In the Galbraithian approach, "planning" or "strategy" refers to the process by which those at the pinnacle of a decision-making process attempt to mould the future across national boundaries while mitigating its uncertain impact, that is, by attempting to control for as many factors as possible that impinge on the processes of accumulation and production. Strategy from this perspective refers to the process by which the technostructure attempts to shape an uncertain future. The practice of strategy is the practice of making crucial decisions and dealing with uncertainty. The strategic decision to move into foreign markets and production, for example, is a crucial decision, which cannot be unmade without cost (cf. Rugman and Verbeke, 2002).[19]

Such a perspective is consistent with Cowling and Sudgen's (1998a: 67) suggestion that their "analysis of strategic decision-making in modern corporations is to some extent focusing … on the proactive shaping of the environment within and without these firms." Moreover it links well with the evolving resource based view of the transnational firm, that descends from Penrose (1956, 1959; see also Kay, 1997, 2000; Pitelis, 2000, 2004, 2007), which describes how the access to routines and capabilities enables a flexible response to an uncertain future. Focusing on uncertainty provides a clearer understanding of the need to access routines and capabilities as well as clarifying the informational foundations of the transaction cost approach (Dunn, 1999, 2000a, 2000b, 2008a).

Such theoretical considerations need to be further explored. The salience of Galbraith's approach is that the boundaries of the firm, or multinational firm, should revolve around the delineation of its power. It should incorporate all market and non-market transactions coordinated from one center of strategic decision-making; for example subcontracting relationships could be viewed as falling within the scope of a single firm depending upon the dependency and contractual conditions binding organizations together.[20] Intra-firm transactions may be conceived as either being composed of market or non-market transactions given that production is coordinated from one center of strategic decision-making. On this view inter-firm transactions represent market transactions although they are different in character to intra-firm market transactions.[21] Inter-firm (market) transactions take place between two centers of strategic decision-makers. Intra-firm (market) transactions originate from one centre of strategic decision-making.[22]

The salience of such an approach is that by narrowly focusing on the type of transaction, market or non-market, one may fail to appreciate fully the scope of a firm's production and the subsequent extent of concentration and influence of the multinational enterprise (Cowling and Sugden, 1998b; Cowling and Tomlinson, 2005; cf. Dugger, 1985b; Grant, 1997; Gatignon and Anderson, 1988). Domestic and overseas outsourcing which appears to reduce the scope and influence of the firm are more likely to be consolidating the power of strategic decision-makers.[23] The subcontracting relationships of the large brand managing firm reflect its global power and reach. As Klein (1999: 24) points out: "Tommy Hilfiger, meanwhile, is less in the business of manufacturing clothes than he is in the business of signing his name. The company is run entirely through licensing agreements, with Hilfiger commissioning all its products from a group of other companies: Jockey International makes Hilfiger underwear, Pepe Jeans London makes Hilfiger jeans, Oxford Industries make Tommy shirts, the Stride Rite Corporation makes its footwear. What does Tommy Hilfiger manufacture? Nothing at all." Thus there may be situations whereby, although the formal relations of the market appear to be in place, the strategic and near exclusive nature of the subcontracting relationships mean that specific relationships and transactions should instead be viewed as coming under the ambit and strategic influence of the multinational firm (see Sugden, 1996; Cowling and Sugden, 1998b).

According to Hipple (1990), 99.4 percent of US trade involves transnational corporations, with nearly 40 percent of US imports being intra-firm, defined in terms of ownership links, e.g. overseas subsidiaries. Similarly Dicken (2003: 53) reports that multinationals account for approximately two-thirds of the worlds exports, with around one-third of trade being interfirm.[24] However, when subcontracting, agency and franchise agreements are taken into account this control and dominance is amplified (Cowling and Tomlinson, 2005). Similarly novel studies such as Cowling, Yusof, and Vernon (2000) highlight the importance of correctly adjusting for import competition. Further studies that aim to ascertain the global reach of the modern corporation would seek to assess the global reach of the technostructure and its direct and indirect influence on other firms and organizations.

A Galbraithian approach to the multinational firm therefore shifts the analytical focus *away* from an *excessive concern for property rights*, to one where power and distributional considerations are central. As Branston, Cowling, and Sugden (2006: 192) point out: "The ... significance of this alternative perspective on the firm is that, unlike mainstream economic theory, it is not associated with a market-centred analysis of impact and policy. Rather, it leads to an understanding of impact based on strategic choice – i.e. governance – and it makes governance the centrepiece of policy."

Galbraith's analysis suggests, moreover, that the modern firm or multinational corporation should not be viewed as an optimal outcome from a collective choice process as typified in the mainstream approach. Strategic decision-makers such as the technostructure may make decisions to benefit themselves, for example yielding distributional gains, at the expense of others, reflecting their exercise of power (cf. Peoples and Sugden, 2000; Coffey and Tomlinson, 2006).[25] A key contribution of Galbraith's, as well as Cowling and Sugden's approach, therefore, is that capitalist firms should not necessarily be conceived as pursuing Pareto efficient decisions.[26]

Cowling and Tomlinson (2000), for example, argue that the process of Globalization pursued by the large firms in the Japanese planning system has been at the expense of small firms in the market system. They note that: "the pursuit of global, corporate interests by Japan's large transnationals has been sub-optimal for Japan's domestic economy. For instance, the increase in outward [Foreign Direct Investment] flows may not only divert new investment from Japan's industrial regions, but also enhances the ability of Japan's large transnationals to outsource their production globally. This has led to a reduction in the demand for intermediate goods supplied by Japan's small business sectors and, in particular, 'the keiretsu' firms who have become 'isolated' due to the increasing trend towards overseas production" (Cowling and Tomlinson, 2000: F359). Such assessments support Galbraith's contention that the strategic decisions of transnational corporations need not operate in the wider public interest (cf. Cowling and Sugden, 1999; Cowling *et al.*, 2005; Branston, Cowling, and Sugden, 2006). It is also why he directs our attention to improving corporate governance and regulation and monitoring the activities of large transnational firms.[27]

Accordingly it would be more appropriate to view competition as a *process* that generates technical and productive advance, produces large oligopolistic firms, and a use and distribution of resources that is skewed toward the interests of those at the apex of its decision-making processes.[28] This has a number of implications. From this perspective power and strategy are always salient analytical categories. Whereas Williamson and Ouchi (1983) separate the power and efficiency approaches, recognizing the salience of power only when efficiency is sacrificed, for Galbraith power is central. From a Galbraithian perspective power and strategy is always fundamental to their approach *even when* efficiency considerations prevail (cf. Cowling and Sugden, 1998a, 1998b).[29] Thus there is a sense in which Galbraith's approach can be viewed as encompassing the salient insights that can be gleaned from the transaction cost perspective into a broader perspective. This clearly calls for innovative empirical studies of the power and reach of firms and how this power is marshaled. In this regard I offer some suggestions, drawn from the pharmaceutical and food industries, for further research in the Galbraithian tradition.

How power is used: the pharmaceutical industry

Galbraith's perspective on the modern firm offers the prospect of a potentially fruitful analysis of the pharmaceutical industry.[30] The pharmaceutical industry is characterized by large multinational firms, such as Pfizer, Roche, Novartis, Sanofi-aventis, and Johnson & Johnson (see table 7). These firms have vast technostructures that undertake huge asset-specific investments in drug development over long periods of time, despite considerable uncertainty about future returns. What is more such investment is undertaken with considerable uncertainty about the future evolution of health policy in different countries and different models of clinical and professional governance.

The fully capitalized cost to develop a new drug can be as high as $897 million, according to the Tufts Center for the Study of Drug Development (DiMasi, Hansen, and Grabowski, 2003). On some calculations it can take up to fourteen years from the point of discovery to bring a drug to market. This fourteen-year period consists of a six-year pre-clinical phase (to assess whether the drug is safe enough to test on humans), a six-year clinical phase of human trials, and a two-year review and approval phase. This process involves a great deal of uncertainty and negotiation with national systems of regulation. According to the Pharmaceutical Research and Manufacturers of America, which may somewhat overstate the case, only five of every 5,000 drugs reach the stage of clinical trials. Of these only 21.5 percent are eventually approved (Tufts Center for the Study of Drug Development, 2002).

Given the high cost of modern drug production, it is natural that the pharmaceutical technostructure would seek to influence consumer response and set prices strategically in a way that allows them to recover their costs across different countries (cf. Goozner, 2004). Drug firms would like to ensure that what they produce (at great cost) is ultimately purchased. Thus it is no surprise that promotional spending is a large share of the industry's total spending, exceeding

Table 7. ***"Big Pharma"***

Corporation[a]	Home economy	Assets		Sales		Employment	
		Foreign	Total	Foreign	Total	Foreign	Total
Sanofi-aventis	France	55,342[b]	102,414	20,266[b]	35,595	71,325	100,289
Pfizer Inc.	USA	53,765	114,837	22,549	48,371	59,818[c]	98,000
Roche Group	Switzerland	52,178	60,980	33,155	33,531	41,554[b]	74,372
Novartis	Switzerland	42,922	68,008	35,630	36,031	52,830[b]	100,735
Johnson & Johnson	USA	32,130	70,556	23,549	53,324	71,756[d]	122,200
Bayer AG	Germany	26,100	73,609	30,650	36,327	48,200[b]	106,000
GlaxoSmithKline	UK	20,194[b]	50,163	28,620[b]	42,732	56,937[b]	102,695

Notes: All figures millions of dollars and number of employees.

[a] All data are based on the companies' annual reports unless otherwise stated. Data on affiliates are based on Dun and Bradstreet's Who owns Whom database.

[b] Data are for activities outside Europe.

[c] Foreign employment data are calculated by applying the share of foreign employment in total employment of the previous year to total employment of 2006.

[d] Foreign employment data are calculated by applying the average of the shares of foreign employment in total employment of all companies in the same industry (omitting the extremes) to total employment.

Source: UNCTAD (2008). UNCTAD/Erasmus University database.

R&D costs by a factor of two or more. In 2002 R&D accounted for "14 percent of total revenue in thirteen of the largest research based pharmaceutical companies ... while selling and general administration absorbed close to 33 percent" (Reinhardt, 2004: 108). Moreover, direct to consumer advertising (DTCA) of pharmaceuticals has become an important element of this strategy, growing from nothing in late 1997, when the US Food and Drug Administration (FDA) eased regulatory restrictions, to US$2.5 billion in 2000 (IMS Health, 2001). Such ramifications have been little explored by the mainstream economics profession.

As we shall explore in more detail in the next chapter, in the conventional wisdom, advertising is usually seen as the provision of information to the consumer, rather than as an attempt to alter consumer preferences. Preferences and prices are taken as exogenous, and consumers and their advocates are presumed or assumed to be able to evaluate the veracity of sellers' claims. Proponents of pharmaceutical advertising argue that it informs and empowers patients, reduces under-diagnosis and under-treatment of disease, de-stigmatizes disease and encourages compliance with regimens. In contrast future research on the pharmaceutical industry in the Galbraithian tradition would not accept the traditional assumption of consumer sovereignty. Recognizing that advertising may have other objectives than the provision of information, we would acknowledge aspects of what Galbraith (1967a) labels the revised sequence: the situation in which consumers and the medical profession are manipulated to meet firm needs, rather than the other way around. The health services research community has also recognized this possibility. They have highlighted the social and medical consequences of efforts by the pharmaceutical industry to manipulate research, as well as influence consumers and providers (see Angell, 2004; Avorn, 2004; Goozner, 2004; Greider, 2003; Abramson, 2004; Moynihan and Cassells, 2005; Petersen, 2008).

For a long time patient advocacy groups, as well as many in the medical profession, have expressed anxiety regarding the fact that drug companies exert undue influence on doctors through a variety of gifts, kick backs, free lunches, and all-expenses-paid conferences at exotic locations. Nevertheless the extent of such payments has been hard to quantify. Some states in the USA, such as Minnesota, however, have passed legislation requiring drug makers to disclose payments to doctors. The Minnesota records, which began in 1997, highlight the extent of the financial ties between pharmaceutical companies and the doctors who prescribe and recommend their products. Harris and Roberts (2007) report that between 1997 and 2005, drug makers paid more than 5,500 doctors, nurses, and other healthcare workers in the state at least $57 million. Another $40 million went to clinics, research centers, and other organizations. More than 20 percent of the state's licensed doctors received money. The median payment per consultant was $1,000, and more than one hundred people received more than $100,000.

This is perhaps only the tip of the iceberg. Marcia Angell (2009), the former editor of the prestigious *New England Journal of Medicine*, estimates "from the annual reports of the top nine US drug companies that it comes to tens of billions of dollars a year." This money is clearly designed to influence the way drugs are prescribed, and medicine is practiced. The "thought leaders" or "key opinion leaders," who write textbooks, practice guidelines, research papers, sit on national advisory panels, and so on, are targeted for "sponsorship", allowing the drug industry to gain influence over medical practice and prescribing, by seeking, for example, to make drugs appear more effective or safer than they actually are. The consequence is that "the pharmaceutical industry has gained enormous control over how doctors evaluate and use its own products. Its extensive ties to physicians, particularly senior faculty at prestigious medical schools, affect the results of research, the way medicine is practiced, and even the definition of what constitutes a disease" (Angell, 2009).

Moynihan (2003a) and Moynihan and Cassells (2005), for example, document industry efforts to create new diseases by encouraging and lobbying for the systematic definition and classification of new medical disorders (see also Petersen, 2008; Lane, 2007). The industry uses a variety of marketing strategies to create wants for ostensibly healthy people by attempting to medicalize ordinary life – a problem that is exacerbated in countries, such as the USA, which permit DTCA. Moynihan *et al.* (2002: 886) highlight the problem of "disease mongering widening the boundaries of treatable illness in order to expand markets for those who sell and deliver treatments." Similarly the many instances of corrupting flows of money between the medical profession and the pharmaceutical industry have been recognized as a threat to the doctor-patient relationship (Angell, 2004, 2009; Moynihan, 2003b; Moynihan and Cassells,

2005; Krugman, 2005c; Harris and Carey, 2008; Harris, 2008; Saul, 2008; Carey, 2008; Harris and Roberts, 2007). Such concerns with the adverse impacts of the revised sequence may illuminate why New Zealand, the only country other than the USA to allow DTCA of drugs, appears to be on the verge in banning it. Pleas for more lenient regulation of pharmaceutical marketing, for example, should not therefore be understood merely as consumer-driven demand for more information.

Future research in the Galbraithian tradition would also identify the symbiosis and contractual nexus of various technostructures and how they can affect the content of medical advertising in ways that conflict with the wider public interest (cf. Angell, 2004; Greider, 2003; Goozner, 2004; Avorn, 2004; Abramson, 2004; Lane, 2007; Petersen, 2008). The tobacco industry, for example, has used its leverage with the chemical and pharmaceutical industries to influence the marketing of anti-smoking drugs. Internal documents from tobacco companies show that from the mid 1980s to the early 1990s they successfully lobbied drug companies to drop or modify their marketing of nicotine replacement therapies (Shamasunder and Bero, 2002). The tobacco industry also used its clout as a buyer of agricultural chemicals from corporations that also produce pharmaceutical products to induce them to modify their anti-smoking messages in ways that undermines public health objectives in specific countries.

Such considerations suggest the need to monitor and regulate some types of advertising and marketing. Once policy makers understand the nature and extent of an industry's influence over the public, that knowledge can be marshaled to serve the development of broader social aims. Policy makers should question whether it is efficient from society's point of view for the pharmaceutical industry to allocate such substantial sums to marketing and R&D and whether alternative institutional and international arrangements should be encouraged (for a discussion of such matters, see Reinhardt, 2004). There is a need to wean off the medical schools and the medical profession from drug industry money and to establish a more robust regulatory response to the problem of medical conflict of interests. For example, Angell (2009) argues that:

> Members of medical school faculties who conduct clinical trials should not accept any payments from drug companies except research support, and

that support should have no strings attached, including control by drug companies over the design, interpretation, and publication of research results. Medical schools and teaching hospitals should rigorously enforce that rule, and should not enter into deals with companies whose products members of their faculty are studying. Finally, there is seldom a legitimate reason for physicians to accept gifts from drug companies, even small ones, and they should pay for their own meetings and continuing education.

Finally, future research would also explore how multinational firms in pursuing protective and affirmative goals use its power internationally to maintain income and prestige. For example, when the New Zealand government sought to take a more strategic approach to purchasing pharmaceuticals, the industry fought a bitter campaign and ultimately withdrew is regional R&D in retaliation. The New Zealand government sought to establish a sole supplier to the whole of the country for a specific class of drugs. It ran a competitive tendering exercise across the drug companies to the exclusive right to supply New Zealand for certain classes of drugs, for example statins. This approach was successful in driving prices down, but drew adverse reaction from the pharmaceutical industry, which threatened and then initiated the withdrawal of regional R&D, with the associated loss of social and intellectual capital that such actions entailed.

The case of agriculture

Galbraith's analysis of the large multinational firm is also instructive in helping to analyze the global food industry. The twentieth century witnessed a technological revolution in the global food supply chain in an effort to manage and mitigate the uncertainties that surround both food production and consumption. There were unprecedented changes in how food is produced, distributed, consumed, and controlled – and this was characterized by a politically aided process of consolidation and concentration.[31] At the turn of the twentieth century, giant machinery "began to replace human labor and 'Fordist' thinking was applied to both plan and animal production. Large-scale experimentation was expended on trying to reduce nature's unpredictability. Agrichemicals replaced the hoe; feedlots replaced grazing; monoculture replaced smallholdings" (Lang and Heasman, 2004: 139).

Table 8. ***World's top seven agrochemical transnational companies, 2001***

Rank	Company	Ag. chem. sales, 2001 ($m)
1	Syngenta	5,385
2	Sanofi-Aventis	3,842
3	Monsanto	3,755
4	BASF	3,105
5	Dow	2,612
6	Bayer	2,418
7	DuPont	1,917

Source: Agrow (2002)

Agriculture has been radically transformed and industrialized by large agrochemical and biotechnology firms, dominated by large technostructures, heavily investing in research and development. The agrochemical industry, which controls the supply of seeds, fertilizers, and pesticides, for example, has become extremely concentrated. As Lang and Clutterbuck (1991) point out, in the late 1980s, the top twenty firms worldwide accounted for around 90 percent of sales. By the late 1990s, the number of firms responsible for this level of sales had halved (Lang, 2004). At the turn of the millennium, seven were responsible for the same level (see table 8). In 2002 biotechnology research was €11.4 billion in the USA, and €5 billion in Europe (Lang and Heasman, 2004: 25). This research is heavily concentrated in the advanced industrial countries, with eight countries representing 83 percent of the total funds spent on biotechnology, and, consistent with Galbraith's thesis of advanced development, a significant proportion of this research is underwritten by governments. Indeed a global science base has emerged to further the goals of increasing output, ranging from universities, colleges of agriculture, extension services, as well as a whole panoply of ancillary support functions (Lang and Heasman, 2004: 19).

The large corporations undertaking such investments have ushered in a series of major revolutions in the growing of food, such as the mass use of agrochemicals, hybrid plant breeding, and genetic modification. The rearing of animals has similarly been subject to a major revolution, with the introduction of factory farming, intensive livestock rearing, and the prophylactic use of pharmaceuticals to increase weight gain.[32] Food processing has also been subject to enormous technological advance, with the increased use of extrusion technology, fermentation, as well as the wholesale use of cosmetic additives to disguise products and yield consistency (Lang, 2004). This transformation has delivered tremendous productive advance, resulting in a relative abundance of cheap, mass-produced food. Again, consistent with Galbraith's thesis, it should be no surprise that this has also given rise to a range of contemporary concerns – which the theoretical framework of *The New Industrial State* and *Economics and the Public Purpose* helps explain, passing the "text of anxiety" (see chapter 4).

The obsession of the global food industry in producing ever-higher yields and ever-larger quantities, has given rise to a variety of environmental and public health costs and concerns. The environmental impact of the rapid industrialization of the global food production chain, for example, has been significant, with the collapse of fish stocks, soil erosion, deforestation, and falling water tables in areas of key agricultural production. There has been increased public concern regarding the impact of pesticide residues, antibiotics and veterinary drugs, food pathogens, environmental toxins, such as lead and mercury, and organic pollutants, such as dioxins, on public health.[33] Nutrigenomics, which aims to unlock the secrets of genes, diet, and lifestyles, is also viewed by some public health specialists, as targeting rich consumers and the worried well, by preying on fears and desires. And there has been further concern over the impact of genetically modified crops and foodstuffs on the food chain. All these concerns call for decisive global regulatory action.[34]

At the same time as agriculture has become increasingly technologically sophisticated, we have also seen the emergence of large firms dominating the global food supply chain (see table 9). Galbraith was aware of such trends. As he pointed out in *American Capitalism*:

> Those from whom the farmer buys and those to whom he sells do, characteristically, have market power. The handful of manufacturers of farm machinery, of accessible fertilizer manufacturers or mixers, of petroleum supplies, of insurance companies all exercise measurable control over the prices at which they sell. The farmer's market for his products – the

Table 9. ***World's top food producers in FT Global 500, 2008***

Sector rank	Global rank	Company	Country	Market value ($m)	Turnover ($m)
1	14	Nestlé	Switzerland	197,215.3	108,313.0
2	60	Unilever	Netherlands/ UK	101,642.1	63,516.8
3	166	Kraft-Foods	USA	47,548.1	37,241.0
4	172	Danone	France	46,027.4	20,192.9
5	341	Archer-Daniels-Midland	USA	26,489.6	44,018.0
6	397	Cadbury-Schweppes	UK	23,228.5	15,996.2
7	462	Kellogg's	USA	20,443.4	11,776.0
8	474	General-Mills	USA	20,062.0	12,442.0
9	498	Wilmar-International	Singapore	19,368.2	16,466.2

Source: FT500 (*Financial Times*, 2008)

meat packing industry, the tobacco companies, the canneries, the fluid-milk distributors – is typically, although not universally, divided between a relatively small number of large companies. There is no more vigorously debated question in economics than that of the measure of jurisdiction that such companies exercise over their buying prices. (Galbraith, 1952a: 159)

It would therefore be no surprise to Galbraith that, for example, in the USA, the market share of the top twenty food manufacturers has doubled since 1967 (Connor, 2003).

Lyson and Raymer (2000) identify the power and control exhibited by the ten largest food and beverage corporations which control over half of the food sales in the United States. Such rise in concentration and power is, however, increasingly masked by traditional analyses (Cowling and Sugden, 1998a, 1998b; Cowling and Tomlinson, 2005; Dunn, 2008a, 2009). As Heffernan, Hendrickson, and Gronski (1999) highlight, conventional measures of concentration do not reveal the extent of vertical integration in the food system in the USA, nor highlight the complex web of global interactions among the top food firms. As noted above, in the conventional wisdom the focus of economic power is usually the individual firm and its market share. The changing nature of the global food system, however, is driving a more complex set of hierarchical power relations between firms and across producers.[35] As Galbraith argued the power of firms can also be exercised through the various relationships in which a firm is involved in, even if it does not hold a majority share. Although acquisition continues to be the dominant strategy for acquiring control of another firm, mergers, joint ventures, partnerships, contracts, and less formalized relationships, such as agreements and side agreements, are also used in the modern food industry to consolidate control and market power (Heffernan, Hendrickson, and Gronski, 1999).

The result is that the global food production system is dominated by large food conglomerates (see table 9). The food supply chain is incredibly complex and technologically sophisticated, starting with involvement in biotechnology, extending through production, and ending with highly processed, heavily marketed, global food brands.[36] Nestlé, for example, produces a range of diverse products, such as soluble, roast, and ground coffee, water and other beverages, dairy products, breakfast cereals, infant food, chocolate and confectionary, food services, pet care, food flavors, and pharmaceutical products, among others. Similarly over the last forty years, McDonald's has emerged as a major global employer and buyer of people, potatoes, beef, chicken, and real estate, with a heavy investment in food science and consumer persuasion. As Eric Schlosser (2002: 4) highlights in *Fast Food Nation*:

> The McDonald's Corporation has become a powerful symbol of America's service economy, which is now responsible for 90 percent of the country's new jobs. In 1968, McDonald's operated about one thousand restaurants. Today it has about twenty-eight thousand restaurants worldwide and opens almost two thousand new ones each year. An estimated one out of every eight workers in the United States has at some point been employed by McDonald's. The company annually hires about one million people, more than any other American organization, public or private. McDonald's is the nation's largest purchaser of beef, pork, and potatoes – and the second largest purchaser of chicken. The McDonald's Corporation is the largest owner of retail property in the world. Indeed, the company earns the majority of its profits not from selling food but from collecting rent. McDonald's spends more money on advertising and marketing than any other brand.

As a result it has replaced Coca-Cola as the world's most famous brand. McDonald's operates more playgrounds than any other private entity in the United States. It is one of the nation's largest distributors of toys. A survey of American schoolchildren found that 96 percent could identify Ronald McDonald. The only fictional character with a higher degree of recognition was Santa Claus.

Over the last twenty years, the large food firms have sought to further consolidate their brands and influence, increasing their market power.[37] This "consolidation of brands" more prosaically alludes to the heavy investment in the persuasion and management of the consumer. Given the technologically sophisticated nature of modern food production, it should be no surprise that the large firms that control and dominate it should seek to manage the responses of the consumer.

To protect their large investments and market dominance, the large food retailers, processors, and agrichemical firms all undertake huge investments in advertising and brand development, targeting "segmented" consumers, and drawing upon a sophisticated array of marketing techniques. The food industry's annual advertising budget, for example, is $40 billion, which is higher than the GDP of 70 percent of the world's nations (Lang and Heasman, 2004: 206). The aim of such advertising and marketing budgets, which ranges from television advertisements aimed at various market segments, including children, to other marketing ploys such as "super size" portions and distributing toys to children, is increased consumption. The global brands, which are marketed by such advertising, however, tend to be excessively refined – high in either salt, sugar, or saturated fats, or all three combined (see table 10).

Nevertheless, the food industry has been slow to respond to the fact that the consumption of its products is driving a range of major public health epidemics.[38] It should be no surprise, therefore, that the increasing global dominance of Coca-Cola, McDonalds, Pizza Hut, KFC, Pepsi and the other large food processing and producing corporations, is coinciding with a range of public health epidemics caused by an excessive consumption of salt, sugar and fat and an under-consumption of fruit and vegetables, that is, the complete opposite of what is recommended as in the public interest by public health officials.[39] It is no surprise that the excessive consumption of energy-dense, high-fat,

Table 10. *Food and beverage companies in the top 100 global brands, 2008*

2008 Rank	Brand	2008 Brand value ($m)	Country of ownership
1	Coca-Cola	66,667	USA
8	McDonald's	31,049	USA
26	Pepsi	13,249	USA
28	Nescafé	13,055	Switzerland
33	Budweiser	11,438	USA
39	Kellogg's	9,710	USA
56	Heinz	6,646	USA
61	Wrigley's	6,105	USA
63	Nestlé	5,592	Switzerland
64	KFC	5,582	USA
66	Danone	5,408	France
81	Pizza Hut	4,097	USA
83	Moët & Chandon	3,951	France
85	Starbucks	3,879	USA
89	Smirnoff	3,590	UK
95	Hennessy	3,513	France

Source: BusinessWeek (2008)

high-salt foods, as well sugary and alcoholic beverages, is driving the contemporary health problems of obesity, alcohol abuse, high blood pressure, and the resultant rise in heart disease, liver disease, stroke, and diabetes.[40] The social costs of this excess consumption, which are significant, are not borne by the food producers who induce it. The US Center for Disease Control, for example, estimates that the cost of obesity in the USA is around $117 billion (CDC, 2002). It is no surprise that we are witnessing an epidemic with childhood obesity given that: "in industrialized countries, food advertising accounts for around half of all advertising broadcast during children's TV viewing times. Three-quarters of such food advertisements promote high-calorie, low-nutrient foods" (Lang and Heasman, 2004: 206).

From a Galbraithian perspective it is unsurprising that the resultant information flow from large firms is uneven, that labeling is arbitrary, or that marketing, advertising, and sponsorship are designed to influence perceptions and mitigate the threat of public challenge. The large transnational firm has a strong financial incentive to manage both the consumer and the flow of information, protecting its investments and pursuing its own objectives, even if it diverges from the wider public interest. But the large firm will not stop there. Instead it will seek to manipulate the public interest, so it aligns with its own interest.

It is therefore to be expected that the food industry will seek to lobby governments and regulators to protect their interests – what contemporary economists refer to somewhat opaquely as "regulatory capture."[41] Meat and diary producers in the USA, for example, have extensively lobbied congress to protect its own interests and have succeeded in diluting the Surgeon General's advice to eat less meat and dairy products (Lang and Heasman, 2004: 114). Similarly the food industry has successfully sought to fight off the threat of tobacco style litigation through the enactment of the 2004 Personal Responsibility in Food Consumption Act, which places responsibility for overeating and obesity firmly with the individual.[42] Paul Krugman (2005a) highlights how the food industry, which promotes excess consumption, and is a key player in the obesity epidemic, is using more sophisticated strategies to mold public opinion and shape regulatory responses:

> Public health activists were successful in taking on smoking in part because at the time corporations didn't know how to play the public opinion game. By today's standards, the political ineptitude of Big Tobacco was awe-inspiring. In a famous 1971 interview on "Face the Nation," the chairman of the board of Philip Morris, confronted with evidence that smoking by mothers leads to low birth weight, replied, "Some women would prefer having smaller babies." Today's food industry would never make that kind of mistake. In public, the industry's companies proclaim themselves good guys, committed to healthier eating. Meanwhile, they outsource the campaigns against medical researchers and the dissemination of crude anti-obesity propaganda to industry-financed advocacy groups like the Center for Consumer Freedom. (Krugman, 2005a)

The resources available to organizations representing consumer interests against the barrage of firm advertising and influence is, however, limited. It is a prime example of social imbalance. As Lang (2004: 12–13) highlights: "The top 20 food brands in the UK spend over £105 million a year on marketing … While the UK Government spends around £5 million on healthy eating advice, Coca-Cola alone spends £27 million in the UK yearly. It spends $1.4 billion on advertising worldwide, as does McDonald's." What is more although public health programmes attempt to alert consumers to the health consequences of their consumption habits, receptiveness to such warnings tends to be contingent upon a mix of education and income (Fine, 2002).

Nevertheless, after a period in which states in developed countries actively promoted the restructuring of supply chains in the name of efficiency and output maximization, adverse public reaction to these changes in the West is now forcing governments to respond differently, driving better food labeling and reductions in fat, salt, and sugar levels in many products. There are calls for new democratically accountable global organizations to understand better and monitor the link between food safety, environment, food security, nutrition, and biotechnology. There is a need for the more rigorous enactment and enforcement of global standards and more comprehensive independent research, monitoring, and assessment. And there is recognition of the need to protect children from junk food advertising, and to follow the lead of both Sweden and Norway, who have banned food TV advertisements aimed at children under twelve.[43]

Future research in the Galbraithian tradition will acknowledge the fact that the model of food production and agriculture that is associated with the emergence of the large agribusiness and food processors has been successful in raising output. But it will also acknowledge and analyze the underlying causes of major public anxieties: "While successfully raising the calorific value of the world food supply, it has failed to address the issue of quality, and as a result, there is now a world wide legacy of externalized health costs" (Lang and Heasman, 2004: 47). And it will also explore the range of regulatory responses that will increase the alignment with the public interest.

The transnational system

Galbraith advanced a view of the multinational corporation which was a logical extension of the theoretical framework detailed in *The New Industrial State*. Otherwise, as Galbraith (1973a: 182) recognized, "all planning would have to stop at the water's edge. Firms might have the requisite domestic power. When they came to do business abroad, they would again be faced with all the uncertainties associated with the market system. To these would be added the extra uncertainties uniquely associated with international trade." In pursuit of protective and affirmative advantage the firm seeks to mitigate the various uncertainties that threaten production and planning, including those associated with international trade.[44]

Galbraith developed an approach to the multinational firm that linked technology, asset-specific capital, money contracts, power, and planning to the peculiar problems of uncertainty that beset international trade. Galbraith's discussion of the multinational firm emphasized the strategic coordinating role of managers, interest groups and other specialists within the firm, that is, the technostructure, and their associated need to plan in an uncertain environment. It is a view that has lasting theoretical and empirical significance.

Galbraith's view of the multinational corporation predates and anticipates aspects of the subsequent internalization arguments of Williamson (1975), Buckley and Casson (1976), and Hennart (1982).[45] Saliently, Galbraith (1973a: 184–5) quotes with approval Hymer's (1970: 441) suggestion that the "Multinational corporations are a substitute for the market as a method of organizing international exchange" noting that they are "islands of conscious power in an ocean of unconscious co-operation." However, and perhaps more importantly, Galbraith is aware that Hymer is paraphrasing D. H. Robertson's (1923: 85) earlier observation and argues saliently that "Since it was made, the islands, it could be said, have become continents" (Galbraith, 1973a: 185; cf. Coase, 1937; Richardson, 1972).

The approach to the multinational firm outlined by Galbraith, however, should not be thought of as a variant of the transaction-cost type of story, such that the firm replaces the market on account of its capacity to minimize the uncertainties and thus the transaction costs that engulf markets. Rather, Galbraith's argument is the reverse, offering a view of the multinational enterprise which incorporates both power and efficiency considerations within an historical and evolutionary conception of economic processes. It represents an original attempt to integrate the study of uncertainty into the theory of the firm. And it provides a basis for further developing and integrating some of the more recent theoretical developments in the transaction cost, monopoly, and resource-based approaches in a more general view of the multinational firm, which acknowledges the role of power and efficiency considerations in impacting on the activities and decision-making structures of the modern corporation.

The view of the transnational corporation developed by Galbraith exists in historical time and presents the firm as an enduring institutional response to the problems of production, accumulation and uncertainty. This also represents a salient contribution not least because transnational theorists of the firm typically do not contemplate the control of markets as a strategic response to the threat of uncertainty. Galbraith also presents us with a rich taxonomy that captures many of the salient strategies pursued by transnational firms to cope with uncertainty – and in doing so anticipates and explains many contemporary concerns that have been raised in the globalization debate. Galbraith offers an original perspective on such matters that differs markedly from the dominant neo-conservative and radical views. That he made such a contribution should no longer be questioned. And that there is a clear need for renewed attention to Galbraith's contribution to the theory of firm and the multinational corporation should now be accepted.

Notes

1 While it is surprising that Galbraith's distinctive contribution to the theory of the firm which was set out in the previous chapter has been neglected, it is perhaps more understandable, although no less tolerable, that his view of the multinational corporation has also slipped from view. In one sense an important exception is Galbraith's youngest son, Jamie (see James Galbraith, 1989). Indeed he noted that: "the rise of international competition and the decline of the great American manufacturing corporation since 1967 are facts often cited by John Kenneth Galbraith's critics, who argue that they render the message of *The New Industrial State* obsolete" (James Galbraith, 1989: 231). However, while James Galbraith provides an otherwise excellent extension of the view of the firm contained with *The New Industrial State* to international trade he ignores the broader contribution detailed below and has perhaps unwittingly contributed to the general neglect of his father's writings on this topic!

2 Indeed Galbraith must also bear some responsibility for this state of affairs. In one of his more prominent contributions on the transnational corporation in the *Harvard Business Review* Galbraith (1978b) ignored his earlier more salient theoretical discussion in *Economics and the Public Purpose* choosing instead to consider the pros and cons of the multinational enterprise largely drawing on the theoretical treatments of Vernon (1977) and Buckley and Casson (1976). Likewise in the fourth edition of *The New Industrial State* he conceded that he: "did not see the development of the foreign, most notably the Japanese, competition to which [the corporation] would be subject ... No one can doubt that in our older industries this competition has substantially impaired the certainty and effectiveness of the planning process" (Galbraith, 1967a: xxxi–xxxii). Equally, in discussion of *The New Industrial State* after twenty years, Galbraith (1988: 375) remarked that "There have also been some important microeconomic developments that I did not foresee. In 1967, my view was, in some measure of a closed American-dominated corporate structure extending its reach internationally by way of American multinational or transnational enterprises. I did not foresee the invasive thrust into this structure by Japan and other countries. This, to put it mildly, has introduced a new element, substantially beyond the influence and control of the firms of the corporate or planning system." Clearly, however, while the nature of international trade undermines the ability of the firm to successfully plan and control it does not diminish its desire to do so. That is to say, it adds to the uncertainty that the firm faces and thus provides further impetus to the pursuit of a variety of strategies that Galbraith considered. It is from this perspective, I would argue, that Galbraith's contribution and continued relevance should be viewed (see also chapter 1 above).

3 Stanfield (1996: 113–15) is one of the few who recognizes the fact that Galbraith extended his analysis to the transnational context. Unfortunately, however, Stanfield does not afford us with an extended reflection on what it means for the theory of the multinational firm, something I dwell on here.

4 That is to say, theorists of the multinational corporations explain typically the emergence of the firm by relaxing the patently unrealistic but "perfect" neoclassical core, drawing on "imperfect" concepts, such as bounded rationality, asset specificity, and opportunism, or highlighting structural "market imperfections" such as monopoly. As argued in more detail in Dunn (2000b, 2001a, 2001c, 2008a), however, both the transaction cost and monopoly approaches implicitly rely on an ergodic conception of economic processes. The import of this assumption is that these imperfections can be overcome in the (very) long run (defined as an

asymptotic end state of a process of learning). Conversely, a Galbraithian-transmutable approach, which exists in historical and uncertain, that is, nonergodic time, is not an imperfectionist account given that there is no pre-programmed omniscience against which present and future configurations can be judged (see the previous chapter).

5 The 2006 UNCTAD report on Foreign Direct Investment (FDI) highlights how the value of cross border mergers and acquisitions (M&As) continues to grow: "Cross-border M&As, especially those involving companies in developed countries, have spurred the recent increases in FDI. The value of cross-border M&As rose by 88% over 2004, to $716 billion, and the number of deals rose by 20%, to 6,134. These levels are close to those achieved in the first year of the cross-border M&A boom of 1999–2001. The recent surge in M&A activity includes several major transactions, partly fuelled by the recovery of stock markets in 2005. There were 141 mega deals valued at more than $1 billion – close to the peak of 2000, when 175 such deals were observed. The value of mega deals was $454 billion in 2005 – more than twice the 2004 level and accounting for 63% of the total value of global cross border M&As" (UNCTAD, 2006: 3).

6 As Galbraith argued (1973a: 185): "Not only is the multinational corporation a precise answer to need, it is an answer that greatly favors the most developed technostructure."

7 It is interesting to note that this appears to be similar to Keynes (1982: 237) who argued that the new techniques of production and associated finance followed the mass migrations to the New World: "At a time when wholesale migrations were populating new continents, it was natural that the men should carry with them into the New Worlds the material fruits of the technique of the Old, embodying the savings of those who were sending them. The investment of British savings in rails and rolling stock to be installed by British engineers to carry British emigrants to new fields and pastures, the fruits of which they would return in due proportion to those whose frugality had made these things possible." Keynes (1982: 237), however, went on to argue that the flow of such technical know-how and finance: "was not economic internationalism remotely resembling in its essence the part ownership of the A.E.G. of Germany by a speculator in Chicago." Keynes believed, as the epigraph at the start of this chapter alludes, that the joint-stock company, in divorcing management from ownership, was undermining the investment decision, reducing it to a short term speculative decision, a situation exacerbated by the development of global finance. For Keynes the rise of the joint stock company and its associated institutions had given rise to a cadre of dilettante investors who are able to alter their

investment portfolios quickly and without appreciable cost, nor consideration of the consequences of their actions upon the wider community. This underpins Keynes (1936: 160) argument that if one were married to one's decisions, as in earlier times, there would not be a market to follow, and one would be compelled to consider a longer time horizon for the prospective yield, rather than focusing on short-term yields and price movements. Galbraith's analysis suggested that the large corporation would increasingly seek to insulate itself from such effects in an effort to minimize the uncertainty that is generated by such market speculation.

8 This results in the pursuit of divide and rule strategies by the large transnational corporation. For a discussion of the wider literature on this and a review of evidence, see Peoples and Sugden (2000) (see also Tomlinson, 2002; Coffey and Tomlinson, 2006).

9 Again such themes are also evident in Keynes (1982: 238): "A considerable degree of international specialization is necessary in a rational world in all cases where it is dictated by wide differences of climate, natural resources, native aptitudes, level of culture, and density of population. But over an increasingly wide range of industrial products, and perhaps of agricultural products also, I become doubtful whether the economic cost of national self-sufficiency is great enough to outweigh the other advantages of gradually bringing the producer and consumer within the ambit of the same national, economic and financial organization. Experience accumulates to prove that most modern mass-production processes can be performed in most countries and climates with almost equal efficiency." Keynes's essay, which appeared in *The New Statesman and Nation* on July 8 and 15, 1933, was a polemic against economic nationalism and national self-sufficiency, and for the need to recognize the defects, as well as the passing, of the *laissez faire* stage of capitalism.

10 As Porter (1990: 18) notes: "estimates suggest that a significant portion of world trade is between subsidiaries of multinationals, and that a meaningful fraction of the imports of advanced national is accounted for by imports from the subsidiaries of a nations own multinationals. National success in an industry increasingly means that the nation is the home base for leading multinationals in the industry, not just for domestic firms that export. In computers, for example, America is the home base for IBM, DEC, Prime, Hewlett-Packard, and other US companies that have facilities and subsidiaries spread widely in Europe and elsewhere."

11 As Galbraith (1979b: 90) remarked in *The Nature of Mass Poverty*: "the rural masses do not work for multinational corporations. They would

invariably improve their incomes if they did. Nor do they sell to them or in appreciable measure buy from them. Their poverty comes less from their adverse terms of trade than from having so little to trade."

12 This explains the point made by Sugden and Wilson (2002) that in the case of developing countries, the development agenda is typically set by a select elite, and influenced powerfully by organizations such as the World Bank, the IMF, and the large transnational corporations, to the exclusion of the people who live in those countries (see also Stiglitz, 2002, 2003).

13 A key culprit here would be Naomi Klein (1999). Nevertheless there is much in Klein that accords with Galbraith's approach.

14 Cowling and Tomlinson (2005) point to the large literature on regulatory capture as evidence that the behavior of governments and regulators is influenced by corporations that they regulate. They also draw our attention to Mercer's (1995) study of how British anti-trust policies have been shaped by powerful business interests and how we are witnessing the emergence of powerful global pressure groups for free trade such as the Trilateral Commission. Cowling and Tomlinson (2005: 12) also highlight that: "one of the consequences of the election of the Bush administration in 2001 was a reversal of US policy to ratify the international Kyoto Agreement on environmental policy. Given that the Bush campaign was largely funded by the US oil industry, we might draw the obvious inference (*Guardian*, 2001)".

15 Similar themes are evident in Baran and Sweezy (1966: 200), who argue that what the giant multinational corporations want is "monopolistic control over foreign sources of supply and foreign markets, enabling them to buy and sell on specially privileged terms, to shift orders from one subsidiary to another, to favor this country or that depending on which has the most advantageous tax, labor and other policies – in a word, they want to do business on their own terms and wherever they choose."

16 As Krugman (1994: 199) notes, "there's a perfectly reasonable argument that says that international trade should be mostly between countries that have very different resource bases and thus can supply [what] each other's lacks. Unfortunately, in the real world most trade is between similar countries; so there's something wrong with the argument (and with any policy conclusion based on it)."

17 In a series of articles I have proposed an extension to the definition of the firm advanced by Cowling and Sugden arguing that centers of strategic decision-makers coordinating production operate under conditions of fundamental uncertainty or non-ergodicity (Dunn, 1999, 2000b, 2001a, 2001c, 2008a). This extension reinforces many of Cowling and

Sugden's central conclusions and, more importantly, extends and clarifies their notion of strategic decision-making. Cowling and Sugden's approach also implicitly suggests a focus on the role of money in production, given that "In the strategic decision-making approach what others have referred to as market exchanges falling outside the ambit of the firm, notably subcontracting relationships, are incorporated inside the firm" (Cowling and Sugden, 1998a: 60–1). From a Post Keynesian perspective, I argue that this link should be made explicit and that by embedding Cowling and Sugden's discussion in terms of uncertainty we underscore the fact that market exchanges are conducted in terms of money denominated contracts as a planning response to an unknowable future (Galbraith, 1967a; Davidson, 1972).

18 As Branston, Cowling and Sugden (2006: 189–90) note: "the idea of firms as units of planning translates into that of corporations making strategic decisions that give rise to their corporate strategies. In line with Zeitlin (1974), the power to make strategic decisions includes the ability to plan a corporation's relationships with other corporations, its relationships with governments and employees, and its geographical orientation."

19 This links to the argument of the previous chapter that the concept of planning articulated by Galbraith should be developed further with respect to the uncertain nature of the environment and not to "market structure" *per se* (see Dunn, 2000b, 2001a, 2001c, 2008a).

20 As Galbraith (1973a: 143) notes: "The contract accorded by the manufacturer or supplier of end products to those that supply him solves, or goes far to solve, the problem of vertical co-ordination in the planning system. The firm producing automobiles or weapons uses its power to plan its own output; by use of contracts it allows those on whom it depends to plan their production and thus ensure that the requisite components are forthcoming when and in the amounts needed."

21 Compare Auerbach (1992: 157), who points out that: "The multinational is often taken to represent the victory of the hierarchical over the market form of governance. But in fact it has emerged ... along with a growth of so-called market relations. Those very conditions which have been conducive to an expansion of trade have also promoted the growth of multinational activity."

22 As Cowling and Tomlinson (2002: 378) argue: "The strategic decision-making approach has a number of implications. In our view, Japanese *keiretsu* relationships fall under the ambit of the core firm with the corporate group. Similarly the boundaries of the Western firm also include activities conducted both in-house and through the market. If activities in each type of organization are coordinated and controlled from the

centre, then there are clear parallels between the command structures in both Western and Japanese firms. This may mean that the hierarchical differences highlighted by Aoki (1990) are somewhat superficial." See also Hamilton and Feenstra (1998); Dyer (1996); and Coffey and Tomlinson (2003).

23 See, for example, Lang (2003), who highlights how many primary producers in the food industry are locked into tight specifications and contracts reflecting the global concentration of market power of the retail sector.

24 See also Maddison (1995a, 1995b, 2001, 2003) for detailed statistical analysis of the changing nature of the world economy.

25 For example, see Coffey and Tominlinson (2006: 559), who follow Cowling and Sugden (1998) in highlighting the non-Pareto aspects of the modern firm and its ability to "take advantage of more devolved forms of organization by outsourcing production to subcontracted units – while retaining an essential monopoly on decision-making at a strategic level."

26 See, for example, Cowling and Sugden (1994, 1998a, 1998b, 1998c), who have explored systemically the consequences of this approach for Pareto efficiency, distribution, employment, trade, and technology.

27 One response to improve the alignment with public interest is to ensure relevant information is widely available to the public and customers. To this end Bailey *et al.* (1994: 316) propose that countries introduce transnational corporation monitoring units "designed to collect information on transnationals' performance and impact, to prepare accounts and to use these to influence economic policy and attitudes of and towards transnationals." Frey and Stutzer (2000) argue, moreover, that greater direct involvement in strategic decision-making might also increase people's well-being. Based on evidence from interview data in Switzerland, they argue that "individuals are *ceteris paribus* happier, the better developed the institutions of direct democracy are in their area of residence" (Frey and Stutzer, 2000: 918).

28 This contradicts the idea employed in the literature that firms are assumed to replace efficiently the market as a result of transaction-type market failure.

29 The decision to economize on transaction costs is a strategic decision in the sense that it is taken by a subset of those involved in production with their motivations and objectives predominating. From this perspective: "the strategic decision-making approach focuses on the objectives and thus decisions of strategic decision-makers as a crucial determinant of activity in modern economies. On some occasions strategic decision makers will make choices with saved transaction costs of paramount

importance ... on other occasions transaction costs are irrelevant ... Whether the issue in any particular case is the distribution of efficiency gains or the existence of Pareto-inefficient outcomes, it is the centrality of strategic decisions and strategic decision makers to the theory of the firm that is the basic insight" (Cowling and Sugden, 1998a: 61).

30 See also Branston *et al.* (2006b: 302), who "consider the health industry in the light of both a strategic decision-making approach to economic development (Sugden and Wilson, 2002) and a corresponding analysis of the theory and the impact of the firm (Cowling and Sugden, 1998a, 1999)."

31 It is a massive industry. As Lang and Heasman (2004: 155) point out: "The food industry is the leading industrial sector in the European Union (with 15 member states), with production estimated at €572 billion accounting for 13 per cent of the total EU manufacturing sector."

32 Gold (2003), for example, highlights how the Indian broiler industry, for example, has grown from 31 million birds a year in 1981 to 800 million two decades later.

33 *Silent Spring* by Rachael Carson (1962) spent several weeks on the *New York Times* bestseller list, and ushered in the now widespread public concerns with pesticides and pollution of the environment. *Silent Spring* contributed to the ban of the pesticide DDT in 1972 in the USA.

34 Lang and Heasman (2004: 181) warn that: "Notwithstanding persistent consumer, environmentalist and (some) expert concerns, the biotechnology industry is quietly making sure that GM [Genetically Modified] crops are almost a *fait accompli* in world food supply; their rapid spread is making it difficult for consumers to avoid them and the trend is possibly irreversible."

35 As Lang (2004: 9–10) points out: "Concentration is strongly linked to power and the concentration of power over the food system is now remarkable, whether one looks nationally, regionally or globally. A web of contractual relationships turns the farmer into a contractor, providing the labor and often some capital, but never owning the product as it moves through the supply chain. Farmers never make the major management decisions."

36 As Schlosser (2002: 121) highlights: "About 90 percent of the money that Americans spend on food is used to buy processed food. But the canning, freezing, and dehydrating techniques used to process food destroy most of its flavor. Since the end of World War II, a vast industry has arisen in the United States to make processed food palatable. Without this flavor industry, today's fast food industry could not exist."

37 Unilever, for example, has reduced its brand portfolio down from 1,200 to 400.

38 It is salient to note that statins are a medicalized and pharmaceutical response to the excessive consumption of cholesterol-inducing saturated fats from dairy products and meat, as well as hydrogenated (trans-) fats.

39 Schlosser (2002: 3) highlights the growth of such brands and the impact on US society: "In 1970, Americans spent about $6 billion on fast food; in 2000, they spent more than $110 billion. Americans now spend more money on fast food than on higher education, personal computers, computer software, or new cars. They spend more on fast food than on movies, books, magazines, newspapers, videos, and recorded music – combined."

40 Schlosser (2002: 240–1) argues, capturing many Galbraithian themes, that although "the current rise in obesity has a number of complex causes, genetics is not one of them. The American gene pool has not changed radically in the past few decades. What has changed is the nation's way of eating and living. In simple terms: when people eat more and move less, they get fat. In the United States, people have become increasingly sedentary – driving to work instead of walking, performing little manual labor, driving to do errands, watching television, playing video games, and using a computer instead of exercising. Budget cuts have eliminated physical education programs at many schools. And the growth of the fast food industry has made an abundance of high-fat, inexpensive meals widely available."

41 In the United States, "the agricultural industry is seen as one of the more powerful lobby groups: in a three-year period, the food sector contributed around $25 million to President George W. Bush's and other politicians' campaigns, and five of the top people running the US Department of Agriculture in 2002 were linked to the meat industry" (Lang and Heasman, 2004: 272). For such reasons Eric Schlosser (2002: 267), in *Fast Food Nation*, concludes that: "The political influence of the fast food industry and its agribusiness suppliers makes a discussion of what Congress should do largely academic. The fast food industry spends millions of dollar every year on lobbying and billions on mass marketing. The wealth and power of the major chains make them seem impossible to defeat."

42 The Food industry appears to have learnt several lessons from the tobacco industry. As Lang and Heasman (2004: 263) highlight: "Often, in the face of emerging activism, the food industry's strategy is to deny links between consumption and ill health, while agreeing to fund scientists to study their product's risk, and to adopt new softer tactics such as corporate social responsibility when confronted with the evidence."

43 It is salient to note that the Judge's decision in the well-publicized "McLibel" case in the UK concluded that "McDonald's did 'exploit' children through its advertising, endanger the health of its regular customers, pay workers unreasonably low wages, and bear responsibility for the cruelty inflicted upon animals by many of its suppliers" (Schlosser, 2002: 247).

44 As Penrose (1959: 42) argued: "Firms not only alter the environmental conditions necessary for the success of their action, but, even more important, they know that they can alter them and that the environment is not independent of their own activities."

45 Arguably, Hymer was influenced by, or had at least read, Galbraith's *The New Industrial State* (see, for example, Hymer and Rowthorn, 1970: 58). For a variety of reflections on Hymer's enduring contribution, see Buckley (2006a), Kindleberger (2002), Pitelis (2002), and Teece (2006).

9 *The management of specific demand*

Speaking broadly therefore, although it is man's wants in the earliest stages of his development that give rise to his activities, yet afterwards each new step upwards is to be regarded as the development of new activities giving rise to new wants, rather than of new wants giving rise to new activities.

Alfred Marshall (1920: 89)

Wants are usually treated as the fundamental data, the ultimate driving force in economic activity, and in a short-run view of problems this is scientifically legitimate. But in the long-run it is just as clear that wants are dependent variables, that they are largely caused and formed by economic activity. The case is somewhat like that of a river and its channel; for the time being the channel locates the river, but in the long run it is the other way round.

Frank H. Knight (1924: 262–3)

In the conventional wisdom the industrial structure is wholly in the service of the individual consumer – what Galbraith calls "The Accepted Sequence." Galbraith challenged this view, arguing that it failed to illuminate reality, obscuring it in the convenient service of vested interests. In *The New Industrial State* Galbraith (1967a) argued that the nature of modern production was such that large corporations would seek to manage the demand for their products. The consequence of the evolution of the modern mode of production was that the market is increasingly managed in the interests of the large firm. Galbraith referred to this as "The Revised Sequence." Galbraith argued that large corporations, with their extensive range of financial commitments, would seek to mitigate the uncertainties they face through a variety of systematic institutional responses such as the management of prices and, more famously, the direct manipulation of consumer response.[1] Galbraith labeled this manipulation "The

Management of Specific Demand," an element within the larger ideological context of "The Revised Sequence."[2]

Although attracting a degree of attention and notoriety around the time of publication, Galbraith's thesis of the management of the consumer has slipped somewhat from view. Economists have either dismissed Galbraith's contribution as an informal expression of the persuasive approach to advertising or have been seemingly content to follow Galbraith (1967a: 23) and point to the "massive growth in the apparatus of persuasion and exhortation that is associated with the sale of goods" as *prima facie* evidence in favor of Galbraith's theory of the management of the consumer. The upshot is that there has been little detailed exploration of Galbraith's ideas by those working both inside and outside the conventional wisdom.[3]

I here reconsider Galbraith's theoretical contribution. I draw attention to the novel aspects of his argument by highlighting how the tobacco industry, which Galbraith (1952a: 57–8, 103–5) identified in *American Capitalism* as exemplifying his analysis of the large firm, has sought to manage demand for its product. Based on an archival exegesis of previously secret industry documents, the range of consumer management techniques used by the tobacco industry is recorded and the correspondence with Galbraith's view is highlighted. Access to the internal tobacco industry documents allows us to move beyond speculation about the intentions of marketers, advertisers, and firm executives; analysis of internal documents reveals such intentions explicitly and in the industry's own words. From this it will be seen that the dominant view of the role of advertising – to provide information and quality signals to consumers – is incomplete and would benefit from renewed engagement with Galbraith's ideas.

The management of specific demand

There are three dominant approaches to advertising and marketing in economics: the informative, complementary, and persuasive views (Bagwell, 2001, 2003). The *informative view*, associated with the Chicago School, holds that advertising affects demand not by altering tastes or preferences, but by conveying information.[4] According to this approach the costs of search may discourage consumers from seeking out a product's existence, price, and quality, resulting in suboptimal choices. Advertising is viewed as an endogenous response of the marketplace which seeks to correct this state of affairs. Through advertising, consumers receive direct information, for example prices or location, and/or indirect information, for example how much the firm is willing to spend on advertising. The firm faces a demand curve that becomes more sensitive to price and quality considerations, that is, more elastic, which is to its competitive advantage given its comparative quality advantage. The informative view suggests that *ceteris paribus* advertised products will be of higher quality such that even seemingly uninformative advertising may provide indirect information that the quality of the advertised product is high (see Nelson, 1974, for an analysis). The tobacco industry advances the informative view in public relations statements, particularly after the cancer scare of the 1950s and the subsequent low-tar boom (Cummings, Morley, and Hyland, 2002; Chaloupka and Warner, 2000).

The *complementary view* postulates that consumers possess a stable set of preferences into which advertising enters directly in a fashion that complements the consumption of the advertised product.[5] Consumers may value social prestige, for example, and the consumption of a product may generate greater prestige through appropriate product advertisement. Under this view advertising does not alter consumers' preferences and need not, although it may, provide information. Thus the complementary view is distinct from the informative view as advertising may affect consumer demand even though it contains no product information. This perspective suggests that the market may under-provide advertising since the firm marketing the product does not benefit from (internalize) the increase in consumer welfare that advertising generates.

Finally, the *persuasive view* maintains that advertising creates artificial product differentiation and brand loyalty by altering consumers' tastes.[6] As a consequence, the demand for an advertising firm's product becomes more inelastic and results in higher prices. In addition, advertising by incumbents may generate barriers to entry, which are exacerbated when economies of scale in production and/or advertising exist (Cowling *et al.*, 1975; Cowling, 1982). The persuasive approach highlights the anti-competitive and adverse welfare effects of advertising. It argues that advertising has no *real* value to consumers but rather induces *artificial* product differentiation, and results in more concentrated markets with higher prices and profits than would otherwise be the case.

Galbraith's thesis is generally viewed as a more literary version of the persuasive view.[7] Accordingly, it is conventionally dismissed as a loose analysis of the social consequences of advertising and subsequently ignored (cf. Bagwell, 2003: 13). Galbraith (1967: 209–12), however, explicitly rejected many of the tenets of what has come to be referred to as the persuasive view.[8] Galbraith's contribution offers a view of the management of consumer demand that is richer and broader in scope than he has typically been given credit for. It is worth reviewing his contribution in more detail.

As noted above in chapter 5, Galbraith maintained that the modern corporation would use an array of marketing and selling techniques to ensure that what was produced was ultimately bought (cf. Packard, 1957).[9] He argued that the nature of modern production, which involves significant up-front costs, imparts a strong incentive for manufacturers to frame information in a manner that induces a favorable response:

> The key to the management of demand is effective management of the purchases of final consumers – of individuals and the state. If these are under effective control, there will then be a comparatively reliable demand for raw materials, parts, machinery and other items going into the ultimate product. If the demand for its automobiles is reliable, General Motors can accord its suppliers the security of long-term contracts. And, in the absence of such contracts, there will still be a reliable and predictable flow of orders which allows planning. (Galbraith, 1967a: 205)

This is a firm-based view that suggests the locus of control over purchasing patterns rests with the firm and not the consumer.[10] What is more it departs quite markedly from the structure-conduct-performance embeddedness of the persuasive view – advertising is necessitated by technology and the nature of planning and not market structure *per se*:

> Were there but one manufacturer of automobiles in the United States, it would still be essential that it enter extensively on the management of its demand. Otherwise consumers, exercising the sovereignty that would be inconsistent with the company's planning, might resort to other forms of transportation and other ways of spending their income. (This is the answer to the orthodox contention that advertising is principally induced by market oligopoly.) (Galbraith, 1967a: 212)

The corollary of this perspective is that consumer demands will be managed not in the service of individual needs, but in the interests of the organization. Though the needs of the consumer and those of the firm need not necessarily be mutually exclusive, Galbraith maintained that the modern corporation seeks to manage needs to promote greater accumulation and maintain the pre-eminence of the technostructure. The firm's top priority is to service its own needs of having a predictable flow of orders, being able to engage in long-term planning, and continuing to cover overhead costs and generate profits.[11] That the firm's needs are paramount makes consumers' needs of secondary importance and, more importantly, possibly in conflict with the corporation's. Indeed we will see that in the case of the tobacco industry the provision of accurate information about the firm's products and consequences of consuming them would thwart the goals of the firm (see Kluger, 1996; Kessler, 2001). The informative view assumes consumer freedom of choice; firms respond to consumer demand by providing information useful to the consumer's autonomous decision-making process. Galbraith, however, suggests that unfettered freedom of choice can damage the firm's long-term success:

> The specific strategy [of managing demand], though it varies somewhat between industries and over time, consists first in recruiting a loyal or automatic corps of customers ... To the extent that it is successful, it means that the firm has a stable body of custom which is secure against the mass defection which might follow from freely exercised consumer choice. (Galbraith, 1967a: 210–11)[12]

Galbraith (1958a) argued in *The Affluent Society*, that it might be thought that increased affluence might result in a reduced propensity to consume; increasingly being sated, individuals spend less of their incomes on additional goods.[13] This presents a problem for the firms that usher in this affluence, however:

> Were they to cease to work after acquiring a certain sufficiency, there would be limits on the expansion of the system. Growth could not then remain a goal. Advertising and its related arts thus help develop the kind of man the goals of the industrial system require – one that reliably spends his income and works reliably because he is always in need of more. (Galbraith, 1967a: 219)

Nevertheless the nature of economic development also makes the modern consumer more vulnerable to persuasion. The affluent society, in satisfying a range of basic human needs, also makes individuals more susceptible to management.[14] And the modern corporation exploits this fact: "as the industrial system develops to the point where it has need for planning and the management of the consumer that this requires, it is also serving wants which are psychological in origin and hence admirably subject to management by appeal to the psyche" (Galbraith, 1967a: 205). After the basics of food, clothing, and shelter have been satisfied, higher-level psychological needs are next in the hierarchy to be satisfied.

That is to say, rising affluence, by moving beyond the satisfaction of basic physical needs, makes individuals more amenable to management through psychological appeals.[15] The modern corporation seeks to take advantage of this fact in securing demand for its products through developing marketing strategies for its products in a manner that is largely *unrelated* to the objective qualities and characteristics of the products that it sells:

> The success of modern industry, however, has meant that goods that are related only to elementary physical sensation – that merely prevent hunger, protect against cold, provide shelter, suppress pain – have come to comprise a small and diminishing part of all production. Most goods serve needs that are discovered to the individual not by the palpable discomfort that accompanies deprivation, but by some psychic response to their possession. (Galbraith, 1967a: 206)[16]

In terms of a theory of the process of advertising, Galbraith's views on the management of the consumer thus embody an important and oft-ignored distinction between primary physical needs and subjective psychological, or in Galbraith's words, "psychic needs" (Dunn and Anderson, 2006). This is important because although we recognize the persuasive nature of advertising, one needs to distinguish *persuasion* (with a lower-case "p") from the *Persuasive* view of advertising. From Galbraith's perspective the psychological or social need pre-exists, but the firm attempts to persuade the consumer that the consumption of its goods will satisfy these psychological or social needs in a way that is unrelated to the actual consumption characteristics that the product confers.[17]

The salience of Galbraith's approach is that it is not that wants (values or psychological needs) are created *per se*, but rather that the corporation identifies such needs and then uses knowledge of them to tailor its marketing strategy to a specific target market to galvanize consumer behavior in service of the firm (cf. Gunter and Furnham, 1992; Hawkins, Best, and Coney, 1998; Heath, 1995, 1996; Weinstein, 1994). Advertisers must generate psychic connections between products and often intangible rewards (Anderson, Glantz, and Ling, 2005). It is this sense in which the consumer is considered to be persuaded – that the demand for a commodity is unrelated to the actual benefits that the product confers, and not that new demands are originated *ex nihilo* by the producer. In *The New Industrial State* Galbraith further elaborated:

> Most goods serve needs that are discovered to the individual not by the palpable discomfort that accompanies deprivation, but by some psychic response to their possession. They give him a sense of personal achievement, accord him a feeling of equality with his neighbors, divert his mind from thought, serve sexual aspiration, promise social acceptability, enhance his subjective feeling of health, well-being or orderly peristalsis, contribute by conventional canons to personal beauty, or are otherwise psychologically rewarding. (1967a: 206)

This analysis echoes Sidney Levy's seminal assertion that "[t]he less concern there is with the concrete satisfactions of a survival level of existence, the more abstract human responses become ... sellers of goods are engaged, whether willfully or not, in selling symbols" (1959: 117). It is also similar to the means-end perspective, which characterizes the marketing discipline. Reynolds, Witlark, and Wirthlin, for example, argue that advertising creates a means-end chain, linking product attributes to consequences deemed desirable, based upon a consumer's values:

> In the means-end framework, product attributes and their functional consequences are just the means to an end. The end is a personal need, goal, or value that reflects the perceptual orientation of the consumer and shows how he or she translates a seemingly inconsequential product into an object having deep personal relevance and importance. (Reynolds, Witlark, and Wirthlin, 2001: 216–17)

It is important to note, however, that the means-end approach is a consumer-based approach that emphasizes the complementary nature of advertising *in the service of the consumer.* Consumers may not always select products in terms of their concrete attributes, but rather in terms of the abstract benefits (or risks) that a product provides. This is clearly different from Galbraith's approach, which focuses on how the consumers' psychological needs are targeted to assure firm ends.

Selecting what is psychologically rewarding for inclusion in advertising messages, is nevertheless a challenge for the technostructure in the context of generating as many consumers for its products as possible. What is compelling or comprehensible to one person may be uninteresting or unintelligible to another. As Galbraith noted, however:

> Technology, once again, solved the problems that it created. Coincidentally with rising mass incomes came first radio and then television. These, in their capacity to hold effortless interest and their accessibility over the entire cultural spectrum, and their independence of any education qualification, were admirably suited to mass persuasion. Radio and more especially television have, in consequence, become the prime instruments for the management of consumer demand. There is an insistent tendency among solemn social scientists to think of any institution which features rhymed and singing commercials; provides intense and lachrymose voices urging highly improbable enjoyments; offers caricatures of the human oesophagus in normal or impaired operation; and which hints implausibly at opportunities for antiseptic seduction, as inherently trivial. This is a great mistake. The industrial system is profoundly dependent on commercial television and could not exist in its present form without it. (1967a: 212–13)

The normative implications of persuasion on this scale are seen in fads, fashions, and the cultural homogenization that accompanies mass marketing (for a discussion of cultural homogenization through global marketing, see Klein, 1999; for a case study see Hafez and Ling, 2005).[18] Galbraith also allows the general climate created by advertising to impact on the aspirations of consumers.[19] Copious advertising for similar products of competing firms elevates not just individual brands but also the product category: "This management performs yet another service. For, along with bringing demand under substantial control, it provides, in the aggregate, a relentless propaganda on behalf of goods in general. From early morning until late at night, people are informed of the services rendered by goods – of their profound indispensability" (Galbraith, 1967a: 214).[20] What Galbraith called a "relentless propaganda on behalf of goods in general" may be likened to Pollay's (1987: 105–6) "chorus":

> Given the common products, goals, and cultural premises of clients and agencies, some notes and themes are echoed by multiple voices. Many ads echo basic behavioral suggestions on who (You!), what (Indulge!), how (Buy!), when (Now!), and where (Here!). The why's (e.g., Pretty, Durable, and Cheap!) vary, but repeat a short list of ideas. Other messages (Fancy and Practical!) provide harmonious counterpoints to augment rather than cancel other messages. Between redundancies and variations, the result may be more a chorus than chaos-noisy, no doubt, but still with intelligible melody and meaning.

Finally, it is important to note that although Galbraith's analytical focus is on this "management" role, he nevertheless acknowledged that not all advertising and selling is directed to managing the consumer (see Galbraith, 1952a: 101–8; 1958a: 150–2; 1967: 208–5). That there is a role for the informative view of advertising is explicitly acknowledged:

> Thus a certain amount of advertising, that of the classified ads and the department store displays, has no great purpose beyond that of conveying information – of advising the public that a particular person or enterprise has a particular item for sale and at what price. Such advertising is seized upon to show that the function of advertising in general is merely to convey information although, as I have noted on other occasions, only a gravely retarded citizen can need to be told that the American Tobacco Company has cigarettes for sale. (Galbraith, 1967a: 208)

This reading of Galbraith suggests the need for a taxonomy of advertising that separates advertisements such as newspaper classifieds from campaigns such as the examples from the tobacco industry presented below (see table 11). The latter class may or may not provide information, but more importantly it may provide antifactual content that misinforms consumers about the product in a way to shore up psychological demands (see Preston, 2002). Stigler and Becker (1977: 84) have stated, a "consumer may indirectly receive utility from a market good, yet the utility depends not only on the quantity of the good but also the consumer's knowledge of its true or alleged properties."

Table 11. *Economic approaches to advertising compared*

Perspective†	Nature of advertising	Consumer tastes and preferences	Advertising content	Marketing	Impact on consumer demand	Impact on firm	Welfare effects of advertising
Information (search): (Nelson, 1970 and 1974)	Endogenous market response to sub-optimal provision of information.	Stable, linked to product attributes.	Direct product attribute information (existence, price, quality, location).	Target consumers who value product most.	More elastic. Information conveys product attributes.	Promote competition, facilitates market entry.	Positive. Augments consumer and (firm specific) producer surplus.
Information (experience): (Nelson, 1970 and 1974)	Endogenous market response to sub-optimal provision of information.	Stable, linked to product attributes.	Indirect product attribute information (existence, high quality).	Target consumers who value product most.	More elastic. Signals quality and product attributes; ascertained through repeat consumption.	Promote competition, facilitates market entry.	Positive. Augments consumer and (firm specific) producer surplus.
Complementary: (Stigler and Becker, 1977, and Lancaster, 1966)	Joint product provision of non-product-related characteristics.	Stable, linked to social (heterogeneous) preferences, e.g. social prestige.	Direct, Indirect &/or unrelated to product attributes.	Target consumers who value consumption characteristics most.	None/derived demand. Uninformative Advertising may be valued directly.	Increase firm costs. Cost of production fully internalized by firm.	Sub-optimal provision (externalities associated with consumption not internalized).

Table 11. (*cont.*)

Perspective†	Nature of advertising	Consumer tastes and preferences	Advertising content	Marketing	Impact on consumer demand	Impact on firm	Welfare effects of advertising
Persuasive: (Chamberlin, 1933, Kaldor, 1950, and Bain, 1956)	Exogenous firm response to maximize profits.	Modifiable, create demand for product attributes.	Direct, Indirect &/or unrelated to product attributes.	Create consumer needs for product attributes.	More inelastic. Artificial product differentiation.	Restrict competition. Creates barriers to entry. Defensive.	Negative. Higher prices and profits. Socially wasteful.
Management: (Galbraith, 1967a)	Endogenous firm response to the technical and time consuming nature of production.	Stable, distinction between objective physical needs and subjective psychological needs.*	Direct subjective needs association, unrelated to objective needs.	Manage and segment consumer psychological needs. Product-marketing strategy. Shift locus of control.	More certain demand, which facilitates higher and growing volumes.	Promote revenue stabilisation. Sustains firm prestige. Intra technostructure competition.	Negative. Misalignment of objective and subjective needs.

Notes:

† The references are the classic references cited in the literature.

* Although such needs may be characterized as stable this is not to imply they are static and immutable. The climate of consumerism and "The Management of Specific Demand" do affect and modify subjective needs. However, it is important to note that such processes work at different levels and across different time periods and thus may be out of synch with the firm's actual attempts to manage demand. It is this sense in which they can be viewed as stable.

Source: author's own analysis

When (1) alleged properties are unrelated to the product and (2) a consumer's attempt to maximize utility is motivated by knowledge gained through antifactual advertising content, it is not the consumer but the firm that is principally benefiting from advertising. A summary of Galbraith's view contrasted with the three dominant economic views is outlined in table 11.

The most robust way of exploring and evaluating Galbraith's thesis, however, is to study historical accounts of firm marketing strategy. Internal industry documents provide a direct means for assessing how firms have sought to influence consumer behavior (Anderson, Dewhirst, and Ling, 2006). In what follows I attempt to illuminate aspects of Galbraith's discussion by considering the experience of the oligopolistic US tobacco industry.[21] Litigation brought by forty-six of the states' Attorneys General against the tobacco industry resulted in the Master Settlement Agreement of 1998 that forced tobacco firms to make their internal documents available for public scrutiny. It is now possible to examine and explore a range of advertising techniques pursued by the tobacco industry and how these have evolved, without having to rely on the circumscribed word of corporate executives. This unique resource offers an unprecedented opportunity for examination of the firm from the inside and thus permits elucidation of the distinctive aspects of Galbraith's thesis of "The Management of Specific Demand."[22]

In what follows, I consider evidence from the tobacco industry illuminating the difference between consumer-based approaches to advertising and marketing and Galbraith's firm-based approach. As we shall see the interests of the tobacco industry – to recruit and retain smokers – are decidedly at odds with the health interests of the consumer. The consequences of consumption in this case are inherently dangerous. It is therefore beneficial to tobacco firms to distract consumers from linking cigarette consumption with outcomes. Rather tobacco advertisements must invoke values, or psychological needs, that are unrelated to cigarette consumption in order to motivate behavior favorable to the firm.

Managing psychological needs

As an American Tobacco Co. document tracing the evolution of the tobacco industry's marketing strategy from 1953 to 1964 noted, it was the "first broadside from the Reader's Digest in January 1950 [that] set alight the smoking-and-health controversy" (American Tobacco, 1964). By 1960 US cigarette manufacturers were faced with burgeoning scientific evidence about the hazards of smoking (US Public Health Service, 1960; US Department of Health Education and Welfare, 1964). The tobacco industry, however, did not quickly disseminate information concerning the health risks of smoking; that is, this new highly salient product information was not swiftly conveyed to its consumers (either directly or indirectly).

The industry's response was to modify both advertising and product design in a way that attempted to temper health concerns without displacing actual demand. With Lorillard's introduction of its "Micronite Filter" in 1952, there followed a sharp rise in offerings of low-tar filter cigarette brands accompanied by advertising campaigns meant to persuade consumers that such brands were healthier alternatives to unfiltered high-tar brands and provided safeguards adequate to make quitting unnecessary. Highlighting practicality and sensibleness, low-tar brands were marketed via "a spate of ads on 'laboratory testing' and 'scientific proof'" (American Tobacco, 1964). Knowing that low-tar cigarettes do not mitigate health risks, tobacco firms sought to expand sales through brand proliferation and public reassurance about the dangers of smoking, as opposed to engaging in direct price competition.

In 1971 tobacco advertising was banned from television and radio, at a time when low-tar cigarettes were beginning to account for an increasing proportion of the US cigarette market. Print advertising then became a more important outlet for tobacco industry messages. Like filtered cigarettes before them, low-tar cigarettes were initially sold on a health and safety platform to a public ever more concerned about the adverse health consequences of cigarette smoke. An advertisement for Kent cigarettes in 1954, for example, claimed "[i]n continuing and repeated impartial scientific tests, smoke from the new KENT consistently proves to have much less nicotine and tar than smoke from any other filter cigarette – old or new" (see Figure 4).

Attempting to capitalize on the publicity about smoking and health, advertisements in the 1970s suggested that switching to low-tar provided adequate health protection and made quitting unnecessary. The True brand advertisement, reproduced in Figure 4, exemplifies this

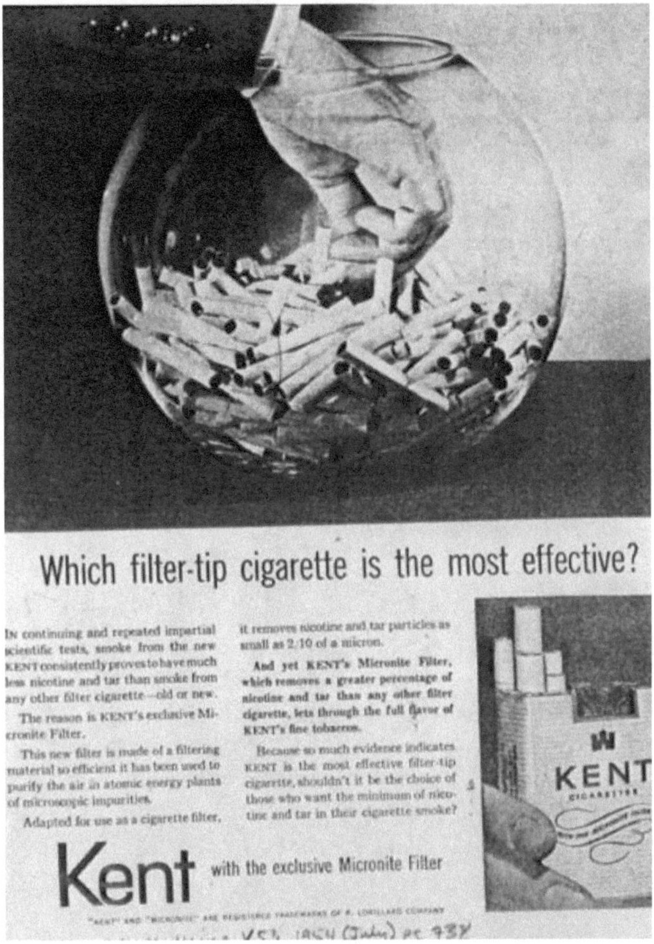

Figure 4. The "low-tar" tobacco lie

strategy, stating: "With all the talk about smoking, I decided I'd either quit or smoke True. I smoke True". This strategy was successful in slowing the upsurge in attempts to quit cigarettes. Low-tar cigarettes share of the US cigarette market, for example, moved from less than 10 percent in 1970 to a nearly 90 percent share in 2001 (Federal Trade Commission, 2003).

Contrary to these advertising claims, however, it is now well-established that low-tar or "light" cigarettes do not offer any meaningful health protection over "regular" cigarettes for either the individual

Figure 4. (Cont.)

or the public. On August 16, 2006, Federal District Judge Gladys Kessler issued her ruling in a lawsuit brought by the US Department of Justice that the major US tobacco companies violated the Racketeer-Influenced and Corrupt Organizations (RICO) Act by defrauding the public regarding the dangers of smoking and deceptively marketing "light" and "low-tar" cigarettes (US District Court, 2005).[23] Judge Kessler concluded:

> In response to this growing body of evidence that smoking caused lung cancer, Defendants and their agents joined together and launched their coordinated scheme in the early 1950s. Defendants developed and

implemented a unified strategy that sought to reassure the public that there was no evidence that smoking causes disease. At the end of 1953, at the urging of the chief executive of the leading cigarette manufacturer at the time, American Tobacco, the chief executives of the five major cigarette manufacturers in the United States – Philip Morris, R.J. Reynolds, Brown & Williamson, Lorillard, and American – met at the Plaza Hotel in New York City with representatives of the public relations firm Hill & Knowlton and agreed to jointly conduct a long term public relations campaign to counter the growing evidence linking smoking as a cause of serious diseases. The series of meetings at the Plaza Hotel spawned an association-in-fact enterprise ("Enterprise") to execute a fraudulent scheme in furtherance of their overriding common objective – to preserve and enhance the tobacco industry's profits by maximizing the numbers of smokers and number of cigarettes smoked and to avoid adverse liability judgments and adverse publicity. The fraudulent scheme would continue for the next five decades. (US District Court, 2005: 5)[24]

Throughout the 1960s and 1970s, tobacco companies also sought to differentiate their brands from others with similar product characteristics through a range of advertising imagery designed to develop brand loyalty and manage the demand for its products. A report by Alan Cox of the RJ Reynolds Tobacco Company (RJR) Marketing Research Department illustrates the shift in cigarette advertising campaigns in the USA from selling products to selling complex user imagery. Specifically, Cox (1984) wrote that the successful marketing of cigarettes should not highlight product characteristics such as a filter configuration or a great tasting tobacco, or even demographic characteristics. Instead, he noted, a brand positioning strategy "should include the main thing(s) the brand wants consumers to think about. It is the brand's unique and meaningful benefit." The objective is to identify, what Galbraith referred to as, a "psychologically rewarding" experience (1967a: 206) for different subgroups in the market and use this to manage product demand.

As Galbraith (1973a: 153) noted, "the management of the private consumer is a task of no slight sophistication; the cost is considerable, and it uses some of the most expert and specialized talent to be found anywhere in the planning system." In order to delineate psychological needs, tobacco firms attempted to identify social or personal aspirations through "psychographic" market segmentation along lines of lifestyle preferences, political and social value systems, life goals, self-concept, and so forth.[25] In a 1994 report, for example, Philip Morris (PM) clustered young male and female markets into segments based upon materialism, sexual interests, leisure time activities, orientation toward future goals, intellectual pursuits, and social aspirations (Ansberry, O'Boyle, and Roberts, 1994). Each segment is tracked into their attitudes about smoking, cigarette purchasing habits, and likelihood of using a particular brand (cf. Hodgson, 1997b). Other tobacco companies have similarly developed their own psychographic market segments, whether principally by similar self-perception variables (Brown and Williamson, 1996) or by perceived congruence between self-concept and brand image (RJ Reynolds, 1981).

As market segmentation research yielded more sophisticated psychographic profiles of different target markets, advertisers moved from simple to complex user imagery that more directly addressed a target-relevant psychological need. Indeed, Cox (1984) noted that "currently a variety of brands are selling primarily psychographic benefits." Explaining "psychographic benefits" to his colleagues in 1982, Richard Nordine, an RJ Reynolds Tobacco Company (RJR) marketing executive, wrote:

> A benefit relates to the consumer's life not to the cigarette product. For example, a benefit obtained from low tar might be to project a rational image to others. A smoker whose most important benefit is to project a rational image would not necessarily be concerned about the alleged hazards of smoking. This person wants to appear to be doing the practical or sensible thing to people around him – to his friends, family, co-workers and so on. In this case, low tar is the means but projecting a rational image to others is the benefit. (Nordine, 1982)

By downplaying the hazards of smoking and instead emphasizing the image a consumer may desire to project to others, Nordine's words highlight how cigarette advertising was intended to exploit psychological needs through communicating psychographic benefits rather than to convey substantive information about product attributes.

Weapons of mass distraction

Galbraith sought to unpack the economists' black box approach to advertising, and marketing more generally. In doing so he explicitly challenged the view that market research was undertaken to ascertain what consumers want and the corollary that the firm is subordinate to such needs:

> A special word is required on market research. This, it has occasionally been argued, is to ascertain what consumers want. In consequence its existence affirms the ultimate power of the consumer and ensures that production is more efficiently subordinated to that power. As often or more often it is to ascertain the effectiveness of different kinds of persuasion or how well different products, brands or packages lend themselves to such persuasion. From this the firm learns how money for persuasion can be most efficiently spent – what sales effort gets the best results and what products lend themselves best to persuasion and how much. Such effort hardly affirms the sovereignty of the consumer. (Galbraith, 1973a: 153–4)

Such considerations can be exemplified by analyzing Project Delta, which was initiated by Brown and Williamson Tobacco Co. (B&W) in 1980 (Brown and Williamson, 1980a). The objective of Project Delta was to develop a low-tar cigarette and accompanying advertising campaign targeting 25–45-year-old, middle or upper-middle class, relatively well-educated women.

A 1981 marketing research report by McCann-Erickson Inc., the advertising agency recruited by B&W at the beginning of Project Delta, identified clusters of important psychological needs among target female smokers; one such cluster was named Personal Experience. The Personal Experience cluster captured women whose "goal involves the maximization of experience and excitement, to them fulfillment equals experience. The means to their goals involve focus-on-self; the psychology of entitlement; and more of a focus on money as a life-style facilitator, rather than a goal in itself" (McCann-Erickson Inc., 1981).

Such profiling was undertaken to identify and categorize the psychological needs of the target market as part of the process of managing consumption of cigarettes. Superficially this might appear to conflict with Galbraith's view, for example consumer needs were being identified in order to create products and advertising that respond to these needs. But the reality supports Galbraith's thesis. The market research was undertaken to identify which needs were amenable to management in the service of the firm. One of Project Delta's proposed brands, Capri, for example, was designed to offer an experience beyond a simple moment of relaxation, promising instead a moment of total escape:

> The trip to a lovely foreign land where there are no phone calls, no kids, no demands ... our appeal is a little more keyed to the experientialist ... someone who is looking for something a little different. ... When we say, Only in Capri, we refer not only to the special benefit that the cigarette brings, but to the unique escape it offers, from the stress of the everyday ordinary world. This is relaxation. It's a special experience; of that we can be sure ... It's exotic ... romantic ... exquisite ... like nothing back home. (Brown and Williamson, 1980b)

In 1986 B&W commissioned Analytic Insight, Inc., a market research firm, to test several proposed advertising campaigns. A 1986 focus group report by Analytic Insight showed the ideals of relaxation and introspection were communicated with varying degrees of success by different prototype campaigns. One campaign, "The Three Faces of Capri," appeared successful in communicating the simultaneous notions of modern femininity and relaxation with two images, "The Professional Woman" and "Dreamer." Focus group respondents saw the Professional Woman as indulging in "a welcome moment at the end of the day when one finally has the time to enjoy a cigarette" (Analytic Insight Inc., 1986a). Analytic Insight noted that respondents:

> found the model in the visual, "Dreamer," somewhat interesting. The mood of quiet relaxation and introspective languor projected by the woman was quite appealing. ... This is the kind of quiet moment for oneself that most busy women have little time to savor. The mood is especially appropriate for enjoying a cigarette. The softness and gentleness projected by the visual is seen as especially consonant with the delicacy of the Capri cigarette and pack. (Analytic Insight Inc., 1986b)

The Management of Specific Demand involves the creation of product features around which a sales strategy can be built (Galbraith, 1967a: 208). According to the focus group facilitator, "Dreamer" was seen as a woman in her twenties and therefore not someone with whom older respondents could easily identify (Analytic Insight Inc., 1986b). The exaggerated slimness of the cigarette and the discreetness of the pack, however, projected "a feminine elegance that most respondents would like to emulate," regardless of age (Analytic Insight Inc., 1986a, 1986b). The especially slim, delicate packaging of Capri had an appeal across age groups in the target psychographic segment (Barenwolt and Thrane, 1986). The ability of the cigarette and pack to communicate femininity led B&W's marketing team to develop a sales strategy based on these product characteristics in spite of the results of focus group research indicating the importance of mood. Contrary to increasing the company's ability to manage demand, however, this initial focus on conveying product attributes proved to hinder the establishment of a deeply involving brand image in Capri campaigns throughout the late 1980s.

Galbraith (1967a: 211) surmised trial and error was not uncommon in attempts to manage demand. This was seen in the subsequent development of advertising campaigns for Capri. The first advertisements for Capri in 1987 and 1988 with the tagline, "Slimmest Slim," were intended to communicate the unusually slim configuration of the cigarette and the fashion consciousness, confidence, and femininity of the brand's users (Analytic Insight Inc., 1986b). The audience's response to the advertisements was generally positive, though many participants in market testing mistook them for Virginia Slims advertisements (Analytic Insight Inc., 1988), a fact that ran counter to the goal of brand differentiation. The Capri brand was also not making gains in market share, showing flat sales at best (Management Science Associates, 1991). After eight years of images similar in tone and style to the "Slimmest Slim" campaigns, B&W's new marketing and advertising consulting firm, Tatham Euro RSCG, developed the "brandscape" for Capri that would position the cigarette in a dramatically different fashion from previous attempts: as an "Escape from the Ordinary":

> The [new] Capri campaign invites women to make this escape through a combination of exotic, romantic visuals in a serene atmosphere; and confident women with a lyrical tone and manner. The women featured in the Capri ads have already made the escape; their objective is to invite like-minded to do the same. The attitude of the Capri woman combines independence, self-confidence, femininity, and comfort with herself. Her

emotional state can best be described as comfortable and quietly joyous – about herself, her surroundings, and her life." (Tatham Euro RSCG, 1995)

In the case of Capri, it appears that stationary or slipping sales was one important motivation behind the shift in marketing strategy from a focus on the product ("slimmest slim") to a focus on consumers' need for a specific emotional state (see Figure 5).

From the mid-1980s to the late 1990s, advertising for Brown and Williamson's Capri brand of cigarettes shifted from emphasizing the uniquely slim character of the product (first image) to positioning the brand as the vehicle by which the target audience could escape to a place of romantic luxury and relaxation (second image). Removal of the product and model from the image and the use of impressionistic print techniques were shown to engage viewers emotionally with the brand.

The new positioning allowed Capri to meet the escapist needs that targets had valued in previous focus groups (Analytic Insight Inc., 1986a, 1986b, 1987, 1988). Tatham Euro's (1995) suggestion was that Capri "signals/owns a uniqueness, elegance and femininity – driven by its slimness – that is emotionally-charged." The campaign itself, however, shifted the focus from emphasizing product characteristics onto the desired mood of the viewing audience. Whereas previous campaigns had featured some description of the slim configuration of the cigarette, the only mention of slimness in the new "She's Gone to Capri" campaign was in the naming of the product itself: Capri SuperSlims. Figure 5 illustrates the shift from product-centrality to mood-centrality in these respective campaigns.

By 1997, Perception Research Services, Inc., another firm working with B&W, concluded: "The current campaign for the Capri brand of cigarettes appears to easily transition/evolve toward the exclusion of models/people in the advertising. In many ways, it appears to strengthen the aspirational feel of the campaign, and make it more personally relevant/compelling" (Perception Research Services, 1997). Joe Schurtz, Vice-President of Perception Research, summarized 1998 focus group testing, noting that the absence of a model "allows each individual to place themselves in the setting and 'I can make it what I want to'" (Schurtz, 1998). The target audience was no longer asked to think about the cigarette, or indeed, about smoking, but rather only

Figure 5. Selling fantasy: the tobacco industry

about a longingly sought-after fantasy. This is the essence of "The Management of Specific Demand":

> Management involves the creation of a compelling image of the product in the mind of the consumer. To this he responds more or less automatically under circumstances where the purchase does not merit a great deal of thought. For building this image, palpable fantasy may be more valuable than circumstantial evidence. (Galbraith, 1967a: 324)

As should be clear, palpable fantasy has dominated the marketing of tobacco. The tobacco industry has actively discouraged critical

Figure 5. (Cont.)

reflection that would negate advertising messages (Pollay, 1995). In purchasing the Capri brand, for example, the consumer was not encouraged to attend to the needs of nicotine addiction, the act of smoking, or the purported benefits of low-tar products, but rather simply to "go to Capri" – where her escapist fantasy lay waiting for her.

The smoking gun?

It is important to note that I have focused here more on "the what" (the marketing process) than on "the why" (why consumers are motivated by it) of advertising. It is clear, nevertheless, that tobacco firms have sought to manage their market and manipulate consumers in a way that supports Galbraith's view of "The Management of Specific Demand." I have not, however, considered the effectiveness of such strategies in stabilizing firm or market demand. An analysis of the tobacco documents, however, uncovers sales reports which seem to suggest a degree of effectiveness following the launch of a new campaign; B&W noted, for example, a slight increase in brand profits following the release of the "She's Gone to Capri" campaign (Brown and Williamson, 1998). Unfortunately, it has not been possible to find a comprehensive record of sales-by-campaign. Even if such analysis were available, it is important to note that the management of the consumer is not a static exercise; rather it requires ongoing development and evaluation:

> When a firm is enjoying steady patronage by its existing customers and recruiting new ones, the existing sales strategy, broadly defined, will usually be considered satisfactory. The firm will not quarrel with success. If sales are stationary or slipping, a change in selling methods, advertising strategy, product design or even in the product itself is called for. Testing and experiment are possible. Sooner or later a new formula that wins a suitable response is obtained. (Galbraith, 1967a: 211)

It is unclear that slipping sales was the prime reason for the shift in Capri advertising, as the change was also instituted after a change in marketing firms. Nevertheless, I consider it telling that the escapist message intended for Capri was conceptualized in the 1980s, but not acted upon until sales were clearly stagnant in the early 1990s.[26]

Similarly the broader literature has not been conclusive about the actual effects of advertising.[27] Although the UK Smee Report (UK Department of Health, 1992) concluded that cigarette advertising has a positive impact on smoking and that bans would reduce demand, there have been several important caveats raised. Chaloupka and Warner (2000: 1592) assert that "there is no 'smoking gun' that proves that advertising and promotion play a significant role in expanding or maintaining the market for tobacco products, or that they do not," but argue, nevertheless that it is more likely than not that advertising and promotion do stimulate cigarette consumption. The tobacco industry, however, clearly believes in its effectiveness. The tobacco industry spends approximately $12.5 billion each year in the USA alone to market cigarettes (Federal Trade Commission, 2003); such an enormous annual expenditure would be counterproductive if it did not significantly benefit the firm.

The current review should not, however, be interpreted as providing conclusive support for the Galbraithian hypothesis. Rather the purpose is to highlight various aspects of Galbraith's thesis of "The Management of Specific Demand" and convey its distinctiveness. What is more, several potential considerations that warrant further analysis and exploration can be identified. First, there is an urgent need to explore more extensively Galbraith's neglected distinction between the appeal to, and management of, subjective psychological needs, as separate from product-related needs. Since at least the 1960s the tobacco industry's intent has been to convey an intangible social or psychological "benefit" associated with a cigarette brand. Such attempts were refined in later decades to exclude cigarettes from the picture altogether. In attempting to manage the consumer, tobacco firms have sought to augment demand by appealing to unrelated psychological needs rather than conveying information regarding the physical attributes of the product.[28] In the context of the health hazards associated with tobacco, such management clearly challenges traditional notions of consumer sovereignty. As Galbraith (1967a: 219) pointed out: "It is true that the consumer may still imagine that his actions respond to his own view of his satisfactions. But this is superficial and proximate, the result of illusions created in connection with the management of his wants." Some of the tobacco industry's marketing strategies have been explicitly designed to downplay health concerns associated with consumption or create an illusory escape from stress, in order to stabilize and grow demand even though it was recognized that product consumption results in adverse welfare effects.

Second, there is a need to consider the historical evolution of actual marketing strategies as they relate to the firm. The information portrayed by cigarette advertisements has been increasingly unrelated to the underlying product attributes. Although tobacco manufacturers have sometimes stressed certain product aspects, such as low tar, this has been designed to appeal to psychological needs and not providing clear, balanced product information. Indeed, low-tar advertising was largely constructed to misinform (Anderson, Pollay, and Ling, 2006; Pollay and Dewhirst, 2002; Leavell, 1999). Such considerations should inform how economists conceptualize tobacco and its advertising. For example, it has been customary to categorize tobacco as an experience good and not as a search good (e.g. Nelson, 1970 and 1974). Tobacco advertising is traditionally viewed as indirectly conveying product information, which perhaps reflects the fact that historically it has conveyed little or no direct product information. What this review highlights, however, is that tobacco firms have instead sought to manage certain psychological needs and limit conscious consideration of the costs and benefits of tobacco consumption either between brands or, more generally, between consuming tobacco or not. Tobacco companies have long recognized the indispensability of addiction to their market success (Dunn, 1972; Teague, 1972). It would seem misleading to interpret the emphasis on marketing (narrow) specific product characteristics as tantamount to conveying substantive product information. For example, communicating lower tar and nicotine numbers in the "scientific" or "clinical" manner popular in the 1960s was intended to lull smokers into complacency with authoritative-sounding jargon rather than provide empirically accurate information about tar, nicotine, smoking, and health. The fact that superficial product characteristics were highlighted in these advertisements is consistent with Galbraith's hypothesis:

> Most goods perform commonplace functions – they suppress hunger, serve alcohol or nicotine addiction, move people gradually through heavy traffic, move waste products more rapidly through the intestinal tract or assist in removing filth. Little or nothing of importance can truthfully be said about the way a product performs these routine functions. Flat lies as to their performance are generally impermissible. But a surrogate for the truth, in which minor or imagined qualities confer great benefits, is essential. (Galbraith, 1967a: 323)

The tobacco industry may be a special case, in that many view the industry with cynicism in light of the growing knowledge about the tobacco industry's political, scientific, and marketing activities. Though the internal corporate documents of other firms are not available, and are less likely to become available, investigation into other industries – such as the food, agrochemical, automotive and pharmaceutical industries – would allow Galbraith's hypothesis to be further explored. Alternatively, the various strategies that are pursued for various market segments could be examined. For example, the recent analysis by Mayo and Nairn (2009) highlights how children are being tracked and targeted by big business, which feeds on their dreams, commodifies their youth and takes advantage of their susceptibility to turn them into demanding consumers that prey on their parents to spend, spend, spend.

Third, the fact that B&W executives appeared to have ignored much of their marketing research by emphasizing the product attributes of Capri raises questions as to the ability of Galbraith's thesis to generate clear testable hypotheses. On the one hand, it appears to support the contention about the indispensability of the management of needs in the management of demand. Yet, on the other hand, it underscores the fallibility of the technostructure and may demonstrate a lack of confidence in the robustness of the "art" of marketing. As the Capri marketing experience highlights, the firm's planning processes are not always successful. The B&W documents reveal substantial trial and error. The imprecision of the marketing process, however, is acknowledged in *Economics and the Public Purpose*:

> Much of what is called market research, it may also be noted, is imprecise. Subjective, random or fraudulent judgments are offered in impressive pseudo-sociometric tables to suggest a precise relationship between outlays on different kinds of persuasion and the resulting sales. This will not be surprising. An industry that employs much carefully tempered mendacity will not be sensitive to its application to itself. (Galbraith, 1973a: 154)

Ultimate success is by no means assured. Galbraith (1967a: 211): "unhesitantly concede[s] ... that it doesn't work perfectly," but this does not mean that it does not work at all. On average one would expect the firm to get it right, but it is by no means inevitable, and to point to failures of marketing need not refute Galbraith's broader contention.

Fourth, it is clear that tobacco industry marketing strategies encompass the whole production planning process, that is, they involve more than just the development of a "concerted media advertising" campaign.[29] Galbraith's thesis is much broader than the black box approach to advertising characteristic of the conventional wisdom, approximating the focus of the contemporary marketing discipline (cf. Fergenson and Fergenson, 1989). It considers the larger process of production covering product development, configuration, and targeting as well as advertising (Gunter and Furnham, 1992; Hawkins, Best, and Coney, 1998; Heath, 1995, 1996; Weinstein, 1994). Accordingly, the firm uses an array of strategies to manage psychological needs in order to assure the requisite demand for its products:

> Advertising will be thought the central feature of this management, [and it] is certainly important ... [but] much more is involved ... The management of demand consists in devising a sales strategy for a particular product. It also consists in devising a product, or features of a product, around which a sales strategy can be built. Product design, model change, packaging and even performance, reflect the need to provide what are called strong selling points. They are thus as much a part of the process of demand management as an advertising campaign. (Galbraith, 1967a: 207–8)

Fifth, once the manner in which the planning system operates is recognized, such knowledge can be marshaled to improve social policy (Anderson, Ling, and Glantz 2007). As research on the tobacco documents makes clear, industry demands for more lenient regulation of tobacco marketing should be understood not as a response to consumers' wishes but as part of a protective response aiming to resist outside interference and as an affirmative response seeking to grow and enlarge the influence of incumbent technostructures.

Persuasion – and power

Galbraith's theory of "The Management of Specific Demand" has much to promote it, both theoretically and empirically. Galbraith makes an oft-ignored yet important distinction between the management of basic needs and abstract needs. This is embedded in a richer view of the process of advertising than is commonly considered. Such aspects of the Galbraithian hypothesis can be highlighted by considering the advertising and marketing strategies of the tobacco industry. Internal industry documents reveal that the modern tobacco corporation has attempted to target psychological needs in order to manage and stabilize demand for its product. The tobacco industry has engaged in extensive market research to identify the psychographic markers of various segments of the population, targeting psychological needs that are salient to different groups of people. Moreover, the targeting of such psychological needs draws attention away from the objective properties conferred by tobacco, i.e., smoke and addiction, and its ultimate welfare consequences, i.e., reduced life expectancy. Tobacco firms do not convey the knowledge needed in order to allow consumers to make informed decisions; quite the contrary, the industry instead presents fantasies that intentionally exclude the information necessary for making an informed, truly utility-maximizing and welfare enhancing decision.

Of course, the specific nature of tobacco with its known harmful effects on health means that such a case study represents an extreme example of the nature and extent of consumer manipulation and its welfare implications (Anderson and Dunn, 2006).[30] It nevertheless provides a unique opportunity to draw out many of the theoretical and empirical implications of Galbraith's thesis in a manner that should promote further study and development (cf. Monbiot, 2006, 2007). In the words of Stigler and Becker (1977: 76): "On the traditional view, an explanation of economic phenomena that reaches a difference in tastes between people or times is the terminus of the argument: the problem is abandoned at this point to whoever studies and explains tastes (Psychologists? Anthropologists? Phrenologists? Sociobiologists?)." This needs to be remedied. Such considerations call for the rehabilitation of Galbraith's approach to the management of the consumer, as well as cross-disciplinary investigation into the precise nature, content, and context of the economics of advertising.

Notes

1 As highlighted at the beginning of the chapter, such themes were also recognized by Knight (1921: 318–19): "It is common to think of the economic process as the production of goods for the satisfaction of wants. This view is deficient in two vital respects. In the first place, the economic process produces wants as well as goods to satisfy existing wants, and the amount of social energy devoted to the former and neglected phase of activity is very large and constantly growing." Similarly Schumpeter (1911, 1939, 1943, 1949) recognized these trends. As he first acknowledged in *The theory of economic development*: "It is ... the producer who as a rule initiates economic change, and consumers are educated

by him if necessary; they are, as it were, taught to want new things, or things which differ in some respect or together from those which they have been in the habit of using. Therefore, while it is permissible and even necessary to consider consumers' wants as an independent and indeed the fundamental force in a theory of the circular flow, we must take a different attitude as soon as we analyze *change*" (Schumpeter, 1911: 65).

2 Galbraith's "Revised Sequence" is broader than "The Management of Specific Demand" and encompasses both the regulation and management of aggregate demand, as well as broader social processes which serve to promote and augment consumption patterns: "The effective management of consumer behavior does not embrace the whole task of controlling demand. An automobile company must ensure that consumers devote a dependable share of their outlays to automobiles in general and to its cars in particular. But its sales will still be highly irregular, if though they spend a constant share of their income on its vehicles, there is a radical fluctuation from year to year in what they have to spend. It follows that effective control of consumer demand requires management not only of how income is spent but also of the amount of income that is available for spending. There must be management of demand both for the specific product and for products in general. Measures to maintain a desired level of aggregate demand are part and parcel of the task of industrial planning" (Galbraith 1967: 205).

3 Although Zinkin (1967) and Wilder (1974) attempt to evaluate Galbraith's thesis with respect to the management of the consumer there has been little attempt to further develop the Galbraithian thesis regarding the management of the consumer. Noteworthy exceptions include Gintis (1972), Petrick and Sheehan (2002), Munier and Wang (2005), Dutt (2008), Lamdin (2008), and, less explicitly, Hodgson (2003). See chapter 7 for a more extensive discussion of Galbraith's broader contribution to the theory of the firm and its fate.

4 The genesis of the informative view can be found in Ozga (1960) and Stigler (1961). Telser (1964) examines several US consumer goods industries and concludes that advertising has served principally to facilitate entry. Nelson (1970) introduced the instructive distinction between experience goods and search goods.

5 The origins of the complementary view are to be found in Stigler and Becker (1977), although, as Bagwell (2003) argues, aspects of this perspective can be found in Telser's (1964) and even Kaldor's (1950) work. A thorough treatment and defense of the complementary approach can be found in Becker and Murphy (1993). Hodgson (2003) provides an important and oft-ignored critique of this perspective.

6 Braithwaite (1928) develops the conceptual foundation of the persuasive view in a perceptive, but somewhat neglected, paper. Indeed the view gained greater momentum with the theoretical contributions on Monopolistic Competition (Bagwell, 2003). For example Chamberlin (1933) accepted that advertising could be persuasive and seek to alter consumer wants. Similarly Robinson (1933) emphasized the fact that advertising may create brand loyalty and deter entry. Kaldor (1950) advanced the view further and argued that advertising can lead to a more concentrated market, owing to the presence of scale economies in advertising. Bain (1956) and Comanor and Wilson (1967), working within the structure-conduct-performance paradigm, offered early empirical support for the persuasive view. As Bagwell (2003) notes, the persuasive view was the dominant view explored by the economic literature in the first half of the twentieth century. At the turn of this century it is perhaps now in the minority, which is surprising given the increasing spend and sophistication of modern marketing.

7 Galbraith's (broader) views about consumer management have been challenged on many occasions for a variety of reasons (see Zeboot, 1959; Johnson, 1960; Hayek, 1961; Solow, 1967; Gordon, 1968; Friedman, 1977; Stigler and Becker, 1977). Stanfield (1996) provides a detailed discussion of these many criticisms.

8 For example, as Galbraith (1973b: 157) argued: "One branch of neoclassical economics has long held that the advertising and persuasion in the typically oligopolistic industry is a purely wasteful exercise in aggression and defense ... were this the case, steps would long ago have been taken to limit advertising outlays by common agreements ... In fact, competitive persuasion serves the common purposes of the planning system. Accordingly, no important effort has ever been made to limit it."

9 Such trends were also recognized by Veblen (1923: 306) who noted: "the fabrication of customers can now be carried on as a routine operation ... such technicians are now diligently bred and trained for this use by all the reputable seminaries of learning." Moreover this salesmanship draws upon the "experts and experimenters in applied psychology, with a workmanlike bent in the direction of what may be called creative psychiatry" (Veblen, 1923: 307n.).

10 Such themes also surface in Knight (1921: 261): "In the field of information for consumers, we have the still more staggering development of advertising ... Only a part of advertising is in any proper sense of the term informative. A larger part is devoted to persuasion, which is

a different thing from conviction, and perhaps the stimulation or creation of new wants is a function distinguishable from either. In addition to advertising, most of the social outlay for education is connected with informing the population about the means of satisfying wants, the education of taste. The outstanding fact is that the ubiquitous presence of uncertainty permeating every relation of life has brought it about that information is one of the principal commodities that the economic organization is engaged in supplying."

11 Similarly Preston (2003: 18) describes "the 'adverse interest' of sellers," which he states, "obligates consumers to know that sellers have purposes, such as making a profit, that prompt them to behave differently than if they were putting the consumer's best interest first."

12 This recruitment of a loyal and automatic corps of customers has been vividly demonstrated by the San Francisco lesbian, gay, bisexual, and transgender (LGBT) community's boycott of Philip Morris (PM) and PM's subsequent courting of the LGBT market (Offen, Smith, and Malone, 2003).

13 Galbraith's approach recognizes the importance of distinguishing between needs and wants, which is poorly accommodated in the approach and methodology of the conventional wisdom. It is similar to the Post Keynesian approach to consumption (Lavoie, 1992, 1994), which begins with the principle of satiable needs, a recognition that (a) there is a fundamental distinction between wants and needs and (b) there are threshold levels of consumption, that is, that beyond certain points, price will have no bearing on the decision to consume. Post Keynesians argue that there is a hierarchy of needs in which some are more basic and fundamental than others. This implies that needs and wants must be satisfied reflecting some degree of prioritisation, with some needs becoming satiated before others.

14 This thesis is related to, but clearly different from, Keynes's distinction in his essay "Economic Possibilities for our Grandchildren." Galbraith (1958: 46) had clearly read this essay and book, quoting it with approval in his discussion of "Economics and the Tradition of Despair" in *The Affluent Society.* Keynes (1972a: 326) noted: "Now it is true that the needs of human beings may seem to be insatiable. But they fall into two classes – those needs which are absolute in the sense that we feel them whatever the situation of our fellow human beings may be, and those which are relative in the sense that we feel them only if their satisfaction lifts us above, makes us feel superior to, our fellows. Needs of the second class, those which satisfy the desire for superiority, may indeed be insatiable; for the higher the general level, the higher still are

they. But this is not so true of the absolute needs – a point may soon be reached, much sooner perhaps than we all of us are aware of, when these needs are satisfied." Galbraith, while emphasizing the emulative nature of psychic needs, focused more on the susceptibility and openness to persuasion. Accordingly it may be more appropriate to view Galbraith's approach as more inspired by Veblen's (1904) critical commentary on "the leisure class."

15 This is similar to Lavoie's (1994) approach to consumer theory, which outlines a realistic view of consumer demand, one that captures many of the concerns voiced by Galbraith.

16 Galbraith's argument is probably inspired by Veblen's "*The Theory of the Leisure Class* ... [which] brilliantly and truthfully illuminates the effect of wealth on behavior. No one who has read this book ever again sees the consumption of goods in the same light. Above a certain level of affluence the enjoyment of goods – of dress, houses, automobiles, entertainment – can never again be thought intrinsic as, in a naïve way, the established or neoclassical economics still holds it to be" (Galbraith, 1979a: 137).

17 On this conception it is worth comparing to Sombart (1913: 74): "To excite interest, to evoke confidence, to awaken the urge to buy – this is the climax of the fortunate trader's endeavor ... It suffices that it is achieved by internal rather than external compulsion, that the other parties to their transaction enter the deal not against their will but by their own resolve. Suggestion must be the aim of the trader. Of the means of inner compulsion there are many."

18 The tobacco industry lost access to these vehicles of mass persuasion in the US in 1971, however, when cigarette advertising was banned from TV and radio. This may have nevertheless accelerated the tobacco industry's use of sophisticated forms of market research and advertising strategies to reach different sub-populations of consumers through print media. The proliferation of print media such as magazines also necessitated improvements in the targeting of advertising messages.

19 Compare Baran and Sweezy (1966: 131–2), who also argued that: "The function of advertising, perhaps its dominant function today, thus becomes that of waging, on behalf of the producers and sellers of consumer goods, a relentless war against saving and in favor of consumption. And the principal means of carrying out this task are to induce changes in fashion, create new wants, set new standards of status, enforce new norms of propriety. The unquestioned success of advertising in achieving these aims has greatly strengthened its role as a force counteracting monopoly capitalism's tendency to stagnation and at the

same time marked it as the chief architect of the famous 'American Way of Life'."

20 With the legal challenges faced by the tobacco industry, the chorus of advertisements for cigarettes as a product category benefits each firm selling its brands within the category. Promotion of cigarettes in general aids individual tobacco firms in the current environment of increasing societal concern for, and legislative responses to, the health effects of smoke and secondhand smoke.

21 The US tobacco industry is dominated by an oligopolistic structure, as Galbraith (1952a: 57–8, 103–5) highlighted in *American Capitalism*. As Gruber (2001: 196–7) notes: "Tobacco is dominated today by four large firms: Phillip Morris (producers of Malboro, Merit, and others who, according to Bulow and Klemperer [1998], control 49 percent of the market); R.J. Reynolds (Camel, Winston; 25 percent of the market); Brown and Williamson (Cool, Carlton; 16 percent of the market); and Lorillard (Kent, Newport; 9 percent of the market). These firms produce over 98 percent of the cigarettes smoked in the United States. As one might expect based on this high level of concentration, the tobacco industry is also very profitable (Bulow and Klemperer, 1998). Profits as a percent of revenue are roughly 38 percent across the industry."

22 The original research presented in this chapter is based on an analysis with Stacey Anderson of documents collected from the Legacy Tobacco Documents Library, Tobacco Documents Online, and the tobacco industry documents websites. These archives contain more than 40 million pages of industry documents related to the advertising, manufacturing, marketing, sales, and industry research of tobacco products. For detailed information on methods for searching and analyzing the documents archives, see Malone and Balbach (2000); Balbach, Gasior, and Barbeau (2002) and MacKenzie, Collin, and Lee (2003). In analyzing Galbraith's thesis, a sample of approximately 200 relevant creative briefs, marketing research reports, focus group transcripts, plans, contracts, and memoranda were analyzed using the methods presented in these guides.

23 The RICO Act was passed by congress in 1970 with the goal of eradicating the public detriment of organized crime (e.g. the Mafia) on the national economy.

24 In addition to elucidating the circumstances surrounding the creation of the TIRC (later renamed the Council for Tobacco research, or CTR, and referred to in the ruling at the "Enterprise") and the profit incentive for its creation, Judge Kessler further described the ultimate intent of the "Enterprise" as one not of scientific research but of public relations.

25 Such consumer profiling typifies other industries and is increasingly being used by Governments, in the form of "social marketing," to counter the effects of excessive consumption of a range of products and promote lifestyle changes.

26 The power of psychographic profiling, however, should not be underestimated. After gathering psychographic information on their consumers and implementing marketing plans tailored to these specific segments, Porche Cars North America in the early 1990s ended a seven-year slump, with sales rising by 48 percent (Taylor, 1995).

27 Early econometric work by McGuiness and Cowling (1975) suggested that total advertising expenditure for cigarettes influences the total spending on cigarettes and is not, as the tobacco industry has argued, frittered away through inter-brand rivalry. Since then the evidence has become more complex (see Chaloupka and Warner, 2000).

28 Just like the tobacco industry other industries, have attempted to divide its consumers into a variety of psychographic segments to manage the demand for its products. The automotive industry typically focuses on four psychographic segments: participants, functionalists, ego show-offs, and do-it-yourselfers (Mitchell, 1994). Similarly the alcoholic drinks market has been divided into three psychographic segments: image seekers, taste seekers, and commodity drinkers (Sampson, 1992). Such approaches, however, are not just restricted to consumption goods. The use of psychographic profiling, for example, has been used to manipulate the demand for agriculture products. For example as part of its "Basis" corn herbicide campaign, DuPont tried to persuade farmers by appealing to their emotional needs to protect family and to enhance their quality of life. The campaign promised to help farmers reduce herbicide costs and increase profits to provide more for their families and, ultimately, to help them pass down the family farm to their children. The "Basis" campaign helped DuPont gain a competitive advantage in an otherwise cluttered marketplace (Bernick, 1996).

29 For example, first of all filter cigarettes and later low-tar cigarettes were advertised to consumers increasingly concerned about the health hazards of smoking (Pollay and Dewhirst, 2002). Similarly as second-hand smoke has also been recognized as a health hazard, the social acceptability of smoking became a concern. This has resulted in tobacco companies experimenting with several ways of modifying the odor and visibility of smoke (though without reducing actual toxicity) with the intention of increasing the social acceptability of smoking (Connolly *et al.*, 2000). Additionally, to increase demand in the young market, the industry has sought to manipulate tobacco blends, additives, and cigarette papers to appeal to young palates (Wayne and Connolly, 2002).

30 Recent advances in economic theory such as Gruber and Koszegi (2001), however, argue that the rationality axiom may be extended (with modifications) to the domain of addiction. Such considerations further suggest that we should be careful in dismissing the experience of the tobacco industry as isolated and unrepresentative.

10 *Money and the real world*

The history of money teaches much or it can be made to teach much. It is, indeed, exceedingly doubtful if much that is durable can be learned about money in any other way ... From the history we can also see more vividly than in any other way, how money and the techniques for its management and mismanagement were evolved and how they now serve or fail to serve. It is from the past that we see how new institutions – corporations, trade unions and the welfare state – have altered the problem of maintaining price stability in the present and how changing circumstances – movement to a class structure in which fewer and fewer people are successfully taught to take less, the changing political interest of the affluent – have greatly complicated the task.

J. K. Galbraith (1975: 13)

Capitalist society ... is defined by the additional phenomenon of credit creation – by the practice, responsible for so many outstanding features of modern economic life, of financing enterprise by bank credit, i.e., by money (notes or deposits) manufactured for that purpose.

Joseph A. Schumpeter (1943: 167)

Although recognized as a prominent Keynesian, little serious reflection has been given to the views of J. K. Galbraith on the nature of money and a monetary economy. While Galbraith's Keynesianism peppered *The Affluent Society* (1958a), *The New Industrial State* (1967a), and *Economics and the Public Purpose* (1973a), and these works contain some commentary about money, their main focus is an analysis of the substantial economic power that the large firm possesses. For this reason, Galbraith appeared less concerned with details of the financial sectors or the nature of money than Keynes or other leading Post Keynesians such as Hyman Minsky or Paul Davidson. However, when these works are seen along other contributions, notably *The Great Crash, 1929* (1955a), *Money* (1975), and *A Short History of*

Financial Euphoria (1990a), Galbraith's monetary economics comes into clearer view.

These contributions warrant further study and reflection. Galbraith's writings on money addressed the fundamental questions that all serious monetary theorists must address, such as: How does money come into existence and what are the conditions that allow for its continued existence? What is its nature and role in an economy? How do the responses to these questions impinge upon our view of the historical development of the banking system? As we shall see Galbraith's answers to these questions were informed by an appreciation of monetary history and are distinctly Post Keynesian.

Galbraith, like the Post Keynesians, highlighted the salience of the financial sector and the distinctive nature of money.[1] Galbraith presented an analysis of money and monetary accumulation that recognized the importance of history, uncertainty, distributional issues and the relevance of political and economic institutions in determining the level of activity in an economy. Moreover, an examination of his writings on money helps explain why Galbraith does not dwell on financial sector and monetary dynamics in his major trilogy. The purpose of this chapter is therefore to consider in depth Galbraith's view of money and assess its continuing relevance.

Money

In the contemplation of economic affairs, money has long been a focal point for discussion and disagreement. However, confusion over the meaning and nature of money continues to plague the economics profession. As Galbraith and others have remarked, money is an enigma, a Holy Grail to which many great minds have turned their attention. Yet there is still no consensus on that most fundamental of questions – what *is* money? Galbraith argued that the nature of modern money and the nature of financial markets and banking can only be understood with reference to history and society.[2] As Harrod has remarked: "Money is a social phenomenon, and many of its current features depend on what people think it is or ought to be" (quoted in Davidson, 1972: 140). Galbraith's (1975) historiography and anthropological analysis of money, and its exemplifications and manifestations over time, identifies the economic, political, and sociological forces that give rise to money and drive its evolution. This analysis reveals that over time many different items have fulfilled the role of money:

> For some four thousand earlier years there had been agreement on the use of one or more of three metals for the purposes of exchange, these being silver, copper and gold ... For brief periods, it should be noted, iron also intruded. And much later tobacco ... had a limited but notable run. More awkward or exotic items such as cattle, shells, whisky and stones, though greatly relished by teachers on money, have never been durably important for people much removed from primitive rural existence. (Galbraith, 1975: 17)

As this analysis makes clear, commodities such as precious metals exhibit a durability that enables them to function as money. It also points to the importance of delineating the essential nature and role of money. The conventional response is that money "is a difficult concept to define, partly because it fulfils not one but three functions, each of them providing a criterion of moneyness ... those of a unit of account, a medium of exchange, and a store of value" (Scitovsky, 1969: 1). What is more these functions are marshaled to derive "illustrative" definitions of money. That is, historically monetary theorists have used exemplifications rather than explanations to define money (by referring to monetary aggregates such as M1, M2, etc.). But, as Post Keynesians have been keen to point out, systematic enquiry "can only occur when definitions are cast not in terms of specific illustrations but are formulated in terms of *essential* features and properties" (Davidson, 1977: 196). Galbraith recognized this, noting that money must possess certain characteristics:

> Writers on money have regularly distinguished between three types of currency: (1) that which owes its value, as do gold and silver, to an inherent desirability derived from well-established service to pride of possession, prestige of ownership, personal adornment, dinner service or dentistry; (2) that which can readily be exchanged for something of such inherent desirability or which carries the promise ... of eventual exchange; and (3) currency which is intrinsically worthless, carries no promise that it will be redeemed in anything useful or desirable and which is sustained at most, by the fiat of the state that it be accepted. In fact, all three versions are variations on a single theme ... It was the fact of scarcity ... that was important. (Galbraith, 1975: 72)

Whatever is to function as money must be scarce at the level of society and not easily reproducible (in real terms) by the use of labor if society increases its demand for it. Technically to remain scarce and hold its liquidity premium, money must be non-producible and other reproducible items cannot easily be substituted for use in the function of money as a means of settling transaction obligations. This is crucial to Post Keynesian explanations of unemployment. Money does not grow on trees; when one is unemployed one cannot just harvest money trees to obtain additional purchasing power (Davidson, 1974, 1981, 1994; Dunn, 2008a).[3] As Keynes (1936: 230–1) pointed out:

> The first characteristic ... is the fact that money has, both in the long and in the short period, a zero, or at any rate a very small, elasticity of production, so far as the power of private enterprise is concerned ... elasticity of production meaning, in this context, the response of the quantity of labor applied to producing it to a rise in the quantity of labor which a unit of it will command. Money, that is to say, cannot be readily produced; labor cannot be turned on at will by entrepreneurs to produce money in increasing quantities as its price rise in terms of the wage-unit ... The second *differentia* of money is that it has an elasticity of substitution equal, or nearly equal, to zero; which means as the exchange value of money rises there is no tendency to substitute some other factor for it.

To say that money does not grow on trees and is non-producible appears to contradict monetary history – the fact that tobacco functioned as money "in Virginia for nearly two centuries and in Maryland for a century and a half" (Galbraith, 1975: 57). Tobacco literally does grow on trees and history would appear to challenge the Post Keynesian analysis. Galbraith, however, recognized that the key to anointing something as "money," even a "producible" shrub such as tobacco, was to ensure that it was scarce, that the crop harvest would not be rapidly expanded by employing additional labor, and that its quality and quantity could be verified over time:

> Initially the tobacco passed from hand to hand in the manner of paper and coins. Apart from being somewhat friable, it had two other characteristics of considerable importance. As a medium of exchange that was grown instead of mined, minted or printed, its supply was uniquely a matter not of luck, organization or state authority but of individual will. And it lent itself with exceptional readiness to depreciation in quality. Both characteristics of tobacco were energetically exploited. (Galbraith, 1975: 57–8)

As a result, the authorities in Virginia and Maryland tried vigorously to limit tobacco production and prevent the debasement of the currency, as evidenced by actions to (1) prevent the use of gold and silver as a means of payment (1642); (2) suspend tobacco production (1666, 1683), and; (3) establish public Warehouses to weigh and grade tobacco (*c.* 1727).[4] "From the earliest days of the Virginia and Maryland settlements, colonial governments were concerned with arrangements for limiting the production of tobacco and thus sustaining its purchasing power" (Galbraith, 1975: 57–8).

In contrast, although precious metals have been mined and minted for most of history, their supply was relatively steady such that for practical purposes it was a non-producible good.[5] The discovery of gold and silver in the New World, however, appears to challenge this view. As Galbraith (1975: 21–2) highlighted, in "the sixteenth and the early seventeenth centuries prices varied upward and greatly with the vast increase in the supply of precious metals available for coinage from across the Atlantic." The increased volume of precious metals available to Europe by the discovery of already produced gold and silver by the natives of Central and South America, according to traditional accounts, led to an increase in the money supply for Europeans and this was associated with inflation. Galbraith, however, was clear that this "profits" inflation, propelled by the movement of these precious metals from the new world to the old world, facilitated and promoted entrepreneurialism and accumulation, that is, the monetary system that evolved during this period had a demonstrative impact on the level of trade (cf. Arestis and Howells, 2001). Even at the dawn of capitalism money was far from a veil, behind which real forces operated.[6] Deeper historical study further brings to light the nexus between accumulation and monetary innovation, and how the pressure for such innovation is driven by the needs of trade:

> In the seventeenth century the [Dutch East India Company] had been an exceedingly solid enterprise, although it often needed short-run accommodation for outfitting ships or until the ships came in. Such loans the [public] Bank [of Amsterdam] came to provide out of the funds on deposit to the account of others. This was a small step towards what, for the modern, everyday commercial bank, is the most orthodox of operations. (Galbraith, 1975: 27)[7]

Galbraith recognized that the legitimization and development of money as a means of contractual payment flowed from historical evolution, from the needs of government and the institutions of business. Money permits production and accumulation and is the means by which exchanges and contracts are settled and discharged over time. Indeed a desire for monetary experimentation, to finance the needs of trade and act as a means of contractual settlement, propelled the development of paper money and fractional reserve banking. Bankers recognized that they could make money through responding to the needs of trade:

> Gold and silver, when deposited at the bank, could be loaned at interest, and borrowers could pay the interest out of what they made from having the loan. And if ... more could be loaned than was on deposit – given the unlikelihood that all depositors would come for their hard money at once – yet more borrowers could be accommodated, yet more interest earned ... From the intrinsic charm of this reward and the resulting improvement in community well-being came an overriding pressure to make loans that increased the outstanding notes and deposits beyond the amount of gold and silver in the vault. Thus, more precisely, the problem of banking: How should lending be limited and other precautions taken against the day when depositors and noteholders would come for the precious metal that, in the nature of banking, wasn't there? (Galbraith, 1975: 39)

Governments and sovereigns also saw an opportunity to ensure the needs of the state were met. In order to relieve the perilous financial condition of France in the early eighteenth century, Louis XIV set up a bank to attract deposits of gold and wealth:

> Under a royal edict of 2 May 1716, [John] Law, with his brother, was given the right to establish a bank with capital of 6 million livres, about 250,000 pounds. The bank was authorized to issue notes. This it did in the form of loans, and, as might be imagined, the principal borrower was the state. The government used the notes in turn to pay its expenses and pay off its creditors. The notes were declared legal tender for payment of taxes. (Galbraith, 1975: 33)

Like private banking, however, the authority of state money rests similarly on the confidence with which the paper was held:

> Government paper in its early manifestations often had the advantage of a rate of interest – a promise of a modest premium when turned in for redemption. It had also back of its promise of redemption the majesty and the integrity of the state, over much of history where money was concerned

two exceedingly dubious assets. Usually, also, it was given a contrived or compelled value. It was declared that, when presented by a debtor to his creditor in adequate amount, the paper legally discharged the debt – it was legal tender. Thus debtors would seek and cherish the money for paying debts. Creditors could not resist. This reinforcement was invariably less potent than hoped. (Galbraith, 1975: 55)

For example, the aversion of the New World colonies to taxation meant that making money legal tender for taxes did not ensure that it became an acceptable form of exchange (Galbraith, 1975: 60). Private banking and private note issue became an acceptable alternative to state paper money.

From this it is clear that Galbraith acknowledged that what is recognized and accepted as money can be linked to the need to pay taxes, or settle contractual obligations, or both, which accords with Keynes's (1930) definition of chartalism in his *Treatise on Money*. Keynes (1930: 3) classifies money as: "that by delivery of which debt contracts and price contracts are *discharged*, and in the shape of which a store of general purchasing power is *held*."[8] It is also important to note that the emergence of "paper" or credit money does not undermine the view that money is non-producible by the use (input) of real resources.[9] To say money possesses a zero elasticity of production does not mean that the money supply is unalterable. As Galbraith (1975) argues throughout *Money*, the money supply may alter endogenously via the banking system or via open market operations performed by the central bank. All a negligible elasticity of production means is that labor cannot easily gain access to, or produce directly with their own hands, that which is deemed to be socially acceptable as money; for example banks do not supply credit to all who demand it.[10]

Liquidity, fast exits, and bank runs

Historically, the problem with the private banking systems that emerged in the New World was its assumption that not everyone would turn up at the bank simultaneously to redeem their claims on the money of ultimate redemption or discharge of contractual obligations:

> The marvel of banks in relation to money – the wonder of creating deposits or issuing notes that so served – was suspended on one silken thread. That was the requirement that depositors or noteholders come in decently small numbers for the hard currency that the bank was under obligation to pay. If all came at once, the bank could not pay, then, often in much haste, all came. (Galbraith, 1975: 31)

To comprehend the need for some form of money that becomes the means of ultimate contractual settlement we must understand the concept of liquidity. In a money-contracting economic system, individuals, and firms have enough liquidity if they have a sufficient quantity of money to meet all future monetary contractual obligations as they come due (or they can obtain enough money, either by borrowing or by readily selling a liquid asset).

Faced with an uncertain future, and hence the possibility that at some point either individuals or firms are unable to meet future contractual obligations, it is quite sensible for individuals or firms to demand and hold an excess of money and other liquid assets (readily resalable for money), over and above the amount of already existing future contractual obligations. Holding money and liquid assets acts as a security blanket; it protects the holder from unpredictable changes that might occur in their future cash flow position. The more uncertain the future appears to businesses and individuals, the more liquidity they will want. In contrast, according to classical theory, all currently produced goods essentially exchange for currently produced goods, and future purchase commitments and earnings are always known with (statistical) predictably, there is no rational need to hold money over any period of calendar time for liquidity purposes (Davidson, 1994).

When a nation is on a commodity standard, for example the gold standard, then the state has announced that the tendering of gold coins or gold certificates issued by the state, where each certificate is "backed" by a specific weight of gold, are the legal tender for discharging all obligations (debts) private and public. Galbraith (1975) noted that, in this system, when banks make loans using deposited gold as reserves, the total obligations of the banking system typically exceed the volume of gold stored in bank vaults. As long as a majority of the community are willing to settle obligations using bank notes and/or checks instead of gold, bank deposits and notes serve as the money in the system. As long as people believe that banks can redeem all their obligations in terms of gold, few will call on the banks for redemption. But if the public fears that the bank cannot redeem all its obligations, a run on the bank will occur as all members of the public attempt to make a "fast exit" from bank deposits to the legal tender money of contractual settlement.

In a fiat money system, where the government declares that central bank notes and obligations are legal tender for all debts – both private and public – the obligations of the central bank to private bankers are the "reserves" similar to gold under the gold standard. A "fast exit" run on a private bank will occur only when the public believes that the banker no longer has sufficient assets on their balance sheet that can be converted into legal tender to meet the public's demand.

Such "runs" precipitate banking collapses. Many painful experiences suggest that if money's "moneyness" is to be preserved, confidence in what is acceptable for discharging contractual obligations must be maintained. As Galbraith (1975: 121) pointed out: "A bank failure is not an ordinary business adventure ... it has not one but two adverse effects on economic activity: Owners lose their capital and depositors their deposits, and both therewith lose their ability to purchase things. But failure (or for that matter fear of failure) also means a shrinkage in the money supply."

Galbraith (1975: 39) argued that, historically, there emerged three solutions to this, of which two or all three could be combined. First, banks could be required to maintain the convertibility of their notes into metallic coins. This solution has been eclipsed by the evolution of modern credit money and banking. Second, banks should have ample reserves available to meet the demand for withdrawals. Third, there should be some special provision for the day when everyone comes to claim their monies. It is in the latter case that the central bank must become the lender of the last resort – something which the Bank of England had to relearn after the Northern Rock debacle in the fall of 2007.

From this need has evolved the central banking role that is now performed through a variety of institutional configurations across modern monetary production economies – to maintain money's standing, that is, to sustain its price and thus its liquidity function.[11] This points to the key roles of the central bank: "As restraint on bank lending during the boom is a basic central-bank function, so serving as a lender of last resort is its main task in the ensuing depression" (Galbraith, 1975: 127). Unfortunately, the experience of 2008 meant that these lessons have had to be re-learnt by policy makers and politicians the hard way. Central banks must take action to ensure that money functions as a means of contractual settlement, facilitating investment and enterprise. They must seek to guard against inflation, which erodes nominal value over time. And they must also ensure that confidence in a bank or a currency is maintained:

> a central bank has three primary functions in relation to commercial banks: It counters the temptation to excessive loans and note issue by the ordinary banks by presenting their notes for redemption; it similarly restrains loan and resulting deposit expansion, perhaps by requiring the commercial banks to keep a specified proportion of their deposits in its vaults, perhaps by pulling loanable cash out of the banks by selling securities and holds the resulting cash itself; and its loans are a source of salvation when too many come to the commercial banks for money. (Galbraith, 1975: 80)

Galbraith was clear that the demands of coordinating exchanges over time – either for trade, production or wars – drove the evolution of the banking system and created the impetus for financial innovation. Moreover, the specific nature of money as a liquid store of wealth underpinned this. Although some other durables may function as a store of wealth, only money functions as a means of contractual settlement (as long as citizens accept the state as the enforcer of the civil law of contracts).[12] As modern economies evolved, both governments and firms increasingly entered "into contracts specifying prices and amounts to be provided or bought for substantial periods of time" (Galbraith, 1967a: 48). In *The New Industrial State*, for example, Galbraith (1967a) identified how large-scale production takes place through (historical) time and that in contemporary capitalism money-denominated contracts facilitate the efficient organization of time-consuming production and exchange activities by providing some assurances to the contracting parties as to the delivery of future commitments (see chapters 7 and 8 above).[13] To finance such trade money is required – because goods buy money, money buys goods, but goods do not buy goods. Money is a "liquid" store of wealth that enables transactions that create contractual obligations to be discharged or postponed.

Expectations, accumulation, and irrational exuberance

Galbraith identified the pathology of modern capitalism in the nexus between the demands of accumulation and the evolving nature of the financial system. Galbraith argued that an unfettered competitive capitalist system operating on pure free market principles was inherently cyclical and unstable.[14] The banking system, through the auspices of money creation, contains the seeds of accumulation, greed, and eventual volatility. "As banking developed from the seventeenth century on, so, with the support of other circumstance, did the cycles of euphoria and panic. Their length came to accord roughly with the time it took people to forget the last disaster" (Galbraith, 1975: 31). Such cycles of euphoria and excess are driven by the desire to accumulate – a love of avarice by both bankers and entrepreneurs:

> The banking and monetary arrangements of the last century ... were admirably designed to respond to euphoria, finance it, enhance it and then add force to the ensuing collapse. Banks and money could be created without effective constraint, to finance the expansion and speculation ... But also essential was the impulse to borrow, invest, risk, speculate. Had this not existed, no bank could have created it. In the United States in the nineteenth century this instinct was highly developed, and for good reason. A new continent rich in land and raw materials was suddenly available for use. (Galbraith, 1975: 124)

In *The Great Crash, 1929* (1955a), *Money* (1975), *A Short History of Financial Euphoria* (1990a) and *The Economics of Innocent Fraud* (2004) Galbraith described the common events preceding and accompanying particular financial crises, including major bubbles such as: the Tulip bulb mania in the 1630s, the South Sea bubble in the early 1700s, the Mississippi bubble, which caused a stock market crash in eighteenth-century France; the Florida real estate bubble in the 1920s; the stock market crash of 1929; the stock market crash of 1987; the Nikkei bubble; the collapse of Barings Bank; and the NASDAQ bubble, which burst in 2000.[15] Indeed as Leathers and Raines (2008: 551–2) point out: "his genius was such that the insights he provided into the nature and social consequences of episodes of speculative bubbles in asset prices stand as a vital part of his legacy to modern economics."

Sentiments of greed, euphoria, frustrated expectations, and panic moved such financial episodes, set off by contemplation and speculation regarding some fundamental change in the economy arousing heightened expectations of return, leading to excess, fraud, and eventually collapse:

> In all the panics there were recognizable constants. First came an expansion in business activity. This usually centered on some dominant form of investment, one that reworked the economic geography of the country. The first such object of investment was the canals; then, and much more important, came the railroads. With canal- and railroad-building went expansion into new lands. Often, although not invariably, prices rose. (Galbraith, 1975: 114)

Expanding business activity feeds entrepreneurial and speculative behavior in the banking sector and financial sectors.[16] "Speculation centers on one or more of those assets, real or fiduciary, that are central to the expansion currently under way" (Galbraith, 1975: 115). It drives monetary innovation and the new forms of credit, financing structures, hedging vehicles, and Enron-type structures that are contrived to allow banks and firms to participate in the boom (cf. Galbraith, 1955a, 1975, 1996b, 2004; see also Minsky, 1982, 1986). Heightened expectations stimulate a credit boom with the banking system keen to lend money in the desire to cash in on the new situation and secure even higher returns:

> The banks, needless to say, provided the money that financed the speculation that in each case preceded the crash. Those buying land, commodities or railroad stocks and bonds came to the banks for loans. As the resulting notes and deposits went into circulation, they paid for the speculative purchases of yet others. (Galbraith, 1975: 120)

Company balance sheets become more precarious as firms borrow more, becoming weighed down with large future commitments to service their debt. With expectations of gain tending to rise with each increase in profits, hedge-financing structures tend to become more speculative; increasingly commitments to make future payments are entered into which can only be covered by issuing new liabilities, that is, borrowing (cf. Minsky, 1986).

New credit vehicles are also introduced to ensure that what is produced is ultimately demanded, reinforcing the link and interdependence between the demand and supply of money. The invention of store credit cards just before World War I and hire purchase in the USA in the 1920s, for example, opened up a new reservoir of credit that drove business activity and expanded the money supply. Galbraith (1958a) further highlighted this tendency in *The Affluent Society* in a chapter entitled "The Bill Collector Cometh," anticipating the explosion and proliferation of credit cards as a result of the Marquette Decision in 1978, which has massively increased consumer debt and endogenously expanded the money supply (see Scott, 2006, 2007):

> One danger in the way wants are now created lies in the related process of debt creation. Consumer demand thus comes to depend more and more on the ability and willingness of consumers to incur debt. An increase in consumer debt is all but implicit in the process by which wants are synthesized. Advertising and emulation, the two dependent sources of desire work across society. (Galbraith, 1958a: 166)

Although credit cards, hire purchase and cheap loans can help underpin an expansion of aggregate demand in the good times, in times of recession, they can accelerate a rapid decline in consumption and aggregate demand, precipitating increased unemployment, personal bankruptcy, and general economic and social misery.

Financial markets and institutions, moreover, are not immune to such innovation and speculation (Toporowski, 2002). Rather they exemplify and amplify it. In *The Great Crash, 1929* Galbraith's discussion echoes Keynes's (1930) *Treatise on Money* argument of how stock market activity affects bank deposits. Keynes argued that when traders are buying and selling in anticipation of capital gains, that is, speculating, stock prices will depend on the balance between "bullish" expectations, that stock prices will rise, and "bearish" expectations, that prices will fall. In a "bullish" market, sustained by "herdish" animal spirits, market sentiment will drive prices and expectations of investment returns to abnormally high levels (Akerlof and Shiller, 2009; Shiller, 2009).[17] The detailed historiography of *The Great Crash, 1929* endorses and provides supportive evidence for this view (cf. Barsky and DeLong, 1990; DeLong and Shleifer, 1991).

The recent revolution in information technology has similarly driven forward monetary innovation and speculation: financial derivatives, auction rate securities, asset-backed securities, and interest rate swaps stand out as contemporary examples.[18] Such speculation leads to euphoria or overtrading – what Alan Greenspan referred to as "irrational exuberance" – in which rising collateral and securities prices encourage speculative excess.[19] As debt accumulates, a situation arises in which debts can only be serviced by the issue of new liabilities. As long as the financial markets are booming it is possible to sustain low levels of cash inflow by issuing new stocks and securities to finance current liabilities:

> Speculation occurs when people buy assets, always with the support of some rationalizing doctrine, because they expect their prices to rise. That expectation and the resulting action then serve to confirm expectation. Presently the reality is not what the asset in question – the land or commodity or stock or investment company – will earn in the future. Rather it is only that enough people are expecting the speculative object to advance in price to make it advance in price and thus attract yet more people to yet further fulfill expectation of yet further increases. (Galbraith, 1975: 116)

Such excess naturally leads to the next phase – when expectations, stock market prices, and financing structures collapse. When the gap between the over-optimistic expectations and the more pedestrian reality is revealed, markets are forced to adjust:

> This process has a pristine simplicity; it can last only so long as prices are rising reliably. If anything serious interrupts the price advance, the expectations by which the advance is sustained are lost or anyhow endangered. All who are holding for a further rise – all but the gullible and egregiously optimistic of which there is invariably a considerable supply – then seek to get out. Whatever the pace of the preceding build-up, whether slow or rapid, the resulting fall is always abrupt. (Galbraith, 1975: 116)

As financial markets slow down, organizations that have covered their future liabilities through issuing more debt are forced to sell assets to meet their liabilities. These "distress" sales cause asset prices to fall, at which point the financial markets, and businesses with excessive liabilities to those markets, collapse. The next phase, in which investors try to get their money back out of the markets, naturally gives way to "panic" (cf. Minsky, 1982, 1986; Toporowski, 2002). At this stage, prices fall precipitously and asset markets break down, unable to cope with the excess of sale orders. Banks collapse and the fall has a very real effect on non-financial sectors:

> Both bank failures and the fear of bank failures ... had the same effect. Both were forces of compelling power to induce deflation – to contract consumer spending, investment spending and therewith sales, output, employment and prices. In these years the monetary system became an engine with such effect. Not that cause and effect ran only from the monetary system to the economy. While failing banks were bringing down the economy, falling prices, output, earnings and employment were ruining good loans, spreading alarm and bringing down the banks. Economic life, as always, is a matrix in which result becomes cause and cause becomes result. (Galbraith, 1975: 203)

Galbraith's analysis highlights how enterprise has been a prime mover in driving forward monetary expansion and innovation and how the unintended consequence of this innovation has been to introduce greater instability into contemporary economies. What is more, Galbraith's analysis of the Great Depression highlights the multiplier effects and downward cumulative spiral that result as a cause and consequence of liquidity preference:

> Once deflation of prices and contraction of output were well under way, further forces converged to keep them going, give them cumulative effect ... frightened individuals reduced their purchases. This affected the prices, output and employment of their suppliers, and that had yet further effect on demand. And singed and frightened investors stopped investing and hung onto cash. So income that was saved was no longer invested and spent, and this too had further effect. And workers lost jobs and reduced their spending. And in consequence prices and output fell, with yet further effect on prices, production and employment. (Galbraith, 1975: 199)

All in all, Galbraith was clear that the banking system both propels and responds to the economy. The financial system matters; it impacts on the economy in a non-neutral way in both the short run and long run (cf. Arestis and Sawyer, 2003, 2004a, 2006).[20]

Financial non-neutrality

For Galbraith, like Keynes (1936: 159), money and finance is neutral neither in the short run nor the long run. A monetary economy operates in a fundamentally different manner to a barter or exchange economy (Cottrel, 1994; Davidson, 1994, 2007; Arestis and Sawyer, 2003, 2004c, 2006, 2008). Galbraith understood that this vision of the economic process went to the very core of economic thinking:

> Where does economic change originate? Does it begin with those who are responsible for money – in this case with those who made loans and thus caused the supply of notes and deposits to increase? (From this then comes the effect on prices and production, including the stimulating effect of rising prices on production and trade.) Or does change begin with the production. Does it originate in business activity and prices with consequent effect on the demand for loans and thence on the supply of notes and deposits, which is to say the money supply? In short does money influence the economy or does money respond to the economy. (Galbraith, 1975: 46)

Indeed the purpose of Galbraith's historical analysis in *Money* was to highlight the institutional evolution of money and its management, in order to explain both the origins of the quantity theory of money as well as its obsolescence. As is familiar to all economists, "the quantity theory of money … holds, in its most elementary form, that, other things being equal, prices vary directly with the quantity of money in circulation" (Galbraith, 1975: 21).[21] This thesis was rehabilitated most famously through Milton Friedman and Anna Schwartz's *A Monetary History of the United States*, where detailed empirical analysis was marshaled to support the argument that expansions in the money supply preceded increases in prices. Nevertheless, Galbraith (1975: 295) raised what are standard Post Keynesian (Davidson, 1972, 1974; Moore, 1988) and Kaldorian (see Kaldor, 1982) concerns: "Professor Friedman's case was not casually advanced; it was supported by massive evidence which, as necessary, was arranged to serve the author's purpose. (Substantial changes in the velocity of money use had especially to be explained away.) There was also the serious and unresolved problem … of what was to be counted as money." While the quantity theory of money and its modern variants have a *prima facie* plausibility at earlier periods in history, that is, it appears conceivable when precious metals function as money and its quantity is somewhat fixed – although this too can be challenged with respect to historical experience, not least through the profits that could be gained from clipping coinage – the evolution of the modern banking system presents a direct challenge to this thesis and affects the conduct of monetary policy:[22]

> Consistent with [Irving] Fisher's [famous Quantity Theory of Money] formula, but not much considered, was a terrible possibility. It was that the supply of money could not be increased. The largest part of the supply of money ... is deposits in banks. These come into existence as people and firms borrow money. If business is sufficiently bad, profit prospects sufficiently dim, gloom sufficiently deep, businessmen may not borrow money. Then no deposits are created, no money comes into existence. The banks can be provided with cash for reserves by purchases of government securities by the Federal Reserve Banks from the banks or their customers. This cash will lie fallow in the banks. Without borrowing and deposit creation there is no effect on prices or through prices on production. (Galbraith, 1975: 221)

Galbraith rejected the quantity theory of money as misleading monetary theory. This is now accepted by the modern "New Consensus" view in macroeconomics, which moves beyond the quantity theory of money. Indeed as Fontana (2006, 2007) identifies, one of the greatest achievements of the "New Consensus" is the assertion of a non-quantity theoretic approach to monetary policy.

According to Galbraith modern money is largely or wholly credit money, created within the private sector by banks (cf. Arestis and Sawyer, 2006).[23] The non-bank public demand loans, and to the extent to which those loans are granted, money is created (and also money is destroyed by the repayment of loans). Increases in expenditure, whether representing a real increase or reflecting higher prices, have to be financed. In this process, the liquidity preference of the banking sector as it interacts with business expectations is key:

> The problem with monetary policy was now clear. It could make reserves available. It could not cause them to be borrowed, bring about the resulting deposit creation. On the old question of how causation ran, it was plain that, in depression at least, it was the state of trade that ruled. The supply of money did not affect prices and trade nearly so much as the state of trade affected the supply of money and the level of prices. (Galbraith, 1975: 227)

Galbraith argued that the money supply expands unevenly to meet the needs of trade and therefore money is not neutral and impacts upon real economic activity.[24] As such, Galbraith challenged the conventional wisdom that money is merely a veil behind which the real economy operates.[25]

Monetary policy and the principle of effective demand

According to Galbraith the nature of a modern credit money economy severely limits the power and potency of monetary policy in both managing the economy and responding to a recession or depression (cf. Arestis and Sawyer, 2004a, 2004b). In the conventional wisdom of the postwar period, the interaction of the demand for money against a fixed money supply was seen to determine the interest rate – this was the Neo-classical Synthesis Keynesian version of Keynes's liquidity preference theory of money. According to this theory, the interest rate is the price that adjusts to bring into balance decisions to save and invest and, with product and labor market flexibility, ensures a sufficient level of aggregate demand to purchase all labor that is willingly supplied at the prevailing rate.

Galbraith recognized that the evolution of the industrial structure and the banking and financial systems meant that this vision of the adjustment process was misleading. First, in modern economies, dominated by large corporations, ensuring that the level of investment was reconciled with the desired level of savings, was more difficult. This adds to system instability:

> The planning system cannot ensure that demand is sufficient to keep the system operating at capacity. Decisions to save and invest are concentrated in a comparative handful of firms – a few thousand. There is no machinery that ensures that the aggregate of the decisions to invest will be sufficient to offset the aggregate of the decisions to save. If investment is insufficient, the system will be subject to a downward spiral of output and income which – by reducing investment more than saving – may for a substantial time be cumulative and persistent. (Galbraith, 1973a: 321)

Second, and more importantly, Galbraith recognized, long before the emergence of the "New Consensus" in macroeconomics that in a modern credit money economy the interest rate is largely fixed by the banking system: "The interest rate, like other prices in the planning system, is now fixed – for practical purposes by the Federal Reserve

System as it influences the rates charged by the banks. The first step towards a proper [monetary] policy consists in accepting the notion of a relatively permanent level and structure of interest rates" (Galbraith, 1973a: 327).

The "New Consensus" view in macroeconomics has several additional features which are worth remarking and reflecting upon in considering the continuing relevance of Galbraith's analysis (Woodford, 2003; see also Snowdon and Vane, 2005; Goodfriend, 2004). First, monetary policy replaces fiscal policy as the main stabilization policy. Second, the main objective of monetary policy is price stability, which practically means a stable inflation rate around 2 percent. Third, this target, which is sometimes implicit, is controlled through the management of interest rate policies by monetary authorities. And fourth, there is no long-run trade off between inflation and unemployment.

Galbraith's view of the transmission mechanism of monetary policy is consistent with the "New Consensus" view. In the "New Consensus" view, when the inflation rate is above the target rate the short-run interest rate is increased to impact on the interest-sensitive components of aggregate demand. But, in contrast to the "New Consensus" view, he emphasized the overriding impact and role of spending in determining the level of output and employment in both the short and long run: "Monetary policy works as it encourages or discourages the spending and respending of borrowed money. It is that spending, nothing else, that has a practical effect on the economy – on prices, production and employment. To bring monetary policy to bear against inflation, the Federal Reserve discourages the lending of money by the banks" (Galbraith, 1981: 348). Galbraith also argued, moreover, that a restrictive monetary policy stance will have differential effects on the planning and market sectors (see Galbraith, 1981: 348). Galbraith's analysis therefore, is quite distinct from the "New Consensus" macroeconomic framework, which variously embodies the classical dichotomy and the notion of a supply side equilibrium. In the "New Consensus" view the appropriate role of monetary policy is to influence the structure of interest rates so as to stabilize output and employment around their long-run trend values. Typically, fiscal policy plays either no role, or has a limited place, for example in dealing with a liquidity trap.[26] Monetary policy is only able to affect aggregate demand in the short run. In the long run prices and wages are viewed as flexible and the monetary authorities are judged as unable to affect the real interest rate.

Although Galbraith's view of the transmission mechanism is similar to the "New Consensus" view, he would nevertheless challenge its key features and underlying assumptions. Echoing Keynes's 1937 finance motive analysis, Galbraith identified an "endogenous" monetary system where banks make new loans and expand deposits in response to business demand for finance to expand production flows.[27] As Galbraith (1958a: 190) acknowledged the "money supply increases or decreases as the result of increases or decreases in commercial bank lending." The money supply reflects the interaction between decisions by households and firms regarding their demand for deposits and loans and the banking system's willingness to hold bank deposits and provide loans and finance investment (cf. Moore, 1988; Davidson, 1994; Wray, 1998). Business expectations about the future will affect the money supply and the level of output, but they do not affect the interest rate. This is the Keynesian view that output, and not the interest rate, adjusts to bring into balance decisions to save and invest:

> What people sought to save, in Keynes's view, had still to be brought to equal what they wanted to invest. But the adjustment mechanism, he argued, was not the rate of interest but the total output of the economy. If efforts to save exceeded the desire to invest, the resulting shortage of purchasing power or demand caused output to fall (Galbraith, 1975: 232).[28]

According to Galbraith it is this shortage of purchasing power, that is, insufficient aggregate demand, that drives unemployment. As was clear from history, modern monetary economies do not automatically achieve, let alone maintain, the full use of existing resources:

> Recognition that the modern economy was subject to severe downward instability, and that this was neither self-limiting nor self-correcting, came in the decade of the thirties. This was the Keynesian Revolution. (Galbraith, 1973a: 199)

According to Galbraith there are no mechanisms which ensure that the level of effective demand will automatically be consistent with full employment. The mature Galbraithian explanation of the level of unemployment was based first and foremost on the principle of effective demand; it was not contingent upon wage rigidity, adaptive expectations, bounded rationality, money illusion, market structure, or any other phenomena that one chooses to identify.[29] Nevertheless

Galbraith (1973a: 342) also argued that there was a pressing need to consider how new and evolving institutions, such as trade unions and large firms, impacted on the operation of the Keynesian system:

> If prices can be held up by the market power of the corporation, it is production that must fall. When production falls, so will employment ... And the reduced spending of those who lose their jobs or who fear that they will lose their jobs can be expected to have a further depressing effect on output and employment. Plausibly this effect on output and employment will be far greater than that which might come, in a competitive economy, from the reduction in prices and wages that Keynes, in the main, envisaged. (Galbraith, 1975: 234)

Galbraith (1975: 233) argued that the "effect of both corporate concentration and union strength was to make radically more unreliable the adjustments which were assumed to sustain Say's law and the full-employment equilibrium." Indeed the unprecedented severity and differential impact of the deflationary spiral of the Great Depression in part reflected the changing institutional structure of the economy:

> In fact, both unions and corporations, as Keynes wrote, were acting to affirm his thesis. He had support for his ideas that he did not use ... In 1920 ... farm prices fell more rapidly and much more severely than did prices of industrial products ... Between 1929 and 1933, the non-farm product of the economy fell from $88.6 billion to $57.8 billion in 1929 prices. Agricultural output rose slightly – from $10.7 billion to $11.0 billion. Non-agricultural employment fell from 37 million in 1929 to 29 million in 1933. Agricultural employment showed only a negligible change – from 10.5 million to 10.1 million. (Galbraith, 1975: 233–4)

The institutional evolution of modern economies also further affects the nature of the operation of the Keynesian system. Large firms, in seeking to escape market uncertainties through developing control over prices, costs, and the consumer, will also seek to insulate themselves from the vagaries of monetary policy – for example, by generating a level of retained reserves that will shield them from untoward movements in the interest rate:

> The second way of reducing demand is by increasing interest rates and otherwise reducing the supply of funds for lending and thus for investment

spending. Here the differential impact on the two systems is forthright. It is central to the protective purposes of the technostructure – the protection of its autonomy – that it minimize its dependence on borrowed funds. Instead it relies extensively for capital on its own earnings; thus the overwhelming importance of business savings as the modern source of capital. (Galbraith, 1973a: 209–10)

Such institutional factors are further compounded by the fact that the rate of interest is also set by central banks – with an oligopolistic banking sector setting their own rates as a direct mark up against this base rate. This diminishes the role of liquidity preference, as long as there are no "fast exit" runs on either banks or financial markets.[30] Together, these factors led to an important policy conclusion – "monetary policy was like a string. You could pull it, though with incalculable results. But you could not shove it at all" (Galbraith, 1975: 226).[31] When expectations about the future are dimmed, no matter how much the rate of interest falls, it will *not* ignite the animal spirits of the technostructure or entrepreneurs (cf. Krugman, 2005b, 2008c).[32] This points to the essence of Keynesianism, for the state and/or the lender of last resort to maintain purchasing power: "The answer – obvious enough here but rather less obvious at the time – was to make the creation and use of money not permissive but obligatory. Money must not only be manufactured but spent – made to operate directly on the state of trade ... This was fiscal as distinct from monetary policy. It is tied irrevocably to the name of Keynes" (Galbraith, 1975: 227). If the problem is insufficient demand for one's products then why would entrepreneurs seek to invest, even if the price of finance – the interest rate – was lowered? What is required is the pull of rising demand, of higher levels of spending, to pump prime the economy.

In terms of the mechanisms to underpin an expansion in the level of aggregate demand to ward off the threat of depression or recession, Galbraith argued that fiscal policy (deficit spending) needs to be combined with monetary policy in order to sustain purchasing power (cf. Arestis and Sawyer, 2004c). Galbraith acknowledged that fiscal policy can affect the level of borrowing and the level of effective demand by influencing business expectations: "Although in a proper policy the interest rate ceases to be the instrument for controlling the volume of borrowing, the volume of borrowing does not remain uncontrolled. Control is exercised through tax and expenditure policy on the volume of demand in the economy" (Galbraith, 1973a: 327).[33] Galbraith argued that the state could, and should, intervene in providing any demand shortfall through spending over and above its income, to prevent recessions and depressions.[34] In arguing that fiscal policy, that is, deficit spending, was an appropriate response to the threat of recession and depression Galbraith rejected the conventional analogy with the individual as misleading:

> An engagingly plausible mode of thought, the fallacy of composition extends the economics of the family to that of the government. A family cannot indefinitely spend beyond its income. So neither can a government. A parent who borrows to live leaves debts, not a competence, to those who come after. A government that borrows does the same. Both are morally deficient. The comparison between family and state, on second thought, is implausible. That anything so massive, diverse, complex, incomprehensible as the United States government (or any national government) should be subject to the same rules and constraints as a wage earner's household is a matter that, to say the least, requires proof. Nor is it proof, as often said, that it *should* be so. Additionally it should be observed that the wealth and solvency of a nation depend on what its national economy produces. If borrowing and spending enhance production, as the Keynesian idea held, then such borrowing and spending enhance solvency. Only rarely do borrowing and spending enhance wealth for a family. (Galbraith, 1975: 244)[35]

As is clear from this passage, Galbraith acknowledged the role government spending has on influencing entrepreneurial expectations and on wealth creation. In times of recession Galbraith maintained that spending on social infrastructure projects, such as building schools, hospitals, universities, metro systems, and bridges, was the best way to pump prime economic recovery.[36] This is acknowledged by the G20 (2009) who note that estimates of infrastructure multipliers vary from 0.5–1.8 compared to 0.3–0.6 for tax cuts. Galbraith nevertheless also argued that progressive taxation should be combined with targeted fiscal policy in order to reduce income inequality and poverty (Stanfield, 1996; Pressman, 2008). It is needed as a response to the social imbalance generated by the new industrial state. And it can help augment consumption and increase effective demand, promoting higher levels of employment than would otherwise be the case.

Galbraith also moved beyond the Keynesian orthodoxy of his day, arguing long before the rise of New Classical Economics and New

Keynesianism that there was a need to understand the microeconomics of macroeconomics, as well as the macroeconomics of microeconomics (cf. Chick, 1995). For Galbraith (1973a: 208) this was an Achilles' heel of the economics profession:

> In the thirty-five years following the publication of Keynes's *General Theory* the continued growth of the great corporation was duly noted by economists, as also its power over prices. A few came to accept its concern with growth as a primary goal. And the less militant character of labor relations was remarked – as also the tendency to settle disputes by passing the costs along in higher prices. But, again these matters belonged to microeconomics or were the concern of specialists in industrial organization or labor relations. Macroeconomics, having to do with the management of aggregate demand, was as always in a different compartment, the work of different scholars. The division of labor, with its implicit assumption that the two parts of the economy could be studied in isolation, fell at exactly the point where it best disguised the impact of corporate and union power.

Galbraith argued that many "redistributive" microeconomic structures, such as trade unions, minimum wages, welfare payments, minimum price regulation, and agricultural subsidies, promote greater macroeconomic stability.[37] Similarly in *The New Industrial State* Galbraith (1967a) argued that the emergence of "The Revised Sequence", where large firms seek to stabilize demand for its products (through the management of the consumer and greater availability of credit), was a natural "planning" response to the absence of factors automatically ensuring a high and stable level of demand for the goods it produced.

"The Revised Sequence" explains why the planning system, by and large, supports public spending programmes and Keynesian policies. The planning system, in undertaking large, technologically sophisticated investments, has a strong incentive to seek a protective response from the state: to assure future demand for its products by buying (directly) its goods, for example the defense industries; or by lobbying for policies that support the (general) demand for its products, for example by pursuing Keynesian macroeconomic policies that support investment and consumption. As Galbraith (1967a: 229) identified, the state regulation "of aggregate demand is necessary to give certainty to this planning and to protect the technostructure." This analysis underlines the symbiotic relationship between the modern corporation and the state, while also explaining the early appearance of Keynesian policies long before the widespread acceptance of the Keynesian theoretical system, as well as the silent Keynesianism of the Reagan and Bush Sr. administrations.[38]

Galbraith further recognized how the institutional structure of the economy affects the precise nature and expression of aggregate demand as it differs across economies, and within the context of a global economic system. The educational structure underpinning an economy, for example, will affect the nature, composition and duration of unemployment and labor market flexibility. As Galbraith (1967a: 246) remarked:

> Unemployment can be both structural and the result of inadequate demand but also something more. It will appear with slackening of aggregate demand and it will be among those who are most inflexibly tied to particular occupations and locations. At the same time there will be vacancies in positions requiring high and specialized qualification. Employment would be higher both with stronger demand and with a better accommodation of preparation to need. But unemployment also reflects the cultural development of the system. It will be smaller, at any given level of demand, the better the *cultural* accommodation to the needs of the industrial system. If this accommodation is good, there will be a smaller core of functional illiterates who cannot be used at all. And there will be a larger number of people not only to fill the vacancies calling for higher qualification but also with the added mobility between occupations and regions that goes with education.

The import of this analysis is that in deciding the most appropriate policy response, the nature and causes of unemployment need to be properly understood:

> The compartmentalization of economics between microeconomics and macroeconomics hides the most stubborn cause of present-day unemployment in the mature industrial countries: the decline of the older industries. And it also hides the relevant solutions. Unemployment as it microeconomically exists can be corrected by some measure by job retraining, provision of public-service jobs, protective tariffs and by action to address suboptimal labor relations and managerial competence. It cannot be remedied in any complete way by a general tax, expenditure or monetary policy. (Galbraith, 1987: 297)

What is more, policies aimed at, say, raising educational attainment can affect the composition and duration of unemployment, as well as future consumption patterns and the structure of aggregate demand. As such, they can affect the historical path of an economy. It is for such reasons that Galbraith (1958a, 1967a) argued in the pursuit of Keynesian policy that there should be a rebalancing of social investment away from defense spending and supporting the needs of private industry, towards investing in health, protecting the environment and broadening both access to, as well as the nature of, higher education.

Inflation, market structure, and economic policy

Galbraith argued that inflation arises from the real side of the economy reflecting rising prices in the non-financial sectors (cf. Arestis and Sawyer, 2003, 2005). On this Galbraith was consistent – controlling inflation requires something more than just the control of the stock of money, even assuming that such control was possible. It requires influencing the price-setting process – either indirectly through changing interest rates, credit, and liquidity, or directly through price and incomes polices. Galbraith's approach to the study of money, moreover, makes clear that the emergence of the large corporation has a significant impact on the nature of the inflationary process.

Galbraith's historical analysis traces the evolution of the industrial structure and its impact on price setting, while integrating it with essential Keynesian insights regarding uncertainty and money. His analysis of "market" inflation approximates what Keynes (1930: 155–6) referred to as "commodity" or "capital" inflation. Market inflation refers to situations whereby increasing demand, against a fixed supply of goods, results in rising prices. Because production takes time there can be no immediate change in the supply of goods to the market, thus the only way to ration demand is by increasing the price of the commodity or asset in question. This also, however, fuels profits and feeds entrepreneurial expectations. And it will also have distributional consequences.

The relevance of such analysis of "market" inflation can be seen clearly at the dawn of capitalism. Galbraith (1975: 22) notes the inflation of the sixteenth and seventeenth centuries had a "profound effect on the distribution of income, with a particular tendency to punish most those who had least. The loss of those who received the lagging wages was in turn the gain of those who paid them and received the high and increasing prices. The result was high profits, and the further result was a general quickening of commercial and, in more elementary manifestation, industrial capitalism." The historical lesson, and the danger, of inflation, is that underpinned by expanding business activity; it feeds and fuels entrepreneurial expectations and adversely impacts on the distribution of income.[39]

Galbraith also followed Keynes (1930: 155–6) in recognizing a second form of inflation – incomes inflation. He argued that the emergence of the modern corporation changes the character and duration of the inflationary process. Market forces no longer temper the ability of large firms to pass cost increases on to the consumer.[40] In the planning sector characterized by large corporations: "the firm has power over its prices. An important purpose of this power ... is to allow wage costs to be passed onto the public" (Galbraith, 1973a: 204). This underscored Galbraith's (1967a: 252 n.) recognition of the cost push dimensions of incomes inflation – what Weintraub (1958) separates into monopoly or profits inflation and factor-price inflation. What is more Galbraith believed his theoretical argument was confirmed by the research of Weintraub (1963).[41]

As noted above in chapter 5, a core part of Galbraith's (1952a, 1952b, 1973a, 1977b) theoretical system is that the development of power blocs makes the economic system more inflationary, with the market power of both firms and unions creating the potential for a wage-price spiral (cf. Arestis and Sawyer, 2005). Indeed a significant consequence of the bimodal image of the modern economic system is its inflationary bias, which, unsurprisingly from a Galbrathian perspective, characterized the postwar period:

> In the [two decades following the second world war] all industrial countries brought the downward instability of the planning system under control. The specter of the cumulative downward spiral in wages, prices and production has receded. Instead industrial countries have uniformly found themselves contending with upward instability – with inflation. (Galbraith, 1973a: 205)

The failure of economists to incorporate the post-World War II emergence of large firms and strong labor unions in their theoretical systems, underpinned their failure to anticipate the emergence of stagflation as a major macroeconomic policy issue. Stagflation challenged the underpinnings of the Philips Curve and the neo-classical synthesis version of the Keynesian revolution, opening the door for the monetarist counter-revolution and the ascendancy of the New Classical Macroeconomics.[42] Galbraith (1975: 235) recognized this, noting that: "The rise of the corporations and unions had another importance for the Keynesian system. They were to be the prime instrument of its failure when inflation, as well as depression, became the problem."

In the 1970s the pursuit of monetary policies that did not acknowledge the changed institutional context only exacerbated the situation and fuelled stagflation:

> Monetary policy could suppress activity and increase unemployment, and especially in those industries – housing, and the construction industry generally, being the leading examples – which depend on borrowed money. The market power of corporations and unions meanwhile could keep prices going up as before. The modern capitalist economy could suffer inflation. And it could suffer recession. And it could, up to a painful level of unemployment, have both at the same time. (Galbraith, 1975: 300)

Conventional anti-inflationary monetary policies constrained aggregate demand, resulting in excess capacity and unemployment, while the more insulated corporate planning system passed on wage increases to the manipulated consumer, resulting in inflation. Galbraith's remedy, however, was not the pursuit of monetarism or the acceptance of a natural rate of unemployment; rather it was the development of appropriate institutions, such as wage and price controls, to minimize inflation and promote the expansion of aggregate demand to achieve full employment (Galbraith, 1973a, 1977b).

As noted several times throughout the course of this book, Galbraith's advocacy of incomes policies, reflected his wartime experience: "Corporate power made comprehensive price control necessary in the Second World War but it also contributed signally and unexpectedly to its success" (Galbraith, 1975: 258). In addition Galbraith highlighted how the changed institutional structure of the economy made price controls easier to administer:

> In the competitive market of small sellers and buyers, controls are very difficult to enforce. With the large corporation everything is vastly easier. There is, first, the effect of excess capacity. The small firm operates, in effect, at capacity. The large corporation, in contrast, usually operates with some excess capacity ... Accordingly, when the prices of the large corporation were fixed, it could continue to expand output and could therefore continue for a substantial period to supply all its customers ... And with the expanding output went expanding profits which removed the justification (though not the plea) for higher prices. Even when capacity operations were reached, controls on the large firm were easier to administer than on the small, competitive enterprise. (Galbraith, 1975: 258–9)

Such considerations have influenced the development of other forms of incomes policies. Weintraub's tax-based incomes policy, for example, targets the corporate income tax structure and penalizes large domestic firms if they acquiesce to wage increases in excess of productivity.

The alternative to such income controls is to manage aggregate demand in order to create a pool of unemployed resources, or an industrial reserve army, to discipline wage and price claims and maintain price stability (Kalecki, 1943). This is tantamount to an *incomes policy of fear* whereby the threat of job losses and falling sales keeps wage and price claims in check (Davidson, 2006). The social consequences and costs of this option fall disproportionately on unskilled and semi-skilled workers. An alternative, more civilized approach, such as the development of institutions that facilitate wage and price control, would certainly be preferable (cf. Galbraith, 1992, 1996b). Unfortunately, the path chosen during the long conservative retrenchment was the path of fear, insecurity, and unemployment.[43]

Whence it came, where it went

Galbraith possessed a sophisticated understanding of a monetary credit money production economy that accords with the Post Keynesian view. For Galbraith, as well as Post Keynesians, money is a human institution organically connected to other economic institutions such as the system of banking and the processes of accumulation and production. Galbraith's views of money and its nexus to the economy and analysis are clear. Economic processes have to be analyzed as taking place in historical time where past experience, as reflected in expectations, beliefs, institutions, and so on, influence present perceptions and decisions which mold what happens in the future. But this future is not a rerun of the past. Galbraith's monetary and financial analysis recognized the "dark forces of time and uncertainty" and the euphoria and speculation that accompany the evolution of financial institutions. As Galbraith (1996b: 34) remarked:

> The cyclical tendency of the basic economic system must be assumed. There are diverse causes, but the evident and reliably persistent one is speculative excess in good times, which results eventually in the curtailment of investment and consumer expenditure; this reduction in the flow of aggregate demand has inevitable consequences for the production and employment thus sustained.

Galbraith dwells significantly on the importance of expectations and how they affect the decision to invest and create new demand in the economy. And Galbraith sought to explore such issues with the general public at a time when little attention was given to them by the mainstream Keynesian literature. Likewise, Galbraith recognized the endogeneity of the money supply, how it feeds and promotes the expansion of trade, and the implications for macroeconomic policy. These are all points which are now firmly embedded within the Post Keynesian literature and deserve wider recognition. The monetary economics of J. K. Galbraith should no longer be ignored by either the mainstream, or by Post Keynesians.

Notes

1 *Money* is a tract aimed at clarifying the nature of paper money and its nexus to the banking system, and exploding the myths associated with convertible money.
2 Galbraith (1975: chapter 2) draws upon the standard treatment of Keynes (1932: 181–2) outlined in *Essays in Persuasion*.
3 Galbraith (1975: 72–3), interestingly from the perspective of Post Keynesian monetary theory, relates his discussion of the scarcity value of money to a discussion of Moon rock, which suggests that Galbraith was aping Keynes's (1936: 235) famous discussion in the *General Theory* and unlike many of his contemporaries had understood the implications of what appeared to many a distracting and impenetrable metaphor. Of

course, Post Keynesians, following Davidson (1972), have long since understood the relevance of this metaphor.

4 What is more, Galbraith (1975: 57–9, 264–5) also writes about how tobacco has the additional advantage of being able to be consumed if its value falls, which in part makes the money supply endogenous.

5 This prompted Keynes' (1930: 298) remark that all the gold produced since biblical times would not fill the cargo space of an ocean ship.

6 Note that Galbraith (1975: 46 n.) was aware of the debates on money as cause and effect and even quotes with approval Weintraub and Habibagahi's (1972) *Journal of Economic Issues* article on money. This is significant given Galbraith's sparse use of references. Weintraub, with Paul Davidson, established the *Journal of Post Keynesian Economics*. What is more, both were good friends with Galbraith.

7 As Galbraith (1975: 56) points out: "The instinct for monetary experiment dates from the earliest days of settlement [in the US]. The colonists, as every history tells, were endemically short of money."

8 Keynes went on to argue that: "the age of chartalist or State money was reached when the state claimed the right to declare what thing should as money to the current money of account ... To-day all civilized money is, beyond the possibility of dispute, chartalist."

9 Moving from commodity to paper and credit money, however, as Moore (1988: 13–14) notes, fundamentally changes its nature: "Because commodity money is a material thing rather than a financial claim, it is an asset to its holder but a liability to no one ... When there is a change in the quantity of commodity money, there is no corresponding change in the stock of financial assets and liabilities. The creation of commodity money is something apart from the world of saving and investment, borrowing and lending. Its supply typically is not highly sensitive to changes in the demand for it. Commodity money carries no price or credit risks, pays no interest, and because it represents immediately available purchasing power, is capital-certain and perfectly liquid ... Credit Money is the liability of the issuing financial institutions and, behind the institution, the institution's borrower. It need not possess all of the key characteristics associated with commodity or fiat money. It may carry a credit risk, it may pay interest, it may be capital-uncertain, and it may not always represent immediately available purchasing power. Most important its supply will be sensitive to the demand for it, as changes in the demand for money are translated into changes in the demand for credit. An excess supply of bank money can be reduced simply through the repayment of bank credit. Credit money thus takes on the characteristics of other financial assets, so that the dividing line between money and non-money assets becomes blurred."

10 From the point of view of society credit money, even from a "horizontalist" perspective, is still non-producible. Indeed, as Davidson (1972: 181) pointed out long ago: "the banking system, by controlling the quantity of bank credit, and financial institutions, by restricting the availability of finance, can constrain the level of economic activity, even when there are idle real resources."

11 As Galbraith (1975: 144) points out: "In the Federal Reserve System they had an instrument for doing all that a modern state needed to do for its money – for monopolizing the note issue, regulating bank lending and the resultant deposit creation and for providing banks with the succoring loans of last resort."

12 Most commentators focus solely on the means of payment role of money to the exclusion of its role as a store of wealth. As Alan Walters (1973: 7) remarked: "things other than money may be, and frequently are, used as a store of value. But in its role as a means of payment (and in its closely related attribute of 'liquidity') one can see the unique role played by money." Yet in ignoring the inseparable nature of money's functions we neglect the study of money: "Money, it is well known, serves two principal purposes. By acting as a unit of account it facilitates exchanges ... In the second place, it is a store of wealth ... But in the world of the classical economy, what an insane use to put it! For it is a recognized characteristic that it is barren; whereas practically every other form of storing wealth yields some interest or profit. Why should anyone outside a lunatic asylum wish to use money as a store of wealth?" (Keynes, 1937: 115–16). The answer to this question relates to the role of money in acting as a link between the past and the future (see Davidson, 1974, 1977, 1994, 2007).

13 Similarly such contracts provide information as to the likely relationship between the current and future costs and commitments and allow agents to plan in the context of an uncertain future. Galbraith's view of the modern corporation emphasizes how contracts are made in terms of non-neutral money.

14 Indeed Galbraith devotes much space in both *The Affluent Society* (1958a) and *The New Industrial State* (1967a) highlighting the various strategies pursued by the firm to emancipate itself from the uncertainties of the market (see chapters 7 and 8 above). Of course, while such strategies might make sense at the level of the firm they can add to instability and the asymmetry of the system, most notably through the dynamics created by the interaction of the planning and market systems (see below for a further discussion).

15 The principal *raison d'être* of *The Great Crash, 1929* (1955a) was to challenge the emerging view of the economy that emerged post-1929

and after World War II in which finance was absent, passive, or significant only for monetary policy.

16 As pointed out by Davidson (1972: 227): "With the income generating-finance motive, an increase in the demand for money induces an increase in supply as long as the bankers are willing and able to expand. This endogenous increase is immediately used to place additional orders for goods and thereby increases the demand for resource services, so that changes in the money supply and changes in resource utilization can be, via this process, directly correlated."

17 See Galbraith (1975: 198) whereby he highlights the fact that business confidence is a fragile phenomena that reinforces the prejudices and outlook of the business class in a way that lends itself to inaction and reinforces the conventional view. That is, the instinct of the herd dominates.

18 These innovations fuel the endogenous growth in the money supply. As Galbraith (1975a: 120–1) notes: "The banking system, as it operated in the last century and after, was well designed to expand the supply of money as speculation required."

19 Krugman (2008c: 142) points out, however, that: "While Greenspan warned against excessive exuberance, however, he never did much about it. He used the phrase 'irrational exuberance' in a 1996 speech in which he suggested, without quite saying it, that there was a bubble in stock prices. But he didn't raise interest rates to curb the market's enthusiasm; he didn't even seek to impose margin requirements on stock market investors. Instead he waited until the bubble burst, as it did in 2000, then tried to clean up the mess afterwards." Krugman (2008c: 139–52), attacks the Greenspan myth and highlights his many failings that Galbraith (1975: 305; 1979a: 29, 105, 245) identified long before. As Galbraith pointed out in an interview with Toru Kunimatsu in 1999: "Those that think that my old friend Alan Greenspan, all by himself, has power to rescue the American Economy are making fools of themselves" (Stanfield and Stanfield, 2004: 210).

20 That is to say: "there is an essential difference between real world monetary economies and mythical non-monetary systems and, therefore, there is a dichotomy of analyses for the two worlds, but in a monetary economy, a dichotomy between the real and monetary sectors is simply illusory" (Davidson, 1972: 213).

21 Regarding Irving Fisher and the Quantity theory, Galbraith (1977a: 194–5) wrote in his book *The Age of Uncertainty*: "He [Fisher] formed an association to promote the regulation of the money supply and thus stabilize prices." Then Galbraith goes on to indicate that although Fisher's idea of increasing the money supply was "the obvious

step" in fixing "depressingly low prices" in the 1930s, when Roosevelt accepted Fisher's idea by reducing the gold content of the dollar so that "for the same gold there would be more dollars ... It didn't work." Thus "Fisher discovered what people, including numerous economists, have been exceedingly reluctant to believe. There are no cheap and easy inventions involving money alone that will solve all, or any, economic problems ... But Irving Fisher's work was not wasted; it paved the way for a much more complex and imaginative step in economic policy. That was to have the government not only create money but also *ensure* its use ... by spending it."

22 What Galbraith (1958a: 187–97) referred to in *The Affluent Society* as "The Monetary Illusion."

23 From this perspective Galbraith should be clearly viewed as a Post Keynesian. Although there are differences amongst Post Keynesian monetary theorists all would accept this proposition. This broad agreement should not be overlooked, and especially when there is such a large gulf between the Post Keynesian approach and the orthodox one. Articles by authors such as Arestis and Howells (1996), Arestis and Sawyer (2006), Cottrel (1994), Dow (1996b), Lavoie (1996, 2003), and Pollin (1991) spell out theoretical differences.

24 This analysis clearly echoes Keynes's (1930: 220) view that bank "credit is the pavement along which production travels, and the bankers if they knew their duty, would provide the transport facilities to just the extent that is required in order that the productive powers of the community can be employed at their full capacity."

25 A key assumption underlying the new consensus macroeconomic framework is the use of a form of the classical dichotomy whereby monetary policy does not have an impact on economic activity in the long run (see Meyer, 2001, for example). For a Post Keynesian discussion critique of the new consensus macroeconomic framework, see Arestis (2006, 2007), Arestis and Sawyer (2003, 2004a, 2004b, 2004c, 2006, 2008), Fontana (2007), and Palacio-Vera (2005).

26 Recently, Bernanke, Reinhart, and Sack (2004) and Krugman (2005b) have highlighted the role that fiscal policy can and should play in the "New Consensus" view. Their argument relates to concerns with what is referred to as "the zero-interest rate bound to monetary policy." Basically, since the short-term interest rate is the principal policy lever in the "New Consensus," once it reaches zero, no further economic stimulus from monetary policy is possible. It is at this point that the role of fiscal policy is contemplated (see also Solow, 2005). As Tcherneva (2008) notes, this is effectively a reformulation of the old liquidity trap problem.

27 Similarly Kalecki (1990: 191) also recognized in 1933 the importance of the banking sector on facilitating the expansion of trade and demand: "the increase in output will result in an increased demand for money in circulation, and this will call for a rise in credits from the central bank. Should the bank respond to it by raising the rate of interest to a level at which total investment would decline by the amount equal to the additional investment caused by the new invention, no increase in investment would ensue, and the economic situation will not improve. Therefore the precondition for the upswing is that the rate of interest should not increase too much in response to an increased demand for credit."

28 See Galbraith (1975: 230–5) for an exposition of the core elements of the Keynesian system.

29 This is clear from Galbraith's own admission below in chapter 12. In 1935 Galbraith began a monograph on the causes of the great depression with the industrialist Henry S. Dennison (see Bruce, 2000, 2001). Dennison argued that adding to demand was the way to remedy the Great Depression whereas Galbraith argued that it was caused by monopoly power and its associated restrictions on output. Galbraith editorially triumphed over Dennison only to be proved wrong by the appearance of *The General Theory* of which he then became one of the most prominent advocates (Davidson, 2005). More recently the Post Keynesian literature has clarified that ultimately it is the existence of money and uncertainty that generates a low level of effective demand and thus "involuntary" unemployment, not the nature of competition or scale economies (Davidson, 1985b; Chick, 1983, 1992; Dutt, 1992; Sawyer, 1992a, 1992b; Shapiro, 1997; Kregel, 1998a). The conclusion that perfect competition would not exhibit unemployment pertains to a neoclassical world of perfect foresight in which Say's Law is operable and money is absent. This is why Post Keynesians argue that it is a pre-Keynes view to argue that "involuntary" unemployment is only possible under oligopolistic or imperfect competition.

30 Although as Chick and Dow (2002) point out banks vary their mark-up depending upon the credit worthiness of borrowers, that is, banks have different degrees of liquidity preference in different circumstances. For a discussion of the role of the non-bank sector impact on liquidity preference, see Arestis and Howells (1996).

31 More technically: "If both money and securities have zero elasticities of production, and if they are good substitutes for each other but poor substitutes with respect to all other durables that have high elasticities of production, then this exogenous increase in the quantity of

money will not be associated with any increased demand for output and resources" (Davidson, 1972: 227).

32 This does not mean that monetary policy has no role. As Galbraith (1973a: 327) argues the role of monetary policy lies elsewhere: "The level at which the interest rate should be set is largely arbitrary – but the bias should be on the low side. Low interest rates favor borrowers rather than lenders. As a broad and not excessively astonishing rule, borrowers have less money than lenders. So lower interest rates contribute to a more equitable distribution of income." For a discussion of the contemporary role of interest rate policy, see Rochon (2007), Rochon and Setterfield (2007), Sawyer (2006), and Smithin (2007).

33 More specifically, Galbraith (1973a: 327) notes that: "Borrowing will be excessive when, along with other sources of demand, it is pulling up prices. It is then curtailed by increasing taxes; this reduces the capacity of people to incur mortgage or other personal debt and, as the demand for goods recedes, it reduces both the incentive and the ability to borrow or use funds for business expansion."

34 As Galbraith (1987: 222) acknowledged: "The modern economy ... does not necessarily find its equilibrium at full employment; it can find it with unemployment – the underemployment equilibrium. Say's Law no longer holds; there *can be* a shortage of demand. The government *can and should* take steps to overcome it. In a depression the precepts of sound public finance must give way to this need."

35 Or as Galbraith (1958a: 41–2) remarked in *The Affluent Society*: "Another interesting instance of the circumstance on the conventional wisdom was that of the balanced budget in times of depression. Almost from the beginning of organized government the balanced budget or its equivalent has been the *sine qua non* of sound and sensible management of the public purse. The consequences of violating this rule had always been unhappy in the long run and not infrequently in the short. Anciently it was the practice of states to cover the deficit by clipping or debasing the coins and spending the metal so saved. The result invariably was to raise prices and the national self-esteem. In modern times the issue of paper money or the obtaining of soft loans from banks had led to the same results. In consequence, the conventional wisdom had emphasized strongly the importance of an annually balanced budget. But meanwhile the underlying reality had gradually changed ... The shattering circumstance was the Great Depression ... A balanced budget meant increasing tax rates and reducing public expenditure. Viewed in retrospect, it would be hard to imagine a better design for reducing both the private and public

demand for goods, aggravating deflation, increasing unemployment, and adding to the general suffering."

36 This is also accepted by Paul Krugman (2008c: 188): "As long as public spending is pushed along with reasonable speed, it should arrive in plenty of time to help – and it has two great advantages over tax breaks. On one side, the money would actually be spent; on the other, something of value (e.g. bridges that don't fall down) would be created."

37 Such considerations were also identified by Schumpeter (1943: 95): "For inasmuch as we may assume that the refusal to lower prices strengthens the position of the industries which adopt that policy either by increasing their revenue or simply by avoiding chaos in their markets – that is to say, so far as this policy is something more than a mistake on their part – it may make fortresses out of what otherwise might be centers of devastation. As we have seen before, from a more general standpoint, total output and employment may well keep on a higher level with the restrictions incident to that policy than they would if depression were allowed to play havoc with the price structure. In other words, under the conditions created by capitalist evolution, perfect and universal flexibility of prices might in depression further unstabilize the system, instead of stabilizing it as it no doubt would under the conditions envisaged by general theory."

38 Such institutional processes do not work precisely and do not conspire to reinstitute Say's Law (indeed the conservative retrenchment saw the state weaken the countervailing power of labor market institutions through reductions in levels of aggregate demand).

39 What is more these lessons are frequently and alarmingly forgotten: "The history of money reveals two highly reliable tendencies. Having recent experience of inflation, people cherish stable prices, and having long experience of stable prices, they become indifferent to the risk of inflation" (Galbraith, 1975: 66).

40 Galbraith (1955a) also noted in *The Great Crash, 1929* the emergence of large corporations which took advantage of their market power and sought to gain competitive advantage through price cuts delivered ostensively through cutting wages thereby maintaining margins (cf. Galbraith, 1975: 199).

41 Galbraith's references are modest by contemporary standards so it is clearly significant that he both read Weintraub's work and sought to highlight its significance: "An important study, affirming the cost-push thesis, to which I am much indebted is Sidney Weintraub's *Some Aspects of Wage Theory and Policy* (New York: Chilton Books, 1963)" (Galbraith, 1967a: 252 n.). Indeed Galbraith (1985: 5) also noted in his eulogy to Weintraub "When the day comes that we restrain the

interacting dynamic of prices and wages by means more benign than unemployment, idle plants, and general hardship, it is Sidney's name that will be cited on both policy and the theoretical underpinning of the need."

42 As Parker (2005: 565) highlights: "Galbraith thought the failure to comprehend the economy's erratic behavior was due to the intellectual 'bargains' that mainstream Keynesians had made. He once again faulted the Neoclassical synthesis for wedding Keynesian macroeconomics to neoclassical microeconomics, rather than developing a clearer role for the influence of power, ideology, and group interests – and a model of policy making that emphasized the complex social and political foundations of choice."

43 The dynamics of the wage price spiral has been therefore weakened in many modern economies; as a result of the conservative retrenchment wages are poorly linked to price changes and trade unions have lost most of their bargaining power.

11 *A man for our times*

In our progress toward a resumption of work we require two safeguards against a return of the evils of the old order; there must be a strict supervision of all banking and credits and investments; there must be an end to speculation with other people's money, and there must be provision for an adequate but sound currency.

Franklin D. Roosevelt, inaugural presidential address (1933)

First of all, we need a rescue plan for the middle class that invests in immediate efforts to create jobs and provide relief to families that are watching their paychecks shrink and their life savings disappear. A particularly urgent priority is a further extension of unemployment insurance benefits for workers who cannot find work in the increasingly weak economy. A fiscal stimulus plan that will jump-start economic growth is long overdue ... Second, we have to address the spreading impact of the financial crisis on the other sectors of our economy: small businesses that are struggling to meet their payrolls and finance their holiday inventories; and state and municipal governments facing devastating budget cuts and tax increases. We must also remember that the financial crisis is increasingly global and requires a global response ... Third, we will review the implementation of this administration's financial program to ensure that the government's efforts are achieving their central goal of stabilizing financial markets while protecting taxpayers, helping homeowners, and not unduly rewarding the management of financial firms that are receiving government assistance.

Barack Obama, first news conference as US president-elect (2008)

Over the course of this book I have sought to strip away the populist cloak from Galbraith's writings in order to highlight the depth of his system of thought. I have attempted to demonstrate the theoretical import of his economic contributions. But Galbraith would not wish to be considered solely in such theoretical terms. He was a practical theorist concerned with practical policy. And the events of 2008 – on the hundredth anniversary of his birth – conspired to make his analysis more relevant than ever. In 2008, wherever one looked, familiar Galbraithian concerns were being wrestled with.

The malfeasance and dominance of the large corporation across the food, tobacco, pharmaceutical, automobile, and alcohol industries were once again a source of public concern and anxiety. The explosion in greed and the cult of superstar celebrity, alongside the increase in national and global poverty, were a staple of the broadsheets. Concern regarding the rise of excessive executive pay and the return of the "robber barons" was being voiced. The loss and erosion of social capital was being lamented. The destruction of the environment and onset of climate change were finally stirring action by global leaders. The reticence of the automobile and oil industries to reduce the reliance on oil, in the face of major and variable price increases, harked back to the oil price hikes and stagflation of the 1970s. The resurgence of the military-industrial complex, after the lull of the ending of the cold war, and the anxiety generated by the first wars of the twenty-first century, in Iraq and Afghanistan, was widespread. The problems of the legacy of African debt, and the reneging of the various G8 Gleneagles commitments, designed to ameliorate this, risked consigning a whole continent to poverty. And to cap it all the financial economic system experienced a global meltdown – what Alan Greenspan, former chairman of the Federal Reserve, called "a once in a half century, probably once in a century type of event." At the turn of the new millennium, the good society did not look very good.

The valid image of the modern economy

As I have argued throughout, Galbraith presented an analysis of the substantial economic power that large firms possess. It is his focus on power and what it means for the firm, how it conditions poverty and its acceptance, and its nexus to the state that embodies Galbraith's principal contribution to our understanding of the modern world. As technology continues to advance, large amounts of time, money, and specialized personnel are required to bring products to the marketplace. Threats to such investments must be protected. To thrive, firms seek to control the market, growing through acquisition and dominating the supply chain. The large firm thus emerges as a planning response to the uncertain nature of markets.

The character of the large corporation continues to dominate the popular consciousness, as well as the economy (see table 12). Exxon Mobil, Wal-Mart, Google, Microsoft, General Motors, Nestlé, Citigroup, and Arcelor Mittal straddle the global economy (see also table 6 in chapter 8 above). Small firms populate the other subservient half of the global economy (see table 1 in chapter 5 above).[1] The market power of smaller firms is held in check by competition and the planning system which dominates them. This power imbalance is the essence of the bimodal view. The social consequences of the concentration of economic power continue to be a constant concern to economists, politicians, social commentators, and the public. As Cowling and Tomlinson (2005: 18) highlight:

> There has been increasing public discontent with the globalization process and the effects of the global concentration of corporate power. The rise of the antiglobalization movement and various international public protests at events such as the meeting of the World Trade Organization in Seattle, are a testament to the view that not all is well with the global economy. We have also seen the emergence of the World Social Forum that aims to promote greater equality of wealth and protection of the environment through dialogue with the global neo-liberal institutions such as the IMF, WTO and World Bank. At the micro-level, consumer groups and antiglobalization protesters have become more vigilant and have begun to use targeted campaigns against high-profile transnationals that have profited from employing poor labor standards or through polluting the environment. Fearful of adverse publicity many global companies have responded by redefining their ethical values or undertaken to sponsor community-based projects under the guise of "corporate social responsibility". Globalization and corporate power have emerged at the forefront of the political agenda.

The lobbying efforts of the major corporations continue to be felt through tax policy, trade policy, environmental policy, foreign policy, and labor policy. It is no surprise, therefore, that the majority of Americans – liberals and conservatives alike, continue to believe that "big business" has too much power in Washington (cf. Carney, 2006). Big firms continue to seek to minimize competition – as exemplified through the US Microsoft antitrust case in the USA (Gilbert and Katz, 2001; Klein, 2001; Whinston, 2001). Market uncertainties continue to be mitigated through mergers and

Table 12. *Top ten largest US firms, 2008*

Rank	Company	Revenues ($m)	Profits ($m)
1	Wal-Mart Stores	378,799	12,731
2	ExxonMobil	372,824	40,610
3	Royal Dutch Shell	355,782	31,331
4	BP	291,438	20,845
5	Toyota Motor	230,201	15,042
6	Chevron	210,783	18,688
7	ING Group	201,516	12,649
8	Total	187,280	18,042
9	General Motors	182,347	–38,732
10	ConocoPhillips	178,558	11,891

Source: Fortune 500, July 21, 2008

takeovers – vertical, horizontal, or conglomerate integration. In 2006 the number of Global Mergers and Acquisitions (M&A) deals reached a record level of 33,100 with a combined value of nearly $4 trillion (Wolf, 2007).

Similarly large firms continue to spend money on advertising in an attempt to control consumer tastes. Over the past century the growth of America's consumer society, the sprawling and malling of the USA, and the growth of advertising have proceeded hand in hand (Dawson, 2003). Although the proportion of GDP devoted to advertising – which is just one facet of the management of specific demand, see chapter 9 – has remained stable at around 2 percent over the last fifty years, this belies the major increase in corporate mendacity that continues to be channeled through Madison Avenue in the interests of the firm.[2] Billions are spent on advertising by large firms to ensure the requisite response from the consumer (see table 13). In 2007 total US measured media spending for all advertisements totaled nearly $150 billion. This equates roughly to the total spend on the English National Health Service, which provides healthcare free at the point for need for the whole English population of 50 million.

The trends that Galbraith identified have accelerated. In *No Logo* Naomi Klein argued saliently that the nature of big business has shifted from making things to marketing things. As she points out:

Table 13. *Advertising spend in the USA, 2007*

Rank	Industry	Spending ($bn)	Rank	Corporation	Spending ($m)
1	Retail	18.70	1	Procter & Gamble Co.	5,230.1
2	Automotive	18.54	2	AT&T	3,207.3
3	Telecom	10.91	3	Verizon Communications	3,016.1
4	Medicine & remedies	9.30	4	General Motors Corp.	3,010.1
5	Financial services	9.22	5	Time Warner	2,962.1
6	General services	8.93	6	Ford Motor Co.	2,525.2
7	Food, beverages & candy	7.46	7	GlaxoSmithKline	2,456.9
8	Personal care	6.31	8	Johnson & Johnson	2,408.8
9	Airlines, hotels, car rentals	5.41	9	Walt Disney Co.	2,293.3
10	Movies, recorded video & music	5.41	10	Unilever	2,245.8

Source: 100 leading advertisers: Annual Advertiser Profile Edition, Advertising www.adage.com, June 23, 2008.

many of today's best-known manufacturers no longer produce products and advertise them, but rather buy products and 'brand' them, these companies are forever on the prowl for creative new ways to build and strengthen their brand images. Manufacturing products may require drills, furnaces, hammers, and the like, but creating a brand calls for a completely different set of tools and materials. It requires an endless parade of brand extensions, continuously renewed imagery for marketing and, most of all, fresh new spaces to disseminate the brand's idea of itself (Klein, 1999: 5).

The contemporary focus on the management of the brand, which is double speak for the manipulation of the consumer, attests to the continued relevance of Galbraith's thesis.

In managing the consumer response, the modern corporation is no longer selling products but lifestyles. The Body Shop sells female identity, ethics, and a concern for the environment. IBM sells business solutions not computers. Nike sells a sporting attitude, not sneakers. Swatch sells time, not watches. Apple sells urbane, technological chic – it sells play, not work. BMW sells the ultimate driving machine, not transportation. Calvin Klein sells lifestyle attitude, not jeans and perfume. Starbucks sells emotional connections, not coffee. As Naomi Klein (1999: 20) records:

> Scott Bedbury, Starbucks' vice president of marketing, openly recognized that 'consumers don't truly believe there's a huge difference between products,' which is why brands must 'establish emotional ties' with their customers through 'the Starbucks Experience.' The people who line up for Starbucks, writes CEO Howard Shultz, aren't just there for the coffee. 'It's the romance of the coffee experience, the feeling of warmth and community people get in Starbucks stores'.

Although fellow Canadian Naomi Klein fails to acknowledge her intellectual debt to Galbraith, many of the concerns and trends that she highlighted in her penetrating book *No Logo* were anticipated in *The Affluent Society* and *The New Industrial State*. As Klein (1999: 3) argues: "The astronomical growth in the wealth and cultural influence of multi-national corporations over the last fifteen years can arguably be traced back to a single, seemingly innocuous idea developed by management theorists in the mid-1980s: that successful corporations must primarily produce brands, as opposed to products."

Galbraith was not, however, anti-business. Rather he was pro-society. It should not be thought, however, that the evolution of the modern corporate giant is wholly malign. The large corporation underpins the vast wealth of modern societies, as well as its unequal distribution. As Galbraith long argued the large firm encourages technological development and, by so doing, continues to contribute to (uneven) improvements in our standard of living. Breaking up such large corporations, as liberals sometimes demand, is not merely futile but would also undermine prosperity. Only big business can make the large-scale investment in new processes, expensive equipment, and basic research required in a modern economy. Better to limit and regulate the power of large firms through better regulation and oversight, rather than destroy the basis of (uneven) advance and development.

Countervailing power

The global food and retail industry also exhibits elements of Galbraith's concept of countervailing power, his bimodal view, and his analysis of "The Revised Sequence." Where once food retail markets were highly fragmented, consisting mainly of small traditional independent retailers, they have since become highly consolidated, driven by a process of organic growth and mergers by leading retailers (see table 14). The result has been the marginalization of small independent retailers, restricted to acting as convenience stores, and market domination by a limited number of large-format, multiple-store retailers that attract the majority of consumer spending. The largest retail corporations have also sought to extend their operations internationally, and, in the process, increased the global concentration of power. For example, over the period from 1993 to 1999, the aggregate concentration of the top ten grocery retailers in the European Union grew by 24.9 percent, whereas the market share of the bottom ten companies in the EU Top 50 fell by 72.2 percent (Dobson, 2003).

Food retailers have consolidated their market position and emerged as main gateways to consumers, using contracts and specifications to gate-keep between primary producers and consumers (Blythman, 2005). This points to the large retailers using their buying power to control a dense, global supply chain to pursue their own ends (cf. Dobson and Waterson, 1999; Clarke *et al.*, 2002).[3] What is more, consistent with the Galbraithian hypothesis, traditional measures of concentration are also likely to understate the global power of the large corporation in the food retailing industry. As Lang (2004: 9–10) points out:

> Concentration is strongly linked to power and the concentration of power over the food system is now remarkable, whether one looks nationally, regionally or globally. A web of contractual relationships turns the farmer into a contractor, providing the labor and often some capital, but never owning the product as it moves through the supply chain. Farmers never make the major management decisions.

Food retailers provide, however, a source of countervailing power that acts as a constraint on the power of large food manufacturers (Dobson and Waterson, 1997; Dobson *et al.*, 2001). This can drive real benefits

Table 14. *World's top ten food retailers, 2005*

Rank	Company	Country	2005 Retail sales ($m)	Countries of operation
1	Wal-Mart Stores Inc.	USA	312,427	Argentina, Brazil, Canada, China, Germany, Japan, Mexico, Puerto Rico, S. Korea, UK, USA
2	Carrefour S.A.	France	92,778	Argentina, Belgium, Brazil, China, Colombia, Dominican Republic, Egypt, France, French Polynesia, Greece, Guadeloupe, Indonesia, Italy, Malaysia, Martinique, Oman, Poland, Portugal, Qatar, Reunion, Romania, Saudi Arabia, Singapore, S. Korea, Spain, Switzerland, Taiwan, Thailand, Turkey, Tunisia, U.A.E.
3	Metro AG	Germany	69,134	Austria, Belgium, Bulgaria, China, Croatia, Czech Rep., Denmark, France, Germany, Greece, Hungary, India, Italy, Japan, Luxembourg, Moldova, Morocco, Netherlands, Poland, Portugal, Romania, Russia, Serbia and Montenegro, Slovakia, Spain, Switzerland, Turkey, Ukraine, UK, Vietnam
4	Tesco plc	UK	68,866	China, Czech Rep., Hungary, Japan, Rep. of Ireland, Malaysia, Poland, Slovakia, S. Korea, Taiwan, Thailand, Turkey, UK
5	Kroger	USA	60,553	USA

Table 14. *(cont.)*

Rank	Company	Country	2005 Retail sales ($m)	Countries of operation
6	Aldi GmbH & Co. oHG	Germany	45,096	Australia, Austria, Belgium, Denmark, France, Germany, Rep. of Ireland, Luxembourg, Netherlands, Slovenia, Spain, Switzerland, UK, USA
7	Rewe-Zentral AG	Germany	44,039	Austria, Bulgaria, Croatia, Czech Rep., France, Germany, Hungary, Italy, Poland, Romania, Russia, Slovakia, Switzerland, Ukraine
8	Albertsons Inc.	USA	40,358	USA
9	Edeka Zentrale AG & Co. KG	Germany	39,445	Austria, Czech Rep., Denmark, Germany, Russia
10	Safeway Inc.	USA	38,416	Canada, USA

Source: Deloitte (2007)

for the consumer. Within ten years of entering the food trade, for example, Wal-Mart drove down market prices by 13 percent (Lang and Heasman, 2004: 160). Although large retailers have provided a countervailing response to the rise of large food and agribusinesses, their impact has not been wholly benign (Blythman, 2005; Lang and Heasman, 2004). It should be no surprise that the UK Government's Competition Commission inquiry in 2000 concluded that industry was "securing a good deal" for the British consumer, but also that UK supermarkets engage in a variety of business practices that operate against the public interest by inducing a climate of fear amongst suppliers, distorting competition, and promulgating consumer confusion (Competition Commission, 2000; see also Blythman, 2005). Similarly in 1999 the United Nations Development Program called for tougher rules on global food governance, concerning labor standards, fair trade, and environmental protection (UNDP, 1999). There have also been some unintended, adverse consequences.

The price of food reflects a mix of production, distribution, and retailing costs – with the later ends receiving the greatest margins, reflecting the dominance of the global retailers and fast food chains. Many of the social, economic, and environmental costs associated with the complex food supply and retail chain – ranging from low pay and poor working conditions, to over-fishing, over-farming, over-watering, excessive use of fertilizers and pesticides, as well as the well-documented contribution of the food industry to climate change, as reflected in the increase in "food miles" – are not, however, reflected into the price that the consumer pays. Although large retailers and fast food chains have succeeded in driving down the relative price of food, this, when combined with the relentless chorus of advertising and marketing messages, has also driven greater consumption. But the fact that typically the dominant global brands are rich in either calories, salt, or saturated fact (or all three) means that excess consumption of such processed food and beverage products is giving rise to a range of health-related problems and fueling an obesity epidemic.

Although food companies and retailers are responding to such concerns, at the present time they appear tokenistic, with little overhaul of the basic business model. The regulatory response so far has also been underwhelming, failing to respond adequately to the tsunami of advertising that drives brand loyalty and excess consumption. As

Lang and Heasman (2004: 206) note: "for every dollar spent by the WHO [World Health Organisation] on preventing the diseases caused by Western diets, more than $500 is spent by the food industry promoting these diets." What is more, much of this advertising is targeted at children and less educated and more gullible groups of consumers. Such anxieties have been raised by Eric Schlosser (2002: 243) in *Fast Food Nation* who noted that: "American children now get about one-quarter of their total vegetable servings in the form of potato chips or french fries. A survey of children's advertising in the European Union (EU) found that 95 percent of the food ads there encouraged kids to eat foods high in sugar, salt, and fat."

Similarly food advertising and labeling does not provide full product information to allow consumers to make real choice. In the European Union, for example, nutritional labeling is only mandatory if a health claim is made. All this calls for a more comprehensive and globally coordinated response to the problems generated by the unquestionable productivity and technological virtuosity of the global food industry.

The environment

Such Galbraithian considerations are also apparent when one reflects on the inadequate response to the challenges of climate change of the large oil and automobile firms.[4] Oil and automobile firms continue to be vast corporations that make-up eight out of the top ten global firms in 2008 (see table 12). General Motors and the other large car and oil firms have massively improved transportation, bringing communities and commuters together, underpinning a major transformation in living standards. But although "General Motors exists to serve the public ... General Motors also serves itself as well or instead" (Galbraith, 1973a: 19).

Automobile companies also have a vested interest in ensuring that there is a high and sustained demand for its products, given its technological investment. As Galbraith (1967a: 205) argued: "An automobile company must ensure that consumers devote a dependable share of their outlays to automobiles in general and to its cars in particular." Thus it is no surprise that the automobile industry continues to be responsible for one of the largest advertising outlays – nearly $19 billion (table 13). Similarly the collusive lobbying of the oil and

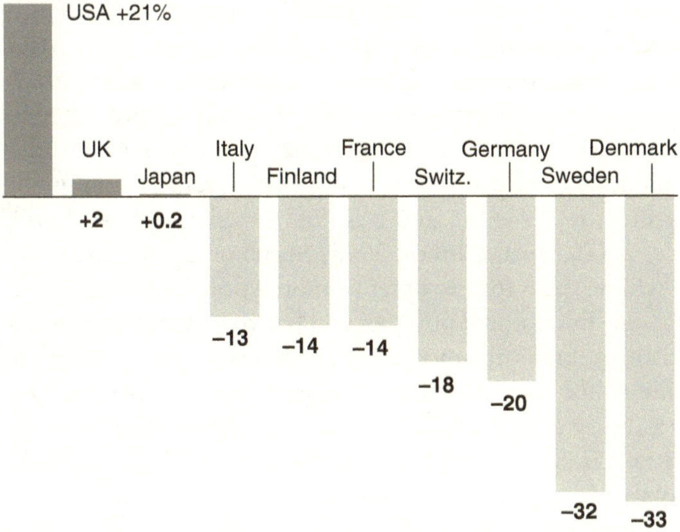

Figure 6. Percentage change in oil consumption between the 1980s and 2007
Source: Mouawad (2008)

automobile technostructures have resisted increased taxes, investment in public transport, improvements in engine efficiency and the development of alternative fuel sources that could have mitigated the rise in oil consumption.[5] They have also been linked to various military and diplomatic interventions designed to secure oil supplies.[6]

Since 1980 the US oil consumption has increased by 21 percent compared to decreases in other major industrialized countries (see Figure 6). As Mouawad (2008) points out:

> The United States is the only major industrialized nation to see its oil consumption surge since the oil shocks of the 1970s and 1980s. This can partly be explained by the fact that the United States has some of the lowest gasoline prices in the world, the least fuel-efficient cars on the roads, the lowest energy taxes, and the longest daily commutes of any industrialized nation. The result: about a quarter of the world's oil goes to the United States every day, and of that, more than half goes to its cars and trucks.

Such energy consumption underpins the increased environmental risk presented by climate change. The USA contains just 5 percent of the world's population (and falling), but it is responsible for 25 percent of the world's greenhouse gas output per annum (Ash, 2005).

Climate change, and the associated need to reduce carbon emissions, represents a challenge to the status and position of the large technostructures that dominate the oil and automobile industries. A protective response was therefore entirely predictable. Just like the tobacco, pharmaceutical, and food industries (see chapters 8 and 9 above), the oil industry has sought to manipulate scientific and public opinion to protect its revenues and position (Oreskes, 2004; David, 2006; Sample, 2007; Mother Jones, 2005; Monbiot, 2006, 2007). As Nobel prize-winner, and former chief economist of the World Bank, Joe Stiglitz (2006) has pointed out: "Exxon has reportedly been funding so-called think tanks to undermine confidence in the science of global warming, just as the tobacco industry funded 'research' to question the validity of statistical findings showing the link between smoking and cancer. Some companies even seem to celebrate the melting of the polar ice cap, because it will reduce the cost of extracting the oil that lies beneath the Arctic Ocean."[7]

The large oil and automobile companies, as well as sections of the media, particularly in the USA, frequently argue that the science and facts of climate change are highly uncertain. However, Oreskes (2004: 1686), in her famous essay in *Science*, makes it clear that this is no substantive disagreement in the scientific community about the reality of human caused climate change: "Politicians, economists, journalists, and others may have the impression of confusion, disagreement, or discord among climate scientists, but that impression is incorrect." Similarly Stern (2007) highlights that there is now clear scientific evidence that emissions from economic activity, particularly the burning of fossil fuels for energy, are causing changes to the Earth's climate. Stern argues that a sound understanding of the economics of climate change is needed in order to underpin an effective global response to this challenge.[8]

When the nexus between the state and the oil and automobile technostructures is understood, the failure of the USA to sign up to the Kyoto Protocol is explainable (cf. *Guardian*, 2001). As noted above, Galbraith argued that the close relationship between the technostructure and the state means that public spending and action will tend to follow and favor the interests of the large corporation. From this arises the requirement of the good society to understand the various claims of the technostructure on public expenditure.[9] It necessitates the securing of the independence of the state through political reform so as to ensure the regulation of the power of the modern corporation is not subject to industry capture.[10] And it underscores the need to understand the potential responses in tackling climate change and environmental destruction and degradation. As Galbraith (1973a: 305–6) identified:

> A substantial part of the remedy for environmental damage consists, simply, in the willingness to spend public money to clean up ... Beyond the provision of such public funds these are three possible strategies for protection of the environment, two of which are irrelevant or impractical. The first solution comes from neo-classical economics, which views environmental damage as a defect in the market system. Wastes are dumped free in the air and water; the community, not the consumer of the eventual product or service, pays for the resulting clean-up. By internalizing such external diseconomies ... the defect in the market is eliminated, and the problem is thereby solved ... The second solution correctly identifies uninhibited growth as the problem and proposes limits to growth. The defect in this solution is that damage to the environment is a clear and present danger ... Additionally, a reduction in growth only becomes a decent remedy as the distribution of income becomes more nearly equal. Otherwise, people or groups are frozen in the consumption they now have. There is now some evidence that protection of the environment is a more appealing proposition to the affluent than to the poor ... The third solution is to continue economic growth but to specify by legislation the parameters within which it can occur ... The setting of these boundaries becomes a major – in some ways *the* major – task of the modern legislature.[11]

It should be clear from this that Galbraith's analysis underscores the need for a renewed regulatory and globally coordinated response to address climate change that is consistent with the public interest.[12]

The opulent society

The Affluent Society was originally to be called "The Opulent Society." Galbraith (1958a: 22) decided, however, that "Opulent has a greasy, unattractive sound." If Galbraith were revising this essay today he might be re-considering this as a title. Since the 1950s the affluent society has got more affluent.[13] Wealth has tripled – with

Table 15. ***Highest-paid chief executives in S&P 500 in the USA, 2007***

CEO	Corporation	Pay ($m)
1. Larry Ellison	Oracle Corp.	$84.6
2. John Thain	Merrill Lynch & Co.	$83.1
3. Leslie Moonves	CBS Corp.	$67.6
4. Richard Adkerson	Freeport-McMoran Copper & Gold Inc.	$65.3
5. Bob Simpson	XTO Energy Inc.	$56.6
6. Lloyd Blankfein	Goldman Sachs Group Inc.	$53.9
7. Kenneth Chenault	American Express Co.	$51.7
8. Eugene Isenberg	Nabors Industries Ltd.	$44.6
9. John Mack	Morgan Stanley	$41.7
10. Glenn Murphy	Gap Inc.	$39.1

Notes: The AP's calculation of total pay figures are based on a compensation formula which includes salary, perks, bonuses, above-market returns on deferred compensation, and company estimates for the value of stock options and stock awards granted.

Source: Associated Press, www.ap.org, August 22, 2008

real per capita GDP at three times the 1958 level. This affluence, however, has been unevenly distributed. In the USA, today, the richest 1 percent holds 38 percent of the wealth (Judt, 2005). The top 10 percent in the USA hold 70 percent of the country's wealth, compared with 61 percent in France, 56 percent in the UK, 44 percent in Germany and 39 percent in Japan (Giles, 2006). In 1973 Galbraith (1973a: 283) noted that: "The head of General Motors or I.T.T. receives some fifty times the compensation of the typical man on the assembly line or factory floor – a considerable differential. The man so rewarded might hesitate to argue, himself, that he was fifty times as valuable. Were it agreed that this pay was a manifestation of his own inspired generosity, there might be complaint." In 2007 the top ten chief executive salaries ranged between $40 million and a massive $85 million, which was paid to Larry Ellison of Oracle Corporation (see table 15).

There can thus be no doubt that income inequalities and its associated problems – a key focus of Galbraith's major trilogy – have got worse over the last few decades (James Galbraith, 1998; James Galbraith and Berner, 2001). This is not something, however, that has lodged in the public consciousness. As Krugman (2002) points out "even bringing up the subject exposes you to charges of 'class warfare,' the 'politics of envy' and so on ... very few people indeed are willing to talk about the profound effects – economic, social and political – of that widening gap."

Nevertheless, a recent OECD (2008a) report found that the gap between the rich and poor has grown in more than three-quarters of OECD countries over the past twenty years (see table 16 below). The report "Growing Unequal?" found that the economic growth of recent decades has benefited the rich more than the poor. In some countries, such as Canada, Finland, Germany, Italy, Norway, and the USA, the gap also increased between the rich and the middle-class. Over the last twenty years, as Figure 7 highlights, income inequality continued to widen.

The OECD report also found that countries with a wide distribution of income tend to have more widespread social problems. It highlighted how social mobility is lower in countries with high inequality, such as Italy, the UK, and the USA, and higher in the Nordic countries where income is distributed more evenly. At the launch of the report in Paris on October 21, 2008, OECD Secretary-General Angel Gurría warned of the dangers posed by inequality and the need for governments to tackle it. Echoing a familiar Galbraithian refrain, Gurría warned that "Growing inequality is divisive. It polarizes societies, it divides regions within countries, and it carves up the world between rich and poor. Greater income inequality stifles upward mobility between generations, making it harder for talented and hard-working people to get the rewards they deserve. Ignoring increasing inequality is not an option" (OECD, 2008b).

The report also highlighted how in developed countries, governments have been taxing more and spending more on social benefits to offset the trend toward more inequality. Again a familiar Galbraithian theme – see chapter 6 above. Without this spending, the OECD report notes, the rise in inequality would have been even more rapid.[14] The OECD has also argued, however, that new ways of tackling income inequalities need to be found, as the tax and benefit system is losing its potency. Raising further Galbraithian concerns, Gurría argued that: "The largest part of the increase in inequality comes from changes in the labor markets. This is where governments must act. Low-skilled workers are having ever-greater problems in finding jobs.

Table 16. *Changes in OECD income inequality and poverty, 1985–2005*

	Mid 1980s to mid 1990s	Mid 1990s to mid 2000s	Mid 1980s to mid 2000s
A. Trends in income inequality (Gini coefficients)			
Significant increase	Czech Republic, Italy, Mexico, New Zealand, Portugal, Turkey, UK	Canada, Finland, Germany	Finland, New Zealand
Small increase	Belgium, Finland, Germany, Hungary, Japan, Luxembourg, Netherlands, Norway, Sweden, USA	Austria, Denmark, Japan, Norway, Sweden, USA	Canada, Germany, Italy, Japan, Norway, Portugal, Sweden, USA
No change	Austria, Canada, Denmark, Greece, Ireland	Australia, Belgium, Czech Republic, France, Hungary, Italy, Luxembourg, New Zealand, Portugal, Spain, Switzerland	Austria, Belgium, Czech Republic, Denmark, France, Greece, Hungary, Ireland, Luxembourg, Mexico, Netherlands, Spain, Turkey, UK
Small decrease		Greece, Ireland, Netherlands, UK	France, Ireland, Spain
Significant decrease	France, Spain	Mexico, Turkey	

B. Trends in income poverty (head-count rates at the 50% median-income threshold)

Significant increase	Germany, Italy, Japan, Netherlands, New Zealand, UK	Austria, Canada, Finland, Germany, Ireland, Japan, Luxembourg, New Zealand, Spain, Sweden	Austria, Germany, Ireland, Japan, Netherlands, New Zealand
Small increase	Austria, Czech Republic, Hungary, Mexico, Norway, Portugal	Australia, Denmark, Netherlands, Switzerland, Turkey	Canada, Czech Republic, Finland, Italy, Luxembourg, Sweden, Turkey, UK
No change	Finland, Greece, Ireland, Luxembourg, Sweden, Turkey	Belgium, Czech Republic, France, Hungary, Norway, USA	Denmark, France, Greece, Hungary,Norway, Portugal, Spain, USA
Small decrease	Canada, Denmark, France, USA	Greece, Portugal	Mexico
Significant decrease	Belgium, Spain	Italy, Mexico, UK	Belgium

Notes: For sub-periods "significant increase/decrease" denotes changes greater than 2.5 points (Gini coefficient) and 1.5 points (headcount); "small increase/decrease" denotes changes between 1 and 2.5 points (Gini coefficient) and between 0.5 and 1.5 points (headcounts); and "no change" denotes changes of less than 1 point (Gini coefficient) and 0.5 points (headcount). For the total period, values are double. Data in the first column refer to changes from around 1990 to the mid 1990s for Czech Republic, Hungary, and Portugal. Data in the second column refer to changes from the mid 1990s to around 2000 for Austria, Belgium, Czech Republic, Ireland, Portugal, and Spain (where 2005 data, based on EU-SILC, are not comparable with those for earlier years); and to changes from 2000 to 2005 for Switzerland.

Source: Computations based on OECD income distribution questionnaire. OECD (2008a)

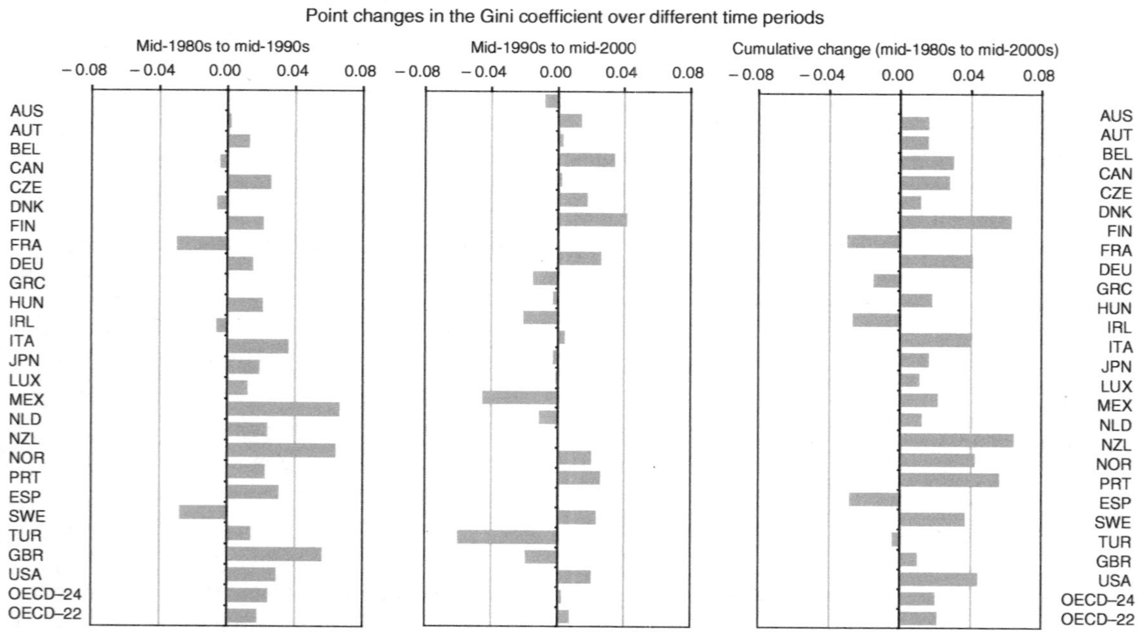

Figure 7. Trends in OECD income inequality, 1985–2005

Notes: In the first panel, data refer to changes from around 1990 to the mid-1990s for the Czech Republic, Hungary and Portugal and to the western länder of Germany (no data are available for Australia, Poland and Switzerland). In the second panel, data refer to changes from the mid-1990s to around 2000 for Austria, the Czech Republic, Belgium, Ireland, Portugal and Spain (where 2005 data, based on EU–SILC, are not deemed to be comparable with those for earlier years). OECD–24 refers to the simple average of OECD countries with data spanning the entire period (all countries shown above except Australia); OECD–22 refers to the same countries except Mexico and Turkey.

Source: Computations based on OECD income distribution questionnaire. OECD (2008a)

Increasing employment is the best way of reducing poverty" (OECD, 2008b). The report, however, also found that investing in education provides an important driver in reducing inequality.

These increasing income inequalities reflect the massive rise in wealth that has accrued at the highest echelons of society. Over the last three decades, for example, the majority of American citizens have received only modest salary increases. As Krugman (2002) highlights in his lengthy *New York Times* magazine essay "For Richer," and which he elaborated upon in his 2007 book *The Conscience of a Liberal*: "the average annual salary in America, expressed in 1998 dollars (that is, adjusted for inflation), rose from $32,522 in 1970 to $35,864 in 1999. That's about a 10 percent increase over 29 years – progress, but not much. Over the same period, however, according to Fortune magazine, the average real annual compensation of the top 100 CEO's went from $1.3 million – 39 times the pay of an average worker – to $37.5 million, more than 1,000 times the pay of ordinary workers."[15]

Since Krugman penned "For richer" such disparities in income have widened. In December 2007 the independent Congressional Budget Office (CBO) published its analysis of increasing income disparities in the USA. The CBO (2007) report highlights how between 1979 and 2005 the after tax incomes of the top 1 percent of families rose in real terms by a staggering 228 percent from $326,400 to $1,071,500 (expressed in 2005 dollars). Over the same period there was only a 21 percent gain for those in the middle of the income distribution with incomes rising from $41,500 to $50,200. The lowest 20 percent saw their incomes rise by only 6 percent from $14,400 to $15,300. The spoils of affluence have thus underpinned the rise of the super rich (see Figure 8).[16] Moreover, as Krugman (2002) argues, by digging behind these broad statistical averages, it becomes clear that the increase in wealth is even more concentrated:

> Most of the gains in the share of the top 10 percent of taxpayers over the past 30 years were actually gains to the top 1 percent, rather than the next 9 percent. In 1998 the top 1 percent started at $230,000. In turn, 60 percent of the gains of that top 1 percent went to the top 0.1 percent, those with incomes of more than $790,000. And almost half of those gains went to a mere 13,000 taxpayers, the top 0.01 percent, who had an income of at least $3.6 million and an average income of $17 million.

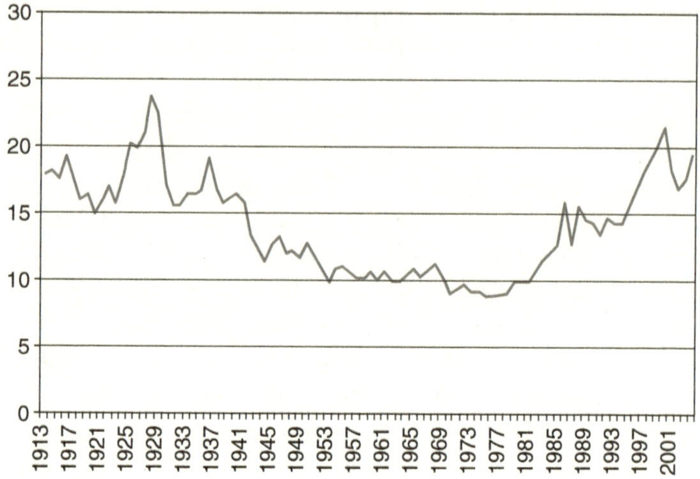

Figure 8. Share of total pre-tax income held by highest-income 1 percent
Source: The Rise of the Super-Rich, Teresa Tritch, NYT, July 19, 2006; based on IRS

Economists advanced three main explanations of what happened to the US distribution of income, relating to the effects of globalization, skill-biased technological change, and the superstar phenomenon. The globalization hypothesis attempted to link the change in the distribution of income to the advance of world trade and increasing imports of manufactured goods from the rapidly industrializing countries. The skill-biased technological change thesis saw change as a result of the information technology revolution, which was driving the increased demand for educated, skilled workers. The superstar hypothesis agued that modern competition often turns into a tournament with large spoils available to the winner. What underpins all these explanations, however, was the belief that one's income reflects what the market is willing to pay. These explanations became, and reflect, the conventional wisdom. The supremacy of the market was not seriously challenged in these debates. And: "Just as truth ultimately serves to create a consensus, so in the short run does acceptability" (Galbraith, 1958a: 35). Paul Krugman (2002), who was a bitter participant in these debates, now accepts, however, that:

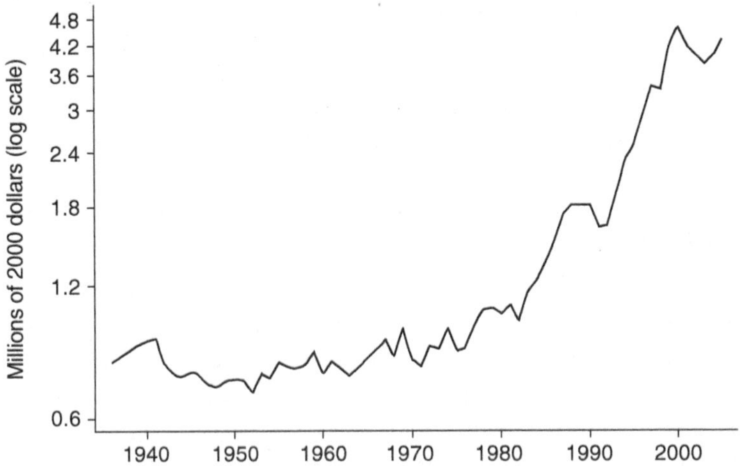

Figure 9. The median value of total executive compensation, 1936–2005
Note: Total compensation is composed of salary, bonuses, long-term bonus payments, and stock option grants. Based on the three highest-paid officers in the largest 50 firms in 1940, 1960 and 1990 (a total of 101 firms).
Source: Frydman and Saks (2008)

there has been a growing sense among economists that none of these hypotheses work ... globalization can explain part of the relative decline in blue-collar wages, but it can't explain the 2,500 percent rise in C.E.O. incomes. Technology may explain why the salary premium associated with a college education has risen, but it's hard to match up with the huge increase in inequality among the college-educated, with little progress for many but gigantic gains at the top. The superstar theory works for Jay Leno, but not for the thousands of people who have become awesomely rich without going on TV.

Krugman (2007) now acknowledges that economists must take seriously the role of power and wider social norms in driving inequality.[17] This insight is long familiar to those versed in Veblen, Keynes, and Galbraith (see James Galbraith, 1998, 2006, 2008a, 2008b). Krugman argues that the impact of the post-New Deal consensus was an attack on the excess of the so-called robber-barons which culminated in the modern executive exercising restraint in the 1950s and 1960s (see Figure 9).[18] Saliently Krugman (2002) cited support for his argument by quoting the following passage from Galbraith (1967: 127–8), who argued:

Management does not go out ruthlessly to reward itself – sound management is expected to exercise restraint ... With the power of decision goes opportunity for making money ... Were everyone to seek to do so ... the corporation would be a chaos of competitive avarice. But these are not the sort of thing that a good company man does; a remarkably effective code bans such behavior. Group decision-making ensures, moreover, that almost everyone's actions and even thoughts are known to others. This acts to enforce the code and, more than incidentally, a high standard of personal honesty as well.

According to Krugman (2002) the: "key reason executives are paid so much now is that they appoint the members of the corporate board that determines their compensation and control many of the perks that board members count on. So it's not the invisible hand of the market that leads to those monumental executive incomes; it's the invisible handshake in the boardroom." This points to the ability of the apex technostructure to set its own pay, reflecting in turn its own dominant power: "Reward depends not on the market but on determination by human agency" (Galbraith, 1973a: 282).[19] Therefore it should be no surprise that a recent study of executive pay between 1936 and 2005 by Carola Frydman and Raven Saks (2008) finds that the steep upward trajectory of pay since the 1970s coincided with similarly large increases in aggregate firm size – see Figure 9.[20]

The analysis of Galbraith (1973a: 283) in *Economics and the Public Purpose* is therefore even more relevant today: "The notion of an impersonally determined salary scale is extremely important to its beneficiaries ... Once the planning system is stripped of its market disguise, the way it arranges its compensation becomes a question of much interest and the proper subject of public policy."[21] Indeed this is why Galbraith (1973a: 284) argued: "Greater equality within the planning system should be the goal of tax policy."

Saliently Krugman (2007), who appears to be metamorphosing into a Galbraithian (even referring to himself as a liberal in the title of his most recent book), also argues that management theorists and economists unwittingly played their part in rationalizing the explosion in inequality – arguing for the alignment of incentives with stockholders. Such management theorists and economists espouse the modern day variant of the conventional wisdom that "as a matter of natural law and equity, what a man has received save by proven larceny is rightfully his" (Galbraith, 1958a: 92).

The long history of financial euphoria

Galbraith, as noted above, tirelessly warned of the dangers of financial excess and speculative manias. In *The Great Crash, 1929* (1955a), *Money* (1975), *A Short History of Financial Euphoria* (1990a), and *The Economics of Innocent Fraud* (2004) Galbraith described the common events that precede and accompany particular financial crises, events that are conveniently forgotten by politicians, regulators, and their advisers in the good times, when financial deregulation takes grip. As Galbraith (1955a: 206) counseled:

> Yet, in some respects, the chances of a recurrence of a speculative orgy are rather good. No one can doubt that the American people remain susceptible to the speculative mood – to the conviction that enterprise can be attended by unlimited rewards in which they, individually, were meant to share. A rising market can still bring the reality of riches. This, in turn, can draw more and more people to participate. The government preventatives and controls are ready. In the hands of determined government their efficacy cannot be doubted. There are, however, a hundred reasons why a government will determine not to use them.

Galbraith, like Keynes before him, identified the instability of modern capitalism in terms of the drive to accumulate excessive wealth and the fragile nature of the financial system.[22] As Galbraith (1971: 104) remarked in his essay "Financial Genius is Before the Fall": "the stock market is inherently unstable, the instability being related to its superbly orchestrated ability to attract people with a promise of effortless riches, give them a taste of such gain, persuade them that it is rewarding their financial acuity (of which they have none) or that of the people who are managing their money (which may be less) and then, usually after overcoming some preliminary setbacks which greatly add to the general state of confidence, destroy these illusions in one mortal thud." Galbraith argued that an unfettered, competitive capitalist system, operating on pure free-market principles, was inherently cyclical and unstable, requiring robust regulation and active government.

Starting with the tulip bulb mania in the 1630s, bubble after speculative bubble has been erased from the popular memory: the South Sea bubble in the early 1700s; the Mississippi bubble, which caused a stock-market crash in eighteenth-century France; the Florida real-estate bubble in the 1920s; the stock-market crash of 1929; the stock-market crash of 1987; the Nikkei bubble, which began in 1991; the NASDAQ bubble of 2000; and the great crash of 2008. These episodes share a theme: a perceived fundamental change in the economy arouses euphoria and heightened expectations of return, leading to excess, fraud, and collapse.[23]

This pattern underpinned the Internet boom and the folly of sub-prime lending, which characterized housing markets across the global economy in recent years, which led to financial contagion and the subsequent credit crunch (see Krugman, 2008c).[24] It characterized the roaring nineties (see Stiglitz, 2003). It also characterizes the recent irrational exuberance of the oil market, which also experienced a speculative bubble not unlike that which has typified the housing market, creating another major anxiety of our time (Davidson, 2008b). As Mouawad (2008) reported: "[Oil] Prices are rising because everyone expects them to do so. We've seen the same thing in the real estate market."[25]

An authoritative report by the Bank of England (2008) charts the recent financial innovation and speculation that Galbraith warned would drive financial instability. In 2001, UK customer lending was comparable to customer deposits, "but by the first half of 2008 the surplus of lending over deposits – 'the customer funding gap' – was £700bn" (Bank of England, 2008: 8). This gap was filled by drawing down on international wholesale markets, which consolidated the financial interdependence of the global economic system. This led to an expansion in banks balance sheets and a broader expansion in risk taking. Heightened expectations stimulated a credit boom with the banking system keen to lend money in the desire to cash in on the new situation and secure higher returns. The expansion in business activity fed entrepreneurial and speculative behavior in the banking, financial, and corporate sectors. It fuelled monetary innovation and the new forms of credit and financing structures, such as hedging vehicles, residential mortgage backed securities, financial derivatives, credit default swaps, and so on. It encouraged Enron, WorldCom, Tyco, Global Crossing, Adelphia-type structures, contrived to allow executives and firms to take part in the speculative orgy. And it also promoted firm growth and consolidation through merger and acquisition. And as Galbraith (1973a: 121) pointed out in *Economics and the Public Purpose*:

> At all times, however, growth by acquisition is a wholly normal tendency of the planning system. Between 1948 and 1965 – years that exclude the frantic mergers of the latter sixties – the 200 largest manufacturing corporations in the United States acquired 2692 other firms with total assets of $21.5 billion. These acquisitions accounted for about one-seventh of all growth in assets by these firms during this period. Excluding the 20 largest manufacturing firms, they accounted for between one-fifth and one-fourth of the growth. During the next three years the 200 largest corporations acquired some 1200 more firms with additional assets of approximately $30 billion.

Since then these trends have only intensified. Global finance and growth through acquisition have exploded exponentially. For example between 1996 and 2006 the value of global mergers and acquisitions increased from $1 trillion to $4 trillion (Figure 10). Similarly the recent revolution in information technology has driven forward monetary innovation with the markets in financial futures and interest rate swaps being more contemporary examples.[26] According to the McKinsey Global Institute, the ratio of global financial assets to annual world output has tripled from 109 percent in 1980 to 316 percent in 2005 (Wolf, 2007). By 2005, the global stock of core financial assets had reached $140,000bn (see Figure 10).

Galbraith warned of the familiar constants that accompany all crashes.[27] Constants that were evident across the collapses of Fannie Mae, Freddie Mac, Bear Stearns, Lehman Brothers, and Merrill Lynch in the USA. Constants that also characterize the experience of Northern Rock, the takeover of Bradford and Bingley by Santander, as well as the predicament endured by HBOS, Lloyds, Barclays, and Royal Bank of Scotland in the UK.

With expectations of gain tending to rise with each increase in profits, hedge-financing structures and stock markets tend to become more speculative, as exemplified by rising price to earnings ratios (see Figure 11). Company balance sheets worsen as they take on more borrowing and become weighed down with debt, with high levels of future commitments and payments that will have to be serviced. Increasingly future financial commitments can only be met by new borrowing. The specter of the great crash looms: "Loans which would

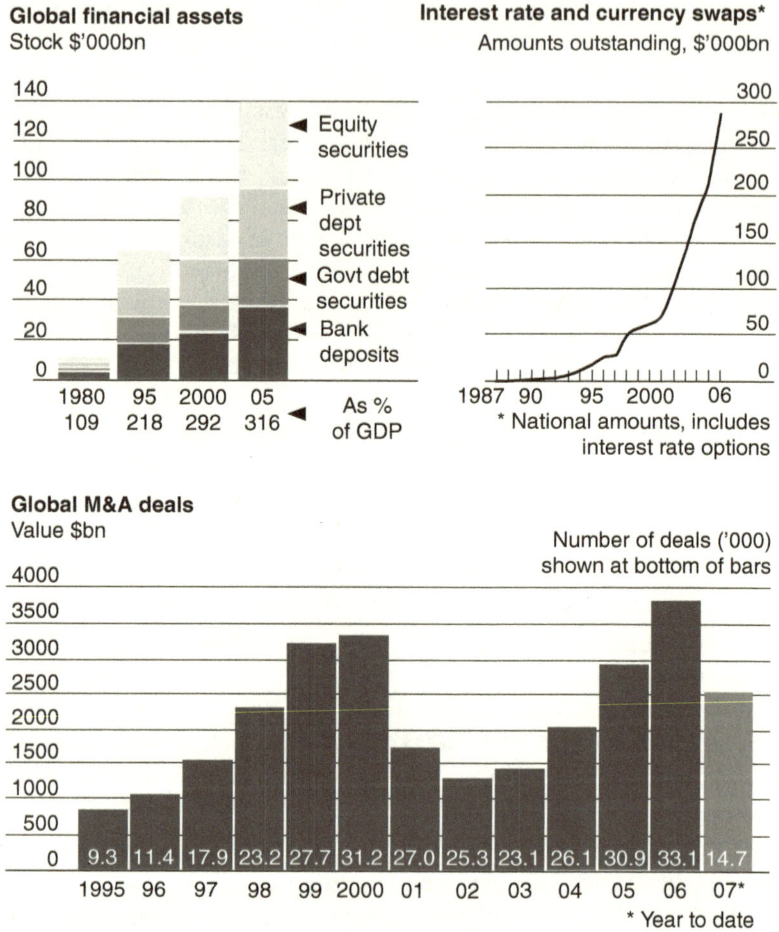

Figure 10. The explosion in global finance
Source: Mckinsey Global Institute, ISDA, Dealogle, Financial Times, June 18, 2007

have been perfectly good were made perfectly foolish by the collapse of the borrower's prices or the markets for his goods or the value of the collateral he had posted ... The bankers yielded, as did others, to the blithe, optimistic, and immoral mood of the times but probably not more so" (Galbraith, 1955a: 196).

As Galbraith, and Keynes before him, warned, such speculation inevitably leads to euphoria or overtrading – "irrational exuberance" in the words of Alan Greenspan – in which rising asset prices encourage

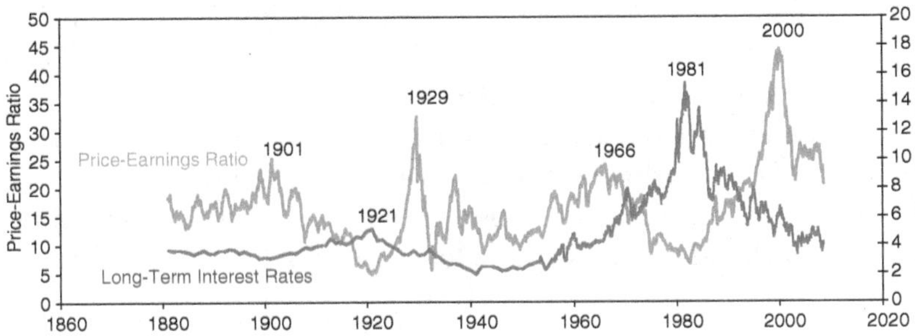

Figure 11. The rise in price-earnings ratios of stocks
Source: Figure 1.3, Shiller (2005)

speculative excess (see Shiller, 2005).[28] As debt accumulates, a situation arises in which debts can only be serviced by the issue of new liabilities. As long as the financial markets are booming, it is possible to sustain low levels of cash inflow by issuing new stocks and securities to finance current liabilities. But when the hangover comes, it hits hard.

Such excess naturally leads to the next phase of when expectations, stock market prices and financing structures collapse. The conventional measure of whether the stock market is overvalued is the price-earnings ratio, which divides stock prices by annual corporate earnings. In 2000 companies in the Standard & Poor's 500 Index were trading at thirty-six times their average earnings over the previous five years (see Figure 11). According to Shiller (2005) this was the highest valuation since at least the 1880s. Similarly in October 2008 the gap between over-optimistic expectations and the more pedestrian reality was once again revealed.

Galbraith repeatedly warned of the risks of such financial euphoria.[29] But politicians and players are all too ready to forget that boom and bust is a result of human greed and not something that can be easily designed out of capitalism. When the financial markets slow their expansion, organizations that have covered their future liabilities through issuing more debt are forced to sell assets to meet their liabilities. These "distress" sales cause asset prices to fall, at which point the financial markets, and businesses with exposure to those markets, collapse. The next phase in which investors try to get their money back out of the markets, naturally gives way to one of "panic." This is the essence of the great crash.[30]

At this stage prices freefall and asset markets break down, unable to cope with the excess of sale orders. Banks collapse and the fall has a very real knock-on effect on non-financial sectors. As Galbraith highlighted, both bank failures and the fear of bank failures have the same effect. Both are "forces of compelling power to induce deflation – to contract consumer spending, investment spending and therewith sales, output, employment and prices" (Galbraith, 1975: 203).

The fall of the masters of the universe

On the eve of Galbraith's hundredth birthday, and following on from the sub-prime crisis, the Dow and the broader Standard & Poor's (S&P) 500-stock index both closed down 18 percent for the week, decimating stock options and wealth.[31] The Dow had never had a week so bad in its 133-year history (Bajaj, 2008). The S&P has fallen slightly more on only two occasions before – in 1929 and 1933. Like 1929, the 2008 story was the same – a speculative orgy, crescendo, climax, and crash. Like 1929 the world economy was weakened by "bad distribution of income ... bad corporate structure ... bad banking structure ... dubious state of the foreign balance ... and poor state of economic intelligence" (Galbraith, 1955a: 194–202).

Once again the lessons of history were forgotten, and the consequences of deregulation and nonregulation were stark. Wall Street had basically reinvented itself after the repeal of the Glass-Steagall Act in 1999, which instituted banking controls in the aftermath of the Great Depression.[32] Glass-Steagall banned banks from underwriting securities – mortgage loans were not to be re-sold. This meant that banks making loans had to do so in the knowledge that they would carry the loan debt over its life. The lender would thus bear the costs, if the borrower defaulted. This provided a strong incentive to avoid bad debtors. Before making loans, lenders would therefore take greater care regarding equity, credit history, and employment prospects. With the repeal of Glass-Steagall, loans could be sold on. Bad debts could be packaged as good debts and sold on. They could be bundled up into Collateral Debt Obligations (CDOs), Structured Investment Vehicles (SIVs), or other mysterious financial vehicles that circumvented banking regulation.[33] And they could then be sold on "to unwary pension funds, local and state revenue funds, individual investors, or other banks domestically or overseas, e.g., Northern Rock in the UK who, led on by the high ratings of these complex financial securities by rating agencies, believe these are safe investment vehicles" (Davidson, 2008a: 2). This financial mystification underpinned the speculative excess that collapsed when rising defaults on sub-prime mortgages started to accelerate.[34]

The love of money was once again man's downfall in the great crash of 2008. The masters of the universe lost all that they had confidently proclaimed was theirs. As the stock markets continued to fall throughout the summer and fall of 2008 hope of a swift correction receded. The experience of the great crash of 1929 was repeated. As Galbraith (1955a: 130) remarked: "The singular feature of the great crash of 1929 was that the worst continued to worsen. What looked one day like the end proved on the next day to have been only the beginning. Nothing could have been more ingeniously designed to maximize the suffering."

The managers who blew a big hole in Lehman Brothers and Morgan Stanley's balance sheets had earned enormous bonuses in the past. Bankers assume that they get paid for their financial genius. They believed they got their just deserts, what the market was willing to pay, what the conventional wisdom variously describes as their marginal productivity.[35] The chief executive of Morgan Stanley, John Mack, received a bonus of $40m in 2006. What is now clear to all, however, was that these bonuses were not tied to increases in productivity or improvements in long term performance. It is also now clear, that shareholders failed to exercise control over financial institutions to prevent the enormous expansion in pay in the banking sector (James Galbraith, 2008a). Banking technostructures had run amok with greed with shareholders and even the bankers themselves believing in their own omniscience and omnipotence: "They were impelled to it by the seminal lunacy which has always seized people who are seized in turn with the notion that they can become very rich" (Galbraith, 1955a: 28)

In 1929, amid the bloodbath, there were buy-backs of stock by investment trusts, desperate to prop up their ailing share prices. This resulted in a massive loss of liquidity, just when cash was at its most needed. As Galbraith (1955a: 146) remarked: "They bought their own worthless stock. Men have been swindled by other men on many occasions. The autumn of 1929 was, perhaps, the first occasion when men succeeded on a large scale in swindling themselves." Unfortunately, it was not the last time, as business journalist Jeff Randall (2008) documents. In 2006 the Royal Bank of Scotland (RBS) spent £1bn buying 54.3m of its own shares at an average price of £18.37. As late as December that year, it paid £141m for 7.1m shares (at an average price £19.79). On October 8, 2008, RBS shares fell by 39 percent to just 90 pence. But the financial genius is before the fall. And RBS was not unique in its wisdom. Even after the credit crunch hit the headlines in September 2008, when Northern Rock crumbled, Halifax-Bank of Scotland was busy buying its own shares at inflated prices. In 2006–7, HBOS spent £1.5bn (at a average share price of £10.01). On October 8, 2008 HBOS's shares fell 37 percent to a fire-sale price of 94 pence.

What impelled HBOS to carry on with such a foolish scheme? As Galbraith (1955a: 145) remarked: "If one has been a financial genius, faith in one's genius does not dissolve at once." It is thus inevitable that the humiliating journey from hubris to nemesis follows as night follows day: "The cash went out and the stock came in, and prices were not perceptibly affected or not for long. What six months before had been a brilliant financial maneuver was now a form of fiscal self-immolation" (Galbraith, 1955a: 145).

Similarly the congressional mortification of Dick Fuld, Lehman's former chief executive on Monday October 6, 2008, and the savaging of Sir Fred Goodwin, the former Royal Bank of Scotland chief executive, and Sir Tom McKillop, the former RBS chairman, by the UK's Treasury Select Committee on February 10, 2009, replayed the experiences that Galbraith chronicled in *The Great Crash*. Dick Fuld's humiliation was orchestrated by Henry Waxman, a veteran Democrat, whose straightforward question about Fuld's alleged $480m of earnings "Is that fair?" epitomized the great inequalities in wealth that now characterize contemporary, affluent societies. Journalists, such as Randall (2008), remarked of the sense of déjà vu at the display of outraged inquisitors wiping the floor with Wall Street's masters of the universe. It was all so wonderfully described by Galbraith (1955a: 136) over fifty years before:

> As the ghosts of numerous tyrants, from Julius Caesar to Benito Mussolini will testify, people are very hard on those who, having had power, lose it or are destroyed. Then anger at past arrogance is joined with contempt

for present weakness. The victim or his corpse is made to suffer all available indignities. Such was the fate of the bankers. They were fair game for Congressional committees, courts, the press and comedians.

The great crash of 2008 also had its share of larceny. On December 11, 2008 Bernard Madoff, the former chairman of the Nasdaq stock market, was arrested, charged, and ultimately convicted of securities fraud, in what is one of the biggest fraud cases ever. Madoff's hedge fund ran up $50bn (£33.5bn) of fraudulent losses, using money from new investors to pay off existing investors. According to the US Attorney's criminal complaint filed in court, it was "basically, a giant Ponzi scheme" – a key feature of the analysis of both Minsky and Galbraith.[36] Similarly on February 17, 2009 Sir Allen Stanford was charged with fraudulently selling $8 billion in high-yield certificates of deposit in a scheme that stretched all around the world. This was all reminiscent of the experiences of the inter-war period. The experience of Richard Whitney, for example, the former vice president of the New York Stock Exchange, in the aftermath of the great crash of 1929, was eerily similar to that of Madoff's:

> Whitney's dishonesty was a casual, rather juvenile sort. Associates of the day have since explained it as the result of an unfortunate failure to realize that the rules, which were meant for other people, also applied to him … In the twenties the Wall Street firm of Richard Whitney and Company was an unspectacular bond house with a modest business. Whitney apparently felt that it provided insufficient scope for his imagination, and with the passing years he moved on to other enterprises, including the mining of mineral colloids and the market of peat humus in Florida …
>
> Nothing is so voracious as a losing business, and eventually Whitney had three of them. To keep them going he borrowed from banks, investment bankers, other Stock Exchange members, and heavily from his brother, George Whitney, a partner of J.P. Morgan and Company. The loans so negotiated, from the early twenties on, totaled in the millions, many of them unsecured. As time passed Whitney was increasingly pressed. When one loan became due he was forced to replace it with another and borrow still more for the interest on those outstanding. Beginning in 1933 his stock exchange firm was insolvent, although this did not become evident for some five years. (Galbraith, 1955a: 178–9)

Ultimately Whitney's deception and incompetence came to light, just like Madoff's, in a falling market. His company bought between ten and fifteen thousand shares in a liquor making company – Distilled Liquors Corporation – at $15 a share in 1933. By the spring of 1934 the stock reached $45 and in January 1935 the firm was listed on the New York Stock Exchange and then used as further collateral for various loans by Whitney. But Distilled Liquors Corporation was not profitable and by June 1936 the price dropped to $11, precipitating a rush of off loading, which, in order to stem the fall, led to Whitney seeking to buy and mop up stock to maintain the price:

> All the other investors unloaded on Whitney. At the time of his failure, of the 148,750 shares outstanding, Whitney or his firm owned 137,672. By then the value had dropped to between three and four dollars a share. Mention has been made of the tendency of people in this period to swindle themselves. Whitney, in his effort to support the stock of Distilled Liquors Corporation, unquestionably emerged as the Ponzi of financial self-deception. As the result of his operation he had all his old debts, many new ones incurred in supporting the stock, all the stock – and the stock was nearly worthless.
>
> As his position become more complex, Richard Whitney resorted increasingly to an expedient which he had been using for several years – that of posting securities belonging to other people which were in his custody as collateral for his loans. By early 1938 he had reached the end of a surprising capacity to borrow money ... The rumor spread he was in poor condition. Still, on 8 March, there was a stunned silence on the floor of the Exchange when President Charles R. Gay announced from the rostrum the suspension of Richard Whitney and Company for insolvency. Members were rather more aghast when they learned that Whitney had been in engaged in theft on a large scale for a long period. (Galbraith, 1955a: 180–1)

That the arrogant should fall so far is not, however, to be celebrated. It is a reflection of the greed and hubris that financial institutions and those that handle money are steeped in.[37] The reality is mundane – the masters of the universe are far from modern alchemists.[38] As Galbraith (1955a: 27) coolly observed: "I have never adhered to the view that Wall Street is uniquely evil, just as I have never found it possible to accept with complete confidence the alternative view, rather more palatable in sound financial circles, that it is uniquely wise." The sooner politicians, regulators, and business journalists realize this, the better.

Are we all Galbraithians now?

As Galbraith pointed out, anticipating the recent global banking meltdown, banking "runs" precipitate banking collapses. And, as has once again been painfully acknowledged, banking collapses matter. This is because "a bank failure is not an ordinary business adventure ... it has not one but two adverse effects on economic activity: Owners lose their capital and depositors their deposits, and both therewith lose their ability to purchase things. But failure (or for that matter fear of failure) also means a shrinkage in the money supply" (Galbraith, 1975: 121). A shrinkage in the money supply means inevitable impacts on demand in the real economy, with the prospect of mass unemployment looming.

In October 2008 the Bank of England (2008) estimated the cost of the global banking collapse to the world's financial firms at $2.8 trillion. The BBC (2008) estimated that global taxpayers had spent nearly $7 trillion to shore up the world's banks and financial institutions.[39] Such interventions were designed to prevent the financial crisis overspilling into the real economy; to avoid another Great Depression following another great crash; and to avoid the re-emergence of the mass unemployment that plagued the interwar years. Lord Turner, the Chair of the Financial Services Authority, which regulates the British banking system, remarked that: "There is no chance of a 1929–33 depression. We know the lessons, and we know how to stop it happening again" (*Guardian*, 2008: 7). It is not clear, however, that the lessons of history have been fully learnt by regulators and politicians. For Krugman (2008c: 182) this hails the return of depression economics:

> What does it mean to say that depression economics has returned? Essentially it means that for the first time in two generations, failures on the demand side of the economy – insufficient private spending to make use of the available productive capacity – have become the clear and present limitation on prosperity for a large part of the world.
>
> We – by which I mean not only economists but also policy makers and the educated public at large – weren't ready for this. The specific set of foolish ideas that has laid claim to the name "supply-side economics" is a crank doctrine that would have had little influence if it did not appeal to the prejudices of editors and wealthy men. But over the past few decades

there has been a steady drift in emphasis in economic thinking away from the demand side to the supply side of the economy.

As already noted above, Galbraith (1973a: 199) long argued "that the modern economy was subject to severe downward instability, and that this was neither self-limiting nor self-correcting." This recognition "came in the decade of the thirties. This was the Keynesian Revolution" (Galbraith, 1973a: 199).[40] The way to avoid another Great Depression is for central banks and the IMF to act as lender of last resort and for the government to maintain demand by increasing public spending (cf. Davidson, 2007; Wray, 2007). "As restraint on bank lending during the boom is a basic central-bank function, so serving as a lender of last resort is its main task in the ensuing depression" (Galbraith, 1975: 127). Across the world regulators and central bankers have clearly failed on the first count. But the major fiscal interventions by governments across 2008 and 2009 appear to have prevented another Great Depression.

Galbraith argued that there are no automatic mechanisms which ensure that the level of demand will be consistent with high employment: "If business is sufficiently bad, profit prospects sufficiently dim, gloom sufficiently deep, businessmen may not borrow money" (Galbraith, 1975: 221). People will not buy all of the goods that the economy produces. This is the lesson that markets do not always self-correct themselves. In the conventional wisdom the interest rate brings into balance decisions to save and invest. Free and flexible markets mean that all that is put on sale is bought. And all who want a job, get one. But as Galbraith was keen to point out throughout his long life, capitalism and its financial and labor markets have changed. The market does not determine the interest rate. The interaction of the demand and supply of money does not set the various interest rates. Rather it is central bankers, monetary policy committees, and a few large banks that set global financial prices.[41] The level of interest rates reflects the decisions of a few, not the needs of the many. And it is the investment decisions of the dominant corporations that largely determine the volume and variability of global spending. Accordingly, there is no guarantee to ensure that investment spending will be enough to provide enough demand across the global economy to sustain high levels of employment.

Financial markets drive the economy. Banks create money. They create money to make a profit. And this oils the wheels and drives demand in the good times. Banks create money by lending to other banks and businesses. Businesses that employ people to make and sell things. These jobs create income to spend on other firms' products. But if banks do not lend and consumers do not spend, businesses go to the wall and demand in the economy dries up.[42] In the fall of 2008, governments across the world started to act by injecting capital into the world's financial institutions, not just to save bankers, but to save the real economy. In doing so, there was a growing recognition that they had to be prepared to spend their way out of trouble (Krugman, 2008b). They had to be prepared for deficits to rise.[43] And in doing so, we must relearn the lessons of history and forever consign the Washington Consensus – which, in response to the various financial crises, urged raising interest rates, slashing spending and increasing taxes – to the dustbin of history. Indeed as Galbraith (1958a: 42) pointed out over fifty years ago, while reflecting on lessons of the Great Depression:

> The conventional wisdom continued to emphasize the balanced budget. Audiences continued to respond to the warning of the disaster which would befall were this rule not respected. The shattering circumstance was the great depression. This led in the United States to a severe reduction in the revenues of the federal government; it also brought pressure for a variety of relief and welfare expenditures. A balanced budget meant increasing tax rates and reducing public expenditure. Viewed in retrospect, it would be hard to imagine a better design for reducing both the private and public demand for goods, aggravating deflation, increasing unemployment, and adding to the general suffering.

In these global times, such action needs to be coordinated by Governments and bankers to make a difference (Galbraith, 1973a: 338–41). This is an important lesson to learn. This means that a federal or a monetary policy committee trying to stave off recession by playing with its national interest rate is only really playing with one club – a key limitation of the New Consensus view in macroeconomics (see the previous chapter). This is why in the Great Depression "monetary policy was like a string. You could pull it, though with incalculable results. But you could not shove it at all" (Galbraith, 1975: 226). And the string is well and truly broken in a global economy.

To maintain spending Galbraith recommended that fiscal policy should be combined with governments' running deficits.[44] As Galbraith (1996b: 40) argued: "The deficit ... must not be seen as a barrier to effective public action, for by stimulating economic activity it increases earnings and tax receipts. Improvements to the public infrastructure – roads, schools, airports, housing – that are made by those newly employed also add to public wealth and income. Public borrowing can, over time, be a fiscally conservative act." This is the way to keep spending high. Galbraith also warned that tax cuts in income, sales, or corporation tax alone will not stimulate the economy:

> Tax cuts have little positive business effect ... Such tax reduction has little immediate effect on either consumer spending or business investment. If profit prospects are good, a corporate tax cut is not needed to encourage investment. If they are bad, no tax cut will make them good. As practical experience with past tax reduction has shown (and as was duly reported by the Council of Economic Advisors), the initial effect of a cut in personal taxes is overwhelmingly to increase savings. Income so saved does not buy goods, and modern business investment, some special pleading to the contrary, proceeds independently of the supply of savings. Only good economic performance – good employment and demand – will encourage borrowing of these funds. (Galbraith, 1979a: 29–30)

At this present time, Galbraith would also urge us to reform international monetary institutions to reduce financial market contagion (cf. Galbraith, 1955a: 197–9, 203; 1975: 268–75).[45] The conventional wisdom of the Washington Consensus, which has been shown wanting through the repeated mishandling of the Mexican, Thai, Indonesian, and Malaysian financial crises, must be rejected (Krugman, 2008c). As Gordon Brown and Nicolas Sarkozy began to acknowledge in the fall of 2008, it is time we changed the international financial architecture (cf. Stiglitz, 2002). The lessons of the postwar period must be re-learned: "In the years following World War II, the international system worked because American policy was reasonably predictable ... Until this arrangement is restored, one thing is certain: the planning systems of several industrial countries will continue, as in the recent past, to stumble from one so-called monetary crisis to the next" (Galbraith, 1973a: 341).[46] Galbraith (1973a: 270–4) would advise us to reconsider the Keynes

Plan of Bretton Woods – which was never properly implemented – or Paul Davidson's International Monetary Clearing Union (IMCU) proposal (see Davidson, 1994: 252–84).[47] These plans permit each nation to pursue full employment without fear of external shocks occurring elsewhere in the global economy.[48]

The liberal hour

October 15, 2008 was the hundredth birthday anniversary of Galbraith. It came in the week of massive Government interventions on both sides of the Atlantic to stem the mounting financial crisis. It came in a year of massive global financial instability. It ensured that Galbraith's analysis of the greed and self-delusion that led to the unraveling of America's stock market and the subsequent Great Depression, acquired renewed prominence. Galbraith was once again being read avidly. He was once again a man for our times (Dunn, 2008b). Once again, as Paul Krugman observed, the limitations of the conventional wisdom were all too apparent:

> Few economists saw our current crisis coming, but this predictive failure was the least of the field's problems. More important was the profession's blindness to the very possibility of catastrophic failures in a market economy ... the economics profession went astray because economists, as a group, mistook beauty, clad in impressive-looking mathematics, for truth ... economists fell back in love with the old, idealized vision of an economy in which rational individuals interact in perfect markets, this time gussied up with fancy equations ... Unfortunately, this romanticized and sanitized vision of the economy led most economists to ignore all the things that can go wrong. They turned a blind eye to the limitations of human rationality that often lead to bubbles and busts; to the problems of institutions that run amok; to the imperfections of markets – especially financial markets – that can cause the economy's operating system to undergo sudden, unpredictable crashes; and to the dangers created when regulators don't believe in regulation ... When it comes to the all-too-human problem of recessions and depressions, economists need to abandon the neat but wrong solution of assuming that everyone is rational and markets work perfectly. (Krugman, 2009)

It should be no surprise that many commentators have sought to return to Galbraith's major works to help explain the major crises of the twenty-first century. Once again the febrile nature of financial markets was reverberating globally. Once again the inequalities and inequities of the market were being laid bare. Once again the whole climate of consumerism, perpetuated through the relentless advertising propaganda, continued to elevate private production over the provision of merit and public goods leading to private affluence amid impoverished and under-provided basic and essential public services. Once again concerns about the social imbalance across our cities, healthcare, the destruction of the environment, the high and variable price of oil, and income inequalities were dominating the US presidential elections. Galbraith (1996b: 76–7) understood these anxieties and long argued for decisive public intervention and a proper regulatory response:

> There is, first, the need for contemporary and long-run protection of the planet, regulatory requirements commonly described as preventing environmental destruction ... Second, there is the need to protect the vulnerable among those employed in the productive apparatus from the adverse effects of the economic machine ... Third, there is the more than occasional propensity of the economy to produce and sell technically deficient or physically damaging goods or services. And, finally, the system incorporates within itself tendencies that are self-destructive of its effective operation. Each of these factors ... produces a sharp conflict with ideological overtones, between those who see the system as a fully independent force and themselves as deservedly rewarded thereby and those who advance the case for protective or corrective action.

It is therefore the continuing, evolving circumstance that conspires to ensure Galbraith's enduring relevance. A lifelong liberal who advised successive Democratic presidents and presidential candidates, Galbraith's economics deserves continued study by economists and policy makers. The flurry of action by governments and central banks around the world in the fall of 2008 suggests that the import of Galbraithian and Post Keynesian analysis is finally recognized by those who inhabit the practical world. The experience of the 1930s must be avoided. Contemporary financial crisis must be met with programmes designed to maintain demand and avoid another Great Depression. With the 100th anniversary of Galbraith's birth passing, his economics matter more than ever.

Notes

1 In Europe 65 percent of jobs in 2002 were in small and medium-sized firms, compared with just 46 percent in the USA (Judt, 2005). Europeans

even appear to be better at generating small and medium-size businesses. There are more small businesses in the EU than in the United States, and they create more employment.

2 Yale professor Robert Shiller (2006) argues that real per capita GDP is three times as high as it was in 1958 when Galbraith published *The Affluent Society*. He considers what US consumers have been spending their affluence on. He argues that: "Americans spent 27% of the huge increase in income between 1958 and 2005 on medical care, 23% on their homes, 12% on transportation, 10% on recreation, and 9% on personal business activities. The kinds of things that advertisers and salesmen typically promote were relatively unimportant. Food got only 8% of the extra money, clothing only 3%, and personal care 1%. Unfortunately, idealistic activities also received little of the extra money: 3% for welfare and religious activities, and a similar share for education. Thus, most of the extra money was spent on staying healthy, having a nice home, traveling and relaxing, and doing a little business." This is a familiar ploy, relying on coarse statistical breakdowns and innocuous labels to obscure the role of large banks, pharmaceutical companies, retail companies, media companies, oil and automobile companies that sell mortgages (homes), drugs (medical care), cars (transportation), entertainment (recreation), computers (personal business activities) and fast food (food). It is a familiar rhetorical ploy that masks the relentless pressure of consumerism.

3 As Eric Schlosser (2002: 149) points out in *Fast Food Nation*: "The industrialization of cattle-raising and meatpacking over the past two decades has completely altered how beef is produced – and the towns that produce it. Responding to the demands of the fast food and supermarket chains, the meatpacking giants have cut costs by cutting wages. They have turned one of the nation's best-paying manufacturing jobs into one of the lowest-paying, created a migrant industrial workforce of poor immigrants, tolerated high injury rates, and spawned rural ghettos in the American heartland."

4 Galbraith (1952a: 97–8) first analyzed the oil industry in *American Capitalism* where he noted the technical advance exhibited by the firms that characterized it: " The oil industry is an unquestioned monopoly; in any market area there are a few large firms and the characteristic fringe of independents. Over the years it has been under repeated attack for violation of the antitrust laws; it has rarely been free of suspicion of holding prices above the level that would be associated with more vigorous competition. Profits have generally been excellent ... The oil industry is clearly progressive ... As the result of its enterprise in petroleum exploration and recovery, in developing new products, and in engineering new

methods of transporting both petroleum and products, the consumer of gasoline and fuel oil has been far more fortunate than the consumer of coal." In *The Affluent Society* and *The New Industrial State* Galbraith sought to highlight the social and environmental imbalance ushered in by the success of the oil and automobile industries.

5 As Galbraith (1973a: 62) remarked of the large firm: "The president of General Motors has a prescriptive right, on visiting Washington, to see the President of the United States. The president of General Electric has a right to see the Secretary of Defense and the president of General Dynamics to see any general. The individual farmer has no similar access to the Secretary of Agriculture; the individual retailer has no entrée to the Secretary of Commerce." In the fall of 2008 this prescriptive right came under intense media scrutiny as the presidents of the major automobile firms sought financial support from the US government to stave off bankruptcy.

6 High oil prices are a net transfer of resources from users who directly or indirectly consume oil-related products, to oil-producing firms and countries who are responsible for the extraction and distribution of oil.

7 Mother Jones (2005) highlights how the oil industry lobby group use tobacco industry tactics to create doubt in the mind of the public that fossil fuel consumption was driving climate change (see also Monbiot, 2006, 2007). It tallies some forty ExxonMobil-funded organizations that either have sought to undermine mainstream scientific findings on global climate change or have maintained affiliations with a small group of "skeptic" scientists who continue to do so. Sample (2007) similarly reports that scientists and economists were offered $10,000 each by the American Enterprise Institute (AEI), an ExxonMobil-funded think-tank with close links to the Bush administration, to undermine the science of climate change. Oil companies have also sought to influence the educational curriculum. In 2006 Exxon Mobil's foundation gave $42 million to key organizations that influence the way children learn about science, from kindergarten until they graduate from high school (David, 2006).

8 The Stern Review was a rigorous and comprehensive analysis of the economic aspects of climate change. It was conducted by Sir Nicholas Stern, head of the UK Government Economic Service, and a former chief economist of the World Bank.

9 For much of the post-World War II era, defense spending as a proportion of the total economy was even higher than it is today (see Gold, 2008). For this reason, some defense analysts say we can afford to raise spending. A Galbraithian response would be that there are more effective channels for public spending, not least addressing the fact that there remain nearly 40 million medically uninsured Americans!

10 In June 2005 a major scandal broke regarding Philip Cooney. Cooney was the chief of staff for President Bush's environmental policy council and was revealed as having previously led the oil industry's fight against limits on greenhouse gases and, more importantly, abusing his position of power by repeatedly editing government climate reports to play down links between such emissions and global warming (Revkin, 2005a). Cooney was a former lobbyist with the American Petroleum Institute, the main lobbying group for the oil industry. Two days after the scandal broke, Cooney resigned. Within a week he had been re-employed by ExxonMobil (Revkin, 2005b).

11 In some ways emissions trading has become more practical in recent years and it might be argued that Galbraith's analysis is now out of date. From a Galbraithian perspective, it could be argued, however, that the development of emissions trading has been made easier by the increased dominance of the global economy by large firms. The major carbon emitters' biggest source of emissions occurs in oligopolistic sectors of the global economy. Consequently, only a thousand or so firms' carbon emissions need to be monitored and traded. Moreover, enforcement is assisted by the fact that large oligopolistic firms are all in the public eye. This perhaps explains the fact that the world's largest emission trading scheme, the European Union Emission Trading System (EU ETS), targets large emitters of carbon dioxide. The ETS currently covers: "over 10,000 installations in the energy and industrial sectors which are collectively responsible for close to half of the EU's emissions of CO_2 and 40% of its total greenhouse gas emissions" (European Union, 2008).

12 As Stiglitz (2007) argues: "The Kyoto Protocol represented the international community's attempt to begin to deal with global warming in a fair and efficient way. But it left out a majority of the sources of emissions, and unless something is done to include the US and the developing countries in a meaningful way, it will be little more than a symbolic gesture. There needs to be a new 'coalition of the willing,' this time perhaps led by Europe – and this time directed at a real danger."

13 For details of the rise in worldwide standards of living since 1800, see Easterlin (2000) and Maddison (1995a, 1995b, 2001, 2003).

14 Galbraith (1992: 158–9), like Keynes, would also allude to the impact of fiscal policy on spending power in the economy: "A reasonably equitable distribution of income is thought by individuals of liberal disposition to be politically virtuous; in fact, it is economically highly functional."

15 In 1980 the average American chief executive earned forty times the average manufacturing employee. By 2000 the top tier of American CEOs, the ratio was 475:1 and, as Krugman's figures suggest, would

be even greater if assets, not income, were accounted for. In other countries the ratio was less, although the gap has been widening. In Britain the gap is 24:1, in France 15:1, in Sweden 13:1 (see Blackburn, 2002: 201, table 3.2).

16 They also make economies more susceptible to another great crash. As Galbraith (1955a: 194–5) points out: "In 1929 the rich were indubitably rich. The figures are not entirely satisfactory, but it seems certain that the five per cent of the population with the highest incomes in that year received approximately one-third of all personal income ... This highly unequal income distribution meant that the economy was dependent on a high level of investment or high level of luxury spending or both ... Both investment and luxury spending are subject, inevitably, to more erratic influences and to wider fluctuations than the bread and rent outlays of the $25-week workman. This high bracket spending and investment was especially susceptible ... to the crushing news from the stock market in October 1929".

17 In a wonderful essay, Duhs (2008) highlights Paul Krugman's recent transformation into a Galbraithian.

18 In his 1936 State of the Union address, President Franklin D. Roosevelt railed against the "entrenched greed"' within American corporations. At that time, the average compensation for the top executive of a big company was about $95,000 equivalent to $1.4 million in today's prices. By 2005 this had grown to over $4 million at today's prices (Frydman and Saks, 2008).

19 In the conventional wisdom there are four dominant explanations of the executive pay. The first set of theories links executive compensation to managers' ability to exploit poor corporate governance and skim profits (Bertrand and Mullainathan, 2001; Bebchuk and Fried, 2004; Kuhnen and Zwiebel, 2007). The second set of theories relates to the firms' competition for scarce managerial talent (Lucas, 1978; Rosen, 1981, 1982; Tervio, 2007). The third set of theories argues that executive pay relates to the increased risk borne by executives (Inderst and Mueller, 2006; Cuñat and Guadalupe, 2006). The fourth set of theories argues that the level of executive compensation reflects the rising demand for general managerial skills (Murphy and Zábojník, 2004).

20 The recent study by Frydman and Saks (2008) provides factual evidence of how in the 1950s and 1960s the level of executive compensation was relatively stagnant and did not keep pace with the growing size of firms. Although their study represents a major contribution to the understanding of executive pay, they fail to consider the fact that executive pay may be linked to the size and power of the firm and social

norms rather than being competitively determined by the nature of the job and the position of the firm.

21 For a discussion of a variety of contemporary options, see Bebchuk and Fried (2004).

22 In *The Economics of Innocent Fraud* Galbraith (2004: 43) noted: "the modern economic system is unpredictable in its movement from good times to bad and then eventually from bad to good. Boom, bubble and inflation go on to declining production, rising unemployment, reduced earnings, stable but lower prices. Then, in time, to a revival – to higher employment, greater earnings, talk if not the reality of inflation."

23 Graham (2008: 28) remarks that: "since the emergence of modern capitalism some three centuries ago, we have seen more than 30 major financial crises – about one every 10 years. In the UK we've had more than 30 years since the last banking rescue (the secondary banks in 1974). One result was a growing belief, now shattered, that banking could be left largely to the private sector."

24 Wray (2008) presents a Minskyian analysis of the history of the current credit crisis (see also Krugman, 2008c: 150). Like Galbraith, followers of Minsky argue that the credit crunch and subprime problems mount to a strong case for greater regulation and a thorough understanding of the limits of markets. For financial fragility to emerge, Minsky argued that specific preconditions must occur such as the explosion of Ponzi financing. For a while many in the media argued that the global financial crisis reflected a "Minsky moment" as epitomized by the fraud of Bernard Madoff, the former chairman of the Nasdaq stock market. Madoff ran up $50bn (£33.5bn) of fraudulent losses in what the US Attorney described as "basically, a giant Ponzi scheme." Although this represents a major fraud, and is reminiscent of those that graced *The Great Crash 1929*, (see Galbraith, 1955a: 152–5, 169–2), this Ponzi scheme is dwarfed by the problems of liquidity that beset the global financial system. Davidson (2008c) argues that the recent financial market instability is not a "Minsky moment" caused by ubiquitous Ponzi financing. Davidson argues that the recent financial market instability is due to an insolvency problem of large underwriters caused by their attempt to "securitize" (make liquid) noncommercial mortgages (where the latter are normally illiquid assets). Governments across the world appeared, however, to side with Davidson (2008a, 2008c, 2008d), who argued that the solution for such an insolvency problem is large direct infusions of new capital in these institutions or removing nonperforming loans from their books. This is precisely what happened on October 8, 2008 in the UK and on October 14, 2008 in the USA.

25 Davidson (2008b) provides an incisive analysis of how speculation has driven oil prices up to current levels. In order to prevent this Davidson argues that the US government should pursue a buffer stock policy, selling oil into the market to reduce the incentives to speculate (see also Davidson, 1991b; Davidson and Davidson, 1996). See also Arestis and Sawyer (2005), who highlight, in a manner that is consistent with the Galbraithian approach, how the price of raw materials, and oil in particular, are key inflationary pressures.

26 It is sobering to note that Galbraith (1990a: 19) warns that what passes as "financial innovation" is, in reality: "the invention of the wheel over and over again, often in a slightly more unstable version. All financial innovations involve, in one form or another, the creation of debt secured in greater or lesser adequacy by real assets."

27 As Leathers and Raines (2008: 563) point out: "The relevance of Galbraith's theory and analyses continues to increase because the 'constants' that he identified in all speculative booms have become continuously active in the financial sector since the 1980s."

28 In Leathers and Raines' (2008: 561) assessment: "Shiller has been involved in both the narrow approach to behavioral finance with his empirical investigations and the broader approach in his book *Irrational Exuberance.* He also published an article on stock prices in January 1987. But whereas Galbraith explained ... why the market was in a speculative bubble that would at some point collapse, Shiller (1987) only provided a theoretical and empirical analysis showing that the volatility of stock prices from 1871 through 1986 challenged the efficient markets models. However, in *Irrational Exuberance*, he essentially emulated Galbraith by applying a behavioral theory of speculative bubbles to the 1990s stock market boom. Curiously, his only reference to Galbraith was superficial and rather dismissive. Quoting a passage from *The Great Crash 1929* that related to the intensity of interest in the stock market during the late 1920s, Shiller (2000: 57, emphasis added) asserted that 'Galbraith's argument contains *some journalistic overstatement*' but was 'on the right track in terms of the direction of change over the 1920s.' But Shiller's analysis of the stock market bubble of the 1990s in terms of the 'structural factors,' 'cultural factors,' and 'psychological factors' effectively amounted to an *incomplete* Galbraithian analysis of psychological and institutional factors that were in play."

29 Galbraith was no doubt influenced by Keynes (1936: 159), who presciently warned: "Speculators may do no harm as bubbles on a steady stream of enterprise. But the position is serious when enterprise becomes

the bubble on a whirlpool of speculation. When the capital development of a country becomes a by-product of the activities of a casino, the job is likely to be ill-done."

30 From a Galbraithian perspective, as Leathers and Raines (2008: 562) point out: "Shiller's analysis of the 'irrational exuberance' of the stock market in the 1990s is incomplete in several critical respects. In regarding institutional investors as influenced by the same factors as non-professional individuals, Shiller (2000: 18–19) ignores Galbraith's observation that those in charge of wealth are assumed to have superior financial intelligence, which they themselves believe. Missing on the psychological side is an explicit recognition of the importance of the speculative mood as being requisite to turning an ordinary bull market in stocks into a speculative bubble. Despite Shiller's attempt to downplay the role of financial euphoria being intensified by the pure instinct of speculation and the vested interest in that euphoria that keeps the bubble inflating, his appropriation of the term 'irrational exuberance' is an implicit admission that the psychological factors must lead to euphoric behavior for a bubble to be explained. The Galbraithian factors most prominently missing in Shiller's 'structural factors' were the importance of debt in financing the speculation and the role of fraud and manipulation. Failing to adhere to the full Galbraithian analytical framework makes Shiller's analysis of the 1990s stock market bubble rather superficial."

31 In an ominous portent Galbraith (1971: 115) identified: "Thursday, 24 October [as] the day history designates as the beginning of the Crash of 1929." Compare the events of October 2008.

32 Davidson (2008a) described the deregulation of US banking activities since the 1970s and the twelve attempts in the last twenty-five years to circumvent Glass-Steagall, which was finally repealed by Congress, with the support of President Clinton, in 1999.

33 As Krugman (2008c: 154–64) highlights, the shadow banking system, which evolved a series of all too clever investment schemes that bypassed more stringent banking regulations, was *de facto* unregulated banking and a major cause of a the financial crash.

34 Davidson (2008a: 2–3) highlights how the forgetting of the lessons of history contributed to the sub-prime crisis. He also highlights how the study of history can provide lessons in how to address the problem: "The Roosevelt Administration's handling of the housing insolvency crisis of the 1930s suggests a precedent for dealing with the US housing bubble distress. In 1933, the Home Owners Refinancing Act created the Home Owners' Loan Corporation (HOLC) to refinance

homes to prevent foreclosures, and also to bail out mortgage holding banks. The HOLC was a tremendous success, making one million low-interest loans which often extended the pay-off period of the original loan, thereby significantly reducing the monthly payments to amounts that homeowners could afford. In its years of operation, the HOLC not only paid all its bills, but it also made a small profit. Other measures might include setting up a government agency to take non-performing mortgage loans off the books of private balance sheets and therefore remove the threat of insolvency for those who took positions in the mortgage-backed securities after being misled by rating agencies. The result will prevent further sell-offs causing financial distress in all financial markets."

35 Foster and Young (2007) highlight the illusory nature of financial genius: "To illustrate how easy it is to set up a hedge fund scam, consider the following example. An enterprising man named Oz sets up a new fund with the stated aim of earning 10 percent in excess of some benchmark rate of return, say 4 percent. The fund will run for five years, and investors can cash out at the end of each year if they wish. The fee is the standard '2 and 20': 2 percent annually for funds under management, and a 20 percent incentive fee for returns that exceed the benchmark. Although he has no investment track record, Oz has a smooth manner, a doctorate in physics and many rich acquaintances. He raises $100 million and opens shop. He then studies the derivatives market and finds an event on which the market places fairly long odds, say 9:1. In other words, it costs $.10 to buy an option that pays $1 if the event occurs and $0 otherwise. The nature of the event is unimportant: it might be a large fall in the stock market, Florida getting hit by a Category 5 hurricane or Russian President Vladimir Putin dying before the end of the year. Next Oz writes some covered options on this event and sells 110 million of them in the derivatives market. This obligates him to pay the option holders $110 million if the event does occur and nothing if it does not. He collects $11 million on the options. To cover his obligations in case the 'bad' event occurs, he uses the investors' money plus the proceeds from the options to buy $110 million in one-year Treasury bills yielding 4 percent, which he deposits in escrow. This leaves $1 million in 'pocket money,' which he uses to lease some computer terminals and hire a few geeks to sit in front of them, just in case his investors drop by. The probability is ninety percent that the bad event does not occur and Oz owes nothing to the option holders. With a gross return (before expenses) of $15,400,000, the investors are thrilled, and so is Oz. He collects $2 million in management fees (of which he has only spent $1 million), plus a performance bonus equal to

20 percent of the 'excess return', namely, 20 percent of $11,400,000. All in all, Oz nets over $3 million for doing absolutely nothing. Oz can then repeat the same gambit next year. When the fund terminates after five years, the chances are nearly 60 percent that the unlucky event will never have occurred. Oz looks like a genius and gets paid like a genius."

36 A Ponzi scheme is a fraudulent investment operation that generates abnormally high returns for investors paid from money put into the scheme by subsequent investors, rather than from real profits generated by share trading. It is named after the swindler Charles Ponzi.

37 As Roosevelt (1933) observed in his Inaugural Presidential Address, which seems amazingly relevant for our present times: "The money changers have fled from their high seats in the temple of our civilization. We may now restore that temple to the ancient truths. The measure of the restoration lies in the extent to which we apply social values more noble than mere monetary profit."

38 As Keynes (1930: 323) remarked: "the vast majority of those who are concerned with the buying and selling of securities know almost nothing whatever about what they are doing. They do not possess even the rudiments of what is required for a valid judgment, and are the prey of hopes and fears easily aroused by transient events and as easily dispelled. This is one of the odd characteristics of the capitalist system under which we live, which, when we are dealing with the real world, is not to be overlooked ... [Hence] it may often profit the wisest to anticipate mob psychology rather than the real trend of events, and to ape unreason proleptically."

39 This is not, however, a bail out of rich bankers, at the expense of the taxpayers. It is designed to stave off a recession, or even another depression. Davidson (2008a: 4) argues that such a view only makes sense in the context of theory that assumes that "macroeconomic activity in the economy will be unchanged whether or not the government takes any positive action to remove distress in financial markets." Galbraithian and Post Keynesian theory, the theory of the real world, makes no such assumption.

40 As noted above Galbraith was a lifelong Keynesian, but he also updated the analysis to take into account the lessons of circumstance.

41 As is to be expected the financial system is not immune to the bimodal view. The dominance of Large Complex Financial Institutions (LCFIs) should not be underestimated. The Bank of England (2008: 8) identifies the major LCFIs to include "Bank of America, Barclays, BNP Paribas, Citi, Credit Suisse, Deutsche Bank, Goldman Sachs, HSBC, JP Morgan Chase & Co., Lehman Brothers, Merrill Lynch, Morgan

Stanley, RBS, Société Générale and UBS." Lehman Brothers dropped out of the LCFI group on September 15, 2008 when it filed for bankruptcy.

42 As Paul Krugman (2008a) points out: "The bursting of the housing bubble has led to large losses for anyone who bought assets backed by mortgage payments; these losses have left many financial institutions with too much debt and too little capital to provide the credit the economy needs; troubled financial institutions have tried to meet their debts and increase their capital by selling assets, but this has driven asset prices down, reducing their capital even further."

43 In summarizing the lessons of *The Great Crash, 1929*, Galbraith (1955a: 200) commented how: "A commitment to a balanced budget is always comprehensive. It then meant there could be no increase in government outlays to expand purchasing power and relieve distress. It meant there could be no further tax reduction. But taken literally it meant much more. From 1930 on the budget was far out of balance, and balance, therefore meant an increase in taxes, a reduction in spending or both." For a discussion of the continuing importance of deficit financing, see James Galbraith (2001), Palley (2001), Godley and McCarthy (1998), and Davidson (2007).

44 Although Galbraith (1996b: 51) long argued for deficit spending, he was not fiscally irresponsible: "There is no law or tradition ... that requires a balanced budget – equal revenues and expenditures on an annual basis. This does not mean, however, that the budget and budget deficits in the modern state can be treated casually; a high measure of intelligence and discretion is always required. What is essential is that the intelligence and discretion be exercised with the relevant framework." Galbraith goes on to distinguish between three types of public expenditures: those that serve no economic purpose; those which enhance or protect the wider social order, such as law enforcement, foreign policy and; those that improve future well-being and drive economic growth. For Galbraith (1996b: 50–8), it is the latter form of public expenditure which justifies a rising budget deficit.

45 Keynes's (1980: 31) famously warned: "Loose funds may sweep round the world disorganizing all steady business. Nothing is more certain than that the movement of capital funds must be regulated."

46 As Davidson (1994: 264) points out that: "The post-war world has conducted several experiments with the international payments system. For a quarter of a century after the war, there was a fixed, but adjustable, exchange rate system set up under the Bretton Woods Agreement. Since 1973 we have operated under a flexible exchange rate system. The period from 1947 to 1973 was 'an era of unprecedented sustained

growth in both developed and developing countries. The growth in real Gross Domestic Product per capita in OECD nations escalated to 2.6 times that of the interwar period (4.9 per cent annually compared to 1.9 per cent) ... Free economies experienced unprecedented real economic growth during the Bretton Woods epoch ... The dismal post-1973 experience of recurrent unemployment and inflationary crisis, slow growth in OECD countries, and debt-burdened growth and/or stagnation (and even falling real GNP per capita) in developing countries contrasts sharply with the experience during the Bretton Woods period."

47 Keynes (1980: 168–9) set out a clear outline of what was required which still resonates: "We need an instrument of international currency having general acceptability between nations ... We need an orderly and agreed upon method of determining the relative exchange values of national currency units ... We need a quantum of international currency ... [which] is governed by the actual current requirements of world commerce, and is capable of deliberate expansion ... We need a method by which the surplus credit balances arising from international trade, which the recipient does not wish to employ can be set to work ... without detriment to the liquidity of these balances."

48 Keynes (1980: 30) argued for a new international system that shifted the burden of adjustment toward surplus countries: "The object of the new system must be to require the chief initiative from the creditor countries, whilst maintaining enough discipline in the debtor countries to prevent them from exploiting the new ease allowed them in living profligately beyond their means."

12 *The origins of the Galbraithian system: talking to John Kenneth Galbraith*

The fact that the general conditions of life are not stationary is the source of many of the difficulties that are met with in applying economic doctrines to practical problems.

Alfred Marshall (1920: 347)

On June 22, 2001 I talked at length with J. K. Galbraith and his wife Catherine – affectionately referred to as Kitty – who was a constant companion and co-organizer throughout his career, about his intellectual history, the origins of his contribution to the theory of the firm and his relationships and experiences with both the two Cambridges and Post Keynesianism. An edited and abridged summary of our discussion is reproduced below.

The origins of the Galbraithian vision

DUNN: How would you describe the Galbraithian system and where do you see its origins? Would it be correct to view it as a reconstruction of economics after the dissolution of the Marshallian system ushered in by Sraffa (1926), Chamberlin (1933), and Robinson (1933) and their recognition of the rise of the modern, large corporation, or would it be more appropriate to view it as part of the old Institutionalist literature and embedded very much in Veblen's (1904) Theory of the Business Enterprise?

GALBRAITH: One of the things about your question that interests me is that I never thought there was a Galbraith system. And in some ways it is a rather new question to me because what I've done all my life is start from the usual starting point, which was a thorough and complete grounding in Alfred Marshall. The first main course I had in economics was at Berkeley; that was after I left Canada where the economics instruction was very poor. E. T. Grether was the dominant economics teacher (not the dominant figure, but the dominant teacher at Berkeley) and I spent the better part of a year going chapter by chapter through Alfred Marshall. There are others too who had a strong influence on me including Thorstein Veblen, but what I did for years to come was to start with Marshall, see the world as it is and make the requisite modifications until there wasn't much of Marshall left, mostly modifications. But that was the process and the modifications I made were piece by piece, chapter by chapter, corporation by corporation, if you will, always from that base until the base disappeared.[1]

My thinking was all in modifications. First of all Keynes, the overwhelming impact of Keynes. I spent one year in Cambridge in '37 to '38 and that was the most intense economic instruction I ever had. You talked about economics, and particularly about Keynes, all day and all night. There was the inevitable conflict between Keynes and Dennis Robertson and the ultimate Keynesians, Richard Kahn and Joan Robinson. Sraffa, who you mentioned, wasn't nearly so important.[2] Sraffa was so hard to understand that people thought Piero had depths of knowledge that they never quite got; and there was that incredible preoccupation of his with Ricardo which lasted year after year, almost decade after decade. But the effect of both Joan and Kahn and Denis Robertson as a counter figure was just enormous. I suppose we talked about that every day and that meant that I came back to Harvard with all the distinction of having been at the center of the Keynesian discussion, even though during that year I never met Keynes; that was the year he had his first heart attack.

So rather than a system, I've never thought of that. I've always thought of the process by which I learn myself and the conclusions I came to. There are a certain number of people who associate themselves with my ideas, but that isn't a large group. People got particular ideas that I urge rather than any comprehensive system. That would be my judgment at least. I've never heard anybody describe himself as a Galbraithian.

DUNN: How did your visit to Cambridge influence your economics and the development of the Galbraithian system?

GALBRAITH: Kitty was with me in 1937 on our great introduction to Keynesian economics.

KITTY: It was pretty awful because before we got to Cambridge, England I had never heard of John Maynard Keynes and *The General Theory* had just been published and all I met were his economist friends. So you know I was quite quiet and so I decided one day after we were talking about *The General Theory*, given I was supposed to be fairly intelligent, to pick it up. I started with the introduction, but early on in the book he explains that he hasn't got quite thought through all his ideas. So I thought I'll wait until he writes his next book and that's where my economics rested. There was a lecture "Is there a rate of interest?" and I thought that if these people don't know there is a rate of interest why do they talk about it? And forty years later that same lecture was on the bulletin board in Cambridge because in a lecture someone asked a lecturer "Is there a rate of interest?"

GALBRAITH: I went down to LSE [London School of Economics] every few weeks to go to Hayek's seminar, which was one of the great centers of discussion at that time. Hayek would come in very tidy and well mannered, sit down at a small desk, and there would be thirty or forty economists there, all of whom disagreed with him. And there was one great day when he came in and said "Now as I indicated last time we will today discuss the rate of interest" and Nicky Kaldor said "Professor Hayek there's no such thing" and that was the last word Hayek got in that day as everybody turned to find out from Nicky why there could be no rate of interest.

I knew Hayek well and saw a lot of him over the years. I sent my son to visit him in Austria once, and shared with him a memorable day in Kirkcaldy recalling Adam Smith.[3] As an aside I always thought Adam Smith's *Wealth of Nations* was one of the most wonderful books of all time. I was giving a lecture three or four years ago in Pennsylvania and tried an experiment to see how a crowd would accept a quote from Adam Smith: "The Quakers of Pennsylvania have recently freed their Negro slaves by which we may judge the slaves were not numerous" but it didn't go over at all well. The Quaker faith is still too strong for a joke like that.

DUNN: Can you describe your process of "conversion" from orthodoxy and to what extent have Veblen, Commons, Mitchell, and Myrdal, the Berkeley Institutionalists and the Cambridge Keynesians influenced you? What works of theirs had the most influence on you? And who else influenced your intellectual development?

GALBRAITH: There are three other influences that were extremely important in my life other than that year in Cambridge. There was first a major job I did in the White House in the late thirties. The economic policies, the Keynesian policies, of the New Deal. I think, remembering the controversy, that I was the first to admit that these were Keynesian, and a major piece of work came out of that on the Keynesian programs, the PWA, the Public Works Administration, and the WPA, the Work Progress Administration. PWA had as its objective what you got built at the end; the Triborough Bridge or something of that sort. The WPA had its focus purely on the number of jobs that it created. This was a source of great conflict in Washington. And I presided over the study of those two programs under the auspices of the National Planning Association and that major study came out just as the war started and got almost no attention because national attention and economic attention had all passed to the problems of the war. And that was the second thing that was very influential in my life because, at a relatively early age, I had what probably could have been the most important of all wartime jobs in economics; I was the Price Czar. I was second in the order of command to Leon Henderson, but I had an enormous delegation. I started with a staff of seven and ended with thousands.[4] You could lower a price without my permission but you couldn't raise one.

General maximum price regulation covered all prices and this had another effect; it was an intimate introduction to the corporate structure of the United States and the discovery, still not fully appreciated, of the extent to which the corporate structure is not capitalist, it is experienced bureaucratic power and intelligence. That's why the word capitalism has to some extent disappeared. It evokes Carnegie, it evokes Rockefeller, it evokes the other wicked capitalists of the past that have been buried and now the innocent reference is to the market system. That is bland and doesn't specify anything as evil as the old capitalist, and it shouldn't, probably because the old-fashioned capitalists couldn't possibly run a modern corporation. That takes a huge bureaucracy and a lot of experience and survival with that. And this was an idea that started to become evident to me when I was running price control. Every afternoon I met with some complaining group of businessmen; business leaders who, making more money than they'd ever made before, were pleading their poverty. It was an introduction to the business community such as very few economists have ever had and that was part of the structure of ideas that became part of my thinking at a relatively early stage.

Then in later years I was editor of *Fortune* magazine. In those days the subject matter of *Fortune* was the anatomy of the big corporations and that was a marvelous introduction to the corporate mind such as it is. Not marvelous but privileged. It reflected a continuing curiosity about the economic process related to that fact that I never had a degree in economics, only in agricultural economics. But that is a detail. I was, at Berkeley, subject to a good economics department at that time and, as I say, the early influence of Keynes before *The General Theory* and the other economists of the time; I've mentioned Marshall, and Veblen. Veblen was the most exciting figure at that time but had nothing to do with agricultural economics!

DUNN: In one sense I find that quite surprising as it only seems that somewhat later the Veblenian influence becomes more prominent in your writing. What were the early influences?

GALBRAITH: This was a process I began with Marshall. Further discussion and further writing elaborated and modified, and one of the modifying influences was Veblen. And the great modifying influence was of course John Maynard Keynes. Kyle Bruce, from Queensland, Australia, is publishing a book next year on an episode in the 1930s.[5] One of the most distinguished businessmen in the United States was Henry Dennison, the manufacturer of paper products. He invited me to join him for a book and I did, coming out at that time still with the basic Marshallian-Taussig view of the world. He was of the impression that a main line of attack in the great depression (he was very close to F. D. R.) should be through taxation, the remitting of taxation, adding to purchasing power. And I talked him out of that to the argument that the depression was caused by the prevalence of monopoly power and the restrictions on output that that imposed. I persuaded him and when I had finished the persuasion that year the General Theory came out and I read that and discovered that Dennison was right and I was wrong so I took steps immediately to halt the book but it was already in print, *Modern Competition and Business Policy*, and I, with some thought, dropped that out of my list of books.[6]

DUNN: Both Dr. Bruce (2001: 26) and I concur in our view that you have long mused on the role and salience of the firm and the large corporation in advanced industrialized economies.

GALBRAITH: I would argue, but I could be wrong, against the influence of the theory of the firm on my thinking, but I never had any doubt on its salience and this is something that one should cite today as a major shortcoming of economic instruction: the concentration on market behavior which still continues and the neglect of the influence of the firm. The United States economy has been dominated, not unsuccessfully in these last years, by the great corporations. If you want to find out what is happening in the country you must look into the decision-making process of the great corporations and how united together they can bring influence to bear on government and the extent to which somebody like George Bush is their unknowing captive. Not knowing any of this, George Bush is in some ways their ideal instrument.

DUNN: Your son, Jamie, wrote a provocative and distinctly Galbraithian newspaper article on how the election of President Bush epitomized

The New Industrial State, with the Supreme Court as the perfidious expression of the corporate structure.[7]

GALBRAITH: Jamie wrote in a small Texas publication called *The Texas Observer* a few days after the election and it was picked up by Internet and attributed to me. I had a lot of correspondence on it which I had to ship off to my son. Jamie once made a birthday speech here at Harvard in which he said it was his ambition in life, hope in life, that I would be seen to have the same stature as John Neville Keynes and he would be then John Maynard.[8] I recall he also mentioned the Mill father and son; he hoped I would be remembered as James Mill. There's no question about that, he's a very good economist.

The influence of contemporaries

DUNN: You write in *A Life in Our Times* (1981: 75) that "an enduring reward from my year at Cambridge [1937–8] was friendship with Michal Kalecki ... the most innovative figure in economics I have known, not excluding Keynes." How did Kalecki influence the evolution of your thought?

GALBRAITH: Well Kalecki of course was a socialist, verging on communism and he was very important to all of us as a continuing critic of the accepted economics. That interposed a much larger role for collective action and the state. It was an escape from the closed apparatus even of Keynesian economics. In Kalecki's thinking social action intervened much more strongly than it did in Keynes's system, and so likewise in his conversation, likewise in his writing. I was impressed by that in Cambridge and years later just before I published *The Affluent Society* I made a visit to Poland and Yugoslavia and spent a lot of time there with Kalecki, who was out of favor. He lived out of favor wherever he was.

DUNN: Did Kalecki influence your bimodal view (Galbraith, 1977b) of the economy?

GALBRAITH: I don't think so; I think that was from my own observations, but I'm not sure. As a footnote when he died he was out of favor in Poland; he lived out of favor with the established view. I wrote a letter to his wife on these matters and she was so grateful; I have somewhere in my files the letter she sent back. So grateful that someone was supporting Kalecki and his somewhat inconvenient behavior. He had gone back to Poland in the hope of a system of economic thought influencing policy, which would be more than he encountered in

Britain or the United States, only to discover there was another one that was equally rigorous.

DUNN: One of the salient contributions you identify with Kalecki was his discussion of the nexus between affluence and attitudes to risk (Galbraith, 1981: 75). Did Kalecki's principle of increasing risk influence your discussion of the modern corporation and its nexus to uncertainty?

GALBRAITH: I suppose so but it's not a connection that I ever made anything from. I've never been sure where ideas came from and that might well have come from Kalecki but I couldn't say yes or no.

DUNN: What was your relationship with Nicholas Kaldor and his influence on your thinking?

GALBRAITH: I wrote one part of *The Affluent Society* in Nicky's house in Cambridge, in his library. But I would have to say generally that through much of my life I have had debt to an enormous number of contemporaries; Nicky was one, Tommy Balogh was one, Paul Samuelson here was one, various others here, but I have never, perhaps this is a very defective behavior, spent a great deal of time identifying those who contributed to my thought. They all did. I have a debt to them all. What I have written has been in some considerable measure the product of my life and association, but I've never mapped it out in detail. I'm sure that any one of my friends reading this would conclude that he had some sort of contribution and he would be quite right.

DUNN: In many respects the Galbraithian system and view of the large corporation has several similarities with that of Joseph Schumpeter. What was the influence of Schumpeter on your own intellectual development and how do you think his vision compares with your own?

GALBRAITH: The difference was that I tried to struggle with the reality, however, dull, and Schumpeter sought the spectacular, however, irrelevant. I learned a lot from Schumpeter, he was a force on all my generation, but he wasn't in any sense a guide to policy. My generation studied economics with a view ultimately to change the economic world, economic policy in Washington, or overwhelmingly the move to Keynesian macroeconomic policy. Schumpeter had no such interest. He had presided in Austria over an inflation and that was enough public life for him. He was a very popular figure here, we all loved Schumpy. He met at a local teahouse every afternoon with a group of students, anybody who wanted to come, and it was a wonderful session, but it was theatrical rather than real.[9]

DUNN: Schumpeter's vision is dominated by large oligopolistic innovating firms who make substantial investments over long periods of time under conditions of uncertainty. This appears to accord well with elements of the vision laid out in *The New Industrial State*.

GALBRAITH: He stood above all this. He would not discuss price theory and policy at all. I don't think he ever made anything, so to speak, of imperfect competition, or what was here called monopolistic competition following Chamberlin (1933). On something like creative destruction he could be quite eloquent. He was a man of driving ideas rather than of great systems.

DUNN: In Richard Swedberg's (1991) biography of Schumpeter he is portrayed as very much an outsider at Harvard, especially in the later years. Was that true?

GALBRAITH: Well everybody tried to be an outsider. He was here during the New Deal years and he wasn't part of the New Deal discussion, the people that went to Washington once a week for some role there, he never dreamed of that, but he was, I would say, the supreme insider. He loved the academic community. He loved the discussions. He loved the audience to which he returned. The audience sought him out. He wasn't an outsider in any sense. There was a dinner in those days of some of the senior faculty once every fortnight. This was a special dinner in Boston to which people went overwhelmingly to hear Schumpeter talk. Seymour Harris would come back from those dinners to tell me what particularly fantastic topic had been under discussion the night before.

DUNN: Did the Oxford challenge to marginalism reach the United States and what was its reception? Did it have any impact at Harvard in the 1940s or at the Office of Price Administration?

GALBRAITH: I don't think so. It didn't have any particular influence on me certainly.

The New Industrial State

DUNN: Where do you see the origins of *The New Industrial State*?

GALBRAITH: That was quite clear. When I finished *The Affluent Society* and it had gone to press and been a major big seller, I was faced with the extremely inconvenient thought that I had published the wrong book, or published only half the book. And the half I hadn't published had to do with the structural behavior of the corporation and including the great corporation as distinct from its purely monopolistic ambitions, which was not something that I emphasized before, and this also included the invasion into the modern corporation the structure of science and technology, the technostructure. And so I set about writing that book to correct what I saw as a major gap in *The Affluent Society.* I had completed a first draft and then the opportunity, the rather agreeable opportunity, of going to India came along, and so I put it away in a safe deposit box for two and a half years. I came back and then finished it. As I worked on it I became more and more involved with the structure of the corporation and the technostructure and its aspirations and that of course became the book.

DUNN: Does the first draft of the manuscript still survive?

GALBRAITH: I doubt it. If it does it's over at the Kennedy library but I wouldn't place any emphasis on it. The first draft is the first flow of ideas and thought and it can be extremely imperfect.

DUNN: Would you agree with the assessment of your son, Jamie (James Galbraith, 1984), who has suggested that the origins of *The New Industrial State* are to be found in the German historical school and organizational theory rather than more orthodox managerial theorists of the firm?

GALBRAITH: No, I wouldn't. I was certainly influenced all my life by German thought from Marx over and on but the major mental incentive on *The New Industrial State* was the actual study of American corporations and their behaviors including my years at *Fortune* magazine. It was one of the rewards of my time at *Fortune* to discover how important were the objectives of the management of the firm, how complex the bureaucracy, and the enormous role of an increasingly deep technology and scientific base and how important that was. Indeed you saw in the case of something like the steel industry the hopeless inadequacy of a corporate management that had no understanding of these matters and didn't even know they existed in some cases.

DUNN: Uncertainty occupies the pivotal role in *The New Industrial State* and underscores the need for the great corporations to plan. How did that arise and come into view?

GALBRAITH: I didn't regard that as anything particularly novel. I think that dealing with economic institutions one must always assume uncertainty because there are enough factors that may by their change or by their interplay be unpredictable and I just took that for granted. I simply assumed uncertainty in all major decision-making and just let it go at that.

DUNN: Were you influenced at all by Keynes or Shackle's view of uncertainty?

GALBRAITH: Oh, Keynes I might have been, but again I get back to the problem that I'm never quite sure where my ideas came from. But Shackle certainly wasn't a major factor in my life.

DUNN: Why did you not return to *The New Industrial State* and undertake further work on it?

GALBRAITH: No question about that. I put everything I write, as I've often said, through four or five revisions, adding the note of spontaneity only in the fifth revision, and by that time boredom has set in, to the point that I don't go back to the topic – I just can't. Not long after I finished *The New Industrial State* I was invited by Rab Butler to spend another year in Cambridge. There I was scheduled to give a term lecture on *The New Industrial State* in the huge new lecture hall where my most important recollection is of Joan sitting in the front seat. Lecturing on that book was so boring that through the year I wrote another book called *Economics and the Public Purpose* which by and large was something of a major mistake because it retraced ground that I had already covered in substantial parts. It reflected only the escape from the boredom of lecturing on *The New Industrial State*, which was I thought an important book, possibly my most important. It has a certain distinction now as one of the first works in economics to deal with the uncertainties of technology although I never had the expectation of technology being the whole basis of entrepreneurship and its disastrous effect.

As an aside my most precious recollection of Joan was going back to Cambridge at the end of the war in the late forties or fifties. I met Joan and we went across the river and sat down for lunch and I opened the conversation by saying "Joan I've been out of touch due to the war, I've been out of touch with my colleagues in this profession. Who are the good people of the new generation?" and Joan's answer was, "Ken, we were the last good generation." She was very firm on that point.

An intellectual legacy

DUNN: You were one of the first Keynesians to be aware of the potentially inflationary consequence of the Keynesian system and to advocate a variety of incomes policies. Why do you think other Keynesians failed to recognize this?

GALBRAITH: To begin with I'm not sure of the point. I think there was a quite general recognition as time passed, in the later years of the New Deal, and under Kennedy for example. But I suppose looking back on it I was somewhat influenced by the enormous concern for inflation in World War II and my responsibilities there went very deep into my thinking and so I was more alert to the problem of inflation than not most, but many of my colleagues. I'd spent the most intense years of my life dealing with inflation.

DUNN: You say in your memoirs (Galbraith, 1981: 170–1) that throughout your time at the Office of Price Administration you managed to keep inflation below 2 percent, which was quite an achievement at that time, and subsequently inflation started to increase when the OPA was dismantled.

GALBRAITH: Broadly speaking there is no memory of inflation in World War II. There was a strong memory of it in the United States in World War I when prices doubled in a matter of two years. When World War II came there was a strong feeling of the danger of inflation and one of the first appointments to the first organizations to deal with the problems of World War II was that dealing with prices, Leon Henderson. It was that tension, that concern, that policy was motivated by in those days. With a strong macroeconomic policy under Morganthau and Harry Dexter White and a strong, very strong, microeconomic policy effectively under me. The tendency, for two or three years during the war, was for me to blame any price increase on the macroeconomic policy and for them to blame any increase on Galbraith. This was a convenient escape, but in fact there is no memory of inflation now in World War II. That problem was solved. It was solved by a strong microeconomic policy, the general maximum price regulation in the Spring of 1942, and by a strong tax policy and to some extent also by a public attitude which restrained price increases even if they might be possible – you didn't want to be a war profiteer!

DUNN: Many economists preserve their ideas via their students – indeed the Cambridge "circus" that surrounded the development of Keynes's *General Theory* served to defend Keynes's ideas from the subsequent orthodox bastardization. Has one of the unintended consequences of your political activities been that you have been unable to devote enough time to teaching and doctoral supervision and create an intellectual vanguard for the Galbraithian system?

GALBRAITH: Well one has to make choices in life. I devoted a lot of time to my lectures which tended to be also what I was writing about. They were I think, safe to say, rather well attended. I did not spend a great deal of my time tutoring disciples. I saw a lot of them but I never saw my main function as having a cadre of students taking my ideas to Washington. That was not a clear decision – it was the way things work out.

DUNN: Would that be a regret?

GALBRAITH: One has to make choices. I couldn't have written *The Affluent Society* if I spent ten hours a day teaching, tutoring, and cultivating.

DUNN: Do you think that the fact that you have not explicitly associated yourself with a school of thought has damaged your intellectual legacy?

GALBRAITH: Well there is a problem of having a legacy, having a Galbraithian view, which is a word that I've taken over from you, if that view changes as the world changes and as your thinking changes. Anybody who wanted to be a student of my views would have had the problem that my views change, as I think an economist must. Most economists having got to a system, got to an idea, stick with it for much of their life – "If you're going to have a view, you'd better keep it even if circumstances change or your view changes." And my basic belief is that I always had to be ready to accommodate myself to two things: the changing of past error, and the appreciation of new events and new knowledge.

DUNN: I would argue that this implies a pragmatic historical approach and as such you could say that the Galbraithian system was very much an appreciation of the evolving processes of capitalism over the twentieth century that would constitute a foundation for building new insights over time and adding to it and subtracting from it in the face of new circumstance, novelty and emerging process.

GALBRAITH: I agree with that – if I understand it. It's my view that the only valid economics is a dynamic economics because one lives in a world where two things are urgent, one is change and one is the correction of past misapprehension. A good example of this is the two people that were associated with the monopolistic flaws in the market. Joan Robinson wrote *The Theory of Imperfect Competition* (1933) and then went onto problems of economic development, problems of the labor left in Britain, a whole range of questions and maintained her role as one of the distinguished figures in the economic profession. My colleague, Ed Chamberlin, a very good man, wrote his book on *Monopolistic Competition* (1933) which appeared almost the same day as Joan's and stayed with that for the rest of his life. Joan remained at the center of the profession, Ed went gradually to one side. And eventually a very unhappy man came to realize this in the later years of his life.

DUNN: I think it relates to the style of your generation. Geoff Harcourt recalls that a characteristic of people like Nicky Kaldor, Joan Robinson, and yourself, was the agility of mind to turn it to a host of new interesting problems and sit down not with the literature, but a pen and one's ideas.

GALBRAITH: Sit down with the pen and the problem. That would be Nicky's approach. Not sit down with a camera – do you remember that Kitty? We were in India together. Nicky went out to get a pictorial record of the whole Indian society and after he came back I was talking to his daughter. I said "How did Nicky's pictures go," and she said "Not good" and I said "Why not?" "Well," she said. "There was one problem. He could never remember to take the cover off the lens."

One terrific night Nicky had something that we all yearned to have. This was in Calcutta at the head quarters of the Institute. We had a big farewell dinner because he had a passport and visa for China along with his wife and we all celebrated their departure, told of our own sorrow that he had got a visa and we hadn't, or had no hope of it evidently. But around midnight they came back, they'd forgotten their passports. They didn't get to China – they had to show their passports to get out of India and discovered they didn't have them. They got in the next day or so later.

DUNN: When did you first meet Paul Davidson and get involved in the founding of the *Journal of Post Keynesian* economics? What influence did he have on the evolution of your thought?

GALBRAITH: Paul Davidson and his wife, Louise, were formerly in New Jersey and moved out to Knoxville with the journal. He was at Rutgers for many years and there were no known economists at that time in Tennessee so he was brought out to teach there. And that brought the journal to Knoxville. Professor Davidson is a long standing friend of mine and we certainly had long discussions, but that's always been a problem in my life. I have discussions, I come away with some new thought which I should possibly attribute to the discussion but it disappears in my memory. Nevertheless Paul's a very important figure in the history of economics, no question about that. The *Journal of Post Keynesian Economics* is very well edited and very perceptive in its choice of articles and gets away from extreme mathematics, which is very good from my point of view because that's my singular weakness. Moreover, mathematics, with respect to the theory of the firm, excludes that as a subject to some extent because for the great structure of economics the firm becomes a dot on the chart and the separate influence of the structure of the firm and the ambitions within the firm and the bureaucratic apparatus has been very largely excluded from professional economic thought. Here at Harvard it is the main subject of the business school across the river but it isn't here.

DUNN: In a recent article in the *Journal of Post Keynesian Economics* (2000a) I argued that part of the future of Post Keynesian economics may lie in business schools and schools of public policy, which is not to denigrate Post Keynesian economics, but to suggest that some of the more salient and insightful contributions to economics that engage the real world are occurring there and that Post Keynesians may find a more receptive audience for some of their ideas in such schools.

GALBRAITH: I agree with that completely. I would only add more emphasis on bureaucratic skills, and give a large place to the particular form of political expression that is sought, which among other things includes a large political support for the revenues of the business structure. We are seeing this in very visible form in the Bush administration but all of the things of influence in the American economy in these last months, in these last years, have been outside of the range of mathematical or technical economics. As I say they come down to a single figure on the chart or a single item, a single letter in the equation.

DUNN: Thank you very much.

Notes

1 Galbraith (1981: 28–9) has remarked: "The Marshallian world is a tidy thing without unemployment, inflation or depression or anyhow not much. Not surprisingly, many who studied Marshall found it pleasant to live in his world forever."

2 The interested reader should also consult Galbraith's (1983b) tribute to Joan Robinson.

3 See Galbraith (1974) on "Scotland's Greatest Son."

4 As Galbraith (1981: 125–6) remarked elsewhere: "Later the Office of Price Administration would employ 64,000 across the country, along with numerous volunteer workers. However, most of those would administer rationing and rent control. The prices staff nationwide was much smaller – about 4,300."

5 See Galbraith (1981: 57–70). Bruce (2000, 2001) further elaborates upon the intellectual impact of Henry Dennison on J. K. Galbraith's theorizing.

6 Historians of Post Keynesian thought should be made aware of the fact that George Shackle (1939: 100) composed a positive and complimentary review of Dennison *et al.*'s (1938) *Toward Full Employment*, noting that: "In a field where useful thinking is strenuous, the several authors of this book have earned admiration and gratitude. Their thinking is almost everywhere rigorous and clear, and the evidence of care and enthusiasm lavished on the book is unmistakable."

7 See "Our New Corporate Republic" by James K. Galbraith, Sunday, January 7, 2001, Boston Globe. A version of this column appeared earlier in *The Texas Observer.*

8 See http://utip.gov.utexas.edu/web/JGarchive/1998/jkg_90th_birthday_party.htm.

9 Swedburg (1991: 115) points out that: "Schumpeter was ... popular with some of the young instructors, especially Paul Sweezy and John Kenneth Galbraith. Sweezy was one of the few sophisticated Marxists in the United States as well as the son of a wealthy banker, a combination that appealed to Schumpeter. Galbraith was very curious about Schumpeter – he, for example, sat in on Ec-11 – but he was also disturbed by Schumpeter's conservatism."

References

Abramson, J. (2004) *Overdo$ed America: The Broken Promise of American Medicine.* New York: HarperCollins.

Adams, J. (1984) "Galbraith on economic development," *Journal of Post-Keynesian Economics*, 7(1), 91–102.

Agrow (2002) "Gap narrows between prospective agrochemical market leaders," *AGROW World Crop Protection News*, 397(29), March, 1.

Akerlof, G. and Schiller, R. (2009) *Animal Spirits: How Human Psychology Drives the Economy, and Why It Matters for Global Capitalism.* Woodstock: Princeton University Press.

Alexander, R. J. (1983) "Contributions of the Galbraith technostructure to the growing crisis of the US economy," *Journal of Economic Issues*, June, 495–502.

Allen, G. C. (1967) *Economic Fact and Fantasy: A Rejoinder to Galbraith's Reith Lectures*, Institute of Economic Affairs Occasional Paper No. 14. London: IEA.

Allsopp, C. and Vines, D. (2005) "The macroeconomic role of fiscal policy," *Oxford Review of Economic Policy*, 21(4), 485–508.

American Tobacco (1964) *Author's Notes On Volume Four, 1953 To 1964: Start Of Filter Age; Battle For Filter Kings; Start Of King Size Filter Menthol; Introduction Of Hi Fi Filtration, Charcoal And Multi Filters; Demise Of Short, Plain Cigarettes; Proliferation Of Brands, Splits And Extensions.* American Tobacco: Bates Number 966068737/8739. http://legacy.library.ucsf.edu/tid/dac70a00.

Analytic Insight Inc. (1986a) *Capri: Creative Development. Consumer Reactions.* Brown & Williamson: Bates Number 465874055/4112. http://legacy.library.ucsf.edu/tid/aib40f00.

(1986b) *Capri: Creative Development Consumer Reactions.* Brown & Williamson: Bates Number 682121824/1939. http://legacy.library.ucsf.edu/tid/sxv03f00.

(1987) *Capri: Second Generation Ads Consumers Reaction to Two Proposed Campaigns.* Brown & Williamson, Bates Number 465645327/5371. http://legacy.library.ucsf.edu/tid/fku60f00.

(1988) *Capri: New Creative Evaluation.* Brown & Williamson: Bates Number 681803027/3087. http://legacy.library.ucsf.edu/tid/pug60f00.

Anderson, S. J., and Dunn, S. P. (2006) "Galbraith and the management of specific demand: evidence from the tobacco industry," *Journal of Institutional Economics*, 2(3), 273–96.

Anderson, S. J., Dewhirst, T., and Ling, P. M. (2006) "Every document and picture tells a story: using internal corporate document reviews, semiotics, and content analysis to assess tobacco advertising," *Tobacco Control*, 15, 254–61.

Anderson, S. J., Glantz, S. A., and Ling, P. M. (2005) "Emotions for sale: cigarette advertising and women's psychosocial needs," *Tobacco Control*, 14(2), 127–35.

Anderson, S. J., Ling, P. M., and Glantz, S. A. (2007) "Implications of the federal court order banning the terms 'light' and 'mild': what difference could it make?" *Tobacco Control*, 16, 275–79.

Anderson, S. J., Pollay, R. W., and Ling, P. M. (2006) "Taking advantage of lax advertising regulations: reassuring and distracting health-concerned smokers," *Social Science & Medicine*, 63(8), 1973–85.

Angell, M. (2004) *The Truth About the Drug Companies: How They Deceive Us and What to Do About It*. New York: Random House.

(2009) "Drug companies & doctors: a story of corruption," *The New York Review of Books*, 56(1), January 15, 2009. www.nybooks.com/articles/22237. Accessed April 9, 2009.

Angeriz, A., Arestis, P., McCombie, J., and Mosler, W. (2008) "The interest rate channel in the new monetary policy framework," *Challenge*, 51(2), March–April, 69–84.

Ansberry, C., O'Boyle, T. F., and Roberts, J. T. (1994) *Today's Adult Young Male Smoker. Wall Street Journal*. Philip Morris: Bates Number 2060127742/7919. http://legacy.library.ucsf.edu/tid/leg76e00.

Ansolabehere, S., Figueiredo, J., and Snyder, J. M. (2003) "Why is there so little money in US politics?" *Journal of Economic Perspectives*, 17(1), Winter, 105–30.

Aoki, M. (1990) "Towards an economic model of the Japanese firm," *Journal of Economic Literature*, 28(1), 1–27.

Arestis, P. (1990) "Post Keynesianism: a new approach to economics," *Review of Social Economy*, Fall, 48(3), 222–46.

(1992) *The Post Keynesian Approach to Economics: An Alternative Analysis of Economic Theory and Policy*. Aldershot: Edward Elgar.

(1996a) "Post-Keynesian economics: towards coherence, critical survey," *Cambridge Journal of Economics*, 20, 111–35.

(2006) "New monetary policy and Keynes," *Intervention: Journal of Economics*, 3(2), 245–62.

(2007) "What is the new consensus in macroeconomics?," in P. Arestis (ed.) *Is There a New Consensus in Macroeconomics?* Basingstoke: Palgrave Macmillan.

Arestis, P., and Karakitsos, E. (2008) "The US housing slump and the consumer," *Journal of Post Keynesian Economics*, 30(3), 335–52.

Arestis, P., and Howells, P. (1996) "Theoretical reflections on endogenous money: the problem with 'convenience lending'," *Cambridge Journal of Economics*, 20(5), 539–52.

(2001) "The 1520–1640 'Great Inflation': an early case of controversy in money," *Journal of Post Keynesian Economics*, 24(2), 181–203.

Arestis, P. and Sawyer, M. C. (1997) *The Relevance of Keynesian Economic Policies Today*. London: Macmillan.

(1998) "Keynesian policies for the new millennium," *Economic Journal*, 108(1), 181–95.

(2001a) "The economic analysis underlying the 'third way'," *New Political Economy*, 6(2), 255–78.

(2001b) (eds.) *The Economics of the Third Way*. Aldershot: Edward Elgar.

(2003) "Does the stock of money have any causal significance," *Banca Nazionale del Lavoro*, 56, 113–36.

(2004a) "Can monetary policy affect the real economy?," *European Review of Economics and Finance*, 3(3), 9–32.

(2004b) *Re-examining Monetary and Fiscal Policies in the Twenty First Century*. Aldershot: Edward Elgar, 210.

(2004c) "On the effectiveness of monetary policy and of fiscal policy," *Review of Social Economy*, LXII(4), 441–63.

(2005) "Aggregate demand, conflict and capacity in the inflationary process," *Cambridge Journal of Economics*, 29(6), 959–74.

(2006) "The nature and role of monetary policy when money is endogenous," *Cambridge Journal of Economics*, 30(6), 847–60.

(2008) "A critical reconsideration of the foundations of monetary policy in the new consensus macroeconomics framework," *Cambridge Journal of Economics*, 32(5), 761–79.

Arestis, P., Dunn, S. P., and Sawyer, M. C. (1999a) "Post Keynesian economics and its critics," *Journal of Post Keynesian Economics*, 21 (Summer), 527–50.

Arestis, P., Dunn, S. P., and Sawyer, M. C. (1999b) "On the coherence of Post Keynesian economics: a comment upon Walters and Young," *Scottish Journal of Political Economy*, 46(3), 339–45.

Ash, T. G. (2005) *Free World: America, Europe, and the Surprising Future of the West*. London: Random House.

Auerbach, P. (1992) "Vertical integration, planning and the market," in P. Arestis and V. Chick (eds.) *Recent Developments in Post Keynesian Economics*. Aldershot: Edward Elgar.

Auletta, K. (1982) *The Underclass*. New York: Random House.

Avorn, J. (2004) *Powerful Medicines: The Benefits, Risks, and Costs of Prescription Drugs*. New York: Knopf.

Bagwell, K. (2001) (ed.) *The Economics of Advertising*. Aldershot: Edward Elgar.

(2003) *The Economic Analysis of Advertising*, mimeo. www.columbia.edu/~kwb8/.

Bailey, D., Harte, G., and Sugden, R. (1994) *Making Transnationals Accountable: A Significant Step for Britain*. London: Routledge.

Bailey, D., Harte, G., and Sugden, R. (1999) "Regulating transnationals: free markets and monitoring in Europe," in K. Cowling (ed.) *Industrial Policy in Europe: Theoretical Perspectives and Practical Proposals*. London: Routledge.

Bain, J. (1956) *Barriers to New Competition: Their Character and Consequences in Manufacturing Industries*. Cambridge, MA: Harvard University Press.

Bajaj, V. (2008) "Whiplash ends a roller coaster week," *New York Times, Business*, October 10, 2008. www.nytimes.com/2008/10/11/business/11markets.html. Accessed October 26, 2008.

Balakrishnan, S. and Wernerfelt, B. (1986) "Technical change, competition and vertical integration," *Strategic Management Journal*, 7(4), 347–59.

Balbach E., Gasior R., and Barbeau E. (2002) "Tobacco industry documents: comparing the Minnesota Depository and internet access," *Tobacco Control*, 11(1), March, 68–72.

Bank of England (2008) *Financial Stability Report, October*, Issue No. 24. London: Bank of England.

Baran, P. A. and Sweezy, P. M. (1966) *Monopoly Capital: An Essay on the American Economic and Social Order*. Harmondsworth: Penguin.

Barsky, R. B. and DeLong, J. B. (1990) "Bull and bear markets in the twentieth century," *Journal of Economic History*, 50(2), June, 265–81.

Baumol, W. (1959) *Business behavior, value and growth*. London: Macmillan.

BBC (2008) "World credit loss '£1.8 trillion'," http://news.bbc.co.uk/1/hi/business/7694275.stm. Accessed October 28, 2008.

Bebchuk, L. A. and Fried, J. M. (2004) *Pay without Performance: The Unfulfilled Promise of Executive Compensation*. Cambridge, MA: Harvard University Press.

Becker, G. (1964) *Human Capital*. Chicago: University of Chicago Press.

Becker, G. and Murphy, K. (1993) "A simple theory of advertising as a Good or Bad," *Quarterly Journal of Economics,* 108(4), 941–64.

Bell, D. and Kristol, I. (1981) (eds.) *The Crisis in Economic Theory.* New York: Basic Books.

Berg. J. (2008) "No rescue for the hungry," *Washington Post*, September 28, 2008; B07, www.washingtonpost.com/wp-dyn/content/article/2008/09/26/AR2008092603265_pf.html. Accessed October 26, 2008.

Berle, A. A. (1953) "American capitalism," *The Review of Economics and Statistics*, February, 81–4.

(1967) "Analyzing the corporate complex," *Saturday Review*, June 24, 29.

Berle, A. A. and Means, G. (1932) *The Modern Corporation and Private Property.* Somerset, NJ: Transaction, 1991.

Bernanke, B., Reinhart, V. R., and Sack, B. P. (2004) "Monetary policy alternatives at the zero bound: an empirical assessment," *Brookings Papers on Economic Activity*, 2, 1–78.

Bernick, K. (1996) "Describing the customer psychographics: hype or hard-hitting strategy ?" *Agri Marketing*, 34, 18–20.

Bertrand, M. and Mullainathan, S. (2001) "Are CEOs rewarded for luck? The ones without principles are," *Quarterly Journal of Economics,* 116(3), 901–32.

Bhaskar, R. (1979) *The Possibility of Naturalism: A Philosophical Critique of the Contemporary Human Sciences.* London: Verso.

Blackburn, R. (2002) *Banking on Death: Or, Investing in Life: The History and Future of Pensions.* London: Verso.

Blaug, M. (1997) "Ugly currents in modern economics," *Options politiques*, 18(September), 3–8.

(2003) "The formalist revolution of the 1950s," in W. Samuels, J. Biddle, and J. B. Davis (eds.) *A Companion to the History of Economic Thought.* Oxford: Blackwell.

Blois, K. J. (1975) "Supply contracts in the Galbraithian planning system," *Journal of Industrial Economics,* 24(1), 29–39.

Blythman, J. (2005) *Shopped: The Shocking Power of British Supermarkets.* London: Harper Perennial.

Bower, J. (1970) "Planning within the firm," *American Economic Review,* 60(2), 186–94.

Bowles, S. (1985) "The production process in a competitive economy: Walraisin, neo-Hobbesian and Marxian models," *American Economic Review*, 75(1).

Bowles, S. and Gintis, H. (1993) "The revenge of homo economicus: contested exchange and the revival of political economy," *Journal of Economic Perspectives*, 7, Winter, 83–102.

Bowles, S., Edwards, R., and Shepherd, W. G. (eds.) (1989) *Unconventional Wisdom: Essays in Honor of John Kenneth Galbraith*. Boston: Houghton Mifflin.

Braithwaite, D. (1928) "The economic effects of advertisement," *Economic Journal*, 38(149), March, 16–37.

Branston, J. R., Cowling, K., and Sugden, R. (2006) "Corporate governance and public interest," *International Review of Applied Economics*, 20(2), 189–212.

Branston, J. R., Sugden, R., Valdez, P., and Wilson, J. R. (2006a) "Generating participation and democracy: an illustration from electricity reform in Mexico," *International Review of Applied Economics*, 20(1), 47–68.

Branston, J. R., Rubini, L., Sugden, R., and Wilson, J. R. (2006b) "The healthy development of economies: a strategic framework for competitiveness in the health industry," *Review of Social Economy*, LXIV(3), September, 301–29.

Brett, W. (1984) "Galbraith and Friedman: two visions of economic reality," *Journal of Post-Keynesian Economics*, 7(1), 18–29.

Brown & Williamson (1980a) *Project Delta, an Ultra Low Tar Cigarette for Women*. Brown & Williamson: Bates Number 544000505/0511. http://legacy.library.ucsf.edu/tid/ngh10f00.

(1980b) No Title. Brown & Williamson: Bates Number 544000497/0504. http://legacy.library.ucsf.edu/tid/mgh10f00.

(1996) *Self Descriptors Female Psychographic Groups*. Brown & Williamson: Bates Number 461234716/4717. http://legacy.library.ucsf.edu/tid/aej81d00.

(1998) *Share data; profit contribution; Capri styles distribution by channel; strong channels for Capri*. Brown & Williamson: Bates Number 502030594/0600. http://legacy.library.ucsf.edu/tid/kut02d00.

Brown, W. B. (1976) "Islands of conscious power: MNCs in the theory of the firm," *MSU Business Topics*, 24, 37–45.

Bruce, K. (2000) "Conflict and conversion: Henry S. Dennison and the shaping of John Kenneth Galbraith's economic thought," *Journal of Economic Issues*, 36(4), 949–67.

(2001) "The making of a heterodox economist: the impact of Henry S. Dennison on the economic thought of John Kenneth Galbraith," in M. Keaney (ed.) *Economist with a Public Purpose: Essays in Honour of John Kenneth Galbraith*. London: Routledge.

Brunton, B. G. (1988) "Institutional origins of the military-industrial complex," *Journal of Economic Issues*, June, 599–606.

Buckley, P. J. (2000) *Multinational Firms: Cooperation and Competition in the World Economy*, London: Macmillan and New York: St. Martin's Press.

(2003) *The Changing Global Context of International Business.* Basingstoke: Palgrave.

(2004) *The Challenge of International Business.* Basingstoke: Palgrave.

(2006a) "Stephen Hymer: three phases, one approach?" *International Business Review,* 15(2), 140–7.

(2006b) *The Multinational Enterprise and the Globalization of Knowledge.* Basingstoke: Palgrave.

Buckley, P. J. and Casson, M. (1976) *The Future of the Multinational Enterprise.* London: Holmes and Meier.

(2007) "Edith Penrose's theory of the growth of the firm and the strategic management of multinational enterprises," *Management International Review,* 47(2), 151–73.

Bulow, J. and Klemperer, P. (1998) "The tobacco deal," *Brookings Papers on Economic Activity: Microeconomics,* 323–94.

Burnham, J. (1941) *The Managerial Revolution.* New York: John Day.

BusinessWeek (2008) *Top 100 Brands,* http://bwnt.businessweek.com/interactive_reports/global_brand_2008/. Accessed March 1, 2009.

Cabinet Office (2008) *Getting on, getting ahead – A discussion paper: analyzing the trends and drivers of social mobility,* Prime Minister Strategy Unit, November 3. www.cabinetoffice.gov.uk/strategy/publications.aspx. Accessed November 8, 2008.

Canterbery, E. R. (1984) "Galbraith, Sraffa, Kalecki, and Supra-Surplus," *Journal of Post-Keynesian Economics,* 7(1), 77–90.

Card, D. and Krueger, A. B. (1994) "Minimum wages and employment: a case study of the fast-food industry in New Jersey and Pennsylvania," *American Economic Review,* 84(4), 772–93.

Carey, B. (2008) "Antidepressant studies unpublished," *New York Times,* January 17. www.nytimes.com/2008/01/17/health/17depress.html. Accessed April 9, 2009.

Carney, T. P. (2006) "Big business and big government," *Cato Policy Report,* XXVIII(4), July/August, 1, 11–14.

Carson, R. (1962) *Silent Spring.* Boston: Houghton Mifflin.

Carter, R. and Hodgson, G. M. (2006) "The impact of empirical tests of transaction cost economics on the debate on the nature of the firm," *Strategic Management Journal,* 27(5), May, 461–76.

Cassidy, J. (1996) "The decline of economics," *New Yorker,* December 2, 50–64.

Castellani, D. and Zanfei, A. (2002) "Multinational experience and the creation of linkages with local firms: evidence from the electronics industry," *Cambridge Journal of Economics*, 26(1), 1–26.

Caves, R. E. (1970) "Uncertainty, market structure and performance: Galbraith as conventional wisdom," in J. W. Markham and G. F. Papnek (eds.) *Industrial Organization and Economic Development: In Honor Of E. S. Mason*. Boston: Houghton-Mifflin, 283–302.

(1971) "International corporations: the industrial economics of direct foreign investment," *Economica*, 38, 1–27.

(1982) *Multinational Enterprise and Economic Analysis*. Cambridge: Cambridge University Press.

CBO (2007) *Historical Effective Federal Tax Rates: 1979 to 2005*, Washington, DC, Congressional Budget Office, December.

CDC (2002) *Physical Activity and Good Nutrition: Essential Elements to Prevent Chronic Diseases and Obesity 2002*. Atlanta, GA: Department of Health and Human Services, Centers for Disease Control and Prevention.

Chaloupka, F. and Warner, K. (2000) "The economics of smoking," in A. J. Culyer and J. P. Newhouse (eds.) *Handbook of Health Economics*, vol. 1B. Amsterdam: Elsevier, 1539–627.

Chamberlin, E. H. (1933) *Theory of Monopolistic Competition: A Re-orientation of the Theory of Value*, 8th edn. Cambridge, MA: Harvard University Press, 1962.

Chandler, A. D. (1962) *Strategy and Structure*. Cambridge, MA: MIT Press.

(1977) *The Visible Hand: The Managerial Revolution in American Business*. Cambridge, MA: Harvard University Press.

(1990) *Scale and Scope: The Dynamics of Industrial Capitalism*. Cambridge, MA and London: Harvard University Press.

Chick, V. (1983) *Macroeconomics after Keynes: A Reconsideration of the General Theory*. Oxford: Philip Allen.

(1992) "The small firm under uncertainty: a puzzle of the General Theory," in W. J. Gerrard and J. Hillard (eds.) *The Philosophy and Economics of J. M. Keynes*. Aldershot: Edward Elgar.

(1995) "Is there a case for Post Keynesian economics?," *Scottish Journal of Political Economy*, 42(1), February, 20–36.

(1998) "Knowing one's place: The role of formalism in economics," *Economic Journal*, 108, 1859–69.

Chick, V. and Dow, S. (2002) "Monetary policy with endogenous money and liquidity preference: a nondualistic treatment," *Journal of Post Keynesian Economics*, 24(4), 587–608.

Chomsky, N. (1989) *Necessary Illusions: Thought Control in Democratic Societies*. London: Pluto Press.

(2002) *Media Control: The Spectacular Achievements of Propaganda*. New York: Seven Stories Press.

Christofides, L. and Tapon, F. (1979a) "Discretionary expenditures and profit risk management: the Galbraith-Caves hypothesis," *Quarterly Journal of Economics,* 93(2), 303–19.

(1979b) "Uncertainty, market structure and performance: the Galbraith-Caves hypothesis revisited," *Quarterly Journal of Economics,* 93(4), 719–26.

Ciscel, D. H. (1984) "Galbraith's planning system as a substitute for market theory," *Journal of Economic Issues,* June, 411–18.

Clark, J. M. (1940) "Toward a concept of workable competition," *American Economic Review*, 30(2), 241–56.

Clarke, R., Davies, S., Dobson, P., and Waterson, M. (2002) *Buyer Power and Competition in European Food Retailing*. Cheltenham: Edward Elgar.

Coase, R. H. (1937) "The Nature of the Firm," *Economica*, 4 (new series): 386–405. Reprinted in G. J. Stigler and K. E. Boulding (eds.) (1953) *Readings in Price Theory: Selected by a Committee of the American Economic Association*. London: George Allen and Unwin.

Coffey, D. and Tomlinson P. R. (2006) "Multiple facilities, strategic splitting and vertical structures: stability, growth and distribution reconsidered," *The Manchester School*, 74(5), 558–76.

Coffey, D. and Tomlinson, P. R. (2003) "Globalisation, vertical relations and the J-mode firm," *Journal of Post Keynesian Economics*, 26(1), 117–44.

Colander, D. (1984) "Galbraith and the theory of price control," *Journal of Post-Keynesian Economics*, 7(1), 30–42.

Comanor, W. S. and Wilson, T. A. (1967) "Advertising, market structure and performance," *The Review of Economics and Statistics*, 49, 423–40.

Commons, J. R. (1934) *Institutional Economics: Its Place in Political Economy*. New York: Macmillan.

Competition Commission (2000) *Report of the Competition Commission on the supply of Groceries from Multiple Stores in the United Kingdom*. London: Competition Commission, Cm 4842.

Connolly, G., Wayne, G., Lymperis, D., and Doherty, M. C. (2000) "How cigarette additives are used to mask environmental tobacco smoke," *Tobacco Control,* 9, Autumn, 283–91.

Connor, J. (2003) "The changing structure of global food markets: dimensions, effects, and policy implications," Paper presented at OECD Conference on Changing Dimensions of the Food Economy, The Hague, February, 6–7.

Cornwall, J. (1977) *Modern Capitalism: Its Growth and Transformation*. New York: St. Martin's Press.

(1994) *Economic Breakdown and Recovery*. Armonk, NY: M.E. Sharpe.

Cottrel, A. (1994) "Post-Keynesian monetary economics," *Cambridge Journal of Economics*, 18(4), 587–606.

Courvisanos, J. (2005) "Technological innovation: Galbraith, the Post Keynesians, and a heterodox future," *Journal of Post Keynesian Economics*, 28(1), 83–102.

Cowling, K. (1982) *Monopoly Capitalism*. London: Macmillan.

(1985) "Economic obstacles to democracy," in R. C. O. Matthews (ed.), *Economy and Democracy*. London: Macmillan.

(2004) "Monopoly capitalism and stagnation," in T. Mott (ed.), *Rethinking Capitalist Development: Essays on the Economics of Josef Steindl*. London: Taylor & Francis.

(2006) "Prosperity, depression and modern capitalism," *Kyklos*, 59(3), 369–81.

Cowling, K. and Sugden, R. (1987a) *Transnational Monopoly Capitalism*. Brighton: Wheatsheaf.

(1987b) "Market exchange and the concept of the transnational corporation: analyzing the nature of the firm," *British Review of Economic Issues*, 9(20), 57–68.

(1990) *A New Economic Policy for Britain: Essays on the Development of Industry*. Manchester: Manchester University Press.

(1992) *Current Issues in Industrial Economic Strategy*. Manchester: Manchester University Press.

(1993) "A strategy for industrial development as a basis for regulation," in R. Sugden (ed.) *Industrial Economic Regulation. A Framework and Exploration*. London: Routledge. Reprinted in D. Parker (ed.) (2000) *Privatization and Corporate Performance*. Cheltenham: Edward Elgar.

(1994) *Beyond Capitalism: Towards a New World Economic Order*. London: Pinter.

(1998a) "The essence of the modern corporation: markets, strategic decision-making and the theory of the firm," *The Manchester School*, 66(1), January, 59–86.

(1998b) "Strategic trade policy reconsidered: national rivalry vs free trade vs international cooperation," *Kyklos*, 51, 339–57.

(1998c) "Technology policy: strategic failures and the need for a new direction," in J. Michie and J. Grieve Smith (eds.) *Globalization, Growth and Governance: Creating an Innovative Economy*. Oxford: Oxford University Press.

(1999) "The wealth of localities, regions and nations: developing multinational economies," *New Political Economy*, 4(3), 361–78.

Cowling, K. and Tomlinson, P. R. (2000) "The Japanese crisis – a case of strategic failure?" *The Economic Journal*, 110(464), F358–F381.

(2002) "Revisiting the roots of Japan's economic stagnation: the role of the Japanese corporation," *International Review of Applied Economics*, 16(4), 373–90.

(2005) "Globalisation and corporate power," *Contributions to Political Economy*, 24, 1–22.

Cowling, K., Cable, J., Kelly, M., and McGuinness, T. (1975) *Advertising and Economic Behavior*. London: Macmillan.

Cowling, K., Sacchetti, S., Sugden, R., and Wilson, J. R. (2005) "The United Nations and democratic globalisation," in M. Di Tommaso and S. Giovannelli (eds.) *United Nations and Industrial Development*. New York: United Nations, 142–60.

Cowling, K., Yusof, F. M., and Vernon, G. (2000) "Declining concentration in UK manufacturing? A problem of measurement," *International Review of Applied Economics*, 14(1).

Cox, A. (1984) *Established Brands Positioning and Evaluation Process Summary*. Lorillard: Bates Number 93285082/5109. http://legacy.library.ucsf.edu/tid/hfl60e00.

Cummings, K. M., Morley, C. P., and Hyland, A. (2002) "Failed promises of the cigarette industry and its effect on consumer misperceptions about the health risks of smoking," *Tobacco Control*, 11(suppl. I), i110–i117.

Cuñat, V. and Guadalupe, M. (2006) "Globalization and the provision of incentives inside the firm: the effect of foreign competition," *Working Paper*. www0.gsb.columbia.edu/faculty/mguadalupe/research.html.

Cyert, R. M. and March, J. (1963) *A Behavioral Theory of the Firm*. Englewood Cliffs, NJ: Prentice-Hall.

Cypher, J. M. (2008) "Economic consequences of armaments production: institutional perspectives of J. K. Galbraith and T. B. Veblen," *Journal of Economic Issues*, 42, March, 37–47.

Dahlman, C. J. (1979) "The problem of externality," *Journal of Law and Economics*, 22(1), 141–62.

Dasgupta, P. (1998) *Modern Economics and its Critics – 1*. Mimeo. University of Cambridge.

Dasgupta, P. and Stiglitz, J. E. (1980) "Industrial structure and the nature of innovative activity," *Economic Journal*, 90, 266–93.

David, L. (2006) "Science a la Joe Camel," *The Washington Post*, November 26, 2006. www.washingtonpost.com/wp-dyn/content/

article/2006/11/24/AR2006112400789_pf.html. Accessed May 7, 2009.

Davidson, P. (1972) *Money and the Real World.* London: Macmillan.

(1974) "A Keynesian view of Friedman's theoretical framework for monetary analysis," in R. J. Gordon (ed.) *Milton Friedman's Monetary Framework: A Debate with His Critics.* London: University of Chicago Press.

(1977) "Money and General Equilibrium." Reprinted in (1990) *Money and Employment: The collected writings of Paul Davidson*, vol. 1. London: Macmillan.

(1981) "Post Keynesian Economics," in D. Bell and I. Kristol (eds.) *The Crisis in Economic Theory.* New York: Basic Books.

(1985a) "Incomes policy as a social institution," in S. Maitak and I. Lipnowski (eds.) *Macroeconomic Conflict and Social Institutions.* Cambridge, MA: Ballinger. Reprinted in (1991) *Inflation, Open Economics and Resources: The Collected Writings of Paul Davidson*, vol. II. London: Macmillan.

(1985b) "Liquidity and not increasing returns is the ultimate source of unemployment equilibrium," *Journal of Post Keynesian Economics*, 7, 373–84.

(1991a) "Is probability theory relevant for uncertainty? A Post Keynesian perspective," *Journal of Economic Perspectives*, 5(1), 129–43. An earlier draft appears in L. Davidson (ed.) (1991) *Inflation, Open Economics and Resources: The Collected Writings of Paul Davidson*, vol. II. London: Macmillan.

(1991b) *Controversies in Post Keynesian Economics.* Aldershot: Edward Elgar.

(1992) "Eichner's approach to money and macroeconomics," in W. Milberg (ed.) *The Megacorp and Macrodynamics.* New York: M. E. Sharpe.

(1994) *Post Keynesian Macroeconomic Theory: A Foundation for Successful Economic Policies for the Twenty First Century.* Aldershot: Edward Elgar.

(1996) "Reality and economic theory," *Journal of Post Keynesian Economics*, 18, 479–508. Reprinted in L. Davidson (ed.) (1999) *Uncertainty, International Money, Employment and Theory: The Collected Writings of Paul Davidson*, vol. III. London: Macmillan, 3–29.

(2005) "Galbraith and the Post Keynesians," *Journal of Post Keynesian Economics*, 28(1), 103–13.

(2006) "Can, or should, a central bank inflation target?" *Journal of Post Keynesian Economics*, 28(4), 689–703.

(2007) *John Maynard Keynes.* London: Macmillan.

(2008a) "How to solve the US housing problem and avoid a recession: a revived HOLC and FTC," *Schwartz Center For Economic Policy Analysis: Policy Note.*

(2008b) "Crude oil prices: 'fundamentals' or speculation?," *Challenge*, 51(4), July–August, 110–18.

(2008c) "Is the current financial distress caused by the sub prime mortgage crisis a Minsky moment? Or is it the result of attempting to securitize illiquid non commercial mortgage loans?," *Journal of Post Keynesian Economics*, 30(4), Summer, 669–76.

(2008d) "Securitization, liquidity, and market failure," *Challenge*, 51(3), May–June, 43–56.

Davidson, P. and Davidson, G. S. (1984) "Financial markets and Williamson's theory of governance: efficiency versus concentration versus power," *Quarterly Review of Economics and Business*, 24 (Winter). Reprinted in L. Davidson (ed.) (1990) *Money and Employment: The collected writings of Paul Davidson*, vol. I. London: Macmillan.

(1996) *Economics for a Civilized Society*, 2nd edn. London: Macmillan.

Davidson, P. and Weintraub, S. (1978) "A statement of purposes," *Journal of Post Keynesian Economics*, 1(1), 3–8.

Davies, A. (1999) *A Strategic Approach to Corporate Governance.* Aldershot: Gower.

Davies, J. E. and Lee, F. S. (1988) "A Post Keynesian appraisal of the contestability criterion," *Journal of Post Keynesian Economics*, 10(1), 3–24.

Davis, J. B., Hands, D. W., and Mäki, U. (eds.) (1998) *Handbook of Economic Methodology.* Cheltenham: Edward Elgar.

Dawson, M. (2003) *The Consumer Trap: Big Business Marketing in American Life.* Champaign, IL: University of Illinois Press.

Deloitte (2007) *2007 Global Powers of Retailing*, report. www.deloitte.com/dtt/press_release/0,1014,cid%253D147895,00.html.

DeLong, J. B. and Shleifer, A. (1991) "The stock market bubble of 1929: evidence from closed-end mutual funds," *Journal of Economic History*, 51(3), September, 675–700.

DeLong, J. B. (2005) "Sisyphus as Social Democrat," *Foreign Affairs*, May/June. www.foreignaffairs.org/20050501fareviewessay84312/j-bradford-delong/sisyphus-as-social-democrat.html. Accessed December 30, 2008.

Demsetz, H. (1974) "Where is the new industrial state?," *Economic Inquiry*, 12(1), 1–12.

Dennison, H. S. and Galbraith, J. K. (1938) *Modern Competition and Business Policy.* New York: Oxford University Press.

Dennison, H. S., Filene, L. A., Flanders, R. E., and Leeds, M. (1938) *Toward full employment*. New York: Whittlesley House.

Dewey, J. (1916) *Democracy and Education*. New York: Macmillan.

(1927) *The Public and Its Problems*. Denver, CO: Holt. Page numbers refer to the reproduction in J. A. Boydston (ed.) (1988) *John Dewey. The Later Works*, vol. II: *1925–1927*. Carbondale, IL: Southern Illinois University Press.

(1948) *Reconstruction in Philosophy*, enlarged edn. Boston: Beacon.

Dicken, P. (2003) *Global Shift: Transforming the World Economy*. London: Sage.

DiMasi, J. A., Hansen, R. W., and Grabowski, H. G. (2003) "The price of innovation: new estimates of drug development costs," *Journal of Health Economics*, 22(2), 151–85.

Dixon, R. (1986) "Uncertainty, unobstructedness and power," *Journal of Post Keynesian Economics*, 8(4), 585–90.

Dobson, P. (2003) "Buyer power in food retailing: the European experience." Paper presented at OECD Conference on "Changing Dimensions of the Food Economy," The Hague, February 6–7.

Dobson, P. W. and Waterson, M. (1997) "Countervailing power and consumer prices," *Economic Journal*, 107, 418–30.

(1999) "Retailer power: recent developments and policy implications," *Economic Policy*, 28, April, 135–64.

Dobson, P. W., Clarke, R., Davies, S., and Waterson, M. (2001) "Buyer power and its impact on competition in the food distribution sector of the European Union," *Journal of Industry, Competition and Trade*, 1(3), 247–81.

Doeringer, P. and Poire, M. (1971) *Internal Labor Markets and Manpower Adjustment*. New York: D.C. Heath.

Dorfman, J. (1934) *Thorstein Veblen and His America*. New York: Viking Press.

Dow, S. C. (1996a) *The Methodology of Macroeconomic Thought: A Conceptual Analysis of Schools of Thought in Economics*. Cheltenham: Edward Elgar.

(1996b) "Horizontalism: a critique," *Cambridge Journal of Economics*, 20, 497–508.

(1997a) "Methodological pluralism and pluralism of method," in A. Salanti and E. Screpanti (eds.) *Pluralism in Economics: Theory, History and Methodology*. Aldershot: Elgar, 89–99.

(1997b) "Mainstream economic methodology," *Cambridge Journal of Economics*, 21(1), 73–93.

(2001) "Post Keynesian Methodology," in R. Holt and S. Presman (eds.) *The New Guide to Post Keynesian Economics*. London: Routledge.

Downie, J. (1958) *The Competitive Process*. London: Duckworth.

Downward, P. and Mearman, A. (2007) "Retroduction as mixed-methods triangulation in economic research: reorienting economics into social science," *Cambridge Journal of Economics*, 31(1), 77–99.

Duesenberry, J. S. (1949) *Income, Saving and the Theory of Consumer Behavior*. Cambridge, MA: Harvard University Press.

Dugger, W. M. (1980) "Corporate bureaucracy," *Journal of Economic Issues*, June, 399–409.

(1983) "The transaction cost analysis of Oliver E. Williamson: a new synthesis," *Journal of Economic Issues*, March, 95–114.

(1985a) "The continued evolution of corporate power," *Review of Social Economy*, (43), 1–13.

(1985b) "The shortcomings of concentration ratios in the conglomerate age: new sources and uses of corporate power," *Journal of Economic Issues*, June, 343–53.

(1987) "An institutionalist theory of economic planning," *Journal of Economic Issues*, December, 1649–75.

(1988) "An institutional analysis of corporate power', *Journal of Economic Issues*, March, 79–111.

Duhs, L. A. (2008) *From Galbraith to Krugman and back: Galbraith, Krugman and 'Good Economics*, University of Queensland, School of Economics Discussion Papers Series(369), www.uq.edu.au/economics/index.html?page=84247. Accessed December 30, 2008.

Dunn, W. J. (1972) Pm PM. Motives and Incentives in Cigarette Smoking. Bates No. 2023193286/3304. http://legacy.library.ucsf.edu/tid/fot14e00.

Dunn, S. P. (1999) "Bounded rationality, fundamental uncertainty and the firm in the long run," in S. C. Dow and P. E. Earl (eds.) *Contingency, Complexity and the Theory of the Firm: Essays in Honour of Brian Loasby*, vol. II. Cheltenham: Edward Elgar.

(2000a) "Whither Post Keynesianism?" *Journal of Post Keynesian Economics*, 22(3), 343–64.

(2000b) "'Fundamental' uncertainty and the firm in the long run," *Review of Political Economy*, 12(4), 419–33.

(2001a) "Uncertainty, strategic decision-making and the essence of the modern corporation: extending Cowling and Sugden," *The Manchester School*, 69, 31–41.

(2001b) "Bounded rationality is not fundamental uncertainty: a Post Keynesian perspective," *Journal of Post Keynesian Economics*, 23(4), 567–88.

(2001c) "A Post Keynesian approach to the theory of the firm," in S. C. Dow and J. Hillard (eds.) *Post Keynesian Econometrics and the Theory of the Firm: Beyond Keynes*, vol. I. Cheltenham: Edward Elgar.

(2003a) "Keynes and transformation," in J. Runde and S. Mizuhara (eds.) *The Philosophy of Keynes's Economics: Probability, uncertainty and convention*. London: Routledge.

(2003b) "Nonergodicity," in J. King (ed.) *The Elgar Companion to Post Keynesian Economics*. Cheltenham: Edward Elgar.

(2004) "Keynes, uncertainty and the competitive process," *Research in the History of Economic Thought and Methodology*, 22A. 65–92.

(2006) "Prolegomena to a Post Keynesian health economics," *Review of Social Economy*, Autumn, 64(3), 273–92.

(2008a) *The Uncertain Foundations of Post Keynesian Economics*. London: Routledge.

(2008b) "Galbraith saw this coming," *Guardian*, October 15, 28.

(2009) "Global food and public health: a Galbraithian perspective," mimeo.

(2012) *John Kenneth Galbraith: The Economic Legacy*, volumes 1–4. London: Routledge.

Dunn, S. P. and Anderson, S. J. (2006) "J. K. Galbraith's challenge to the accepted sequence: the management of the consumer," *Economica*, 8(2), 337–51.

Dunning, J. H. (1988) *Explaining International Production*. London: Unwin Hyman.

(1993) *Multinational Enterprises and the Global Economy*. Wokingham: Addison Wesley.

(1997) *Governments, Globalization and International Business*. Oxford: Oxford University Press.

(2006) "Towards a new paradigm of development: Implications for the determinants of international business activity," *Transnational Corporations*, 15(1), 173–228.

Dutt, A. (1992) "Keynes, market forms and competition," in B. Gerrard and J. Hillard (eds.) *The Philosophy and Economics of J.M. Keynes*. Cheltenham: Edward Elgar.

Dutt, A. K. (2008) "The dependence effect, consumption and happiness: Galbraith revisited," *Review of Political Economy*, 20(4), 527–50.

Dyer, J. H. (1996) "Does governance matter? Keiretsu alliances and asset specificity as sources of Japanese competitive advantage," *Organization Science*, 7(6), 649–56.

Earl, P. E. (2000) *The Legacy of Herbert A. Simon in Economic Analysis*. Cheltenham: Edward Elgar.

Easterlin, R. A. (2000) "The worldwide standard of living since 1800," *Journal of Economic Perspectives*, 14(1), 7–26.

Edwards, F. and Heggestad, A. (1973) "Uncertainty, market structure, and performance: the Galbraith-Caves hypothesis and managerial motives in banking," *Quarterly Journal of Economics,* 87(3), 455–73.

(1979) "Comment on uncertainty, market structure and performance: the Galbraith-Caves hypothesis revisited," *Quarterly Journal of Economics,* 93(4), 727–29.

Eichner, A. S. (1976) *The Megacorp and Oligopoly: Microfoundations of Macro Dynamics.* Cambridge: Cambridge University Press.

Eichner, A. S. (ed.) (1978) *A Guide to Post Keynesian Economics.* Armonk, NY: M.E. Sharpe.

(1983) *Why Economics Is Not Yet A Science.* London: Macmillan.

Eichner, A. S. and Kregel, J. (1975) "An essay on Post Keynesian theory: a new paradigm in economics," *Journal of Economic Literature*, 13, 1293–314.

Ellwood, D. T. (2000) "Anti-poverty policy for families in the next century: from welfare to work – and worries," *Journal of Economic Perspectives*, 14(1), 187–98.

European Union (2008) "Questions and answers on the Commission's proposal to revise the E.U. Emissions Trading System," *MEMO/08/35*, Brussels, January 23, 2008. http://europa.eu/rapid/pressReleasesAction.do?reference=MEMO/08/35&format=HTML&aged=0&language=EN&guiLanguage=en. Accessed January 31, 2009.

Evans, J. C. and Leathers, C. G. (1980) "Veblen on owners, managers, and the control of industry: a reply," *History of Political Economy*, 12(3), 441–48.

Federal Trade Commission (2003) Federal Trade Commission Cigarette Report for 2001 Federal Trade Commission. 20 pp.

Fergenson, P. E. and Fergenson, L. (1989) "Galbraith on marketing and the marketplace: An interview," *Review of Business,* 11, 29–36.

Financial Times (2008) "FT500 2008," *Financial Times*, www.ft.com/cms/s/0/d61a3e3e-413b-11dd-9661-0000779fd2ac,dwp_uuid=4ca4e366-413b-11dd-9661-0000779fd2ac.html?nclick_check=1. Accessed March 1, 2009.

Fine, B., Heasman, M., and Wright, J. (1996) *Consumption in the Age of Affluence: The World of Food.* London: Routledge.

Fine, B. (2002) *The World of Consumption.* London: Routledge.

Folbre, N. (1994) *Who Pays For the Kids? Gender and the Structures of Constraint.* London: Routledge.

Folbre, N. and Bittman, M. (2004) *Family Time: The Social Organization of Care.* London: Routledge.

Folbre, N. and Nelson, J. (2000) "For love or money – or both?," *Journal of Economic Perspectives*, 14(4), 123–40.

Fontana, G. (2006) "The 'New Consensus' view of monetary policy: a new Wicksellian connection?," *The Levy Economics Institute Working Paper No. 476*.

(2007) "Why money matters: Wicksell, Keynes, and the new consensus view on monetary policy," *Journal of Post Keynesian Economics*, 30(1), 43–60.

Fontana, G. and Venturino, E. (2003) "Endogenous money: an analytical approach," Scottish *Journal of Political Economy*, 50(4), 1–19.

Forelle, C. and Bandler, J. (2006) "The perfect payday: some CEOs reap millions by landing stock options when they are most valuable; luck – or something else?" *Wall Street Journal*, March 18, A1.

Forstater, M. (2003) "Public employment and environmental sustainability," *Journal of Post Keynesian Economics*, 25(3), 385–406.

(2004) "Green Jobs: addressing the critical issues surrounding the environment, workplace and employment," *International Journal of Environment, Workplace and Employment*, 1(1), 53–61.

(2006) "Green jobs," *Challenge*, 49(4), 58–72.

Foss, N. J. (1993) "The theory of the firm: contractual and competence perspectives," *Journal of Evolutionary Economics*, 3, 127–44.

(1994a) "The theory of the firm: the Austrians as precursors and critics of modern theory," *Review of Austrian Economics*, 7, 127–44.

(1994b) "The two Coasian traditions," *Review of Political Economy*, 6, 37–61.

(1996a) "Whither the competence perspective?," in N. J. Foss and C. Knudsen, *Towards a Competence Theory of the Firm*. London: Routledge.

(1996b) "Firms, incomplete contracts, and organizational learning," *Human Systems Management*, 15, 17–26.

(1997a) "Research in strategy, economics, and Michael Porter," *Journal of Management Studies*, 33, 1–24.

(1997b) *Resources and Strategy: A Reader*. Oxford: Oxford University Press.

(1997c) "Austrian insights and the theory of the firm," *Advances in Austrian Economics*, 4, 175–98.

(1997d) "The resource-based perspective. An assessment and diagnosis of problems," *Danish Research Unit for Industrial Dynamics Working Paper No. 97-1*.

Foster, D. P. and Young, H. P. (2007) "Hedge fund wizards," *Washington Post*, December 17. www.washingtonpost.com/wp-dyn/content/

article/2007/12/18/AR2007121801642_pf.html. Accessed October 25, 2008.

Foster, J. F. (1981) "The papers of J. Fagg Foster," *Journal of Economic Issues*, 15(4), December, 857–1012.

Freeman, C. and Soete, L. (1997) *The Economics of Industrial Innovation*, 3rd edn. London: Pinter.

Frey, B. and Stutzer, A. (2000). "Happiness, economy and institutions," *The Economic Journal*, 110, 918–38.

Friedman, M. (1953) *Essays in Positive Economics*. Chicago: University of Chicago Press.

(1977) *From Galbraith to Economic Freedom*. London: Institute of Economic Affairs.

Friedman, M. and Schwartz, A. (1963) *A Monetary History of the United States*. Princeton, NJ: Princeton University Press.

Frydman, C. and Saks, R. E. (2008) "Executive compensation: A new view from a long-term perspective, 1936–2005," *NBER Working Paper No. 14145*.

G20 (2009) *Group of Twenty: Meeting of the Deputies*, January 31–February 1, 2009, London, UK. Note by the Staff of the International Monetary Fund. www.g20.org/pub_further_pubs.aspx. Accessed March 30, 2009.

Galbraith, J. K. and Salinger, N. (1978) *Almost Everyone's Guide to Economics*. Mount Vernon, NY: Consumers Union.

Galbraith, J. K. (1934) *California County Expenditures*, Giannini Foundation of Agricultural Economics, 55, bulletin 582. Berkeley, CA: Agricultural Experiment Station.

(1936) "Monopoly power and price rigidities," *The Quarterly Journal of Economics*, 50(3), 456–75.

(1938) "Rational and irrational consumer preference," *The Economic Journal*, 48(190), 336–42.

(1941) "The selection and timing of inflation controls," *Review of Economic Statistics*, 23(2), 82–85.

(1943) "Price control: some lessons from the first phase" (in Price Control), *The American Economic Review*, 33(1), Papers and Proceedings, 253–59.

(1945) "Germany was badly run," *Fortune*, 32(6), 173–200.

(1946a) *Recovery in Europe*. Washington, DC: National Planning Association.

(1946b) "Discussion" (in New Frontiers in Economic Thought), *The American Economic Review*, 36(2), Papers and Proceedings, 139–53.

(1946c) "Reflections on price control," *The Quarterly Journal of Economics*, 60(4), 475–89.

(1947) "The disequilibrium system," *The American Economic Review*, 37(3), 287–302.

(1949a) "Monopoly and the Concentration of Economic Power," in H. E. Ellis (ed.) *A Survey of Contemporary Economics*. Philadelphia: The Blakiston Company.

(1949b) "Appraisal of marketing research" (in Commodity Marketing – Going Where?), *The American Economic Review*, 39(3), Papers and Proceedings, 415–16.

(1952a) *American Capitalism: The Concept of Countervailing Power*. London: Hamish Hamilton.

(1952b) *A Theory of Price Control*. Cambridge, MA: Harvard University Press.

(1954) "Countervailing power" (in Fundamental Characteristics of the American Economy: Degrees of Competition, of Monopoly, and of Countervailing Power; Theoretical Significance), *The American Economic Review*, 44(2), Papers and Proceedings, 1–6.

(1955a) *The Great Crash, 1929*. Boston: Houghton Mifflin.

(1955b) *Economics & the Art of Controversy*. New Brunswick, NJ: Rutgers University Press.

(1957) "Market structure and stabilization policy," *The Review of Economics and Statistics*, 39(2), 124–33.

(1958a) *The Affluent Society*, 2nd edn. Harmondsworth: Penguin, 1967.

(1958b) "Galbraith on market-structure and stabilization policy – comment," *Review of Economics and Statistics*, 40(2), 168.

(1958c) "A Comment on Market Structure and Stabilization Policy: Reply" (in Notes and Book Reviews), *The Review of Economics and Statistics*, 40(4), 415–16.

(1959) "Mr. Hunter on Countervailing Power: A Comment" (in Notes and Memoranda), *The Economic Journal*, 69(273), 168–70.

(1960) *The Liberal Hour*. Boston: Houghton Mifflin.

(1961) "A positive approach to economic aid," *Foreign Affairs*, 39(3), 445–57.

(1962) *Economic Development in Perspective*. Cambridge MA: Harvard University Press.

(1963) *The Mclandress Dimension*. Boston: Houghton Mifflin.

(1964a) *Economic Development*. Boston: Houghton-Mifflin.

(1964b) *The Scotch*. Boston: Houghton Mifflin.

(1966a) "The new industrial state, Reith Lectures: Lecture 1," *The Listener*, LXXVI(1964), November 17, 711–14.

(1966b) "The modern corporation, Reith Lectures: Lecture 2," *The Listener*, LXXVI(1965), November 24, 755–58.

(1966c) "Control of prices and people, Reith Lectures: Lecture 3," *The Listener*, LXXVI(1966), December 1, 793–95, 812.

(1966d) "The role of the state, Reith Lectures: Lecture 4," *The Listener*, LXXVI(1967), December 8, 841–43, 853.

(1966e) "The bearing on socialist development, Reith Lectures: Lecture 5," *The Listener*, LXXVI(1968), December 15, 881–84.

(1966f) "The cultural impact, Reith Lectures: Lecture 6," *The Listener*, LXXVI(1969), December 22, 915–18.

(1967a) *The New Industrial State*. Penguin, Harmondsworth. 2nd edn, 1972, 4th edn, 1985. (References are to the 2nd edn unless stated.)

(1967b) *How to Get Out of Vietnam: A Workable Solution to the Worst Problem of Our Time*. New York: New American Library.

(1969a) *Ambassador's Journal: A Personal Account of the Kennedy Years*. London: Hamilton.

(1969b) *How to Control the Military*. Garden City, NY: Doubleday.

(1969c) "Professor Gordon on 'The Close of the Galbraithian System'," *The Journal of Political Economy*, 77(4), Part 1. 494–503.

(1970a) "Economics as a system of belief" (in Economics in the Industrial State: Science and Sedative), *The American Economic Review*, 60(2), Papers and Proceedings of the Eighty-second Annual Meeting of the American Economic Association, 469–78. Reprinted as chapter 4 in Galbraith (1971).

(1970b) *Who Needs the Democrats, and What it Takes to be Needed*. Garden City, NY: Doubleday.

(1971) *Economics, Peace and Laughter: A Contemporary Guide*. Harmondsworth: Penguin.

(1973a) *Economics and the Public Purpose*. Harmondsworth: Penguin.

(1973b) "Power and the useful economist," *American Economic Review*, 63(1), 1–11.

(1973c) "Controls or Competition – What's at Issue? A Comment" (in Notes), *The Review of Economics and Statistics*, 55(4), 524.

(1973d) *A China Passage*. Boston: Houghton Mifflin.

(1974) "Scotland's Greatest Son," *Horizon*, Summer. Reprinted in Galbraith (1979) as "The founding faith: Adam Smith's *Wealth of Nations*."

(1975) *Money, Whence It Came, Where It Went*. Harmondsworth: Penguin.

(1977a) *The Age of Uncertainty*. London: British Broadcasting Corporation.

(1977b) "The bimodal image of the modern economy: remarks upon receipt of the Veblen–Commons Award," *Journal of Economic Issues*, 11(2), 189–200. Reprinted in Galbraith (1979a) as "The Valid Image of the Modern Economy." References are to the reprint.

(1977c) *The Galbraith Reader: From the Works of John Kenneth Galbraith*. Ipswich, MA: Gambit.

(1978a) "On Post Keynesian economics," *Journal of Post Keynesian Economics*, 1(1), 8–11.
(1978b) "The defense of the multinational company," *Harvard Business Review*, March/April. Reprinted in Galbraith (1979a) as "The Multinational Company: How to put your worst foot forward or in your mouth." References are to the reprint.
(1979a) *Annals of an Abiding Liberal*. London: Andre Deutsch.
(1979b) *The Nature of Mass Poverty*. Cambridge, MA: Harvard University Press.
(1981) *A Life in Our Times: Memoirs*. Boston: Houghton Mifflin.
(1983a) *The anatomy of power*. London: Corgi Books.
(1983b) "Joan Robinson: a word of appreciation," *Cambridge Journal of Economics*, 7, 211.
(1983c) *The Voice of the Poor: Essays in Economic and Political Persuasion*. Cambridge, MA: Harvard University Press.
(1985) "Eulogy – a tribute to Sidney Weintraub," *Journal of Post Keynesian Economics*, 7, 508–9.
(1986) *A View from the Stands*. Boston: Houghton Mifflin.
(1987) *A History of Economics: the Past as the Present*. Harmondsworth: Penguin.
(1988) "Time and the New Industrial State" (in The New Industrial State After Twenty Years), *The American Economic Review*, 78(2), Papers and Proceedings of the One-hundredth Annual Meeting of the American Economic Association, 373–76.
(1989) "A look back: affirmation and error," *Journal of Economic Issues*, 23(2), 413–16.
(1990a) *A Short History of Financial Euphoria*. Knoxville, TN: Whittle Direct Books.
(1990b) *A Tenured Professor: A Novel*. Boston: Houghton Mifflin.
(1991) "Economics in the Century Ahead," *The Economic Journal*, 101(404), 41–6.
(1992) *The Culture of Contentment*. Boston: Houghton Mifflin.
(1994a) *A Journey Through Economic Time: A Firsthand View*. Boston: Houghton Mifflin.
(1994b) *The World Economy Since the Wars*. London: Mandarin.
(1996a) "John Kenneth Galbraith," in D. C. Colander and H. Landreth (eds.) *The Coming of Keynesianism to America: Conversations with the founders of Keynesian Economics*. Cheltenham: Edward Elgar.
(1996b) *The Good Society: The Humane Agenda*. Boston: Houghton Mifflin.
(1998) *Letters to Kennedy*. Cambridge, MA: Harvard University Press.
(1999) *Name-dropping: From F.D.R. On*. Boston: Houghton Mifflin.

(2001) *The Essential Galbraith*. Boston: Houghton Mifflin.

(2004) *The Economics of Innocent Fraud: Truth for Our Time*. Boston: Houghton Mifflin.

Galbraith, J. K., Jarrett, H., and Future, R. F. T. (1958) *Perspectives on Conservation: Essays on America's Natural Resources*. Baltimore, MD: Johns Hopkins Press.

Galbraith, James K. (1984) "Galbraith and the theory of the corporation," *Journal of Post Keynesian Economics*, 7(1), 43–60.

(1989) "Trade and the planning system," in Bowles, S., Edwards R., and Shepherd, W. G. (eds.) *Unconventional Wisdom: Essays in honor of John Kenneth Galbraith*. Boston: Houghton Mifflin, 231–56.

(1998) *Created Unequal: The Crisis in American Pay*. New York: The Free Press.

(2001) "The meaning of a war economy," *Challenge*, November–December, 44(6), 5–13.

(2006) *Unbearable Cost: Bush, Greenspan and the Economics of Empire*. New York: Palgrave Macmillan.

(2008a) *The Predator State: How Conservatives Abandoned the Free Market and Why Liberals Should Too*. New York: The Free Press.

(2008b) "The abiding economics of John Kenneth Galbraith," *Review of Political Economy*, 20(4), 491–99.

Galbraith, James K. and Berner, M. (2001) *Inequality and Industrial Change: A Global View*. New York: Cambridge University Press.

Gambs, J. S. (1975) *John Kenneth Galbraith*. Boston: Twayne.

Gatignon, H. and Anderson, E. (1988) "The multinational corporation's degree of control over foreign subsidiaries: an empirical test of a transaction cost explanation," *Journal of Law, Economics, and Organization* 4(2), 305–36.

Gerrard, W. J. (1989) *Theory of the Capitalist Economy: Towards a Post-Classical Synthesis*. Oxford: Basil Blackwell.

Giddens, A. (2000) *The Third Way and Its Critics*. Cambridge: Polity Press.

Gilbert, R. J. and Katz, M. L. (2001) "An Economist's guide to US v. Microsoft," *Journal of Economic Perspectives*, 15(2), 25–44.

Giles, C. (2006) "Two per cent hold half of world's assets," *Financial Times*, December 5.

Gintis, H. (1972) "Consumer behavior and the concept of sovereignty: Explanations of social decay" (in The Future of Consumer Sovereignty), *American Economic Review*, 62(2), 267–78.

Glantz, S., Slade, J., Bero, L., Hanauer, P., and Barnes, D. (1996) *The Cigarette Papers*. Berkeley CA: University of California Press.

Godley, W. and McCarthy, G. (1998) "Fiscal policy will matter," *Challenge*, January–February, 41(1), 38–54.

Godley, W. (2000) "Drowning in Debt," *Policy Notes*, 2000/6, Jerome Levy Economics Institute.

Gold, D. (2008) "How much defense can we afford?" *Challenge*, 51(5), September–October, 65–9.

Gold, M. (2003) M-Eatless. Petersfield, UK: Compassion in World Farming.

Goodfriend, M. (2004) "Monetary policy in the new neo-classical nynthesis: a primer" *Economic Quarterly*. Federal Reserve Bank of Richmond, Summer, 21–45.

Goozner, M. (2004) *The $800 Million Pill: The Truth Behind the Cost of New Drugs*. Berkeley, CA: University of California Press

Gordon, S. (1968) "The close of the Galbraithian system," *Journal of Political Economy*, 76(4), 635–44.

(1969) "The Galbraithian system: Rejoinder," *Journal of Political Economy*, 76(4), 635–44.

Graham, A. (2008) "If China spends its trillions, recession could be averted," *Guardian*, October 15, 28.

Granovetter, M. (1998) "Coase revisited: business groups in the modern economy," in Dosi, G., Teece, D. J. and Chytry, J. (eds.) *Technology, Organization and Competitiveness: Perspectives on industrial and corporate change*. Oxford: Oxford University Press.

Grant, R. R. (1997) "Measuring corporate power: assessing the options," *Journal of Economic Issues*, 31(2), 453–60.

Greider, K. (2003) *The Big Fix: How the Pharmaceutical Industry Rips Off American Consumers*. New York: PublicAffairs.

Gruber, J. (2001) "Tobacco at the crossroads: the past and future of smoking regulation in the United States," *Journal of Economic Perspectives*, 15(2), 193–212.

Gruber, J. and Koszegi, B. (2001) "Is addiction rational? Theory and evidence," *Quarterly Journal of Economics*, 116(4), 1261–305.

Gruchy, A. G. (1984) "Uncertainty, Indicative Planning, and Industrial Policy," in M. R. Tool (ed.) *An Institutionalist Guide to Economics and Public Policy*. Armonk, NY: M.E. Sharpe.

Guardian (2001) "George Bush's favours to Big Business – all the president's businessmen," *Guardian*, April 27.

(2008) "Lord Turner: Our Touch will be heavier. We have to focus on the risks," *Guardian*, October 17, 6–7.

Gunter, B. and Furnham, A. (1992) *Consumer Profiles: An Introduction to Psychographics*. New York: Routledge.

Hafez, N. and Ling, P. (2005) "How Philip Morris built Marlboro into a global brand for young adults: implications for international tobacco control," *Tobacco Control*, 14, August, 262–71.

Hall, P. (1994) *Innovation, economics and evolution: Theoretical perspectives on changing technology in economic systems.* London: Harvester Wheatsheaf.

Hamilton, G. G. and Feenstra, R. C. (1998) "Varieties of hierarchies and markets: an introduction," in G. Dosi, D. J. Teece, and J. Chytry (eds.) *Technology, Organization and Competitiveness: Perspectives on Industrial and Corporate Change.* Oxford: Oxford University Press.

Harcourt, G. C. (1980) "Discussion: of Tarshis (1980)," *American Economic Review*, 70(2).

(1987) "The legacy of Keynes: theoretical methods and unfinished business," in D. A. Reese (ed.) *The Legacy of Keynes*, Nobel Conference XXII, Harper & Row, San Francisco. Reprinted in C. Sardoni (ed.) (1992) *On Political Economists and Modern Political Economy: Selected essays of G. C. Harcourt.* London: Routledge.

Harcourt, G. C. and Kenyon, P. (1976) "Pricing and the investment decision," *Kyklos*, 29, 449–77. Reprinted in C. Sardoni (ed.) (1992) *On Political Economists and Modern Political Economy: Selected essays of G. C. Harcourt.* London: Routledge.

Hargreaves Heap, S. P. (1986–87) "Risk and culture: a missing link in the Post Keynesian tradition," *Journal of Post Keynesian Economics*, 9(2), Winter, 267–78.

Harrington, M. (1962) *The Other America.* Baltimore, MD: Penguin Books.

Harris, G. (2008) "Top Psychiatrist Didn't Report Drug Makers' Pay," *New York Times*, October 8, www.nytimes.com/2008/10/04/health/policy/04drug.html. Accessed April 9, 2009.

Harris, G. and Carey, B. (2008) "Researchers fail to reveal full drug pay," *New York Times*, June 8, www.nytimes.com/2008/06/08/us/08conflict.html?_r=1&partner=rssnyt. Accessed April 9, 2009.

Harris, G. and Roberts, J. (2007) "Doctors' ties to drug makers are put on close view," *New York Times*, March 21, www.nytimes.com/2007/03/21/us/21drug.html. Accessed April 9, 2009.

Hawkins, D. I., Best, R. J., and Coney, K. A. (1998) *Consumer Behavior: Building Marketing Strategy*, 7th edn. Burr Ridge, IL: Irwin/McGraw-Hill.

Hayek, F. A. von, (1961) "The non sequitur of the Dependence Effect," *Southern Economic Journal*, 27, 346–48.

Heath, R. P. (1995) "Psychographics: Qu'est-ce que c'est?" *American Demographics: Marketing Tools Supplement*, 74–9.

(1996) "The frontiers of psychographics," *American Demographics*, 18, 38–43.

Heffernan, W., Hendrickson, M., and Gronski, R. (1999) *Consolidation in the Food and Agriculture System* Report to the National Farmers Union, http://web.greens.org/s-r/gga/heffernan.html. Accessed April 5, 2009.

Heilbroner, R. (1989) "Rereading *The Affluent Society*", *Journal of Economic Issues*, June, 367–77.

Heilbroner, R. and Milberg, W. (1995) *The Crisis of Vision in Modern Economic Thought*. Cambridge: Cambridge University Press.

Hennart, J-F. (1982) *A Theory of the Multinational Enterprise*. Ann Arbor: University of Michigan Press.

(1991) "The transaction cost theory of the multinational enterprise," in Pitelis, C. N. and Sugden, R. (eds.) *The Nature of the Transnational Firm*, 1st edn. London: Routledge.

Herman, E. S. and Chomsky, N. (1998) *Manufacturing Consent: The Political Economy of the Mass Media*. London: Vintage.

Hession, C. H. (1972) *John Kenneth Galbraith and His Critics*. New York: New American Library.

Hipple, F. S. (1990). "The measurement of international trade related to multinational companies," *American Economic Review*, 80(5), 1263–70.

Hodgson, G. M. (1986) "Behind methodological individualism," *Cambridge Journal of Economics*, 10(3), September.

Hodgson, G. M. (1988) *Economics and Institutions*. Oxford: Polity Press.

(1989) "Post Keynesianism and institutionalism: the missing link," in J. Pheby (ed.) *New Directions in Post Keynesian Economics*. Aldershot: Edward Elgar.

(1996) "Corporate culture and the nature of the firm," in J. Groenewegen (ed.) *Transaction Cost Economics and Beyond*. Boston: Kluwer, 249–69.

(1997) "The ubiquity of habits and rules," *Cambridge Journal of Economics*, 21(6), November, 663–84.

(1998) "The approach of institutional economics," *Journal of Economic Literature*, 36(1), March, 166–92.

(1999) *Economics and Utopia: Why the Learning Economy Is Not the End of History*. London: Routledge.

(2001a) *How economics forgot history: The problem of historical specificity in social science*. London: Routledge.

(2001b) "From Veblen to Galbraith: What is the essence of institutional economics," in M. Keaney (ed.) *Economist with a Public Purpose: Essays in Honour of John Kenneth Galbraith*. London: Routledge.

(2003) "The hidden persuaders: institutions and individuals in economic theory," *Cambridge Journal of Economics*, 27(2), 159–75.

(2004) *The Evolution of Institutional Economics: Agency, Structure and Darwinism in American Institutionalism*. London: Routledge.

(2006) *Economics in the Shadows of Darwin and Marx: Essays on Institutional Themes*. Cheltenham: Edward Elgar.

(2007) "Meanings of methodological individualism," *Journal of Economic Methodology*, 14(2), June, 211–26.

Hofstadter, R. (1944) *Social Darwinism in American Thought*. Boston: Beacon.

Holmstrom, B. and Kaplan, S. N. (2001) "Corporate governance and merger activity in the United States," *Journal of Economic Perspectives*, 15(2), 121–44.

Holt, R. P. F. and Pressman, S. (eds.) (2001) *The New Guide to Post Keynesian Economics*. London: Routledge.

Home Affairs Committee (2009) *Knife Crime: Seventh Report of Session 2008–09, House of Commons, HC 112-I*. London: The Stationery Office.

Horst, T. (1972) "Firm and industry determinants of the decision to invest abroad: an empirical study," *Review of Economics and Statistics*, 54, 258–66.

Humbert, M. (2005) "With John Kenneth Galbraith: a 'political and moral philosophy' conception to study economic activities," *Journal of Post Keynesian Economics*, 28(1), 47–64.

Hymer, S. and Rowthorn, R. (1970) "Multinational corporations and international oligopoly: the non-American challenge," in K. P. Kindleberger (ed.) *The International Corporation*. Cambridge, MA: MIT Press.

Hymer, S. H. (1970) "The Efficiency (Contradictions) of Multinational Corporations," *American Economic Review*, Papers and Proceedings, 60(2), May, 441–8.

(1976) *The International Operations of National Firms*. Cambridge, MA: MIT Press.

IMS Health (2001) US Leading Products by DTC Spend. January 2000 – December 2000, IMS Health Incorporated. www.imshealth.com/public/structure/dispcontent/1,2779,1203–1203–143221,00.html.

Inderst, R. and Mueller, H. M. (2006) "CEO Compensation and Private Information: An Optimal Contracting Perspective," *Working Paper*.

Jacoby, R. (1987) *The Last Intellectuals: American Culture in the Age of Academe*. New York: Basic Books.

Jensen, M. C. (1986) "The agency costs of free cash flow: corporate finance and takeovers," *American Economic Review*, 76(2), May,

323–9. Reprinted in M. Wright (ed.) (1994), *Management Buy-Outs*, part of the series *International Library of Management*, K. Bradley (ed.). UK and Vermont: Dartmouth Publishing, 3–9.

(1988) "Takeovers: their causes and consequences," *Journal of Economic Perspectives*, 2(1), Winter, 21–48. Reprinted in P. A. Gaughan, (ed.) (1993), *Readings in Mergers and Acquisitions*. Oxford: Blackwell.

(1989) "Eclipse of the public corporation," *Harvard Business Review*, September–October, 5, 831–80. Reprinted in D. A. Oesterle (ed.) (1991) *The Law of Mergers, Acquisitions, and Reorganizations*. St. Paul, MN: West.

(1993) "The modern industrial revolution, exit, and the failure of internal control systems," *The Journal of Finance*, 48(2), July, 831–80. Reprinted in the *Journal of Applied Corporate Finance*, Winter 1994, 6(4), and in *Finanzmarkt und Portfolio Management* (January 1993), 7(3). Reprinted in M. C. Jensen (2000) *Theory of the Firm: Governance, Residual Claims, and Organizational Forms*. Cambridge, MA: Harvard University Press.

Johnson, C. (1982) *MITI and the Japanese Miracle*. Stanford, CA: Stanford University Press.

Johnson, H. G. (1960) "The Consumer and Madison Avenue," *Current Economic Comment*, 22(3), 3–10.

Joskow, P. L. (1985) "Vertical integration and long-term contracts: the case of coal-burning electric generating plants," *Journal of Law, Economics, and Organization*, 1(1), 33–80.

(1987) "Contract duration and relationship specific investments: empirical evidence from coal markets," *American Economic Review* 77(1), 168–85.

(1988) "Asset specificity and the structure of vertical relationships: empirical evidence," *Journal of Law, Economics, and Organization* 4(1), 95–117.

(1991) "The role of transaction cost economics in antitrust and public utility regulatory policies," *Journal of Law, Economics, and Organization*, 7, September, 53–83.

Judt, T. (2005) "Europe vs. America," *The New York Review of Books*, 52(2), February 10.

Kahn, J. (1974) *The Political Economy of Thorstein Veblen and John Kenneth Galbraith*, Humanities Honors Program, Stanford University.

Kaldor, N. (1950) "The economic aspects of advertising," *Review of Economic Studies*, 18, 1–27.

(1970) "The case for regional policies," *Scottish Journal of Political Economy*, 17(3), 337–48.

(1972) "The irrelevance of equilibrium economics," *Economic Journal*, 82.

(1978) *Further Essays on Economic Theory*. London: Duckworth.

(1982) *The Scourge of Monetarism*. Oxford: Oxford University Press.

(1983) "Keynesian Economics after fifty years," in Worswick, D. and Tevithick, J. (eds.) *Keynes and the Modern World*, Cambridge: Cambridge University Press.

(1985) *Economics without Equilibrium*. Cardiff: University College Press.

Kalecki, M. (1935) "A macrodynamic theory of business cycles," *Econometrica*, 3(3), 327–44.

(1939) *Essays in the Theory of Economic Fluctuations*. London: Allen & Unwin.

(1940) "The supply curve of an industry under imperfect competition," *Review of Economic Studies*, 7, 91–112.

(1943) "Political aspects of full employment," *Political Quarterly*, 14(4), 322–31.

(1954) *Theory of Economic Dynamics*. London: Allen & Unwin.

(1968) "Trend and the business cycle," *Economic Journal*, 78, 263–76.

(1971) *Selected Essays on the Dynamics of the Capitalist Economy*. Cambridge: Cambridge University Press.

(1990) *Capitalism: Business Cycles and Full Employment Collected Works*, vol. I, ed. J. Osiatynski. Oxford: Clarendon Press.

Kay, N. M. (1984) *The Emergent Firm: Knowledge, Ignorance and Surprise in Economic Organisation*. London: Macmillan.

(1997) *Pattern in Corporate Evolution*. Oxford: Oxford University Press.

(2000) "The resource-based approach to multinational enterprise" in C. N. Pitelis and R. Sugden (eds.) *The Nature of the Transnational Firm*, 2nd edn. London: Routledge.

Kaysen, C. (1957) "The social significance of the Modern Corporation," *American Eocnomic Review*, 47(20).

(1965) "Another view of Corporate Capitalism," *Quarterly Journal of Economics*, 79(1).

Keaney, M. (2001) (ed.) *Economist with a Public Purpose: Essays in Honor of John Kenneth Galbraith*. London: Routledge.

Kennedy, P. (2009) "Read the big four to know capital's fate," *Financial Times*, March 12, 2009. http://blogs.ft.com/capitalismblog/. Accessed March 15, 2009

Kenyon, P. (1980) "Discussion: of Tarshis (1980)," *American Economic Review*, 70(2).

Kessler, D. (2001) *A Question of Intent: A Great American Battle with a Deadly Industry*. New York: Public Affairs.

Kesting, S. (2005) "Countervailing, conditioned, and contingent – the power theory of John Kenneth Galbraith," *Journal of Post Keynesian Economics*, 28(1), 1–25.

Keynes, J. M. (1921) *Treatise on Probability*. London: Macmillan.

(1919) *The Economic Consequences of the Peace*. London: Macmillan.

(1926) *The End of Laissez Faire*, London: Hogarth Press. Reprinted in J. M. Keynes (1973) *The Collected Writings of J. M. Keynes*, vol. IX, *Essays in Persuasion*. London: Macmillan, for the Royal Economic Society.

(1930) *A Treatise on Money*, vol. II. London: Macmillan.

(1931) *Essays in Persuasion*. Reprinted in J. M. Keynes (1972) *The Collected Writings of J. M. Keynes*, vol. IX. London: Macmillan, for the Royal Economic Society.

(1932) *Essays in Persuasion*. New York: Harcourt, Brace.

(1936) *The General Theory of Employment, Interest and Money*. New York: Harcourt Brace.

(1937) "The General Theory of Employment," *Quarterly Journal of Economics*, 51(2), 209–23.

(1940) *How to Pay for the War*. London: Macmillan.

(1971) *A Tract on Monetary Reform*, vol. IV, *The Collected Writings of John Maynard Keynes*. London: Macmillan, for the Royal Economic Society.

(1972a) *The Collected Writings of J. M. Keynes*, vol. IX, *Essays in Persuasion*. London: Macmillan, for the Royal Economic Society.

(1972b) *The Collected Writings of J. M. Keynes*, vol. X, *Essays in Biography*. London: Macmillan, for the Royal Economic Society.

(1973) *The Collected Writings of J. M. Keynes*, vol. XIV, *The General Theory and After: Part II Defense and Development*. London: Macmillan, for the Royal Economic Society.

(1980) *Activities 1940–1944: Shaping the Post-War World: The clearing union, The Collected Writings of John Maynard Keynes*, vol. XXV. London: Macmillan, for the Royal Economic Society.

(1981) *The Collected Writings of J. M. Keynes*, vol. XIX, *Activities 1922–1929: The Return to Gold and Industrial Policy, part II*. London: Macmillan, for the Royal Economic Society.

(1982) *The Collected Writings of J. M. Keynes*, vol. XXI, *Activities 1931–1939: World Crises and Policies in Britain and America*. London: Macmillan, for the Royal Economic Society.

Kindleberger, C. P. (1969) *American Business Abroad.* New Haven, CT: Yale University Press.

(2002) "Stephen Hymer and the multinational corporation," *Contributions to Political Economy*, 21, Special Issue, 5–7.

(1973) *The World in Depression 1929–1939.* London: Allen Lane.

King, J. (2002) *A History of Post Keynesian Economics Since 1936.* Cheltenham: Edward Elgar.

Klaes, M. (2000a) "The history of the concept of transaction costs: neglected aspects," *Journal of the History of Economic Thought*, 22(2), 191–216.

(2000b) "The birth of the concept of transaction costs: neglected aspects," *Industrial and Corporate Change*, 9(4), 567–93.

(2004) "Evolutionary economics: in defense of vagueness," *Journal of Economic Methodology*, 11(3), 359–76.

Klein, B. (2001) "The Microsoft case: what can a dominant firm do to defend its market position?" *Journal of Economic Perspectives*, 15(2), 45–62.

Klein, N. (1999) *No Logo: Taking Aim at the Brand Bullies.* New York: Picador.

Klein, P. A. (1992) "Institutionalists, radical economists, and class," *Journal of Economic Issues,* June, 535–44.

Kluger, R. (1996) *Ashes to Ashes: America's Hundred-year Cigarette War, the Public Health, and the Unabashed Triumph of Philip Morris.* New York: Alfred A Knopf.

Knight, F. H. (1921) *Risk, Uncertainty and Profit.* Boston: Houghton Mifflin. Reprinted (1946). London: London School of Economics.

(1924) "The limitations of scientific method in economics," in R. Tugwell (ed.) *Trend of Economics*, 229–67. Reprinted in Knight (1935).

(1935) *The Ethics of Competition and Other Essays.* New York: Harper.

Knight, K. G. and Sugden, R. (1990) "Efficiency, economic democracy and company law," in K. Cowling and R. Sugden (eds.) *A New Economic Policy for Britain: Essays on the Development of Industry.* Manchester: Manchester University Press.

Knoedler, J. T. (1995) "Transaction cost theories of business enterprise from Williamson and Veblen: convergence, divergence, and some evidence," *Journal of Economic Issues*, June, 385–95.

Kregel, J. A. (1998a) "Keynes and the new Keynesians on market competition," in R. J. Rotheim (ed.) *New Keynesian Economics/Post Keynesian Alternatives.* London: Routledge, 39–50.

Krugman, P. (1979) "Increasing returns, monopolistic competition, and international trade'" *Journal of International Economics*, 9, 469–79.

(1994) *Peddling Prosperity: Economic Sense and Nonsense in the Age of Diminished Expectations*. New York: Norton.

(1998) "Knowing one's place: the role of formalism in economics," *Economic Journal*, 108(451), 1829–1836.

(2002) "For richer," *New York Times Magazine*, October 20. http://query.nytimes.com/gst/fullpage.html?res=9505EFD9113AF933A15753C1A9649C8B63. Accessed October 25, 2008.

(2005a) "Free to choose obesity?" *New York Times*, www.nytimes.com/2005/07/08/opinion/08krugman.html. Accessed December 30, 2008.

(2005b) "Is fiscal policy poised for a comeback?" *Oxford Review of Economic Policy*, 21(4), 515–23.

(2005c) "Drugs, Devices and Doctors," *New York Times*, December 16, 2005. http://select.nytimes.com/2005/12/16/opinion/16krugman.html?_r=1&sq=Drugs,%20Devices%20and%20Doctors&st=nyt&oref=slogin&scp=1&pagewanted=print. Accessed March 10, 2009.

(2006) "Our sick society," *New York Times*, http://select.nytimes.com/2006/05/05/opinion/05krugman.html. Accessed December 30, 2008.

(2007) *The Conscience of a Liberal*. New York: Norton.

(2008a) "Gordon Does Good," *New York Times*, October 12, www.nytimes.com/2008/10/13/opinion/13krugman.html. Accessed October 26, 2008.

(2008b) "Let's Get Fiscal," *New York Times*, October 16, www.nytimes.com/2008/10/17/opinion/17krugman.html. Accessed October 26, 2008.

(2008c) *The Return of Depression Economics and the Crisis of 2008*. London: Penguin.

(2009) "How Did Economists Get It So Wrong?," *New York Times*, The Times Magazine, September 2. www.nytimes.com/2009/09/06/magazine/06Economic-t.html. Accessed September 13, 2009.

Kuhn, T. S. (1970) *The Structure of Scientific Revolutions*, 2nd edn., enlarged. Chicago: University of Chicago Press.

Kuhnen, C. M. and Zwiebel, J. H. (2007) "Executive Pay, Hidden Compensation and Managerial Entrenchment," *Working Paper*.

Lamdin, D. J. (2008) "Galbraith on advertising, credit and consumption: a retrospective and empirical investigation with policy implications," *Review of Political Economy*, 20(4), 595–611.

Lancaster, K. (1966) "A new approach to consumer theory," *Journal of Political Economy*, 74, 132–57.

Lane, C. (2007) *Shyness: How Normal Behavior Became a Sickness.* New Haven, CT: Yale University Press.

Lang, T. (2006) "Food, the law and public health: Three models of the relationship," *Public Health*, 120, October, 30–41.

(2003) "Food industrialisation and food power: implications for food governance," *Development Policy Review*, 21(5), 555–68.

(2004) *Food Industrialisation and Food Power: Implications for food governance*, International Institute for Environment and Development, IIED gatekeeper series no. 114, 1–25.

(2007) "Functional foods," *British Medical Journal*, 334 (1015–16). May 19.

Lang, T. and Clutterbuck, C. (1991) *P is for Pesticides.* London: Ebury.

Lang, T. and Heasman, M. (2004) *Food Wars: The Global Battle for Mouths, Minds and Markets.* London: Earthscan.

Langlois, R. N. (1984) "Internal organisation in a dynamic context: some theoretical considerations," in M. Jussawalla and H. Ebenfield (eds.) *Communication and Information Economics.* Amsterdam: North-Holland.

(1988) "Economic change and the boundaries of the firm," *Journal of Institutional and Theoretical Economics*, 144, 635–57.

(1992) "Orders and Organizations: Toward an Austrian Theory of Social Institutions," in B. Caldwell and S. Boehm, (eds.) *Austrian Economics: Tensions and New Directions.* Boston: Kluwer.

(1995a) "Transaction costs, production costs and the passage of time," in S. G. Medema (ed.) *Coasean Economics.* Dordrecht: Kluwer. (Page references are to the mimeo.)

(1995b) "Do firms plan?," *Constitutional Political Economy*, 6, 247–61.

Langlois, R. N. and Everett, M. (1992) "Complexity, genuine uncertainty, and the economics of organisation," *Human Systems Management*, 11, 67–76.

Langlois, R. N. and Foss, N. J. (1998) "Capabilities and governance: the rebirth of production in the theory of economic organization," *KYKLOS*, 52, 201–18.

Langlois, R. N. and Robertson, P. (1995) *Firms, Markets and Economic Change.* London: Routledge.

Laperche, B. and Uzunidis, D. (2005) *John Kenneth Galbraith and the Future of Economics.* London: Palgrave Macmillan.

Laperche, B., Galbraith, James K., and Uzunidis, D. (2006) *Innovation, Evolution and Economic Change: New Ideas in the Tradition of Galbraith.* Cheltenham: Edward Elgar.

Lavoie, M. (1992) *Foundations of Post-Keynesian Economic Analysis.* Aldershot: Edward Elgar.

(1994) "A Post Keynesian approach to consumer choice," *Journal of Post Keynesian Economics*, 16(4), 539–62.

(1996) "Horizontalism, structuralism, liquidity preference and the principle of increasing risk," *Scottish Journal of Political Economy*, 43(3).

(2003) "A primer on endogenous credit money," in L-P. Rochon and S. Rossi (eds.), *Modern Theories of Money*. Cheltenham: Edward Elgar.

Lawson, T. (1989) "Abstraction, tendencies and stylized facts: a realist approach to economic analysis," *Cambridge Journal of Economics*, 13(2), March.

(1995) "A realist perspective on contemporary 'economic theory'," *Journal of Economic Issues*, 29(1), March, 1–32.

(1997) *Economics and Reality*. London and New York: Routledge.

(2003) *Reorientating Economics*. London and New York: Routledge.

Lazonick, W. (1991) *Business Organization and the Myth of the Market Economy*. Cambridge: Cambridge University Press.

Leathers, C. G. and Evans, J. C. (1973) "Thorstein Veblen and the New Industrial State," *History of Political Economy*, 5, 420–37.

Leathers, C. G. and Raines, J. P. (2008) "John Kenneth Galbraith's contributions to the theory and analysis of speculative financial markets," *Review of Political Economy*, 20(4), 551–68.

Leavell, N. (1999) "The low tar lie," *Tobacco Control*, 8, Winter, 433–37.

Lee, F. S. (1988) "A new dealer in agriculture: G. C. Means and the writing of industrial prices," *Review of Social Economy*, 46.

(1989) "G. C. Means's doctrine of administered prices," *Thames Papers in Political Economy*, Summer. Reprinted in P. Arestis and Y. Kitromilides (eds.) (1990) *Theory and Policy in Political Economy: Essays in Pricing Distribution and Growth*. Cheltenham: Edward Elgar.

(1990) "The modern corporation and Gardiner Mean's critique of neoclassical economics," *Journal of Economic Issues*, 24(3), 673–93.

(1994) "From Post Keynesian to historical price theory, part I: facts, theory and empirically grounded pricing model," *Review of Political Economy*, 6(3).

(1998) *Post Keynesian Price Theory*. Cambridge: Cambridge University Press.

Lee, F. S. (ed.) (2000a) "On the genesis of Post Keynesian economics: Alfred S. Eichner, Joan Robinson and the founding of Post Keynesian economics," in (2000) *Research in the History of Economic Thought and Methodology*, vol. XVIII-C, *Twentieth-Century Economics*. JAI, Elsevier.

Lee, F. S. (2000b) "The social history of Post Keynesian economics in America, 1971–1995," *Journal of Post Keynesian Economics*, 23(1), 141–62.

Lee, F. S., Irving-Lesman, J., Earl, P., and Davies, J. (1986) "P. W. S. Andrews' Theory of Competitive Oligopoly: a new interpretation," *British Review of Economic Issues*, 8(19), 13–40.

Levy, S. (1959) "Symbols for sale," *Harvard Business Review*, 37, July/August: 117–19.

Loasby, B. J. (1976) *Choice, Complexity and Ignorance: An Enquiry into Economic Theory and Practise of Decision Making*. Cambridge: Cambridge University Press.

Lublin, J. S. and Thurm, S. (2006) "Behind soaring executive pay, decades of failed restraints: instead of damping rewards, disclosure, taxes, options helped push them higher return of golden parachutes," *The Wall Street Journal*, Thursday, October 12, A16.

Lucas Jr., R. E. (1978) "On the size distribution of business firms," *The Bell Journal of Economics*, 9(2), 508–23.

Lyson, T. A. and Raymer, A. L. (2000) "Stalking the wily multinational: power and control in the US food system," *Agriculture and Human Values*, 17(2), June, 199–208.

MacKenzie, R., Collin, J., and Lee, K. (2003) *The Tobacco Industry Documents: An Introductory Handbook and Resource Guide for Researchers*. London: Centre on Global Change and Health, London School of Hygiene and Tropical Medicine.

Maddison, A. (1992) "A long-run perspective on savings," *Scandanavian Journal of Economics*, 92, 181–96.

(1995a) *Explaining the Economic Performance of Nations: Essays in Time and Space*. London: Edward Elgar.

(1995b) *Monitoring the World Economy, 1820–1992*. Paris: OECD Development Centre.

(2001) *The World Economy: A Millennial Perspective*. Paris: OECD Development Centre.

(2003) *The World Economy: Historical Statistics*. Paris: OECD.

Malcolmson, D. (1984) "Efficient labour organisations: incentives, power and the transaction cost approach," in F. Stephen (ed.) *Firm Organisations and Labour*. London: Macmillan.

Malone, R. and Balbach, E. (2000) "Tobacco industry documents: Treasure trove or quagmire?," *Tobacco Control*, 9, Autumn, 334–38.

Malthus, T. (1798) *An Essay on the Principle of Population as it Affects the Future Improvement of Society, with Remarks on the Speculations of Mr. Godwin, M. Condorcet, and other Writers*. Ann Arbor: University of Michigan Press, 1959.

Management Science Associates (1991) MSA Annual Industry National Volume and Share Trend Summary 820000 910000. Management Science Associates. Lorillard: Bates Number 88917099/7270. http://legacy.library.ucsf.edu/tid/cst90e00.

Marris, R. (1964) *The Economic Theory of Managerial Capitalism.* London: Macmillan.

(1968) "Review of The New Industrial State," *American Economic Review*, 58(1), 240–47.

Marris, R. and Wood, A. (1971) *The Corporate Economy: Growth, Competition, and Innovative Potential.* Cambridge, MA: Harvard University Press.

Marshall, A. (1920) *Principles of Economics.* London: Macmillan.

Martin, J. B. (1976) *Adlai Stevenson of Illinois.* Garden City, New York: Doubleday.

Masten, S. E. and Saussier, S. (2000) "Economics of contracts: an assessment of developments in the empirical literature on contracting," *Revue d'économie industrielle,* 92(2/3), 215–36.

Masten, S. E., Meehan J. W. Jr., and Snyder, E. A. (1989) "Vertical integration in the US auto industry," *Journal of Economic Behavior and Organization*, 12, 265–73.

Masten, S. E., Meehan, J. W. Jr., and Snyder, E. A. (1991) "The costs of organization," *Journal of Law, Economics, and Organization* 7(1), 1–25.

Masten, S. E. (1984) "The organization of production: evidence from the aerospace industry," *Journal of Law and Economics* 27, October, 403–17.

(1996) "Empirical research in transaction cost economics: challenges, progress, directions," in J. Groenewegen (ed.) *Transaction Cost Economics and Beyond.* Boston: Kluwer, 43–64.

Mayo, E. and Nairn, A. (2009) *Consumer Kids: How Big Business is Grooming our Children for Profit.* London: Constable.

McCann-Erickson Inc. (1981) Social Trends among Female Smokers Application to Project Delta. Brown & Williamson: Bates Number 677046078/6107. http://legacy.library.ucsf.edu/tid/wzj13f00.

McCloskey, D. (1994) "Fun in Econ 101: The Surprisingly sensible, never boring words of John Kenneth Galbraith," *Chicago Tribune*, September 25, 4, section 14.

(2000) *Economical Writing.* Prospect Heights, IL: Waveland Press.

(2007) "Creative Destruction vs. the New Industrial State', *Reason, October*, www.reason.com/news/show/122024.html. Accessed May 27, 2009.

McFadzean, F. (1968) *Galbraith and the Planners*. Strathclyde: Strathclyde University Press.

(1977) *The Economics of John Kenneth Galbraith*. London: Centre for Policy Studies.

McGuinness, T. and Cowling, K. (1975) "Advertising and aggregate demand for cigarettes," *European Economic Review*, April.

McManus, J. (1972) "The theory of the multinational firm," in G. Piaquet (ed.) *The Multinational Firm and the Nation State*. London: Macmillan.

Meade, J. E. (1968) "Is 'The New Industrial State' Inevitable?," *Economic Journal*, 78, June, 372–92.

Means, G. C. (1936) "Notes on Inflexible Prices," *American Economic Review*, 26, Supplement.

(1972) "The administered price thesis reconfirmed," *American Economic Review*, 62, 292–306.

Mearman, A. (2002) "To what extent is Veblen an 'Open-Systems Theorist'?," *Journal of Economic Issues*, 36(2), 573–80.

Mercer, H. (1995) *Constructing a Competitive Order: The Hidden History of British Antitrust Policies*. Cambridge: Polity Press.

Meyer, L. H. (2001) "Does money matter?," *Federal Reserve Bank of St. Louis Review*, 83(5), 1–15.

Minsky, H. P. (1975) *John Maynard Keynes*. New York and London: Macmillan.

Minsky, H. P. (1982) *Can It Happen Again?* Armonk, NY: M.E. Sharpe.

(1986) *Stabilizing an Unstable Economy*. New Haven, CT: Yale University Press.

(1992) "The financial instability hypothesis," Working Paper No. 74, Annandale-on-Hudson: The Levy Economics Institute.

(1996) "Uncertainty and the institutional structure of capitalist economies," Working Paper No. 155, Annandale-on-Hudson: The Levy Economics Institute.

(1996) "Uncertainty and the institutional structure of capitalist economies," *Journal of Economic Issues*, 30(2), 357–68.

Mitchell, V. W. (1994) "How to identify psychographic segments: Part 1" *Marketing Intelligence & Planning*, 12(7), 4–10.

Monbiot, G. (2000) *Captive State: The Corporate Takeover of Britain*. London: Macmillan.

(2006) "The denial industry," *Guardian*, Tuesday 19 September 2006, www.guardian.co.uk/environment/2006/sep/19/ethicalliving.g2. Accessed May 27, 2009.

(2007) *Heat: How We Can Stop the Planet Burning*. London: Penguin.

Moore, B. (1988) *Horizontalists and Verticalists*. Cambridge: Cambridge University Press.

Morris, M. D. (1979) *Measuring the Condition of the World's Poor: The Physical Quality of Life Index*. New York: Pergamon.

Mother Jones (2005) "Some like it hot," *Mother Jones*, May/June, www.motherjones.com/environment/2005/05/some-it-hot. Accessed May 7, 2009

Mouawad, J. (2008) "The big thirst," *New York Times, Week in Review*, April 20.

Moynihan, R. (2003a) "The making of a disease: female sexual dysfunction," *British Medical Journal*, 326, 45–7.

(2003b) "Who pays for the pizza? Redefining the relationships between doctors and drug companies. 2: Disentanglement," *British Medical Journal*, 326, 1193–96.

Moynihan, R. and Cassells, A. (2005) *Selling Sickness: How the World's Biggest Pharmaceutical Companies Are Turning Us All into Patients*. London: Nation Books.

Moynihan, R., Heath, I., and Henry, D. (2002) "Selling sickness: the pharmaceutical industry and disease mongering," *British Medical Journal*, 324, 886–91.

Munier, F. and Wang, Z. (2005) "Consumer sovereign and consumption routine: a reexamination of the Galbraithian concept of the dependence effect," *Journal of Post Keynesian Economics*, 28 (1), 65–82.

Munro, C. L. (1977) *The Galbraithian Vision: The Cultural Criticism of John Kenneth Galbraith*. University Press of America.

Murphy, K. J. and Zábojník, J. (2004) "CEO pay and turnover: a market based explanation for recent trends," *American Economic Review* 94, 192–96.

Murray, C. (1984) *Losing Ground: American social policy 1950–1980*. New York: Basic Books.

Myrdal, G. (1939) *Monetary Equilibrium*, translated from the Swedish edition of 1931 and the German edition of 1933. London: Hodge.

(1944) *An American Dilemma*. New York: Harper & Brothers.

(1957) *Economic Theory and Underdeveloped Regions*. London: Duckworth.

(1968) *Asian Drama: An Inquiry into the Poverty of Nations*. New York: Pantheon Books.

(1972) *Against the Stream: Critical Essays in Economics*. New York: Pantheon Books.

(1978) "Institutional Economics," *Journal of Economic Issues*, 12(4), December, 771–84.

Nelson, P. (1970) "Information and consumer behavior," *Journal of Political Economy,* 78(2), 311–29.

(1974) "Advertising as information," *Journal of Political Economy,* 82, August, 729–54.

Nordine, R. (author inferred) (1982) Brand Family Positioning in the Cigarette Market. (Presentation Script). RJ Reynolds: Bates Number 507549813/9843. http://legacy.library.ucsf.edu/tid/gir28c00.

North, D. C. (1981) *Structure and Change in Economic History.* New York: Norton.

(1990) *Institutions, Institutional Change and Economic Performance.* Cambridge: Cambridge University Press.

Obama, B. (2008) "'I'm going to confront this economic crisis,' Obama says," Transcript of first news conference as US President Elect, November 7, http://edition.cnn.com/2008/POLITICS/11/07/obama.conference.transcript/. Accessed November 8, 2008.

OECD (2008a) *Growing Unequal?* Paris: OECD.

(2008b) "Income inequality and poverty rising in most OECD countries," press release, www.oecd.org/document/25/0,3343,en_2649_201185_41530009_1_1_1_1,00.html. Accessed February 3, 2009.

Offen, N., Smith, E., and Malone, R. (2003) "From adversary to target market, the ACT-UP boycott of Philip Morris," *Tobacco Control,* 12, 203–7.

Olson, M. (2000) *Power and Prosperity: Outgrowing Communist and Capitalist Dictatorships.* New York: Basic Books.

Oreskes, N. (2004) "Beyond the ivory tower: the scientific consensus on climate change," *Science*, December 3, 306(5702), 1686.

Ormerod, P. (1994) *The Death of Economics.* London: Faber and Faber.

(2000) "The *Death of Economics* Revisited," Keynote address to the Association of Heterodox Economics, London, June.

Osborn R. N. and Baughn, C. C. (1990) "Forms of interorganizational governance for multinational alliances," *Academy of Management Journal*, 33(3), 503–19.

Ozga, S. A. (1960) "Imperfect markets through lack of knowledge," *Quarterly Journal of Economics,* 74(1), 29–52.

Packard, V. (1957) *The Hidden Persuaders.* London: Longmans, Green.

Palacio-Vera, A. (2005) "The 'modern' view of macroeconomics: some critical reflections," *Cambridge Journal of Economics*, 29(4), 747–67.

Palley, T. (2001) The case against Budget Surpluses, *Challenge*, November–December, 44(6), 13–28.

(2007) "Macroeconomics and monetary policy: competing theoretical frameworks," *Journal of Post Keynesian Economics*, 30(1), 61–78.

Parker, R. (1993) "Can economists save economics?," *The American Prospect*(13), Spring.

(1999) "Early influences on Galbraith's worldview and economics," in H. Sasson (ed.) *Between Friends: Perspectives on John Kenneth Galbraith*. Boston: Houghton Mifflin, 147–59.

(2005) *John Kenneth Galbraith: His Life, His Politics, His Economics*. New York: Farrar, Straus & Giroux.

Patel, R. (2008) *Stuffed and Starved: The Hidden Battle for the World Food System*. London: Portobello Books.

Peach, J. (2008) "Galbraith and the problem of uneven development," *Journal of Economic Issues*, 42, March, 25–35.

Penrose, E. T. (1955) "Research on the business firm: limits to the growth and size of firms," *American Economic Review*, 45, 531–43.

(1956) "Foreign investment and the growth of the firm," *Economic Journal*, 66, 220–35.

(1959) *The Theory of the Growth of the Firm*. London: Macmillan.

(1960) "The theory of the growth of the firm: a case study: the Hercules Powder Company," *Business History Review*, 34, 1–23.

(1968) *The Large International Firm in Developing Countries: The International Petroleum Industry*. London: Allen and Unwin.

Peoples, J. and Sugden, R. (2000) "Divide and rule by transnational corporations," in C. N. Pitelis and R. Sugden (eds.) *The Nature of the Transnational Firm*. London: Routledge.

Perception Research Services (1997) A Qualitative Exploration of the Capri Print Advertising Campaign; #143 24 Fg 697. Brown & Williamson: Bates Number 502030531/0551. http://legacy.library.ucsf.edu/tid/hut02d00.

Peteraf, M. A. (1993) "The cornerstones of competitive advantage: a resource-based view," *Strategic Management Journal*, 14, 179–91.

Petersen, M. (2008) *Our Daily Meds: How the Pharmaceutical Companies Transformed Themselves into Slick Marketing Machines and Hooked the Nation on Prescription Drugs*. Sarah Crichton/Farrar, Straus and Giroux.

Peterson, W. C. (1989) "Market Power: the missing element in Keynesian economics," *Journal of Economic Issues*, 23, 379–91.

Petrick, K. and Sheehan, B. (2002) "Galbraith's management of specific demand." Paper presented at the Seventh International Post-Keynesian Conference, University of Missouri, Kansas City, USA, June 29–July 3, 2002.

Pitelis, C. N. (2000) "A theory of the (growth of the) transnational firm: a Penrosean perspective," *Contributions to Political Economy*, 19, 71–89.

(2002) "Stephen Hymer: life and the political economy of multinational corporate capital," *Contributions to Political Economy*, 21, Special Issue, 9–26.

(2004) "Edith Penrose and the resource-based view of (international) business strategy," *International Business Review*, 13(4), 523–32.

(2007) "Edith Penrose and a learning-based perspective on the MNE and the OLI," *Management International Review*, 47(2), 207–19.

Pitelis, C. N. and Sugden, R. (2000) (eds.) *The Nature of the Transnational firm*, 2nd edn. London: Routledge.

Poire, M. and Sabel, S. (1984) *The Second Industrial Divide*. New York: Basic Books.

Pollay, R. (1995) Faculty Of Commerce UBC, History Of Advertising A. Sackman vs. Liggett Group Inc., Case No. 93 Civ. 4166 (Ads) Report of Richard W. Pollay, the History of Advertising Archives Faculty of Commerce, UBC. Bates No. 2046832662/2666. http://legacy.library.ucsf.edu/tid/jyw06c00.

(1987) "On the value of reflections on the values in the distorted mirror," *Journal of Marketing* 51(3), 104–10.

Pollay, R. and Dewhirst, T. (2002) "The dark side of marketing seemingly Light cigarettes: successful images and failed fact," *Tobacco Control*, 11(Suppl. I.), i18–i31.

Pollin, R. (1991) "Two theories of money supply endogeniety: some empirical evidence," *Journal of Post Keynesian Economics*, 13(3), 366–96.

Porter, M. E. (1990) *The Competitive Advantage of Nations*. London: Macmillan.

Portney, P. R. (2000) "Environmental problems and policy: 2000–2050," *Journal of Economic Perspectives*, 14(1), 199–206.

Pratson, J. (1978) *Perspectives on Galbraith: Conversations and Opinions*. Boston: CBI.

Pressman, S. (2006) *Fifty Major Economists*, 2nd edn. London & New York: Routledge.

(2008) "John Kenneth Galbraith and the Post Keynesian tradition in economics," *Review of Political Economy*, 20(4), 475–89.

Pressman, S. and Scott, R. (2007) "Three million Americans are debt poor," *Dollars and Sense*, July/August, 10–13.

Preston, I. (2002) "A problem ignored, dilution and negation of consumer information by antifactual content," *Journal of Consumer Affairs*, 36(2), 263–83.

(2003) "Dilution and negation of consumer information by antifactual content, proposals for solutions," *Journal of Consumer Affairs*, 36(3), 1–21.

Rajan, R. (2008) "Bankers' pay is deeply flawed," *Financial Times*, January 8.

Ramamurti, R. (2004) "Developing countries and MNEs: Extending and enriching the research agenda," *Journal of International Business Studies*, 35(4): 277–83.

Randall, J. (2008) "Remember 1929 – what seemed to be the end was only the beginning," *Daily Telegraph*, October 9.

Randhawa, M. S. and Galbraith, J. K. (1968) *Indian Painting: The Scene, Themes, and Legends*. Boston: Houghton Mifflin.

Reich, R. (2009) *Supercapitalism: The Battle for Democracy in an Age of Big Business*. London: Faber and Faber.

Reinhardt, U. E. (2004) "An information infrastructure for the pharmaceutical market," *Health Affairs* 23(1), 107–12.

Reisman, D. (1980) *Galbraith and Market Capitalism*. London: Macmillan.

(1990) "Galbraith on ideas and events," *Journal of Economic Issues*, 24, 733–60.

Revkin, A. C. (2005a) "Bush aide softened greenhouse gas links to global warming," *The New York Times*, June 8, 2005, www.nytimes.com/2005/06/08/politics/08climate.html?pagewanted=print. Accessed May 7, 2009.

(2005b) "Former Bush aide who edited reports is hired by Exxon," *The New York Times*, June 15, 2005, http://query.nytimes.com/gst/fullpage.html?res=9D0DE2DF163BF936A25755C0A9639C8B63. Accessed May 7, 2009.

Reynolds, P. (1990) "Kaleckian and Post Keynesian theories of pricing: some extensions and implications," in P. Arestis and Y. Kitromilides (eds.) *Theory and Policy in Political Economy: Essays in Pricing Distribution and Growth*. Cheltenham: Edward Elgar.

Reynolds, T., Whitlark, D., and Wirthlin, R. (2001) "Effectively translating in-depth consumer understanding into communications strategy and advertising practice," in T. J. Reynolds and J. C. Olson (eds.) *Understanding Consumer Decision Making: The Means-End Approach to Marketing and Advertising Strategy*. Mahwah, NJ: Erlbaum.

Richardson, G. B. (1959) "Equilibrium, expectations and information," *Economic Journal*, 69, 223–37.

(1960) *Information and Investment*, 2nd edn. Oxford: Clarendon Press.

(1964) "The limits to a firm's rate of growth," *Oxford Economic Papers*, 16, 9–23.

(1972) "The organization of industry," *Economic Journal*, 82, 883–96.

RJ Reynolds (1981) 1981 (810000) Segmentation Study Presentation. RJ Reynolds: Bates Number 503014504/4665. http://legacy.library.ucsf.edu/tid/bor68d00.

Robertson, D. H. (1923) *The Control of Industry*. Cambridge: Cambridge University Press.

Robinson, J. V. (1933) *Economics of Imperfect Competition*. London: Macmillan.

(1972) "The second crisis of economic theory," *American Economic Review*, Papers and Proceedings, May.

(1974) "History versus equilibrium," in *Contributions to Modern Economics*, Oxford: Blackwell, 1978.

(1977) "What are the questions?," *Journal of Economic Literature*, 15(4), 1318–39.

Rochon L.-P. (2007) "The state of Post Keynesian interest rate policy: where are we and where are we going?," *Journal of Post Keynesian Economics*, 30 (1), 3–12.

Rochon L.-P. and Setterfield, M. (2007) "Interest rates, income distribution, and monetary policy dominance: Post Keynesians and the 'fair rate' of interest," *Journal of Post Keynesian Economics*, 30(1), 13–42.

Roosevelt, F. D. (1933) Inaugural address, Washington, DC. http://avalon.law.yale.edu/20th_century/froos1.asp. Accessed October 25, 2008.

Rosen, S. (1981) "The economics of superstars," *American Economic Review*, 71, 845–58.

(1982) "Authority, control and the distribution of earnings," *Bell Journal of Economics*, 13, 311–23.

Rosenberg, N. (1982) *Inside the Black Box: Technology and Economics*. Cambridge: Cambridge University Press.

(1994) *Exploring the Black Box: Technology, Economics and History*, Cambridge: Cambridge University Press.

Rotheim, R. (1999) "Post Keynesian economics and realist philosophy," *Journal of Post Keynesian Economics*, 22, 71–104.

Rothschild, K. W. (1947) "Price theory and oligopoly," *Economic Journal*. Reprinted in G. J. Stigler and K. E. Boulding (eds.) (1953) *Readings in Price Theory: Selected by a Committee of the American Economic Association*. London: George Allen and Unwin.

Rugman, A. M., and Verbeke, A. (2002) "Location, competitiveness and the multinational enterprise" in A. M. Rugman and T. L. Brewer (eds.) *The Oxford Handbook of International Business*. Oxford: Oxford University Press.

Rutherford, M. H. (1980) "Veblen on owners, managers, and the control of industry," *History of Political Economy*, 12(3), 434–40.

(1984) "Thorstein Veblen and the processes of institutional change," *History of Political Economy*, 16(3), Fall, 331–48.

(1992) "Thorstein Veblen and the problem of the engineers," *International Review of Sociology*, 3, 125–50.

Sachs, J. (2009) "The case for bigger government," *Time*, Thursday, January 8, www.time.com/time/printout/0,8816,1870268,00.html. Accessed March 15, 2009.

Saint-Paul, G. (1997) *Dual Labor Markets: A Macroeconomic Perspective*. Cambridge, MA: MIT Press.

Sample, I. (2007) "Scientists offered cash to dispute climate study," *Guardian*, Friday, 2 February 2007, www.guardian.co.uk/environment/2007/feb/02/frontpagenews.climatechange. Accessed May 7, 2009.

Sampson, P. (1992) "People are people the world over: the case for psychological market segmentation," *Marketing and Research Today*, 20, 134–48.

Samuels, W. J. (1984) "Galbraith on economics as a system of professional belief," *Journal of Post Keynesian Economics*, 7(1), 61–76.

Samuelson, P. (1989) "Galbraith as artist and scientist" in S. Bowles, R. Edwards, and W. G. Shepherd (eds.) *Unconventional Wisdom: Essays in honor of John Kenneth Galbraith*, Boston: Houghton Mifflin, 231–56.

Sasson, H. (ed.) (1999) *Between Friends: Perspectives on John Kenneth Galbraith*. Boston: Houghton Mifflin.

Saul, S. (2008) "Merck wrote drug studies for doctors," *New York Times*, April 16, www.nytimes.com/2008/04/16/business/16vioxx.html. Accessed April 9, 2009.

Sawyer, M. C. (1979) *Theories of the Firm*. London: Weidenfeld and Nicolson.

(1982) *Macroeconomics in Question: The Keynesian-Monetarist Orthodoxies and the Kaleckian Alternative*. Sussex: Wheatsheaf.

(1985a) *The Economics of Industries and Firms*, 2nd edn. London: Croom Helm.

(1985b) *The Economics of Michal Kalecki*. London: Macmillan.

(1988) "Theories of monopoly capitalism," *Journal of Economic Surveys*, 2(1), 47–76.

(1989) *The Challenge of Radical Political Economy*. London: Harvester Wheatsheaf.

(1990) "On the Post Keynesian tradition and industrial economics," *Review of Political Economy*, 2(1), 43–68. Reprinted in M. C. Sawyer, *Unemployment, Imperfect Competition and Macroeconomics: Essays in the Post-Keynesian Tradition*. Aldershot: Edward Elgar.

(1992a) "Keynes's macroeconomic analysis and imperfect competition," in W. J. Gerrard and J. V. Hillard (eds.) *The Philosophy and Economics of J.M. Keynes*. Aldershot: Edward Elgar.

(1992b) "On imperfect competition and macroeconomic analysis," in A. del Monte (ed.) *Recent Advances in the Theory of Industrial Organization*. London: Macmillan. Reprinted in M. C. Sawyer, *Unemployment, Imperfect Competition and Macroeconomics: Essays in the Post-Keynesian tradition*. Aldershot: Edward Elgar.

(1993) "The nature and role of the market," in C. Pitelis (ed.) *Transaction costs, markets and hierarchies*. Oxford: Basil Blackwell.

(1995) *Unemployment, Imperfect Competition and Macroeconomics: Essays in the Post Keynesian Tradition*. Aldershot: Edward Elgar.

(2006) "Inflation targeting and central bank independence: we are all Keynesians now! or are we?," *Journal of Post Keynesian Economics*, 28(4), 639–52.

Scaperlanda, A. (1992) "The European Community and multinational enterprises: lessons in the social control of industry," *Journal of Economic Issues*, June, 421–32.

(1993) "Multinational enterprises and the global market," *Journal of Economic Issues*, June, 605–16.

Scherer, F. M., and Ross, D. (1990) *Industrial Market Structure and Economic Performance*. Boston: Houghton Mifflin.

Schlesinger, A. Jr. (1984) "The political Galbraith," *Journal of Post Keynesian Economics*, 7(1), 7–17.

Schlesinger, A. M. (1999) "Galbraith and politics," in H. Sasson (ed.) *Between Friends: Perspectives on John Kenneth Galbraith*. Boston: Houghton Mifflin.

Schlosser, E. (2002) *Fast Food Nation: What the All-American Meal is Doing to the World*. London: Penguin.

Schmookler, J. (1966) *Invention and Economic Growth*. Cambridge, MA: Harvard University Press.

Schor, J. (1991) *The Overworked American: The Unexpected Decline of Leisure*. New York: Basic Books.

Schuler, D. A., Eden, L., and Lenway, S. (2006) "Multinational corporations through the uneven development lens," in S. Jain and S. Vachani (eds.) *Multinational Corporations and Global Poverty Reduction*. Cheltenham: Edward Elgar, 301–19.

Schultz, T. (1993) *The Economics of Being Poor*. Oxford: Blackwell.

Schumacher, E. F. (1973) *Small is Beautiful*. Harmondsworth: Penguin.

Schumpeter, J. A. (1911) *The Theory of Economic Development*. Cambridge, MA: Harvard University Press.

(1939) *Business Cycles*, vol. I. New York: McGraw-Hill.

(1943) *Capitalism, Socialism and Democracy.* London: Allen and Unwin.

(1949) "English economists and the state-managed economy," *Journal of Political Economy*, LVII(5), 371–82.

(1954) *A History of Economic Analysis*. London: Routledge.

Schurtz, J. (1998) *Summation of Capri Post Shoot Qualitative. P. R. Services.* Brown & Williamson: Bates Number 432201822/1830. http://legacy.library.ucsf.edu/tid/ine11c00.

Scitovsky, T. (1943) "A note on profit maximization," *Review of Economic Studies*, 11.

(1969) *Money and the Balance of Payments*. London: Allen and Unwin.

(1987) "Growth in an affluent society," *Lloyds Bank Review*, January, 1–14.

(2000) *The Joyless Economy*, 2nd edn. Oxford: Oxford University Press.

Scott, R. (2006) "An analysis of credit card default," in R. Holt and S. Pressman (2006) *Empirical Post Keynesian Economics: Looking at the real world.* New York: M. E. Sharpe.

(2007) "Credit card use and abuse: a Veblenian analysis," *Journal of Economic Issues*, 61(2), 567–74.

Seidman, L. (1990) *Saving for America's Economic Future.* Armonk, NY: M.E. Sharpe.

Sen, A. (1999) *Development as Freedom*. New York: Random House.

Shackle, G. L. S. (1939) "Review of: H.S. Dennison and others," *Toward Full Employment, Economic Journal*, 49(193), 100–2.

(1955) *Uncertainty in Economics: and other reflections.* Cambridge: Cambridge University Press.

(1967) *The Years of High Theory: Invention and Tradition in Economic Thought 1926–1939.* Cambridge: Cambridge University Press.

(1972) *Epistemics and Economics.* Cambridge: Cambridge University Press.

Shamasunder, B. and Bero, L. (2002) "Financial ties and conflicts of interest between pharmaceutical and tobacco companies," *JAMA*, 288, 738–44.

Shapiro, N. (1997) "Imperfect competition and Keynes," in Harcourt, G. C. and Riach, P. (eds.) *General Theory "Second Edition".* London: Routledge, 83–92.

Sharpe, M. E. (1973) *John Kenneth Galbraith and the Lower Economics.* London: Macmillan.

Shiller, R. (2005) *Irrational Exuberance*, 2nd edn. Princeton, NJ: Princeton University Press.

(2006) "The rising wealth of nations," *Project Syndicate*, www.project-syndicate.org/commentary/shiller42. Accessed October 28, 2008.

(2009) "A failure to control the animal spirits," *Financial Times*, March 8, www.ft.com/cms/s/0/453e55ca-0c0c-11de-b87d-0000779fd2ac.html. Accessed March 15, 2009.

Simon, H. (1955) "A behavioral model of rational choice," *Journal of Political Economy*, 69, 99–118.

Simon, H. A. (1957) *Models of Man: Social and Rational.* New York: Wiley.

(1959) "Theories of decision-making in economics," *American Economic Review*, 49, 253–83. Reprinted in P. E. Earl (ed.) (1988) *Behavioural Economics*, vol. 1. Aldershot: Edward Elgar.

(1961) *Administrative Behaviour*, 2nd edn. New York: The Free Press.

(1972) "Theories of bounded rationality," in C. B. McGuire and R. Radner (eds.) *Decision and Organisation*. London: North-Holland.

(1976) "From substantive to procedural rationality," in S. Latis (ed.) *Method and Appraisal in Economics*. Cambridge: Cambridge University Press.

(1979) "Rational decision making in business organisation," *American Economic Review*, 69, September, 493–513.

Skidelsky, R. (1992) *John Maynard Keynes*, vol. II, *The Economist as Saviour, 1920–1937.* London: Macmillan.

Smith, R. J. and Birnbaum, J. H. (2007) "Drug Bill demonstrates lobby's pull: Democrats feared industry would stall bigger changes," *Washington Post*, January 12, A01.

Smithin, J. (2007) "A real interest rate rule for monetary policy?," *Journal of Post Keynesian Economics*, 30(1), 101–18.

Snowdon, B. and Vane, H. R. (2005) *Modern Macroeconomics: Its Origins, Development and Current State*. Cheltenham: Edward Elgar.

Solow, R. M. (1967) "The New Industrial State, or son of affluence?", *The Public Interest* (9).

(2005) "Rethinking fiscal policy," *Oxford Review of Economic Policy*, 21(4), 509–14.

Sombart, W. (1913) *Der Bourgeois: zur Geistesgeschichte des modernen Wirtschaftsmenschen*. Munich and Leipzig.

Spencer, D. A. (2000a) "Braverman and the contribution of labour process analysis to the critique of capitalist production – twenty-five years on," *Work Employment and Society*, 14(2), 223–43.

(2000b) "The demise of radical political economics? An essay on the evolution of a theory of capitalist production," *Cambridge Journal of Economics*, 24(5), 543–64.

(2008) *The Political Economy of Work*. London: Routledge.

Sraffa, P. (1926) "The laws of return under competitive conditions," *Economic Journal*, 36.

Stanfield, J. R. (1973) *The Economic Surplus and Neo-Marxism*. Lexington, MA: Lexington Books.

(1979) *Economic Thought and Social Change*. Carbondale and Edwardsville: Southern Illinois University Press.

(1983) "The affluent society after twenty-five years," *Journal of Economic Issues*, September, 589–607.

(1989) "Veblenian and Neo-Marxian perspectives on the cultural crisis of late capitalism," *Journal of Economic Issues*, September, 717–34.

(1990) "Keynesianism, monetarism, and the crisis of the state: a review article," *Journal of Economic Issues*, December, 1139–46.

(1991) "The dichotomized state," *Journal of Economic Issues*, September, 765–80.

(1994) *Economics, Power and Culture: Essays in the Development of Radical Institutionalism*. London: Macmillan.

(1995) "Institutions and the significance of relative prices," *Journal of Economic Issues*, June, 459–66.

(1996) *John Kenneth Galbraith*. London: Macmillan.

(2001) "The useful economist," in M. Keaney (ed.) *Economist with a Public Purpose: Essays in Honour of John Kenneth Galbraith*. London: Routledge.

Stanfield, J. R. and Carroll, M. (1997) "The monopoly capital school and original institutionalist economics," *Journal of Economic Issues*, 31(2), 481–89.

Stanfield, J. R. and Stanfield, J. B. (1997) "Where has love gone? Reciprocity, redistribution, and the nurturance gap," *The Journal of Socio-Economics*, 26(2), 111–26.

Stanfield, J. R. and Stanfield, J. B. (eds.) (2004) *Interviews with John Kenneth Galbraith*. Jackson: University Press of Mississippi.

Stanfield, J. R. and Wrenn, M. (2005) "John Kenneth Galbraith and original institutional economics," *Journal of Post Keynesian Economics*, 28(1), 26–45.

Steindl, J. (1945) *Small and Big Business: Economic Problems of the Size of Firms*. Oxford: Blackwell.

(1952) *Maturity and Stagnation in American Capitalism*. Oxford: Blackwell.

Stern, N. (2007) *The Economics of Climate Change: The Stern Review*. Cambridge: Cambridge University Press.

Stigler, G. J. (1954) "The economist plays with blocs," *American Economic Review*, 44(20, 7–14.

(1961) "The economics of information," *Journal of Political Economy*, 69, June, 213–25.

Stigler, G. and Becker, G. (1977) "De gustibus non est disputandum," *American Economic Review*, 76(2), 76–90.

Stiglitz, J. (2002) *Globalization and Its Discontents*. New York: Norton.

(2003) *The Roaring Nineties*. New York: Norton.

(2006) "A cool calculus of global warming," *Project Syndicate*, www.project-syndicate.org/commentary/stiglitz77. Accessed October 28, 2008.

(2007) "The changing climate on climate change," *Project Syndicate*, www.project-syndicate.org/commentary/stiglitz80. Accessed October 28, 2008.

Sugden, R. (1996) *Multinational Economies and the Law of Uneven Development*, Research Centre for Industrial Strategy, Occasional Papers in Industrial Strategy (37), May.

(1997) "Economías multinacionales y la ley del desarrollo sin equidad" (Multinational economies and the law of uneven development), *FACES Revista de la Facultad de Ciencias Económicas y Sociales*, 3(4), 87–109.

(2003) "Internationalism and economic development: transnational corporations, small firm networking and universities," in M. Waterson (ed.) *Competition, Monopoly and Corporate Governance: Essays in Honour of Keith Cowling*. Cheltenham: Edward Elgar.

(2004) "A small firm approach to the internationalisation of universities: a multinational perspective," *Higher Education Quarterly* 58(2/3), 114–35.

Sugden, R. and Wilson, J. R. (2002) "Development in the shadow of the consensus: a strategic decision-making approach," *Contributions to Political Economy* 21, 111–34.

(2003) "Economic 'prosperity' and 'globalisation': an agenda and perspective," in R. Sugden, R. Hartung Cheng and G. R. Meadows (eds.) *Urban and Regional Prosperity in a Globalised, New Economy*. Cheltenham: Edward Elgar.

(2005) "Economic globalisation: dialectics, conceptualisation and choice," *Contributions to Political Economy*, 24, 13–32.

Swedberg, R. (1991) *Schumpeter: A Biography*. Princeton, NJ: Princeton University Press.

Sweezy, P. M. (1942) *The Theory of Capitalist Development*. New York: Monthly Review Press, 1970.

(1939) "Demand under conditions of oligopoly," *Journal of Political Economy*, 65.

Targetti, F. and Thirlwall, A. (1989) *The Essential Kaldor*. New York: Holmes and Meier.

Tarshis, L. (1980) "Post Keynesian economics: a promise that bounced?," *American Economic Review*, 70(2), 10–14.

Tatham Euro RSCG (1995) Brand Equity Exploration Capri Superslims. Escape From the Ordinary. Brown & Williamson: Bates Number 433010333/0403. http://legacy.library.ucsf.edu/tid/yhd90f00.

Taylor, A. (1995) "Porsche slices up its buyers," *Fortune*, January 16, 24.

Tcherneva, P. R. (2008) "The return of fiscal policy: can the new developments in the new economic consensus be reconciled with the post-Keynesian view?" *The Levy Economics Institute Working Paper No. 539*.

Teague, C. J. (1972) Research Planning Memorandum on the Nature of the Tobacco Business and the Crucial Role of Nicotine Therein. Bates No. 500898378/8386. http://legacy.library.ucsf.edu/tid/nnv59d00.

Teece, D. J. (2006) "Reflections on the Hymer thesis and the multinational enterprise," *International Business Review*, 15(2), 124–39.

Telser, L. (1964) "Advertising and competition," *Journal of Political Economy*, 72(6), 537–62.

Tervio, M. (2007) "The difference that CEOs make: an assignment model approach," Working Paper.

Time (1968) "The Great Mogul," *Time*, February 16.

Tirole, J. (2001) "Corporate governance," *Econometrica*, 69(1), 1–35.

Tomlinson, P. R. (2002). "The real effects of transnational activity upon investment and labour demand within Japan's machinery industries", *International Review of Applied Economics*, 16(20), 107–29.

Toporowski, J. (2002) *The End of Finance: Capital Markets Inflation, Financial Derivatives and Pension Fund Capitalism*. London: Routledge.

Trebing, H. M. (1989) "Restoring purposeful government: the Galbraithian contribution," *Journal of Economic Issues*, June, 393–411.

Tufts Center for the Study of Drug Development (2002) *Impact Report: Analysis and Insight into Critical Drug Development Issues*, 4(5), September/October.

UK Department of Health (1992) *Effect of Tobacco Advertising on Tobacco Consumption: A Discussion Document Reviewing the Evidence*. London: Economics and Operational Research Division, Department of Health.

UK Government White Paper (2003) *The Future of Higher Education*. London: HMSO.

UNCTAD (2003) *World Investment Report: Policies for Development: National and International Perspectives*. New York and Geneva: United Nations.

(2005) *World Investment Report: Transnational Corporations and the Internationalization of R&D*. New York and Geneva: United Nations.

(2006) *World Investment Report: FDI from Developing and Transition Economies: Implications for Development*. New York and Geneva: United Nations.

(2008) *World Investment Report: Transnational Corporations and the Infrastructure Challenge*. New York and Geneva: United Nations.

UNDP (1999) *Human Development Report 1999*. New York: Oxford University Press and UNDP.

(2003) *Human Development Report 2003*. New York: Oxford University Press and UNDP.

(2007) *Human Development Report 2007/2008*. Basingstoke: Palgrave Macmillan.

United Nations (1952) *Preliminary Report on the World Social Situation*. New York: United Nations.

United Nations Research Institute for Social Development (1970) *Contents and Measurement of Socio-economic Development: An Empirical Enquiry*, Geneva, Switzerland, United Nations Research Institute for Social Development.

UNU-WIDER (2006) *The World Distribution of Household Wealth*, December 2006, World Institute for Development Economics Research of the United Nations University, www.wider.unu.edu/events/past-events/2006-events/en_GB/05–12–2006/. Accessed March 16, 2009

US Department of Health and Human Services (2001) Women and Smoking: A Report of the Surgeon General – 2001. Washington, DC: US Department of Health and Human Services, Centers for Disease Control and Prevention, National Center for Chronic Disease Prevention and Health Promotion, Office on Smoking and Health.

US Department of Health Education and Welfare (1964) Smoking and Health. Report of the Advisory Committee to the Surgeon General of the Public Health Service. Washington, DC: US Department of Health, Education, and Welfare, Public Health Service, Communicable Disease Center.

US District Court (2005) *United States of America et al vs Philip Morris Incorporated, et al*. United States District Court, for the District Of Columbia, Final Proposed Findings Of Fact (Incorporating Errata of August 16, 2005), www.usdoj.gov/civil/cases/tobacco2/index.htm.

US Public Health Service (1960) Smoking And Health, Report Of The Advisory Committee To The Surgeon General Of The Public Health Service. American Tobacco: 968034326/4715.

US Strategic Bombing Survey (U.S.SBS) (1945) *The Effects of Strategic Bombing on the German War Economy*, October 31.

(1946) *The Effects of Strategic Bombing on Japan's War Economy*, December.

Veblen, T. B. (1898a) "Why is economics not an evolutionary science?," *Quarterly Journal of Economics*, 12(3), July, 373–97. Reprinted in Veblen (1919a).

(1898b) "The instinct of workmanship and the irksomeness of labor," *American Journal of Sociology*, 4(2), September, 187–201. Reprinted in Veblen (1934).

(1898c) "The beginnings of ownership," *American Journal of Sociology*, 4, November, 352–65. Reprinted in Veblen (1934).

(1899) *The Theory of the Leisure Class: An Economic Study in the Evolution of Institutions*. New York: Macmillan.

(1900) "The preconceptions of economic science: III," *Quarterly Journal of Economics*, 14(2), February, 240–69. Reprinted in Veblen (1919).

(1904) *The Theory of Business Enterprise*. New York: Charles Scribners.

(1906) "The place of science in modern civilization," *American Journal of Sociology*, 11(1), March, 585–609. Reprinted in Veblen (1919).

(1909) "The limitations of marginal utility," *Journal of Political Economy*, 17(9), November, 620–36. Reprinted in Veblen (1919).

(1914) *The Instinct of Workmanship, and the State of the Industrial Arts*. New York: Macmillan.

(1915) *Imperial Germany and the Industrial Revolution*. New York: Macmillan.

(1918) *The Higher Learning in America: A Memorandum on the Conduct of Universities by Business Men*. New York: Huebsch.

(1919) *The Place of Science in Modern Civilization and Other Essays*. New York: Huebsch.

(1921) *The Engineers and the Price System*. New York: Harcourt Brace and World.

(1923) *Absentee Ownership and Business Enterprise in Recent Times*. New York: Huebsch.

(1925) "Economic theory in the calculable future," *American Economic Review (Papers and Proceedings)*, 15(1), March, 48–55. Reprinted in Veblen (1934).

(1934) *Essays on Our Changing Order*, ed. Leon Ardzrooni. New York: Viking.

Vernon, R. (1977) *Storm Over the Multinationals: The Real Issues.* Cambridge: Cambridge University Press.

Voorhies, E. C., Galbraith, J. K., and Todd, F. E. (1933a) "Economic Aspects of the Bee Industry," *Giannini Foundation of Agricultural Economics*, Paper No. 39, Bulletin No. 555. Berkeley: Agricultural Experiment Station.

Voorhies, E. C., Galbraith, J. K., and Todd, F. E. (1933b) "Honey marketing in California," *Giannini Foundation of Agricultural Economics*, Paper No. 38, Bulletin No. 554. Berkeley, CA: Agricultural Experiment Station.

Waligorski, C. (2006) *John Kenneth Galbraith: The Economist as Political Theorist.* New York: MD: Rowman & Littlefield.

Walker, C., Bloomfield, M., and Thorning, M. (1990) *The US Savings Challenge.* Boulder, CO: Westview Press.

Waller, W. (2008) "Galbraith and Robinson's Second Crisis of Economic Theory," *Journal of Economic Issues*, 42, March, 13–24.

Walters, A. (1973) "Introduction: Money and the economy," in Walters, A. (ed.) *Money and Banking: Selected Readings.* Harmondsworth: Penguin.

Wayne, G. F. and Connolly, G. (2002) "How cigarette design can affect youth initiation into smoking: Camel cigarettes 1983–93," *Tobacco Control,* 11(Suppl. I), i32–9.

Weinstein, W. (1994) *Market Segmentation: Using Demographics, Psychographics, and Other Niche Marketing Techniques to Predict and Model Customer Behavior.* Chicago: Probus.

Weintraub, S. (1958) *An Approach to the Theory of Income Distribution.* Philadelphia: Chilton Books.

(1963) *Some Aspects of Wage Theory and Policy.* New York: Chilton Books.

Weintraub, S. and Habibagahi, H. (1972) "Money supplies and price-output indeterminateness: the Friedman puzzle," *Journal of Economic Issues* 6(2–3).

Whinston, M. D. (2001) "Exclusivity and tying in US v. Microsoft: what we know and don't know," *Journal of Economic Perspectives*, 15(2), 63–80.

(2003) "On the transaction cost determinants of vertical integration," *Journal of Law, Economics and Organization*, 19(1), 1–23.

White, E. N. (1990) "The stock market boom and crash of 1929 revisited," *Journal of Economic Perspectives*, 4, 67–83.

Wilder, R. (1974) "Advertising and inter-industry competition: testing a Galbraithian hypothesis," *Journal of Industrial Economics,* 22(3), 215–26.

Williamson, O. E. (1964) *The Economics of Discretionary Behavior.* Englewood Cliffs, NJ: Prentice-Hall.

(1970) *Corporate Control and Business Behavior.* Englewood Cliffs, NJ: Prentice-Hall.

(1971) "The vertical integration of production: market failure considerations," *American Economic Review*, 6(1), 112–23.

(1975) *Markets and Hierarchies: Analysis and Anti-trust Implications: A Study in the Economics of Internal Organization.* New York: Free Press.

(1979) "Transaction-cost economics: the governance of contractual relations," *Journal of Law and Economics*, 22, 233–61.

(1981) "The modern corporation: origins, evolution, attributes," *Journal of Economic Literature*, 19, 1537–68.

(1985) *The Economic Institutions of Capitalism: Firms, Markets, Relational Contracting.* London: Macmillan.

(1987) *Antitrust Economics.* Oxford: Basil Blackwell.

(1989) "Transaction-cost economics," in R. Schmanesee and R. D. Willig (eds.) *Handbook of Industrial Organization*, vol. I. Amsterdam: Elsevier Science B.V.

(1996) *The Mechanisms of Governance.* Oxford: Oxford University Press.

(1999) "Strategy research: governance and competence perspectives," *Strategic Management Journal*, 20, December, 1087–108.

(2000) "The new institutional economics: taking stock, looking ahead," *Journal of Economic Literature*, 38, September, 595–613.

(2004) "Herbert Simon and organization theory," in M. Augier and J. March (eds.), *Models of a Man: Essays in Memory of Herbert A. Simon.* Cambridge, MA: MIT Press, 279–95.

(2005) "The economics of governance," *American Economic Review*, 95, May, 1–18.

(2008) "Corporate boards of directors: in principle and in practice," *Journal of Law, Economics, and Organization*, 24(2), 247–72.

Williamson, O. E. and Ouchi, W. G. (1983) "The markets and hierarchies program of research: origins, implications, prospects," in A. Francis, J. Turkj and P. Willman (eds.) *Power, Efficiency and Institutions: A Critical Appraisal of the 'Market and Hierarchies Paradigm.* London: Heinemann.

Wilson, W. J. (1987) *The Truly Disadvantaged: The Inner City, The Underclass, and Public Policy.* Chicago: University of Chicago Press.

Winslow, E. G. (1986a) "'Human logic' and Keynes 's economics," *Eastern Economic Journal*, 12, 413–30.

(1986b) "Keynes and Freud: psychoanalysis and Keynes's account of the 'animal spirits' of capitalism," *Social Research*, 53, 549–78.

(1989) "Organic interdependence, uncertainty and economic analysis," *Economic Journal*, 99, 1173–82.

(1990) "Bloomsbury, Freud, and the vulgar passions," *Social Research*, 57, 785–819.

(1992) "Psychoanalysis and Keynes's account of the psychology of the trade cycle," in W. J. Gerrard and J. V. Hillard (eds.) *The Philosophy and Economics of J.M. Keynes*. Cheltenham: Edward Elgar.

(1993) "Keynes on rationality," in W. J. Gerrard (ed.) *The Economics of Rationality*. London: Routledge.

Wolf, M. (2006) "A new gilded age," *Financial Times*, April 25.

(2007) "Unfettered finance is fast reshaping the global economy," *Financial Times*, 18 June.

Woo-Cumings, M. (1999) *The Developmental State*. Ithaca, NY: Cornell University Press.

Woodford, M. (2003) *Interest and Prices: Foundations of a Theory of Monetary Policy*. Princeton, NJ: Princeton University Press.

Wray, L. R. (1998) *Understanding Modern Money: The Key to Full Employment and Price Stability*. Edward Elgar: Cheltenham.

(2001) "Money and Inflation," in R. Holt and S. Pressman (eds.) *A New Guide to Post Keynesian Economics*. London and New York: Routledge, 79–81.

(2007) "A Post Keynesian view of central bank independence, policy targets, and the rules versus discretion debate," *Journal of Post Keynesian Economics*, 30(1), 119–46.

(2008) "Lessons from the subprime meltdown," *Challenge*, 51(2), March–April, 40–68.

Wrenn, M., Stanfield, J. R., and Carroll, M. (2008) "Galbraith and Robinson's second crisis of economic theory," *Journal of Economic Issues*, 42, March, 5–11.

Young, A. A. (1928) "Increasing returns and economic progress," *Economic Journal*, 38(4), December, 527–42.

Zanfei, A. (2000) "Transnational firms and the changing organization of innovative activities," *Cambridge Journal of Economics*, 24(5), 515–42.

Zeboot, C. A. (1959) "Economics of affluence," *Review of Social Economy*, September, 112–25.

Zeitlin, M. (1974) "Corporate ownership and control: the large corporation and the capitalist class," *American Journal of Sociology*, 79(5), 1073–119.

Zinkin, M. (1967) "Galbraith and consumer sovereignty," *Journal of Industrial Economics*, 16(1), 1–9.

Additional works by Galbraith

Baran, P. A. and Galbraith, J. K. (1947) "Professor Despres on effects of strategic bombing on the German war economy," *Review of Economic Statistics*, 29(2), 132–34.

Chamberlin, E. H., Wright, D. M., Abramson, V., Harris, A. L., and Galbraith, J. K. (1946) "Discussion," *American Economic Review*, 36(2), 139–53.

Clapham, B. I. and Galbraith, J. K. (2000) "John Kenneth Galbraith: world of ideas," *Canadian Investment Review*, 13(4), 17.

Dean, V. M. and Galbraith, J. K. (1950) *Can Europe Unite?* New York: Foreign Policy Association.

Dennison, H. S., Filene, L. A., Flanders, R. E., Leeds, M., and Galbraith, J. K. (1938) *Toward Full Employment*. New York: Whittlesley House.

Eliot, T. H. and Galbraith, J. K. (1992) *Recollections of the New Deal: When the People Mattered*. Boston: Northeastern University Press.

Flanders, R. E., Galbraith, J. K., Mason, E. S., Neal, A. C., Phillips, C. F., and Wright, W. (1947) *Pricing Problems and the Stabilization of Prosperity*. Washington, DC: Chamber of Commerce of the USA.

Galbraith, J. K. (1934) "Branch banking and its bearing on agricultural credit," *Journal of Farm Economics*, 16(2).

(1934) "Some aspects of the overseas market for Canadian honey," *Scientific Agriculture*, December.

(1937) "The farmers' banking system: four years of F.C.A. operations," *Harvard Business Review*, 15(3), 313–20.

(1937) "The Federal land banks and agricultural stability," *Journal of Farm Economics*, 19(1), 48–58.

(1939) "Fiscal policy and the employment–investment controversy," *Harvard Business Review*, 18(1), 24.

(1939) "Hereditary land in the Third Reich," *Quarterly Journal of Economics*, 53(3), 465–76.

(1941) "Defense financing and inflation: some comments on Professor Hansen's article," *Review of Economic Statistics*, 23(2), 78–93.

(1946) "Reflections on price control," *Quarterly Journal of Economics*, 60(4), 475–89.

(1949) "Appraisal of marketing research," *American Economic Review*, 39(3), 415–16.
(1949) *Beyond the Marshall Plan*. Washington, DC: National Planning Association.
(1949) "Commodity marketing – going where?" *American Economic Review*, 39(3), 415.
(1950) *America and Western Europe*. New York: Public Affairs Committee.
(1951) "The strategy of direct control in economic mobilization," *Review of Economic Statistics*, 33(1), 12–17.
(1953) "Farming an abandoned farm," New York Times Magazine. (Reprinted in Galbraith (1960) *The Liberal Hour*, 144–50. Boston: Houghton Mifflin).
(1953) "Appraisals of new Fabian essays," *Review of Economics and Statistics*, 35(3), 200–10.
(1953) "The poor countries," *Encounter*, 1, 68–72.
(1954) "Countervailing power," *American Economic Review*, 44(2), 1–6.
(1954) "The defense of business: a strategic appraisal," *Harvard Business Review*, 32(2), 37–43.
(1954) "Economic preconceptions and the farm policy," *American Economic Review*, 44(1), 40–52.
(1954) "Perils of the big build-up," *New York Times Magazine*, March 7, 12 and 39–40.
(1955) "The businessman as philosopher," *Perspectives USA*, 13, 57–9.
(1956) "Can we solve the farm problem Mr Benedict?" *Journal of Farm Economics*, 38(3), 878–82.
(1956) "On the economics of F D R," *Commentary*, 22(2), 172–75.
(1956) *Inequality in Agriculture: Problem and Program*. Guelph: University Press, Department of Agricultural Economics and Ontario Federation of Agriculture.
(1957) "Are living costs out of control?" *Atlantic Monthly*, 199(2), 37–41.
(1957) "Gray on caricature," *Journal of Farm Economics*, 39(2), 539–41.
(1957) "Market structure and stabilization policy," *Review of Economic Statistics*, 39(2), 124–33.
(1957) "A note on Wilcox review," *Journal of Farm Economics*, 39(4), 1045.
(1958) "The days of boom and bust," American Heritage. Reprinted in Galbraith (1960) *The Liberal Hour*. Boston: Houghton Mifflin, 82–97.
(1958) *Journey to Poland and Yugoslavia*. Cambridge, MA: Harvard University Press.

(1958) "The mystery of Henry Ford," *Atlantic Monthly*, 201(3), 41–7.

(1958) "Rival economic theories in India," *Foreign Affairs*, 36(4), 587–96.

(1959) "Developed economic attitudes and the underdeveloped economy," *Public Policy*, 9, 73–83.

(1959) "Heresy revisited," *Encounter*, 12(1), 45–53.

(1959) "Mr. Hunter on countervailing power: a comment," *Economic Journal*, 69(273), 168–70.

(1959) "The pleasures and uses of bankruptcy," *The Reporter*. Reprinted in Galbraith (1960) *The Liberal Hour*. Boston: Houghton Mifflin, 138–44.

(1959) "Royalty on the farm", *The Reporter*. Reprinted in Galbraith (1960) *The Liberal Hour*. Boston: Houghton Mifflin, 151–59.

(1959) "The social balance," *Educational Record*, 40(3), 183–88.

(1960) "The age of the wordfact," *Atlantic Monthly*, 206(3), 87–9.

(1960) "For public and potent building," *New York Times Magazine*, October 9, 34, 64, 68, and 70.

(1960) "Introduction," in R. Shaplen (ed.) *Kreuger, Genius and Swindler*. New York: Knopf.

(1960) "Mr. Nixon's Remedy for Inflation," *Harper's Magazine*, February, 29–34.

(1961) "Economic power and the survival of capitalism," in S. Tsuru (ed.) *Has Capitalism Changed?* Tokyo: Iwanami Shoten.

(1961) "Ed O'Connor," New Yorker, 24 June. Reprinted in Galbraith (1971) *A Contemporary Guide to Economics, Peace, and Laughter*. Boston: Houghton Mifflin, 231–37.

(1961) *On Criticism in the Open Society*. New Delhi: United States Information Service.

(1962) "The approach to poverty," *Department of State Bulletin*, 46(1200), 1024–27.

(1962) "Dissent in a free society," *Atlantic Monthly*, 209(2), 44–8.

(1962) "Economic-development – rival systems and comparative advantage," *Department of State Bulletin*, 47(1201), 13–17.

(1962) "The language of economics," *Fortune*. Reprinted in Galbraith (1971) *A Contemporary Guide to Economics, Peace, and Laughter*. Boston: Houghton Mifflin, 32–44.

(1962) "The poverty of nations," *Atlantic Monthly*, 210(4), 47–53.

(1963) "Introduction," in G. Steinem (ed.) *The Beach Book*. New York: Viking Press.

(1963) "A communication," *Washington Post*, November 25, A13.

(1963) "John Strachey," *Encounter*, 21(3), 53–4.

(1963) *The Mclandress Dimension*. Boston: Houghton Mifflin.
(1963) "On our quarrel with success," *Department of State Bulletin*, 49, 52–56.
(1964) "The balance of payments: a political and administrative view," *Review of Economic Statistics*, 46(2), 115–22.
(1964) "Economics and the quality of life," *Science*, 145(3628), 117–23.
(1964) "Experiment in India," *Saturday Review*, August 15, 20–3.
(1964) "Reflection on the Asian scene," *Journal of Asian Studies*, 23(4), 501–4.
(1965) *Economic Policy Since 1945: The Nature of Success*. New York: Graduate School of Business Administration, New York University.
(1965) "Economics vs the quality of life," *Encounter*, 24(1), 31–9.
(1965) "Foreign policy: the stuck whistle," *Atlantic Monthly*, 215(2), 64–8.
(1965) "Galbraith's reply," *Encounter*, 24(6), 92.
(1965) "US embassy geese," *New York Times*, June 14, 32.
(1966) "Agenda for American liberals," *Commentary*, 41(6), 29–34.
(1966) "Planning ahead – reply," *Commentary*, 42(3), 14.
(1966) "The starvation of our cities," *The Progressive*, December. Reprinted in Galbraith (1986) *A View from the Stands*, Boston: Houghton Mifflin, 19–25.
(1966) "William F. Buckley, Jr.," *New York Herald Tribune*, October 16. Reprinted in Galbraith (1971) *A Contemporary Guide to Economics, Peace, and Laughter*. Boston: Houghton Mifflin, 237–40.
(1967) "Capitalism, socialism, and the future of the industrial state," *Atlantic Monthly*, 219(6), 61–7.
(1967) "Interview: the public sector is still starved," *Challenge*, 15(3), 18–21.
(1967) "Market planning and the role of government," *Atlantic Monthly*, 219(5), 69–79.
(1967) "The new industrial state: planning and the modern corporation," *Atlantic Monthly*, 219(4), 51–7.
(1967) *The Non-potable Scotch: A Memoir on the Clansmen in Canada*. Harmondsworth: Penguin Books.
(1967) *Planning, Regulation and Competition: Evidence to the Subcommittees of the Select Committee on Small Business*. US Senate, 90th Congress, 1st Session. Washington, DC: US Government Printing Office.
(1967) "The polipollutionists," *Atlantic Monthly*, 219(1), 52–4.

(1967) "Review of a review," *Public Interest*, 9, 109–18.
(1967) "Vietnam – a way out of Vietnam – thoughts and possibilities for revision of American politics," *Europa Archiv*, 22(23), 851–63.
(1967) "Vietnam: the moderate solution," *Christianity and Crisis*, 27, 185–90.
(1968) "The case for constitutional reform at Harvard," *Harvard Alumni Magazine*, December 23. Reprinted in Galbraith (1986) *A View from the Stands*. Boston: Houghton Mifflin, 109–13.
(1968) "The future of the industrial system," *McKinsey Quarterly*, 5(1), 26.
(1968) "Introduction," in J. Mill (ed.) *The History of British India*. New York: Chelsea House.
(1968) *The Triumph: A Novel of Modern Diplomacy*. Boston: Houghton Mifflin.
(1969) "1929 and 1969 – financial genius is a short memory and a rising market," *Harper's*, 239(1434), 55–62.
(1969) "The affluent society after ten years," *Atlantic Monthly*, 223(5), 37–44.
(1969) "The American ambassador," *Foreign Service Journal*. Reprinted in Galbraith (1971) *A Contemporary Guide to Economics, Peace, and Laughter*. Boston: Houghton Mifflin, 147–59.
(1969) "Berkeley in the thirties," *Atlantic Monthly*. Reprinted in Galbraith (1971) *A Contemporary Guide to Economics, Peace, and Laughter*, Boston: Houghton Mifflin, 259–70.
(1969) "The big defense firms are really public firms and should be nationalised," *New York Times Magazine*, November 16, 50 and 162–70.
(1969) "The consequences of technology," *Journal of Accountancy*, 127, 44.
(1969) "John Steinbeck," *Atlantic Monthly*, 224(5), 65–7.
(1969) "Professor Gordon on 'The Close of the Galbraithian System'," *Journal of Political Economy*, 77(4), 494–503.
(1969) "Remarks on planning and market," *Politicka Ekonomie*, 17(11), 1048–49.
(1969) "Reply," Harvard Alumni Magazine, February 24. Reprinted in Galbraith (1986) *A View from the Stands*. Boston: Houghton Mifflin, 113–16.
(1970) "Dwight D. Eisenhower, General, Book World," Washington Post, 28 June (reprinted in Galbraith (1971) *A Contemporary Guide to Economics, Peace, and Laughter*. Boston: Houghton Mifflin, 212–16.
(1970) "Economics as a system of belief," *American Economic Review*, 60(2), 469–78.
(1970) "The Nixon administration and the great socialist revival," New York, September 21. Reprinted in Galbraith (1971) *A Contemporary*

Guide to Economics, Peace, and Laughter. Boston: Houghton Mifflin, 86–97.

(1970) "Odyssey of a friend, W. Chambers letters to W. F. Buckley, Jr, 1954–1961," *New Republic*, 162(13), 17–19.

(1970) "Plain lessons of a bad decade," *Foreign Policy*, 1, 31–45.

(1970) "Richard Nixon," *Life*, March 27. Reprinted in Galbraith (1971) *A Contemporary Guide to Economics, Peace, and Laughter.* Boston: Houghton Mifflin, 216–20.

(1970) "Wage–price controls – the cure for runaway inflation," New York Times Magazine, June 7, 25 and 104–5.

(1970) "Why do you go to Gstaad?," Holiday, January. Reprinted in Galbraith (1971) *A Contemporary Guide to Economics, Peace, and Laughter.* Boston: Houghton Mifflin, 253–59.

(1970) "Winning in November is not enough," *New Republic*, 162(24), 13–14.

(1971) "Albert Speer was the man to see," *New York Times Book Review*, January 10, 2–3 and 30–1.

(1971) "The day Nikita Khrushchev visited the establishment," Harper's Magazine, February. Reprinted in Galbraith (1971) *A Contemporary Guide to Economics, Peace, and Laughter.* Boston: Houghton Mifflin, 199–207.

(1971) "Do you sincerely want to be rich?," *Washington Post*, August 15. Reprinted in Galbraith (1979) *Annals of an Abiding Liberal*, Boston: Houghton Mifflin, 311–17.

(1971) "East Pakistan: we can help – but without arms," *New York Times*, August 19, 35.

(1971) "Galbraith answers Crosland," *New Statesman*, January 22, 101.

(1971) "Introduction," in J.-J. Servan-Schreiber and M. Albert (eds.) *The Radical Alternative.* New York: Norton.

(1971) "Patterns from difficult decade in American foreign policy," *Europa Archiv*, 26(5), 159–70.

(1971) "Preface," in R. A. Butler (ed.) *The Art of the Possible.* Boston: Gambit.

(1971) "The United States," New York, November 15. Reprinted in Galbraith (1986) *A View from the Stands.* Boston: Houghton Mifflin, 215–29.

(1971) "Who's minding the store?," in P. Nobile (ed.) The Con III Controversy: The Critics Look at the Greening of America. New York: Pocket Books.

(1971) *The American Left and Some British Comparisons.* London: Fabian Society.

(1972) "Buckly v. Vidal," *Esquire*, October 13, 1113–15.

(1972) "The case for George McGovern," Saturday Review, July 1.

(1972) "Competing with government," *New York Times*, September 17, E10.

(1972) "Contemporary capitalism and the problem of unequal growth," *Acta Oeconomica*, 9(2), 117–26.

(1972) "Eleanor and Franklin revisited," *New York Times Book Review*, March 19, 2.

(1972) "The emerging public corporation," *Business & Society Review*, 1, 54.

(1972) "Foreword," *American Economic Review*, 62(2), R7–R8.

(1972) "Galbraith has seen China's future and it works," *New York Times Magazine*, November 26, 38–9 and 88–94.

(1972) "Recent economic policy: the deeper perspective," *SAM Advanced Management Journal*, 37(4), 13–21.

(1973) *A China Passage*. Boston: Houghton Mifflin.

(1973) "Controls or competition – what's at issue?" *Comment, Review of Economics and Statistics*, 55(4), 524.

(1973) "Conversation with an inconvenient economist," *Challenge*, 16(4), 28–37.

(1973) "Economics: unequal development and the theory of social action," *Proceedings of the Royal Society of Medicine*, 66(6), 559–64.

(1973) "Introduction," in T. Veblen (ed.) *The Theory of the Leisure Class*. Boston: Houghton Mifflin.

(1974) "Across Australia by train," Travel and Leisure. Reprinted in Galbraith (1979) *Annals of an Abiding Liberal*. Boston: Houghton Mifflin, 221–9.

(1974) "Corporations in the eighties," *Annals of Public & Cooperative Economics*, 45(3/4), 267.

(1974) "Diplomat," *New York*, October 21, 130–1.

(1974) "The higher economic purpose of women," *MS Magazine*, May. Reprinted in Galbraith (1979) *Annals of an Abiding Liberal*. Boston: Houghton Mifflin, 36–46.

(1974) "Hindsight," *New Republic*, 171(8), 8.

(1974) "Neuroses of the rich," Playboy, February. Reprinted in Galbraith (1979) *Annals of an Abiding Liberal*. Boston: Houghton Mifflin, 148–52.

(1974) *Of Men and Foreign Policy*. Santa Barbara, CA: Center for the Study of Democratic Institutions.

(1974) "The paintings of Husain," Boston Globe, December 1. Reprinted in Galbraith (1986) *A View from the Stands*. Boston: Houghton Mifflin, 162–4.

(1974) "Richard Nixon," Boston Globe, August 18. Reprinted in Galbraith (1986) *A View from the Stands*. Boston: Houghton Mifflin, 393–6.
(1974) "Scotland's greatest son," Horizon. Reprinted in Galbraith (1979) *Annals of an Abiding Liberal*. Boston: Houghton Mifflin, 86–102.
(1974) "Solving unemployment without inflation," *Social Policy*, 5(3), 4–5.
(1974) "The technostructure," *New York Certified Public Accountant*, 44, 75.
(1974) "Vesco and the joy of swindling," New York, November 18. Reprinted in – Galbraith (1979) *Annals of an Abiding Liberal*. Boston: Houghton Mifflin, 317–22.
(1974) "What comes after General Motors?" *New Republic*, 171(18). Reprinted in Galbraith (1979) Annals of an Abiding Liberal. Boston: Houghton Mifflin, 73–85.
(1975) "Apothegms of avarice," *Harpers*, 251(1503), 64–5.
(1975) "Capitalism's failures: tasks for the democratic left," *New Republic*, 173(7/8), 18.
(1975) "The coming of J. M. Keynes," *Business & Society Review*, (15), 32–8.
(1975) "The conservative-majority fallacy," New York, December 22. Reprinted in Galbraith (1979) *Annals of an Abiding Liberal*, Boston: Houghton Mifflin, 47–53.
(1975) "Diplomats all," The CPA, 45, 12.
(1975) "The Downing Street papers," *New Statesman*, December 12, 758–9.
(1975) "The economics of the current anxiety," *McKinsey Quarterly*, 3, 31.
(1975) "Pros and cons of controls," *Fortune*, 91(5), 130.
(1975) "Recessional," *Harvard Gazette*, June 12. Reprinted in Galbraith (1986) *A View from the Stands*. Boston: Houghton Mifflin, 129–36.
(1975) "Seymour Edwin Harris," *Review of Economic and Statistics*, 57(1), vi–vii.
(1975) *Socialism in Rich Countries and Poor* (Ahmedabad Bombay: Ajit Bhagat Memorial Trust; distributed by Commerce Publications Division).
(1975) "Will the answer be controls," *The Listener*, January 30, 130–1.
(1976) "Conservative majority myth," *Dissent*, 23, 123–6.
(1976) "Economic logic – reply," *New Republic*, 174(17), 27.
(1976) "Preface," in S. Tsuru (ed.) *The Collected Works*. Tokyo: Kodansha.
(1976) "The halls of ivory," *New York Times*, April 30, 22.

(1976) "Political novels past and present," *New York Times Book Review*, 12 September. Reprinted in Galbraith (1979) *Annals of an Abiding Liberal*, Boston: Houghton Mifflin, 279–85.

(1976) "Tempted to say boob," *Fortune*, 93(4), 70.

(1976) "Wherein a tax cut is termed 'obscene'," *New York Times*, December 3, 27.

(1977) "Capitalism, socialism and democracy – Schumpeter, J A," *New Society*, 40(758), 74–5.

(1977) "Crime and no punishment," *Esquire*, December. Reprinted in Galbraith (1979) *Annals of an Abiding Liberal*. Boston: Houghton Mifflin, 323–30.

(1977) "Economic choices," *Harpers*, 254(1523), 8–10.

(1977) *The Galbraith Reader: From the Works of John Kenneth Galbraith*. Ipswich, MA: Gambit.

(1977) *The Age of Uncertainty*. London: Book Club Associates.

(1977) "Galbraithian guide to economic folkways of Americans," *Fortune*, 96(2), 97.

(1977) "Humble quislings," *New Republic*, 177(1), 7.

(1977) "It started with Adam Smith," *New York Times Magazine*, May 15, 23–4.

(1977) "My forty years with the F.B.I.," *Esquire*, October. Reprinted in Galbraith (1979) *Annals of an Abiding Liberal*. Boston: Houghton Mifflin, 155–81.

(1977) "The seven wonders of the modern world," *New York Times*, November 27, 322–3.

(1977) "A very specific guide to the economic folkways of American business and businessmen," *Fortune*, August. Reprinted in Galbraith (1986) *A View from the Stands*. Boston: Houghton Mifflin, 230–3.

(1978) "Advice to Exxon," *Challenge*, 21(4), 58–9.

(1978) "Alger Hiss and liberal anxiety," *Atlantic Monthly*, May. Reprinted in Galbraith (1979) *Annals of an Abiding Liberal*. Boston: Houghton Mifflin, 303–10.

(1978) "All Washington's gone AVOL ... voluntarily," *New York Times*, 4 April, F3.

(1978) "Defending the multinational corporation," *The CPA Journal*, 48, 64.

(1978) "Defense of multinational company," *Atlantic Community Quarterly*, 16(2), 193–207.

(1978) "The defense of the multinational company," *Harvard Business Review*, 56(2), 83–93.

(1978) "Further on Churchill and the Churchill style," Esquire, October 24. Reprinted in Galbraith (1986) *A View from the Stands*. Boston: Houghton Mifflin, 306–9.

(1978) "The investment balance," *Modern Office Procedures*, 23(6), 12.
(1978) "Labor, leisure, and the new class," *Modern Office Procedures*, 23(10), 10.
(1978) "The North Dakota plan," *Atlantic Monthly*, 242(2), 24–5.
(1978) "On security and survival," *Modern Office Procedures*, 23(11), 12.
(1978) "The position of poverty," *Modern Office Procedures*, 23(9), 12.
(1978) "Production and price stability," *Modern Office Procedures*, 23(4), 12.
(1978) "The theory of social balance," *Modern Office Procedures*, 23(5), 12.
(1978) "The transition to new goals," *Modern Office Procedures*, 23(7), 12.
(1978) "The trouble with economists," *New Republic*, 178(2), 15–22.
(1978) "Writing, typing & economics," *Atlantic Monthly*, 241(3). Reprinted in Galbraith, J. K. (1979) *Annals of an Abiding Liberal*. Boston: Houghton Mifflin, 285–94.
(1979) *Annals of an Abiding Liberal*. Boston: Houghton Mifflin.
(1979) "Are public libraries against liberty?," *American Libraries*, 10(8), 482–5.
(1979) "Being a diagnosis of inflation: causes and cures," *New York Times*, 12 January, A23.
(1979) "The great Wall Street crash," *New Republic*, 181(15), 17–25.
(1979) "How to get ahead," *New York Review of Books*, 26, 4–6.
(1979) "The origin of the document," *Atlantic Monthly*, 244(1), 50.
(1979) "Socialism for corporations," *Washington Post*, October 3, A22.
(1980) "Foreword," in C. Worswick (ed.) *Princely India: Photographs by Raja Deen Dayal, 1884–1910*. New York: Knopf.
(1980) "Henry Robinson Luce – and *Fortune* magazine," in *Writing for Fortune*. New York: Time.
(1980) "H. L. Mencken: the Baltimore oracle," Book World, *Washington Post*, 14 September, 1–3.
(1980) "Two pleas at Berkeley," *New York Review of Books*, 27, 25–6.
(1981) "Barabara Ward: in memory," *The Economist*, June 6. Reprinted in Galbraith (1986) *A View from the Stands*. Boston: Houghton Mifflin, 95–7.
(1981) "The conservative onslaught," *New York Review of Books*, 27, 30–5.
(1981) "The economics of the arms race – and after," *Bulletin of the Atomic Scientists*, 37(6), 13–16.

(1981) "Galbraith on Galbraith," *Fortune*, 104(4), 21.
(1981) "The language is an alibi," *Washington Post*, September 27, C8.
(1981) "The management problem of the 80s," *Management International Review*, 21(1), 4–6.
(1981) "The market and Mr. Reagan," *New Republic*, 185(12), 15–18.
(1981) "Marketing's changing economic climate," *Marketing Times*, 28(1), 10.
(1981) "Musings of a (relative) conservative," *New York Times*, May 31, F3.
(1981) "The old left strikes back: what has the new right got right? Not much, says its favorite foe," *Canadian Business*, 54(9), 133.
(1981) "A policy divided against itself cannot stand – the market and Reagan," *New Republic*, 185(12), 15–18.
(1981) "Up from monetarism and other wishful thinking," *New York Review of Books*, 28(3), 27–31.
(1981) "The uses of excuses for affluence," *New York Times Magazine*, May 31, 10–13.
(1982) "The budget and the bust," *New Republic*, 186(11), 9–13.
(1982) "The confident speculators," *Atlantic Monthly*, 249(5), 100.
(1982) "Recession economics," *New York Review of Books*, 29, 34.
(1982) "The second imperial requiem," *International Security*, 7(3), 84–93.
(1982) "The social consensus and the conservative onslaught," *Millennium Journal of International Studies*, 11, 1–13.
(1982) "The way up from Reagan economics," *Harvard Business Review*, 60(4), 6–12.
(1982) "The wonders of Robertson Davies," *New York Times Book Review*, 14 February, 7–8.
(1983) "The anatomy of power: interview," *Challenge*, 26(3), 26–33.
(1983) "David Niven," *Boston Globe*, August 3. Reprinted in Galbraith (1986) *A View from the Stands*. 406–8. Boston: Houghton Mifflin.
(1983) "Economics and the arts": The W. E. Williams Memorial Lecture given at the National Theatre on January 18, 1983. London: Arts Council of Great Britain.
(1983) "Eleanor Roosevelt," *Esquire*, December. Reprinted in Galbraith (1986) *A View from the Stands*. Boston: Houghton Mifflin, 389–92.
(1983) *Essays from the Poor to the Rich*. Bombay: Bharatiya Vidya Bhavan.
(1983) "From drips to digitals," *New Republic*, 189(15), 34–6.
(1983) "Further on economics and the arts," Ethos. Reprinted in Galbraith (1986) *A View from the Stands* Boston: Houghton Mifflin, 144–51.

(1983) "Joan Robinson: a word of appreciation," *Cambridge Journal of Economics*, 7(3/4), 211.
(1983) "Preface," in A. Trollope, *Barchester Towers*. Harmondsworth, UK: Penguin.
(1984) "Corporate man," *New York Times Magazine*, January 22, 39.
(1984) "The heartless society," *New York Times Magazine*, September 2, 20–1 and 44–5.
(1984) "Keynes, Roosevelt, and the complementary revolutions," *Challenge*, 26(6), 4–8.
(1984) "Money in American fiction," *New York Times*, 21 October. Reprinted in Galbraith (1986) *A View from the Stands*, 67–74. Boston: Houghton Mifflin.
(1984) "Reading about the rich," *New York Times Book Review*, October 21, 1 and 54–5.
(1984) "Reagan vs. the military," *New York Times*, February 5, E19.
(1984) "Russia," New Yorker, 3 September. Reprinted in Galbraith (1986) *A View from the Stands*, 264–75. Boston: Houghton Mifflin.
(1985) "The compleat politics of arms control: the American context," Proceedings of the Groupe de Bellerive. Reprinted in Galbraith (1986) *A View from the Stands*. Boston: Houghton Mifflin, 8–18.
(1985) "The concept of work as a species of fraud," *Parade*, 10 February. Reprinted in Galbraith (1986) A View from the Stands, 42–5. Boston: Houghton Mifflin.
(1985) "Eulogy: a tribute to Weintraub, Sidney," *Journal of Post Keynesian Economics*, 7(4), 508–9.
(1985) "How to get the poor off our conscience," *Humanist*, 45(5), 5.
(1985) "Humanistic economics," *The Progressive*, 49(8), 41–2.
(1985) "Let's be plain about politics and money," *New York Times*, November 28, A27.
(1985) "Reagan's 'facts' – artistic license," *New York Times*, September 27, A27.
(1985) "Russia's big problem," *Fortune*, 111(3), 15.
(1985) "Taking the sting out of capitalism," *New York Times*, May 26, F1.
(1986) "A journey to Argentina," *New Yorker*, 62(9), 70–7.
(1986) "Let the politicians run foreign policy," *Washington Post*, December 24, 15.
(1986) *Revolutions Reconsidered*. Sackville, NB: Mount Allison University.
(1986) "The Scotch: an excursion backward in time," *Reader's Digest*, February. Reprinted in Galbraith (1986) *A View from the Stands*. Boston: Houghton Mifflin, 276–84.

(1986) "The year of the spy," *New York Times*, January 5, E19.
(1987) "The 1929 parallel," *Atlantic Monthly*, 259(1), 62–6.
(1987) "The American economy now – and when the returns come in," *Business Forum*, 12(3), 8–11.
(1987) "Economic development: engine of democracy," *New York Times*, August 25, A21.
(1987) *A History of Economics: The Past as the Present.* London: H. Hamilton.
(1988) "Baseball: socialist as apple pie," *New York Times*, August 7, E23.
(1988) "Coolidge, Carter, Bush, Reagan ... no wonder people don't bother to vote," *New York Times*, December 18, A19.
(1988) "Critical issues of the twenty-first century," *Vital Speeches of the Day*, 54(6), 185.
(1988) "The future of global economic systems," *Asian Finance*, 14(12), 22.
(1988) "How businesses behave," *New Republic*, 198(25), 42.
(1988) "Interest groups by any other name," *New York Times*, 29 May, E17.
(1988) "Interview: the political asymmetry of economic policy," *Eastern Economic Journal*, 14(2), 125–28.
(1988) "Time and the new industrial state," *American Economic Review*, 78(2), 373–76.
(1988) "Tribute," in *The Proceedings of the Archibald Macleish Symposium,* May, 1982. Landam, MD: University Press of America.
(1989) "Friendly advice to a shrinking military," *New York Times*, 22 November, A25.
(1989) "Ideology and economic reality," *Challenge*, 32(6), 4–9.
(1989) "A look back: affirmation and error," *Journal of Economic Issues*, 23(2), 413–16.
(1990) "(Class) war in the Gulf," *New York Times*, November 7, A31.
(1990) "Galbraith defends Galbraith," *Fortune*, 121(3), 161.
(1990) "Interview: John Kenneth Galbraith," *Aurora Online*, http://aurora.icaap.org.
(1990) "The rush to capitalism," *New York Review of Books*, 37(16), 51.
(1990) "What's wrong with this picture?," *American Heritage*, 41(8), 57–64.
(1990) "Which capitalism for Eastern Europe?," *Harper's Magazine*, 280, 19–21.
(1991) "Economics in the century ahead," *Economic Journal*, 101, 41–6.

(1991) "In tribute to Del Paine," *Fortune*, 123(4), 152.
(1991) "Let's borrow more money: that's the way to end this recession," *New York Times*, May 16, A23.
(1991) "Reflections – 1960," *Grand Street*, 10(1), 26.
(1991) "The sting of truth," *Scientific American*, 264(5), 136.
(1991) "What sort of capitalism is best for former communist nations?" *Utne Reader*, 43, 106–7.
(1991) "Writing and typing," *Nieman Reports*, 45(1), 32–4.
(1992) "Culture of contentment," *New Statesman & Society*, 5(201), 14–16.
(1992) "The economic hangover from a binge of greed," *Business and Society Review*, 81, 6–7.
(1992) "The functional underclass," *Proceedings of the American Philosophical Society*, 136(3), 411–15.
(1992) "Introduction," in T. H. Eliot (ed.) *Recollections of the New Deal: When the People Mattered*. Boston: Northeastern University Press.
(1992) "Toeing the hard line," *New Statesman & Society*, 5(192), 14.
(1992) "The university: reflections over the years," *Academe*, 78(5), 10–12.
(1992) "What monuments the religious have wrought!," *New Choices for Retirement Living*, 32(8), 26.
(1993) "The autonomous power of organization," in J. Brauer and M. Chatterji (eds.) *Economic Issues of Disarmament: Contributions from Peace Economics and Peace Science*, 43–6. New York: New York University Press.
(1993) "Countervailing power: memoir and modern reality," in C. Kerr and P. Staudohar (eds.) *Labor Economics and Industrial Relations: Markets and Institutions*. Cambridge, MA: Harvard University Press, 431–34.
(1993) "Foreword," in S. Tsuru (ed.) *Japan's Capitalism, Creative Defeat and Beyond*. Cambridge: Cambridge University Press.
(1993) "Foreword," in A. Gregory (ed.) *The Gilded Age: The Super-rich of the Edwardian Era*. London: Cassell.
(1993) "Introduction to the American Journal of Agricultural Economics' 75th anniversary issue," *American Journal of Agricultural Economics*, 75, 1.
(1993) "Raising Keynes," *Washington Monthly*, 25(12), 46.
(1993) "Recession? Why worry?" *New York Times*, May 12, A19.
(1993) "The return of Keynes," *NPQ: New Perspectives Quarterly*, 10(2), 10.
(1994) "The autonomous military power: an economic view," in M. Chatterji, H. Jager, and A. Rima (eds.) *The Economics of*

International Security: Essays in Honour of Jan Tinbergen. London: Macmillan Palgrave, 9–13.
(1994) "Capitalism's dark shadows," *Washington Monthly*, 26(7/8), 20.
(1994) "False economies," *New Statesman & Society*, 7(290), 24.
(1994) "The good life beckons," *New Statesman & Society*, 7(287), 14–16.
(1994) "The good society considered – the economic dimension," *Journal of Law and Society*, 21(2), 165–70.
(1994) "The 'living industry' and the environment," *EPA Journal*, 20(3/4), 41.
(1994) *The World Economy Since the Wars: A Personal View.* London: Sinclair–Stevenson.
(1995) "Blame history, not the liberals," *New York Times*, September 19, A21.
(1995) "Our forked tongue," *New York Times,* February 6, A17.
(1996) "Foreword: the indebted society," in J. Medoff and A. Harless (eds.) *The Indebted Society: Anatomy of an Ongoing Disaster.* Boston: Little, Brown.
(1996) "The good society: the economic dimension," in P. Arestis and M. Sawyer (eds.) *Employment, Economic Growth, and the Tyranny of the Market: Essays in Honour of Paul Davidson*, vol. 2. Aldershot: Edward Elgar.
(1996) "Interview: John Kenneth Galbraith," in D. C. Colander and H. Landreth (eds.) *The Coming of Keynesianism to America: Conversations with the Founders of Keynesian Economics.* Cheltenham: Edward Elgar.
(1997) "Globalisation and the politics of resistance: preface," *New Political Economy*, 2(1), 5–9.
(1997) "The imperatives of consumer demand," in M. Casson (ed.) *Culture, Social Norms and Economics: International Library of Critical Writings in Economics*, vol. 83. Cheltenham: Edward Elgar.
(1997) "Mr. Galbraith's Principle," *Across the Board*, 34(6), 14.
(1997) "The new internationalism: the fact and the response," *UN Chronicle*, 34(3), 62.
(1998) "Evading the obvious," *New York Times*, October 12, A19.
(1998) "John Maynard Keynes: from retrospect to prospect," *Journal of Post Keynesian Economics*, 21(1), 11–13.
(1998) *Letters to Kennedy.* Cambridge, MA: Harvard University Press.
(1998) *The Socially Concerned Today.* Toronto and Buffalo: University of Toronto Press.
(1998) "To a market Pollyanna," *Civilization*, 5(6), 61–9.

(1999) "The affluent society 40 years on," *Dollars & Sense*, 226, 49.
(1999) "Challenges of the new millennium," *Finance and Development*, 36(4), 2–5.
(1999) "The commitment to innocent fraud," *Challenge*, 42(5), 16–20.
(1999) "The epic years," *Washington Monthly*, 31(3), 42.
(1999) "Free market fraud," *Progressive*, 63(1), 54.
(1999) "How Keynes came to America," in L. Tarshis, O. F. Hamouda, and B. B. Price (eds.) *Keynesianism and the Keynesian Revolution in America: A Memorial Volume in Honour of Lorie Tarshis*. Cheltenham: Edward Elgar, 8–17.
(1999) "A liberal's debt to Canadians," *Maclean's*, 112(31), 40.
(1999) "Peace through patience, not air power," *New York Times*, April 15, section 4, 17.
(1999) *The Unfinished Business of Our Century*. Bryn Mawr: American College.
(1999/2000) "Why diplomats clam up," *Nieman Reports*, 53/54(4/1), 189–90.
(2000) "Foreword: the social left and the market system," in B. K. Gills (ed.) *Globalization and the Politics of Resistance*. Basingstoke: Macmillan.
(2000) "Preface," in B. Kreisky, M. P. Berg, J. Lewis, and O. Rathkolb (eds.) *The Struggle for a Democratic Austria: Bruno Kreisky on Peace and Social Justice*. New York: Berghahn Books.
(2001) "Economic delusion, political disaster," *New York Times*, March, 11, section 4, 15.
(2001) *The Essential Galbraith*. Boston: Houghton Mifflin.
(2001) "What happened to the good society? Interview with John Kenneth Galbraith," *Challenge*, 44(4), 5–13.
(2002) "The clumsy multinational," *Harvard Business Review*, 80(9), 128.
(2002) "Foreword – globalization: what it is and what to do about it," *Annals of the American Academy of Political and Social Science*, 581, 6–7.
(2003) "Afterword: a Japanese social initiative – the relevant view," in J. M. Harris and N. R. Goodwin (eds.) *New Thinking in Macroeconomics: Social, Institutional, and Environmental Perspectives*. Cheltenham: Edward Elgar.
(2003) "What has the new right got right: not much, says its favorite foe," *Canadian Business*, 76(17).
(2004) "Innocent fraud," *Across the Board*, 41(2), 10.
Galbraith, J. K. and Baker, J. F. (1975) "Interview: John Kenneth Galbraith," *Publishers Weekly*, August 18, 10–12.

Galbraith, J. K. and Basco, S. (2003) "On Bush, greed, and God's minister: John Kenneth Galbraith speaks out," *TomPaine.Com*, April 4.

Galbraith, J. K. and Black, J. D. (1935) "The quantitative position of marketing in the United States," *Quarterly Journal of Economics*, 49(3), 394–413.

(1936) "The production credit system of 1933," *American Economic Review*, 26(2), 235–47.

(1938) "The maintenance of agricultural production during depression: the explanations reviewed," *Journal of Political Economy*, 46(2), 235–47.

Galbraith, J. K. and Blanton, K. (1996) "Interview: a conversation with John Kenneth Galbraith," *Boston Globe*, April 28 (City edn), A97.

Galbraith, J. K. and Canadian Broadcasting Corporation (1965) *The Underdeveloped Country.* Toronto: Canadian Broadcasting Corporation.

Galbraith, J. K. and Conway, L. (1997) "Interview: the Ken Galbraith (and Bill Buckley Show)," *Nieman Reports*, 51(4), 53–5.

Galbraith, J. K. and Davis, W. A. (1995) "Interview: The Lion in Winter: the Harvard prof's latest lesson: how to age wisely," *Boston Globe*, October 24, 55.

Galbraith, J. K. and Dietrich, M. (2003) "Interview: J. K. Galbraith: liberal politics and the economics of the modern business firm," *New Political Economy*, 8(3), 385–400.

Galbraith, J. K. and Dunn, S. P. (2002) "The origins of the Galbraithian system: Stephen P. Dunn in conversation with J. K. Galbraith," *Journal of Post Keynesian Economics*, 24(3), 347–65.

Galbraith, J. K. and Evans, F. (1987) "Interview: a conversation with John Kenneth Galbraith," *Business Forum*, 12(3), 12–17.

Galbraith, J. K. and Holton, R. H. (1955) *Marketing Efficiency in Puerto Rico.* Cambridge, MA: Harvard University Press.

Galbraith, J. K. and Karier, T. (1992) "Interview: John Kenneth Galbraith looks back at the Reagan–Bush era," *In These Times*, June 10–23, 18–19.

Galbraith, J. K. and Kaur, H. (1998) "Interview: a gentler, kinder approach – the Galbraith way," *Business Times*, 12(51), 4.

Galbraith, J. K. and Kunimatsu, T. (1999) "Interview: Galbraith says capitalism will prevail," *Daily Yomiuri*, January 10, 1.

Galbraith, J. K. and Laurence, M. (1968) "The Playboy interview: John Kenneth Galbraith," *Playboy*, June, 63–178, 138, 164–74.

Galbraith, J. K. and Lewis, A. (1966) "Interview: the world through Galbraith's eyes," *New York Times Magazine*, December 18, 25, 88–92.

Galbraith, J. K., Macy, R. M., and Malenbaum, W. (1937) "Farm mortgage loan replacement," *Journal of Farm Economics*, 19(4), 764–82.

Galbraith, J. K. and McClaughry, J. (1973) "Interview: Galbraith and his critics," *Business & Society Review*, 8, 12–16.

Galbraith, J. K. and McCracken, P. W. (1983) *Reagonomics: Meaning, Means, and Ends*. New York: Free Press.

Galbraith, J. K. and MacNeil, R. (1992) "Interview: conversation with John Kenneth Galbraith," MacNeil/Lehrer News Hour, July 1 (transcript 4368), 12–16.

Galbraith, J. K. and Menshikov, S. (1988) *Capitalism, Communism and Coexistence: From the Bitter Past to a Better Prospect*. London: Hamish Hamilton.

Galbraith, J. K. and Navasky, V. S. (1967) "Interview: Galbraith on Galbraith," *New York Times Book Review*, June 25, 2–3.

Galbraith, J. K. and Olsen, W. (1987) "Interview: America will feel the crunch of Reagan revolution," *Tribune, Business*, 1–6.

Galbraith, J. K. and Peterson, G. M. (1932) "The concept of marginal land," *Journal of Farm Economics*, 14(2).

Galbraith, J. K. and Pressman, S. (1989) "Interview: conversation," *Review of Political Economy*, 1, 381–86.

Galbraith, J. K. and Solo, C. S. (1953) "Puerto Rican lessons in economic development," *The Annals of the American Academy of Political and Social Science*, 285, 55–9.

Galbraith, J. K. and University of London. (1967) "A Beginner's Guide to American Studies: An Address Given on the Occasion of the Official Opening of the Institute of United States Studies," University of London, on May 12, 1967. London: University Institute of United States Studies.

Galbraith, J. K. and Wallace, M. (1978) *A Guide to Today's Economy*. New York: Encyclopedia Americana/CBS News Audio Resource Library.

Galbraith, J. K., Fergenson, P. E., and Fergenson, L. R. (1989) "Galbraith on marketing and the marketplace: an interview," *Review of Business*, 11(3), 29.

Galbraith, J. K., Grether, E. T., Mason, E. S., Neal, A. C., Sumner, J. D., and Heflebower, R. B. (1947) "Content and research uses of price control and rationing records," *American Economic Review*, 37(2), 651–66.

Galbraith, J. K., Higgins, B. H., Woytinsky, W. S., and Brownlee, O. H. (1948) "Discussion," *American Economic Review*, 38(2), 443–51.

Galbraith, J. K., Kuh, E. and Thurow, L. C. (1971) "The Galbraith plan to promote the minorites," *New York Times Magazine*, August 22, 9, 35, and 38–9.

Galbraith, J. K., Ulmer, H., Weidenbaum, M. J., and Murray L. (1976) "The case for and against national economic planning," *Challenge*, 19(1), 30.

Gauhar, A. and Galbraith, J. K. (1983) "North–South dialog: an interview with J. K. Galbraith," *Third World Quarterly*, 5(2), 263–69.

Levine, D. and Galbraith, J. K. (1970) *No Known Survivors: David Levine's Political Plank*. Boston: Gambit.

Moraes, F. R., Galbraith, J. K., and Howe, E. (1974) *John Kenneth Galbraith Introduces India*. London: Deutsch.

Rudenstine, N., Galbraith, J. K., and Thomson, J. C. J. (1995) "Rudenstine, Galbraith and Thomson Talks," *Nieman Reports*, 49(3), 37.

Samuelson, P. A. and Galbraith, J. K. (1975) "Economic policy – where is it leading?," *Boston University Journal*, 23(1), 30–6.

Yadin, Y., Maeda, Y., and Galbraith, J. K. (1962) *Guildhall Lectures*. Manchester: Granada TV Network.

Index

www.ingramcontent.com/pod-product-compliance
Lightning Source LLC
LaVergne TN
LVHW102007210926
848483LV00009B/121
* 9 7 8 0 5 2 1 5 1 8 7 6 5 *